EXPOSITION

OF THE

GRAMMATICAL STRUCTURE

OF THE

ENGLISH LANGUAGE;

BEING AN ATTEMPT TO FURNISH

AN IMPROVED METHOD OF TEACHING GRAMMAR.

FOR THE USE OF SCHOOLS AND COLLEGES.

BY

JOHN MULLIGAN, A. M.

NEW YORK:
D. APPLETON AND COMPANY,
549 & 551 BROADWAY
1874.

PREFACE.

In the following treatise, we have adopted a plan of arrangement entirely different from that of preceding grammarians; and we trust that, to all judicious teachers, this innovation will appear an improvement. We commence by calling the attention of the student to the purposes served by language, the facts which render grammatical contrivances necessary in language, to the formation of propositions to convey our thoughts;—all subjects useful and important, independent of the design with which we introduce them. Our statements in reference to these points can be readily comprehended by every student, of average capacity and average application. Having thus established a mutual understanding with the student, as regards the nature of our subject and the purposes which we have in view, we endeavor to maintain this common understanding, and a rational acquiescence in the correctness of our deductions unimpaired through the whole treatise, by carefully guarding against taking any step in advance which he cannot readily follow. We thus hope to secure through the whole course, a clear perception of the practical utility of what is already explained, and adequate preparation (if not awakened desire) for the further prosecution of the inquiry. By pursuing this method, the student will feel conscious at every step that he has made sensible progress in the acquisition of a knowledge of the structure of language, and that even if he were to suspend his studies at this step, his labor in attempting to learn grammar would not be entirely lost. We need not advert to the manifest defects of the old methods of grammatical instruction in these respects.

We shall not dwell in this place on the other peculiarities which distinguish the following treatise. These peculiarities cannot be advantageously described or defended in a preface. They can be best seen and best appreciated in the regular perusal of the work. We may possibly, hereafter, find an opportunity of examining the defects of the old systems of grammatical instruction, and of explaining and defending our own views, more fully than we have been able to do in the notes interspersed through this volume. Manifest proofs are exhibited, in the complaints of teachers and grammarians, that the friends of education are sensible of the defects of our old systems, and ardently desire a reformation. And, in this connection, we feel pleasure in acknowledging that much has been done by the efforts of our immediate predecessors to introduce, and to prepare the way for the reception of an improved method of grammatical instruction.

The importance of a thorough reformation of the method of teaching grammar to the general intellectual progress of the age, can scarcely be over-estimated. We may form some notion of this importance, if we reflect that this science not only lays (or, at least, should lay) the foundation of all sound logic and all true eloquence—has the closest connection with correct thinking, as well as with the correct transmission of the products of thought from mind to mind—but serves as a natural and indispensable introduction to our courses of intellectual training, and the first step in a philosophical education. (How much may the future success of the young student depend, on the manner in which this first step is taken?) Besides this, a thorough knowledge of grammar is the great preparation for the easy and correct acquisition of ancient and modern languages, enabling us with greatly diminished labor to comprehend clearly the laws of their structure, and fix these laws indelibly in our memory for ready recollection.

After what we have already said, we need not assure the intelligent reader, who may do us the favor of perusing our treatise regularly from the commencement, that he can find no difficulty in following our steps. But, looking to the nature of the subject, and to the method of treating it which we have adopted, and to some necessary innovation (we have studiously avoided all *unnecessary* innovation) in the use of terms, &c., we deprecate all attempts to take up our treatise in the middle, or to pronounce judgment on a part without a complete knowledge of our whole system.

We have expended much labor in adapting this book to the purpose of giving instruction to classes. With this end in view, we have prepared a course of questions, placed for the greater convenience of the teacher and student at the foot of the page; and we have secured a ready reference, by numbers, to the part of the text in which the answers are found. For the same purpose a series of exercises is prescribed, consisting chiefly of written examples (to be furnished by the student) of the forms of construction treated in each section. We think this kind of exercise better suited than any other to secure the rapid progress of pupils in acquiring a knowledge of the principles of grammar, and at the same time (what is one of the most valuable literary accomplishments) experience in the correct construction of sentences. We trust that the pains taken to accommodate the book to the practical purposes of instruction will be appreciated by intelligent teachers.

It will be observed that the arrangement is such that, by omitting the parts included in brackets, and generally indicated by smaller type, a first course in the most essential (and, at the same time, most easily comprehended) principles of grammar can be given in a rapid manner. We recommend a first course of this kind, exhibiting a general outline of the Structure of the English Language, in all cases where the student is not already familiar with the subject of grammar. When in such a course the student comes to the chapter on Compound Propositions, he may return to the beginning, and in a second course be required to answer all the questions. Satisfactory answers to these will generally include all that the young student is expected to learn. The notes are designed chiefly for the satisfaction of teachers and inquisitive adepts in the science of grammar.

If the method of teaching grammar here proposed should be received with a share of public approbation, we shall soon furnish an abridgment suited for the use of those who are only commencing their grammatical studies. The book now presented might, we think, be profitably employed, in the manner above recommended, with the youngest classes in grammar. But the details necessary to explain and justify our method, and our views, when they differ from those commonly received, have swelled the book to a degree which may seem to render it unfit, both as to size and price, for the use of beginners. These details will be interesting and serviceable to more advanced students, who may wish to perfect their knowledge of grammar,—the class for whose special use we design the present treatise. We hope that the work in its present shape will also prove acceptable to teachers of youth, and to such gentlemen as take interest in the progress of education, and in this class of literary subjects.

CONTENTS.

INTRODUCTION.

CHAPTER I.

OF PROPOSITIONS.

CHAPTER II.

OF NOUNS.

CHAPTER III.

OF VERBS.

CHAPTER IV.

MODIFICATION OF THE SUBJECT AND PREDICATE BY NOUNS.

CHAPTER V.

OF PREPOSITIONS.

CHAPTER VI.

OF ADJECTIVES.

CHAPTER VII.

OF ADVERBS.

CHAPTER VIII.

OF INTERROGATIVE AND IMPERATIVE PROPOSITIONS.

CHAPTER IX.

OF COMPOUND PROPOSITIONS.

CHAPTER X.

COMBINATION OF INDEPENDENT PROPOSITIONS.

CHAPTER XI.

OF INTERJECTIONS AND EXCLAMATORY WORDS AND PHRASES.

STRUCTURE OF LANGUAGE.

INTRODUCTION.

§ 1. The signs employed in making known to others our feelings, emotions, and thoughts, may be divided into two distinct classes, (1) NATURAL SIGNS and ARTIFICIAL SIGNS.

(2) In the class of *natural signs* we include, 1st, signs addressed to the ear—the various sounds indicative of the emotions of our minds; as, sighs, groans, cries. 2d, Signs addressed to the eye—the various indications of emotion by the expression of the countenance, by smiles, frowns, &c., or by various gestures of the head, arms, and other members of the body. And, 3d, a more limited number of signs addressed to the sense of touch; as the grasp and pressure of the hand, &c.

(3) Between this class of signs and the feelings or emotions which they indicate there exists a *natural* bond of association. They do not, like the class of *artificial signs*, owe their origin in any degree to human contrivance, to the consent of men, to an arbitrary agreement that they shall be used to express exclusively certain feelings, or certain emotions. On the contrary, they flow spontaneously from nature, are not acquired by human industry, and are intelligible alike to men of every nation. (4) The signs of this class constitute what has been called *natural language*. (5) It may be remarked, in pass-

§ 1. (1) What two distinct classes of *Signs* are employed in conveying our thoughts and feelings to others?

(2) Enumerate some of the *Natural Signs* employed for this purpose.

(3) What distinguishes these signs from those of the second class? (4) What do these signs constitute? (5) What are they best fitted to express?

ing, that this species of language is much better adapted to express feeling, or emotion, than to express thought; and that it is possessed, in a greater or lesser degree, by the lower animals.

§ 2. In the class of *artificial signs* we include (1) those (in some sense, at least) arbitrary, acquired signs, which constitute the endless variety of dialects employed for the interchange of thought amongst men. (2) These signs, unlike those of *natural language*, have no *necessary* connection with the ideas which they represent, but owe their significance to the contrivance, or to the consent of the distinct races of men who employ them. This class of signs for the communication of thought is distinguished (3) by the name of *artificial* or *articulate language* (*a*).

§ 3. The signs of natural language have (1) the advantage of being universally understood by all mankind. They serve as the only means of communication between those who have not a common dialect. They also express the stronger emotions in the most vivid and impressive manner. (2) But, on the other hand, only a limited portion of our feelings, and few of our thoughts, can be *clearly* conveyed to the minds of others by these signs. (3) We must have recourse to *articulate—artificial language*, for the purpose of communicating to others the nicer shades of feeling, and the various products of our thinking powers with a satisfactory degree of perspicuity and fulness.

§ 4. (1) Such a means of communication as articulate language affords, is indispensable both to the complete development and to the proper use of man's rational powers. (2) It is an instrument necessary for the improvement and advancement of reason, for giving precision and fixity to human thought, and securing its retention in the memory of the inquirer, as well as for the mutual interchange of the products of thought among men. (3) Our gracious

(*a*) See Appendix to this Introduction.

---

§ 2. (1) What are *Artificial Signs?* (2) What is the distinguishing characteristic of this class of signs? (3) By what name are they called?

§ 3. (1) Point out the advantages of natural language. (2) Point out its defects. (3) Mention some purposes which cannot be effected without recourse to artificial language.

§ 4. (1) To what particular purpose is articulate language indispensable? (2) Repeat what is said in illustration. (3) How has our Creator displayed his bounty towards man in regard of this matter?

Creator has, accordingly, to complete his bounty to his rational offspring on earth, added to the gift of reason the gift of organs adapted to enunciate distinctly the truths which reason discovers.

§ 5. It is proper here to observe, that (1) the combination of natural with artificial language is requisite to the most effective communication of our thoughts. (2) Emphasis, inflexions of the voice, tones, expression of the countenance (especially of the eyes), gestures, &c. (all borrowed from natural language), when united with *artificial language*, contribute much to render it perspicuous, as well as impressive. Hence, chiefly, the superior charms, and the greater power of *spoken* compared with *written* discourse. (3) The accomplished and skilful orator combines with the arbitrary signs of artificial language other signs from a language which addresses every class of minds. Even when, on account of the ignorance of his hearers, artificial signs are imperfectly comprehended, *natural signs*, which are universally intelligible, serve to interpret their meaning. They infuse spirit and life into the *dry bones* of articulate speech, and may be said to endow it with a living soul.

§ 6. (1) The grammarian's researches are exclusively directed to artificial or articulate language. (2) Some few signs, belonging properly to natural language, are found mixed with the signs of artificial language. (3) But these signs—commonly called, in our grammars, interjections—do not come under the laws of grammar. The grammarian has only to distinguish them from other signs, give them a name, and pass them by.

(4) To explain the *laws* of artificial language is the particular province of him who proposes to teach the *science* of grammar. (5) To guide to the proper *use* of the signs of artificial language, and to the correct interpretation of the thoughts of others embodied in

---

§ 5. (1) What is requisite to the most effective communication of human thought? (2) Illustrate this assertion. To what are the superior charms and the greater power of *spoken* discourse attributable? Answer. Chiefly, if not exclusively, to the combination of natural with artificial language. (3) Illustrate this assertion.

§ 6. (1) To which of these languages are the grammarian's researches directed? (2) Are the signs of natural language ever found mixed with those of artificial language? (3) If so, what are they called—do they come under the laws of grammar, and what has the grammarian to do with them?

(4) What is the province (or peculiar business) of him who teaches the science of grammar? (5) Of the teacher of grammar as an *art*? (6) What is the course pursued in

language, so far as this can be effected by reference to the *laws* and *usages* of language, is the province of him who proposes to teach grammar as an *art*. (6) In practical treatises for the instruction of the young, the *science* and the *art* are usually taught together. The *laws* of language, to some extent, are explained in connection with their practical application to a particular language. (7) It seems the most judicious course to teach the elementary principles of *universal grammar* (the *science* of grammar) in connection with the *particular grammar* of our mother tongue, and with the aid of illustrations drawn, as much as possible, from that language of which the forms, usages, and significance are most familiar to us.

§ 7. (1) Artificial language is presented to us in two distinct forms, viz., *spoken language* and *written language*. It is often necessary, in grammatical researches, to keep steadily in view the distinction between these two forms of language. (2) A neglect of this precaution has frequently led to confusion of thought and inaccuracy of expression. (3) *Spoken language* consists of *signs of thought*, expressed by the organs of speech, and addressed to the ears. These signs are called *words*. (4) *Written language*, on the other hand, consists of *signs of these signs*; that is, of *signs* of *words*. (5) We call both classes of signs *words*; and hence frequent confu sion. (6) It is to be wished that we had a special name for a *written word*, to distinguish it, where necessary, from a *spoken word*, and also a name for a *written letter*, to distinguish it from a *spoken sound*.

§ 8. (1) It is not by the use of separate unconnected words, repeated in succession without rule or law, but by the properly regulated *combination of words*, that we, in almost every case, communicate our thoughts to one another. Though it is not to be denied that every word has significance of some sort (2), a single word is seldom in our language the sign of a complete thought. (3) We cannot

---

grammars intended for the instruction of the young? (7) What method is recommended as judicious?

§ 7. (1) In what two distinct forms is artificial language presented to us? (2) Why is it necessary to keep this distinction in view? Ans. Because "a neglect," &c. (3) Of what does spoken language consist? (4) Of what written language? (5) By what common name are the signs of spoken and written language designated? (6) What is to be wished in order to avoid the danger of confounding *spoken signs* and *written signs?*

§ 8. (1) Do we generally express our thoughts by unconnected words, or by combinations of words? (2) Are single words often in our language the signs of complete

announce clearly in the English language even the simple fact that we are cold, without the use of more than one word. The shortest form of expressing this simple thought requires the use of three words, *I am cold.* Each of these words is, no doubt, a significant sign, but, at the same time, incapable alone of communicating a clear declaration of thought to those around us. (4) Again, every combination of words will not express thought. A combination made at random generally expresses nothing but nonsense.

(5) Hence the necessity of paying attention to the principles which regulate, in each particular language, the *combination* of words, in order to express thought clearly and forcibly. The investigation of these principles is the purpose proposed in a treatise on grammar. (6) It is to the fact that the artificial signs, which unite to express our thoughts, are complicated, and require skilful combination, that the Laws of Grammar owe their origin. (7) If every word served as the sign of a complete thought, whilst the number of words requisite for the purpose of communicating our thoughts (contrary to what might, at first sight, be expected) would be greatly increased, Grammar would either be altogether useless, or its province would be greatly limited, and entirely changed. This may be illustrated by referring to some few words in our language which express a complete thought: (8) for example, *Yes* and *No.* Such words fall not within the ordinary rules, nor even within the ordinary classifications and *nomenclature* of grammar. All complexity is here excluded, since a single sign expresses a complete thought; consequently, the application of all laws of combination is excluded. Grammatical science and art, as now understood, are null and useless, so far as concerns such signs.

§ 9. After these preliminary remarks, the reader will be prepared to find that (1) WORDS—THE CLASSIFICATION OF WORDS, THE MODIFICATION OR CHANGES OF FORM which WORDS undergo in order

---

thoughts? (3) Repeat the illustration. (4) Do all combinations of words, or combinations *made at random*, express thought?

(5) What is the inference drawn from these facts? (6) To what do the laws of grammar owe their origin? (7) If every word were to serve as the sign of a complete thought, what consequences would follow in reference to the number of words necessary to form a copious language, and in reference to systems of grammar? (8) Illustrate this position.

§ 9. (1) Enumerate the subjects which are to engage our attention in the following pages.

to express a MODIFIED MEANING, and, especially, THE LAWS OF PRINCIPLES which regulate THE COMBINATION OF WORDS for the purpose of expressing THOUGHT, form the subject matter of the following pages.

APPENDIX TO INTRODUCTION.

Till recently, two opinions, in reference to the origin of language, have divided the learned. According to the one, *the original language* was the direct gift of God to our first parents. According to the other, language is the invention of man himself—the work of his conscious reason.

According to the first opinion, man must have been taught the words of language, as a scholar is taught a foreign language at the present day. Such instruction presupposes a knowledge of what is to be expressed by language. If this opinion is correct, all man's first knowledge, as well as the language in which to express it, must have been a direct revelation. It may be objected that all this is inconsistent with the mode in which God has treated man in other things. He has bestowed on man powers of research and invention, and generally left these to find their natural development, under the circumstances in which he has placed him. The opinion now stated seems also inconsistent with the language employed in Genesis 2 : 19, where we are informed that God brought the animals "unto Adam, to see what he would call them; and whatsoever *Adam* called every living creature, that was the name thereof." In accordance with the opinion we are considering, we should expect rather to have been told that God gave the names and taught them to Adam, and that whatsoever God called every living creature, that was the name thereof. On the contrary, Adam is represented as already possessed of the power of speech, and as spontaneously inventing names for the objects around him.

According to the second opinion, man is the inventor of language, in the same sense in which he is the inventor of the various contrivances which distinguish civilization; and it is consistent with this opinion, as held by the ancients, to suppose that man may have remained for a long time after his appearance on earth without the advantage of language, as we know that he did in fact remain destitute of many of the most valuable inventions which he now possesses. The poet, in accordance with this view, describes men, when they first *crawled* from the earth, as devoid of articulate speech: "*Mutum et turpe pecus.*" This theory gives to man the glory of contriving language, in the same sense as he claims the glory of other human inventions.

It is objected to this view of the origin of language, that it is inconceivable how men, without some considerable advance in civilization, without some progress towards social order, could invent and agree upon a language, and equally inconceivable how they could have made any advance towards social order without the help of language. It might, indeed, be answered that the invention of language and the progress of civilization advanced simultaneously—*pàri passu.* But another and more serious objection is, that this theory, at least in its boldest form, is inconsistent with what is recorded in the Scriptures in regard of the primitive condition of man; and perhaps it is equally inconsistent with all that we can discover of the history of our race from other resources, and with the conjectures of a sound and enlightened philosophy.

Another theory of the origin of language has been more recently proposed; first, we believe, by the philosophical grammarians of Germany, viz., that language is a *spontaneous growth*—the result of that organization bestowed by our Creator on his rational offspring on earth. This theory, subjected to proper modifications, we think less objectionable than either of the preceding. It is more reconcileable, both with what is said in reference to this matter in Genesis, and with all the historical facts which bear upon this subject. It is more conformable, also, with what we see every day subjected to our observation in the progressive growth of language.

According to this theory, language is a *growth*—an organized growth, because the product of an organization—just as the intellectual improvement of our race is a *growth*—a development of powers lodged in man at his creation—a growth, progressive according to our wants. As our knowledge is enlarged, the vehicle of communication is simultaneously enlarged. According to this theory, every thought of a being organized as man is, naturally labors to find utterance, and calls into exercise his powers of articulation.

This theory accounts for the conformity discovered in the general laws of structure in all languages, and for the resemblance of many of the original words in these languages to the things which they represent. This is especially exemplified in words which express sounds, and in the names given to animals and to actions distinguished by some peculiarity of sound. (See Introduction to Becker's *Ausführliche Deutsche Grammatik.*)

Viewed according to this theory, articulate language is natural, as well as what has been distinguished from it by the name of *natural language.* Still, it is in some sense arbitrary and artificial. It is subjected, as regards its external form, to human volition, to human choice, to human caprice if you will, as is manifest from the manner in which we see languages daily grow under our eyes, as well as from the vast variety and diversity of the languages which we find in the world. No such diversity is found in those natural signs which constitute what has been called natural language. These are invariably always the same in the same race of animals, and instantly alike intelligble to each individual of the race.

CHAPTER I.

OF PROPOSITIONS.

§ 10. (1) WE employ artificial language, 1st. To assert (that is, to say or speak) our opinions, or declare our thoughts, feelings, emotions, &c. 2nd. To question, or interrogate others in order to obtain information. 3rd. To express commands, entreaties, exhortations, &c. (2) Distinct forms of expression are employed in discourse for these three several purposes; and, though, by supplying what is suppressed in the form of the expression (because manifestly implied in the sense), we might readily reduce all questions and commands to the form of assertions, still it is convenient to consider these forms separately.

§ 11. (1) Any combination of words which expresses an assertion, a question, a command, &c., or, more generally, any combination of words which expresses *complete sense* is called a PROPOSITION. (2) Those combinations by which an assertion, a question, a command (including entreaty, request, &c.), are expressed, may be called respectively *assertive* or *declarative*, *interrogative* or *questioning*, and *imperative* or *commanding propositions*. These three are usually recognized as distinct forms of propositions (*a*).

NOTE (*a*).—This classification includes all *independent propositions*. *Dependent propositions* (that is, propositions employed to modify or complete other propositions) sometimes express neither assertion, interrogation, nor command. As, for example, *If the men come*, I will let you know. Here the proposition, *if the men come*, asserts nothing. It expresses merely the condition on which the assertion, "*I will let you know*" rests; it is simply here a modification of this latter proposition. But it differs no way in *form* from an assertive proposition,

---

§ 10. (1) Enumerate the purposes for which language is employed. (2) Why is a classification of the purposes for which language is employed important in a grammatical point of view? Ans. Because distinct *forms of expression* are employed for these several purposes.

§ 11. (1) What is a proposition? (2) Enumerate the different kinds of propositions.

and therefore requires no separate place in a classification of propositions having reference to their *grammatical forms.* In fact, when you withdraw the word "*If*" (which is no part of the proposition, but serves merely to indicate its connection, and the purpose of this connection with another proposition), the proposition becomes at once assertive. Or, perhaps, rather, *if* is the verb of an imperative proposition, and "*the men come*" is the objective to it.

Since interchange of thought is effected through the medium of propositions, and discourse consists almost wholly of propositions of one or other of the kinds above mentioned, it follows (3) that the chief business of the grammarian is the *analysis of propositions,* and the explanation of the manner in which words are combined to form them.

(4) The assertive or declarative proposition claims our first and chief attention. (5) It is the most simple; it is complete, containing all the parts essential to every form of proposition fully expressed; it recurs most frequently in discourse; and even were *interrogative* and *imperative* propositions not reducible (as they seem to us to be) to the *assertive* form, they differ from it only in the arrangement, or in the suppression of some of their constituent parts. After the assertive form is explained, the few points in which the others differ from it will be easily explained and readily understood.

§ 12. (1) It is manifestly essential to an assertion that *something* should be asserted—that is, said or spoken—of *some person,* or *some thing,* and as an *assertive proposition* is an assertion clothed in language, the three following parts may be distinguished in every such proposition when fully expressed. (2) First, *some means of indicating the person or thing* of which we speak, or make the assertion. This is called the SUBJECT of the proposition. (3) Second, *a means* of expressing what is intended to be *said* or *asserted* of the subject. This is called the PREDICATE of the proposition. (4)

---

(3) What is the chief business of the grammarian?

(4) Which kind of propositions claims our first and chief attention? (5) Enumerate the reasons assigned for considering this form first.

§ 12. (1) How many parts may be distinguished in every completely expressed proposition? (2) What is the *subject* of a proposition? Ans. That about which the assertion contained in the proposition is made. (3) What is the *predicate* of a proposition? Ans.

The word *predicate* means what is *said* or *asserted.* [(5) The subject and predicate are called by logicians the *two terms* of the proposition.] And, third (6), *a means* of indicating that the *predicate* is *intended* to be *asserted* of the subject. This is what the logicians call the COPULA—that is to say, what *couples,* connects, or unites the subject and predicate.

§ 13. [(1) In some languages (the Latin and Greek, for example) all the parts of a proposition, *subject, predicate,* and *copula,* are sometimes expressed by a *single word;* but *a word* including *a combination of significant signs.*] (2) In our language, the subject, however simple and unmodified, is usually expressed by at least one separate word in assertive propositions. (3) The copula is never (as we view the matter, see § 46, and note) expressed in the English language, nor in any language, which we know, by a *separate word.* (4) The copula and predicate (or the *leading part* of the predicate) are united in the same word. Otherwise, the word which expresses the predicate, or leading part of the predicate, is so modified—assumes such a form, or receives such place in the arrangement of the proposition, as, in accordance with the usages of language, to *indicate assertion* in assertive propositions, *interrogation* in interrogative propositions, &c.

NOTE.—There are a few, very few exceptions; and even these occur in forms of expression now rarely employed—such as, for example, *methinks, meseems, melisteth.* These we intend to consider in their proper place. (See §§ 66: 8; and 79: 18.) On the contrary, in imperative propositions (if the analysis commonly given of them is to be followed) the subject is usually suppressed; for example, *Go to the door; Bring me a book,* &c. In such propositions as these, no mistake can arise from the suppression of the subject, since the party addressed—the person or persons spoken to—is in our language almost always the subject. The subject of an imperative proposition must be ex-

---

That which is asserted of the subject. (4) What does the word predicate mean? [(5) What are the subjects and predicates of propositions called by logicians?] (6) What is meant by the copula of a proposition? Ans. That which indicates that the predicate *is asserted* of the subject.

[§ 13. (1) How are the three parts of a proposition sometimes expressed in certain languages?] (2) How is the subject of an *assertive* proposition usually expressed in our language? (3) Is the copula expressed by a separate word? (4) How then is it indicated? Ans. "The predicate is so modified," &c.—repeating as above.

pressed, when it does not coincide with the party we address. This happens rarely in modern speech.

(5) The predicate and copula united, since they are essential constituents of the proposition, must always be fully expressed in every complete *independent* proposition by a word of that class which the usage of language has assigned for that purpose. (6) Two words, then, are necessary, in our language, to the full expression of an assertion, or to constitute a complete proposition—one to express the subject, and another to express the united predicate and copula.

[(7) When two or more propositions, having the same common subject, or the same predicate, are united together, the common subject or predicate is very generally suppressed in one or more of them. (8) For example, *John reads and writes*=to *John reads*, and *John writes.* Here the subject of the latter proposition is suppressed by the usage of language, and left to be supplied from the preceding one. John and James write=to John writes, and James writes. Here the predicate and copula are only once expressed, but in such a form as to indicate that the assertion reaches both subjects. Sometimes, in a proposition connected with a preceding proposition, only the modifying words are repeated, and both subject and predicate with copula, are to be supplied from the other propositions. For example: "*They* (power and riches) *keep* off the summer shower not the winter storm"=to They keep off the summer shower, they keep not off the winter storm. (9) But this forms no real exception to what we have asserted above. The subject or predicate, in such cases, is simply *suppressed*, left to be supplied by the *understanding* of the hearer. It is not *indicated* or *contained* under the form of the part of the proposition *expressed.* They are not, therefore, complete independent propositions. (10) When, in certain languages, a whole proposition is expressed by a single word, the

---

(5) Are the united predicate and copula always expressed in an independent proposition? (6) How many words are necessary in our language to the full expression of an assertion, or to constitute a complete proposition?

(7) What sometimes happens when two or more propositions having the same subject or the same predicate are united together? (8) Give examples. (9) Show that this is not a real exception to what is said above. (10) When a whole proposition, as in some languages, is expressed by a single word, how is the subject indicated?

subject of the proposition is indicated by the form and inflexion of the word which expresses the united predicate and copula.]

§ 14. We are now prepared to commence the *analysis* of the most simple form of propositions; namely, those which consist of two words, one representing the subject, and the other the united copula and predicate of the proposition. [(1) By the *analysis* of a proposition we mean the separation of its parts for the purpose of distinct examination.] Let us take, as an example for analysis, the expression, *Snow melts.* (2) These two words form a proposition, because they express a complete assertion. (3) The word "*snow*," in this proposition, represents the *subject*, because it expresses *the thing* concerning which the *assertion* is made. (4) The word "melts" includes both the *predicate* and *copula*, because it both expresses *what is asserted* of the subject, and indicates that *it is intended to be asserted.*

[We may carry our analysis still fárther, and separate the predicate from the copula. For, though we have no means in language of expressing the copula alone (5), we can express the predicate separately by a word that gives no indication of assertion. In the proposition "*snow melts*," the word *melting* exactly expresses the predicate; for the action expressed by the word melting is manifestly what is asserted of the "*snow.*"

(6) It may be remarked here, that the predicate-word *melting*, preceded or followed by the subject-word *snow*, *asserts* nothing—that is, these two words cannot constitute a proposition. *Snow melting* and *melting snow*, though significant phrases—that is, words properly arranged to enter into discourse, and form *part* of a proposition—are neither of them *complete propositions*, because they do not express an assertion. (7) But, on the other hand, the word *melts*—at once, in accordance with the usage of our language, indicating assertion and expressing the action of *melting*—joined to the

---

§ 14. (1) What is meant by the analysis of a proposition? (2) Why are the words "*snow melts*" said to form a proposition? (3) In the proposition "*snow melts*" point out the word which represents the subject, and give the reason for so considering it. (4) Which word represents predicate and copula, and why is it said to represent these?

[(5) Can the predicate of a proposition be exhibited separately? What is the predicate of the proposition "*snow melts*" disconnected from the copula? (6) Show that this predicate-word or sign joined to a subject will not form a proposition. (7) Repeat what is said above of the word *melts.*]

subject *snow*, constitutes a proposition; that is, expresses an assertion, or, what is the same thing, a complete thought.]

(8) In the arrangement of an *assertive* proposition, the subject is generally placed before the assertive word. This may be considered the *natural* order (9), though it is often inverted by poets to suit their measure, and by orators for rhetorical effect. (10) The contrary arrangement also prevails in some few forms of expression in ordinary use; as, "*says I*," "*said he*," and the now obsolete form of expression, "*quoth he*," and perhaps a few other forms of assertion.

§ 15. (1) In the analysis of propositions, the learner should always direct his attention first to the *assertive* word. (2) This we recommend, first, because this is the most important part of every proposition; and, secondly, because it is the part most easily recognised. This results from the fact, that the assertive word is always employed for one and the same purpose (except it should be a word of double meaning—see § 16, below), whereas the class of words employed to represent the subjects of propositions (without any change of meaning) perform other functions, serve other purposes besides expressing the subjects of propositions. (3) The answer to the question, formed by the assertive word preceded by *what*, gives the subject. For example, *Beauty fades. What fades?* Ans., *Beauty*, the subject.

It is now time to exercise the pupil in pointing out the words which express the subjects, and the words which express the combined predicates and copulas, or what, for the sake of brevity, we may call the *assertive words*, in the following and similar propositions.

Exercise I.—Beauty fades. Virtue flourishes. Memory decays. Time fleets. Day dawns. Corn grows. Rain falls. Water freezes.

---

(8) What is the usual or natural order of arrangement of the subject, and the assertive word (or combined predicate and copula) in an *assertive* proposition? (9) Mention classes of writers that sometimes invert the usual order, and the purposes for which they take this liberty with the arrangement in common use. (10) Mention some of the inverted expressions in ordinary use.

§ 15. (1) To which part of a proposition should the learner first direct his attention in attempting an analysis? (2) State the reasons assigned for recommending this course. (3) Tell how to form a question to which the answer is the subject of a given proposition. Illustrate by an example.

Gunpowder explodes. Men walk. Reptiles creep. Birds fly. Fishes swim. Boys play. Children talk. Laborers work, &c. &c.

The pupil may be questioned on these examples according to the following *model*. Example: "*Beauty fades*." Do these two words form a proposition? Ans. Yes. Why? Ans. Because they express an assertion. What is the assertive word in this proposition, and why is it so called? Ans. "*Fades*" is the assertive word, because it expresses the predicate, and indicates assertion. Point out the subject-word of the proposition, and tell why you call it the subject. Ans. "*Beauty*" expresses the subject, because it is in regard of beauty (*about beauty*) that the assertion expressed by the word "*fades*" is made. Can the predicate of this proposition be expressed alone—separate from the copula? Ans. Yes, it may be expressed by the word *fading*. *Fading* is exactly what is here asserted of beauty. Can the copula be expressed separately? Ans. No; the copula is never expressed by a separate word, but is always combined with the predicate, or the *leading part* of the predicate, to form the *assertive word*.

The teacher can add more examples, if he pleases. But it is better, we think, to encourage the pupil to form examples for himself, in the manner prescribed in the following exercises. A good exercise may also be given by selecting a passage from any book, or taking one of the exercises in the more advanced part of this work, and requiring the learner to point out the subject and assertive word of each proposition.

Exercise II.—Form propositions, by uniting such other assertive words as will make sense with the subjects in Exercise I.

Under this, and some of the following exercises, the pupil may be required to construct a given number of propositions for a lesson; and he may continue the exercise so long as he finds he can supply appropriate assertive words to unite with the given subjects.

Exercise III.—Form a given number of propositions by uniting other subjects with the assertive words in Exercise I.

Exercises IV., V., &c.—Let the pupil now form *two-worded* propositions from his own resources, without having either subject or assertive word suggested to him.

In a class, let each pupil try who can construct the greatest number of appropriate propositions consisting of two words.

NOTE.—These exercises must be continued till the learner clearly comprehends what constitutes a proposition, and can readily distinguish the terms which form its essential parts. Here let a sure foundation for the work of *grammatical analysis* be laid. This being done, we trust the learner will be able, on the plan we propose, to pursue this study with ease, satisfaction, and rapid improvement.

In performing these exercises, and all the exercises prescribed hereafter, let the pupil be strictly enjoined to offer no proposition that is not consistent with truth, and which does not express an appropriate thought—in other words, *good sense.* If this suggestion is duly regarded, the performance of these tasks will lead to the easy development and improvement of the rational powers of younger pupils; it will help them to acquire facility in that difficult and most valuable accomplishment—the correct and clear expression of their thoughts in writing, whilst they are pursuing, at the same time, what we believe to be the most effective and systematic course of training in the grammatical knowledge of their own language.

§ 16. (1) *The use or purpose which a word* (or a class of words) *serves in discourse,* that is, in forming propositions, we shall hereafter, for the sake of greater precision and brevity, call the FUNCTION of the word, or class of words. (2) Words are divided into several classes, in reference to the distinct *functions* which they perform. (3) These classes are commonly called "THE PARTS OF SPEECH."

(4) In our survey of the essential parts of an assertive proposition in its most simple form, two of these classes of words (and these *the two most important*) have been brought under our view; namely, those which perform the *function* of subjects of propositions, and those which perform the *double function* of indicating assertion and expressing (in whole or in part) the predicate or thing asserted. (5) These two classes of words are essentially distinct, and never interchange functions with each other. The words which express subjects cannot be employed, at least in the same sense, to express

---

§ 16. (1) What is meant by the function of a word? (2) On what principle, or in reference to what fact, are words classed by grammarians? (3) What are these classes of words usually called?

(4) Tell how many kinds, or classes of words are used in the most simple proposition, and the functions which they perform. (5) Can these classes of words exchange places?

assertion, nor those which express assertion to express the subjects of propositions. The learner will find no difficulty in distinguishing these two kinds of words when presented together. (6) There are, indeed, many words in our language which, having a double meaning, are employed for both purposes. (7) For example, *cook*, the name applied to the person who prepares food by fire, and *cook*, employed to assert the *act* of *cooking*, or preparing food by fire, as in the assertion, *Men cook their food; work*, the name applied to that which is the effect or result of working, and *work*, employed to assert the *act* of working, as, for instance, in the proposition, *These honest men work faithfully*. (8) The marked difference of *function*, and the position in the arrangement of the parts of the proposition, prevent all danger of being deceived by these signs of double meaning.

§ 17. [(1) The names *subject*, *predicate*, and *copula*, which we have used above to indicate the parts of propositions, refer properly to the things signified by the words employed to express these parts —not to the words, or signs themselves. (2) Sometimes, indeed, they are employed to indicate the word or sign, as well as that which it expresses. Or rather the terms *subject* and *predicate* are employed in an ambiguous manner to express both at once, neglecting the discrimination between the sign and the thing signified. Such employment of these terms naturally leads to confusion of thought. We require for the purposes of grammatical analysis such names for the classes of words, as shall indicate with precision that we intend to refer to the *signs* or words themselves, and not to the things signified by these words.]

(3) Grammarians have called that class of words which expresses the subjects of propositions, NOUNS—that is, NAMES. [(4) *Noun* (*nom*), is a term borrowed from the French language, in which it means simply *name*. The grammars of many languages

---

Answer. No; they "are essentially distinct," &c. (6) Do words the same, as to sound, sometimes perform both *functions*? (7) Illustrate by examples. (8) What prevents the danger of being deceived by these signs of double meaning?

§ 17. [(1) To what do the names Subject, Predicate, and Copula properly refer? (2) Why are other names necessary for the classes of words which express the several parts of Propositions?]

(3) What name have grammarians given to the class of words which expresses the subjects of Propositions? [(4) Tell the origin and explain the meaning of the term NOUN.]

indicate this class of words by the term which in those languages signifies *name.* It would perhaps conduce to perspicuity, if we also called this class of words by our own plain English term NAMES. But long usage has given a kind of prescriptive right to the term *noun.*] (5) Sometimes the Grammarians call them SUBSTANTIVE NOUNS, to distinguish them from another class of nouns, which is not used to express the *subjects* of propositions. We shall call them simply *nouns*, and sometimes substantives, employing these terms (perhaps improperly), like most of the Grammarians of the present day, as of equivalent meaning.

§ 18. (1) Those words which are used to express assertion, or to represent the copula and the predicate, in whole or in part, are called by the Grammarians VERBS. (2) VERB is a term derived, like most of our grammatical terms, from the Latin language, and means WORD. This name is intended to indicate that the kind of sign to which it is applied is pre-eminently THE WORD (*a*).

As *verbs* are employed always in assertive propositions only for the purpose of expressing the assertive part, we may in our analysis of propositions designate them simply by their name—*verbs.* But as nouns perform a variety of functions in the construction of propositions (3), whenever a noun is employed as *subject*, or *leading part* (*nucleus*) *of the subject* of a proposition, we shall call it the SUBJECT NOUN, to distinguish it from nouns employed for other purposes. (4) In writing the analysis of a proposition, it will be convenient to express the word *subject* by the abbreviation or symbol *S.; subject noun* by the abbreviation *S. N.*, *verb* by *V.*, and *predicate* and *copula*, when we have occasion to use them in written exercises, by *P.* and *C.*

The pupil should now learn to point out the *subject noun* and the *verb* in the assertive propositions contained in any of the exercises given in the subsequent pages, or in his reading book. Let this exercise be continued with pupils beginning the study of grammar, till

NOTE (*a*). The old grammarians gave the name *verb* to this class of words, because the force and energy of every assertion—of all discourse—is contained in the *assertive word.* "*Videlicet quod in* VERBIS *vim sermonis* * * * * * * * * *esse judicaverunt.*"—Quintilian, I: 4: 18.

---

(5) By what other name are nouns sometimes called?

§ 18. (1) What name is given to the class of words which expresses assertion?

(2) What does the term VERB mean, and what does it indicate in reference to the class of signs to which it has been applied by the ancient grammarians?

they can, without hesitation, indicate the *subject noun* and the *verb* in each proposition. When these parts of a proposition can be promptly discovered, the first step (and the most important step of all) in grammar is fairly accomplished—a step essential to all satisfactory progress, and which prepares the way for every step that follows. After having spent months—sometimes, after having spent years—in attempting to learn grammar, young pupils do not succeed in accomplishing so much as this. Yet we hope that every intelligent pupil will be surprised to find this important step so easily made by the method here recommended, and under the guidance of a skilful and persevering instructor.

§ 19. (1) *Nouns* and *verbs* are, in all respects, by far the most important classes of words in every language. (2) As we have already seen, they serve to constitute a considerable number of complete propositions, without the assistance of any other kind of words. But this is not all. They enter as the essential parts into every proposition, which we use in discourse. They form, as it were, the framework on which all propositions are built. No proposition can be formed without a *subject noun* (or what for the time performs the function of a subject noun), and a *verb* expressed or implied. (3) The first things, therefore, to be sought in the analysis of every proposition, are the *verb* and the *subject noun*. (4) In fact, all the words employed in constructing even the most complicated propositions, are either 1st, *The subject noun*, or *the verb*; or, 2nd, Words designed to *modify*, *limit*, *explain* either the subject noun or the verb—that is, to *complete* the subject and predicate respectively; or, 3d, Words employed to *connect* propositions with one another; and this also, most frequently, for the same purpose of completing the subject or the predicate of the proposition, with which the attached proposition is united by these connective words. More briefly, if we except connectives employed to unite independent propositions, *all discourse*, so far as it consists of propositions, *is made up of nouns and verbs, and the words which are employed to*

---

(3) How is a noun distinguished when employed as *subject* or leading part of the subject of a proposition? (4) By what abbreviations are *subject*, *subject noun*, *verb*, *predicate* and *copula* to be represented respectively in written analyses?

§ 19. (1) What is said of the importance of nouns and verbs compared with other classes of words? (2) Tell what is said to illustrate the importance of *nouns* and *verbs*. (3) What are the first things to be sought in the analysis of a proposition? (4) For what purposes

modify nouns and verbs. (5) It will be found presently that nouns not only perform the function of expressing the subjects, or leading part of the subjects of propositions, but are also largely employed for the purpose of *modifying* or *completing* the subjects and the predicates of propositions. (6) When, in addition to this, we consider that the *verb* is the predicate with an assumed *assertive* form, and that the predicate itself is a noun of a particular kind (see § 27), we may judge how largely nouns figure in the formation of propositions, and (what is nearly the same thing) in constituting discourse.

To present the names and definitions of all the parts of speech to the young learner at this stage of his progress, appears to us injudicious, and is inconsistent with our plan. These strange names and definitions cannot but appear unmeaning and repulsive till the want of them is felt, till the pupil has occasion to employ them to facilitate his progress. To burden the memory with unknown terms, and definitions as yet incomprehensible, is needlessly to render the study of grammar disgusting to the youthful mind. In conformity with these views, we shall confine our attention, for some time to come, exclusively to the two important classes of words already presented—the *nouns* and the *verbs.*

The *noun* we proceed to consider first, and for the present, only in its *main function* of *subject noun.* The *manner of distinguishing nouns from other words; the classification of nouns* so far as it appears important for grammatical purposes; and the *modifications of form to which they are subjected,* whilst employed as *subject nouns,* must come briefly under our notice. Our attention must also be incidentally directed to another class of words serving to modify nouns, namely, *determinative adjectives,* as without reference to these, some of the peculiar uses of nouns cannot be fully explained. For more extended discussion of these points, we must refer the reader to § 91; and *Additional Observations on Determinative Adjectives,* § 158.

---

are other words, besides the *subject noun* and *verb*, employed in propositions? (5) What other functions do *nouns* perform in the construction of propositions besides that of *subject noun?* (6) Is the noun, besides this, a constituent part of *verbs?* Yes; all verbs may be considered as nouns (of a particular class) with an assertive form.]

CHAPTER II.

OF NOUNS.

DEFINITION OF NOUNS.—CLASSIFICATION OF NOUNS.—MODIFICATION OF THE FORM OF THE SUBJECT NOUN TO EXPRESS PLURALITY.

§ 20. [(1) A *complete* definition of nouns ought to embrace all the functions which they perform in discourse. (2) But as a full definition of this sort would be unmanageable in practice on account of its length, we substitute for the present one embracing only the great distinguishing function of nouns. This definition follows naturally, and will be easily understood from what we have said in the preceding chapter.]

(3) *Nouns are words which express the subjects of propositions.* Any single word which, without another sign implied, customarily serves to represent the subject, or the *leading part* of the subject of a proposition, is to be classed as a *noun.* (4) This definition will include all *names* of persons, places, things, notions or conceptions of the human mind, of which we ever have occasion to make an assertion—to say any thing. (5) When words, not commonly used or recognized as nouns, serve to express the subjects of propositions, they are said to be employed *substantively;* they perform on such occasions the functions of nouns. Whatever may be their more common use, and their generally received name and classification, they are, *for the time, nouns,* and, in the analysis of language, must be considered and treated as nouns. (6) A *phrase* or an entire proposition sometimes serves as the subject of another proposition, and is then said to be used *substantively*—that is, em-

---

§ 20. [(1) What should a complete definition of nouns embrace? (2) State the objection to a complete definition.]

(3) Give a definition embracing the main function of nouns. (4) What will this definition include? (5) What is meant by words *employed substantively?*

(6) What is meant by a phrase, or a proposition being used substantively?

ployed as a *noun*. (7) For example, To SEE THE SUN *is pleasant.* The subject of this proposition is the phrase, "*To see the sun.*" *Being pleasant* is asserted of that which this phrase expresses. Again, in the proposition, *That vanity is ridiculous is generally admitted,* the subject of the main proposition is, "*Vanity is ridiculous,*" which words themselves form a complete proposition, because they contain an assertion.

(8) It will be observed that we have here used the term *phrase,* to designate a regularly arranged combination of words, which does not constitute a complete proposition, or express an assertion. We may sometimes find occasion to use this term again, in the same sense.

§ 21. In making the assertion that all words, which, singly employed, express the subject of an assertion, are nouns, we contemplate words only, as used for the proper purpose which they are designed to serve in language, namely, as *signs of thought.* Every word whatever, or even any syllable or letter of a word, when employed merely to indicate the spoken or written *sign* itself, and not that which it usually signifies, may serve as the subject of a proposition. Thus we may say of the verb *think* considered merely as a *vocable* or *word, Think is a verb; think is a word of one syllable; think is a word expressed in writing by five letters,* &c. But the word *think,* employed *alone,* and as *significant of what it usually indicates,* cannot be made the subject noun of any proposition. We can neither say that *think* (with its proper significance) *is,* or that *think does* any thing.*

When a word is used in grammatical and philological discussions,

* We have used the limitation, "*employed alone,*" because, if we place the little particle *to* before *think,* it becomes what we shall call a *verbal noun,* and may be used as the subject, or leading part of the subject, of an assertive proposition; as, *To think correctly is a rare accomplishment.* Here, *To think correctly* is the subject of the proposition, and *To think* the leading part of the subject, to which "correctly" is superadded as a modification. Again, a proposition, of which *think* is the verb, might be employed as subject of another proposition; as, *That William thinks his brother to be wrong,* is well known to his intimate friends. Here the proposition, "*William thinks his brother to be wrong,*" is used *substantively,* and, as subject of the assertion, "*is well known to his intimate friends.*"

(7) Give examples.
(8) What is the difference between a phrase and a proposition?

not as the sign of the conception which it usually indicates, but, as above, to represent the sign or word itself, it is said to be taken or employed *materialiter* or technically. Employed in this way, every word becomes for the time a *noun*, that is, the name of itself, the name of the uttered or written sign, not of that which it has been invented to represent.

We are not to be understood as asserting universally that every single word, entitled to the name of *noun*, is capable of serving as the *subject noun* of a proposition. A word which performs any of the *functions* (to be enumerated hereafter) peculiar to *nouns*, must be classed among nouns. For example, we would class the word *while* among nouns (though in modern English it is never used, and could not now with propriety be used, as the *subject noun* of a proposition), because it manifestly performs the function of a noun in completing the predicates of certain propositions: as, He remained *a while*, I will come after *a while*, &c. When a *subject noun*, of the same meaning with *while*, is wanted, we employ the word *time*. That *while* serves not as a *subject noun*, is to be attributed to a rare accident in language.

A full definition of nouns, as we have already said, ought to embrace all the functions which they perform in discourse. The defini tion above given we do not offer as complete, but as *sufficient* for the learner's guidance in distinguishing nouns. There are very few nouns, indeed, which cannot be readily ascertained to be such by the *test* we have adopted; and if they cannot, it is only because, like the word *while*, they have fallen into disuse in their prominent function of serving as *subjects* of propositions, and, in this respect, have given place to some more modern term.

§ 22. When the learner meets a word manifestly intended to express the subject of an assertion, or the leading part of the subject—that part which all the words making up the complete subject regard, modify, limit or describe—he can have no room to doubt what he should call it. It is a *noun*, or a word or combination of words, for the time used as a noun. Whether a word, employed for a different purpose from that of subject noun, is a noun, may be readily ascertained, in nearly all cases, by trying whether it can *serve* as the subject noun of a proposition, or, in other words, by trying whether an assertion can be made in regard to that which it expresses—whether it can be said of it, that it *is*, or *is not* something, or that it *does*, or *does not do* something.*

---

* A practical rule, commonly given for the purpose of distinguishing

The rule to determine whether a word is to be classed among nouns may be given in the following brief form: (1) *Every word which, alone and without any word implied, expresses what can be made the subject or leading part of the subject of a proposition or assertion, is a* NOUN.*

EXERCISE.—Let the learner point out the nouns in the following passage, and show that the test given in the above rule applies to each of them:—

"Columbus was not ignorant of the mutinous disposition of his crew, but he still maintained a serene and steady countenance; soothing some with gentle words; endeavoring to stimulate the pride or avarice of others, and openly menacing the refractory with signal punishment, should they do any thing to impede the voyage."

MODEL OF EXAMINATION.—Point out the first noun in this passage. Ans. *Columbus.*—How do you ascertain that Columbus is a noun? Ans. From the fact that it expresses the subject of the proposition, "*Columbus was not ignorant*," &c.—Point out the next noun in the passage. Ans. "Disposition."—Why class this as a noun? Ans. Because it will serve to express the leading part of the subject, or, in other words, serves as subject noun, for example, in the following proposition, *The disposition of his crew was mutinous.* "*Crew*" is a noun; we can say, *The crew was mutinous*, &c. In the next proposition, *He*

---

nouns, is, to try whether they will make sense when united with a determinative or descriptive adjective—classes of words which we shall come to consider hereafter—in other words, to try whether they admit of being *modified* by these classes of words. This rule, besides the objection that it is indirect and mechanical, fails in regard of at least one large class of words now recognized by the best grammarians as nouns, viz., those words which have usually been called the *infinitives of verbs;* and it applies very clumsily to many proper names of persons, places, &c. It will exercise the rational powers of the learner to much better purpose to apply the *test, Is this word the subject noun of the proposition which I am analyzing, or,* if not, *can it* (stripped, if necessary, of case ending or inflexion) *be made the subject noun of some other proposition*—that is, *can any thing be asserted of it?*

* The learner will find afterward that for some purposes nouns take certain inflexions, of which they must be stripped before they can serve as subject nouns. This fact will, in the end, present little difficulty, and it is unnecessary, at this point of our progress, to perplex the pupil by embracing it in our rule.

---

§ 22 (1) Repeat the rule to determine whether a given word is a *noun.*

is a noun, according to our definition (and may be so called till the learner finds a special name for it), because it expresses the subject of the proposition, "He still maintained a serene and steady countenance." The word "*his*" in the preceding proposition may be passed over for the present, though, if an inflected form of *he*, it has claims to be classed as a noun.

§ 23. Classification of Nouns.—Some knowledge of the *classification* of nouns is necessary in order to comprehend certain modifications, of which they are susceptible, by a change of form, or by the addition of other words, to fit them to express the various subjects of human thought. But it may be useful, thus early, to dwell longer on the *classification* of nouns, than would be absolutely necessary for the purpose mentioned, because, next to a careful application of the *test* already given, a review of the several kinds of nouns will, more than any thing else, assist the young learner in distinguishing readily this important class of words. Besides, it is requisite for other reasons connected with our method of treating grammar to give in this place more extended notice to some of the classes which we shall designate.

§ 24. First Class: Concrete Nouns, or Names of Substances.—(1) The names of *substances*, material and immaterial, constitute the most prominent class of nouns. (2) We use the word substance here in the philosophical sense to indicate what *subsists by itself*—what has, or is conceived to have, *an independent existence.* (3) This class includes the names of all persons, animals, places, of all the objects around us in the universe, whether formed by our Creator, or by the skill, industry, and contrivance of man—in a word, every thing which appears to our senses as a separate independent object of contemplation, or which is conceived by the mind as such, as God, angels, souls of men, &c. (4) These are called *concrete nouns*, or *names of substances.*

Exercise I.—Let the pupil point out the *concrete nouns*, or *names of substances* in the following extract:—

"On the right, amid a profusion of thickets, knolls, and crags, lay the bed of a broad mountain lake, lightly curled into tiny waves by the breath of the morning breeze, each glittering in its course under

§ 24. (1) What words constitute the most prominent class of nouns? (2) In what sense is the word *substance* here used, and what does it mean or indicate? (3) Enumerate some of the kinds of names which belong to this class. (4) What is the name given to this class of nouns?

the influence of the sunbeams. High hills, rocks, and banks waving with natural forests of birch and oak, formed the borders of this enchanting sheet of water; and, as their leaves rustled in the wind, and twinkled in the sun, gave to the depth of solitude a sort of life and vivacity."

EXERCISE II.—Let the pupil write a given number of examples of concrete nouns. This exercise, in the case of young pupils, may, with advantage, be often repeated. Each time it may be prescribed to give a number of examples from one subdivision of these names. 1st, names of persons; 2d, names of animals; 3d, names of places; 4th, names of things of natural production, as minerals, plants, &c.; 5th, names of things of artificial production; 6th, names of spiritual, or immaterial substances.

§ 25. COLLECTIVE NOUNS.—What are called *collective nouns* may be regarded (1) as a peculiar subdivision of the *names of substances.* (2) The *collectives* claim our notice, because some of them are occasionally so employed as to give rise to certain peculiarities of construction, as we shall find hereafter; (§ 56, rule II.) (3) They are called *collectives,* because they express an *assemblage* of objects contemplated by the mind as forming a single conception, and capable of being embraced collectively under the same assertion. The individual objects which form such assemblages are contemplated as united together by some common bond, or for some common purpose, and we appropriate to them, as thus united, a collective name. (4) We have examples in the words, *army,* meaning an *organized collection of soldiers; navy,* a *collection of ships and seamen; society, party, parliament, congress, council, mob, group, crowd, horde, host,* &c.

EXERCISE.—Let the pupil give a written list of collective nouns.

§ 26. (1) SECOND CLASS: ABSTRACT NOUNS.—The names given to *qualities, properties,* or *attributes,* ABSTRACTLY considered; that is, considered separately from the substances, or objects in which they are found, constitute a *second class* of nouns very distinct from the former. (2) Some of these qualities, or properties, are perceived by the

---

§ 25. (1) How may collective nouns be regarded? (2) Why does this subdivision of nouns claim a share of our notice? (3) Why are these nouns called collectives? (4) Give examples of collective nouns.

§ 26. (1) What words constitute the *second class* of nouns? (2) Recite the illustra-

senses, as, for example, the properties of external bodies—*hardness*, *softness*, the various *colors*, &c. Others are made known to us by the help of an intellectual process, as, for example, the various properties or attributes of human minds—*emotions*, *passions*, *feelings*, *affections*, *virtues*, *vices*, &c. These attributes or properties, whether of matter or of mind, have obviously no *independent existence*. They all subsist only in connection with substances, and, apart from these, they have no real being. (3) But we often find it convenient to contemplate these properties separately, or *abstracted* from the substances in which they exist, and to discourse of them as thus viewed. Hence we give them names, and express our thoughts of them in propositions, in the same manner as we do of substances. (4) To distinguish this class of names from the names of *substances*, they are commonly called ABSTRACT NOUNS. Or they may be called NAMES OF ATTRIBUTES; that is, of those qualities or properties which we *attribute* to *substances*.

EXERCISE I.—Point out the nouns in the following sentences, and distinguish the *abstract names* from the *names of substances*:—

"Whatever promotes and strengthens virtue, whatever calms and regulates the temper, is a source of happiness. Devotion produces these effects in a remarkable degree. It inspires composure of spirit, mildness and benignity; weakens the painful, and cherishes the pleasing emotions; and, by these means, carries on the life of a pious man in a smooth and placid tenor"

The pupil will call "whatever" a noun, since it expresses the subject of several propositions in the beginning of this passage, but he need not give himself any trouble for the present to determine to what class of nouns it belongs.

EXERCISES II. III., &c.—Write out a given number of *abstract nouns*. 1st. Names of *sensible* or *external* attributes. 2d. Names of *spiritual* or *mental* attributes, or such as are perceived by the help of an intellectual process.

§ 27. (1) VERBAL NOUNS.—What are called *verbal nouns* may be considered as a peculiar subdivision of abstract nouns, or names

---

tions and examples given above and suggest others. (3) Account for the formation of this class of nouns. (4) By what names are they called?

§ 27. (1) How may *verbal nouns* be considered?

of attributes subjectively employed.* (2) These are called *verbals*, because they express *substantively*, or *subjectively*, that which is expressed assertively by their kindred verbs.

The name verbal seems intended to imply that these nouns are derived from verbs. But, on the contrary, *verbs themselves* may, with more propriety, be considered as these (so called) *verbal nouns* with an assumed assertive form. "A verb is a noun and something more." It is a noun with an indication of assertion superadded. This indication is usually expressed by the *form* of the verb in most languages; but in English for want of verbal terminations, or, rather, through disuse of those formerly employed, we are often left to determine from the construction whether a word is assertively used or not—that is, whether it is a verb or not. It is easy, however, to distinguish the verbal nouns we are now considering from the verb. The one is generally marked by its prefixed particle *to*, and when this is omitted, as after certain verbs (chiefly those called auxiliary), its relation to these verbs prevents all mistake; the other verbal is distinguished by its invariable termination *ing* from the verb, though not from the verbal adjective or participle.

(3) We have in the English language two of these *verbals* for every verb, with the exception of four or five very peculiar verbs of the class called auxiliary verbs—*may*, *can*, *shall*, *must*. These and *will* in its auxiliary sense have no correspondent *verbals*.

(4) One of these verbals consists of what is called the *root*, or *radical form* of the verb, generally, with the particle *to* prefixed. The other consists of the radical form with the termination *ing* affixed. For example, from the *root read* we have the two *verbals*, *to read* and *reading*; from *print*, *to print* and *printing*. (5) When

* That is, if *being* and *acting* are to be admitted among properties or attributes of things *substantial*. If not, the *verbals* are entitled to be admitted as a separate class. But whether we regard them as a subdivision of *abstract nouns*, or as a distinct class, they claim the particular attention of the learner on account of the peculiar modes of expression and forms of construction which arise from their use in language.

---

(2) Why is this class of words called *verbals*?

(3) How many *verbal nouns* are connected with each verb? (4) Describe these *verbals* and give examples. (5) Notice the exception in forming the *written* verbal in *ing*.

the written radical form of the verb ends in an *e* mute (that is, not sounded), this *e* is omitted before the termination *ing*.

(6) The form consisting of the *root* with the particle *to* prefixed, is commonly called the infinitive mode of the verb. (7) But it cannot be classed as a verb, consistently with the definition already given, since it does not express assertion. (8) On the contrary, it is always employed to perform the function of a noun—sometimes that of a *subject noun*, most frequently that of *modifying* or *completing* a *verb*. (9) In performing this latter function after some few verbs (mostly *auxiliaries*), the particle *to* is omitted, and the bare *root* employed; as, *he can* READ=*he is able* TO READ. *He must go; men dare* UNDERTAKE, &c.,=*men dare* TO UNDERTAKE. (10) As this class of words has been so long known by the name of *infinitives of verbs*, we shall continue to call them *infinitives*, whenever we have occasion to distinguish them from other nouns; but by so doing we must not be understood as admitting them to be *verbs*.

(11) The verbal in ING (as we have remarked in § 14: 5),* very exactly expresses in English that which is predicated—that part of the predicate, which is contained in the kindred verb. (12) For example, *John writes*. What is asserted of John in this proposition, is precisely that *action*, which is expressed by the noun *writing*. In other words, writing expresses a well-known act *substantively*, or *subjectively*—that is, in the form to be employed as the *subject* of an *assertion*. *Writes* expresses the same act assertively. (13) In many languages the *infinitives* express precisely in a *substantive*, or *subjective* form, that which is expressed assertively

* The first number, when we use two numbers in a reference, is the number of the section, and the second is the number intended to direct the learner to the answers of the subjoined questions. We may find it convenient to use these numbers, sometimes, to refer more exactly to the part of the section which explains any point under consideration.

(6) By what name is the first of these two verbals called? (7) State the objection to classing it as a verb. (8) What functions does it perform? (9) Is it always preceded by the particle *to*? Mention exceptions. Give examples. (10) When we call this class of verbals *infinitives*, do we admit them to be verbs? (11) What does the *verbal* in ING express? (12) Give example and illustrate. (13) What do the Infinitives of many languages

by the verb. (14) The verbal in ING, employed as *subject noun* of a proposition, sometimes admits of being interchanged with the infinitive; as, SEEING *the sun is pleasant*, or TO SEE *the sun is pleasant*. (15) With this exception, these *verbals* generally perform distinct functions (as we shall see hereafter), and the one cannot (with propriety) be substituted for the other. (16) The verbal in *ing* is sometimes called the *gerund*. This is the name given to a form of like use and signification in the Latin language, and it may sometimes be conveniently employed to distinguish this class of verbals, as the term *infinitives* is used to distinguish the other.

(17) These verbals differ from other nouns, in being capable of taking the same forms of complements, or the same kinds of words to modify them as their kindred verbs. This fact will be considered and accounted for in treating of complements or modifications. (See § 76 : 32, et seq.)

(18) There are sometimes other nouns formed from the verbs, or perhaps we should rather say in most cases from these verbals, which might from their connection with verbs be also called verbal nouns. Both verbs and verbals sometimes originate from a noun that has nothing to do in its proper sense with the expression of action; as from the *noun eye*, we have the *verb to eye*, from *hand to hand*, &c. But such nouns are in no sense *verbals*. We only call those verbals which express in some form the action of their kindred verbs. For example, *act*, *actor*, *action*, *agent*, all connected with the *verbal to act* in form, and borrowing an essential part of their significance from it; and *command*, *commandment*, *commander*, connected with the *verbal to command*. It is not, however, necessary to form verbals of this kind into a distinct class, or to give them any special notice, as there is nothing peculiar in their grammatical functions, and as all grammarians agree in arranging them among the nouns.

(19) It may also be observed, to guard against mistakes, that

---

express? (14) Can verbals in ING and infinitives be interchanged, or substituted for each other, and, if so, under what circumstances? (15) Can the one *verbal* be generally substituted for the other? (16) By what name is the verbal in *ing* sometimes called?

(17) What peculiarity distinguishes these *verbals* from other nouns?

(18) Are there other verbals besides the *infinitives* and *gerunds*? Tell what is said of them, and give examples.

(19) Are all nouns formed by the union of the roots of verbs with the termination *ing* to

all nouns made by the union of the roots of verbs and the termination *ing*, do not belong to the class of *verbals* in *ing* or *gerunds*, though exactly agreeing with them in form. *Concrete* nouns are sometimes formed by adding *ing* to the root of the verb, as *building*, a something built; altogether distinct in meaning from the *gerund building*, the act asserted by the verb *build;* in the same manner many of these words in *ing* are used both as verbals and in another and often a concrete sense; for example, *lodging*, *beginning*, *painting*, &c. Let it be remembered that the *verbals*, which alone merit special attention on account of their peculiar relation to the verbs in *meaning* and in the *modifications* which they admit in common, are those which express that *substantively* which the verbs express *assertively*.

(20) Care must also be taken to distinguish these verbal nouns in *ing* from the verbal adjectives or participles which in modern English agree with them in form.

NOTE.—The forms were originally distinct in our language, as the corresponding forms are still in the sister dialects. The *verbal* is not the participle usurped substantively, as most grammarians have incorrectly asserted. The *verbal nouns* had a place in the language in their present form—ending in ING or UNG centuries before verbal adjectives or participles had assumed or *borrowed* this ending.

The present, or rather *imperfect* participle, in Anglo-Saxon terminates in *ende*, and the termination *ende* or *end*, more frequently written *ande* or *and*, was retained in old English, and consequently the distinction in form between these participles and the verbal nouns in *ing* till near the times of Wiclif and Chaucer. Participles in *and* occur in authors who wrote in the northern parts of Britain till a much later period. We subjoin examples from an old *gloss* which we find quoted in *Bagster's Hexapla*, p. 7: "And he prechyde *sayande*, a stalworther thane I schal come efter me, of whom I am not worthi *downfallande* or *kneelande*," &c. "And pleside to Harowde, and also to the *sittande* at mete," &c. Observe that in the last quotation the participle *sittande* is employed substantively to mean the *persons sitting* at meat. If our nouns in *ing* had been, as supposed by the gram-

---

be classed as *gerunds?* Tell what is said of other nouns so formed, and how the *gerund* may be distinguished from them.

(20) What other class of words has assumed the same form with the *gerunds*, and how are the *gerunds* to be distinguished from these?

marians, participles used substantively, this, of which we have here an example, must have been their use, viz., to indicate, not the abstract action of the verb, as they in fact do, but, as here, the agent or actor. This is invariably the use of the corresponding participle, employed substantively in all other languages. We select from Mr. R. Taylor, to whom we are indebted for a complete elucidation of this matter, a few examples in which the verbal noun and the participle both occur in their distinct forms:

"——— Such thyngis that are lik*and*
Tyll mannys her*yng* are ples*and*."—Barb. Bruce (1357), b. 1, l. 9.

"Hors, or hund, or othir thing,
That war ples*and* to thar lik*ing*."—Barb. Bruce, l. 207.

"Full low inclin*and* to their queen full clear,
Whom for their noble nourish*ing* they thank."—Dunbar.

See more examples, and a full and (to me) satisfactory exposition of this matter in Mr. Taylor's valuable additional notes to the Diversions of Purley.—*T. Tegg*, *Lond.* 1840.

The learner will distinguish the *verbal noun* from the *verbal adjective*, by the test given above (§ 20: 3), and from the other nouns in *ing*, by attending to the remarks we have just been making on these nouns.

Exercise I.—Let the learner distinguish the *gerunds* from the other nouns in *ing*, and from the *verbal adjectives* in the following sentences. To assist in distinguishing the nouns from the verbal adjectives, we use the former only in their function of subject nouns. If, therefore, the word in *ing* is *subject* or main part of the subject of the proposition, it is a noun (whether *gerund* or not remains for the pupil to determine); if, on the contrary, some other word is the main part of the subject, the word in *ing* is a *verbal adjective*. When the word in *ing* can take an *infinitive* as a substitute, it is a *gerund*.

This writing is blotted. The boy writing to his father told him, &c. Writing is a fatiguing employment. The beginning of the exercise is better than the end. Beginning a good course requires effort. Telling falsehoods is mean. Speaking the truth is commendable. The man saying this departs. Saying and doing are very different things. This saying is hard. Loving our enemies is a difficult duty. Reading is less laborious than writing. Wasting time is as bad as wasting money. Giving is sometimes easier than forgiving; and forgiving is easier than forgetting.

In going through the preceding exercise, it will be proper

to point out the verb first in each proposition, and next the *subject noun.* Next show to which class the word ending in *ing* belongs.

MODEL.—"This writing is blotted." Which is the verb, or assertive word? Ans. *Is.* Which is the *subject noun?* Ans. "*Writing*," because it is about *writing* that the assertion in the proposition is made. Is writing here the *gerund?* Ans. No; because it does not mean the action writing, but something that is written. It is here a *concrete noun* or name of a substance. Observe that several of the propositions at the end are double propositions, one of the verbs being suppressed. "Reading is less laborious than writing." Supply *is* after *writing;* and so of the rest.

EXERCISE II.—Point out, or rather write out all the *infinitives* and *gerunds* in a given portion of any book used by the pupil or by a class of pupils.

EXERCISE III.—Form a given number of propositions with *infinitives* or *gerunds* for their *subjects.* Let the learner continue these exercises till he becomes perfectly familiar with this class of words.

§ 28. THIRD CLASS: PRONOUNS. (1) Another class of words comes under our definition of *nouns* (that is, of words which serve to express the subjects or leading parts of the subjects of propositions), which, because of their peculiar function in language, have been generally treated as a distinct *part of speech.* Some have called them, very appropriately, *nouns of the second order;* but they are commonly known by the name of PRONOUNS. (2) This class of words, as the name indicates (*pro-noun*=to the English *for-noun*), is employed for nouns; that is, to represent nouns, or names. [(3) Let it be remembered that all the nouns, hitherto noticed, are the representatives, or signs of things existing in nature, or conceived by the mind as existing in nature. (4) These *nouns,* or *names,* are so associated with the *things, classes of things, substances,* attributes, existences, &c., which they represent, that, when uttered, they serve to recall them to the minds of those who understand the particular language to which these names belong. (5) The *pronouns,* on the

§ 28. (1) What is said of a third class of words, which come under our definition of nouns; and what have they been commonly called? (2) Tell what the name *pronoun* signifies, and the purpose for which this class of words is employed? [(3) Of what are the *nouns* hitherto noticed the signs? (4) What is said in illustration of the connection between these *nouns* and what they represent? (5) Of what are pronouns the representa-

contrary, are only the *representatives* of *nouns*, not the direct *signs of things*. (6) As the same *pronoun* may be used to represent an unlimited number of *nouns*, that is, the *names* of an unlimited variety of things, the *pronouns* are not associated in the memory, by the use of language, with any objects or classes of objects exclusively, but are used to represent the names, now of one, now of another object, or class of objects. (7) Thus every man employs the pronoun *I* to represent his own name—to indicate himself, when he has occasion to express any assertion of which he is the subject. We use *thou* or *you* to represent any individual whom we address. Thus *I* is employed to represent the unlimited number of individuals who may have occasion to speak of themselves; and *thou* or *you* to represent the unlimited number of persons, to whom others may have occasion to address any assertion having the person or persons addressed for its *subject*. *He*, again, represents the names of all beings in the universe recognised as *males*, when (not addressed, but) spoken of individually to others; *she* the names of all the *females;* and *it* all objects that are not recognised as either *male* or *female*. So that these three little words, *he*, *she*, *it*, together, represent the names of all persons and things in the universe singly or individually considered; and the single *pronoun they* represents them all, when assertions are to be made in regard to a number of them taken together.

(8) It follows from this account of the functions of pronouns, that the mind must always refer back from the *pronoun* which represents the person spoken of, to the *noun* which it represents, in order to know what is intended to be designated. (9) When language is skilfully employed, this reference can always be readily made by proper attention to the connection and arrangement of the words in discourse, and to the recognised usages of speech. (10) If on any occasion we cannot determine to what particular noun a pronoun has reference, we fail completely of catching the meaning of the speaker or writer.

---

tives? (6) What farther is said of the pronouns? (7) Illustrate; and tell what the pronouns *I*, *thou* or *you*, *he*, *she*, *it*, and *they*, may severally represent. Divide the question. What does *I* represent? &c.

(8) How do we ascertain what is designated by a pronoun? (9) In what case is the reference of a pronoun readily made, and how is it made? (10) If we fail *altogether* in dis-

(11) If we cannot determine this reference with certainty and with promptitude, we complain justly of obscurity. Our mind, in this case, is diverted from the subject matter of the discourse to the irksome occupation of unravelling the perplexities of the construction—a result fatal to the success of either orator or author, except his matter is possessed of more than common interest, and the hearer or reader possessed of more than common patience. Even then, such obscurity occasions annoyance and waste of time, and sometimes greatly diminishes the effect of sound argument and profound research. (12) Let us here add, that there is nothing in which inexperienced writers more frequently fail, than in securing by a lucid arrangement the certain and easy reference of pronouns of the third person, as they are called, to the *nouns* which they are intended to represent. (13) If a writer wishes to be easily and clearly understood, let him take care never to employ a *pronoun* in such a way, that an intelligent reader can hesitate to decide to what it refers. (14) It is particularly in the use of the pronouns, *he*, *she*, *it*, and *they*, that this precaution is necessary. The other pronouns can scarcely be so employed as to occasion obscurity.]

NOTE.—Much of what is said about the pronouns seems to apply more strictly to what are called the pronouns of the third person—*he*, *she*, *it*, and *they*—than to those of the first and second persons, those which represent the speaker and the party addressed, *I*, *we*, *thou*, *you*. It may even be questioned whether the name *pronoun* (*representative* of noun) can with strict propriety be given to these last. They can scarcely be said either to *stand for nouns* or to *refer to nouns*. They are signs as directly indicating the parties engaged in discourse, as the names of these parties would be: they indicate them more clearly, more explicitly, than their proper names in the circumstances would do. There is no need of a *reference to the names* of the parties in order to understand who is designated. Nay, the names may be unknown, and yet no want of perspicuity be occasioned; as when persons enter into conversation on the road, who do not know each

---

covering the reference of a pronoun, what is the consequence? (11) What is the consequence if we cannot discover it promptly? (12) In what is it alleged that inexperienced writers often fail? (13) Mention the precaution to be observed by a writer, that he may be easily and clearly understood. (14) In reference to what pronouns is this precaution particularly required?]

other's names, nor perhaps wish to know them, or when the author or orator addresses unknown readers or hearers, or, as often happens in our periodicals, when the name of the author and the names of those whom he addresses are mutually unknown. There is then a marked distinction in some respects between these two classes of pronouns—those of the first and second persons, as they are called, and those of the third person. But in this they agree, and in this they are both unlike nouns, that they are not appropriated exclusively to express one object or one class of objects. The pronouns of the first and second persons are made to designate all persons who are for the time speakers or parties addressed, as those of the third designate all persons and things spoken of, exclusive of the speaker and the party addressed. Those of the first and second persons especially, besides expressing the subject, indicate the part which the subject performs in the discourse—a service which could not be performed so readily by the use of the nouns which these pronouns are said to represent; but which they certainly do more than *merely represent.*

(15) The *pronouns* employed as subject *nouns* of propositions, are of two distinct classes, called *personal pronouns*, and *relative pronouns.* Some grammarians have given to this latter class the more appropriate because more characteristic name of *conjunctive pronouns.* We confine our attention for the present to the *personal pronouns.* The *conjunctive pronouns* will come under our notice in a more suitable place, when we shall have occasion to show their use in the construction of compound propositions.

§ 29. The Personal Pronouns.—(1) This class of pronouns is called *personal* because, besides performing the functions of nouns in the subjects of propositions, they indicate the PERSON or *part* which what they represent sustains in discourse.*

* The ancient grammarians seem to have borrowed the term *person* from the language of the stage, in which the players were called the *dramatis personæ, persons* of the drama. (Originally *persona* meant the mask through which the actor spoke, afterwards it was employed also as a name for a player, for him who wore the mask and sustained the character of a party in the drama.) Among the actors a first, second, &c., *persona,*

(15) How many kinds of pronouns are employed as subjects, and by what names are they called?

§ 29. (1) Why are the personal pronouns called by this name?

(2) These performers enacting distinct parts in discourse are, *first*, the *speaker*—in his own name alone, or in his own name, and that of others for whom he undertakes to speak—who is called the FIRST PERSON, as sustaining the *first*, or chief part in discourse; *second*, the *party* (or *parties* when more than one) *addressed*, called the SECOND PERSON, as sustaining the *second part*, or part of hearers in discourse; and, *third*, the *party*, or parties *spoken of* in discourse, when *distinct* from the speaker and the party addressed, called the THIRD PERSON. [(3) Under the first and second persons are included only what are called *persons* in the common modern sense of the word *person*, or what, for the time, are conceived as performing the functions of *persons*, that is, the functions of rational beings using or at least understanding speech; that is, such as alone can sustain a part in discourse. (4) When we speak to animals, they are recognised as sustaining the part of a *second person*, as listening to human discourse, and are, in such cases, addressed by the pronoun of the *second person;* as, "Sing'st thou, sweet Philomel, to me?" (5) The same happens in the use of the figure called personification, when we conceive, or represent insensible objects, as if they possessed reason, and could listen to our discourse. Sometimes such mute objects are represented as performing the part of *speaker* or *first person*. (6) Under the *third person* the grammarians comprehend every class of beings that can become the subject of thought—both persons (properly so called) and things.]

The extension of the term person, in treating of the pronouns of the *third person*, so as to comprehend beings which not only are not by common usage called persons, but excluded from the class of persons, has led to an ambiguous and inconsistent employment of this word by the grammarians. In speaking of *nouns*, and especially of the *personal pronouns*, we are told that all *animals* and *things*, as well as *per-*

---

person or actor, was recognised; and this fact also seems to have been present to the thoughts of the grammarian who first adopted the terms *first person, second person, third person*, in treating of these pronouns.

---

(2) What is the part sustained in discourse by what is called in grammar the FIRST PERSON? What by the SECOND PERSON? What by the THIRD PERSON? [(3) What class of beings alone is generally included under the *first* and *second* persons? (4) Mention an exception. (5) Mention a second apparent exception. (6) What classes of beings are comprehended under the *third person*?]

sons, are of the third *person*, when merely spoken of; manifestly including animals and things in the class of *persons*, as comprehended with them under the *third person*. Again, when it becomes necessary to distinguish the conjunctive pronouns, *who* and *which*, we are told that *who* applies to *persons*, and *which* to *animals* or *inanimate things*, manifestly excluding *animals* and *inanimate things* (in accordance with the commonly received usage of the term) from the class of *persons*. In these two cases the word person is employed in two senses not only different, but strikingly inconsistent. We cannot free ourselves effectually from this inconsistent employment of the term *person*, without a considerable change in the language employed in treating of the persons of nouns, pronouns, and verbs; or, in other words, of the parts which subjects sustain in discourse. A reformed nomenclature is perhaps needed in this, as in some other departments of grammar. Let us, in the mean time, mark and admit the extension beyond its usual and proper sense given to the term *person*, when we speak of the *third person* of *nouns* or *pronouns*, and guard against any confusion of thought which might arise from the ambiguous or inconsistent employment of this term.

§ 30. (1) The *first person*, or *speaker* (when the *subject* of a proposition) is expressed by the pronoun I; or, if he speaks in the name of others, as well as in his own name, by the pronoun WE. *I* serves instead of the speaker's own proper name, and WE instead of the speaker's name and the names of those whom he represents. (2) The *second person*, or the party addressed (when the subject of a proposition), is represented by the pronoun THOU, or YOU, if a single individual; if a number of individuals, by YOU, or YE. (3) THOU, except in addresses to the Deity, and in the *solemn style*, is almost out of use in the English of the present day. The same may be said of YE. (4) The form YOU has come to be universally employed in ordinary discourse, both in addressing an individual and a number of persons, except among the Friends. (5) The *pronoun* of the THIRD PERSON (or party spoken of, exclusive of speaker and hearers), representing a single individual, has three distinct forms, according as the party spoken of is recognised as being of the *male*

---

§ 30. (1) What pronoun represents the *speaker* as subject of a proposition? What pronoun is used when the speaker speaks for others with himself? (2) What are the pronouns of the *second person?* (3) What is said of the use of THOU? (4) What of the employment of YOU? (5) What is said of the pronoun of the *third person?*

sex, or of the *female sex*, or as belonging to the class of *things without sex*, or in which sex is not recognised in the ordinary use of language. (6) HE is employed in speaking of an *individual male*, SHE of an individual female, and IT in speaking of things without life, and of animals when we do not know or do not choose to mark the sex. (7) When we speak of more than one individual THEY is employed, as *subject noun*, to represent all classes of beings—persons, animals, and things, without distinction.

(8) We may notice here the classification of nouns on the basis of the distinction of the two sexes, and of the absence or non-recognition of sex, commonly called by grammarians the GENDERS of NOUNS. (9) The word *gender* (*genus*) means, simply, kind or class. (10) In English we have three *genders*, that is, *three kinds* of nouns in reference to sex: 1st, all males recognised as such in ordinary discourse (as God, angels, men, the male heathen deities, and the males of the nobler, and of the more conspicuous and best known animals), are arranged in the MASCULINE GENDER, or *class of males;* 2d, all females (as women, goddesses, and the more conspicuous female animals), are, in like manner, arranged in the FEMININE GENDER, or class of females; and, 3d, all things without animal life, or in which sex, in the ordinary usage of language is not recognised, are arranged under the NEUTER (or *neither*) *gender*, that is, the class which is *neither* male nor female. (11) This classification is of little use in English, save in reference to the employment of the pronouns of the third person, HE, SHE, and IT, and some words of their family. (12) *He*, as will be seen from what is said above, represents nouns of the *masculine gender*, and may be called the *masculine pronoun;* *she*, in like manner, represents nouns of the *feminine gender*, and may be called the *feminine pronoun;* and *it* represents *neuter nouns*, and may be called the *neuter pronoun*. (See § 157.)

---

(6) What pronoun represents an individual *male* in the *third person?* What represents a female in like manner? What represents individually or singly things without life, and animals in which the sex is not known or not regarded in language? (7) For what purpose is the pronoun THEY employed?

(8) What is said of the classification of nouns called the GENDERS? (9) What does the term *gender* mean? (10) Describe this classification, as regards our language. (11) Is this classification of much importance in English? (12) Tell what *gender* or class each of the pronouns *she, he, it*, represents.

(13) The learner will please remember that in all *propositions*, *I* and *we* alone are used to represent the first person or speaker, singular and plural. Thou or you, alone to represent the second person or party addressed, singular or plural. (14) Nouns are never used to express the subjects of assertions in reference to these parties. (15) But in making assertions of parties distinct from the speaker and the party addressed, we use either the noun—the *name* of the *person* or *persons*, the *thing* or *things* spoken of—or we can use their representatives, the pronouns *he*, *she*, *it*, and *they* (when no obscurity is occasioned), as *subject nouns* of propositions. (16) From this it follows that all nouns *employed as the subjects of propositions* are to be classed under the third person; they are only used to express parties merely spoken of.

(17) There is another pronoun of the *third person* which we must notice here; namely, the word *one*. This word seems to be the French *on*, borrowed, likely, from the *Normans*. It is used to represent an *indefinite* third person, and can scarcely be said to be the representative of a name, but rather of that which is *nameless*. ONE *thinks*=any person thinks. (See § 155 : 25.)

EXERCISES ON THE PERSONAL PRONOUNS.—I. Analyze the following propositions: I think. We live. Thou standest. You run. He sleeps. She learns. It decays. They work. We prosper. He plays. I study. It snows. Man toils, he suffers, &c.

MODEL OF ANALYSIS.—Example: "*We live.*" Point out the verb in this proposition. Ans. The word "*live.*" Why do you call "*live*" a verb? Ans. Because it is the assertive word of the proposition. What is the *subject* of this proposition? Ans. The word "*we.*" What do you mean by the subject of a proposition? Ans. The subject is that of which the assertion contained in the proposition is made. What kind of word is "*we*"? Ans. A *noun* of the *second order*, or a *personal pronoun* of the *first person*. What is meant by a *pronoun* or *noun* of the *second order?* Ans. A word

---

(13) What words are always used in propositions to represent the speaker and the party or parties addressed? (14) Are nouns ever employed for this purpose? (15) What *subject nouns* are employed in propositions having reference to parties distinct from speaker and hearer? (16) Under what person then are all nouns *employed as subjects of propositions* to be classed?

(17) Repeat what is said of the indefinite pronoun ONE.

which stands instead of a *noun*, or which represents a noun, without being the definite or fixed name of any particular object or class of objects. What does the pronoun "*we*" here represent? Ans. The names of the person who speaks (who utters the proposition), and of those for whom, in connection with himself, he speaks.

These questions may be increased or diminished, according to the capacity and the progress of the learner. It will generally be best to analyze a few examples very fully, and afterwards abbreviate the process, as in the model which follows:

MODEL SECOND.—Example: "*She learns.*" The *verb* is "*learns*," for "*learns*" expresses the assertion contained in the proposition. The *subject* is the pronoun SHE. This pronoun is of the *third person* and *feminine gender;* for it represents an *individual merely spoken of*, and that individual a *female.* Or, more briefly still, the subject is the *feminine pronoun* SHE *of the third person.*

Example: *Man toils, he suffers*, &c. The subject of the second proposition is HE, the *masculine pronoun* of the *third person.* This pronoun represents the noun "*man*"—the *subject* of the preceding proposition.

In written analyses, the following abbreviations may be adopted: *pron.* for pronoun, *persl.* for personal, *pers.* for person, the numerals 1, 2, 3 to express the number of the person, *mas.* for masculine, *fem.* for feminine, *neut.* for neuter. It may be useful, in writing, to draw a line under all the grammatical terms and abbreviations employed to indicate the analysis, in order to distinguish them more clearly from the words of the example analyzed. In the printed book we exhibit the words employed to express the analysis in *Italics*, to distinguish them from the words analyzed, which are exhibited in *Roman* type.

MODEL OF A WRITTEN EXERCISE.—Example: He sleeps (He, *mas. pron.* 3 *pers.*) *s.* sleeps, *v.* That is, He, *the masculine pronoun of the third person, is the subject*, sleeps *is the verb.*

EXERCISES II. III., &c.—Let the pupil form a given number of written propositions having *personal pronouns* for their subjects.

§ 31. PROPER NOUNS AND COMMON NOUNS.—We must now attend to another classification of nouns, founded on a different principle—a classification of considerable importance in a grammatical point of view, as many of the contrivances of language have reference to the fact or principle on which it rests. The fact to which we allude is the extent of the signification of nouns. (1) In reference to this, Grammarians have divided them into two classes, called by them *proper nouns* and *common nouns.*

(2) Some nouns are names appropriated to certain persons or things, as the names of men and women, names given to some of the domestic animals, as dogs, horses, &c., by which we recognise only a single individual. To this class belong also the names of countries, regions, cities, towns, mountains, rivers, states, nations, or races of men, languages, days, months, festivals, great events, ships, &c., &c. (3) These are called *proper nouns*, because they are names *proper*—that is, *peculiar* or *appropriated* to *individual persons, places*, &c., of which they are the spoken signs. *Proper* has, in this use, the sense it retains in the word *property.* These names are, as it were, the property of the individuals they represent. Examples: George Washington, Maria Edgeworth, Europe, the Canadas, London, New-York, the Alps, the Potomac, Pennsylvania, the Germans, the Celts, French, English, Monday, May, Christmas, Easter, the Revolution, &c.

(4) There are other names which are used to designate, not a single individual, but a whole class of objects: as, *animal, man, tree.* These are sometimes employed to designate the whole class taken together, sometimes to designate any individual or any number of individuals of the class. (5) Without the help of some other sign, they never indicate any *determinate* individual or *determinate* individuals of the class. (6) They are sometimes called *general terms*, because some of them serve to indicate a whole *genus* or class. In grammar, they are generally and more properly called COMMON NOUNS; because they are names *common* to a whole class of objects.

The following description of the manner in which men may have

---

§ 31. (1) Name the two classes into which nouns are divided in reference to the extent of their signification.

(2) What nouns, or names are included in the first class, or class of *proper nouns?* (3) Why are they called *proper nouns?* Give examples. (4) Describe the other class of *nouns.* (5) Do these nouns alone serve to indicate a determinate individual? (6) What are these nouns sometimes called, and for what reason? What are they usually called by

been led to the invention of *common names*, will serve to elucidate the distinction between these classes of words. We subjoin it for the perusal of the learner. The account of the matter here given rests on the supposition that the first names invented would naturally be proper names. We know that this is disputed, perhaps justly; we enter not into the controversy. But whether the supposition is correct or not, the statement given below will tend to explain the distinction between proper and common names, to exhibit clearly the use and importance of common names, and to fix the subject in the memory of the learner.

Let us suppose that we are commencing the formation of a language. Our first effort, so far as names of substances is concerned, would be to give names to the objects around us, by which names we might recall the conception of these objects (when absent) to our own minds, and to the minds of others. In commencing this task, we would likely attempt to give a separate name to every conspicuous and interesting object (a sign exclusively appropriated to it), which, when uttered, would, with unfailing certainty, recall its image to the mind. Thus we might call each individual of our own species by a distinctive name; our favorite animals, as dogs, horses, &c., we might designate in the same way; and every river, mountain, hill, valley, and conspicuous or notable place might have an appellation appropriated to itself.

But when we come to name the trees of the forest, or the grass of the fields, or the ears or kernels of grain, and the other products of the teeming earth, or the pebbles on the sea-shore, or the more diminutive swarms of living insects, we should find it utterly impossible to proceed as before, and to give a peculiar name to each individual tree, blade of grass, &c. These objects, though sometimes collectively considered highly interesting to man, individually considered, are not of sufficient account in our view to require each a separate name. The attempt to give such names would frustrate the most valuable purposes of language by introducing an innumerable host of signs of individual objects—singly considered, of little or no importance to us—which the longest life would not be sufficient to master, and the strongest memory could not retain. Were it possible to give names to every single plant in a piece of fertile land of a few acres' extent, these names would be more numerous than the words contained in the most copious language of civilized man.

We should, therefore, soon find ourselves obliged to proceed—as mankind in the formation of languages have in fact proceeded—to give names to CLASSES of these objects, and relinquish the absurd attempt to give a separate name to each individual object. Thus, all plants agreeing in certain characteristics we would call by the general name tree. Another class grain; another grass, &c. These again we might divide into other inferior classes, possessing certain characteristics or marks distinguishing them from the rest of the greater class. Thus, trees might be divided into sub-classes, with distinctive names, as ash, beach, oak, pine, &c., each class so named being distinguished from all other trees by obvious characteristics. By this device, we avoid the endless labor of inventing a new name for every distinct object, as well as the confusion arising from a language so crowded with words as to be wholly unmanageable, or, at least, unsuitable to the purpose of readily communicating our thoughts.

Even where every individual of a class has a proper name, as is the case in regard of our own kind, still a common or general name (a *class* name) in addition becomes indispensable whenever we wish to make an assertion embracing the whole kind or class. It would be not merely inconvenient, but impossible, to enumerate by their proper names all the individuals of the class, in order to make an assertion embracing them together. Such an assertion as, "Man is mortal," or, "Men are mortal," could never be made, were we obliged to express the *proper* names of all the parties included under the assertion. So that, even if we had a *proper* name for every object, we could not dispense with the use of common names.

[(7) This division of nouns into *proper nouns* and *common nouns* has reference chiefly, if not exclusively, to *concrete nouns*, or *names* of *substances*, including *collective nouns.* (8) All *proper nouns* are names of substances, and the name *common nouns* applies chiefly and most appropriately to signs of classes of substances. (9) The *collectives* are chiefly *common nouns*, names *common* to kinds of collections of individuals, as *party*, *assembly*, &c., each of these representing a class of those collections, or unions into which individuals are sometimes formed. (10) Sometimes collectives are employed as proper names; as, when we use the word *Parliament*, to mean the Parliament of Great Britain; or Congress,

grammarians? [(7) To what kinds of nouns does this division into proper and common extend? (8) To which of the classes of nouns already enumerated do proper nouns exclusively belong? and to what nouns does the name *common* most appropriately apply? (9) What class are chiefly *common* nouns? (10) Are any of the *collectives* to be considered as proper nouns? (11) Give examples of plural proper nouns.

to indicate the Legislature of the United States; *Parliament met for business—Congress adjourned.* (11) Such expressions as the Romans, the Stuarts, the Bourbons, the Cæsars, &c., may be considered as a kind of collective or plural proper nouns.

(12) The grammarians generally designate all nouns which are not *proper nouns* (that is, names appropriated to individual persons or things, or determinate collections of persons or things), as *common nouns.* (13) It would perhaps be better to restrict this classification to the names of *substances.* (14) Many, indeed, of the *abstract nouns* may, in some sense, and as sometimes employed, be considered, like *common nouns,* the names of classes. (15) For example, *whiteness* may, in some sort, be considered as the name of a class of attributes, for there is one *whiteness* of snow, another *whiteness* of milk, another *whiteness* of paper, &c. *Virtue,* too, is the name of a numerous class of moral qualities, and *vice* in like manner. (16) Yet even these words are not, in their general usage in language, contemplated as names of classes of qualities or attributes, but as names of *single* attributes, or qualities, found, indeed, in various and large classes of objects, and in various degrees of intensity, but, in the mind's conception of them, possessed of a sort of individuality. When intended to be employed as names of classes, some variation of expression is generally necessary to announce this fact. (17) Some of these nouns are expressive of qualities which admit of no variation, as *mortality, perpetuity, equality,* &c. The conceptions of which these are the signs have all the individuality of those represented by *proper nouns.* (18) Upon the whole, as the manner in which all *abstract* and *verbal nouns* and the pronouns are employed in language, is more like that in which proper nouns are used, than that in which common nouns are used, we think it best not to class them with *common nouns,* but to restrict the division of nouns into proper and common *to names of substances.*]

---

(12) How do grammarians generally designate all nouns that are not proper nouns? (13) What restriction of this classification is suggested? (14) May *abstract* nouns ever be considered as common nouns? (15) Illustrate this point. (16) Are *abstract* nouns in their general usage contemplated as names of classes of attributes? (17) What is said of the qualities or attributes expressed by some abstract nouns? (18) To what kind of nouns does it seem best to restrict the division into proper and common?]

(19) Let the learner remember that, in writing *proper names* and words derived from them, we always begin the word with a large letter, or, as it is commonly called, a *capital letter*. (20) Thus, *England* is spelled with a large *E*, and *English*, though not a noun, because it is derived from, and has reference to, a *proper name*, is spelled with a capital *E*. The same may be said of *America* and *American*. (21) In the beginning of the last century it was customary, in our printed books, to distinguish every noun, whether *proper* or *common*, by a capital letter. This custom is still retained by the Germans. In their language every *noun*, and every word *employed as a noun*, is distinguished by a capital.

Let the learner tell to which class *proper nouns* or *common nouns*, each word in the following exercise, belongs, giving, in each case, the reason for so classing it. In this exercise we have not employed capitals in spelling the proper nouns, lest we should distinguish them from the common nouns. After repeating the exercise, as an oral lesson, the learner may be required to write it, distinguishing the proper nouns by an initial large letter.

Exercise.—Plant, town, country, india, franklin, man, england, president, america, king, soldier, hero, st. paul's, trinity church, general, mountain, the rocky mountains, philadelphia, liverpool, country, kingdom, state, bristol, stranger, horse, day, thursday, april, stephen, boston, city, &c.

Model of Examination.—What kind of word is plant? Ans. *A noun*, or substantive. Why do you call it a noun? Ans. Because it belongs to that class of words which serve as subjects of propositions. What kind of noun? Ans. A concrete common noun. Why call it a concrete noun? Ans. Because it is the name of a substance, or of that which possesses independent existence. Why a common noun? Ans. Because it is a name *common* to a class of things, and not appropriated to a single individual thing.

The young learner may now be required to give twenty (or more, according to circumstances) examples of concrete nouns as a written exercise, distinguishing each proper noun in the usual manner, by beginning it with a large letter. After this exercise has been ex-

(19) How are proper nouns and nouns derived from proper names written? (20) Illustrate this by examples. (21) What was the practice in former times in writing nouns?

amined, let the pupil be questioned according to the above model, on each example. These exercises must be repeated till the learner can promptly distinguish proper and common nouns from one another, and from all other classes of words.

§ 32. (1) In employing *common nouns*—that is, words which designate classes of things—we may have occasion either to speak, 1st, of the whole class; 2d, of an individual of the class; or, 3d, of a number of individuals of the class without comprising the whole class. (2) The noun, in its simplest form, without any modification of any kind, is sometimes employed in English to indicate the whole class of objects to which the name is applicable. (3) Thus, the word *man* is employed to signify the whole race of men, or all mankind, as when we say *Man is frail*, *Man is mortal*, The proper study of mankind is MAN. By *man*, in all these cases, we mean the whole human race, or humanity in general. (4) When we wish to indicate, by a common noun, a single individual, we must, in our language, have recourse to the use of one of a class of words which we shall call DETERMINATIVES; as, *a man*, *one man*, *any man*, *some man*, &c. (5) The term *man* cannot with propriety be used *alone* in our language to indicate a single individual man. And the same holds of other common nouns.

(6) When we wish to indicate more than one individual of a class or species, without indicating the whole species, we must use what is called the *plural form* of the noun, and a determinative or descriptive word besides, to restrict or limit the noun. (7) As examples we may take the phrases, *some men*, *many men*, *good men*, *wise men*, &c. Here we use *men*, the plural form of *man*, and add the limiting words, *some*, *many*, *good*, *wise*. (8) The plural form of the word *man*, as well as the singular form, is used without any modifying word to express the whole race; as, *Men are frail*, *Men are mortal*, &c. [(9) Indeed it is generally the plural form of *com-*

---

§ 32. (1) Mention the purposes for which we may have occasion to employ common nouns. (2) For what purpose is the common noun in its simplest form sometimes employed in English? (3) Give illustrations of this fact. (4) To what contrivance must we have recourse in English in order to indicate a single individual by a common noun? (5) What is said of the term man?

(6) How do we indicate more than one of a class without indicating the whole class? (7) Give examples. (8) For what purpose is the *plural form* without any modifying word employed? [(9) What form of a *common* noun is *generally* employed to express the

mon nouns which is employed to express the whole class collectively. (10) It is only in the case of certain words that we can with propriety employ the singular form to express the whole class; and when we do use it, it does not so much indicate the class, or individuals taken collectively which form the class or species, as the combined qualities or attributes which constitute or distinguish the class. (11) Thus, *man* means, when used alone or unmodified, the combined qualities, properties, distinguishing attributes which constitute *man*, or nearly the same which is sometimes indicated by the term *humanity;* as in the example already given, The proper study of mankind is MAN—that is, the properties, attributes, &c., which belong to or constitute *man*. (12) We cannot use such words as *tree* or *animal* to express the whole class of trees or animals; nor such words as *oak* or *ash*. These last, when used without a determinative, signify a very different thing from the species which they indicate collectively considered. Thus used, they serve to indicate the kind of wood which they afford, considered as a material for human uses, not the collective species of trees.]

§ 33. We are now brought to consider an important modification of the *subject noun*, effected (at least partly) by a change of the form of the word. (1) We use the unaltered form of the noun (accompanied generally, in the case of names of substances, by a determinative word) to indicate *a single individual* of the class to which the noun serves as a common name, and we employ a modified form, when we intend to indicate *more than one individual* of the class. (2) These two forms may be called the *singular form* and the *plural form*—the *singular* indicating a *single* thing, the *plural* a *plurality of things*, or more than one. [(3) For the sake of brevity, we may henceforth call the original, unmodified, uninflected form of *nouns* and *verbs* the *root* of the noun or verb.] (4) The gram-

---

whole class collectively? (10) What is said of the employment of the singular form to express a whole class? (11) Illustrate by an example. (12) Can such words as *tree*, or *animal*, &c., be used to express the class of trees, &c.; and what do such words as *oak* and *ash* used alone signify?]

§ 33. (1) What form of the noun is used when we speak of a single object of a class, and what when we speak of more than one? (2) What may these forms be called? [(3) What is meant by the *root* of a *noun* or *verb*?] (4) What have grammarians called this modification of nouns?

marians generally call this modification of nouns NUMBER, and say that nouns have *two numbers*, the *singular* and the *plural.*

As this manner of expression has been so long employed, we shall feel obliged (through a regard to convenience, and to avoid the appearance of making unnecessary innovations), to adopt it on some occasions, though it is liable to serious objection, because it implies that *unity* is a number, whereas *number* consists of the aggregation or sum of two or more units. The difficulties which have occurred to some of the grammarians, and the less scientific writers on arithmetic, in attempting to define *number*, and the glaring absurdities which have been sometimes produced as definitions, are all to be traced to the improper extension (an extension unwarranted by the common usage of language, and reprobated by philosophers as early as the times of Aristotle) of the word *number*, so as to embrace under it the conception of *unity* as well as of plurality. It is not to be expected that any serviceable definition can be given embracing in the same terms conceptions so diverse—so opposed as *unity* and *plurality.* In other words, while a *unit* is considered one of the *numbers*, there can be no rational or logical definition of *number.* We may, indeed, have such jargon as "number is the consideration of an object as one or more;" or, "number is that property of a noun, by which it expresses one, or more than one," &c. When number is considered as made up of the aggregation or sum of units, the proper definition obviously presents itself. But then to talk of the *singular number* is absurd—a contradiction of terms. This use of the term number by most grammarians, and by a host of writers on arithmetic, is also altogether inconsistent with the current usage of language in speaking of every thing except grammar and arithmetic. When we use the word *number* in common discourse we always intend to *indicate* a *plurality*, and to *exclude unity* (except in such colloquial expressions as "*number one*"). A *number of men*, a *number* of *things*, always implies plurality, and is equivalent to *several men*, several things.

When we have occasion hereafter to speak of the singular form of nouns, we shall call it simply the *singular form*, and not the *singular number;* but as there is no other name in our language to express that modification or *accident* of nouns which we are considering, we are obliged to employ the term *number*, or *numbers of nouns*, for this purpose, whilst we admit its want of strict appropriateness, except as applied exclusively to the *plural form.* At the same time, we shall endeavor to guard our readers and ourselves against any misconception to which the use of this term might possibly lead.

§ 34. In coming to treat of the formation of the *plural* of nouns, a class of the contrivances of articulate language distinct from what we have yet had under consideration, and a class which will employ much of our attention in the remainder of this treatise, is presented to our notice. (1) Hitherto we have contemplated nouns and verbs as performing their respective functions in propositions without any species of modification, whether effected by a change of their form, or by the assistance of other words. (2) Very few of the purposes which language now serves can be accomplished without advancing a step beyond this. With unmodified nouns, and unmodified verbs, we could form but a very small number of propositions, and express a very limited portion of our thoughts. (3) The learner will, no doubt, have discovered this fact already in attempting to form rational propositions consisting of two words—a simple unmodified noun, and an unmodified verb. (4) For example, of the subject expressed by the noun *man* without any modification, we can by the use of bare verbs make only a very limited number of assertions consistent with truth, and deserving the attention of rational beings. *Man lives*, *man thinks*, *man speaks*, *talks*, *sings*, *walks*, runs, &c., &c. Such propositions, though all true, contain truths so well known by mankind generally, that we seldom find occasion to employ them in this naked form in conversation or in writing, and even when we do, in order to give our assertion more appearance of weight, we usually employ some more dignified mode of expression, as *man is endowed with thought*, *with speech*, &c.

(5) Even, if we are allowed to modify at pleasure the verbs we employ, we can make only a limited number of true and rational assertions about the subject expressed by the naked term MAN. (6) But, when we are allowed to *modify* this term by the assistance of additional words, and, at the same time, to modify the verb, we

---

§ 34. (1) What is said of the manner in which we have been contemplating nouns and verbs hitherto? (2) Can the purposes of language be effected by unmodified nouns and verbs? (3) What will the learner have already discovered in regard to this matter? (4) Give example, and go through the illustration.

(5) When allowed to modify the verbs we employ, can we make a large number of assertions in regard to the subject expressed by the bare word man? (6) How is it, when we are allowed to modify the subject noun and the verb? (7) Illustrate by examples.

can readily increase our stock of propositions. (7) For example, we cannot say with truth, *man is happy*, for many men are far from being happy. We cannot say, *man is esteemed*, *man is loved*, *man is admired*, *man is envied*, &c., because these predicates do not apply to every man indiscriminately. But we can say without offending against truth or propriety, *a virtuous man is happy*, *an upright man is esteemed*, *a good man is loved*, *a great man is admired*, *a rich man is envied*, &c. (8) In these propositions, it will be observed, the assertions are not made of man generally—of man considered as possessing only the necessary and essential characteristics of the human family—of any, or every man; but of *a* man—some individual man possessing a superadded quality, which does not necessarily, or in reality, belong to all men. The real subject of the foregoing propositions is not the bare word *man*, but the modified or completed subjects, *a virtuous man*, *a good man*, &c. (9) The modifying words *virtuous*, *good*, &c., together with the little determinative sign *a*, are added to the noun (which forms, as it were, the *basis* or *nucleus* of the subject), and these together constitute the *complete subject*.

(10) Various contrivances are employed to complete the subjects of propositions; that is, to express with its proper limitations, qualifications, &c., the *exact subject* of which we make an assertion. In like manner, there are also various contrivances for expressing the proper limitations, qualifications, &c., of the predicates of propositions.

(11) All these contrivances, for want of a better name, we may, for the present, call MODIFICATIONS of *nouns* and *verbs*. (12) They may be divided into two general classes: 1st, modifications effected on the form of the noun or verb; and 2d, modifications effected by the assistance of other words. (13) The first class we shall call simply modifications. When we come to treat of the latter class, we shall call them, after the French manner, COMPLEMENTS (that is,

---

(8) Of what are the assertions in the examples made—of man expressive of the human race, or of what? (9) What constitutes the *real* subjects of these propositions?

(10) What is said of the contrivances employed to *complete* propositions?

(11) What name may be given to these contrivances? (12) Describe the two general classes of these modifications. (13) How shall we designate the first, and how the second class?

completements) of the *subject* and *predicate* respectively, or sometimes *modifications* of the *subject-noun* and *verb* respectively.

REMARK.—(14) The young learner will please remember that the word complement means that which *fills up*, or *completes*, and that it is not to be confounded with the more common word compliment, which is wholly unlike it in meaning, though similar in sound.

§35. (1) Our attention for the present is to be exclusively directed to the first *class* of *modifications*—those which are indicated by some change effected on the form of the noun or verb; and first, to the change of the form of the noun employed as *subject-noun* to express *plurality*. (2) It may here be remarked that these modifications of the forms of both nouns and verbs—especially of the verbs—are of two distinct kinds; first, those which consist of a change of what is called the *root*, or *radical part* of the word without any thing being added to the word; for example, *man* is changed into *men* to form the plural. Here the sound of the root is changed or modified, but nothing is added. The second kind of modification is effected by adding a sound to the root; as, for example, the plural of the word *book* is formed by adding the sound of *s*; singular *book*, plural books, the first used to express a single book, the latter a number of books.

(3) There are now only a few nouns in our language that form their plurals by a modification of the sound of the root, or by what we shall call for the sake of distinction a *radical modification*.*

* We have got no appropriate distinctive name in our language for these two kinds of modification. Indeed the fact, on which this distinction rests, has been noticed by few of our grammarians. They have rid themselves of all trouble with nouns and verbs which undergo the *radical modification*, by setting them aside as *irregular*. This is a very convenient way of disposing of these words, but it is neither fair, nor philosophical to treat in this manner what is apparently the most ancient species of modification in our own language, in its mother the Anglo-Saxon, and in all the sis-

(14) What is the meaning of the word complement, and from what word must it be distinguished?

§ 35. (1) To which class of these modifications are we to attend first? (2) What subdivision may be made of this first general class of modifications? Describe each subordinate class.

(3) What distinctive names may be given to these modifications?

We shall add a list of these after we have treated of the formation of the plural by the more usual process, namely, by an addition made to the root or radical form of the word. This for distinction's sake we may call the *flexional modification.*

(4) Before we proceed to treat farther of these modifications of the forms of words, and in particular of the formation of the plurals of nouns, it will be necessary to give some account of the *elementary sounds* which constitute words, and of the written signs employed to represent these words to the eye. (5) Without some knowledge of these matters the learner will not be prepared to follow us readily in treating of the variations of form which words undergo in order to accomplish the purposes of language. In fact, we find that without presupposing such knowledge on his part, we cannot treat these modifications in a clear or satisfactory manner. We cannot refer to the different classes of sounds and of letters, without first briefly considering these classes, and putting the pupil in possession of their names.

REMARK.—It is usual to introduce something on the sounds of the language in the beginning of grammars. We think it better not to introduce this discussion till such time as it is *needed,* and must be applied in treating of the contrivances of speech. Though its introduction here must for a short time suspend our remarks on the modification of nouns, the course we pursue saves the pupil the trouble of learning, first a number of dry facts apparently unconnected with the subject of the construction of language, and being again compelled to learn them a second time, when they come to be of practical use.

REMARKS ON THE ELEMENTARY SOUNDS OF THE ENGLISH LANGUAGE, AND ON THE SIGNS USED TO REPRESENT THESE SOUNDS.*

§ 36. (1) Words consist either of a single sound uttered by a

---

ter dialects. Our cousins, the Germans, who have gone far ahead of us in grammatical and philological research, have given these two species of modification distinctive names.

* In pursuing our inquiries on this subject, we must never lose sight

---

(4) To what subject is it necessary to call the attention of the learner before we treat farther of the modification of the forms of words? (5) State the reasons for introducing this subject, and suspending our remarks on the formation of the plural, &c.

§ 36. (1) How are words constituted?

single effort of the organs of speech, or of a combination of two or more such sounds. (2) Every single sound thus uttered is called a syllable. (3) The term *syllable* means so much of a word as is *taken together;* that is, so many letters in *written language*, as are taken together to form one single sound, or *voice*—the name by which some have chosen to call human utterances to distinguish them from ordinary sounds.*

(4) A word of *one* syllable is called a *monosyllable;* a word of *two* syllables a *dissyllable;* a word of *three* syllables a *trisyllable;* and a word of *four* or more syllables a *polysyllable.*

(5) The sounds employed in *articulate* language to form syllables are produced by the breath passing through the throat and mouth, and acted upon, in some cases, during its passage by the several organs of speech—especially the tongue, teeth and lips. [See Latham's Eng. Gram. p. 17.]

(6) These sounds are constituted of two kinds of elements, *vocal*, or vowel sounds, and *consonantal modifications* of sound. (7) The letters which represent these vocal sounds and consonantal modifications of sound, are called *vowels* and *consonants.*

§ 37. (1) VOWELS.—The vocal or vowel sounds are formed by the passage of the breath through the mouth kept in a particular position, without any interference of the tongue, lips, or teeth. (2) These sounds admit of being continued so long as we choose to

---

of the distinction between a *sound* and a *letter*. A letter is the sign or representative of a sound—often only of a part of a complete sound or utterance. Obvious as this distinction may seem, it has been sometimes overlooked in treating this part of grammar, and both confusion of thought and confusion of language, as might have been expected, have been the result.

* This employment of the term *voice*, is not sanctioned by the common usage of our language; though in Latin *vox*, from which voice is derived, is frequently employed to denote a sound emitted by the human voice.

---

(2) What is the name given to a single sound? (3) Explain the meaning of the term *syllable.*

(4) What name is given to a word of one syllable? To a word of two syllables? &c.

(5) How are the sounds employed in *articulate language* formed? (6) What two kinds of elements constitute these sounds? (7) What are the letters which represent these distinct elements of articulate sounds called?

§ 37. (1) Describe the manner in which vowel sounds are formed? (2) What is said of

keep the mouth in the same position, and pass the breath through it. (3) They can be uttered alone, being complete sounds, and hence may constitute a syllable or a word.

(4) The vowel sounds are represented in the *written* English language by the letters, *a*, *e*, *i*, *o*, *u*; which are hence called vowels. (5) The letter *y* also represents a vowel sound—the same sound as *i* or *e*—when found in the middle or end of a syllable. (6) *W*, also, in the middle or in the end of a syllable is generally considered a vowel. Sometimes it represents the sound of *u*, as in *now*, *cow*, *vow*, &c.

[(7) In many cases it is, as the language is now pronounced, a mere *quiescent* or *otiose* (*idle*) *letter* in the written language, having no corresponding sound in the spoken language. This hap pens when it follows the vowel *o*; as, in *low*, *blow*, *flow*, *follow*, &c. Sometimes it indicates the particular sound which the preceding vowel represents. This happens when it follows *a*; as in *law*, *bawl*, *raw*, &c. And sometimes it combines with the vowel *e*; in which case it is sounded nearly like *u*. In our language it can never stand alone in a syllable. It must be supported by another vowel. In this it differs from *y*, as well as from all the other vowels.]

(8) *W* and *y* are commonly reckoned consonants when they begin a syllable. [(9) Semivowels—the name given to them, when they occupy this position, by some modern grammarians—is a much more appropriate appellation, if the older grammarians had not already applied it to another class of sounds, or rather—as we have ventured to consider and treat them—modifiers of sounds.

(10) The vowel *sounds* in the English language are much more numerous than the letters which are used to represent them. (11) The letter *a* represents three or four distinct sounds, as may be seen in the words *late*, *man*, *far*, *ball*. *E* represents the two distinct sounds found in the words, *me* and *met*; *i* the two found in the

---

our power of continuing these vowel sounds? (3) Can these be uttered alone? What follows as a consequence?

(4) By what letters are the *vowel sounds* represented? (5) What is said of *y*? (6) What of *w*?

[(7) What further is said of *w*?]

(8) When are *w* and *y* reckoned consonants? [(9) What other name has been applied to them by some grammarians, and what is said of this other name?

(10) Have we a distinct letter to represent each distinct vowel sound in our language? (11) How many distinct sounds does the letter *a* represent? How many the letter *e*? &c.

words *pin* and *pine*; *o* the three found in *no*, *not*, *move*, &c. (12) It is reckoned that there are from ten to twelve distinct simple vocal sounds used in the English language. (13) From these we must exclude the sound represented by *i* in *pine*, as being a compound, and not a simple sound. (14) Some others, which we have mentioned above, may be considered as distinguished only by a more or less protracted pronunciation.]

§ 38. (1) Two vowel sounds are sometimes pronounced in combination by a single impulse of the voice, or in one syllable. Such combinations are called *diphthongs*, that is, *double sounds.* (2) Examples are found in the words *voice* and *ounce*, in which two sounds represented by different letters are united in the same syllable. [(3) We have also an example in *pine.* Here two sounds—the sound of *a* in man and of *i* in *pin*, or, as some think, of the semivowel *y* in *yet*—are distinguishable, though the combined sound is represented by the single character *i*.

(4) On the other hand, two vowel characters, or letters, are often found united in the same syllable in the written language, when the syllable, in our modern pronunciation, contains but one simple vowel sound. We have examples in the words *head*, *field*, *great*, *lead*, &c. (5) Those combinations which represent a double sound in the *spoken language* are commonly called by grammarians *proper diphthongs*, and those which do not represent a double sound are called *improper diphthongs*—by some, more properly, *digraphs.* (6) This distinction, it will be noticed, has reference only to the written language. (7) There are no improper diphthongs in the *spoken language.** (8) Sometimes in written language we find

* As the term diphthong, in its proper sense, can apply only to spoken language, the expressions *proper* and *improper* diphthongs, meaning diph-

(12) How many distinct simple vowel sounds are reckoned in English? (13) What sound represented by a single letter must be excluded from the number of the simple vowel sounds? (14) By what alone do some of the vowel sounds above enumerated seem to be distinguished from each other?]

§ 38. (1) What is said of the combination of vowel sounds, and what are such *combinations* of simple sounds called? What does the term *diphthong* mean? (2) Furnish examples. [(3) What is said of *i* in such words as *pine*?

(4) Do two vowel characters in the same syllable always represent a double sound in spoken language? Give examples. (5) What is a *proper* diphthong? What an *improper diphthong*? (6) What is said of this distinction? (7) Are there any improper diphthongs in spoken language? (8) Are three *vowel characters* ever united in the same syllable in the

three vowel characters combined in one syllable; as in the words *beauty*, *beau*, *lieutenant*, &c. These have been called triphthongs (9), perhaps improperly, as it is more than doubtful whether, in our spoken language, such a thing as the combination of three sounds in one syllable ever occurs. (10) The *eau*, for example, in *beau*, represents but a single vocal sound in the pronunciation of the word; and *eau* in *beauty*, and *ieu* in *lieutenant*, represent certainly nothing more complex than a diphthongal sound.]

§ 39. CONSONANTS.—(1) The consonants are sounds, or, more properly, modifications of sounds, which cannot be pronounced alone, but only in connection with a vowel.* (2) And hence the name

thongs which are a combination or coalescence of two vowel sounds, and diphthongs which are *not* a combination of two vowel sounds (that is, which are not diphthongs at all), involve an absurdity. The grammarians have been led into this absurdity by the confusion of vowel sounds with the characters which represent them, both of which they have called by the same name—*vowels*. We much need a term to express a *vowel character or letter* distinct from the term used properly to express a *vowel sound*, and a term to express a written word distinctly from a spoken word. Improper diphthongs are more properly called *digraphs*—that is, sounds represented by two letters in the written language.

* The vowel in a syllable may be considered as the basis of the sound, and the so called consonantal sounds as modifications applied to this sound (*vox*) as it passes through the mouth. Every entire syllable is a single sound or utterance, either *simply vocal* or *modified*. The consonantal modifications effected by the tongue, lips, teeth, &c., produce that boundless copiousness and variety of articulations which distinguish artificial language. With the vowels *alone* we could form only a dozen or so, distinct syllables, and even these ill adapted for the purpose of combination to form words. But, by the combination of *vowel sounds* with *consonantal modifications*, we can form a great variety of syllables; and by the further combination of two or more of these syllables in words, we obtain the countless number of signs which are employed in the various dialects spoken by the races of mankind.

Since writing the preceding part of this note, we have found a remark in an article on Comparative Philology in the North British Review for November, 1851, which we introduce here as confirmatory of our views.

written language, and if so, what are such combinations called? (9) Are there any *triphthongs*, that is, combinations of three *vowel sounds*, in the *spoken* language? (10) What is said of such combinations of vowel *letters* as *eau* in *beau* and in *beauty*, and *ieu* in *lieutenant?*]

§ 39. (1) What is said of *consonants?* (2) What does the term consonant mean?

consonant—sounding-with. (3) Alone, they can, of course, never form a word or syllable. All the remaining letters of the alphabet, after we have subtracted the vowel characters above enumerated, are called consonants. (4) These have been divided by the grammarians into two classes, *mutes* and *semivowels.*

Mutes and Semivowels.*—(5) The distinction drawn between these is, that the mutes cannot be sounded at all without the aid of a vowel, whereas the semivowels have a sort of imperfect sound without the aid of a vowel.

(6) The consonantal sounds, classed under the name of *mutes*, are represented in our alphabet by the letters *b*, *c* hard, *d*, *g* hard, *k*, *p*, *q*, and *t*. [(7) To these may be added the two distinct sounds represented by *th* in the words *thing* and *though*, which are simple sounds, or simple modifications of vocal sounds, though both—awkwardly and improperly—represented in our *present* written language by the two characters *t* and *h*. In the Anglo-Saxon alphabet these sounds had each an appropriate representative. (8) From the mutes above enumerated we may, as regards *sounds*, deduct two, since the letters *c* hard, *k*, and *q*, represent only a single sound, and *c* soft has the same sound as *s*.]

(9) The *semivowels* are represented by the letters *f*, *l*, *m*, *n*, *r*, *s*, *v*, and *c* and *g* soft. (10) We have omitted *x* and *z* in enumerating the mutes and semivowels, because each of them is the representative of a combination of two consonantal sounds, *x* of *k* combined

"Alphabets are the result of analysis; syllables are really the units of sound. The Chinese and, we believe, the Mandschur, have really only syllabaries, the former significant, and the latter phonetic as well."

* This classification is of little practical use in our language, and is founded on, what seems to us, a rather doubtful distinction. Still, as it is old, and commonly adopted, it deserves some passing notice.

---

(3) Can a syllable be formed of *consonants* alone? (4) Tell the classes into which most grammarians have divided the consonants?

(5) State the distinction between *mutes* and *semivowels.*

(6) Enumerate the mute consonants. [(7) What is said of the sounds represented by *th*? (8) What is said of the sounds of *c*, *k*, and *q*?]

(9) Enumerate the *semivowels.* (10) What reason is assigned for omitting the sounds represented by *x* and *z*? (11) What other letter has been excluded from the enumeration? [(12) What is said of the propriety of excluding *h*?] (13) What is said of the *liquids*?

with *s*, and *z*, as commonly supposed, of *d* with *s*.* (11) *H* has also been excluded from this enumeration, because it is said to represent only an aspiration or breathing. [(12) This is, perhaps, unjust treatment of our strong aspirated English *h*, since it seems to serve the same purpose with all the other consonantal sounds—the purpose, namely, of so modifying the utterance of a vowel as to form a distinct syllable. The sound represented by *hat*, for example, when well pronounced, is nearly as distinct from *at* as the sounds *cat*, or *fat*, or *mat*, and serves as well the purpose of a distinct sign in articulate language.] (13) Four of the *semivowels* are distinguished by the name of *liquids*, from their smoothness, and their consequent easy union in the same syllable with other consonants. The *liquids* are *l*, *m*, *n*, and *r*.

§ 40. [(1) Another, and more practically useful, classification of the consonantal sounds, is into *sharp* and *flat*, or *hard* and *soft*. (2) This classification claims our notice, because the fact on which it is founded exercises an important influence on the inflexion of many words in the English language—I mean the *spoken* language. It accounts, also, for some of the irregularities of our pronunciation of the written letters; or, in other words, for some of the numerous inconsistencies between our orthography and our pronunciation. We are indebted to Dr. Latham for what follows:

(3) When two or more mutes of different degrees of sharpness or flatness come together in the same syllable, they form a combination of sounds that is incapable of being pronounced. (4) This may be understood by practising a few combinations according to the following table. The sharp mutes are arranged on the left, the flat ones on the right side of the line.

(5) Sharp or hard.		(6) Flat or soft.	
p . .	f	b . .	v.
t . .	th (*in thin.*)	d . .	th (*in thine.*)
k . .		g . .	
s . .	sh.	z . .	z (*as in azure.*)

* Whether *d* is a component of the sound of *z*, as now pronounced in the English language, may well be doubted.

§ 40. [(1) What other classification of the consonantal sounds is mentioned? (2) State the claims which this classification has on our notice.

(3) What happens when mutes of different degrees of sharpness or flatness come together? (4) What mode of illustration is adopted and recommended? (5) Name the sharp

(7) Now, taking whatever letter we may from the one side of the line, and joining it in the same syllable, with any letter whatever from the other side of the line, we find the combination unpronounceable. For example, *avt*, *agt*, *ags*, *ads*, *apd*, &c., &c. (8) Of course, combinations of this sort can be written, and they can be spelt (indeed, in the English, as written combinations, they occur very frequently; for example, *stags*, *lads*, &c., &c). They cannot, however, be pronounced, each sound remaining unchanged.

(9) In order to become pronounced, a change must occur: one of the sounds changes its character, and so accommodates itself to the other (10) This change takes place in one of two ways; either the first of the two sounds takes the degree of sharpness or flatness of the second, or the second the degree of sharpness or flatness of the first: for instance, *abt* becomes pronounceable either by *b* becoming *p* or by *t* passing into *d*; in other words, it changes either to *apt* or to *abd*. And so with the rest.

(11) *avt* becomes either *aft* or *avd*.
agt " " *akt* or *agd*.
ags " " *aks* or *agz*.
apd " " *apt* or *abd*, &c., &c.

(12) This change is necessary and universal. It holds good, not for the English alone, but for all languages. (13) The only difference is, that different languages change different letters; that is, one accommodates the first letter to the second, and so turns *agt* into *akt*; the other (another) accommodates the second letter to the first, changing *agt* into *agd*.]—*Latham's Elem. Eng. Gram.*, pp. 19–21.

We add in this place some further extracts from Dr. Latham, for the satisfaction of our readers, and in order to do full justice to the author:—

---

or hard consonantal sounds. (6) Name the soft sounds on the right side of the line. (7) What is said of combinations formed of sounds from different sides of the line—that is, combinations of hard with soft sounds? (8) Are combinations of this kind ever written; and when written can they be pronounced?

(9) What change must take place in pronouncing words formed in writing by the combination of sharp and flat, or hard and soft sounds? (10) Describe the two ways in which this change is effected. (11) Tell what *avt*, *agt*, *ags*, &c. become in pronunciation? (12) Is this change universal, or is it confined exclusively to the English language? (13) What is the only difference between different languages in this respect?]

"In order to understand this difference" (the difference between the sharp and the flat sounds), "it is necessary to take some mute consonants (*p, b, f, v, t, d, th, k, g, s, z, sh, zh*), and to pronounce them as independently of any vowel as it is possible to do. We must try to give a sound to such single consonants as *p'*, *t'*, &c. In attempting this, we shall succeed in making an imperfect sound.

"Now, if the mute consonant so taken and uttered be one of the following, *p, f, t, th* (as in *thin*), *k, s*, or *sh*, the sound will be that of a whisper. The sound of *p'*, *t'* (such as it is), is that of a man speaking under the natural pitch of his voice, and at a whisper.

"But if the mute consonant so taken and uttered be either *b, v, d, th* (as in *thine*), *g, z*, or *zh*, the sound will be that of a man speaking at the natural pitch of his voice, and with a certain degree of loudness and clearness. This difference in the nature of the mute is highly important to be familiar with. Those that are sounded like *p'* and *f'*, &c., are called the flat mutes.

"When two or more mutes of different degrees of sharpness or flatness come together in the same syllable, they form a combination of sounds that is incapable of being pronounced." And so on in continuation follows the passage quoted, with some slight abridgment in our article on the sounds and letters. After which the author proceeds as follows:

"There is no fact that requires to be more particularly known than this." (Namely, the fact which forms the subject of the latter part of the extract introduced under the article just referred to.) "There are at least three formations in the English language where its influence is most important. These are, *a*) the possessive forms in *-s*; *b*) the plurals in *-s*; *c*) the preterites in *-d* and *-t*.

"Neither are there many facts in language more disguised than this is disguised in English. The *s* in the word *stags* is sharp; the *g* in the word *stags* is flat. Notwithstanding this, the combination *ags* exists. It exists, however, in the spelling only. In speaking, the *s* is sounded as *z*, and the word *stags* is pronounced *stagz*. Again, in words like *tossed, plucked, looked*, the *e* is omitted in pronunciation. Hence the words become *tossd, pluckd, lookd;* that is, the flat *d* comes in contact with the sharp *k* and *s*. Now, the combination exists in the spelling only, since the preterite of *pluck, look*, and *toss*, are, in speech, pronounced *pluckt, lookt, tosst.*

"For the sake of fixing the attention of the reader on the point, I will indicate in this place the reason for the difference between the spelling and the pronunciation, which has just been alluded to. This is as follows: For the possessive case singular, for the nominative plural, and for the preterite tense of verbs, the forms in Anglo-Saxon were fuller than they are in the present English. The possessive singular ended not in *-s* only, but in *-es;* and the nominative plural in *-as*. Similarly the preterite of the verbs ended either in *-od*, or *-ed*, not in *-d* only. *E. g. wordes=of a word* (*word's*), *flódes =of a flood* (*flood's*), *landes=of a land* (*or land's*), *thinges=of a thing* (*or* *thing's*), *endas*=*ends*, and so on throughout the language. In this case the vowel separated the two consonants, and kept them from coming together. As long as this vowel kept its place, the consonants remained unchanged, their different degrees of sharpness and flatness being a matter of indifference. When the vowel, however, was dropped, the consonants came in contact. This reduced a change on one side or the other to a matter of necessity.

"Next to knowing that two mutes of different degrees of sharpness or flatness cannot come together in the same syllable, it is important to know that two identical letters cannot come together in the same syllable.

"In illustration of this, we may take a word ending in *p*, *t*, or *s*, and try to add a second *p*, *t*, or *s* to the first one; *e. g. tap*, *bat*, *mis*. To add a second *p* to *tap*, a second *t* to *bat*, or a second *s* to *mis*, is impracticable. At the first glance this statement seems untrue. Nothing, apparently, is commoner than words like *tapp*, *batt*, *miss*. However, like the combinations indicated above, these are, in reality, combinations in spelling only; they have no existence in pronunciation. We have only to attempt to pronounce *bat 't*, *sap 'p*, &c., &c., to prove this."—(Latham's El. Eng. Gram. pp. 18, 19, 21, 22.)

§ 42. Formation of the Plural of English Nouns.

I. (1) The plural of English nouns is generally formed by adding either the sharp, hissing sound represented by the character *s* (the sound in *son* and *hiss*), or the soft sound (the sound of z), often represented in our language by the same character. (2) Examples. *Roof*, *roofs*; *book*, *books*; *cup*, *cups*; *boot*, *boots*; *smith*, *smiths*. All these, and all words terminating in similar sounds (viz., in the sounds represented by *f*, *k*, *p*, *t*, and *th* hard), add the sharp sound of *s* to the root to form the plural. (See the reason of this in § § 40.) (3) All nouns terminating in the vowel sounds represented by *a*, *e*, *i* or *y*, *o*, *u*; and in the consonantal sounds represented by *b*, *d*, *g*, *l*, *m*, *n*, *r*, *v*, and *th* soft, add the soft sound of *s* (the same as that represented in English by z), to the root to form the plural. (4) Examples. *Bay*, *bays*; *bee*, *bees*; *tie*, *ties*; *bow*, *bows*; *virtue*, *virtues*; *cab*, *cabs*; *lad*, *lads*; *stag*, *stags*; *hill*, *hills*; *drum*, *drums*; *pen*, *pens*; *star*, *stars*; *wave*, *waves*; *tithe*, *tithes*. These plural

§ 42. (1) How is the plural of English nouns generally formed? (2) What nouns take the sharp sound of *s* to form the plural? Give examples. (3) What nouns take the soft sound like *z*? (4) Give examples, and tell how they are pronounced.

forms are pronounced as if spelled *bayz*, *beez*, *cabz*, *stagz*, &c. These sounds are always represented by the letter *s*.

II. (5) When the noun ends in an *s* sound—that is, in *s*, *ss*, *x* (which is equal to ks), *sh*, the soft sound of *ch* as in *church*, *se*, or *ce*, the syllable *es* (sounded *ez*) is added to form the plural.*

(6) Examples. *Kiss*, *kisses*; *box*, *boxes*; *brush*, *brushes*; *church*, *churches*; *phrase*, *phrases*; *face*, *faces*. We have scarcely any original English noun which in the singular form ends in a single *s*. We have from the Latin *isthmus*, *fungus*, *rebus*, *omnibus*, and a few others, which have the plurals *isthmuses*, *omnibuses*, &c. All these plurals are pronounced with the soft sound of *s*, *kissez*, *boxez*, *isthmusez*, &c.

III. (7) Nouns ending in *fe* form plurals by the change of this termination into *ves*, as *wife*, plural *wives*; *knife*, *knives*; pronounced *wivez*, *knivez*. *Strife*, plural *strifes*, is an exception, retaining the hard sound of *f*, and the hissing sound of *s*, which serves to distinguish this plural from the verb *strives*; also, *fife*, plural *fifes*. (8) Many nouns, also ending in a single *f*, form plurals by changing the *f* into *v* and adding *es*=*ez*; as, *loaf*, *loaves*; *leaf*, *leaves*; *half*, *halves*; *sheaf*, *sheaves*; &c.† (9) Words ending in *ff* form their plurals regularly by adding the sharp sound of *s*; except *staff*, plural *staves*.

* The reason of this is that we cannot utter the sound of *s* after another *s* without the interposition of a vowel sound. In regard of words ending in an *s* sound, we must, therefore, either be contented to employ the same form in expressing a single object and a plurality of objects—that is, fail in distinguishing the plural from the singular noun—or interpose a vowel sound between the two *s* sounds, and thus add a syllable to the word. The first of these alternatives has been followed in the French language in the case of words ending in *s* sounds, the second in the English.

† The words in *f* and *fe* which form plurals in *ves* are said to be all of Anglo-Saxon origin, except *beef*, plural *beeves*; and writers on Anglo-Saxon grammar agree that *f* in the end of Anglo-Saxon words was pronounced with the softened sound of *v*. This fully accounts for the formation of these plu

(5) In what cases do we add the syllable *es* to form the plural, and how is the *s* in this syllable pronounced? (6) Give examples.

(7) How do nouns ending in *fe* form *plurals?* Mention exceptions. (8) How do many nouns ending in *f* alone form their *plurals?* Examples. (9) How do nouns ending in *ff* form the *plural?* Mention exceptions.

IV. (10) Nouns ending in *o* preceded by a consonant generally add the termination *es* to form the plural; as, *hero*, plural *heroes; cargo, cargoes; wo, woes; echo, echoes;* &c. Exceptions: *canto, grotto, junto, portico, quarto, tyro, solo,* add only *s*. (11) When the *o* is preceded by a vowel, *s* alone is added, as *folio*, plural *folios;* &c.

V. (12) Nouns ending in *y* preceded by a *consonant* change the *y* into *ies* in the plural, as *city*, plural *cities; lady, ladies.**

(13) There are some few plurals, of old English words, which are not formed on the same general principle with the classes of nouns already enumerated: viz., by the addition of an *s* sound, but by a modification of the vowel sound of the root (see § 35: 2). We subjoin a list of the principal nouns of this class, as some of them are familiar words, frequently employed in discourse, and we may find it necessary to introduce them in the construction of examples.

Singular.	*Plural.*	*Singular.*	*Plural.*
Man,	Men.	Foot,	Feet.
Woman,	Women.	Tooth,	Teeth.
Mouse,	Mice.	Goose,	Geese.
Louse,	Lice.		

We may add the personal pronouns and their plural forms used as subjects.

	Singular.	*Plural.*		*Singular.*	*Plural.*
1st person,	I,	We.	3d per.	He, *mas.* She, *fem.* It, *neut.*	They, *all genders.*
2d person,	(Thou or) You,	You.			

rals in *ves*. The word *dwarf*, though Anglo-Saxon, forms its plural by adding the sharp sound of *s*.—(See Latham's Eng. Gram. p. 61.)

* In the beginning of the 17th century, the singular forms of these nouns ended in *ie*, for which *y* has since been substituted. In the *early editions* of the authorized English version of the Bible, *city* is spelled *citie; mercy, mercie;* &c. The present plurals of these nouns are the regularly constructed plurals of these ancient singular forms. Nouns ending in *y* preceded by a vowel add *s* soft to form the plural.

(10) How do nouns ending in *o* preceded by a consonant form their plurals? Give exceptions. (11) What happens when the *o* final is preceded by a vowel?

(12) What is said of the formation of the plural of nouns ending in *y* preceded by a consonant? Give examples.

(13) What is said of exceptions? What is the *plural* form of man? &c.

Exercises on the Formation of the Plural.—Exercise I Let the pupil furnish a list of a certain number of nouns which form their plurals by adding the sharp sound of *s*, and give the reason—viz., because they end in one of the sharp consonantal sounds, *f*, *k*, *p*, *t*, *th* hard.

Exercise II. Give a similar list of nouns forming the plural by the addition of the soft sound of *s* = z; and assign the reason—viz., because they end in one of the vowel sounds, or in one of the flat consonantal sounds, *b*, *d*, *g*, *l*, *m*, *n*, *r*, *v*, and *th* soft.

Exercise III. A similar list of nouns ending in an *s* sound with their respective plurals.

Exercise IV. Nouns in *f*, and *fe*, forming plurals in *ves*.

Exercise V. Nouns in *o* preceded by a consonantal sound, taking the addition *es* in the *written* plural.

Exercise VI. Nouns in *y* preceded by a consonantal sound, and taking *ies* in the plural.

What we have said above will be sufficient for the student to learn on first passing through the book. We subjoin some additional remarks to be studied on a second perusal, together with a table of irregular forms. The pupil will remember that plurals are almost universally formed by adding either *s* or *es*, soft or hard. The exceptions are not very numerous, though they give the grammarian considerable trouble, on account of their various forms.

[§ 43. Additional Remarks on the Formation of Plurals.—(1) A few English nouns form their plurals by the addition of *en* to the root. This plural termination was more common in Anglo-Saxon than in English. It seems to have been in earlier use than the formation in *s;* which, however, superseded it (in *living use*) even in Anglo-Saxon long before the Norman invasion. (2) The only plurals of this form, in current use at the present day, are *oxen*, plural of *ox; children*, plural of *child;* and *brethren*, one of the plural forms of *brother*.

Dr. Latham has justly observed (Eng. Language, p. 220, 2d edit.), that the irregularity (if it may be so called) of the formation of the plurals, both of nouns ending in *o* preceded by a consonant, and of nouns ending in *y*, is a matter of orthography rather than of etymology—of spelling rather than of grammar. In the *spoken language*, all these plurals are regularly formed by the addition of the soft sound of *s* to the noun. For more on the subject of the formation of the plural, exceptions, &c., see Additional Remarks, § 43.

[§ 43. (1) What is said of the formation of plurals in *en?* (2) Name the plurals of this form in current use.

(3) *Children* seems to exhibit a combination of two ancient plural forms. Or, rather the *en*, in the case of this word, has been added to a form already in use as a plural. *Childer*, as the plural of *child*, is still in common use among the uneducated classes, in many parts of the British empire. The present plural seems to have been formed by adding *en* to this more ancient plural. The Anglo-Saxon plural was cildru or cildra. So, here, as in a thousand other cases, the aberration from the real analogies, and old established rules of language—*the blunder*, if you please—is chargeable to the educated and *fashion-following* class, not to the common people.

(4) According to present custom, the plural form *brothers* is employed, when we intend to express the natural relation subsisting between children of the same parents; and *brethren*, when we apply the word figuratively to designate the fellow members of the same profession, or society; as *Christian brethren*; *masonic brethren*, &c. (5) In the earlier language, and particularly in the authorized version of the Bible, the form *brethren* is employed in the literal sense to express the relation of sons of the same parent; as, *Joseph's brethren*, &c.

(6) Plurals in *en* were much more common in old English. We find such forms as *hosen*, plural of *hose*; *shooen*, or *shoon* (not yet altogether out of use in some parts of Britain), plural of *shoe*; *bischopen*, plural of *bischop*—now written *bishop*, &c.

(7) We have noticed already that a few nouns form the plural by a *radical* change—a change of the vowel sound of the *root*. This method of formation is likely of earlier date than any of which traces have come down to the present time. We have already enumerated the few nouns which still retain plurals of this form; § 42 : 13.

(8) The word *penny* takes *pence* for plural, when we mean to express a *sum of money*; but *pennies*, when we mean to refer to the *pieces of coin*. The words *six pence* mean so much money—it may be contained in a single silver coin—but the words *six pennies* mean six of the copper coins, of which we call each one a penny.*

---

* The word *pence*, accompanied by a numeral, assumes a plural form; as, two *six pences*, &c. Here, as to form, we have a double plural. As re

---

(3) What remarks are made in regard of the plural form *children*?

(4) What is said of the use of the plural forms *brothers* and *brethren*? (5) How was the form *brethren* used in former times?

(6) Repeat what is said of plurals in *en* in Old English.

(7) Repeat what is said of plurals formed by a *radical change*.

(8) Mention the plural forms of *penny* and their distinct uses. Give the illustration.

(9) *Dice* is the plural form of *die* used in play; but *die*, a stamp, has the regular plural form *dies*.

(10) The nouns, *deer* and *sheep*, are the same in the singular and in the plural. Swine, often given as the plural of sow, generally means the species. When we speak of a number of the animals, we use the regular form, two sows, &c.

(11) Many words of foreign origin retain the plural form of the language from which they are adopted. (12) Some have two plural forms, one their original form, the other, a regular English form; as, *cherub*, plural *cherubim* or *cherubs*—the first the Hebrew, the second the English plural. In the same manner *genius*, a *spirit*, has the plural *genii;* but *genius*, a person of extraordinary intellectual power, has for plural *geniuses*. *Index*, an algebraic term, has *indices* for plural; *index*, a table of reference, has the English form, *indexes*.

We subjoin a list of the principal words which commonly take foreign plurals. To those which have sometimes a plural of the English form we add E. pl.=English plural:

(13) *Singular.*	*Plural.*	*Singular.*	*Plural.*
Alumnus.	Alumni.	Arcanum.	Arcana.
Amanuensis.	Amanuenses.	Axis.	Axes.
Analysis.	Analyses.	Bandit.	Banditti, E. pl.
Animalculum.	Animalcula.	Basis.	Bases.
Antithesis.	Antitheses.	Beau.	Beaux.
Cherub.	Cherubim, E. pl.	Medium.	Media, E. pl.
Crisis.	Crises.	Memorandum.	Memoranda, E. pl.
Criterion.	Criteria.	Metamorphosis.	Metamorphoses.
Datum.	Data.	Nebula.	Nebulæ.
Effluvium	Effluvia.	Oasis.	Oases.
Ellipsis.	Ellipses.	Parenthesis.	Parentheses.
Erratum.	Errata.	Phenomenon.	Phenomena.
Focus.	Foci.	Radius.	Radii.
Formula.	Formulæ.	Seraph.	Seraphim, E. pl.
Fungus.	Fungi, E. pl.	Speculum.	Specula.
Genius.	Genii, E. pl.	Stimulus.	Stimuli.

---

gards thought, our mind contemplates a sixpence as a single object. The *conception* is of a *unit*, and hence susceptible of *plurality*.

---

(9) State the facts in regard of the word *die*.

(10) The facts in regard of the words *deer*, *sheep*, *swine*.

(11) What is said of some words of foreign origin? (12) What further fact in regard of some of these? Give examples.

(13) What is the plural form of alumnus? &c.

Singular.	*Plural.*	*Singular.*	*Plural.*
Genus.	Genera.	Stratum.	Strata.
Hypothesis.	Hypotheses.	Thesis.	Theses.
Index.	Indices, E. pl. (11)	Vertebra.	Vetebræ.
Lamina.	Laminæ.	Vertex.	Vertices.
Magus.	Magi.	Vortex.	Vortices.

We might add to this list, as words of this description are daily increasing in the language. But as such words are generally (especially those newly imported) only used by persons who understand the languages from which they come, it is less necessary to give a complete enumeration. (14) We now commonly use Messieurs—by contraction Messrs. as the plural of Mr.; as the *Messrs.* Thomson, or *Messrs.* Thomson and Adams. The old fashion was to say the Mr. Thomsons; and Mr. Thomson and Adams. In the same manner we now say the two Misses Thomson. Formerly it was more common to say the two Miss Thomsons. Mesdames for the plural of Mrs., so far as we know, occurs rarely, if at all.

(15) In regard to compound words, such as take after the principal word in the compound another word or words (as a modification or complement) form the plural by adding the *s* sound to the principal word ; as, *commander-in-chief*, pl. *commanders-in-chief.* Here, *in-chief* is a mere complement of *commander*. The same applies to the words *father-in-law*, *son-in-law*, *aide-de-camp*, &c.

(16) When the principal word comes last, it of course takes the plural modification. (17) Sometimes both words assume the plural form, but in such cases the words are scarcely to be reckoned compounds, but rather nouns in apposition. We have examples in men-servants, women-servants, knights-templars.

(18) Nouns used only in the Plural Form.—Some nouns, being the names of things formed double by nature or by art, are used only in the plural; as, *bellows*, *lungs*, *scissors*, *tongs*, *pincers*, &c.

(19) Nouns used only in the Singular Form.—Proper names, when used strictly as such, that is, when used appropriately to a single individual, have necessarily no plural form. When nouns, originally

(14) What is said of the plural of Mr.? &c.

(15) What of compounds, when complementary words follow the principal word?

(16) What when the principal word comes last in the *compound?* (17) What is said of compound words in which both words take the plural form?

(18) Describe the nouns which are used only in the plural form; and give examples.

(19) Tell the first class of nouns used only in the singular form. Notice apparent exceptions.

proper, are usurped to name a class, they have plurals; as, The Cæsars, The Tudors, &c.

(20) Most *abstract nouns* are never used in the plural. Some of them are occasionally employed as names of *classes* of abstract attributes, and then assume a plural form, being used for the time in the same manner as *common nouns;* for example, we say the *virtues* of *justice* and *benevolence.* But this is a deviation from the special use of abstract nouns, which is to express an attribute regarded in all its universality as a single conception. When we speak of virtue, we mean the attribute virtuous in its whole extent, and this admits of no plural; but when we say the virtue of prudence, we imply that the conception of virtue admits of subdivision of parts, and consequently the name must admit a plural form. (See § 26.)

(21) The names of substances which are not divided into perceptible parts or portions, and of which, consequently, we cannot determine the quantity, by mere enumeration of these parts, but only by measure or weight, are seldom used in the plural form. (22) Such words as, *butter*, *lard*, *pitch*, *wax*, *gold*, *silver*, *iron*, &c., are for this reason never used in the plural form.*

(23) Several nouns having plural terminations are employed in the construction of propositions, sometimes with the singular, sometimes with the plural form of the verb. (24) The nouns, *means*, *wages* (see

* For the same reason assigned above, namely, that the quantity of the substances which they represent is always ascertained by weight, the nouns *wool, tea, sugar,* &c., are never used in the plural form, except when we speak of different sorts of these commodities. Thus, we speak of the *wools* of Spain, and the *wools* of Saxony; of *green teas* and *black teas,* &c. Many things, such as the large fruits, *apples, pears, peaches, plums,* though their quantity is generally ascertained by measure, present themselves in a form which suggests the ideas of unity and plurality. They are capable of being counted, and are, in fact, usually retailed by number. But the metals, and some other substances never present themselves in such a manner as to suggest the notion either of *unity* or *plurality,* except when formed into regular masses, or manufactured into useful or ornamental articles; and then these masses or manufactured articles are known by their own appropriate names; as *ingots* of *gold,* or *silver, bars* of *iron, guineas, dollars, cups, goblets,* &c., &c.; so that a plural form of the name of the material is wholly unnecessary.

(20) Repeat what is said of *abstract nouns* in reference to this matter.

(21) Describe a class of names of *substances* used only in the singular. (22) Give examples.

(23) Repeat what is said of some nouns having plural terminations. (24) Give exam-

Gen. 30 : 28; Hag. 1 : 6; Rom. 6 : 23), *amends*, are of this class, with *ethics*, *mathematics*, *physics*, and many similar names of sciences. (25) News, though a plural form, is treated in construction as singular. (26) The noun *pains*, in the sense of *trouble*, *labor*, is employed in construction, sometimes as singular, sometimes as plural. (27) Modern usage inclines to the employment of this word exclusively as plural. (28) *Riches*, originally a singular noun (*richesse*) introduced from the French language, seems to have been taken by the uneducated for a plural, because it ends in an *s* sound, and hence it has come to be treated as a plural form in grammatical construction. (29) The word always takes plural verbs, and is represented by plural pronouns: "Riches certainly *make themselves* wings; *they* fly away," &c.

(30) The word *alms* is also originally a singular form. This word has come in the same way to be treated generally in the language of the present day as a plural. (31) It is (at least, sometimes) recognised as a singular form by older writers; for example, "Asked *an alms*." (Acts 3 : 3.)

Exercise I., II., &c.—Let the learner form propositions having for their subject a given number of the above exceptions to the general rule for the formation of plurals.]

---

ples. (25) What of the noun *news?* (26) What of *pains*, in the sense of *trouble?* (27) What is said of modern usage in this matter? (28) What is said of the word *riches?* (29) What form of verbs does it take, and what pronouns represent it? Give example.

(30) What is said of the word *alms?* (31) Has it ever been treated as *singular?* Ex-

CHAPTER III.

OF THE VERB.

§ 44. PRELIMINARY REMARK.—(1) It is the usual practice, both in Grammars and in Dictionaries, to employ the *infinitive* (the *verbal noun* with the prefix *to*, noticed in § 27) to designate any particular verb. (2) Thus, the word which asserts *being* is called the verb *to be*, the word which asserts *writing* the verb *to write*, &c. (3) It will be convenient in compliance with universal usage to retain this manner of indicating verbs; though apparently inconsistent with the definition of verbs which we have given, since the verbal with the prefix *to* is not assertive, and therefore *not* a verb, according to our definition. (4) The learner will therefore please remember that when we use this form of expression, *the verb to write*, *the verb to think*, &c., we do not mean that the words *to write*, *to think*, are themselves verbs, but to express concisely (what may be more fully expressed) *the verb which asserts the action to write, or of writing—the verb which expresses the action to think*, &c.

(5) We here repeat the definition of the verb which we have adopted: viz., THE VERB IS THAT WORD IN A PROPOSITION WHICH EXPRESSES ASSERTION. As we arrange in the class of verbs *all* the words and *only* the words which perform the peculiar and readily recognised function of *asserting*, the learner, after a little practice, can find no difficulty in distinguishing them.

CLASSIFICATION OF VERBS IN REFERENCE TO THEIR MEANING.—(6) The first striking distinction, in reference to meaning which arrests our attention, is that between verbs, which express *alone* a *complete* predicate—form a full rational assertion respecting the

---

§ 44. (1) How are particular verbs designated in *grammars* and *dictionaries?* (2) Illustrate by an example. (3) What is said of the practice of indicating verbs in this manner? (4) Repeat the caution given to the learner.

(5) Repeat the definition of a *verb* and the remark which follows.

(6) Mention a striking distinction among verbs in reference to their meaning. (7) Illus-

subject of the proposition—and those which do not express a predicate without the help of other words to *complete* them. (7) For example, the verbs *grow* and *sleep* express a *complete predicate*—a *complete assertion*. Uniting the *subject nouns*, CORN and BOYS, with the verbs GROWS and SLEEP respectively, we form two complete propositions containing rational assertions; CORN GROWS; BOYS SLEEP. But such verbs as MAKE and GIVE will not form complete predicates, or complete assertions. If I say MEN MAKE, or MEN GIVE, I express no complete sense. Some completing word must be placed after them in order to form a proposition; as, *The man makes ploughs; the man gives lessons*, &c. (8) Regarded in this point of view, verbs might be divided into *complete* or *perfect verbs*, and *incomplete* or *imperfect verbs*.

Perhaps the most complete classification of verbs founded on their meaning (as distinct from their form), and having reference to constructional arrangements, would be one which should distribute them according to the *forms* of the *complements* or *modifications* of which they are susceptible. Following this method, we should have a class of verbs which, without any *complement* or modification, express a rational predicate, a class of verbs which require a complement indicating a *passive* or *suffering object*, a class of verbs which require complements, indicating both a *passive* and a *personal object*, a class of verbs which take a *passive* and a *factitive object* to complete them, a class of verbs which require an *adverb*, &c. Such a classification would lead to details unsuited to the present stage of our progress in grammatical analysis. All the useful purposes which it could effect will be effected, whilst we examine and discuss hereafter the several complements of verbs. When our discussion is completed, a classification founded on this principle can, if requisite, be more readily made, and more easily comprehended by the learner.

But though the division of verbs into *complete* and *incomplete verbs*, subdividing the *incomplete* into classes in reference to the forms of *complements* necessary to constitute them rational predicates, is perhaps the most philosophical, we defer (for the reasons assigned) introducing it for the present, (9) and confine ourselves to the old and generally received classification, which is exclusively used in all our dictionaries as well as grammars, and for this reason claims the

---

trate this distinction by examples. (8) Into what classes might verbs be divided in reference to this fact?

attention of the learner. (9) It claims attention also as preparatory to the explanation of what is called the passive voice of verbs.

§ 45. (1) This classification divides verbs (on the principle of their requiring or not requiring one particular form of complement) into *intransitive* and *transitive*, or, to use the more ancient names, *neuter verbs* and *active verbs*. (2) The distinction between these two classes is this, in what are called *intransitive* or neuter verbs, that which is asserted or predicated *terminates* in the *subject* of the assertion—affects only the subject. (3) Thus, when we say, "*Corn grows*," we predicate the action of *growing* of the subject corn, as terminating in the corn. The act of growing is not such as affects directly any other object beyond the subject of which it is asserted. (4) Hence, this class of verbs has been appropriately called, by some modern grammarians, *subjective verbs*, as the action which they express terminates in the *subject.*

(5) On the contrary, the *transitive* or *active* verbs express an action which does not terminate in the subject, but passes over on some other object either expressed or implied in the proposition. (6) Thus in the example used above, "the man makes a table," the action of making passes over upon the object made—"*the table*," which undergoes or suffers the action. (7) The object which undergoes the action expressed by the verb is called, to distinguish it from other objects of the verb's action, the *suffering* or *passive* object. (8) From the fact that the action of these verbs *passes over*, they have been called *transitive verbs*. *Transitive* means that *passes over*. (The reason for which they have been called *active verbs* is to be explained presently.) (9) These verbs have also been appropriately named *objective verbs*, because the action which they express has always reference to some *object* external to the subject, and a word expressive of this object is necessary to complete them—that

---

(9) What reasons are assigned for giving attention to the old classification?

§ 45. (1) Give the names of the two divisions of verbs according to this classification. (2) State the peculiarities which distinguish *neuter* or *intransitive* verbs. (3) Illustrate by examples. (4) By what name have these neuter verbs been appropriately called by some modern grammarians?

(5) Describe the active or transitive verbs. (6) Illustrate by example. (7) What name is given to the object which undergoes the action of the verb? (8) What does the term *transitive* mean, and why is it applied to this class of verbs? (9) What other name has

is to enable them to form a rational *predicate.* (10) We shall retain the old names *neuter* and *active*, or *intransitive* and *transitive*, which, as we understand and use them, are equivalent, viz., intransitive to neuter, and transitive to active.

(11) Every verb that always expresses a complete predicate belongs of course to the class of *neuter* or *intransitive verbs.* (12) But many verbs which cannot make complete sense without modifying words belong also to the class of *neuter verbs*—that is, of verbs expressing an action terminating in the subject of which it is asserted. (13) Thus the verb *behaves* will not form a complete assertion without the help of another word. The *boy behaves* is not a complete assertion. To express complete sense, we must say, *the boy behaves well* or *behaves ill*, or use some other words expressive of the manner of his behavior. [(14) Still this verb requires no *passive* object. The action of *behaving* passes over upon no other object; it terminates in the *subject.* If we place after it a word in the form of an *objective complement*, it must be a word expressive of the same person with the *subject noun;* as in the example, *the boy behaves* HIMSELF *well.* Here *himself* refers to the same individual expressed by the *subject noun—boy.* We cannot say that, the boy *behaves any other person* or *any other thing*, well or ill, &c. That is, the verb *behaves* can take after it no *suffering* or *passive* object distinct from the subject of which it is asserted. In other words, the *action terminates* in *the subject.*]

(15) It has been already noticed that all the verbs of the class which we have ventured to name *complete verbs*, *admit* of modifying or completing words, but none of them admit of the modification of a *passive object;* they do not express an action which can pass over on an object distinct from the subject of which they are employed to make an assertion. The importance of this distinction among verbs will be better understood, when we come to treat of the various forms of modifications or complements which we attach

---

been given to them? And why? (10) What names do we adopt? (11) To which of these classes do the complete verbs belong? (12) Are any of the incomplete verbs also neuter? (13) Illustrate by an example. [(14) Repeat what is said in further illustration of the example.]

(15) Do the verbs which we have called complete verbs admit of completing words? Can they be completed by a noun expressive of a passive object?

to them in order to form complete predicates; and when we come to consider the passive form.

[(16) The nature of the distinction between active and neuter verbs may perhaps be rendered more intelligible by the exhibition of examples of neuter verbs which are manifestly equivalent to certain other active verbs, together with a noun expressing a particular passive object. *Participate*, for instance, is equivalent to the verb *take* with the noun *part* employed as its passive object. *Participate, to take part.* Here *take*—the active verb—is obviously the *less complete* of the two, since it requires the complementary word *part* in order to render it equivalent to participate.*]

* We may here notice the advantage gained in language by employing, as we commonly do, verbs expressive of incomplete predicates, instead of always employing verbs expressive at once of an action and the object which this action immediately affects. The word *participate*, means exclusively to *take part.* Indeed it is a compound of two Latin words, the one of which means *part* and the other *take.* But the word *take* may have a vast number of other modifications designating passive objects attached to it besides this, and with each of these it will express a distinct assertion; as *take advice, take courage, take counsel, take time*, &c., &c. And, it will be observed that all the words employed to express these modifications are necessary for other purposes besides this. They are not invented and added to the language for this sole purpose, but already previously existed as names to be used for *subject nouns.* This is only a secondary use to which they are applied. Now if we had a separate form, as in the case of the word *participate*, to express the verb *take* with each of the *passive objects* which may modify it, we should have a considerable number of words added to the language to express assertions which are sufficiently expressed by the verb *take*, repeated with certain words already in use for other necessary purposes. When we reflect that what we have now said of the verb *take* applies to a host of other verbs, we shall be able to conceive what vast economy of words has been effected by the subdivision of thought in the process of forming signs to give it expression. Were not only verbs modified by *objective* complements, but verbs modified by all the other complements (of which we shall treat presently), serving to make up full and perfect predicates, to be expressed by separate distinct forms corresponding to each several modification, the increase of words would be still immensely greater. The next step in a *retrograde* direction would be to express every distinct proposition, subject, predicate, and all their several modifications by one dis-

[(16) Illustrate the distinction between *active* and *neuter* verbs by the example of the verb participate.]

[(17) We must not omit to notice that frequently the same word is used both as an *active* and a *neuter verb*—but, let it be remembered, with very different meanings. (18) Thus, *The ship sinks*, and *The pirate sinks the ship.* In the first case the word *sinks* expresses an action which terminates in the *subject*, in the latter case an action which necessarily passes over upon a *suffering* or *passive object;* that is, an object which *suffers*, or *receives*, or is *affected* directly by the action. (19) We have similar examples in *Glass breaks*, and *John breaks the glass; The wood burns*, and *The man burns the wood; William feels warm*, and *The physician feels the patient's pulse*, &c. (20) Here the verbs, "*breaks*," "*burns*," "*feels*," are used both *transitively* and *intransitively*, in an *active* and in a *neuter* sense, but the meaning of these words, when employed transitively and intransitively, is totally different; the actions asserted in the two cases are altogether unlike. (21) The action of *burning* asserted of the *wood* in the one case, and the action of *burning* asserted of the man who uses wood as fuel in the other case, are as unlike as almost any other two actions. Both agree in being attended by the same phenomenon—the combustion of wood, and from this come to be expressed by the same word, the same sign. The verb *burns* has a third meaning distinct from the two already mentioned; as, for example, when we say, *The fire burns any substance placed near it, The fire burns the boy's clothes.* (22) In regard to most of these verbs doubly employed, as active and as neuter verbs, the neuter seems to be the primitive or original use, and the active a secondary use usurped in the progress of the language. (23) Many

---

tinct sign. A language of this kind would be wholly unmanageable and nearly useless in the intercourse of life. We reap much advantage from the complex method adopted for the purpose of expressing thought—the method of employing propositions consisting of numerous signs (words) orderly arranged. We should not, therefore, complain, if this complex arrangement sometimes occasions a little trouble in grammatical analysis, and often renders great care necessary on the part of the speaker and writer to avoid ambiguity and obscurity.

[(17) What is said of the same word being employed both in a *neuter* and in an active sense? (18) Illustrate by an example. (19) Give other examples. (20) What is said of the difference of meaning in all these examples between the active and neuter verb? (21) Illustrate in the case of *burn* in a *neuter*, and *burn* in an *active* sense. (22) Which ap-

of these verbs, in their usurped, active, or transitive use, belong to the class which the grammarians have called *causatives*. In the active use they signify *to cause to do* that which the neuter verb expresses. For example, *The pirate sinks the ship*, that is, *The pirate* CAUSES *the ship to sink*. *The farmer burns wood*, that is, *causes wood to burn for fuel*.]

EXERCISE I.—Let the learner point out the verbs in a given lesson, distinguishing the neuter and active verbs, assigning his reason for calling them verbs, and his reason for classing them among the active or neuter verbs, as the case may be.

MODEL OF ANALYSIS.—EXAMPLE 1.—*Commerce and manufactures flourish together*. The verb in this proposition is *flourish*, because *this word expresses* the *assertion*. Flourish is a *neuter* or *intransitive* verb, because it expresses an action terminating in the *subject*, and not passing over upon any *object* suffering that action, or directly affected by it. We cannot say that commerce or manufactures flourish any person or any thing.

EXAMPLE 2.—*Perseverance overcomes difficulties*. The verb or assertive word here is "*overcomes*." This verb is *active* or *transitive*, since it expresses an action which passes over directly on a passive *object*. In this case, the object is expressed by the word difficulties. The action expressed by "*overcomes*" does not terminate in the subject.

EXERCISE II.—Let the learner furnish a written list of twenty or more neuter verbs, and give his reasons for assigning them to this class.

EXERCISE III.—A similar list of active verbs, with reasons assigned for the classification.

EXERCISE IV.—A list of verbs used both in an active and in a neuter sense.

These exercises to be repeated till the learner understands completely how to distinguish neuter and active verbs.

§ 46. [(1) Among the *intransitive* verbs there is one which merits our special notice on account of its frequent employment in language, and yet more on account of its peculiar significance—we mean the verb which is used to assert existence or *being*, commonly called the verb TO BE. (2) This verb assumes, when employed assertively, the forms *am*, *is*, *are*, *was*, *were*, &c., according to the

---

pears to be the primitive use of most of these verbs? (23) What is said of the active sense of many of these verbs?]

§ 46. [(1) What intransitive verb merits special notice? Tell the reason. (2) What

person and number of the *subject noun.* (3) The verb *to be* has been generally considered as THE VERB, by way of pre-eminence, and has hence been called the *substantive verb.* (4) These distinctions have been bestowed on this word because it has been supposed not only to possess peculiar significance, but to perform a *peculiar function* in propositions. (5) It has been recognised, both by logicians and grammarians, as ordinarily expressing the *simple copula*, and therefore essential to all propositions, and always *implied* when not expressed in every assertive word. (6) According to this view all other verbs imply this *copula* or verb, *to be*, and express, at the same time, an *attribute*, and from this fact are called *adjective verbs*, being, as is supposed, made up of the *substantive verb* and an attribute or adjective. (7) This opinion of a *peculiar grammatical function* pertaining to the verb, expressive of existence, though almost universally admitted since the days of Aristotle, we think, will appear, on careful examination, destitute of a solid foundation. (8) And, so long as it is maintained, it stands, as it seems to us, a serious obstacle in the way of those who attempt a lucid and consistent analysis of language. (9) *The verb* IS, in our opinion (an opinion not rashly formed), *expresses a predicate*, or *partial predicate* (namely, BEING), *and indicates a copula, like all other verbs.* (10) The real difference, the only difference is between *the predicate* which this verb asserts and the predicates asserted by other verbs. (11) Other verbs are nearly all used to assert action (we mean action in the most enlarged sense), this to assert *being* or existence, which it must be acknowledged is a very peculiar conception, and which has intimate relation with the subject matter of our other conceptions. (12) Were we to attempt to explain the conception of *being* or *entity*, and its relation with other conceptions, we might, like many who have gone before us, readily involve ourselves in a maze of metaphysical subtleties. (13) Happily this task does not lie in our way.

---

are the usual assertive forms of the verb *to be?* (3) In what light has this verb been generally regarded? (4) Why have such distinctions been bestowed upon this word? (5) What peculiar function does it exclusively perform according to the notions of grammarians and logicians? (6) What do all the verbs according to this view imply, and what have they in consequence been called? (7) What is said of this notion? (8) What is the effect of maintaining it? (9) What opinion is here expressed of the verb IS? (10) What appears to be the real and only difference between the verb *to be* and other verbs? (11) Illustrate this view of the subject. (12) What is said of explaining the conception of being? (13) Has

(14) We simply contend that the *verb* TO BE *has, grammatically considered, no function that distinguishes it from other verbs;* whatever may be the metaphysical mysteries connected with the *conception* which it expresses. (15) In the proposition, for example, *The steward is faithful*, what we assert of the steward is the *predicate* BEING, modified or completed by the word *faithful*. "*Being faithful*" is asserted in the proposition, and not simply "*faithful*," as the logicians and grammarians generally have inadvertently maintained.]

NOTE.—The doctrine in regard to the verb *to be*, presented above, may seem novel to some of our readers, who have been taught to consider this verb as expressing the naked *copula*. We were taught so to consider it, and never doubted till recently of the soundness of the ancient and common doctrine in reference to this subject. We had written a large part of a treatise on *grammatical analysis* in conformity with the common view of this matter. In the progress of the work we encountered difficulties which we could not surmount, inconsistencies which we could not reconcile, whilst we adhered to the current opinion entertained of the verb *to be*. Though the distinction stated above, and the innovation proposed in the manner of analyzing propositions may appear of small moment to a superficial observer, we are assured that it will not so appear to intelligent and well-informed grammarians. Such will anticipate that very important changes in the mode of conducting grammatical analysis will necessarily follow from this new view of the so called *substantive verb*. And they will readily trace these changes in other parts of this treatise. We appeal to the judgment of our readers, as we have heretofore appealed to the judgment of others in conversation, without ever once failing of obtaining a verdict in favor of our view of the matter, when fully and plainly stated. We put to them the following simple question; their answer will decide whether they hold to the old doctrine, or agree with our views: In the proposition, "*The steward is faithful*," is it simply "*faithful*" that is asserted of the steward, or is it "*being faithful*," that is asserted of him? If the latter, as we maintain, and as all to whom we have presented the subject, after deliberation have admitted; then the verb IS, *grammatically considered*, differs in no respect from other intransitive verbs. It may be modified,

---

the grammarian any thing to do with this task? (14) What is here asserted of the verb *to be?* (15) Illustrate by an example.]

as we shall presently see, by the same kind of complements as other neuter verbs, and by no kind of complement different from those which *some* of them admit. The analysis of the propositions in which it is used as the assertive word, presents, under this view, no peculiarity. Owing to its peculiar *meaning*, it is more frequently used than any other verb. And owing also to this peculiar meaning it happens, that in the English language every kind of action asserted by all the other verbs, with a few exceptions (see § 62), can be asserted by this verb, completed by the verbal adjective in *ing* (or perhaps rather the *verbal noun*) formed from the other verbs respectively. (See § 64). This capability of such universal application, and especially of serving with the help of a verbal to assert *substantially* the same predicates which are asserted by the other verbs, has, no doubt, originated, or at least given greater currency to the notion so generally entertained, that this verb is simply a *copula*—an instrument to indicate assertion—and, consequently, that it is implied in all other verbs. The action, for example, of *growing* can be predicated either by using the word *grows*, or by using the words *is growing*. *The corn grows*, or *the corn is growing*. But when we come to the close analysis of the latter proposition, we find that it contains an element which the other does not. In the proposition, *corn grows*, *growing* simply is asserted of the corn; but in the proposition, *corn is growing*, *being growing* is asserted. These two propositions, in the current usage of the language, are employed for different purposes, as having a recognised difference of meaning. The one cannot, with propriety, in all cases be substituted for the other. *Corn grows*, is a proposition always true, but *corn is growing*, is only true in the season when corn is actually in a state of growth. In the former case *growing* is asserted *indefinitely*, in the latter it is asserted as *actually existing* and *progressive*.

We may notice here, that a large proportion of all the propositions which we have occasion to use in the intercourse of life, are those in which the existence of some quality or property is asserted of some subject. In constructing all such propositions, the verb which predicates existence performs a part. Add to this, what we have just mentioned above, that the same verb is used with the verbals in *ing*, to express *action* in actual existence, or going on at a time indicated, besides (what we are about to consider) that the passive form in our language is made by means of this verb, and we shall not be surprised to find that the several assertive forms of the verb *to be* come into constant use in discourse.

Before we conclude this note (perhaps not unnecessarily long for the vindication of the course which we have pursued in the treatment of the verb *to be*, and the copula of propositions, &c.), we may mention briefly, for the benefit of those who are curious in these matters, some of the difficulties which we encountered in pursuing our analysis on the old method (namely, considering the verb *to be* as the real copula of all propositions), and which difficulties have been the occasion of leading us first to *doubt* of the soundness of the common views of the copula, and finally, to *reject* these views.

One of these difficulties arose from matters already presented in this note. How shall we establish a distinction, according to the common theory, that IS constitutes simply the copula (or simply indicates predication), between such assertions as, 1st, *corn grows*, and 2d, *corn is growing?* What is asserted of corn in the first of these propositions? Is it not plainly the act expressed by *growing?* And if IS merely indicates assertion, what but growing is asserted in the second? And yet all must admit that the two propositions are not equivalent, are not always, or (what is the same thing) completely interchangeable. It may be replied, that *growing*, which we assert is predicated in the first case, is a noun; and *growing*, in the second example, is a participle. Suppose we admit this, how will it help the objector and the advocate of the old view? Is an action expressed in the second proposition? If so, how comes it to be expressed by a participle, and not by a *substantive* name of that action? Here is a new difficulty. But, waving this, how will this plea that *growing* in the second proposition is a participle, help to explain the difference between the two propositions? The difficulty, it will be seen already, is easily solved, if we admit *is* to be, like other verbs, a predicate, or partial predicate, indicating at the same time assertion. *Is*, according to this view, as we have seen above, asserts *being*. And in the assertion, corn is growing, *being growing* is what is asserted of the corn, that is, *being*, *or existence in that qualified state expressed by the attributive word growing.* But we suspect that *growing* is, in the above use, rather the noun in *ing* than a participle. (See § 64.)

Again, in many cases, IS is employed as a complete predicate. As in the examples, *God is*, "*Joseph is not*, *Simeon is not;*" "TIME WAS, but time shall be no more." In the first of these examples, *being* without any modification is asserted of God—to God exists; in the last, *being* in the past is asserted of time. The cases in which the verb *to be* is employed to express a full predicate in our language, are far more numerous, than at first sight appears. The propositions in our language where the verb *to be* expresses the complete predicate, are generally introduced by the words *it* or *there*. Examples, *It is winter*, *It was autumn.*

" '*Twas* All-Souls' Eve, and Surrey's heart beat high."

There are men who think, &c.=men who think, &c., are; that is (the predicate), *being* is asserted of "*men who think*" *so and so.* The fact that the verb *to be* in such instances expresses a full predicate, is somewhat disguised by the form of expression. But surely *it*, in the first class of examples, serves only as a substitute for the real subject which immediately follows the verb, and neither *it* nor any thing else serves as a complement of the predicate. In the first example, simple existence in an implied present time, is predicated of winter, and in the second, past existence is predicated of autumn. In the examples commencing with *there* (whatever may have been the origin of this form of expression, whether it is an imitation of the French *Il-y-a*, occasioned by the importation of French idioms after the Norman conquest, or an *insensible extension* of the use of the word *there*, till it came to be employed in cases where its original meaning was obscured, and finally lost), one thing is plain, that now this word adds no modification to the predicate, but serves much the same general purpose as the word *it* does in the preceding examples; that is, it serves to enable us to throw the subject after the verb, and thus bring the *subject noun* into contact with the proposition ("men who think," &c.) which modifies it. This is the form of expression which we generally adopt to predicate mere *being* or *existence.* To say, *Men who think so and so* are, to express the mere existence of such men, is a manner of expression unsanctioned by usage, contrary to our idiom, and which seems feeble and void of all harmony. The feebleness and want of harmony are, perhaps, the reason for rejecting it, and adopting the form commencing with *there*, in which the original meaning of *there*, namely, *in that place*, is wholly suppressed, and the word comes to serve a sort of pronominal function. In many other languages, simple existence in such cases is expressed by the verb equivalent to our *to be* (by what in those languages is called the *copula* by logicians), without any accompanying word; as for example, in Latin *sunt* (supply homines) *qui putent*, &c. We subjoin a few more examples, from the authorised version of the Scriptures, of the verb TO BE, used to express a complete predicate: "That they are double to that which IS." Job 11: 6. "The grass of the field, which to-day IS." Matt. 6: 30. "He that cometh to God must believe that He IS." Heb. 11: 6. "From him which *is* and which *was.*" Rev. 1: 4. "And there are seven kings; five are fallen, and one *is*," &c. Rev. 17: 10. "And the beast that *was*, and *is* not." Rev. 17: 11.

Another difficulty which presented itself whilst, in our attempts to give a satisfactory analysis of the structure of the language, we recognised the verb *to be* as performing the function of a mere copula, was to ascertain the distinction between the grammatical functions performed by *is*, for example, in the proposition, The *man* is *old*, and the function performed by *becomes* in the proposition, The man *becomes* old, or by *grows* in the proposition, The man *grows* old, or by *seems* in the proposition, The man *seems* old. The difference of *meaning* of all these verbs is abundantly clear, but we could not discover or assign any *grammatical* distinction. Till this was done, we felt bound, if we called *is* the copula, to call *becomes*, *grows*, *seems*, &c., *copulas*. In this case, copulas would be numerous enough, since every verb which can take an adjective after it as a modification (and we shall find hereafter that there are many such) might claim this name. This was the difficulty which actually arrested our progress, and the attempt to solve it has led to the conclusion, already stated, that between is and the other verbs mentioned above, there is NO GRAMMATICAL, NO FUNCTIONAL DIFFERENCE WHATEVER; that both it and they alike express a predicate, whilst, in common with all verbs, they *indicate predication*, that is, serve as *copula;* consequently that there is no word in our language (and question, is there one in any other?) which expresses a mere naked copula.

§ 47. THE PASSIVE VOICE.—(1) Besides the other uses of the verb *to be*, what is called the passive voice is formed in English, as in many other languages, by the combination of this verb with a class of *verbals* expressive of *completed* action formed from the other verbs. (2) For example, we say, using the *active* form, *The son loves the father*, and using the *passive* form, *The father is loved by the son. Is loved*, made up of the assertive form of the verb *to be*, with the word *loved*, a *verbal adjective* (or, as it is commonly called, participle), expressive of *completed* action, constitutes, as we see here, the *passive form* of *loves.*

(3) The *passive voice* or *passive form* is confined to that class of verbs which we have above named transitive or active verbs. (4) The passive form of these verbs affords us another way of expressing the same proposition, that is expressed by the active form. (5) When we employ the passive form, we make the word which, when we use the *active* form of the verb, represents the *passive* or *suffer-*

§ 47. (1) How is the passive voice in English formed? (2) Illustrate by an example. (3) To what class of verbs is the passive voice or passive form confined? (4) What does this form enable us to do? (5) What change do we make in the subject noun, when

ing object, the *subject noun* of the proposition. (6) Thus, using the active form, we say, *The carpenter* MAKES *a table*, and, using the passive form, *A table* IS MADE *by the carpenter*. (7) This passive form of the verb is convenient when, as often happens, we wish to express that some person or thing suffers, or undergoes an action performed by an agent unknown to us, and we cannot, therefore, supply a definite *subject* for the proposition expressed actively. (8) For example, we can say, *The man is killed*, without knowing who has killed him; *The house was set on fire*, without knowing the incendiary, whose name would serve as the definite subject of the proposition made with the verb in the active form. (9) We have other means, it is true, of expressing the same fact by an active form. (10) We can assume an indefinite subject, such as is expressed by the indefinite words, *somebody*, *something*, and say, *Somebody killed the man*, *Somebody or something set the house on fire.* This form of expression is preferred in some languages. (11) But the passive form is not only often the most convenient in such cases as now described, but also sometimes useful for the purpose of securing greater variety and greater smoothness of expression.

EXERCISES.—REMARK.—In the following exercises, the learner may be allowed to modify his subject noun by a determinative such as *a*, *an*, *the*, *this*, *that*, *one*, and *these*, *those*, *two*, *three*, &c., with plural nouns; or by any descriptive adjective, such as *good*, *bad*, *faithful*, &c. After the verb *to be* he may use any adjective, and after the active verb any noun necessary to complete its meaning, and after the *passive form* of the verb, the noun which serves as subject of the *active* form with the word *by* before it. The liberty of using these modifications will facilitate his task in forming propositions. These modifications will all be explained afterwards in their proper places. In the mean time, they cannot perplex the pupil who knows English. Use the word *is* in forming the passive when the *subject noun* is singular, and *are* when the *subject* noun is plural.

EXERCISE I.—Change the following propositions into propositions expressing the same meaning, and having verbs of the passive form.

---

we employ the passive form? (6) Illustrate by an example. (7) When is the use of this form convenient? (8) Illustrate by an example. (9) Can we effect the same purpose by an active form? (10) Describe the way of employing an active form? (11) For what other purposes is the *passive voice* convenient?

John writes a letter. Somebody strikes William. James sends a message. The servant kindles a fire. The soldiers plunder the country. the army vanquishes the enemy. He praises good men. He loves good boys. John detests dishonest practices. That man assists worthy persons. That man keeps three horses. Vice produces immense suffering.

EXERCISES II. III., &c.—Write ten propositions, each expressed both actively and passively. Model: John keeps a gardener. A gardener is kept by John. We give the perfect participles of the verbs used above. These participles are to be used in the formation of the passive. Write, *written;* strike, *struck;* send, *sent;* keep, *kept.* The rest all end in *ed.* See list of those which do not end in *ed*, § 67.

[(12) We may here observe that it is to the existence of a passive form of the verb in the Greek and Latin languages—a form constituted, to some extent, of the root of the verb modified by *flexion* without the aid, as in our language, of an additional word—that we owe the origin of the terms active, passive, and neuter, applied to verbs. (13) The *transitive* verbs were susceptible both of an active form and a passive form; that is, a form in which the subject of the proposition is the actor or agent, and a form in which the subject represents the recipient of the action, and is passive. (14) These verbs, when used in the one form, were called by the ancient grammarians *active*, and when used in the other form, *passive.* (15) Or one form of the transitive verb was called by them the *active voice*, the other form the *passive voice* of the verb. (16) All *active verbs*, and none but active verbs, according to this classification, are susceptible of a passive use and passive form. (17) All other verbs, not admitting of a passive object, and, consequently, not of a passive voice, they called *neuter* verbs; that is (for *neuter* means *neither*), *neither active* nor *passive verbs.* (18) The subject of these verbs is by them *neither* asserted to act on an object distinct from itself, nor to be the passive recipient of an action.]

NOTE.—The foregoing remarks are the more necessary, because some modern grammarians seem to have misunderstood the principle

[(12) To what do we owe the origin of the terms *active*, *passive*, and *neuter?* (13) Of what two forms are *transitive verbs* susceptible? (14) How are they called when used in the one form, and how when used in the other? (15) Express this otherwise. (16) What verbs alone are susceptible of a passive form? (17) What are all other verbs called, and what does the name by which they are called mean? (18) What is said of the subject of *neuter verbs?*]

on which the ancient division is founded. They have, in consequence of this misunderstanding, in some cases suggested, in some cases adopted, a classification of verbs into "active transitive, active intransitive, passive and neuter;" not observing that the term *active* is used by the ancient grammarians to indicate the same thing which is now indicated by transitive, and that, with the sense which the word active assumes in the old grammars, an *active intransitive* verb is an absurdity, and *active transitive* a useless repetition of equivalent terms.

The ancient classification is (properly) founded on the basis of a distinction in the *grammatical* susceptibilities of verbs; but the division into *active transitive*, *active intransitive*, &c., is founded on two bases—the grammatical susceptibilities of verbs, and their meaning as signs of thought. Verbs are called *active* from their meaning, their significance, and *transitive* or intransitive from the fact that they are susceptible, or, on the contrary, not susceptible of being modified by a passive object. A classification of this kind is illogical, and serves only to create confusion of thought, and difficulty and embarrassment to the learner.

Were it not that many of our dictionaries retain the old names, *active* and *neuter*, we should feel disposed to discard these names altogether, and employ exclusively the more significant and less objectionable names, *transitive* and *intransitive*, now generally used by grammarians. But, whilst, in most dictionaries, the old names *active* and *neuter* are still used to designate this division of the verbs, and, in some more recent dictionaries, the terms *transitive* and *intransitive* are employed for the same purpose, it is necessary for the guidance of the learner in consulting dictionaries, that these two sets of terms should be familiar to him, and that he should remember that though the names are different, the classification designated by them is the same.

§ 48. TENSES OF VERBS.—(1) The most important modification of form which verbs undergo in our language is that employed to indicate the different *times*, to which an assertion has reference. (2) These forms are called the TENSES of the verb. (3) The term *tense* is derived from the French language, in which it is the word to express time.*

* The Latin word *tempus* used to express this same modification of verbs

§ 48. (1) What is the most important modification of the form of verbs? (2) What name is given to this modification? (3) Tell the derivation of the term *tense*.

SUPPOSED HISTORY OF THE FORMATION OF TENSES IN THE NORTHERN DIALECTS.

The following remarks in reference to the history of the formation of tenses, especially in the Teutonic family of languages, may interest the inquisitive student of English Grammar:

We may conceive the history of the formation of tenses to be this. First, the verb in its primary form (the root) was employed to make all kinds of assertions, whether in reference to the present, past, or future; that is, it was employed altogether *indefinitely* as regards *time*. But as past transactions (past events) form a large class of the subjects about which men have occasion to speak, it would be found convenient to have a form specially appropriated to this purpose, leaving all assertions about all other except past occurrences, to be expressed by the ancient *indefinite* form. As mankind generally, and especially in a rude age, do not make the future so much the theme of conversation as the past, which embraces all that traditionary and legendary lore which forms the whole literature of rude nations, a future tense would be a later invention. In fact, the ancient Teutonic dialects appear never to have arrived at this stage of progress. They had no future tense. The modern languages founded on these dialects have supplied this defect, though generally in a somewhat clumsy and awkward manner.

The first step towards a tense in the ancient Teutonic tongues, seems to have been to modify the vowel sound of the original verb, when the assertion had reference to a past event. Afterwards, they began to express the same distinction by an addition to the root—by what is called inflexion. This addition likely in the first instance, consisted of some significant word appended to the root. But this in time came to be so incorporated with the root, as to form with it a single word. In this state, we find the Anglo-Saxon, at the period when the old English begins to be formed from it. It possesses only one tense distinct from the original verb, formed in the words in most common use, and likely of most ancient origin, by a modification of the vowel sound of the root, and in the rest, by a termination. Besides this it possessed means less or more complete of distinguishing the *conjunctive* from the *independent* use of both these tenses, or what is called the *subjunctive* from the *indicative mode*. Our future

---

in that language, and from which the French *temps*, English tense, is derived also signifies time.

tense and all the other compound tense forms, whether expressive of *time*, or of the *condition of the action*, or of both, are the fruits of the (rather bungling) efforts of an age posterior to the Anglo-Saxon period, to express what is generally expressed in the languages ancient and modern of the South of Europe, by a complicated system of inflexions.

These historical remarks throw light upon several grammatical peculiarities. For example, the use of the *indefinite tense* on some occasions, and especially in colloquial forms of expression in speaking of what is past and future; as, when we say, Plato writes beautifully, or reasons well, &c., and, I go to the country to-morrow. Such forms of expression will not surprise us, when we remember, that the form of the verb here employed was anciently used for assertions relating to all times, and till a comparatively recent period, *always* used to express the *future*. The more recent forms appropriated to express past time and future time, can in such instances be dispensed with, as the distinction of time is either not important to be considered, or sufficiently indicated by the sense, if not by the accompanying modifying words.

[(4) In most languages, by what are called the tenses of verbs, more than mere time is indicated. (5) If time alone were indicated, we could have only four modifications at the most, viz., one to indicate that the assertion is made without reference to time, a second to indicate present time, a third to indicate past time, and a fourth to indicate future time (that is time to come).

(6) For verbs by means of the forms called *tenses* do not generally indicate *time* more definitely than this. (7) When greater precision in indicating time is required, recourse is had to additional modifying words expressive of the definite time intended. (8) Many languages have not forms of verbs sufficient to indicate distinctly the three grand divisions of *present*, *past*, and *future* time. (9) And most languages have no separate form to be used when there is no reference to time intended. (10) They employ for this purpose the same form by which *present time* is expressed. (11)

[(4) Is more than mere *time* indicated by *tense* forms? (5) If time alone were indicated, how many *tenses* should we have? (6) State the reason assigned. (7) How do we indicate time with greater precision? (8) Have all languages forms sufficient to distinguish *present*, *past*, and *future*? (9) Have languages generally a distinct form to use when there is no reference to time? (10) What form usually serves this purpose? (11) If time alone

Such languages, if time alone were indicated by the forms called *tenses*, should have only three *tenses*. (12) Yet some of these lan guages have six or more forms *called* tenses. (13) The reason of this is that another modification of the sense of the verb, besides *time*, and distinct from time, is expressed by what are called tenses or *tense forms* in most languages. (14) This fact seems, from the terms *perfect* and *imperfect* used in naming certain tenses, to have been recognised by the old grammarians, though it has been overlooked by the majority of modern grammarians. (15) *Verbs*, as we have already observed, generally express action, and all *actions*, and *being* also (that is all conceptions asserted by verbs), may come to be spoken of either first, as *progressive* (that is, going on), or *incomplete* at any time *past*, *present* or *future*, or, secondly, as *completed* at a *present* or *past* time, or to be completed at a future time. (16) This element we may call the *condition* of the action as *completed* or *perfected*, or, on the contrary, incomplete and progressive. (17) Now to express distinctly all the varieties of modification occasioned by the union of these elements—the *complete* and *incomplete condition* of *the action* expressed by the verb, with the element of *time*, we should require ten separate forms.

(18) We should require, 1st, A form to express an assertion indefinitely—without reference either to the time, or the condition of the action asserted.

(19) 2d. A form to express an assertion that has reference to the *present time* alone, without indicating either the *complete* or *incomplete* condition of the action.

(20) 3d. A form to express an assertion that has reference simply to the *past*, without indicating whether the action is *completed* or not *completed.*

(21) 4th. A form to express an assertion that has reference, in like manner, simply to *future time*—the time to come.

---

were indicated by *tense* forms, how many tenses should such languages have at most? (12) How many forms *called tenses* have some of these languages? (13) Tell the reason of this. (14) What leads us to suppose that this fact was recognised by the ancient grammarians? (15) Describe the different manners in which the action of verbs may come to be spoken of. (16) How may the element described as connected sometimes with the action of verbs be called? (17) To express fully the various combinations of the two elements of the time and the condition of the action of the verb, how many separate forms are required? (18) Describe form 1st. (19) Form 2d. (20) Form 3rd. (21) Form 4th. (22) Forms 5th,

Forms to express assertions in reference to

(22) 5th,	Present time,	Action progressive.
6th,	Past time.	
7th,	Future time.	
(23) 8th,	Present time.	Action completed.
9th,	Past time.	
10th,	Future time.	

(24) In English we express only two of the above modifications of the sense of the verb, by means of the *root* and *inflexion*, without the help of other words. Or, to express the same thing otherwise, we have only two *simple* tense forms in our language; and it is doubtful, as we shall see, whether one of these two can properly be called a tense.]

§ 49. (1) We call those SIMPLE TENSES which consist either of the root of the verb alone, or of the root after undergoing some modification of its form. (2) When any modification of the *time* or of the *condition* of the action asserted by a verb is expressed by the help of other words, we call this combination a *compound tense.* We shall first consider the simple tenses.*

(3) We use the simple root of the verb, subject to certain modifications to indicate the *person* of the subject (§ 52), to express an assertion without reference either to the *time* or the *condition* of the action. Examples: *I write, he writes, the man thinks*, &c. (4) This may be called the INDEFINITE FORM of the verb—*indefinite*, we mean, as relates both to *time* and to *progressive* or *completed* action. (5) For the sake of uniformity, we shall call this the INDEFINITE TENSE.† [(6) This form has been generally, but improperly, as we

* It may admit a doubt whether what we have called the compound tenses should be considered as proper tense *forms* of the respective verbs to which they are assigned in our grammars.

† This name, we admit, is not strictly proper, for this form of the verb is really no *tense*, because it does not indicate *time.* We may here observe,

6th, and 7th. (23) Forms 8th, 9th, and 10th. (24) How many of these modifications of the sense of the verb do we express in English by modified forms of the root?]

§ 49. (1) What are called *simple tenses?* (2) What *compound tenses?*

(3) What form is employed to express an assertion without reference either to the *time* or to the condition of the action? (4) What may this form be called? (5) What name is adopted for the sake of uniformity? [(6) Why has this form been called the *present tense?*

think, called the present tense of English verbs, because it is very commonly used in assertions that have reference to present existing events or facts (7), but it certainly does not *indicate* any necessary connection with the present or any other time. (8) This form is employed in asserting all general truths—truths which exist independent of all time; as, *God* IS *eternal; Truth* IS *unchangeable; A triangle* HAS *three sides and three angles;* and all mathematical and physical truths that are of an immutable nature. (9) It is, in fact, used precisely for the purpose described above, under form 1st; namely, to assert all kinds of action and existence, when we do not intend to limit the action definitely to either *past, present,* or *future,* nor to indicate whether it is *completed* or *progressive.* (10) So far is this form from being confined to the assertion of actions or states of being connected with present time, that it is often employed to express what is manifestly past or manifestly future; as, *Plato* THINKS *profoundly, Cicero* WRITES *with great elegance.* (11) Here the actions asserted are past. *John* WRITES *to his father next Saturday. He* GOES *to town to-morrow.* Here the action is future. (12) Now, although neither the past existence of

---

that the more philosophical grammarians have applied the terms definite and *indefinite* very vaguely to tenses. They are not even agreed which tenses are *definite* and which *indefinite.* Some call the past tense definite and the perfect indefinite; others, on the contrary, call the past tense indefinite and the perfect definite. This disagreement has arisen from confounding the two distinct elements or modifications indicated by the forms called tenses; namely, *time* and the condition of the predicate as completed or incomplete. A reference to this, and to the fact that no tense ever expresses a definite point of time, would at once have settled the controversy. When the past tense is called *definite,* it is meant that it expresses that which is *definitely past.* When the perfect is called definite, it is meant that it expresses what is *definitely completed,* not what is *definitely past.* The name imperfect, most improperly given to the *past tense,* seems to have led to the error of calling it indefinite. It certainly expresses the *past* definitely. We have nothing to do with this dispute, as we see no use in applying this term either to the past or the perfect tense. We apply it only to the tense before us, and only

---

(7) State the objection. (8) For what is this form said to be employed? Give the examples. (9) Describe the precise purpose for which this form is employed. (10) What is said to show that this form is not confined to the expression of present actions? (11) Illustrate by examples. (12) State the conclusion drawn from such examples, &c.

the actions in the one case, nor the future existence in the other is indicated by the verb, but either left to be inferred from the nature of the subject matter, or rendered manifest by the accompanying words expressive of time; yet, if it were the proper and inherent function of this form to assert present time (that is, if it were, as most grammarians teach, a *present tense*), it could never be employed in this manner.

(13) Again, on the other hand, we cannot employ this form to express, in an explicit manner, that an agent actually performs an action in the present time. (14) For this purpose we must have recourse to a different form of expression. (15) If I am asked what John actually does at present, I do not answer, *He writes*, but *He is writing*. For the explanation of this form of expression, see § 62)*].

§ 50. (1) We employ in English a *modified* form of the roots of our verbs to express an assertion that has reference simply to the PAST, without indicating whether the action was progressive or completed at the past time referred to. (2) Examples: *The boy*

---

in the sense indicated, namely, indefinite as to both time and the state of the action.

* It may be added, in confirmation of the views expressed above, that in the Anglo-Saxon, the basis of the present English, there is nothing except this indefinite form to express *future* action. Whether an assertion in that language is indefinite as to time, or present, or future, is not to be learned from the *form* of the verb, but by some other means—from the nature of the assertion, the connection of the discourse, or modifying words added to indicate time. For proof of this the inquisitive reader is referred to satisfactory examples in the following passages of the Anglo-Saxon translation of the Gospels:—Matt. 25: 46. Luke 13: verses 24, 25, 26, 27, 28, 29, 30. In all these places (and we might add an indefinite number of similar examples) the Greek future (or perhaps the Latin future, for the translation appears to have been made from a Latin version) is invariably rendered by the Anglo-Saxon indefinite form—the form from which our indefinite form (incorrectly called the present tense) has manifestly descended, and which it, to a large extent, represents.—See Remarks, § 48.

---

(13) Can we by this form express action in the present explicitly? (14) How do we express such action? (15) Give an example.]

§ 50. (1) Describe the purpose for which we employ a modified form of the roots of our verbs. (2) Give examples, and tell what the form of the verb employed indicates. [(3)

wrote yesterday; The man thought differently; The poet lived in the country. In these expressions it is simply indicated *by the form* of the verb employed, that the action asserted is past. [(3) The action may have been in progress or completed; and owing to the *nature of the action*, we may be able from such an assertion to infer its condition, whether progressive or completed at the time past; but this condition in such cases is *only inferred*; it is not *indicated by the form* of the expression. (4) This is the only tense properly so called; that is, expressed in English by a modification effected on the root or original form of the verb without other auxiliary words. (5) What we have called the indefinite tense, is expressed by the unchanged *root* of the verb; and, as regards indication of time, is properly *no tense*. Or, if we employ tense as a *grammatical term* for a particular *form* of the verb, this might be called *tense no tense*—the tense that excludes the element of time.]

(6) The *tense* formed by a modification of the root of the verb, and which expresses simply past time, we shall call the PAST TENSE, or PRETERIT TENSE; and verbs of this form PRETERITS. [(7) This form has been very commonly, but very improperly, called in our grammars the *imperfect tense*. (8) Except that it is used to express what was customary or habitual in past time, it has nothing in common with what is called the imperfect tense in other languages.]

NOTE.—We might object, not without reason, to the name *imperfect tense*, that strictly speaking it involves an absurdity, since *perfect*, or *imperfect* cannot, with propriety, be asserted of time, or attributed to *time*, that is, to *tense* (*temps, tempus*) in its original signification. The absurdity will appear, if we propose the questions, what do you mean by *imperfect* time? What kind of time is *imperfect*, or *perfect* time? It will not do for the grammarian who calls the tense under consideration the *imperfect*, to attempt to rid himself of this absurdity, by saying that *perfect time* means *finished* time, and *imperfect time* unfinished time; because, unfortunately for him, it is what is called the *perfect tense* in our own, and in other languages, and *not* the *imperfect*

When this tense is used, may we sometimes *infer* the condition of the action? And how may we infer it? (4) State what is remarked in regard of this tense. (5) What is here said of the *indefinite tense*?]

(6) What name is given to the *tense* formed by a modification of the root of the verb? [(7) By what name has this tense been improperly called? (8) Has this tense any thing in common (in regard to its use) with the imperfect tense in other languages?

tense, which is used *exclusively* in asserting actions performed in a period of time not yet fully elapsed or finished. We say, *John has written a letter this day, this week, this year, to his father*, employing the (so called) perfect tense for the very reason (as grammarians universally admit) that the period of time referred to—*the day, the week, the year*, is yet present, and *not finished*. On the contrary, if the assertion referred to *yesterday, last week, last year*—a period of time completely past and *finished*, we must employ what has been improperly called the *imperfect tense; John* WROTE *a letter yesterday*, &c. Our objection to *imperfect* employed as an attribute of time, obviously applies equally to *perfect* and to *pluperfect*, which last is, independently of this objection, an absurd and barbarous term.

But we waive the objection now stated to the use of the terms perfect and imperfect tense deduced from the proper etymological meaning of the word tense, though we do not see how those, who explain all the tense forms found in the verbs of all languages, as used "to mark time more precisely," can get over this objection. With our views of the functions of tense forms, we can get over it readily, and without inconsistency, and shall use (one if not both) the terms perfect and imperfect, for the convenience of being more readily understood, and to avoid as much as possible unnecessary innovation by the introduction of new terms. Still, we shall employ these terms, unlike the *great mass* of English grammarians, in a manner consistent with the views presented above; that is, with recognition of the fact, that two distinct modifications are expressed by what are called tense forms; in other words, that the term *tense* has, in grammatical usage, lost its exclusive, special, and etymological reference to time, and is now employed as the name of certain forms of the verb, which indicate sometimes *time* alone, sometimes *time* in combination with the *condition* of the action as completed, or remaining incomplete and progressive, and sometimes, as in the case of the English *indefinite tense* (or indefinite *form*), indicative of the absence of restriction from either modification. And, as to the terms perfect and imperfect, when we come to use them, we shall consider them, as the grammarians who first introduced them seem to have done, as referring exclusively to the condition (as above described), not to the time of the action; *perfect* (*perfectum, done, accomplished*, fully *finished*), being applied to forms which express completed action, and imperfect (imperfectum) to forms which express incomplete or progressive action.

In conformity with these views, and in accordance with the practice of some recent grammarians, we reject the name *imperfect tense*, as altogether inappropriate to what we have called above the past tense, since it is no part of the function of this tense to give any indication whatever of the *condition* of the action expressed by the verb. In fact, it is most generally used in speaking of that which is completed (perfectum); but this is not necessarily indicated, nor intended to be indicated by the form. It is inferred from the nature of the action, combined with the fact that it is past; or, sometimes, from accompanying words limiting the action to a specified time past; examples: *Noah* BUILT *an ark; John* WROTE *a letter yesterday.* On the contrary, in the example, "*The village master* TAUGHT *his little school,*" we have an action expressed that was *incomplete—progressive* at the past time referred to. But this fact, again, we learn by *inference,* not by any thing distinctly indicated by the past form of the verb. We shall see hereafter the propriety of carefully distinguishing, what is explicitly indicated by a grammatical form, from that which may, in some cases, be *inferred* from what it indicates, either alone, or combined with other modifying or completing words.

There is another very strong objection to the employment of the name *imperfect tense,* in designating the form of the verb now under consideration. And this is, that this improper appellation occasions much confusion of thought, and consequent embarrassment to young learners, when, after having studied the grammar of their own language, they begin to acquire a knowledge of any of the ancient or modern languages of southern Europe. In these they find an imperfect tense, which, unlike what most of our grammars call the imperfect tense in English, does really indicate, according to its name, *imperfect,* or unfinished action (that is, action unfinished at the past time intended to be indicated), and which, the young scholar finds, cannot, generally, be properly translated by what he has been taught to call the English imperfect tense. On the contrary, he has to be taught that, in writing these languages, our past tense (which he has been allowed to call the imperfect) can seldom be represented by their imperfect tense. In asserting a past action that was *customary, habitual,* oft *repeated,* or a *continuous* state of being, and therefore not definitely, and, once for all completed, the ancient and modern languages referred to properly employ their imperfect tense. In such assertions we loosely employ our past (*improperly* called imperfect) tense. In such assertions as, *The poet* LIVED *in the country,* "*The village master* TAUGHT *his litle school,*" the imperfect would be employed in those languages, and not the tenses to which our past tense is generally equivalent. It is rarely, except in the case now mentioned, that our past tense can, with propriety, be rendered by the imperfects of other languages.

This employment of our past tense to express what, in other languages is expressed more appropriately by their imperfect, has naturally arisen from the poverty of our language in *simple tense forms.* Having only one *simple* form to express *past time,* it was natural, that it should be used for every assertion relating to past time, which did not *absolutely* require more definite modification. In fact, we cannot express the distinction noticed above between a single past occurrence, and customary action, or continuous being, even with the help of our *compound* tenses. The compound tense, expressive of past progressive action, which usually represents the imperfect of other languages, cannot be properly used here. We must either leave the fact of customary action to be inferred from the *nature* of the action, as we generally do, where more precision is unnecessary, or employ a less concise form o. expression; as, for example, The poet *was in the habit of living* in the country; "The village master" *was accustomed to teach* "his little school," instead of the more usual mode of expressing these assertions employed above.

In connection with this we may remark, that, the form under consideration being our *great tense* (our only *simple tense*) form for *past time*, it sometimes happens (as it does also in reference to the correspondent tense in other languages) that assertions which might be expressed with more precision by some of those combinations called *compound tenses*, are often expressed by this tense, when the further modification given by the *compound tense* is not important to the sense. This may account for, and, perhaps, justify such as sertions as, "*I* WAS *this morning with the secretary*," *I wrote this morning*, &c., instead of, I *have been* this morning with the secretary, &c.

§ 51. FORMATION OF THE PAST TENSE.—We now come to explain the formation of the simple tenses. (1) And here our task is confined to a statement of the modifications which the root undergoes to express *past time*, since, as we have already remarked (§ 49 : 3), the *indefinite tense* is the root itself—the simplest form of the verb.

(2) The *past tense* of English verbs is formed from the root in two distinct ways (already noticed, § 35 : 2), by *inflexion*, and by a *radical modification*. (3) The learner will remember that inflexion is the name given when some addition by way of *termination* is made to the root, and that *radical modification* is the name given when a change is effected in the vowel sound of the root, or original word. (4) We have examples of the formation of the *past tense* by *inflexion* in the following verbs; *act*, past tense *acted ; talk, talked ; call, called ; paint, painted*, &c. And of the formation by a *radical modification* in *write*, past tense, *wrote ; see, saw ; speak, spoke ; give, gave*, &c., &c.

(5) The *past tense* of the greatest part of our verbs is formed by inflexion. (6) This inflexion consists of the addition (in the present spoken language) of the *sound* of *d*, or *ed*, or, sometimes, *t* to the root of the verb. (The causes, which determine whether the *d*,

§ 51. (1) To what is our task confined in explaining the formation of the simple tenses, and why is it so confined? (2) In how many ways is the past tense formed from the root of the verb? (3) Repeat what is said of inflection and radical modification. (4) Illustrate by examples.

(5) How is the past tense of the greatest part of English verbs formed? (6) What ad-

or the *t* sound must be added in any particular case are described in § 40 and 41.) (7) In the written language, when the root of the verb happens to end in *e*,* we add the letter *d*, and when the root has any other ending we add *ed* to form the past tense. (8) Thus the past tense of this whole class in the written language ends in *ed*, except a few which have undergone contraction; such as *leapt*, contracted from *leaped; knelt*, from *kneeled; wept*, from *weeped; spelt*, from *spelled*, &c.

[(9) This termination (*ed*) was, no doubt, universally pronounced fully, so as to form a complete additional syllable in the spoken language of our early ancestors. (10) It is still sometimes fully pronounced in reading the sacred Scriptures and on solemn occasions; but both in the language of conversation, and in ordinary reading and public speaking the vowel sound is suppressed, and the *d* sound alone attached to the root, wherever this is possible. (11) It is not possible (see § 41), when the root ends in a *d*, or a *t* sound;

* We doubt whether it is altogether proper to consider the final *e* in such verbs as *love, write*, &c., as a part of the root. The roots of these verbs are properly *lov* and *writ*, and the *e* is a fragment of the original personal termination retained, in order, perhaps, to indicate (as it does in most cases) that the long sound is to be given to the radical vowel. The final *e* in such words as *hate, revere, write, move, fume*, &c., shows the reader how he is to pronounce the radical vowels, viz., with the long sound of each vowel respectively. There are some exceptions, as in the words *have* and *love*, as they are now pronounced. On the other hand, the final mute *e* is retained in many words, where it is altogether unnecessary for the purpose above mentioned; for example, in such words as *perceive, receive, rejoice*, &c., where the diphthong sufficiently indicates that a long sound is to be given to the radical syllable. But these are only small samples of the great want of consistency in the mode of representing our spoken signs which has become established in our written language—or, in other words, small samples of our anomalous *orthography*—anomalous, we mean, in reference to the present spoken language.

In reference to the final *e* mute of our verbs, it is altogether unnecessary,

dition is made to the root of the verb in the spoken language to form the past tense? (7) Describe what is done in the written language. (8) What is the ending of the past tense of this whole class of verbs in the written language? Mention exceptions.

[(9) What is said about the pronunciation of the termination *ed* in ancient times? (10) What is the modern custom in reference to the pronunciation of this final *ed*? (11) What must be done when the *root* ends in a *d*, or a *t* sound? Illustrate by examples.]

and in such cases we add in speaking the full sound represented by the *ed* to the root; as, for example, in the verbs *end*, past tense, *ended; add, added; act, acted;* &c.]

(12) Verbs forming their *past tense* in this manner, we may hereafter call verbs of the *modern class* or *modern conjugation*.

(13) Those verbs which form their past tense by means of a *radical modification*, are commonly (but, we think, improperly) called *irregular verbs*, because it has been found difficult to detect any general law governing the changes to which their roots are subjected. (14) We may call them verbs of the *ancient* or *primitive conjugation*. [(15) Some have called this the *strong* conjugation, or the *strong* order of verbs, and what we have called the modern conjugation, the *weak* conjugation or order.

(16) The verbs which belong to the ancient conjugation are not so numerous as those which belong to the modern conjugation, but they constitute perhaps the most ancient part of the language, and many of them are more used for the ordinary purposes of speech, than any other verbs. (17) This method of formation has been long obsolete—obsolete even in the Anglo-Saxon times. (18) The modern method of formation is the *current* one—the only one which for many centuries has been employed in the case of verbs newly adopted into the language. No new past tense would now be formed by a radical modification. (19) On the contrary, a tendency to extend the modern formation to verbs which belong to the ancient conjugation, is observable in the usage of our language; for example, in substituting the modern form *digged* for the ancient past tense *dug* of the verb to *dig; hanged, shined, strived, weaved,* &c., for the ancient forms, *hung, shone, strove, wove,* &c. (20) Still

---

for the purposes of the grammarian, to trouble the learner with any distinction between verbs which have it, and those which have it not. If it be a fragment of a personal termination, it now serves no flexional purpose in the language—it indicates no modification of sense whatever.

---

(12) By what name do we distinguish verbs which form the past tense in this manner?

(13) What name is generally given to verbs which form the past tense by a radical modification? (14) How do we name them? [(15) What other name has been given to them?

(16) What is said of the verbs of the *ancient conjugation?* (17) Repeat the remark in reference to the ancient method of formation. (18) Repeat the remarks in reference to the modern method of formation. (19) What tendency in reference to this matter is observed

many of the past tenses of the ancient formation have obtained such fast hold in general usage, that this tendency in favor of the modern and current formation has not in centuries been able to supersede them, nor is it likely to be able to supersede them all for ages to come.]*

(21) The verb *to be* may be considered irregular or rather defective, being made up apparently of fragments of several ancient verbs, "each of which is defective in several of its parts. The parts, however, that are wanting in one verb, are made up by the inflexions of one of the others."† (22) The same may be said of the verb *to go.*

REMARK.—We shall give at the close of this chapter an alphabetical list of all the verbs which do not form their preterits by the addition of *ed* or *d*, including all the verbs of the ancient conjugation, and such verbs of the modern conjugation as by contraction or otherwise have come to assume an *apparently* irregular form, together with the few really irregular or defective verbs.

EXERCISES I., II., &c.—Form propositions with verbs of the past tense.

§ 52. OF MODIFIED FORMS OF THE VERB EMPLOYED TO INDICATE THE NUMBER AND PERSON OF THE SUBJECT.—[(1) Some lan-

* In the lapse of ages, however, the modern formation has made great encroachments on the domain of the ancient or strong conjugation. A very considerable number of verbs which in Anglo-Saxon had preterits of the *ancient* or *strong* form, have in our present language preterits of the *modern* or *weak* form.—(See a list of these in Latham's English Language, p. 340, 2d ed.)

† See Latham's Eng. Language, 2d ed., chapters 26th and 28th, for some judicious remarks on the distinction between *irregularity* and *defectiveness*, and the impropriety of classing all verbs which do not form their preterits in *ed* or *d* as irregular. See also in the last mentioned chapter a useful distinction drawn between *vital* (what we have called above *current*), and *obsolete* processes of formation. The ancient process by which strong preterits were formed is *obsolete;* the modern process of adding the *d* sound (*ed* or *d* in the written language) is the *vital* process—the one in actual use. So the vital process of forming plurals of nouns is by adding *s*, &c., to the singular form. The process of adding *en*, as in the case of *ox* plural oxen, or changing the vowel sound as in *man men*, is obsolete.

in our language? Illustrate by examples. (20) Are preterits of the ancient formation likely to be entirely superseded?]

(21) What is said in reference to the verb *to be?* (22) What of the verb to go?

§ 52. [(1) How many distinct forms in each tense are employed in some languages to in-

guages—the Latin, for example—have six distinct forms in each tense to indicate each of the three persons singular, and the three persons plural. (2) Many other languages retain a less or more complete set of forms of this kind; in some languages, these forms are so incomplete as to be of little or no practical service.

NOTE.—In those languages which possess a distinct termination to express each person singular and plural, the subject noun of the first and second persons, both singular and plural, can always be suppressed without occasioning obscurity, and, generally, whenever the subject of the third persons singular and plural may be represented by a pronoun, the pronoun can be suppressed. Let us take, for example, the present tense indicative of the Latin verb *stare, to stand; sto, stas, stat, stamus, statis, stant. Sto,* being invariably and exclusively employed to express the action of standing, predicated of the first person, as clearly indicates the subject noun as if it were preceded by *ego*=I, since nothing but this can serve as subject to this form of the verb. *Stas* indicates its subject with equal clearness. *Stat*, also, indicates with certainty that something of the third person singular must be the subject; and whenever the reference is so clear that a pronoun may represent the subject, and that the expression of gender can add nothing to this clearness, *stat* alone will serve to express both subject and verb. (In this way, a single word comes in some languages to express a complete proposition.) The same may be repeated in reference to the plural terminations. The suppression of the pronouns is very generally practised in those languages which have a complete set of personal terminations, such as the Latin, Greek, Spanish, Italian. The power of doing this is a considerable advantage in point of style. In languages that have not a complete set of these terminations, the few which they retain seem to be of no use whatever. Where we must always use the pronoun to escape ambiguity, the personal terminations serve no purpose that we can discover. They seem to be of no use in the present English. This may account for the fact that they have nearly all disappeared. We once had more of them, as will be seen in what follows. At a remote period our language, or rather the languages from which it is descended, had, likely, complete sets of personal terminations, and could suppress the subject when a pronoun in the same manner as the Latin or modern Spanish. The Gothic, as it is found in Ulphilas' version of the New Testament, agrees in this respect with the Greek and Latin. It has personal terminations as complete as they have, and even dual persons like the Greek, and admits similar suppression of pronouns. Indeed, it is probable that personal terminations had precedence, in the date of their origin in language, to personal pronouns. That is to say, that such forms as *sto* (I stand), had existence before words were invented to express the elements *I* and *stand* separately.

---

dicate the *number* and *person* of the subject? (2) What is said of other languages in re

It may here be remarked, that though in the *written* French there are separate terminations for most of the persons, yet, because the *spoken* language confounds in pronunciation many of the persons which are written differently, in using French, we have always, as in English, to repeat the pronominal subjects before the verbs. The apparatus of personal terminations serves no practical purpose in that language. When the (subject) pronouns must be used, they secure a degree of perspicuity, to which the use of personal terminations can make no addition.

(3) In the earlier stages of the English language, these personal terminations were more numerous than at the present time. (4) A form distinct from all the singular persons was used for the three persons plural, in both the indefinite tense and the past tense. (5) This form was made by adding the termination *en* to the root of the verb, or *n* only when the root ended in *e;* as, for example, *We dwellen, You dwellen, They dwellen,* where we now say, *We dwell,* &c. *We wenten,* where we say, *We went;* "*Peter and John* WENTEN *up into the temple.*" (Acts 3 : 1; Wiclif's translation.) (6) This plural form seems to have been generally employed in the age of Wiclif and Chaucer. It was not yet completely obselete in the times of Spenser, since he occasionally employs it.*]

(7) At present, there remains in our language no distinctive termination for the plural of any of our verbs, except the verb *to be.* (8) This verb has a plural form in the past tense, *We were, Ye were,*

* Another form of the plural of the indefinite tense is found in writings as late as the end of the fourteenth century, that is, as late as Chaucer and Wiclif. This form ends in *eth,* which differs little from the Anglo-Saxon plural termination of the indefinite tense *ath.* We give the following examples from a sentence of Trevisa, as quoted by Mr. Tyrwhitt, in his "Essay on the Language and Versification of Chaucer": "In alle the gramer scoles of Englond children *leveth* Frenche, and *construeth* and *lerneth* an English, and *haveth* thereby," &c There are many other examples of this form in the same piece. (Chaucer, Ed. E. Moxon, Lond., 1847. Essay, p. xxii., n. 21.)

ference to these forms? (3) What remark is made in reference to the earlier stages of our language? (4) Illustrate this remark. (5) How was the ancient plural of verbs formed? Give examples. (6) To what period did this form continue in use?]

(7) Have we any plural form of our verbs in present use? (8) What is said of the past tense of the verb *to be?*

They were; anciently, and down till the times of Spenser, *We weren, Ye weren,* &c.

(9) This verb has also *apparently* a plural form in the indefinite tense, *We are, Ye are,* &c. But it may be doubted whether this is really a plural form, or only the unmodified root from which the singular forms *am* and *art* are made. (10) Whether intended originally for the purpose or not, this form now serves to distinguish the plural of this verb, being different from all the singular personal forms.

(11) As to personal terminations, there is no distinction whatever of form between the three persons plural in any tense of any of our verbs. (12) In the English of the present day, the root (or radical form) of the verb without change is used for the first person singular, and for all the three plural persons of the indefinite tense. (13) For example, these persons of the verb to call, are, 1st person singular, *I call;* plural persons, 1st, *We call,* 2d, *You call,* 3d, *They call,* or *Men,* &c., *call.* (14) The only exception occurs in the forms of the verb *to be,* in which the 1st person singular differs from the plural persons: 1st person singular, *I am;* plural persons, *We are, You are, They are.*

(15) The simple form of the past tense (already described) is used for the 1st and 3d persons singular, and for all the plural persons; as, 1st person, *I called,* 3d person, *He, She, It, The man,* &c., *called;* plural 1st pers., *We called,* 2d, *You or ye called,* 3d, *They, Men,* &c., *called.* (16) The only exception to this again occurs in the past tense of the verb TO BE, in which *was* is the form for the 1st and 3d persons singular, and *were* for the plural persons: 1st person singular, *I was,* 3d, *He,* &c., *was;* plural 1st, *We were,* 2d, *You or ye were,* 3d, *They,* &c., *were.*

(17) The second person of both tenses, indefinite and past, is formed by adding the termination *st*—to the *root* for the indefinite,

---

(9) What is said of the indefinite tense of the verb *to be* in reference to a plural form? (10) What is said of the purpose which the form ARE actually serves, whether originally intended, or not?

(11) Mention the general remark about personal terminations. (12) What persons does the root of the verb express in the indefinite tense? (13) Give example. (14) State exception.

(15) What persons singular and plural are expressed by the simple past form? (16) Mention an exception, and give full explanation.

to the *past form* for the past tense—when this can readily coalesce with the root or past form respectively; when it cannot, *est* is added. (18) Examples: 2d person, indefinite tense, *Thou call*EST, *Thou mov*EST, &c.; 2d person, past tense, "*Thou called*ST *us not when thou went*EST" (Judges 8: 1). (19) Remark: These second persons singular, of both tenses, are now rarely used, except in the solemn style (§ 30).

(20) The third person singular of the indefinite tense is formed in two ways: 1st, by adding the sound represented by *eth* to the root—in the written language, by adding the letters *eth* to the root, or *th* only when the root ends in *e*, mute; 2d, by adding an *s* or *z* sound to the root—in the written language, by adding the letter *s*. (21) Examples: *He call*ETH, or *He calls; He mov*ETH, or *He moves*. (22) The form in *eth* is rarely used at present, except in the solemn style; but it was very generally employed by many of the best writers (especially by Scottish writers) of the last century. (23) Remark: The form in *s* being made in the same way as the plural form of nouns, is subject to many of the same rules of formation. (24) For example; when the root of the verb ends in an *s* sound, we add *es*, sounded *ez;* as, *I miss, He miss*ES; *She blush*ES; *He march*ES, &c. When the verb ends in *o* we add *es;* as, *He go*ES, *He do*ES, &c. And, when the verb ends in *y*, *preceded by a consonant*, in the written language, we change the *y* into *i* and add *es;* as, *He cries*, from *cry; It flies*, 3d person of the verb *to fly*. (25) Whether an *s* or a *z* sound is to be added to a verb to form the third person, is determined by the same principles referred to in treating of the formation of the plural of nouns. (See § 41 and § 42.)

The following are exceptions to the rules now given for the formation of the 2d and 3d persons singular of verbs. (26) The verb *have* has for its 2d and 3d persons the forms *ha*ST and *ha*TH or *has*, evidently contractions for *have*ST and *have*TH or *haves*. (27)

---

(17) How is the second person of both the indefinite and past tense formed? (18) Give examples. (19) Repeat the remark.

(20) How is the third person singular of the indefinite tense formed?

(21) Give examples. (22) Repeat the observation in reference to the form in *eth*. (23) Repeat the remark in reference to the form in *s*. (24) Illustrate this remark by examples of verbs ending 1st in an *s* sound; 2d in *o*, and 3d in *y*, preceded by a consonant. (25) Repeat what is said about determining whether an *s*, or a *z* sound shall be added to form the 3d person. (26) What is said of the 2d and 3d persons singular of the verb *have?* (27)

Will (used as an auxiliary to indicate *futurity*) and *shall* form the second person singular by adding the sound of *t* instead of *st* to the root. In writing them we drop one *l*; as, *Thou shalT go*, *Thou wilT go*. (28) *Will* (auxiliary), *shall*, *may*, *can*, *must*, and (generally) *dare* (=to have courage, and followed by the *infinitive* or *verbal*), take no addition to the root in the third person singular; as, *He* WILL *come; He* SHALL, MAY, CAN, MUST, DARE *go*.*

We have now, we believe, noticed all the changes of form which English verbs, in the present state of the language (and for some centuries backward) exhibit. We except a few forms of the verb *to be*, omitted because they can be best learned from the table below, in which all the variations of this verb—or rather the fragments of several verbs, employed to assert *being*—are presented.

The essential part of the formation of the persons (all that cannot be learnt from the tables of the tenses to be presently given) may be summed up briefly as follows:

(29) The *second persons singular* of both tenses are formed by adding *st* or *est* to the *root* and to the *past tense form* respectively; and the *third person singular* of the *indefinite tense* is formed by adding an *s* to the *root*. In the other persons of the indefinite tense the *unmodified root* is employed; and, in the other persons of the past tense, the *past tense form*, without further modification, is employed.

(30) Remark: The formation of the third person singular of the

* When *will* is used in its original sense, to express determination, resolution, purpose of mind, or volition, sometimes the second, and generally the third, person is regularly formed. Examples of the second person of *will* thus used and regularly formed are rare. Lowth has produced two from one of Atterbury's sermons. (Intr. to Eng. Gram. p. 70. Lond. 1788.) Examples of wilt, used in the original sense of will, are found in the New Testament. Examples of the third person regularly formed are easily found. "*It is not of him that will*ETH." (Rom. 9: 16.) "Because *he can walk if he wills*." (Locke, as cited by Webster. Dict. sub voce.) *Dare* = to challenge, followed by a noun, we believe, always takes the regular termination of the third person; as, *He dares the enemy to fight* = he *challenges* the enemy.

What of the 2d persons of the verbs *will* and *shall*? (28) What of the 3d persons of *will*, auxiliary,) *shall*, *may*, *can*, *must*, and *dare*?

(29) Repeat the summary account of the formation of the persons. (30) Repeat the remark.

indefinite tense merits the chief attention. The second persons singular of either tense come rarely into use.

§ 53. (1) We may here notice the formation of the two *verbal adjectives*, commonly called *participles*, which, we shall presently find, are employed in forming some of the *compound tenses*. (2) One of these verbals ends in *ing*. In the usage of the language at the present day (and for several centuries past), it always corresponds exactly in form with the verbal *substantive* in *ing*, already considered. (See § 27.) (3) It is formed by adding *ing* to the root of the verb; as, from *call* is formed *call*ING. (4) When the verb, in the written language, ends in *e* mute, the *e* is rejected; as, for example, from *move*, rejecting *e*, is formed *mov*ING. (5) When an *i* precedes the *e* mute, the *i* is changed into *y*, the *e* rejected, and *ing* added; as, for example, *die*, *dy*ING; *lie*, *ly*ING.*

(6) This form is most commonly called the *present*—but by some more properly the IMPERFECT PARTICIPLE. (7) It expresses the action of the verb in an *imperfect*, *unfinished*, or *progressive condition*, not assertively, like the verb properly so called, but *attributively*; that is, in the form suited to be employed as an *attribute* of a noun, or as the *complement* of a predicate. (8) By the fact that it always performs *attributive functions*, it is readily distinguished from the *verbal noun* in ING, which is always employed to perform some function of a *substantive*.

* When a word of one syllable, or a word of more than one syllable accented on the last syllable, ends in a single consonant preceded by a single vowel, we double the final consonant in forming the imperfect participle; as, *get, getting; stop, stopping; beset, besetting; compel, compelling;* &c. The object of so writing this, and other formations from words ending in this manner, is to indicate that the short sound of the last syllable of the *root* is to be retained in the word when the inflexion is added. If we wrote *stoping* it might appear that we intended the *o* to be sounded long, as in *no*, instead of short, as in *not*. This, as well as the remark about verbs ending in *e mute*, applies only to the *written*, not to the *spoken* language. As regards the spoken language, the sound of *ing* is added to every verb root (without exception) to form the imperfect participle.

§ 53. (1) What is said of verbal adjectives, or *participles?* (2) What is said of the form of the first of these *verbal adjectives?* (3) How is this verbal formed? (4) How formed when the verb ends in *e* mute? (5) How when an *i* precedes the *e* mute?

(6) What is this form called? (7) In what condition and in what manner does it express the action of the verb? (8) How may it be distinguished from the verbal noun?

(9) The second verbal adjective, or *participle* in verbs of the *modern conjugation* corresponds in form with the past tense—that is, it always ends in *ed*, except in a few cases of contraction. (See § 51.) (10) For example; *call* has for its past tense *called*, and for verbal adjective also *called;* as "*There was a certain man in Caesarea* CALLED *Cornelius, a centurion of the band* CALLED *Italian.*" (11) In the verbs of the *ancient conjugation* this *participle* has generally a form peculiar to itself—distinct from the past tense form. (12) In the most remote times it seems to have been formed by adding the termination *en* sometimes to the *root*, sometimes to the *past tense form.* (13) Many of these participles in *en* still remain in the language, others have gradually become obsolete. (14) As examples of participles in *en* we may mention *broken, eaten, forgotten, laden, risen, written*, &c. (15) The form of this *participle*, as well as the form of the *past tense* in the verbs of the *ancient conjugation*, is so various that the learner must in all doubtful cases be referred to the table of this class of verbs at the end of this chapter, in which we shall give the participle as well as the past tense of each verb.

(16) This verbal is appropriately called the *perfect participle*, as it expresses the action of the verb in a *completed* or *perfect* (*perfected*) *condition.* Like the other participle it is always employed attributively.*

---

*Some call this verbal very improperly the past participle; neither this, nor the participle in ING give any direct indication of the time of the action which they express; they simply indicate the condition of the action—the *imperfect participle*, as *unfinished*, or *progressive*, and the *perfect participle*, as *finished*, or *completed.* Hence they are both employed in forming compound tenses—*past, future*, and *indefinite* as regards time. This proves sufficiently that the names present and past participles do not accurately express the significance of these forms. The name passive, sometimes given to the perfect participle, is also improper for similar reasons.

---

(9) What is said of the second verbal adjective? (10) Give example. (11) What is said of the form of this participle in verbs of the *ancient conjugation?* (12) How does it seem to have been formed in the most remote times? (13) Do forms ending in *en* still remain in the language? (14) Give examples. (15) Repeat the remark about the way of ascertaining the form of these participles in verbs of the ancient conjugation.

(16) What name is given to this participle, and how is it employed?

§ 54. Of Modes.—(1) Of the modifications which we have considered, the tenses have reference to the predicate—to the action expressed by the verb. (2) For example, in the proposition, *the boy called his father*, *calling his father at a past time* is asserted of the boy. The predicate *calling*, asserted without modification in the indefinite tense, is asserted in the *past tense* with a modification indicating that the action of calling is past. (3) The modifications indicative of person and number have reference to the subject of the verb.

(4) There is still another modification which has reference to the *manner* of predication, and the purpose for which a proposition is used. (5) The modification to which we refer is called *mode*, that is, the manner or way in which what the verb indicates is *said.*

(6) Mode, correctly speaking, is a property of propositions. At least it is in the different purposes for which propositions are employed, that we can best and most readily trace the nature of *modes.*

(7) Hitherto our attention has been directed exclusively to one species of propositions—those employed to assert or declare directly what is predicated as matter of fact of the subject. (8) These may (to distinguish them) be called *declarative* or *indicative* propositions; and if we had a form of the verb used exclusively, or chiefly to express propositions of this kind, it might be called the *declarative* or *indicative mode.* (9) In some languages a particular form of the verb is employed chiefly for the purpose of expressing assertions as matter of fact, and this form is in such languages distinguished by the name of the *indicative* or *declarative mode.*

(10) Again, a proposition may be employed, not for the purpose of directly declaring the assertion as matter of fact, but for the

---

§ 54. (1) To what have tense modifications reference? (2) Illustrate by an example. (3) To what have the modifications indicative of number and person reference?

(4) Describe another species of modification. (5) What is this modification called, and what does the name signify? (6) What is mode properly speaking, and where can its nature be most readily traced?

(7) To what species of propositions has our attention been hitherto directed? (8) What may these be called, and what the form of verbs used chiefly to express them? (9) Is there such a form in some languages?

(10) Describe another purpose for which a proposition may be employed. (11) Have

purpose of expressing some condition on which an assertion made in another proposition depends; or for the purpose of modifying in some way a proposition to which it is attached or subjoined. (11) Some languages have a form of their verbs employed for this special purpose, which is called, from the nature of its function, the *conditional*, *conjunctive*, or *subjunctive mode.* (12) The last is the name most commonly given to it—the *subjunctive mode* meaning the mode used in a *subjoined* proposition. (13) For example: *You will not act in that manner, if you think on the consequences.* (14) The first proposition here is declarative, but the assertion made in it depends upon a condition expressed in the subjoined proposition. (15) *I sent the messenger that he might inform you of your danger.* Here the proposition, *I sent the messenger*, is modified or completed by the subjoined proposition—*he might inform you*, &c. (16) In languages which have a subjunctive form of the verb, this form is employed in such subjoined propositions.

(17) Remark.—We include both the declarative and the subjoined propositions under the class of *assertive propositions*, though a subjoined proposition very often makes no *direct* assertion. (18) It is always, however, of the same form, and if we remove the connecting word, (which is what in our language, with a few exceptions, alone indicates that the proposition is used for the purpose of expressing a condition or a modification,) the proposition at once becomes declarative. (19) Remove the words *if* and *that* from the subjoined propositions in the above examples, and they become at once declarative assertions.

(20) Another way or *mode* in which a proposition may be used, is to express a *command*, *request*, *entreaty*, &c. (21) A form of the verb used exclusively in such propositions, is called the *imperative* or *commanding mode.* (22) It will be remembered that we recog-

---

some languages a form of the verb to be used in such propositions? What is this form called? (12) Which name is most commonly used? (13) Give example. (14) Repeat the explanation. (15) Give second example, and repeat explanation. (16) What mode of the verb is employed in such subjoined propositions?

(17) Repeat the remark in regard to the manner in which we have classed declarative and subjoined or complementary propositions. (18) Do these two kinds of propositions agree in form? (19) Give the illustration.

(20) Describe another mode of employing propositions. (21) What is the form of verbs employed in such propositions called? (22) Repeat the remark.

nised propositions of this kind as a distinct class under the name of imperative propositions.

We recognised also another class of propositions—interrogative propositions—the form employed in asking questions. (23) This may be considered as another mode of the proposition. (24) There is no form of the verb in any language, which we know, employed exclusively for this purpose. (25) In our language the interrogative proposition is in most cases distinguished by a peculiar mode of arrangement—by placing the subject noun after the verb. (26) For example, we say assertively or declaratively, *John has a book;* and interrogatively, *Has John a book?* (27) This we may call, if we please, a *mode.* (28) The exceptions to this mode of expressing interrogation by inversion of the subject noun and verb, as well as some other peculiarities of this form of speech, we shall consider in their proper place. (See § 98.)

(29) The *negative* proposition (that is, the proposition which asserts that a predicate does not apply to a certain subject) is attended in our language sometimes with peculiarities which do not belong to *affirmative* propositions, such as we have hitherto adduced as examples. (30) This again might be called a mode of propositions, though the verb has no form intended exclusively to serve this purpose.*

§ 55. Of the Modes of English Verbs.—The observations already made will help the learner to comprehend what is meant

* (31) Most grammarians call the verbal noun, to which we have, in accordance with long established usage, given the name infinitive, the *infinitive mode* of the verb. But, as we do not admit that this verbal is a verb, we cannot admit the propriety of calling it a *mode* of the verb. It is certainly, we admit, a *mode of expressing the action of the verb*—the mode of expressing it *substantively*—and a mode, too, that is sometimes employed to express more compactly that which is otherwise expressed by a *subjoined* or *subjunctive* proposition. This we shall see, when we come to treat of infinitives and propositions employed as *modifications* or *complements.*

(23) What is said of the *interrogative* proposition? (24) Have verbs an *interrogative* form? (25) How is interrogation or questioning generally indicated in our language? (26) Give example. (27) What may this inverted arrangement be called? (28) Repeat the remark about exceptions.

(29) What is said of *negative* propositions? (30) What might the negative form of expression be called? (31) What is said in the note of the so called *infinitive mode?*

by the *modes* of verbs. We are next to examine to what extent this modification of verbs exists in the English language.

(1) If we admit that verbs have *modes*, only when they indicate by a distinct form the *manner* in which a proposition is employed, we have *very little* of *mode* remaining in our language—*very little*, even when we take into account not only the *radical* and *flexional* modifications of the forms of our verbs, but also those modifications effected in the compound tenses (hereafter to be considered) by employing auxiliaries. (2) Hence some have maintained that we have now no modes in the English language—no variation whatever in our verbs indicative of the manner in which predication is made, whether *declaratively*, *conditionally*, *subjunctively*, or *imperatively*, &c.

(3) Of a *conditional* or *subjunctive mode*, *differing in form* from the verb when employed in the simple assertion of a fact, we have at present no remains save a *past tense conditional* of the verb *to be*. (4) The peculiarity of this conditional form extends only to the three *singular* persons. The *plural* persons correspond entirely with the same persons of the past tense used *declaratively*. (5) In this single instance, we have retained the *subjunctive* or *conditional*, from the Anglo-Saxon.

(6) Most grammarians recognise in our language a present *subjunctive* distinct from the present (or what we call the indefinite tense) indicative, or declarative. (7) This subjunctive indefinite differs from the *declarative* indefinite only in suppressing the terminations *st* and *s* in the second and third persons singular, and using the simple unmodified root for all the persons singular and plural. (8) For example, "*Though He* SLAY *me*, *yet will I trust in Him.*" Here the verb "*slay*" is employed without the usual modification (*eth* or *s*) of the third person used *declaratively*. "*Though He slay me*," is only a conditional proposition, expressing not a *fact*, but a *supposition*, and serves to complete the other proposition, "*yet will I trust in Him.*" (9) The unmodified root *be*, is used for all

§ 55. (1) Repeat the substance of the remark. (2) What have some grammarians maintained in reference to modes in the English language?

(3) What remains have we of a *conditional mode?* (4) How far does the peculiarity of this form extend? (5) Repeat remark.

(6) What do most grammarians recognise in our language? (7) In what does this *subjunctive indefinite* differ from the *declarative indefinite?* (8) Give the example, and explanation. (9) Repeat remark in reference to the subjunctive of *to be*.

the persons singular and plural of the *indefinite subjunctive* of the verb *to be*, instead of the variety of forms employed for these persons in the declarative mode.

We believe that this unmodified form of the second and third persons singular is now seldom used (and perhaps should never be used), except as an elliptical expression with a manifest suppression of some auxiliary, such as *shall* or *should*. Some have called it a future tense contingent. We think the so called *subjunctive present* in such cases, when our analysis is carried to its legitimate limits, will be found an infinitive, having the verb, which it is intended to complete, suppressed. The example, for instance, above introduced, when fully expressed, would read thus: "*Though He* SHALL *slay me*," or "*Though He* SHOULD *slay me*," &c. On the improper use of this unmodified form—this so called subjunctive mode—there is much said, and to good purpose, in the Introduction to Webster's Dictionary, pp. 52–54. Ed. Springfield, 1848.

If we were to adopt fully the course indicated by the remarks now made, we should recognise no conditional or subjunctive mode in the language, save the fragments of a subjunctive or conditional past tense of the verb *to be* But as what has been called the present subjunctive form occurs often, especially in our early writers, we shall give it a place in our tabular arrangements of the verbs; calling it the subjunctive indefinite, or future contingent. We shall also exhibit the mode of expressing a command, called the imperative mode; and the peculiarities of *interrogative* and negative propositions, without insisting on calling these forms modes of the verb.

(10) In expressing commands, &c., we employ the root of the verb without any modification. (11) This is called the *imperative mode.* We have only one person, the second singular and plural (in common use) in this mode, since we generally *command* or *entreat* only those to whom our discourse is addressed; and we have no variation for tense. (12) In the *imperative* form of a proposition we generally omit the subject noun, since this subject noun is always the pronoun *you*, and the party to whom we address the *command*, &c., is sufficiently indicated by circumstances independent of articulate language. When the subject noun is expressed (as sometimes it is in the more ancient style), it is placed after the verb: as "Follow thou me;" "Tarry ye."

---

(10) What form of the verb do we employ in expressing commands? (11) What is this form of the verb when thus employed called? (12) What is said of the omission of the subject noun in imperative propositions, and when the subject noun is expressed, where is it placed?

In some languages there are distinct forms of the verb for the third persons, both singular and plural, of the imperative mode; and in many of our grammars the combinations of words usually employed to translate these third persons imperative of other languages, are exhibited, as English third persons imperative. First persons formed in the same manner as these (so called) third persons are also supplied. In grammars which adopt this plan, the whole imperative mode is thus presented:

	Singular.	*Plural.*
1st person,	Let me call,	Let us call,
2d person,	Call, or call thou,	Call, or call ye or you,
3d person,	Let him call.	Let them call.

Our later grammarians generally retain only the second persons, and analyze the forms given above as first and third persons, as consisting of the second person imperative of the verb *let*, completed by the infinitive of another verb—for instance, in the example above, the infinitive of the verb *call.*

There is a form of the third persons singular and plural, and of the first person plural (we have found no well sanctioned example of the first person singular), sometimes found in prose, and freely employed by the poets, which is exactly similar to the second persons imperative. It consists like them of the root of the verb with the subject noun usually placed after it. We subjoin examples, borrowed partly from the grammar of Mr. G. Brown. It would be easy to multiply these. "Blessed *be he* that blesseth thee." "Thy *kingdom come.*"

"*Fall he* that must beneath his rival's arms,
And *live the rest* secure of future harms."—POPE.

"For me, when I forget the darling theme,
Be my tongue mute, *my fancy paint* no more,
And, dead to joy, *forget my heart* to beat!"—THOMSON.

"——— *Be these* my theme."—IDEM.

"*Be* thine *despair* and sceptred *care.*"—GRAY.

"My soul turn from them—*turn we* to survey."—GOLDSMITH.

Though these ancient or poetical forms seldom occur, we assign them a place in the conjugations below, that when the learner happens to meet with any of them he may find no difficulty in disposing of them satisfactorily. We join the other grammarians in discarding the forms made with the verb *let;* and in treating *let* in such cases as the real verb, and of the *second person,* instead of the *first* or *third.* (See § 99.)

§ 56. (1) We shall now exhibit the regular arrangement of the numbers and persons of a few verbs, through the several modes and the simple tenses. (2) This kind of arrangement is called the Con-

§ 56. (1) Tell what is now proposed. (2) What is such an arrangement as is proposed

jugation of Verbs. (3) We have already noticed the division of verbs into two conjugations, in reference to the manner in which they form their past tenses and perfect participles. We shall present examples of both conjugations. (4) We arrange with them the verbal noun, called the infinitive, and the two verbal adjectives (formed from each verb) as adjuncts or accompanying forms, but not (the learner will remember) as coming within our classification or definition of verbs. (5) We write them in this manner with the conjugation of the simple tenses, because, with the help of the simple tenses of certain other verbs, called *auxiliaries*, they are employed in forming the compound tenses. (6) We shall also prefix to the tenses of some of the verbs first conjugated the predicate asserted in each tense respectively.*

(7) Conjugation of the Verb To Call.

INDEFINITE TENSE. PREDICATE, CALLING.

No.	*Pers.*	*Indicative Mode.*	*Subjunctive Mode.*	*Imperative Mode.*
Sing.	1.	I call,	If I call,	
	2.	Thou call*est*,	If thou call,	Call, or call thou,
	3.	He call*s* or call*eth*.	If he call.	Call he, &c. (*poetic*).
Plu.	1.	We call,	If we call,	Call we, "
	2.	You or ye call,	If you or ye call,	Call, or call you or ye,
	3.	They call.	If they call.	Call they (*poetic*).

PAST TENSE. PREDICATE, PAST CALLING.

Sing.	1.	I call*ed*,	Same as indicative.	Wanting.
	2.	Thou call*edst*,	"	"
	3.	He, &c., call*ed*.	"	"
Plu.	1.	We call*ed*,	"	"
	2.	You or ye call*ed*,	"	"
	3.	They call*ed*.	"	"

* We employ the conjunctive IF to indicate the subjunctive mode. This mode is very generally preceded by the conjunctions *if* or *though*.

called? (3) How many conjugations are admitted, and by what are the conjugations distinguished? (4) What other words do we arrange with the verbs in these forms of conjugation? (5) For what reason are these words arranged with the verbs? (6) What is prefixed to the tenses of some of the verbs?

INFINITIVE.—To call, or call.

PARTICIPLES { Imperfect, Call*ing*.
Perfect, Call*ed*.

We here subjoin two rules, to be observed in the construction of propositions :—

(7*a*) RULE I.—The verb in a proposition must always agree in number and person with the subject noun.

RULE II.—Collective nouns, when the collection of individuals which they represent is regarded simply as a collective unity—"as a whole"—have verbs of the singular form; but when reference is made in the assertion to plurality in the subject—"when the collective expresses many as individuals"—the verb is sometimes of the plural form. (See § 25.)

EXAMPLES.—The society *is* numerous. The army *was* victorious. The parliament *is* prorogued. The meeting *was* unanimous. The meeting *were* divided into different parties = the members of the meeting were divided.

Except when there is a decided reference to plurality of subjects in the assertion, we think it is safest to employ the singular form with collectives. Usage in this matter is very far from being fixed, in regard to several nouns of this class. For example, the word *people* is used by the translators of the Bible, indiscriminately, as singular and as plural: "My people doth not consider." "My people, they who lead *thee*," &c. "My people *is* foolish." "O my people, what have I done unto *thee*." "O my people, that *dwellest* in Zion," &c. Again we have *a* people, *any* people, &c. On the contrary, we can produce any number of examples of the use of a plural verb with the subject people. "My people *are* gone into captivity." "My people *love* to have it so," &c., &c.

The use of these rules is confined chiefly, except in the verb *to be*, to the third persons of the indefinite tense; since the second person singular is rarely used. The learner will remember that a violation of Rule I. is reckoned the grossest and most inexcusable of all grammatical blunders.

Nouns, singular in form, when manifestly plural in sense, take plural verbs; as, *Ten* HEAD *of cattle* ARE *in the field; Ten sail are in sight*, &c.

EXERCISE I.—Let the verbs *live*, *love*, *command*, &c., be conjugated after the model above given.

---

(7) Repeat the verb call regularly as arranged above. (7*a*) Repeat the rules.

Exercises II., III., &c.—Give complete propositions with verbs of the *modern* conjugation, and subject nouns or pronouns of each person singular and plural through both tenses, and all the modes. Let the verbs be as various as possible. Let the active verbs have after them a noun to complete their meaning. The neuter verbs may also be accompanied by any expression necessary to complete their sense; as, for example, *He lives*, may be completed by *in the country*, *in the city*, *at home*, &c. *He walks*, by *in the fields*, *often*, *rapidly*, &c. This exercise may, if necessary, be divided, and repeated (in the case of young pupils) till they are perfectly familiar with this conjugation.

Conjugation of the verbs *to write* and *to see*, the irregular verb *to go*, and the auxiliaries *to do* and *to have*. (8) We omit the subjunctive indefinite, and the imperative, as they always consist of the *root* of the verb. The past tense subjunctive does not differ from the past indicative.

(9) Indefinite Tense. Predicates, Writing, &c.

Sing.	1. I	Write,	See,	Go,	Do,	Have,
	2. Thou	Write*st*,	See*st*,	Go*est*,	Do*st*,	Hast,
	3. He, &c.	Write*s*.	See*s*.	Go*es*.	Do*es*.	Has, or Hath.
Pl.	1. We	Write,	See,	Go,	Do,	Have,
	2. You	Write,	See,	Go,	Do,	Have,
	3. They	Write.	See.	Go.	Do.	Have.

Past Tense. Predicates, Past Writing, &c.

Sing.	1. I	Wrote,	Saw,	Went,	Did,	Had,
	2. Thou	Wrote*st*,	Sawe*st*,	Went*est*,	Did*st*,	Had*st*,
	3. He, &c.	Wrote.	Saw.	Went.	Did.	Had.
Pl.	1. We	Wrote,	Saw,	Went,	Did,	Had,
	2. You	Wrote,	Saw,	Went,	Did,	Had,
	3. They	Wrote.	Saw.	Went.	Did.	Had.

---

(8) What *modes* are omitted in the following table? Mention the reason assigned for the omission. (9) Repeat the conjugation of the verbs *to write*, *to see*, &c. Which of these verbs are active, and which neuter? Tell how you know this fact.

Infinitives.	To write.	To see.	To go.	To do.	To have.
Imp. Participle.	Writ*ing*.	See*ing*.	Go*ing*.	Do*ing*.	Hav*ing*.
Perf. Participle.	Writt*en*.	See*n*.	Go*ne*.	Do*ne*.	Ha*d*.

Exercises I., II., III., &c.—Form propositions, as in the last prescribed exercises, with the verbs in the above table, through each person in each tense, using a completing noun with the active verbs, and such words as *slowly*, *speedily*, *into the house*, *city*, *country*, &c., *by railroad*, *by coach*, &c., with the neuter verbs.

Write similar exercises with the verbs, *lie*, *lay*, *put*, *pay*, &c., distinguishing, first, the active verbs from the neuter. See *past form* in list § 67. The teacher will select those verbs in most common use, and in the use of which mistakes most frequently occur.

Conjugation of the irregular verb *to be*, through the simple tenses of each mode. (10) *To be*, like *to do* and *to have*, besides its other uses, serves also as an *auxiliary verb*.

(11) Indefinite Tense. Predicate, Being.

No.	*Per.*	*Indicative Mode.*		*Subjunctive Mode.*	*Imperative Mode.*
Sing.	1.	I am,	I be,	If I be,	
	2.	Thou art,	Thou beest,	If thou be,	Be, or Be thou,
	3.	He, &c., is.	He be.*	If he, &c., be.	Be he, &c.
Pl.	1.	We are,	We be,	If we be,	Be we,
	2.	You or ye are,	Ye be,	If ye or you be,	Be ye or you,
	3.	They are.	They be.	If they be.	Be they.

The form in the second column is not at present in use.

Past Tense. Predicate, Past Being.

Sing.	1.	I was,	If I were,	Wanting.
	2.	Thou was*t*,	If thou wert,	"
	3.	He. &c., was.	If he, &c., were.	"
Pl.	1.	We were,	If we were,	"
	2.	Ye or you were,	If ye or you were,	"
	3.	They were.	If they were.	"

* This third person is rarely found. We have an example in Shakspeare (cited by Dr. Lowth.) "I think *it be* thine indeed; for thou liest in it."—

(10) What purpose does the verb *to be*, in common with the verbs *to do* and *to have*, serve? (11) Repeat the conjugation of the verb to be. What is said of the form in the second column of the indefinite tense?

Infinitive,	To be.
Imperf. Participle,	Being.
Perf. Participle,	Been.

EXERCISES I., II., &c.—Form propositions in the same manner as in the preceding exercises, with the *verb to be*, through all the persons of each tense and mode. The pupil will use any word (adjective) necessary to form complete sense with the verb *to be;* as, *George is generous, You are industrious*, &c. Such complements will be explained in their place, but they may be now employed by the pupil, guided by his own judgment. This kind of exercise will prepare him to attend more intelligently to their explanation.

ADDITIONAL EXERCISES IN THE USE OF COLLECTIVES. See Rule II.—Form a given number of propositions with the verb *to be*, in both tenses, and with the following nouns for subjects: *party, council, group, crowd, horde, host, mob, people, nation, parliament, congress, assembly, army, navy*, &c. Such word, as is necessary to complete the sense of the verb, to be used. Other verbs may be employed at the pleasure of the pupil.

Hamlet. Some of the other persons of this now obsolete form occur frequently in our older writers. It may be observed that this form (the *obsolete* form presented in the 2d column) of the indefinite tense, indicative of this verb, agrees, except in the second person singular, with the subjunctive indefinite. This renders it difficult in some cases to assure ourselves whether an author, in employing those persons which correspond in the two modes, intended the indicative or the subjunctive form. The following may be given as undoubted examples of the obsolete form of the *indicative* indefinite. "If thou *beest* he."—Milton. "We *be* twelve brethren."—Gen. 42: 32. "These *be* they who separate themselves."

When we call this an obsolete form, we do not mean that it is older than the form *am, art, is*, &c., and that this latter has been adopted to supply its place. On the contrary, the two forms existed together, side by side, in the Anglo-Saxon period. Our verb to be, as now used, is partly formed from both. The indefinite tense of the subjunctive given above, as well as the infinitive, and two participles, have descended directly from the obsolete verb. In the Anglo-Saxon there was another indefinite subjunctive of the same meaning, of which no trace remains in modern English. This consisted of *sy* for the singular persons, and *syn* for the plural persons. Our verb to predicate *being* is, as we have before remarked, patched up out of the fragments of three or four verbs.

Conjugation of the Auxiliary Verbs, Will, Shall, May, and Can.

INDEFINITE FORM.

Sing.	1.	I	Will,	Shall,	May,	Can,
	2.	Thou	Wil*t*,	Shal*t*,	May*st*,	Can*st*,
	3.	He, &c.	Will.	Shall.	May.	Can.
Plur.	1.	We	Will,	Shall,	May,	Can,
	2.	You	Will,	Shall,	May,	Can,
	3.	They	Will.	Shall.	May.	Can.

PAST FORM.

Sing.	1.	I	Would,	Should,	Might,	Could,
	2.	Thou	Would*st*,	Should*st*,	Might*st*,	Could*st*,
	3.	He, &c.	Would.	Should.	Might.	Could.
Plur.	1.	We	Would,	Should,	Might,	Could,
	2.	You	Would,	Should,	Might,	Could,
	3.	They	Would.	Should.	Might.	Could.

(13) We have already noticed the peculiarity in the formation of the second persons singular of *will* and *shall* (§ 52 : 27). (14) It will be observed that none of these verbs takes the termination *s* in the third person singular. (15) In fact the verbs *shall*, *may*, *can*, and *will* too, when a mere auxiliary, have, according to present usage, invariably the same form in all the persons, except when in the solemn style the second person singular is, on some rare occasions, employed.

[(16) *Shall*, *may*, *can*, and *will* (auxiliary) have no corresponding *infinitives* or *participles*. (17) The same peculiarity belongs to *must* and *ought*, which have, perhaps, nearly equal claims with *may* and *can* to be recognised as *auxiliaries*. (18) *Will*, employed not as an auxiliary to indicate the futurity of what is asserted in a proposition, but in its original sense, to express *determination*, *volition*, &c., has both

---

(12) Repeat the conjugations separately of *will*, *shall*, &c.

(13) Mention the peculiarity referred to in regard of *will*, and *shall*. (14) Repeat the observation made in regard of the 3d person singular of all the verbs above conjugated. (15) Repeat the general remark in regard to all the persons of these verbs in common use.

[(16) What is said of shall, will, auxiliary &c. in reference to infinitives and participles. (17) Repeat the remark in reference to *must* and *ought*. (18) Repeat the remark in reference to *will* in its original use.

infinitive and *participles*, and, as we have already observed (§ 52: 28, note), generally the same terminations, at least in the third person in definite, as other verbs.*

(19) It is peculiar to all these verbs (except *will*, not auxiliary) that they require, to complete them, the *verbal nouns* commonly called *infinitives*. As now used, they express no *distinct predicate;* or, rather, perhaps, language affords us no means of expressing the predicate which they serve to assert; since, in their case, the *verbal noun*, which expresses the simple predicate without assertion, is wanting, as well as the *infinitive* and *verbal adjectives*. (20) We have no such *verbal nouns* as *shalling*, *maying*, *canning*, *musting*, &c., no more than we have *to shall*, *to may*, &c. (21) We have *willing* and *to will*, but in the proper original sense of the verb, not in its auxiliary sense. (22) In this respect they differ from the other auxiliaries, *to be*, *to do*, *to have*, for these serve not only as auxiliaries, but also to express the independent predicates, *being*, *doing*, *having*. (23) The modifications of verbal meaning expressed by these words, *will*, *shall*, &c., are, in many languages, indicated by a modification of the *form* of the verb. (24) For this reason, and because they contain no *expressible* predicate, without the addition of an infinitive to complete them, the combinations formed by connecting these verbs with the infinitives of other verbs are commonly recognised (not without apparent cause) as COMPOUND TENSES of the verbs to which the complementary infinitives belong. We shall exhibit these *compound tenses* afterwards in their proper place.]

§ 57. (1) We next come to treat of the compound tenses.

Some have contended that these forms of expression are not tenses of the verb. If nothing is to be considered a tense, except what is

* *Shall*, it is said, was formerly used, like *will*, as a transitive verb, taking after it an *objective modification.* "*Shall* is the Saxon *scealan*, Gothic *skallan*, (scealc denoting a *servant*,) which signifies *to owe*, and consequently implies duty; as, "Hu mycel *scealt* thu?" (Luke 16: 5, 7,) that is, "How much owest thou?" It was used transitively down to Chaucer's time; thus, "The faith I shall to God;" *i. e., owe.* Grant's Eng. Gram. p. 74. Lond. 1813. We suspect that examples of *shall* thus used are rare, even in the earliest times.

(19) Repeat what is stated to be peculiar to all these verbs. (20) Are there verbal nouns and verbal adjectives or participles corresponding to these, as to the other verbs? (21) In what sense are *willing* and to *will* used? (22) What is said of the auxiliaries *to be*, *to do*, *to have*, in reference to this matter? (23) Repeat the remark in regard to other languages. (24) Repeat what is said of these verbs in relation to the formation of compound tenses.]

§ 57. (1) What subject comes next to be treated?

expressed by a modification of the root of the verb, then, certainly these are not tenses. They are, however, very peculiar forms of expression, and even those grammarians who have rejected their claim to be recognised as distinct tenses, have found themselves compelled to exhibit them to the learner, and investigate their origin, structure, significance and functions, as well as those who have given them a name and place in their arrangement of modes and tenses. The controversy about this matter among the grammarians, therefore, seems in a great measure a controversy about terms and names. We take no part in this controversy. We have so arranged our book, that it may be conveniently used either by the advocates of the one or the other opinion. We have done this, not for the purpose of suiting the views of those who discard the compound tenses, but, partly, because we think it will conduce to give the learner clearer notions of the inflexion of our verbs to exhibit, as we have done, the simple tenses first, and *apart*. When the learner is perfectly familiar with these, he will find no trouble in mastering the compound tenses, since he has already become acquainted, in learning the simple tenses of the auxiliaries, with all that is necessary to the flexion of the compound tenses. He has only to add a participle or an infinitive to a simple tense of the auxiliary, to form a compound tense. The task of learning the simple tenses alone does not appear so formidable to the pupil as when the whole conjugation, including both simple and compound tenses, is at once presented to his view, and yet when he has mastered the simple tenses, his work is nearly accomplished.

The language could be analyzed without any reference to the compound tenses. Every verb may be considered as belonging to one of the tenses and modes which we have already exhibited—the final result of a complete analysis will reduce all verbs to one of these forms. But it is inconvenient on every occasion to go through all the steps of this analysis, though the student of grammar should be able to go through them when required, and should be trained in reference to this purpose. Our plan of exhibiting the tenses of the verb will render this an easy task. But it is not merely for the purpose of abbreviating the process of analysis that we present the compound tenses. It is because some of the combinations called compound tenses are in our language employed in a sense different from the natural and original sense made up of the elements of which they are composed. The compound has come in the progress of language to convey a meaning distinct from that conveyed by the united elements in their proper separate sense. So that when we have pushed our analysis to the farthest, we have overshot the mark—we have got separate words having separate proper meanings, which meanings combined are not the exact meaning now attached by common consent to the compound expression. This will appear more clearly when we come to examine the compound tenses separately, and trace their formation and account for their present meaning. Still we may now illustrate what we have said by a single example. *The river will overflow its banks to-morrow.* Now if we resolve the words "*will overflow*" into *will*, indefinite tense of the verb *to will*, and the infinitive "*overflow*," we have two separate meanings, which combined will not express what is intended by the combination "will overflow." These words do not mean that the river *determines* or *has a will to overflow* its banks, but predicate of the river the *future* action of overflowing. The compound has come to express or imply a new meaning, not made up of the combined original meanings of "*will*" and "*overflow.*" But more of this when we come to treat of the future tense.

(2) The learner will take notice that we here pass from one to another of those general classes of *modifications* of the *subject noun* and the *verb* mentioned above in § 34; namely, from those which are effected by some change of the *form* of the subject noun or the verb, to those which are effected by the employment of distinct modifying words.

[(3) It may here be remarked that though the compound tenses about to be presented are classed as tenses or forms of the several verbs whose infinitives and participles are combined with the auxiliaries to form these compounds, and though logically considered, they may be regarded as modifications of the meanings of these *verbs*, yet, as regards their grammatical form, they are all really modifications of the *auxiliaries* which enter into these combinations. (4) The auxiliary is in all cases the real verb—the word which possesses the assertive force, and the infinitive or participles of the verb under which the grammarians arrange these forms, and to which they refer them in analysis, are, grammatically considered, *complements* of the *auxiliaries.*]

(5) These complements or modifications of the auxiliaries, which with them form compound tenses, are of three distinct kinds;

---

(2) Give a statement of the fact which the student is requested to notice.

[(3) Repeat the observation in reference to the compound tenses. (4) Which part of the compound expression is really the verb?]

(5) How many distinct kinds of these complements or modifications of the auxiliary are

namely: (6) I. The infinitive belonging to the particular verb to which the compound tense is referred by those who allow them to rank as distinct tenses. This is employed with the auxiliaries, *do, will, shall, may, can, would, should, could.* We might add, if we please, *must* and *dare*, and *ought.* (7) With all these, except *ought*, the form of the infinitive, which consists of the bare *root* of the verb without the particle *to*, is combined to form the compound tenses. For example, *I do call, I will call*, &c.

(8) II. The second form of these *modifications* of the *auxiliaries* consists of a participle employed to complete the predicate expressed by the auxiliary. (9) This form is employed with the verb *to be.* (10) Both the imperfect and the perfect participles of verbs are united with the several tenses of this verb for purposes to be explained hereafter.* (11) Example, *The man is calling.* Here *being*, the predicate asserted by *is*, is completed by the imperfect participle *calling;* what is asserted of the man is *being calling.* As a second example we take *the man is called.* Here the perfect participle is used, and the predicate asserted is *being called.*

(12) III. The third form of modification or complement is that employed with the verb *have.* This is the perfect participle, the same as with the verb *to be*, but employed in a peculiar manner, which we shall describe when we come to the compound tenses formed by the help of the verb *to have.*

§ 58. Compound Tense formed with Shall and Will.—We shall first present the compound form employed to express an assertion that has reference simply to the *future*—to a *time to come.* (1) This is called the Future Tense. It is formed by the combi-

* It will be seen afterward that we are inclined to think that it is not unlikely the verbal noun, and not the imperfect participle, which is used to form *compound tenses* with the verb *to be.* (See § 64.)

enumerated? (6) Mention the first kind, and name the auxiliaries with which it is used. (7) What form of the infinitive is employed with these auxiliaries respectively?

(8) Mention the second form of these modifications employed with auxiliaries. (9) Name the auxiliary with which this form is employed. (10) Which participles are employed with the verb *to be?* (11) Give examples and illustration.

(12) State what is said of the third form of modification, and the auxiliary with which it is employed.

§ 58. (1) How is the future tense formed? (2) Give example. (3) Repeat the remark in reference to the verbal in this tense.

nation of the auxiliary *shall*, or the auxiliary *will* with the infinitive or verbal noun. (2) For example, *I shall write*, and *I will write.* (3) The verbal in this tense is never preceded by the particle *to.*

(3*a*) REMARK. The name *auxiliary* is given to *shall, will, do,* &c., because they *help* in forming the compound tenses.

The *conjugation* or arrangement of the singular and plural persons of the *future tense* of the verb *to write* is exhibited below in two columns distinguished as Nos. I. and II. (4) We employ No. I. when we refer chiefly or exclusively "to futurity of event;" (5) and No. II. when the *speaker* indicates his determination in reference to a future event. (6) If he speaks of himself, his determination of doing or being what is expressed by the predicate of the proposition, if of himself and associates, using the first person plural, his and their joint determination. If he speaks of those whom he addresses, or of third parties, his determination that they shall *do* or *be* whatever is expressed by the verb.

(7) FUTURE TENSE OF THE VERB TO WRITE.

Subjects.		*Predicate, Future Writing.* I.	II.
Sing.	1. I	Shall write,	Will write,
	2. Thou	Wilt write,	Shalt write,
	3. He, &c.	Will write.	Shall write.
Plur.	1. We	Shall write,	Will write,
	2. You	Will write,	Shall write,
	3. They, &c.	Will write.	Shall write.

EXERCISES I., II., &c.—Form propositions in the same manner as prescribed before with the verbs in the *future tense*, and modified as in the preceding exercises by any word necessary to complete the sense. These exercises may be multiplied at pleasure. Especial attention should be given to the distinction between *shall* and *will.* Questions should be asked from time to time in reference to the subjects and predicates of the propositions presented, that what has been taught in reference to propositions may be well fixed in the memory of the pupils.

[(8) Originally, at least, these combinations did not *directly* express futurity. (9) *Shall*, in its original use, expressed some kind of

---

(3*a*) Repeat the remark on the name *auxiliary.*

(4) When do we employ the form in column I.? (5) When the form in column II.? (6) Repeat the illustration. (7) Repeat separately the two forms of the *future tense.*

[(8) Did these combinations originally express futurity directly? (9) What did shall and

necessity arising from duty, obligation, or external compulsion, and *will*, determination, intention, purpose, choice, volition, &c. (10) *I shall write*, implied, originally, *I am under some necessity to write.* (11) From this it would naturally be inferred that *I am about to write at some future time.* (12) *I will write*, properly expresses (or, at least, once expressed) in a direct manner that *I determine* or *purpose*, or *have a will to write.* (13) From this, in like manner, it may be inferred that *I am about to write.* (14) The reference to the future now implied—perhaps now directly suggested—by these forms, must in the beginning have been an *inference* of the understanding, the result of an act of reasoning, not of the simple apprehension of the direct signification of the terms.*

(15) The original force of *shall* and *will* is in a great measure disguised, since, in the vicissitudes of language, they have come to be so generally used to indicate future time. (16) Still they retain so much of there original force, that the one cannot be employed for the other without impropriety—without a violation of the idiomatic usage of the language.† (17) Those who have been brought up in England, or

* What is said above in regard of the manner in which *shall* and *will* come to indicate *futurity*, is worthy of the careful attention of the grammarian and the philologist. It frequently occurs that what was at first an *inference* —a *deduction* of *reason*—comes in the progress of a language to be recognised as the proper and direct sense of particular words and phrases. A reference to this fact may sometimes enable us to explain forms of expression, constructions and idioms, which cannot readily be explained in any other way. For example, "I have been young," comes by inference to equal "Now I am old." In the same way, in Latin, *vixit*, "he has lived," comes to imply "he is dead;" and "*Fuit Ilium*," "Troy has been," to imply, *Troy is no more. Living*, in the one case, is declared to be completed, and *being* or *existing* in the other; and from the fact that these states of *living* and of *being* are finished, the inference is obvious.

† If these words had once come to indicate simple futurity, without retaining any thing of their original distinct significance—of *necessity* in the case of *shall*, and of *purpose* or *volition* in the case of *will*—they would naturally have come afterwards to be used indifferently; or, perhaps, rather one of them would have fallen into disuse.

will originally express? (10) Give example of shall. (11) What would naturally be inferred from this expression? (12) What does will directly express? (13) What may be naturally inferred from this expression? (14) What is remarked of the reference to the future now implied or suggested by these forms?

(15) What is remarked of the original force of shall and will? (16) What proof is given that they still retain part of their original force? (17) What is said of the natives of Eng-

New England, or any colony of pure English descent, seldom employ these two words improperly. (18) On the contrary, it is very difficult even for the educated natives of Scotland and Ireland, and of many parts of the United States, to avoid inaccuracies in the use of these words, because, in the conversation of the uneducated classes—familiar to their ears from early infancy—the proper distinction is not observed. The same difficulty is felt by all foreigners in the use of *shall* and *will*.*

(19) The rule commonly given for the employment of *shall* and *will*, is, that when future time alone is intended to be indicated *shall* is employed with the first persons singular and plural, and *will* with the second and third persons singular and plural. (20) On the contrary, *will*, used with a subject of the first person singular or plural, indicates a promise or a threat, together with a reference to the future; and *shall*, used with the second and third persons, indicates a threat—some species of compulsion.† (21) In other words, a speaker indicates future action, &c., on the part of himself, or on the part of himself and others, whom he represents, by employing *shall*—importing that he, or he and his associates, are under *constraint* to perform the action, &c.; and he indicates future voluntary action, &c., on the part of those whom he addresses, or others, by declaring, not that they are under constraint (this might be discourteous), but that they are *willing*, *disposed* to perform the action, &c. Again, when the speaker promises or threatens the future performance of an action, &c., on his

* The speech attributed to the Scotchman, who had the misfortune to fall into a deep ditch in a dark night, is a good example of the misuse of *shall* and *will*. "I *will* be drowned; nobody *shall* save me." The man understood himself as imploring the assistance of the passers-by. The Englishman, on the contrary, who heard his cries, concluded from his language that he was resolved to drown himself, and that he deprecated all officious interference with his purpose.

† This rule has been expressed in the following doggerel lines:

In the first person simply *shall* foretells;
In *will* a threat, or else a promise dwells;
Shall, in the second, and the third, does threat·
Will simply then foretells the future feat.

land, New England, &c., in reference to the correct usage of *shall* and *will*? (18) What of the natives of Scotland, Ireland, aud many parts of the Unites States?

(19) What is the rule for the employment of *shall* and *will*, when future time alone is intended to be indicated? (20) What does *will* used with a subject of the 1st person indicate? And what *shall* used with subjects of the 2d and 3d persons? (21) State the rule in another form and more at length.

own part, or on his own part and the part of others, he asserts *will* or *determination*, to perform the action, &c., employing the auxiliary *will*. And when he wishes it to be understood that those whom he addresses, or others, are under constraint (whether exercised by him, or resulting from any other cause), to perform an action, &c., he asserts this constraint by using *shall*, which imports necessity from obligation or compulsion.*

(22) It may be useful to subjoin a few examples for the purpose of illustration. *I* SHALL *go to the country to-morrow; I* WILL *go to the country to-morrow*. The first of these forms is properly used when circumstances render it necessary that I should go to the country, and I merely indicate that I am about to go; the second, when I *voluntarily determine* to go, or *promise* to go. (23) *I* SHALL *never see him again; I* WILL *never see him again*. The first is appropriately employed, when I despair of seeing a friend again; the latter, when I determine never to see a person again, because I am displeased with his conduct. We subjoin a number of examples from good authors, selected from those given by Mr. D'Orsey. The learner may be profitably exercised in trying to assign a reason for the use of SHALL or WILL in each of them. (24) "When I am forgotten, as I *shall* be."—Shaks. "I *shall* win, for I know she *will* venture there now."—Southey. "I *shall* forget myself."—Shaks. "Hear me, for I *will* speak."—Shaks. "You *shall* digest the venom of your spleen." "For them no more the blazing hearth *shall* burn."—Gray. "The stars *shall* fade away."]

NOTE.—As it is important to all who would speak English correctly, to be able to decide with certainty and readiness, where they should employ the auxiliary *shall*, and where the auxiliary *will*, we subjoin some additional

* We have spoken above of *future action*, &c. What we have said will apply whatever may be the predicate asserted, whether *action* or *being*. It will be observed in all this that the true key to the proper use of these two forms of the future tense is to be found by attending carefully to the original signification of the words *shall* and *will*. The only case in which nothing of their original force can be traced, is when we use *will* in speaking of subjects incapable of determination or volition. Then it implies nothing but futurity, as in the example, *The river will overflow its banks*. This may be considered an *insensible extension* of the use of *will*, from being predicated of persons to be predicated of things, if we may not consider it as originating from a sort of *personification*.

(22) Tell the different purposes for which we employ *I shall go*. and *I will go*. (23) Tell the difference between *I shall never see him again*, and *I will never see him again*. (24) Why is shall employed in this example? And so of the other examples.]

remarks from D'Orsey. We have made a few alterations to adapt these remarks more perfectly to our purpose and to our opinions.

Place an emphasis on *shall* second and third, and *will* first person, and *determination* is expressed on the part of *the speaker*. For example, *I* WILL *go*, with emphasis on *will* expresses the determination of the *speaker* to go. *You* SHALL *go*, *he* SHALL *go*, *they* SHALL *go*, with emphasis on SHALL express *positive command*, or *intention*, on the part of the speaker, to *force compliance*.

Mistakes, in the use of *shall* and *will*, are more likely to be made in asking questions than in declarative propositions. "A Scotchman says, WILL *I do it?* WILL *we go?* that is, AM I WILLING *to do it?* ARE WE WILLING *to go?* Such questions are obviously absurd, as no one can answer except the speaker. The forms should be, *Shall I do it? shall we go?* thus asking permission," or whether it is incumbent on the party represented by the first person in the one case to *do it*, in the other to *go*. We can call to mind at present but one case in which the auxiliary *will* can, with propriety, be employed with the first persons in an interrogative proposition. This is when the interrogative form is employed to express negation in an emphatic or impassioned manner. For example, suppose I am solicited to assist in some undertaking which appears to me dishonorable. The party soliciting inquires, WILL *you assist us in this undertaking?* "WILL *I assist in such a base undertaking?* No." Here I use *will*, either taking it up and repeating it from the question addressed to me; or I may intend to propound the question to my own conscience, *Am I willing*, can I possibly have a *will* to assist, &c? Except in such extraordinary cases, we presume, *will* should never be employed with the **first** persons in an interrogative proposition. "SHALL *you go?* means, *Do you intend to go?*" (rather, we say, *Is it incumbent on you to go?*) "whereas, WILL *you go?* implies that the person asking is anxious you should go. SHALL *they go?* has" (may have) "for reply, *Yes, if you give them leave. Will they go?* may be answered, *I cannot tell; ask them. Will* sometimes expresses a simple question as to what may happen, thus, *Will it rain?* WILL *the dog come out of his kennel?* means, *Do you think he will?* SHALL *the dog come out?* means, WILL *you let him?*" or *Do you require that he shall? or think it necessary that he should?*

(25) Much of what has been said of *shall* and *will* applies with equal force to *should* and *would*, and may assist the learner in determining which is proper to be employed in any particular case.]

§ 59. COMPOUND TENSES FORMED WITH THE AUXILIARY HAVE.—(1) We next present the compound tenses formed by means of the auxiliary HAVE. These are:

I. (2) The PERFECT TENSE, formed by combining the indefinite

---

(25) What is remarked in reference to *should* and *would?*]

§ 59. (1) Which *compound tenses* are next to be presented? (2) How is the perfect

tense of HAVE with a PERFECT PARTICIPLE. (3) This tense is used to express an action or event that is *perfected* or *finished.* (4) That the action or event is *past,* is generally *implied* by the fact that it is finished, but this form gives no *direct indication* of *time.* (5) Examples: "Persius *has given* us a very humorous account of a young fellow," &c.—Addison. "A friend of mine whom I *have* formerly *mentioned.*"—Idem. "Cicero *has written* orations." "Moses has told us many important facts in his writings."

II. (6) The PAST PERFECT TENSE, formed by combining the past tense of the verb HAVE with a PERFECT PARTICIPLE. (7) This *tense* is used in a proposition expressing an action or event *perfected* or *finished* at a past time. (8) This is usually connected with another proposition expressing some other action or event, which determines the past time intended. (9) Example: *John* HAD FINISHED *his letter, when his father arrived.**

III. (10) The FUTURE PERFECT TENSE formed by combining the future tense of HAVE with the PERFECT PARTICIPLE. (11) This *tense* is used to express that of two future actions or events, one will be completed prior to the occurrence of the other. (12) Ex-

* This form is often used to express a condition on which the assertion in another proposition depends. The proposition in which it is used thus, is generally preceded by the conditional sign IF. But the *if* is sometimes omitted. Example: "HAD *I but* SERVED *my God with half the zeal.*"—Shak., instead of the fuller expression, *if I* HAD *but* SERVED.

This form is also used for *would have,* or *should have,* as in John 11: 32, "*Lord, if thou hadst been here, my brother* HAD *not* DIED."

In the following passages from Sterne and Byron, quoted by D'Orsey, (see D'Orsey's English grammar, Part I., p. 92,) we have both these uses exemplified. "HAD *I* MET *it in the plains of Hindostan I* HAD REVERENCED *it.*" —Sterne.

"*Oh!* HAD *my fate* BEEN JOINED *with thine,*
As once this pledge appeared the token;
These follies HAD *not then* BEEN *mine—*
My early vows HAD *not* BEEN BROKEN."—Byron.

---

tense formed? (3) What is this *tense* used to express? (4) What further is generally implied by this tense? (5) Repeat examples.

(6) How is the *past perfect* formed? (7) In what kind of proposition is it employed? (8) With what is this proposition generally connected? Ans. "With another proposition," &c., as above. (9) Example.

(10) How is the *future perfect tense* formed? (11) What is it used to express? (12) Give example. State exception with example.

ample: When you *shall have completed* your task, I *will permit* you to play. We sometimes by this tense express the completion of an action at a present time; as, *Your brother will have finished his task by this time.*

(13) REMARK.—We cannot readily imagine a case in which WILL could be employed with propriety with the first person in this *tense;* and SHALL, on the contrary, is very seldom employed in the second and third persons. We now exhibit the conjugation of these three *tenses.*

(14) TO WRITE. PERFECT TENSE. PREDICATE, HAVING WRITTEN.

Singular.	*Plural.*
I have *written,*	We have *written,*
Thou hast *written,*	You have *written,*
He has *written.*	They have *written.*

(15) PAST PERFECT TENSE.

Singular.	*Plural.*
I had *written,*	We had *written,*
Thou hadst *written,*	You had *written,*
He had *written.*	They had *written.*

(16) FUTURE PERFECT TENSE.

Singular.	*Plural.*
I shall have *written,*	We shall have *written,*
Thou wilt or shalt have *written,*	You will or shall have *written,*
He will or shall have *written.*	They will or shall have *written.*

COMPOUND INFINITIVE. To have written.

COMPOUND PARTICIPLE. Having written.

(17) Let it be remembered that *have* itself has all these tenses, formed by the combination of its *indefinite, past* and *future* tenses, with its *perfect participle,* thus: perfect, *I have had;* past perfect, *I had had;* future perfect, *I shall have had.*

EXERCISES I., II., &c.—Let a given number of propositions with

(13) Repeat the remark.

(14) Repeat the *perfect tense.* (15) Repeat the *past perfect tense.* (16) Repeat the *future perfect tense.*

(17) What remark is made in reference to the compound tenses of HAVE itself?

verbs in the perfect, past perfect, and future perfect tenses, be formed by the pupil, till he is found perfectly familiar with the formation and use of these tenses. Let the reason be given for using the particular tense employed; viz.: because he intended to express *completed action*, *action completed at a past time*, or *to be completed at a future time*, according as the case may chance to be.

From the combination of the *indefinite tense* of *have* with the *perfect* participle, we might call this form, with propriety, the indefinite perfect—that is, a form *indefinite* as regards *time*, and *perfect* or *perfected* as regards the condition of the action. But since this form, as we think, gives no *direct* indication of time, but simply indicates that what is predicated by the verb is *completed*, we omit the epithet *indefinite* as superfluous. Some grammarians have called this form the *present perfect*. Holding, as these grammarians do, that what we have called the *indefinite tense* is a *present tense*, the name *present perfect* is appropriately given by them to the form under consideration. Similar reasons to those which we have given for rejecting the name Present Tense as an improper designation of what we have called the Indefinite Tense, lead us in like manner to reject the name of Present Perfect. We question the accuracy of the common assertion of grammarians that this tense *always* "represents an action or event as perfect or completed in *present time*, expressed or implied; that is, in a *period* of which the *present* forms *a part*." We admit that when "an action or event completed in" "a period of time of which the present forms a part" is to be expressed, this tense is almost universally employed, if the period of time is mentioned. (We have noticed some exceptions at the end of Note, § 50.) But we do not admit that present time is necessarily and always implied, if not expressed, when this tense is used. Is there any reference to present time in the following examples? "I *have been* young, and *now* am old." "And where the Atlantic rolls, wide continents *have bloomed*."—Byron. "Privileges *have been granted* to legislators in all ages."—Lord Mansfield. "Many, who *have been saluted* with the huzzas of a crowd one day, *have received* their execrations the next; and many who, by the popularity of their times, *have been held* up as spotless patriots, *have*, nevertheless, *appeared* upon the historian's page, when truth *has triumphed* over delusion, the assassins of liberty."—Idem. In fact, we can discover no example to justify the assertion that this tense, of itself, *necessarily* or *directly*, indicates any connection with the present period of time, or any other period. When no period of time is expressed in the proposition in which this tense is used, a past time—a time before the present moment, but otherwise indefinite—is, as we think, *generally* understood by *inference* from the *completed condition* of the action or event. When a period of time is expressed in the proposition, it must be such as is described above—one "of which the present forms a part." It can never, we believe, be used with propriety, when a period of time definitely past is expressed. Such expressions as, I *have written* to my friend *yesterday*, are rejected as inaccurate by all the grammarians. Our definition of this tense—*perfect*, as to *condition of the action*, *indefinite* as to *time*—will, if we mistake not, be found much more conformable to the actual usage of the language than the one commonly given, which seems to be more appropriate to the Greek perfect tense than to ours. The grammarians have taken much trouble to reconcile the actual use of this tense with their definition. Their success, in our opinion, has not equalled their ingenuity and their industry. Perhaps the misapprehension (such we certainly think it) in reference to the use of this form has originated, partly in recognising what we call the *indefinite* tense as a *present* tense, and partly in an unthinking application of what has been taught, in reference to the *Greek* perfect tense, to the *English* perfect tense.

We may notice one example—we presume more might be found—in which this tense is employed, in speaking of a *future event:* "The cock shall not crow, till thou *hast denied* me thrice." Now certainly the future time is not here indicated by the form of the verb, but by the conjunctive adverb of time TILL, and the connection with another proposition explicitly declaring a future event; still it will be hard to account for such employment of this form, if we adopt the definition of its use commonly given by grammarians.

Substantially the same views which we have given above were presented to the public sixty years ago by the late Dr. Noah Webster.

We quote from his Dissertations on the English Language, published in Boston, 1789: "*I have loved*, or *moved*, expresses an action performed and completed, generally within a period of time not far distant; but leaves the particular *point* of time wholly *indefinite* or *undetermined*. On the other hand, I *loved* is necessarily employed when a particular *period* or *point* of time is specified. Thus, it is correct to say, *I read a book yesterday, last week, ten years ago*, &c.; but it is not grammatical to say, *I have read a book yesterday, last week*, &c."

Had the doctor perceived, when he wrote this, that the so called present tense is altogether *indefinite*, it would have contributed to the clearness and precision of his views in reference to the perfect tense.

Dr. Crombie, in speaking of what he calls the *present tense*, uses the following language "The first (the form *I write*) is indefinite as to time and action. If I say, *I write*, it is impossible to ascertain by the mere expression whether be signified, *I write now, I write daily*, or, *I am a writer in general.*" —Crombie's Eng. Grammar, London, 1809, p. 167.

Strange, that after this, he should persist in calling this form a *present* tense, and should, in consequence, involve himself in a mist, when he comes to speak of the *perfect tense*. We quote part of his remarks on the *perfect tense*, accompanied by our commentary in parentheses:

"*I have written*, expresses an action completed," (so far sound,) "in a time supposed to be continued to the present, or an action, whose consequences extend to the present time." (Does not agree with all the facts; unsound, expressed in this unmodified manner.) "As a tense, it derives its character from the tense *I have*," (excellent,) "significant of present time;" (all wrong, and wholly inconsistent with his own assertion above, that this tense "is *indefinite* as to *time* and action;") while the perfection of the action is denoted by the *perfect* participle." (All right.)—Crombie's Eng. Gram., p. 169.

This perfect tense seems to have been little, if at all used with its present significance in the Anglo-Saxon. Where we employ the *perfect*, the Anglo-Saxons employed the *past tense*. The reader may find many examples to illustrate this point in the Anglo-Saxon version of John, ch. 17. This chapter abounds with instances of the use of the perfect tense in the original Greek, and in our authorised version. They are all rendered in the Anglo-Saxon version by the *past* tense. Wiclif, in 1380, used the perfect as we do at present. It may be here noticed that in Latin, also, the past and perfect are expressed by the same form.

We are not prepared to trace the introduction and extension of the use of this form in our language. It is likely that it was first employed only in the case of *active* or *transitive* verbs, followed by a *passive object*, to which the participle was attached as a modification. Thus, at first, it is probable that the words, *I have written a letter*, meant the same as, *I have a letter written;* I possess a letter in the written state. In the progress of the language, the original connection of the participle with the object must, on this supposition, have been gradually overlooked or forgotten, and the form have come *insensibly* to express, as it now does, the predication of HAVING WRITTEN (in the present sense of these words), and this modified by the object—*a letter*, instead of expressing the predication of *having or possessing a letter*—and the letter modified by the word *written*. This step being made, the *insensible extension* of the use of this form to *neuter verbs* was easy. Before this step, the use of the verb indicating possession, in connection with a perfect participle would have appeared absurd. It would have been, for instance, in such an expression as, *The man has gone*, to assert possession, where there is nothing possessed.

In corroboration of the views now expressed, we adduce the fact that many of our neuter verbs are still, as the French express it, conjugated with the verb *to be* as well as with the verb *to have*. For example, we say both *He is gone* and *He has gone*, *is come* and *has come*, *is arrived* and *has arrived*, *is fallen* and *has fallen, is descended* and *has descended*, &c. In French, most *neuter verbs* are conjugated to this day with *être*. The same remark applies to other languages. Is it not likely that all our neuter verbs were originally compounded with the verb *to be*, and that the usage in regard of the more numerous class of active verbs was *insensibly* extended to them, after the proper and original force of the verb Have in these active compounds had ceased to be recognised?

§ 60. Compound Tenses formed with the Auxiliary Do.—We next proceed to exhibit the *compound tenses*,* formed by the help of the auxiliary do.

(1) Do is a very *energetic* little word, and the *compound tenses* formed by combining its *indefinite* and *past* tenses with an infinitive are used, as the indefinite and past tenses of the verb whose infinitive is thus combined; 1st, To express either strong assertion, or contradiction of an assertion, or the answer to a question; 2d, In asking a question; and 3d, In negative propositions. A form with *do* is also sometimes used in imperative propositions. (2) These forms are employed for the purposes mentioned instead of the indefinite and past tenses of all the verbs in the language which have infinitives, except the auxiliaries, *to be*, and *to have*. *Shall, will, may, can, must, ought*, it will be recollected, have no infinitives. (3) The verb *do* itself has these compound tenses formed by the combination of its indefinite and past tenses with its own infinitive; thus, *He* does do *so; He* did do *so;* Does *he* do *so?* Did *he* do *so?* (4) The learner ought to guard against combining do with have. (5) *He does have*, and *He did have, Does he have*, and *He don't have*, &c., are incorrect forms of expression, and yet often used in some parts of the United States.† (6) No person accustomed to use the English language from childhood is in danger of combining *do* with *be*.

* Perhaps we should rather call these forms modes.

† This form of expression is unphilosophical—incongruous as regards meaning—since the verb Have does not express energy, but mere passive possession. When we wish to express active or energetic *having*, we employ the verbs *to possess*, or *to hold*. And with both these, do can with propriety be combined. But it is sufficient to condemn these combinations of *do* with *have*, that they are unsanctioned by respectable usage. No correct writer

§ 60. (1) What is said of do, and for what purposes are the compound tenses formed by it used? (2) For what tenses are these forms employed? (3) What is said of the compound tenses of *do* itself? (4) Repeat the caution to the learner. (5) What is said of such expressions as, *He does have, he did have*, &c.? (6) Repeat remark about *do* and *be*.

(7) We present the compounds formed by DO in three *modes*, the emphatic, the interrogative and the negative. (8) The interrogative form is distinguished by the fact that the subject is arranged after the auxiliary; and the negative form takes the negative particle NOT after the auxiliary. (9) According to the present usage of our language we rarely employ the simple indefinite or past tense, except of the verbs *to be* and *to have*, in an interrogative or negative proposition. (10) Such forms of expression as *Writes he? Goes he? He writes not, He goes not*, are now scarcely used, except in poetry. We say now universally, DOES *he write?* DOES *he go? He* DOES *not write*, &c. We shall mention an exception in interrogative forms presently. (11) By turning to the authorised English version of the Bible, or any book written in the same or any preceding age, we shall find the simple tenses very generally employed both in interrogative and negative propositions. "*Believest* thou not?" "Know ye what?" "What went ye out to see?" "Why stand ye here?" "Went not." "Repented not." Instead of these expressions we now use, *Dost thou not believe? Do ye know what? What did ye go out to see? Why do ye stand here? Did not go.*

---

or speaker on either side of the Atlantic ever employs them. So far as we know, they are used by no class of persons, whether educated or uneducated, in the British Isles. The following caution therefore, has exclusive reference to the citizens of the United States.

Great care should be taken by all who wish to speak good English, to guard against the use of these combinations, which persons even of good education are subject to adopt insensibly in colloquial intercourse with the uneducated. Some attention should be given to this grammatical impropriety by teachers, wherever it prevails, not only by calling the attention of the learner to the nature of the mistake, and correcting it whenever it is made, but by exercises so constructed as to render the correct usage familiar in cases where such blunders would most likely be committed. We think it the more necessary to call the attention of teachers to these ungrammatical forms of expression, because in some places the use of them is so prevalent, that careless writers begin to introduce them in works prepared for the press, and because, so far as we know, this solecism is not noticed in the grammars in common use.

---

(7) Name the several compounds formed with DO. (8) How is the interrogative form distinguished? And how the negative form? (9) Repeat the remark in reference to the present usage of our language. (10) Repeat the illustration. (11) Describe the usage com-

Did not repent. (12) The forms with *do* are also employed in the Bible and in writings of that age; but they had not yet completely superseded the simple tenses in interrogative and negative propositions.

THE VERB TO WRITE.

		EMPHATIC FORM.	INTERROGATIVE FORM.	NEGATIVE FORM.
			(13) *Indefinite Tense.*	
Sing.	1.	I do write,	Do I write?	I do not write,
	2.	Thou dost write,	Dost thou write?	Thou dost not write,
	3.	He does write.	Does he write?	He does not write.
Plur.	1.	We do write,	Do we write?	We do not write,
	2.	You do write,	Do you write?	You do not write,
	3.	They do write.	Do they write?	They do not write.
			(14) *Past Tense.*	
Sing.	1.	I did write,	Did I write?	I did not write,
	2.	Thou didst write.	Didst thou write?	Thou didst not write.

All the other persons are the same, except as to the subject, with the first person singular.

(15) *Imperative Emphatic Form.*

	Singular.	*Plural.*
2d Person,	Do thou write.	Do ye or you write.

(16) When the *compound tenses* are used interrogatively, the subject is placed after the *first auxiliary* word; and when used negatively, the negative particle is placed after the *first auxiliary* word. (17) *The first auxiliary word* in all compound tenses is really the verb—the *assertive word*, and always to be regarded as such. (18) Hence the subject in interrogation and the negative

---

mon in the authorised version of the Bible, and illustrate by examples. (12) Are the interrogative forms with DO employed in the Bible and writings of the same age?

(13) Repeat the indefinite tense of the *emphatic form*. Of the *interrogative form*. Of the negative form. (14) Repeat in like manner the *past tense* of the same *forms*. (15) Repeat the *emphatic imperative form*. (16) Where is the subject placed when compound tenses are used interrogatively? And where the *negative particle* when they are used *negatively?* (17) Repeat the remark in reference to the *first auxiliary word*. (18) Repeat the inference.

particle in negation regularly follow it, and have precedence of all the other parts of the combination.*

(19) REMARK.—In interrogative propositions *generally*, the subject follows the verb. EXCEPTION: (20) When the *subject noun* is an interrogative word, or is modified by an interrogative word, it is placed before the verb, like the subject in assertive propositions; (21) and, in this case, the simple indefinite and past tenses, and *not the compounds with* DO, are employed. (22) Examples: WHO GOES *to the post-office this morning?* WHICH HORSE RUNS *fastest?* WHAT HOUSE FELL? We shall consider the interrogative subject nouns in another place. (§ 98.)

(23) COMPOUND TENSES USED INTERROGATIVELY.

	With an Ordinary Subject.	*With an Interrogative for Subject.*
Future.	Shall I write? &c.	Who will write?
Perfect.	Have I written? &c.	Who has written?
Past Perf.	Had I written? &c.	Who had written?
Future Perf.	Shall I have written? &c.	Who shall have written?

(24) In the same manner questions are made with the compound tenses (yet to be considered) formed with the help of the verb *to be* and other auxiliaries. (25) The subject of the interrogative proposition, *if not an interrogative word*, is placed after the auxiliary; *Is he writing? Is he called? Can he go?* &c. With an interrogative word for subject, the order of arrangement is, *Who is writing? Who is called? Which party can go?* &c.

EXERCISES IN INTERROGATIVE, EMPHATIC AND NEGATIVE PROPOSITIONS. EXERCISE I.—Write a given number of interrogative propositions, using the indefinite and past tenses interrogative. This and all the following exercises to be repeated till the pupil is perfectly familiar

* In negative interrogation, the negative follows the subject; thus, *Do I not write?*

(19) Repeat the remark about the place of the subject in *interrogative propositions*. (20) Repeat the *exception*. (21) What form of the verb is employed in this case? (22) Repeat examples.

(23) Repeat the *future tense interrogatively* through all the persons. The *perfect* in like manner. The *past perfect*. The *future*. And the 3d persons of each tense with an interrogative word for subject. (24) What is said in reference to questions made with the compound tenses (yet to be considered) formed with *to be* and the other auxiliaries? (25) Repeat the illustration, and the examples.

with the form of the verb employed, and with the use of this kind of proposition.

EXERCISE II.—Write a given number of interrogative propositions employing verbs in the compound tenses.

EXERCISE III.—A given number of *emphatic* propositions in the indefinite and past tenses.

EXERCISES IV., V., &c.—Negative propositions in the indefinite and past tenses, and in the compound tenses.

EXERCISE VI., &c.—Write imperative propositions with the imperative *emphatic form.*

§ 61. COMPOUND TENSES FORMED BY THE COMBINATION OF INFINITIVES WITH MAY, CAN, MIGHT, COULD, WOULD, SHOULD.—(1) These tenses are usually represented as constituting what is called the POTENTIAL MODE. (2) They are generally used as before stated (§ 54 : 10), either in the construction of the principal proposition in a *conditional* assertion, or in expressing the *condition* on which a conditional assertion depends. (3) The following sentences afford examples of both uses: *I would go to the country, if you would go with me. I can follow, if you can lead. I may do it, if you may do it,* &c. (4) The first proposition in each of these sentences contains an assertion dependent on a condition expressed in the second. (5) The first proposition in each is *declarative*, but in a conditional manner; the second performs the function of a subjoined or *complementary* proposition. (6) But all these compound tenses, and especially that formed with CAN, are employed sometimes to make unconditional assertions. (7) Examples: *The boy* CAN WRITE. *John* MAY PLAY *to-morrow. Exercise* WOULD *greatly* IMPROVE *his health. Industry* SHOULD BE *rewarded. The young man* MIGHT *study more diligently. Socrates* COULD *govern his temper.*

[(8) If we call these forms the conditional tenses, or the conditional mode, it is only because they are *most frequently* employed in connexion with a condition, or to express a condition, not because

---

§ 61. (1) What do the tenses formed with may, can, might, &c., constitute? (2) How are they generally used? (3) Repeat the examples. (4) What is said of the first proposition in each of these sentences? (5) What further is said of the first proposition? What of the second? (6) Repeat the remark made in regard to all these *compound tenses?* (7) Repeat the examples.

[(8) What reason is assigned for calling these the *conditional tenses*, or *conditional mode?* and what in fact indicates conditional assertion? See note.

they are exclusively so employed.* (9) We shall now exhibit these tenses as they are commonly arranged; but we present in the table § 64, what we consider a more correct arrangement founded on the fact that *might, could, would* and *should*, are generally equally indefinite, as regards time, with *may* and *can*. See § 63. (10) In the common grammars, and in the arrangement below, it is assumed that *may* and *can* form *present* (what we call *indefinite*) tenses, and *might, could, would*, and *should*, past tenses.]

Conditional (or Potential) Mode.

(11) *Indefinite Tense.*

I, He, We, You, They, may write, or can write.
2d *Person Singular*, Thou mayst write, or canst write.

(12) *Past Tense.*

I, &c., might, could, would, or should write.
Thou mightst, couldst, wouldst, or shouldst write.

(13) *Perfect Tense.*

I, &c., may or can have written.
Thou mayst or canst have written.

(14) *Past Perfect.*

I, &c., might, could, would, or should have written.
Thou mightst, couldst, wouldst, or shouldst have written.

---

* It is not by a form of the verb that we indicate, in our language, that an assertion is made conditionally, but by means of conjunctive words; as, *if, lest, unless, though*, &c. We sometimes suppress the conditional conjunctive word, especially with the words *had* and *were*, whether used as principal verbs or auxiliaries, and indicate the suppression or the conditional nature of the assertion by a transposition of the *subject* and *verb*. For example, *Had I a horse*, for *If I had a horse. Were I as rich as that man*, for *If I were as rich*, &c. *Should he arrive in time*, for *If he should arrive*, &c. Still *were* (used with a singular subject) may with propriety be called *conditional*, as it is exclusively used in expressing conditions; and the forms under consideration made with *may, can, might*, &c. may also be called *conditional*, because they most frequently express either a condition or an assertion which depends on a condition.

We use both *if I were* (or were I) and *if I should be*, conditionally, or

---

(9) How are these *compound tenses* here arranged? What is said of the arrangement in table § 64? (10) What is assumed in the common grammars and in the arrangement here given?] (11) Repeat all the persons in each number of *I may write*. Of *I can write*. (12) Repeat in the same manner, *might write, could write*, &c. (13) In the same manner *may have written*, and *can have written*. (14) In the same manner *might have written*, &c.

(15) The second person singular is seldom used. The form used with all the other persons is invariably the same. (16) MUST may be united in the conjugation with CAN and MAY, if the teacher pleases. The young learner ought to inflect each form separately; thus, *I may write, Thou mayst write*, &c. *I can write, Thou canst write*, &c.

EXERCISES ON THE CONDITIONAL OR POTENTIAL MODE. EXERCISES I., II., &c.—Write propositions similar to the preceding, with the verbs in the different tenses of the conditional mode.

§ 62. COMPOUND FORMS MADE WITH THE VERB TO BE.—(1) The verb *to be* has the same compound tenses as other verbs, except that it does not admit of the forms compounded with the verb DO; neither the emphatic, the interrogative, nor the negative form. It has *besides the simple tenses already exhibited*, the perfect tense, *I have been;* the past perfect, *I had been;* the future, *I shall or will be;* the future perfect, *I shall have been;* the conditional tenses *I may or can be, I may or can have been;* and the hypothetical tenses, *I might, could, would, or should be, I might*, &c., *have been.* It is not necessary to exhibit all these tenses at full length, as they will be sufficiently exhibited in the conjugation of the two compound forms, made by uniting the various tenses of this verb with the imperfect and the perfect participles. If it is thought necessary to go through the whole conjugation of the verb *to be* separately, it can be learnt from these compound conjugations, by omitting the participles.

THE PROGRESSIVE FORM OF THE VERB.—(2) By combining the imperfect or progressive participle with the tenses of the verb TO BE, we constitute what may be called the progressive form of the several verbs. (3) This form combines the significance of the several tenses of the verb TO BE with the action of the verb (whose participle is united with them) in its incomplete or progressive condition. (4) In

---

rather hypothetically, but with this difference, that *were* implies strongly *that the condition does not exist, should be* implies *contingency.* The last is little different from the future with *shall.* It may be regarded as a kind of

---

(15) Repeat the remark in reference to the 2d person singular. The remark in reference to the other persons. (16) Repeat the remark in reference to *must.* And in reference to the mode of inflecting these forms.

§ 62. (1) Repeat the substance of what is said about the compound tenses of the verb *to be?*

(2) Describe the progressive forms of the verb. (3) What is said of the significance of these forms? (4) What does this form in fact amount to?

fact it amounts to nothing more or less, than the completing of the verb TO BE by the imperfect or progressive participle (or perhaps rather by the verbal noun, see below, § 64), precisely as it is completed by any other adjective.

We exhibit the passive form of the verb, together with the progressive form, since they differ only as to the participle employed in combination with the several tenses of the verb to be. In the passive form we employ the perfect participle. For remarks on the purposes which the passive form serves, see § 47.

We have arranged the following table so as to exhibit at once the conjugation of the verb *to be*, so far as is necessary to enable the learner to repeat the whole. We stop in each tense when we come to that point beyond which there occurs no further variation of the form. The learner will supply what is omitted by repeating the proper subject for each person, with the form last presented to the end of the tense. The conjugation of the verb *to be* should first be repeated by itself, and afterwards with each of the participles separately through all the tenses; thus making three distinct conjugations to be prepared and recited separately.

VERB TO BE, AND PROGRESSIVE AND PASSIVE FORMS OF TO CALL.

	Indefinite Tense.	*Progressive.*	*Passive.*
Sing.	1. I am	Calling,	Called,
	2. Thou art	"	"
	3. He is	"	"
Plur.	1. We are	"	"
	Past Tense.		
Sing.	1. I was	Calling,	Called,
	2. Thou wast	"	"
	3. He was	"	"
Plur.	1. We were	"	"
	Perfect Tense.		
Sing.	1. I have been	Calling,	Called,
	2. Thou hast been	"	"
	3. He has been	"	"
Plur.	1. We have been	Calling,	Called,

---

softened future, a future with a doubt implied. "*I will deliver your message, if* I SHOULD ARRIVE *in time*, expresses, perhaps, more uncertainty of my arrival than *if I shall*, &c.

Past Perfect Tense.	*Progressive.*	*Passive.*
Sing. 1. I had been	Calling,	Called,
2. Thou hadst been	"	"
3. He had been	"	"
Future Tense.		
Sing. 1. I shall or will be	Calling,	Called,
2. Thou wilt or shalt be	"	"
3. He will or shall be	"	"
Future Perfect Tense.		
Sing. 1. I shall have been	Calling,	Called,
2. Thou wilt or shalt have been	"	"
3. He will or shall have been	"	"
Imperative Mode.		
Sing. 2. Be, or be thou	Calling,	Called,
Plur. 2. Be, or be you or ye	"	"
Subjunctive Indefinite.		
Sing. 1. If I be	Calling,	Called,
Past Tense Subjunctive.		
Sing. 1. If I were	Calling,	Called,
2. If thou wert	"	"
3. If he were	"	"
Plur. 1. If we were	"	"
Conditional Form.		
Sing. 1. I may or can be	Calling,	Called,
2. Thou mayst or canst be	"	"
3. He may or can be	"	"
Plur. 1. We may or can be	"	"
Conditional Perfect.		
Sing. 1. I may or can have been	Calling,	Called,
2. Thou mayst or canst have been	"	"
3. He may, or can have been	"	"
Plur. 1. We may or can have been	"	"
Hypothetical Form.		
Sing. 1. I might, could, would, or should be	Calling,	Called,
2. Thou mightst, couldst, &c.,	"	"
3. He might, could, &c.,	"	"
Plur. 1. We might, &c	"	"

	Hypothetical Perfect.	*Progressive.*	*Passive.*
Sing.	1. I might have been	Calling,	Called,
	2. Thou mightst, &c.,	"	"
	3. He might, &c.,	"	"
Plur.	1. We might, &c.,	"	"

We add the verbals formed by the combination of the verbals of TO BE with the perfect participles of other verbs.

PASSIVE INFINITIVES.

Indefinite. To be called.
Perfect. To have been called.

PARTICIPLES.

Being called.
Having been called.

REMARK.—What we have called the *passive form* is generally called the *passive voice* of verbs.

We have given above and in the conjugation of the *perfect tenses* the compound infinitives and the compound participles. We may here add that the verbal in *ing* is also often compounded in the same way, and for the same reason as the verbs and participles, viz., because of the nature of the conception which all three in common express. As the auxiliary is the real verb in compound tenses, so in infinitives, participles and verbals in *ing* the first auxiliary is that which gives the grammatical name to the compound. It is that which serves as the basis of the expression, the participles or infinitives added are really *modifications.* We give examples of compound verbals in *ing.* BEING *excessively* PRAISED *is injurious, especially to the young.* Here the compound verbal *being praised,* is the subject noun. HAVING PRACTISED *obedience, is an excellent preparation for exercising authority over others.* Here *having practised* is subject noun, modified by obedience—objective modification. (See § 76 : 32.)

A verbal in *ing* analogous to the passive compound infinitive, is sometimes employed. *The having been educated in that institution, affords a presumption in favor of his scholarship.* We may give examples of these compound verbals used in other functions. "Much depends on the rule's *being observed,* and error will be the consequence of its *being neglected.*" Most of these forms are clumsy, and therefore avoided by writers of delicate taste.

EXERCISES I., II., &c.—Write a given number of propositions formed with the compound tenses of the verb *to be.*

Exercises III., IV., &c.—Write a given number of propositions with the tenses of the progressive form of the verb.

Exercises V., VI., &c.—Write a given number of propositions with the passive form of the verb.

The verbs in all these exercises to be varied as much as possible. The exercises to be repeated according to the judgment of the instructor.

The learner may pass over the following observations on the auxiliaries, and on the use of the past tenses in hypothetical propositions, till he comes to the subject of *conditional* and *hypothetical* propositions in the chapter on *accessory* propositions. Both the *conditional* and *hypothetical* forms given in the table § 64, and the following remarks, are to be carefully studied in connection with what we shall say on the latter subject. See § 137.

§ 63. Additional remarks on the auxiliaries Will, Shall, May, Can, and their past forms, Would, Should, &c., and on their use in Conditional and Hypothetical Propositions.

Will (auxiliary) and *shall*, though of the indefinite form, are employed, as is seen in treating of the *future tense*, to predicate future actions or events. *Would* and *should* retain the original sense of *will* and *shall;* that is to say, *would* expresses *determination*, or *volition*, and *should duty*, *obligation*, generally, but not always, in propositions either *expressing a condition*, or *depending on a condition*. For example, *I would go*, or *I should go*, if *I could;* and *I could go*, if *I would*. In the same manner *may* and *might* are used to express *possibility*, or *the having permission*, *license*, &c., and *can* and *could* to express *power;* as, *I may help him, if I can find him; I might help him, if I could find him;* both propositions expressing the *possibility* of helping the person indicated by *him*, on condition of possessing the power to find him. The difference in the meaning between the condition expressed by *if I can*, and *if I could*, will be considered presently.

It is important to remark that, what we have presented (both in the conjugation of will, shall, may, can, separately, and in the conjugation of the compound conditional tenses (§ 61) formed with may, can, might, &c.), as *past forms* are generally only *past* in *form*, not in *signification*. They rarely, *of themselves, indicate past time*, though they are often employed in speaking of *past events*. That the time of the events is past is usually indicated either by a word expressive of past time, or by the tense of the verb in the accompanying proposition; as, *Last year he could do that; John said he might, could, would, should do so.* Here, in both examples, a *past time* is indicated, but in the one by the words *last year*, and in the other by the tense of the verb *said.* We can equally say, *He could do so* NOW, provided this proposition is to be followed by a condition; as, *He could do so now, if he would.* Hence in the conjugation of these words singly, we have abstained from calling the *past form* a *past tense. Would, should, might, could,* and we may include *ought* (past tense of *owe*) and *were* (*subjunctive* or *conditional form* of *to be*), are all generally used indefinitely as to time. And whatever may be the difference in meaning between *may* and *might, can* and *could*, it does not, as is generally the case in other verbs, consist in this, that *might* and *could* always express as *past*, that which *may* and *can* express *indefinitely* in reference to time.

It is to be remembered, however, that these past forms are generally used in propositions *subjoined* to other propositions having their verbs in the *past tense.* For example, *He told them he would, should, might, or could come.* Here, because *told* is the past tense, the past forms *would, should,* &c., must be employed in the subjoined propositions.* Yet if *would, should,* &c., indicate any time here, it must be a *time future* in reference to the time indicated by *told.* We do not say, *He told them that he may come, or he can come.* The same remark holds good when one of these *past forms, would, should, might, could,* is used in the leading proposition; for example, *I would go, if I could.* We cannot say, with propriety, I would go *if I can.* These past forms naturally, like all past tenses, accompany each other. *May* and *can* also, in *conditional* propositions, and their accessories, which express the *condition*, are used together; as, *He may go, if he can;* and *He can go, if he may. May* and *can* are also used in the same way in expressing a condition on which an assertion in the *future form* depends; as, *He will go, if he can,* &c.†

---

* There is an apparent exception in such cases as the following: *I said to them, I can go.* Such an expression is not to be accounted incorrect, because I may be understood as quoting myself—as repeating the very words used on the occasion referred to. *He said, he can go,* cannot be defended in the same way. We must here use *could, He said, he could go.* Or we might say, without impropriety, but with some stiffness, *John* (or *he*) *said* "*I can go;*" repeating the very words supposed to have been employed by John.

† A similar law regulates the *sequence* of the tenses in other languages. In Latin, for example, a tense of the subjunctive mode which accords *in time* with the tense of the principal verb (the verb of the proposition which the subjunctive proposition modifies), must always be employed; namely, either a *present*, or a *present perfect* of the *subjunctive*, must follow *presents, present perfects,* and *futures* of the indicative; and either imperfect or past per-

Because we have said that the past forms, *would*, *should*, &c., are generally employed in propositions subjoined to assertions having reference to the past, it is not to be inferred that they can never be subjoined to propositions, in which the verb is of the indefinite tense, nor that they may not be *followed* by *modifying* propositions having verbs of the indefinite tense. It commonly occurs that propositions in which these past forms are used, are connected with preceding assertions, and with assertions following them made by verbs in the indefinite tense. Examples, I THINK *your father* WOULD FEEL *pleased to see your young friend.* *I* WISH *that I* COULD APPROVE *his conduct.* *I* BELIEVE *you* MIGHT PREPARE *your lessons better.* *Your brother* SAYS *you* SHOULD *not* ACT *as you* DO. In fact other verbs, as well as these, might be used in the past tense, under the same circumstances in which these are employed in the above examples. Some of our writers have followed too servilely and inconsiderately the Latin rule, that conjunctions couple like tenses. They have, in so doing, committed gross blunders, especially where *that* is used (or is supposed to be implied) for the conjunctive word, as in all the above examples. We have an interesting collection of these blunders in Dr. Webster's Dissertations, from which we select a few specimens:

"Suppose I were to say, that to every art there *was* a system of such various and well-approved principles."—Harris.

"If an atheist would well consider the arguments in this book, he would confess there *was* a God." 'Why not,' remarks Dr. Webster, 'confess that there *is* a God?'

"Two young men have made a discovery that there *was* a God."—Swift. 'A curious discovery indeed!' says Dr. Webster. 'Were the Dean still alive, he might find there *is* a great inaccuracy in that passage of his works.'—Dissertations, p. 270, et seq.

We may here see a strong confirmation of the propriety of the course we pursue in reference to the *indefinite* (improperly called the *present*) *tense.* As we have described it, it is exactly the form which suits in the above passages. A misapprehension of the true force of this form (confounding it with the present tense of other languages), together with the prejudice derived from familiarity with the Latin rule about *similar tenses*, has, no doubt, betrayed the learned authors into the use of the above absurd forms of expression—equally at variance with the English idiom and with good sense.

---

fect tenses must follow imperfect, past, and past perfect tenses of the indicative. Whether the present or perfect, the imperfect, or the past perfect, is to be used depends upon the condition of the action, and is not determined by the form of the verb in the principal proposition.

When employed in a proposition expressing the condition on which another assertion depends, there is a marked difference in the sense implied by *may* and *can* on the one hand, and *might* and *could* on the other, though both forms are as thus employed altogether *indefinite* in reference to *time*. This will be readily understood if we examine the sense expressed in the following examples: *I will go, if I* CAN. Here, *if I can*, implies that I do not know whether I shall be able to go or not. *I would go, if I* COULD. Here it is intimated that *I cannot go*. The same may be said of the conditional propositions, *I will go, if I may;* and *I would go, if I might*. The condition in the first intimates that I am ignorant whether I shall obtain permission to go or not, and the condition in the second that I have not permission or liberty to go. *The same applies to I might go, if I would, and I would go, if I should*. The first condition implies that I have not a will to go, the second that I do not think it *incumbent* on me to go.

In the first case, when we use the *indefinite forms*, we express the intention to act in a certain manner dependent on a certain contingency; in the second, when we use the *past forms*, we express what our conduct would be on the supposition of a state of circumstances different from that which actually exists.

We may call the whole proposition, including assertion and condition, a *conditional proposition*, when the condition is uncertain or contingent; and a *hypothetical proposition* when it is implied that the supposed condition has no existence. These terms being well understood, we may, from the above observations, deduce the following rule, for the use of the indefinite and past tenses of these verbs, including *will* and *shall*, as well as *may* and *can*.

RULE.—We employ the *indefinite forms* in the *conditional proposition*, and the *past forms* in the *hypothetical proposition*.*

What we have said in regard to the employment of *past forms* in hypothetical propositions, applies to other verbs as well as to the auxiliaries *might*, *could*, *would*, *should*. In hypothetical propositions having *would*, *should*, &c., for verbs in the *principal* proposition, when other verbs are employed in the *accessory* proposition, it is the past form of these verbs which is used. Like *would*, *should*, &c., they are used indefinitely—without reference to time; and the proposition of the affirmative form implies that the condition which it expresses *does not* exist, and that of the negative form, on the contrary, implies that

* For a further account of *hypothetical* and conditional propositions, see the chapter on *accessory propositions*, § 137.

it does exist. We believe Dr. Noah Webster was the first who called attention, at least in our language, to this fact. See his Dissertations on the English language. We borrow a few of his examples and illustrations:—

"A servant calls on me for a book which his master would borrow. If I am uncertain whether I have that book or not, I reply in this manner: 'If the book *is* in my library, or if I *have* the book, your master shall be welcome to the use of it.' But if I am certain I do not possess the book, the reply is different: 'I have not the book you mention; if I *had*, it should be at your master's service.' What is the difference between these two forms of speaking? It cannot be in *time*, for both refer to the same. The ideas both respect present time: 'If I *have* it *now*, it shall be at your master's service.' 'If I *had* it *now*, it *should* be.' The distinction in the meaning is universally understood, and is simply this: the first expresses *uncertainty*, the last implies *certainty*, but in a peculiar manner; for an affirmative sentence implies a positive negation; and a negative sentence implies a positive affirmation. Thus, *if I had the book*, implies a positive denial of having it; *if I had not the book*, implies that I have it; and both speak of possessing or not possessing it at this *present* time.

"The same distinction runs through all the verbs in the language. A man, shut up in an interior apartment, would say to his friend, '*If it rains*, you cannot go home.' This would denote the speaker's uncertainty. But on coming to the door and ascertaining the fact, he would say, '*If it rained*, you should not go;' or, '*If it did not rain*, you might go.' Can these verbs be in *past* time? By no means. *If it did not rain now you could go*, is present, for the present existence of the fact prevents the man from going.

"These forms of speech are established, by unanimous consent, in practice." . . .

"We have not these antiquities; and if *we had* them, they would add to our uncertainty."—Bolingbroke on History, Let. 3.

"Whereas, *had* I (if I had) still the same woods to range in, which I once *had*, when I was a fox-hunter, I should not resign my manhood for a maintenance."—Spect., No. 16.

"Whatever these verbs may be in declaratory phrases, yet, after the conditional conjunctions *if* and *though*, they often express present ideas, as in the foregoing examples. In such cases, this form of the verb may be denominated the *hypothetical* present tense." (We would rather say, This may be called the *hypothetical use* of the Past Form.) "This would distinguish it from the same form, when it expresses uncertainty in the past time; for this circumstance must not be passed without notice. Thus, 'If he *had* letters by the last mail,' denotes the speaker's uncertainty as to a past fact or event. But, 'If he *had* a book, he would lend it,' denotes a present certainty that he has it not. The times referred to are wholly distinct."

The example "If he had letters by the last mail," is not given above with sufficient clearness. Whether it "denotes the speaker's uncertainty" or not, depends on what may follow it to complete the sense, which remains manifestly incomplete. *If he* HAD *letters by the last mail, he did not say so to me.* Here *uncertainty* and past time are denoted. *If he had letters by the last mail, he would tell me.* Here it is implied that he had no letters by the mail; the whole proposition is merely *hypothetical*, and the time indefinite. Again, if we remove the *hypothetical accessory*, from "If he *had* a book," and replace it by a different form of proposition, the verb will resume its past signification, and uncertainty will be denoted. Thus, *If he had a book, I did not see it.*

Dr. Webster seems not to have observed that this usage of past tenses in hypothetical propositions is not *peculiar* to the English language, and he has made no attempt to account for it, perhaps regarding it as a mere idiomatic use, and as not coming within the province of universal grammar. We have not been so happy as to meet with any explanation of this use of past tenses in *hypotheticals*—a use prevalent in many languages—nor even with an attempt at an explanation. Most probably, attempts, and perhaps successful attempts, to explain this matter, have been made in some of the innumerable treatises on our own and on other languages, though we have overlooked them. We subjoin our own conjectures regarding the origin of a usage so prevalent in different languages:

We suspect that the cause of the past forms *might*, *could*, *would* and *should* having come to be employed so generally in an indefinite manner—indefinite as regards time—may be traced to their frequent use in hypothetical propositions. From being used in these without definite reference to past time, or to any time, they may have come very naturally to be used for other purposes in the same manner. (It is to be remembered all along that they are still used sometimes with the proper force of preterits.) If, then, we can account for the use of a past form in a hypothetical proposition, the whole matter will be explained. We are not sure that we can give all the reasons for this use, but we can suggest something that may help to account for it. Let us propose an example of a hypothetical proposition, to which reference may be made as we proceed in our remarks. *I would gladly accompany you, if I could.* What is to be expressed by this form is *my willingness to accompany you upon a* SUPPOSED *condition.* Now, what tense form shall we employ, for the purpose of expressing this kind of condition? Not the *indefinite form.* From this, we are precluded by the fact that this has been employed to express a *condition* that is *contingent*, unknown to me as yet, but which the future will determine.

I will gladly accompany you if I can. This form is already appropriated. There was no future originally in the language; and if there had been, it would not have served our purpose; it rather serves the purpose of expressing the contingent. In fact, the conditional proposition, though the *condition* is expressed by an indefinite form, has regard to a future act or event. Hence, there was no form left to use but the past, except we should invent one for this special purpose.

Farther, it may be argued that the selection of the past tense for this purpose is peculiarly appropriate. We have already said that there is perhaps always in a hypothetical proposition a *foregone conclusion* implied—an admission that what is *hypothetically* asserted is only a supposed case—a case beyond the confines of reality. This is naturally inferred from the very fact that the proposition is stated hypothetically. If the condition on which the principal proposition is made to depend, really existed, either there would be no need of adverting to it at all, or it would be stated as a fact; and if the condition were contingent, it would coincide with the conditional proposition. The hypothesis then relates to that which has no existence at present, and is not expected to exist in the future; it has no connection with time, and if by possibility with any time, it must be with the past. Being precluded, then, from the use of other forms, we dispose of the hypothetical among the facts that are *by gone*. As we say, I have been young, or, I was young, to imply that I am no longer young, so we say, I would accompany you, if I could, or if I were able, implying that I am no longer able, though I might have been able at a *past time*.

The classical reader will remember that the use of past tenses to express hypothetical propositions is not peculiar to the English language. The Latin language adopts past forms for the same purpose. The Greek has a peculiar mode which is employed to express the hypothetical accessory, but which shows its connection with past tense forms by its inflexions, and which is preceded by a past tense in the *main* proposition. But, in fact, it is in the nature of the *principal* proposition, and not in the *accessory* of hypotheticals, that we must seek for the cause of the use of past tenses. The tense of the accessory is determined here by the tense of the principal proposition. The above observations may help to account for the use of past forms in hypothetical propositions, and, at the same time, for the fact that *would*, *should*, *might*, *could*, and *were*, which constantly occur in hypotheticals, are so often apparently indefinite as regards time. This indefinite use has, no doubt, extended beyond the limits of absolutely hypothetical propositions. These forms are used sometimes to express an assertion in a softened or mitigated form, through politeness or through modesty on the part of the speaker. *I would rather not accompany you.* This is less blunt than to say, *I will not accompany you. I would desire always to do what is right.* This is more modest than to assert positively, *I desire always to do what is right.* Often these past forms are used because there is, in fact, a hypothetical accessory implied. Perhaps there is one implied in the examples above. *I would rather (if you allow me to choose) not accompany you. I would desire (if I understand myself)* always to do what is right.

§ 64. Remarks on the Forms of Conjugation presented in the Synoptical Table. (*See pp.* 152, 153.)

There is an apparent contradiction of terms in the name *perfected progression,* given to the form, *I have been writing.* The reader, in order to account for this, will remark, that the term perfected applies to the whole predicate, *having been writing,* especially to the condition of the action as expressed by the words *have been,* and *progression* only to that part of the predicate expressed by the word *writing.* The *being writing*—that is, the *act* of *being engaged in writing*—is expressed by means of *have,* as *completed, finished, perfected;* but not so the *writing* itself. This is not, by the form of expression, declared to be completed. In the form, *I have* written, on the contrary, both the writing itself, and the *being engaged in* writing are declared *finished, completed.* The learner will, therefore, please remember, that in the above noticed form, the term *progression* applies only to the part of the *predicate* over which it directly stands, and which is in similar type; viz., the part expressed by the *progressive* participle (or rather noun), and not to the whole predicate taken together.

Some remarks seem necessary in reference to what are called in the *Synoptical Table,* the progressive tenses of the passive form, namely, *is building, was building,* &c.; or, with a subject noun, *the house is building, the house was building,* &c. This tense, it will be noticed, is exactly the same in the *active* and *passive* forms. The only difference is in the subjects, and a *modification* of which one of them, and not the other, is susceptible. The active form has the *builder* for its subject, and takes the name of the building after it to complete the predicate; but, in the passive, the building itself is the subject, and no *objective modification* can be applied to the predicate. *The* ARCHITECT *is building a* HOUSE *on the hill. A* HOUSE *is building on the hill.* The word building is employed (apparently) actively in the one case and passively in the other. Hence some grammarians have classed the imperfect or progressive participle both among what they call the active and the passive participles. The word is certainly, whatever we may call it, employed in constructing both active and passive progressive forms. This ambiguous use has been regarded as a blemish in our language. To remedy the evil many writers and speakers have, since the commencement of the present century, adopted a substitute for the passive progressive form exhibited in the table. The substitute is likely enough, from present appearances, to obtain currency, though hitherto (we think) it has been avoided by authors of the most approved taste, has received no encouragement from the more respectable grammarians, and is in itself an awkward, clumsy, and, according to our notion, *barbarous* form of expression. This innovation consists in substituting for the forms of expression, *The house is building*, &c., the form *The house is being built*, *The house was being built*, &c.

If our method of analysis is correct, a new objection will arise to this innovation. The predicate in the form *The house is being built* would be, according to our view, BEING BEING built, which is manifestly an absurd tautology.

We have insinuated, once and again, a doubt whether this word in *ing*, employed in the progressive tenses, is a *participle*, as all grammarians seem to take for granted. It is time that we should plainly say, that we think that the *progressive passive especially*, is *not* compounded with the imperfect participle, but with the verbal noun in ING, which Mr. Taylor has triumphantly proved to be a form entirely independent of the participle. The original form of expression used by our forefathers, from which the present passive progressive has grown, was, it seems to us, not *the house is building*, but *the house is* A *building; a* here being a preposition contracted from *on* and *in*. (See § 81: 8.) In Anglo-Saxon ON had the same signification with our IN. IN seems to have been at first only a form of *on*.

We submit a few examples of this old mode of construction, from which we suspect that the passive progressive form is derived by a suppression of the preposition. "While the ark *was a preparing*."—1 Pet. 3: 20. Compare with this, "While his humble grave *is preparing*."—Blair. We are indebted to Mr. Taylor (see additional notes to Diversions of Purley, p. 48) for a number of examples in which the preposition *in* appears without contraction. "While these sentences *are in reading*."—Com. Service. "Whiles that *is in singing*."—Coronation of Henry VII. "While the flesh *was in seething*."—1 Sam. 2: 13. The modern way of expressing all these propositions is by dropping the preposition, and then we have the *passive progressive*. While the sentences *are reading*, While the flesh *is seething*, &c. Or, according to the still more modern innovation, While these sentences *are being sung*, &c.

We do not assert it as a positive fact, but we repeat again our strong suspicion that the passive progressive has originated from these more ancient forms of expression, and that the word in *ing*, found in it, is not a verbal *adjective* (a participle) but a verbal *noun*. This view, if adopted, disposes of the argument employed by those who favor the innovation which we have been considering, that it is an abuse of language to employ the same participle both actively and passively. Still, we admit, the ambiguity which arises from the use of the same form to express predicates so different in sense remains. But, before we attend to it, we may further remark, that we are

SYNOPTICAL TABLE OF ENGLISH TENSE FORMS.

ACTIVE VOICE.

Tenses Proper.		*Condition of the Action.*		
INDICATIVE MODE.		Progressive.	*Perfected.*	*Perfected* Progression.
INDEFINITE,	I WRITE.	I AM writing.	I HAVE *written.*	I HAVE *been* writing.
Emphatic,	I do write.			
PAST,	I WROTE.	I WAS writing.	I HAD *written.*	I HAD *been* writing.
Emphatic,	I did write.			
FUTURE,	{I SHALL / I WILL} WRITE.	BE writing.	HAVE *written.*	HAVE *been* writing.
IMPERATIVE MODE.				
INDEFINITE,	WRITE.	BE writing.		
Emphatic,	Do write.			
SUBJUNCTIVE MODE.				
INDEFINITE,	IF I WRITE.	If I BE writing.	If I HAVE *written.*	If I HAVE *been* writing.
PAST,	IF I WROTE.	If I WERE writing.	If I HAD *written.*	If I HAD *been* writing.
CONDITIONAL MODE.				
INDEFINITE,	{I MAY / I CAN} WRITE.	BE writing.	HAVE *written.*	HAVE *been* writing.
HYPOTHETICAL MODE.				
INDEFINITE,	{I MIGHT / I COULD / I WOULD / I SHOULD} WRITE.	BE writing.	HAVE *written.*	HAVE *been* writing.

PASSIVE VOICE.

INDICATIVE MODE.

INDEFINITE	It IS *built*.*	It IS building.	IT HAS *been built*.	It HAS *been* building.
PAST,	It WAS *built*.	It WAS building.	It HAD *been built*.	It HAD *been* building.
FUTURE,	{ It SHALL / It WILL } BE *built*.	BE building.	HAVE *been built*.	HAVE *been* building.

IMPERATIVE MODE.

INDEFINITE,	BE *called*.			

SUBJUNCTIVE MODE.

INDEFINITE,	If it BE *built*.	If it BE building.	If it HAS *been built*.	If it HAS *been* building.
PAST,	If it WERE *built*.	If it WERE building.	If it HAD *been built*.	If it HAD *been* building.

CONDITIONAL MODE.

INDEFINITE,	{ It MAY / It CAN } BE *built*.	BE building	HAVE *been built*.	HAVE *been* building.

HYPOTHETICAL MODE.

INDEFINITE,	{ It might / It could / It would / It should } BE *built*.	BE building.	HAVE *been built*.	HAVE *been* building.
Infinitives,	{ To BUILD. / To BE *built*. }	To BE building. To BE building.	To HAVE *built*. To HAVE *been built*.	To HAVE *been* building. To HAVE *been* building.
Participles,	{ }	Building. Being building.	Having *built* and *built*.† *Built*, being *built*, and having *been built*.	Having *been* building. Having *been* building.

It will be observed that the *simple* tenses, the *progressive*, and the *perfected* are given throughout in distinct type.

* For the subject IT, the learner may substitute *The house*, *The palace*, &c.

† The learner will remember, that this participle is used in forming both the active and the passive voice.

inclined to think that the active progressive form also has a similar origin, and that the word in *ing* here, as in the other case, is the verbal noun, and not (as seems to be tacitly admitted by the grammarians) the participle. We believe that this tense form, as it is now considered, has arisen from the frequent combination of the verbal with the tenses of the verb *to be* as a *noun and preposition modification.* (See § 81 : 18.) The preposition here used was also *a*, which, as in the other case, has been retrenched in the language of books, and of the educated classes. The use of the preposition still lingers with the uneducated classes, among whom we may often trace the origin, and find the explanation of forms of speech, when it might be difficult to discover any light by researches in our written literature. There is nothing more common at the present day among the less educated, than to say I *am a coming*, I *am a going*, I *am a thinking*, He *is a staying with his friends*, &c. By way of illustration we give an extract from Bulwer's "My Novel, or Varieties of English Life," which, we believe, represents fairly the dialect of the uneducated classes (at least, so far as regards the expression in question), not in a single locality alone, but in most places where the English language is spoken.

"'The gallus!' answered Solomons—" he *be a goin* to have it hung from the great elm tree. And the Parson, good man, *is a quotin* Scripter agin it—you see he's *a takin* off his gloves, and *a puttin* his two hans together,'" &c.

In this form of expression, used by that class with which the genuine idiomatic constructions of a language remain generally longest, and often least adulterated, we think, we discover the origin of what is called the active progressive tense. If our conjecture is right, the active and passive forms have come to coincide, not by our ancestors' rudely usurping the same participle passively which was already used actively, but by taking after the tenses of the verb *to be* a modification, consisting of a preposition and verbal noun, for two distinct purposes. The coincidence of the two forms seems to have been perfectly accidental, and not the result of violently straining a form of speech from its established and legitimate use to a new, and very dissimilar, if not opposite, use. The whole ambiguity, if this explanation is admitted, arises from the fact that the verbals in ING are employed to express both an action and a condition. *Building*, for example, expresses both the *action* of the *builder* and the *condition* of the house, while the builder is erecting it.

After all we have said, the ambiguity still remains, whatever way we choose to explain the origin of these tense forms. But in any case, in which the passive progressive is ever employed, the ambiguity disappears when the proposition is completed. It is only the partial predicate consisting of the verb *to be*, and the verbal in *ing* which presents ambiguity. When the subject of the proposition is presented, or the objective modification necessary to the active form, there is no more uncertainty in reference to the sense. *The architect is building a house*, can never be mistaken for a passive form, nor *The house is building*, for an active form; because a house cannot perform the *action* of building. The same may be said of the *Man is writing a letter*, and *The letter is writing*. And so, of all cases in which any one who understands the language would think of employing the passive progressive tenses. Whenever the same word might serve as subject noun both of the active and passive form of a verb, it becomes improper to employ the passive progressive forms exhibited in the table. It would not, for example, be allowable to use the expression, *The man is killing*, in a passive sense, because the same subject may serve for the active form. Here the new passive progressive has the advantage. The expression, *The man is being killed*, does not lie exposed to the same objection.

If a less objectionable form of expression had been invented, as a substitute for the old form, we should have accepted it thankfully, as removing even the appearance of ambiguity, and extending the use of the *passive* to cases in which the old form cannot, with propriety, be used. But as the matter now stands, we think that all who would aim at purity and elegance of diction, will eschew all forms of the passive progressive, and in all possible cases express their meaning by the active form. Instead of saying, *A house is building*, or *A house is being built in such a street*, we should prefer to say, *They are building*, or *Somebody is building a house in such a street*, employing the pronoun *they* indeterminately, if the parties building are not known by name. When the party who builds is known, it is best for all purposes—for securing perspicuity, elegance, vigor, and liveliness of expression—to make the name of the party the subject noun, and use the active form.

We may here notice, as having connection with this subject, that there is a difference in the nature of the actions expressed by verbs and by verbal words, which, under certain circumstances, influences the choice of the tense form employed in our language. Some actions are, from their nature, incapable of indefinite continuation. They are either momentary in their duration, or completed in a limited time, whether longer or shorter. Other actions are, on the contrary, in their nature indefinitely continued, or habitual. Now, in the use of the former class, we have often occasion to distinguish between action completed and action incomplete; for example, between the sense expressed by *The architect built a house*, and *The architect was building a house*; *The house was built*, and *The house was building*, or in progress of construction. *Building, writing, reading, ploughing*, &c., and most words which express external acts, are of the first class. Those which express continuous movements of the mind, or habitual acts, are of the second class; as, *loving, fearing, hating*, &c., and *living, dwelling*, &c. Such of these latter verbs, as are active, are very seldom (some of them perhaps never) used in the progressive forms active, and none of them, we think, can be used with propriety in the progressive form passive. Such as are neuter, are more rarely than other verbs employed in the progressive form. The reason is, that, the action being in its nature continuous, we find no occasion to distinguish progressive from completed action, or, rather, that in all forms these verbs express an action in its own nature progressive, and requiring no grammatical indication of this fact. *When I knew that man he* LOVED *to read poetry and fiction.* Here is continuous and progressive action. The action of loving, though *complete* in one sense, is not indicated by this expression to be *finished;* the contrary is inferred from the nature of the action, which is capable of indefinite continuation in its *complete* state. The proposition expresses a continuous or habitual occupation of the man's mind. On the contrary, if we wish to express the continuous occupation or engagement of a man in building a house, we cannot express it in the same way. We must, for example, say, *When we knew that man, he was building a house,* if we intend to express the manner in which he was then occupied, not *When we knew that man, he built a house.* If I wish to express that *building* was his habitual occupation, I can do it by a past tense, He *was* a builder. Observe, also, we can never say passively, *The reading of poetry and fiction was loving;* we must say *was loved.* A progressive form passive, is wholly unnecessary to this class of verbs. So in regard of neuter verbs, we say, *He* LIVED *in the city,* when *I knew him,* because the action is in its own nature *continuous.* We can here say also, *He was* LIVING *in the city when I knew him,* but the other is the more usual form of expression.

The facts here noticed account for the coincidence on some occasions of our *past tense* with the imperfect tense of other languages. *He lived,* or *He dwelt in the country when I knew him,* because the *living* or *dwelling* is habitual and not indicated as *finished,* would be expressed by the *imperfect tense* in Latin, French, &c.—in all languages which have a proper imperfect tense. In the same manner, *He loved the reading of poetry,* when I was acquainted with him, would also be expressed by the imperfect. Except in the use of this kind of verbs, our *past tense* never coincides with the *imperfect* of other languages.

§ 65. OF DEFECTIVE VERBS. (1) We may here notice a class of verbs, which have been called by the grammarians *defective,* because they fail in certain tenses, either *simple* or *compound.* We have noticed the chief of these among the auxiliaries. We subjoin a list of the whole class. (2) They all fail, or are defective, in the compound tenses, because they have neither infinitives nor participles. They have, therefore, only the two simple tenses.

	Indefinite.	*Past.*	*Indefinite.*	*Past.*
(3)	Can,	Could.	Shall,	Should.
	May,	Might.	Will,	Would.
	Must,	———	Wis, (*b*)	Wist.
	Ought, (*a*)	———	Wit, (*c*)	Wot.
	Quoth,	Quoth.	Wot,	

§ 65. (1) Describe the defective verbs. (2) In what tenses do these verbs all fail, and for what reason? (3) Repeat the list of these verbs

(a) (4) We have said enough already of *can, may, shall, will,* in another place. Ought was originally the past tense of *owe,* but is now used indefinitely as regards time; as, *I ought now to go.* When used to express past duty or obligation, it is followed by the perfect form of the infinitive—a use peculiar to itself; as, *I ought to have gone there yesterday.* With other verbs, when we do not intend to express the action indicated by the com pleting infinitive, as *perfected, finished,* we always use the simple infinitive· as, *I intended* TO GO *yesterday. Yesterday I determined* TO SEND, &c.

(b) This verb is now out of use in the current language. It was formerly employed in a sense equivalent to "I think," "I imagine."

(c) Wit is now only used in the phrase *to wit.* Both *wit* and *wot* are found in the translation of the Bible and in our earlier authors. Its meaning is equivalent to that of the word *know.*

§ 66. OF IMPERSONAL VERBS.—(1) There remains still another peculiar kind of verbs to consider; namely, those commonly called *impersonal,* but sometimes, perhaps more properly, *unipersonal* verbs. Of these verbs there are several distinct classes.

1st. (2) There are a few verbs, such as, *It rains, It snows, It hails,* &c., expressing natural phenomena or operations, of which men in the early ages did not understand the causes, and of which we could not, even in the present improved state of natural science, express the causes (which causes would naturally form the subject nouns of the above verbs) by a single term, or in any convenient way; while the phenomena or operations themselves are of common occurrence and of general interest, and therefore need to be expressed both substantively and assertively. (3) In English, we place before the verbs which express such operations the neuter pronoun IT, which here serves the peculiar function of representing, not a known noun, but a cause *unknown,* or that cannot be conveniently expressed every time we have occasion to express the natural phenomenon assertively. (4) These verbs admit of being conjugated, like other verbs, through all tenses, but only in the third person singular.

2d. (5) There is another class of what are commonly called impersonal verbs, which admit only of a proposition for their subject, and are therefore necessarily *unipersonal.* Only a few of these now remain in our language. (6) We have, though now rarely used, *It behooves or behooveth, It irks or irketh,* and perhaps some others. (7)

---

(4) Repeat what is said of the verb *ought.*

§ 66. (1) What kind of verbs remains to be considered, and how more properly named? (2) Describe the first class of these verbs. (3) What word is usually placed before these verbs? Describe the function which it performs in this case.

(5) Describe another class of impersonal verbs. (6) Give examples. (7) Repeat what is said of other verbs employed in the same way.

Many other verbs are employed in the same way, having a proposition for their *real* subject, and the pronoun *it* for a *substitute* subject (see § 103 : 7), but the same verbs, unlike those mentioned above, are also employed with nouns both singular and plural, and sometimes with pronouns of the first and second persons for their subjects. We mean such verbs as, *It becomes*, *It suits*, &c. These present no difficulty. All that is peculiar in them, is the fact that a proposition may serve as their subject, and that matter comes under our consideration elsewhere. (See § 103.)*

3d. (8) There is still another very peculiar class of impersonal verbs now obsolete—altogether out of use—but which claim notice, because they sometimes occur in our more ancient authors, and present a form of expression which puzzles inexperienced grammarians. (9) Those which occur most frequently in authors of the seventeenth century, are *methinks*, past tense *methought*, and *meseems.* The list might be much enlarged by having recourse to authors of an earlier date. (10) Such forms as *melisteth*, *meliketh*, &c., were once common. We find "us ought," in Chaucer. (11) Some grammarians consider these the only *impersonal* verbs in the language, because they have nothing in the shape of a *subject noun*, not even the substitute *it.* But in so doing, they employ the term *impersonal* in a peculiar sense of their own, unsanctioned by general use, to mean verbs which have neither a noun for subject, nor a substitute pronoun to represent the proposition which serves as their real subject. (12) For these verbs are all verbs having a proposi-

* We may perhaps find in some *boyish* translations of Latin authors, instances of the use of another class of *impersonals* or *unipersonals*, peculiar to the Latin language, viz., the third person singular of neuter verbs, with a passive form. The following may serve as an example of the form to which we allude. It was fought *on both sides with the greatest bravery till the evening,* instead of the battle was continued, or the conflict was maintained, &c. This *unipersonal* form is not likely to be employed by those who really understand English. It is uncongenial to our language.

(8) What claim has the third class of impersonal verbs on our attention? (9) Name the verbs of this kind which occur most frequently in authors of the 17th century. (10) Name others which occur in more ancient authors. (11) Repeat what is said of the grammarians who have considered these as the only really impersonal verbs in our language. (12) What distinguishes these from other verbs, which have a proposition for their subject?

tion for their subject, and are like other verbs of the same kind, save that they are not preceded by the substitute subject *it*. (13) In this they resemble verbs in other languages, which employ no word equivalent to *it* with a verb having a proposition for subject.* (14) The pronouns which in this form precede the *impersonal verb*, *me* for example in *methinks*, are real *datives*. See further explanation of these forms when we come to treat of the dative modification, § 79 : 18–21.

§ 67. We subjoin a list of the verbs of the ancient conjugation, with the verbs of the modern conjugation, which have contracted preterits. This list is intended to include all the verbs of which the past tenses and perfect participles do not always end in *ed;* or what are (we think, improperly) called in most grammars, *irregular verbs.* We might have given a separate list of the contracted forms belonging to the modern conjugation, and we might have classified the verbs of the ancient conjugation in reference to the different ways in which their preterits and participles are formed from the root. Had we done so, we must have presented several distinct lists, and this would have rendered our tables less convenient for the purpose of reference in cases of doubt. Instead of presenting separate lists, we mark with *con.* (= contracted) those words which are manifestly contracted from a *modern* form, leaving all about which there is room for doubt to be accounted as of the ancient conjugation; and we subjoin notes where we think any additional remark necessary.

When a verb has a preterit or participle of the *regular* modern form in use, besides the ancient or the contracted form exhibited in the list, we indicate this fact by placing *-d* or *-ed* after the form in the list. This *-d* or *-ed* is to be added to the root. The forms printed in *italics* are either out of use, or seldom used, or not used by reputable authors, and therefore to be avoided. In the column for perfect par-

* The employment of the pronoun IT before this class of verbs, seems to have orginated from the loss of the *personal* terminations, which once distinguished our verbs. A pronoun became absolutely necessary in cases where the subject noun was not expressed to distinguish the *person* intended. The use of pronouns for this purpose being once generally introduced, extended naturally to cases like this, where they are not absolutely necessary; for here the subject *is* expressed, though by a proposition, and after the verb.

(13) Repeat what is said of their resemblance to ***impersonal*** verbs in other languages. **(14)** What is said respecting the pronouns which **precede these verbs**?

ticiples, we give all those which differ from the past tense in form, omitting those which coincide in form with that tense. We have occasionally used the mark of interrogation (?) to indicate a form, in our opinion, questionable.

LIST OF VERBS OF THE ANCIENT CONJUGATION, WITH THOSE OF THE MODERN CONJUGATION WHICH HAVE THE PAST TENSE CONTRACTED.

Indefinite Form.	*Past Tense.*	*Perf. Participle.*
Abide	Abode	
Am	Was	Been
Arise	Arose	Arisen
Awake	Awoke, -d	Awaked
Bake	Baked	Baked, *Baken*
Bear, *to bring forth*	Bore, *Bare*	Born
Bear, *to carry*	Bore, Bare	Borne
Beat	Beat	Beaten, Beat
Begin	Began	Begun
Behold	Beheld	Beheld, *Beholden* (*a*)
Bend	Bent *con.*, -ed	
Bereave	Bereft *con.*, -d	
Beseech	Besought	(See remark at the end of List.)
Bid	Bade or Bid	Bidden, Bid
Bind	Bound	
Bite	Bit	Bitten, Bit
Bleed	Bled *con. ?*	
Blend	*Blent con.*, -ed (*b*)	
Blow	Blew	Blown
Break	Broke, *Brake*,	Broken, *Broke* (*c*)
Breed	Bred, *con. ?*	
Bring	Brought	(See remark.)
Build	Built *con.*, -ed	
Burn	Burnt *con.*, -ed	
Burst	Burst	
Buy	Bought	(See remark.)
Can	Could	No participle.
Cast	Cast *con.*, -ed (*d*)	
Catch	Caught, -ed	(See remark.)
Chide	Chid, *Chode* (*e*)	Chid, Chidden
Choose	Chose	Chosen
Cleave, *to split*	Cleft, *Clave* (*f*)	Cleft, Cloven
Cleave, *to adhere*	-d, *Clave* (*g*)	-d
Cling	Clung	
Climb	-ed, *Clomb* (*h*)	-ed

Indefinite Form.	*Past Tense.*	*Perf. Participle.*
Clothe	-d, *Clad*	-d, *Clad* (*i*)
Come	Came	Come
Cost	Cost *con.*	
Creep	Crept *con.*	
Crow	Crew, -ed	-ed.
Cut	Cut *con.*	
Dare, *to venture* (*j*)	Durst, -d	-d.
Deal	Dealt *con.*, -ed ?	
Dig	Dug, *-ged*	
Do	Did	Done
Draw	Drew	Drawn
Dream	-ed, Dreamt *con.*	
Drink	Drank, Drunk	Drunk, *Drunken* (*k*)
Drive	Drove	Driven
Dwell	-ed, Dwelt *con.*	
Eat	Ate, *Eat*	Eaten
Fall	Fell	Fallen
Feed	Fed *con.*	
Feel	Felt *con.*	
Fight	Fought	
Find	Found	
Flee	Fled *con.*	
Fling	Flung	
Fly	Flew	Flown
Forbear	Forbore	Forborne
Forget	Forgot	Forgotten, Forgot
Forsake	Forsook	Forsaken
Freeze	Froze	Frozen
Get	Got, *Gat*	Got, Gotten
Gild	Gilt *con.*, -ed	
Gird	Girt *con.*, -ed	
Give	Gave	Given
Go	Went	Gone
Grave	Graved	-ed, Graven
Grind	Ground	
Grow	Grew	Grown
Hang	Hung, -ed (*l*)	
Have	Had *con.*	
Hear	Heard *con.*	
Heave	-d, Hove	
Help	-ed	-ed, *Holpen*
Hew	-ed	-ed, Hewn
Hide	Hid	Hidden, Hid

Indefinite Form.	*Past Tense.*	*Perf. Participle.*
Hit	Hit *con.*	
Hold	Held	Held, *Holden*
Hurt	Hurt *con.*	
Keep	Kept *con*	
Kneel	Knelt *con.*, -ed ?	
Knit	Knit *con.*, -ed	
Know	Knew	Known
Lade	-ed	-ed, *Laden*
Lay, *to place*, (act.)	Laid *con.*	
Lead	Led *con.* ?	
Lean	-ed, Leant *con.*	
Leave	Left *con.*	
Lend	Lent *con.*	
Let	Let	
Lie, *to recline*, (neut.)	Lay	Lain, *Lien* (*m*)
Light	-ed, Lit *con.* ?	
Load	-ed	-ed, *Loaden*
Lose	Lost *con.*	
Make	Made	
May	Might	No participle
Mean	Meant *con.*, -ed. ?	
Meet	Met *con.*	
Melt	-ed	-ed, *Molten*
Mow	*-ed*	-ed, Mown
Pay	Paid *con.*, -ed ?	
Pen, *to enclose*	Penned, Pent *con.*	
Put	Put *con.*	
Quit	Quitted, Quit *con.*	
Rap, *to transport*	Rapped	Rapped, Rapt *con.*
Read	Read (*sounded red*)	
Reave, *to rob*	Reft *con.*, -ed ?	
Rend	Rent *con.*	
Rid	Rid *con.*	
Ride	Rode, Rid ?	Ridden, *Rid*
Ring	Rang, rung	Rung
Rise	Rose	Risen
Rive	-d	Riven, -d ?
Rot	Rotted	Rotten, -ed
Run	Ran	Run
Saw	-ed	-ed, Sawn
Say	Said *con.*	
See	Saw	Seen
Seek	Sought	(See Remark.)

Indefinite Form.	*Past Tense.*	*Perf. Participle.*
Seethe	-d, sod	-ed, Sodden
Sell	Sold	
Send	Sent *con.*	
Set	Set	
Shake	Shook	Shaken
Shall	Should	No participle.
Shape	-d	-d, *Shapen*
Shave	-d	-d, Shaven
Shear	-ed, *Shore*	-ed, Shorn
Shed	Shed *con.*	
Shine	Shone, -d	
Shoe	Shod *con.*	
Shoot	Shot *con ?*	Shot, *Shotten*
Show or shew	-ed	-ed, Shown
Shrink	Shrunk, Shrank	Shrunk, *Shrunken*
Shred	Shred *con.*	
Shut	Shut *con.*	
Sing	Sung, *Sang*	Sung
Sink	Sank, Sunk	Sunk, *Sunken* (*n*)
Sit	Sat, *Sate*	Sat, *Sitten*
Slay	Slew	Slain
Sleep	Slept *con.*	
Slide	Slid *con. ?*	Slid, Slidden
Sling	Slung, *Slang*	
Slink	Slunk	
Slit	Slit *con.*	Slit, Slitted ?
Smite	Smote	Smitten, *Smit*
Sow	-ed	Sown, -ed
Speak	Spoke, *Spake*	Spoken, Spoke ?
Speed	Sped *con.*	
Spell	Spelt *con.*, -ed	
Spend	Spent	
Spill	-ed, Spilt *con.*	
Spin	Spun, *Span*	Spun
Spit	Spit, *Spat*, -ed ?	Spit, Spitten -ed
Split	Split *con.*	
Spread	Spread *con.*	
Spring	Sprung, Sprang	Sprung
Stand	Stood	
Stay	Staid *con.*, ed ?	
Steal	Stole	Stolen
Stick	Stuck	
Sting	Stung	

Indefinite Form.	*Past Tense.*	*Perf. Participle.*
Stride	Strode, Strid	Stridden
Strike	Struck, *Strook*	Struck, Stricken
String	Strung, -ed	
Strive	Strove, -d?	Striven, -ed?
Strow or strew	-ed	-ed, Strown
Swear	Swore, *Sware*	Sworn
Sweat	Sweat, -ed, *Swet*	-ed, *Sweaten*
Sweep	Swept *con.*	
Swell	-ed	-ed, Swollen
Swim	Swam, Swum	Swum
Swing	Swung	
Take	Took	Taken
Teach	Taught	(See remark.)
Tear	Tore, *Tare*	Torn
Tell	Told	
Think	Thought	(See remark.)
Thrive	Throve, -d	Thriven, -ed
Throw	Threw	Thrown
Thrust	Thrust *con.*	
Tread	Trod, *Trode?*	Trodden, Trod
Wake	Woke, -d	-d
Wax	-ed	Waxen, -ed
Wear	Wore	Worn
Weave	Wove, -d	Woven, *Wove*
Weep	Wept *con.*	
Wet	Wet *con.*, -ed	
Whet	Whet *con.*, -ed	
Will	Would	No participle.
Win	Won, *Wan*	Won
Wind	Wound	
Work	-ed, Wrought,	(See remark.)
Wring	Wrung, -ed	Wrung
Write	Wrote, *Writ*	Written

NOTES AND REMARKS ON THE LIST OF VERBS.

(*a*) Beholden is used in a different sense. It means *indebted, obligated,* 'Little are we *beholden* to your love."—Shak. This form, we think, is seldom employed in the current English of the present day.

(*b*) "In one red burial *blent,*"—Byron, as quoted by Mr. D'Orsey, to whom we are indebted for many of the examples introduced in these notes.

(*c*) "The deer is *broke.*"—Scott.

(*d*) "Thou *castedst* them down into destruction."—Ps. 73: 18.

(*e*) "Jacob *chode* with Laban."—Gen. 31: 36.

(*f*) "The ground *clave* asunder."—Numb. 16: 31.

(*g*) "Certain men *clave* unto him," &c.—Acts 17: 34.

(*h*) "So *clomb* this first grand thief into God's fold."—Milt.

(*i*) "Was clad with zeal."—Is. 59: 17.

(*j*) Dare *to challenge* has always the form of the mod. conjugation *dared.*

(*k*) Drunken is most generally used adjectively. It was formerly sometimes used to form compound tenses. "Thou hast *drunken* the dregs," &c.—Is. 51: 17.

(*l*) There is, perhaps, a tendency in the use of this verb to prefer the form in *ed.* In speaking of suspension for the purpose of taking life, we now always use the form in *ed,* both as past tense and participle.

(*m*) The form *lien* is found in the early editions of the authorized version. It may be found in the current editions in Gen. 26: 10. In other instances it has been replaced by *lain.* We suspect that *lain* is to be traced to a modern innovation—a change of fashion—in pronunciation (perhaps having some connection with the confusion of this verb with *lay*), which has come to be represented in the written form of the language. In Tyndale, Cranmer, and the Geneva version, the word is written *lyne.* These old forms retain the vowel sound of the root, which is not the case with *lain.*

(*n*) Sunken is still sometimes used adjectively.

REMARK.—(1) There are some verbs in the above list which neither belong properly to the ancient conjugation, nor are they *contracted* forms of the second. They, in fact, partake apparently of the character of both conjugations, since there is both a change of the vowel sound, and a *t* added in the formation. They really belong to the modern conjugation, and have been placed here because they differ from the usual forms of that conjugation, though they are not, properly speaking, *contracted forms.* We enumerate the chief of these verbs: *beseech, besought; bring, brought; buy, bought; catch, caught; seek, sought; teach, taught; think, thought.* To these we may add *work, wrought,* in which there is, besides the peculiarity common to the rest, a transposition.

REMARKS ON THE VERBS OF THE ANCIENT CONJUGATION.—In verbs of the ancient conjugation there is, as we have before observed, generally a change of the vowel sound. The changes which take place are chiefly the following:

1. (2) A few verbs of this conjugation form preterits by changing *o* into *e.* In most of these the *o* is followed by *w,* as *blow, blew; crow,*

---

§ 67. (1) Repeat the substance of the first remark, and name the verbs to which it ap-

crew, &c. In like manner, *hold* and its compounds make *held*. *Fall*, *fell*, and *draw*, *drew*, having a vowel sound approaching that of *o*, may come within this class. *Slay* and *fly* have preterits similar to the verbs in *ow*, viz., *slew* and *flew*.

2. (3) The preterits of many verbs of this conjugation are formed by changing *ea* of the *root* into long *o*. Some of these have a second form in *a*. Example, *speak*, *spoke*, *spake* ; *bear*, *bore*, *bare*.

3. (4) A few preterits are formed by changing *a* long into *oo* as, *take*, took, and its compounds. We may place here also *stand*, stood. Others change *a* long into *o* long, as, *awake*, *awoke*.

4. (5) The preterits of many verbs are formed by changing *i* long into *o* long, as *rise rose*, &c.

5. (6) *I* short is usually changed into *a* short; as, *swim*, *swam* ; *sit*, *sat*, &c. The short *i* in *give* is changed into the long sound of *a*, *gave*. Many of the verbs have a second form in *u* ; as, *swim*, *swam*, and *swum* ; *sing*, *sang*, and *sung*. This second form seems to owe its origin to the fact that in Anglo-Saxon preterits, the vowel was often changed in forming the plural persons, and the second person singular; for example, they said in the singular, *Ic sang*, I sung; and in the plural, *we sungon*, we sung. In our language we have, in some instances, retained both forms, but use them indiscriminately, either as singular or as plural.

Nearly all the verbs of the ancient conjugation come within one or other of these classes. *Get*, *got* ; *bite*, *bit* ; *beat*, which is the same in the preterit, and perhaps a few other solitary forms, do not admit of classification.

(7) When the perfect participle has a form distinct from the past tense, it most generally consists of *en* or *n* added, sometimes, to the root, sometimes to the preterit form. This seems to have been the usual termination of the perfect participles of verbs of the ancient conjugation in Anglo-Saxon.

Remarks on the Contracted Modern Preterits.—(8) These forms are generally easily accounted for, by a reference to the principles which govern the combination of sounds in language. (See §§ 40 and 41.)

1. (9) In a number of the words which we have marked contracted, there is rather a total defect of inflexion than contraction. This is

plies. (2) Describe the first class of the verbs of the ancient conjugation. (3) The second class of these verbs. (4) The third class. (5) The fourth class. (6) The fifth class; and tell how the second form of their preterits is accounted for. (7) Repeat the remark on the perfect participle of these verbs.

(8) What is said of the contracted modern preterits? (9) Describe the first class and

occasioned by the fact that the root ends in a *d* or *t* sound. To this no second *d* or *t* sound could be added without lengthening the word by one syllable. To this lengthening (though contrary to the natural tendency of our language to curtailment) we have submitted in some cases; for example, in *add*, *added; print*, *printed*, &c.; but, in other cases, rather than add a syllable, we have dispensed altogether with the inflexion peculiar to the preterit; for example, in *cut*, *cost*, *hit*, &c. (10) Sometimes a final *d* is changed into *t* in the preterit; as in *bend*, *bent; spend*, *spent*, &c. Sometimes the syllable is shortened in the preterit for the sake of distinction, as in *bleed*, *bled; feed*, *fed; read*, *read;* the root is pronounced *long*, the preterit *short* as if written *red*.

2. (11) Another class of these contracted forms has merely a *t* substituted for a *d* in their preterits, in accordance with the principle explained in § 40. In these the *e* which precedes the *d* in the usual inflexion is omitted, and the *t* is joined to the final consonant of the root; the vowel sound of the root is also usually shortened, because followed now by two consonants. Examples, *dream*, *dreamt; sleep*, *slept; deal*, *dealt*, &c. The verb cleave, which would naturally coalesce with the *d* sound, exchanges its *v* for an *f*, and takes *t* like the rest of these contracts; *cleave*, *cleft*.

This last class is not to be considered *irregular*, since nothing has happened to them, except what follows necessarily from the laws which govern the utterance of sounds. The only really anomalous class of these verbs of the modern conjugation, is that considered under our first remark, viz., *beseech*, *besought;* catch, caught, &c.; and even the preterits of these are not so capriciously formed, as might seem at first sight. See more on this subject in Latham's English Language, from which we have borrowed largely in the preceding remarks.

The learner may be questioned in the usual way upon the list given above, asking him to tell the preterit and participle of each verb separately. A much more effectual way of learning these verbs thoroughly, is to write lists of the distinct classes in the manner which we prescribe below in the exercises.

Exercises I., II., III., &c.—Form a complete enumeration from the list of all the verbs of the ancient conjugation, coming under class 1, 2, 3, &c., and afterwards the same with the contracted forms of the

---

give examples. (10) What changes in sound do some of these undergo without receiving any additional inflexion? Give examples. (11) Describe the second class. Show how their preterits are formed, and give examples.

modern conjugation. Each class to be described, and then the enumeration written after the model of the list—roots, preterits and participles.

Then follows a course of exercises in forming propositions with certain prescribed tenses of a prescribed number of the verbs from the list. By this plan the learner may be made as familiar as we please with these verbs, while he is acquiring practice in the formation of propositions, and in the use of the tenses. Let him be especially enjoined to form propositions with the different tenses of those verbs in which he is most likely to make mistakes; such as *come*, *do*, *drink*, *go*, *lay*, *lie*, *see*, *sit*, *write*, &c. These exercises to be extended according to the wants of the pupil.

CHAPTER IV.

MODIFICATION OF THE SUBJECT AND PREDICATE BY NOUNS.

§ 68. (1) Hitherto we have treated of such modifications of the subjects and predicates of propositions as are effected by a change of the *form* of the subject noun, or of the verb; namely, the change of the form of the noun, intended to indicate plurality, and the changes of the form of the verb, intended to indicate plurality, person, time, and mode. (2) We now proceed to consider the

Modifications of the Subject Noun and Verb effected by the employment of Complementary or Modifying Words.

(3) Before we introduce any new class of words employed for the purpose of modification, we intend to consider the several modifications of both subject and predicate, effected by the instrumentality of one of the the two classes of words already familiar to the learner—we mean by the instrumentality of nouns. (4) The words belonging to the class of verbs never perform this kind of function. (5) According to the definition we have adopted, verbs are always assertive, and can never *alone*—or, except as forming the assertive part of an *accessory* proposition—modify other words.

(6) Nouns are employed in three distinct ways to modify other words; namely, 1st. Without any change of their form, except what they undergo when used as subject nouns; 2d. With an inflected form, distinct from that employed as *subject noun;* And, 3d. Accom-

---

§ 68. (1) Mention the kind of modifications heretofore treated. (2) What kind do we now propose to consider?

(3) What special class of these modifications comes first under notice? (4) Do verbs ever perform the function of modifying other words? (5) Tell why they are not employed *alone* for the purpose of modification?

(6) Mention the three distinct ways in which nouns are employed for the purpose of

panied by a word which serves as an *intermediate* to the complementary noun and the word which it completes, and forms an essential part of the complement. (7) Each of these classes of complements formed by nouns we shall treat separately. (8) And, first, the

MODIFICATIONS EFFECTED BY THE EMPLOYMENT OF THE NOUN IN THE SAME FORMS—SINGULAR AND PLURAL—AS WHEN IT SERVES AS SUBJECT NOUN OF A PROPOSITION.

(9) REMARK.—For convenience sake we may call the noun *modified* the PRINCIPAL NOUN.

§ 69. (1) THE NOUN IN APPOSITION MODIFICATION OR COMPLEMENT. (2) This form of modification is restricted to *nouns*, or to words or phrases taken *substantively*. It is never applied to verbs. (3) It consists of another noun *apposed*—that is, *placed to* or *by*—the *principal* noun. (4) The *noun in apposition* usually expresses some attribute — something descriptive — or some appellation of that which is signified by the principal noun. (5) It is the addition of another name applicable to the object designated by the *principal noun*, generally for the purpose of rendering the expression more clear and definite, but sometimes merely for the purpose of ornament or of emphasis. Example: (6) *William, the* FARMER, *is an honest man.* Here the noun *farmer* is *apposed*, or placed by the noun *William*, to render the subject of the assertion more clear and definite. (7) This *apposition* indicates that the subject of our assertion, in the present instance, is not any man whatever called William, but the particular person to whom both the name *William* and the name *farmer* are applicable—the man known to the person whom we address as, *The farmer*.

[(8) This modification is most frequently, though not exclusively, applied to the *proper* names of persons and places. (9) It is applied to nouns, whether they serve as subject noun of a proposition, or are employed in any of the functions to be hereafter described. (10) Per-

---

modifying words. (7) How is it proposed to treat these several forms of modification? (8) Which special division is considered first? (9) Repeat remark.

§ 69. (1) What name is given to the modification first treated? (2) To what class of words is this modification restricted? (3) Of what does it consist? (4) What does it express? (5) State the additional explanation. (6) Give example, and point out the *apposition*. (7) What does the *apposition complement* in this case indicate?

[(8) To what class of nouns is this modification most frequently applied? (9) Is it applied only to nouns employed as subjects of propositions, or to nouns whatever may be their

haps the only exception is, that it would be improper, or at least inelegant, to modify a noun itself placed in *apposition* by another *noun in apposition*, thus adding *apposition* to *apposition*.]

(11) The noun in apposition is most generally, though not always, placed after the noun which it modifies. In such expressions as My *brother William*, *General Washington*, &c., the nouns *brother* and *general* are the modifying nouns, and precede the nouns with which they stand in apposition.*

[(12) In languages which have case terminations, the noun in apposition must be in the same case with the principal noun. (13) In English it does not always take the *case termination* of the *principal noun*, as will be seen hereafter. (See § 75: 26, 27.)†

* It may be doubted whether in such examples as General Washington, Queen Victoria, &c., the modifying word should not be called *a noun adjectively employed.* There is often not much difference between the two forms of modification; but *the noun employed adjectively*, as we shall see, can generally be resolved into some other form of modification, made by the case of a noun, or by a *noun* and *preposition*, from which modification it is contracted; but the noun in apposition can be resolved into no other form but that of an *adjective accessory proposition;* and in this, such modifications as *general*, in the expression General Washington, are like other nouns in apposition. The word *general* cannot be resolved into a *genitive case modification*, a *noun* and *preposition modification*, an *adjective modification*, &c., but only into a modification formed by an accessory proposition, as *Washington, who was general.*

† It may be here observed, that this species of modification effects very nearly the same purpose which is effected by an *adjective modification.* The noun in apposition is necessarily a *common noun* or name of a class, and not only *denotes* objects of its kind, but at the same time *connotes* (as the logicians say) the distinguishing qualities and characteristics of the class. Hence, when placed in *apposition* with another noun, it serves to indicate the presence of these *connoted* qualities or characteristics. For example, when I use the expression, *Plato, the philosopher*, the noun in apposition, *philosopher*, indicates that the Plato intended was the one who possessed the characteristics, properties, attributes of a philosopher—the person distinguished from all others of the name, by the possession of these attributes, &c. It would be incorrect, however, to say that the noun thus used becomes an adjective.

function? (10) Is there any exception?] (11) Where is the noun in apposition placed? [(12) What is said of the noun in apposition in languages which have case terminations? (13) In English does it always take the case *termination* of the principal noun?] (14) What

(15) A noun in apposition is sometimes employed to modify a *proposition* (or perhaps rather in many cases, to *represent* a proposition), and, on the other hand, a *proposition* is sometimes placed in apposition with a noun to modify or explain it. This might be expected, since propositions often perform the functions of nouns, or, to use the current language of our grammars, are *used substantively*. (16) As example of a noun in apposition with a proposition, take the following: TO BE GOOD IS TO BE HAPPY—TRUTH *never to be forgotten by those commencing the journey of life.* (17) In this example (as indeed in every instance of apposition, and perhaps in the use of every form of modification or complement employed with a noun), there is a suppressed predication, a tacit assumption of the assertion, that *to be good is to be happy, is a truth never to be forgotten*, &c. (18) We have an example of a proposition used as an apposition modification in the following sentence: *The* APOLOGY, *often pleaded by the slaves of vicious habits*, THAT THEIR VICES INJURE NONE BUT THEMSELVES, *is generally inconsistent with truth, and even if strictly consistent with truth in some cases, is no adequate justification of their conduct.* Here the proposition, "Their vices injure none but themselves," is placed in *apposition* with the noun "apology," and serves to explain it.

(19) It is unnecessary to observe that *infinitives* (alone, or with their accompanying modifications or complements) are often used as apposition modifications, since we consider infinitives as a peculiar class of nouns.

(20) A noun is often repeated (with, or without accompanying modification), for the purpose of emphasis, and thus placed in a sort of apposition with itself. (21) This occurs chiefly, though not exclusively, when the noun is used in what is called the *case of address*. (See § 99 : 9.) (22) For example: "O Jerusalem, *Jerusalem*, which killest the prophets," &c. "My people have hewed out cisterns, *broken cisterns*," &c. (23) We should in practical analysis rather call this EMPHATIC REPETITION.

(24) "A plural term is sometimes used in apposition after two or

---

is meant by the terms *principal noun?* Ans. The *noun which is modified* by the noun placed in apposition.

(15) Mention a purpose for which a noun in apposition is sometimes employed. (16) Give the example. (17) Repeat the remark. (18) Give an example of a proposition used as an apposition modification; and point out the words in apposition.

(19) Repeat the remark in reference to infinitives.

(20) What is said of the repetition of a noun? (21) When does this chiefly occur? (22) Repeat the example. (23) What would we call this in analysis?

(24) Repeat the remark in reference to the use of a *plural* term in *apposition;* and give the example.

more substantives singular, to combine and give them emphasis; as, "*Time*, *labor*, *money*, *all* were lost."

(25) Distributive words are sometimes put in apposition with a plural substantive; as "*They* went *each* of them on his way." In the construction of a sentence, the distributive word is sometimes omitted. Of this character are such expressions as the following: "*They* stood in *each other's* way—that is, *they* stood *each* in the other's way."—(*Bullion's Eng. Gram.* secs. 671–673.)*

(26) An adjective used substantively (that is, with its noun suppressed), is often employed as an *apposition modification* of a noun; as, *Charles the Bold*, *Alexander the Great*, *William the Third.* In these phrases, there is (perhaps) a suppression of the name after the adjective, as *Charles the Bold*, for Charles, the bold Charles; or of the title of the person; *Duke*, in the first example, *Conqueror*, in the second, and *king* of that name in the third. The determinative, or article, we suppose, may, in such cases, be regarded as indicating a suppressed noun. If not, this must be considered a peculiar use of the *adjective.*]

(27) In written exercises, the *noun in apposition*, *modification*, or *complement*, may be represented by the following contraction: *Ap. modn.*, or *Ap. com.* In our examples, and in the exercises, we use some of the determinative words, as *a*, *the*, *this*, *that*, &c., which have not been yet explained. In analysis, the learner may pass over these for the present.

Model of a Written Exercise.—Cicero, the orator, flourished, &c. Cicero, *S. N. mod'd by* orator, *N. Ap.* Read thus—*Cicero* is the subject noun of the proposition, and is modified by *orator*, a noun in apposition. The noun *Cicero*, thus modified, is the *complete* subject.

Let the learner point out, or, in a written exercise, *underline*, the apposition complements, in the following examples:

* In some cases, where a *noun in apposition* would seem to be the most natural modification, we employ a noun with the preposition *of;* as, *The City of Rome*, *The month of June;* not, *The City Rome*, *The month June*, as in Latin and German. This usage is confined chiefly to names of towns, countries, and months. The French and some other modern languages agree nearly with ours in this matter.

(25) What remark is made in reference to *distributive* words put in apposition ?

(26) What is said of an apposition modification formed by an adjective used *substantively?* Illustrate by examples.]

(27) By what contractions may the *noun in apposition modification* or *complement* be represented in written exercises ?

"The gentle Spenser, fancy's pleasing son."

"Let Newton, pure intelligence, whom God
To mortals lent," &c.

"Raleigh, the scourge of Spain."

"Nor can the muse the gallant Sydney pass,
The plume of war!"

"His friend, the British Cassius, fearless bled."

"Nature! great Parent! whose unceasing hand."

"Scipio, the gentle chief."

"Where art thou Hammond? thou, the darling pride,
The friend, and lover of the tuneful throng!"

"The watery deep, an object strange and new,
Before me rose."

"Emblem of peace, the dove before thee flies."

"A stranger to superior strength,
Man vainly trusts his own."

"Thou Sun, of this great world both eye and soul."

"Come peace of mind, delightful guest."

EXERCISE I.—Let the learner find ten or more examples of nouns placed in apposition. This exercise may be repeated, till this construction becomes familiar.

EXERCISE II., III., &c.—Form a given number of propositions, having subjects modified by a *noun in apposition modification.*

Let the verbs in these and the following exercises be selected from the list of verbs of the ancient conjugation. When the pupil is once sufficiently familiar with these verbs, and especially with those in which he might be most subject to commit blunders, let him be required to use verbs of the modern conjugation regularly inflected. In one exercise, let it be required that all the verbs shall be in a certain tense simple or compound; in the next, in a different tense, that the learner may become perfectly acquainted with all the forms of the verb. Perseverance in these exercises will secure a thorough knowledge of grammar; serve as an introduction to English composition, which consists of propositions properly arranged to express thought and call the pupil's powers of invention into full action.

(28) The learner must be careful not to confound this *apposition complement* with the peculiar species of complement of the predicate which we are soon to consider. (29) For this purpose, let him remember, first, that the word in *apposition* is always employed to

(28) What warning is given to the learner? (29) What two facts is he enjoined to re-

modify *a noun* (including the few instances in which a proposition considered *substantively* is thus modified), never a verb. Second, that the modified noun, and the noun in apposition, are always in the same member; that is, both in the subject, or both in the predicate of the proposition. (30) In such examples as "John fell a victim to his ungovernable passions," "Hortensius died a martyr," the construction is entirely different from that which we have been considering. (31) The words *victim* and *martyr* are not in apposition with John and Hortensius, but manifestly make up a part of what is asserted of them respectively. (32) What is asserted of John, is *falling a victim to his passions*, and of Hortensius, *dying a martyr*—a very different construction (conveying a different meaning) from *Hortensius, the martyr, died.* (33) In the following passage, we have an example of each of these distinct species of construction: "My wife, sweet *soother* of my cares, fell * * * * * * * a *victim* to despair." Here *soother*, with its modifications, is placed in apposition with *wife*, the *subject noun*, but *victim* is a complement of the predicate—a part of what is asserted of *his wife, the sweet soother of his cares.*

MODEL ANALYSIS—NOUN IN APPOSITION.—EXAMPLE : *John, the carpenter*, fell, &c. *John is modified by the noun* CARPENTER *placed in apposition.* Till the learner thoroughly understands this construction, the question should be put, whenever a noun in apposition occurs, What do you mean by a *noun in apposition?* The answer to this is, *It is a noun expressing an attribute or an appellation (some other name) placed by another noun, generally, in order to denote more definitely the object represented by the principal noun, sometimes, merely for the purpose of ornament or emphasis.*

(34) A noun in apposition, when it follows the *principal* noun, is separated from it, and from the rest of the proposition, by commas. (See Appendix on Punctuation.)

§ 70. (1) We may here notice another way in which a *noun* without any change of form, or connecting word expressed, is employed to modify another noun. (2) It consists in attaching a *modifying* noun to a *principal* noun (as we do an adjective, see § 86) to limit or describe it. (3) We have examples in such combinations as,

---

member? (30) Give examples of a construction sometimes confounded with apposition. (31) What is said in reference to the words *victim* and *martyr* in these examples? (32) What is asserted of John and Hortensius respectively in the examples? (33) Give an example containing both forms of construction, point out these separate forms, and tell how they are distinguished. (34) What is said of the punctuation or interpunction?

§ 70. (1) Is the noun unchanged and without a connecting word employed in any other way, save apposition, to modify other nouns? (2) How? (3) Give examples. (4) What

window shutters, a wine cellar, a gold watch, a gold pencil case, &c. (4) Here the words *window, wine, gold, gold pencil*, perform a function similar to that of descriptive adjectives. (5) Indeed the word *gold*, used as in the examples above, is commonly recognised as an adjective, as well as *golden*, which is formed from it, and always employed *attributively*. (6) But for considering the word *gold* an adjective, we see no more reason than for considering the words *window, wine*, &c., as employed above, adjectives. (7) They all alike perform, as here used, the function of attributives or adjectives.

(8) We shall call this THE MODIFICATION BY A NOUN ADJECTIVELY EMPLOYED.

[(9) This species of construction is very prevalent in our language, and has given origin to a large class of our compound words. (10) We might enumerate some dozens of these compounds, formed from the single noun *horse*, used *adjectively* before other words; as, *horseback, horsebean, horseblock, horseboat, horseboy, horsebreaker*, &c., &c. (11) Some of these compounds are written as one word, some with a *hyphen-mark* (-) between the component parts; sometimes the two words are written separately. (12) The usage in regard to the manner of writing many words thus formed is not perfectly settled; some writing them with, and some without a hyphen, and some writing words as separate, which others unite by the hyphen. (13) It is plain that all such compounds must have originated from what we have called the *adjective* use of the noun; and this adjective use has itself, we suppose, generally originated from an elliptical mode of expressing various complements formed by the noun. (14) For example, *horseboat* is equal to *boat for horses*, that is, to carry horses, or a *boat moved by horses;* for this compound word has these two distinct meanings. *Horse breaker = one who breaks horses*, *Horse* being here originally *objective* complement to the verbal word *breaker*. *Horse-courser, horse-keeper, horse-stealer* are all similar to horse-breaker. *Horse-hair, horse-flesh*, &c. = *horse's hair, horse's flesh*, or *the hair of a horse*, &c.

---

kind of function do the words *window, wine*, &c., perform in these examples? (5) What is said of the word *gold?* (6) What further remark about gold as an adjective? (7) What remark in reference to all these words?

(8) What name is given to this species of modification?

[(9) Repeat the remark in reference to this species of construction. (10) What is said of the number of compound words thus formed? (11) What is said of the spelling of these compounds? (12) Repeat remark in reference to the usage in this matter. (13) What is said in reference to the origin of these compounds? (14) Illustrate by examples. (15) Re

(15) When the two nouns have completely coalesced into a single word, it will be unnecessary in practical analysis to have recourse to our mode of naming the modifying noun. The compound may be treated as a single noun. (16) We have noticed this species of modification that the learner may be able to give a satisfactory account of the cases in which the nouns are either universally, or occasionally written separately. (17) If there were no cases of this kind now to be found, it would still be proper that we should notice the fact that this species of modification once prevailed extensively in the language, and gave birth to a host of our compound terms.]

§ 71. There is yet another species of modification sometimes applied to nouns which we may as well treat in this place. (1) It consists of the verbal noun, commonly called the *Infinitive.** (2) This form of *modification* is placed after the *principal* word. (3) We have examples in such phrases as, *A desire to learn. A propensity to find fault. The wish to excel. The desire to please.* (4) *He has a heart to pity, a hand to help.* The infinitive here expresses a purpose = a heart for the purpose of pitying, a hand for the purpose of helping. (See § 77 : 6, and Note.) (5) *An action to be condemned.* Here there is perhaps an ellipsis of the word *worthy*, or some similar adjective. *It is time to rise.* An *opportunity to enrich* himself. (6) This kind of modification occurs less frequently than some others, and has received slight notice from grammarians. (7)

* Since these words are preceded in this case by the particle *to*, this modification might perhaps be placed among those united to the *principal* word by an *intermediary*. But there is good reason to doubt whether the word TO is really in this use a mere *intermediary;* and we have already, waiving all dispute about the matter, presented the *infinitive* with its accompanying particle as a noun, because, thus accompanied, it performs the function of *subject noun*. We must, therefore, in consistency, treat the combination of the particle with the verbal root, here as elsewhere, as if it were a single word. Indeed, there is no other course open to us, till it has been

---

peat remark in reference to the mode of analysis, when this kind of compounds occurs. (16) What reason is assigned for noticing this species of modification? (17) What further is said about noticing this species of modification?]

§ 71. (1) Mention another species of modification applied to nouns. (2) Where is this modification placed in reference to the principal word? (3) Repeat the first four examples. (4) Repeat the next example and the observation. (5) Repeat remark on example, "*an action to be condemned.*" (6) Repeat remark in reference to this kind of modification. (7) What name may be given to this form of modification?

We may call it the INFINITIVE MODIFICATION OF THE NOUN. In the analysis of such a phrase as, *A desire to learn*, the scholar will simply say that the noun *desire* is modified by the infinitive *to learn.**

EXERCISE.—Let the learner select a given number of examples from some book. Or, what is better, and in this case perhaps easier, let him form a given number of propositions containing appropriate examples of this species of modification.

§ 72. (1) We next direct attention to such modifications of verbs as consist of a noun in the same form as it is employed for subject noun, and without the aid of an *intermediary* word. (2) Nouns are thus employed, both in the singular and plural form, to modify, or, rather, to complete many *neuter verbs*—especially the verb *to be.* (3) We may call this species of modification (till we can find a better name) the NOUN COMPLEMENTARY OF THE NEUTER VERB.†

---

settled what is the precise function (or functions, if more than one) of the particle *to* in the *infinitive form* of verbals. Whether it is to distinguish the *Infinitive use*, the termination originally marking this *verbal* being lopped away in the progress of the language, we leave others to inquire. Enough for our present purpose that these combinations perform the main function of nouns. It may be remarked that the particle *to* was not employed in the Anglo-Saxon with the infinitive form, but with a kind of gerundive; for example, infinitive, *Lufian* (never preceded by the particle *to*), to love; gerundive, *to Lufigenne* (always preceded by *to*), to love, to loving, &c.

* These infinitives after nouns bear some resemblance to apposition modifications. They may generally be expanded into accessory propositions which serve as appositions; as, *The boy has a desire to learn* = *The boy has a desire that he may learn.* (See §§ 105 and 106.)

† There are several other forms of modification nearly allied to this, which we are not ready as yet to bring under the notice of the learner. When we have got them all before us, we intend to explain our views of the whole class at the same time, and give our reasons for adopting the names by which we call them. These constructions have never been *satisfactorily* explained, so far as we know, in any of our English grammars. The laborious Germans have gone farthest in the investigation of this form of modification.

---

§ 72. (1) To what is our attention next directed? (2) Repeat what is said in reference to the modification of *neuter verbs.* (3) What name may we give to this species of modification?

EXAMPLES.—*Knowledge is power. Wealth is power.* "Thy *word is truth.*" "*Wisdom is* a *defence.*" "The *fear* of the Lord *is* the *beginning* of wisdom." "The *love* of money *is* the *root* of all evil." *Demosthenes was* an *orator.* The *men were Athenians.* "This *man seems* the *leader* of the whole party." *He continued steward.* "*Hortensius died* a *martyr.*" "The gentle *Sydney lived* the shepherd's *friend.*" *He reigned* absolute *monarch. He stood candidate* for that office. "There the *pitcher stands* a *fragment.*" *John becomes* a *man.*

Let the learner analyze all the words printed in italics in the preceding examples, as a *first* exercise on the use of this modification. MODEL OF EXAMINATION.—EXAMPLE, *Knowledge is power.* Point out the subject of this proposition? Ans. *Knowledge*, for of this the assertion is made. Point out the predicate as it here stands assertively expressed. Ans. *Is power*, for this forms the assertion. Can you express the predicate alone freed from assertion? Ans. Yes. *Beiny power*, for this is what, in the proposition, is asserted of KNOWLEDGE. Point out the *verb*, name the class to which it belongs, and tell tense, number, and person. Ans. *Is* is the verb, because it makes the assertion; it belongs to the class of neuter verbs; and is in the indefinite tense, singular number, third person. What is the subject noun? Ans. Knowledge. Is it modified? Ans. No. How is the verb modified? Ans. By the *complementary noun* POWER.

MODEL OF A WRITTEN EXERCISE.—Knowledge *S. N.* is *V. n. indf. sing.* 3. *md. by* power *comp. N.* To be read thus: *knowledge* is the subject noun; *is* the verb. It is of the neuter or intransitive class, indefinite tense, singular number, third person, and modified by the complementary noun *power.* EXERCISE II.—Write the above examples after this model.

EXERCISE III., IV., &c.—Let the learner endeavor to find, or to construct a given number of examples embracing one or more of the

---

Yet we cannot follow their footsteps exactly, since our mode of analysis differs considerably from theirs in other things, but especially in reference to the verb *to be.* We are happy to shelter ourselves under the authority of Becker, and to acknowledge our obligations to him for much information on the subject of this class of modifications, which he calls the *factitive object.* Though our *method* differs materially from his, we believe our opinions on this subject are consistent with his, except in reference to the verb *to be.* This verb he treats, like all other grammarians, as being the naked copula; we reduce it in a grammatical point of view—that is, in reference to its constructional functions—to a level with other intransitive verbs.

preceding forms of modification. This exercise may be repeated till the learner is familiar with the forms of construction already exhibited.

§ 73. (1) We might proceed to treat of several other *modifications* of the verb, or *complements* of the predicate, consisting of nouns which, in the present state of the language, are used for this purpose without any change of their form. (2) There is a class of words, however, recognised as nouns, namely, the pronouns, which assume a form distinct from the subject form, when they are employed in some of these modifications. (3) And in the language from which the English descends, as well as in many of the ancient and modern languages, a distinct form of the noun is generally employed for the purposes referred to. (4) Besides, these complements stand in a different relation to the subject of the proposition, from that in which the noun complementary of the neuter verb stands.* This distinction it may be useful to mark by treating these modifications as belonging to separate classes. (5) We therefore propose to suspend for the present the enumeration of the various species of modifications, in order to consider briefly the particular changes which the noun undergoes in our language, that it may serve certain functions as a *modifying* or *completing* word.

* The *noun complementary* of the neuter verb expresses something which is contemplated by the speaker as having its seat in the subject, in such manner as the verb indicates. For example, "Knowledge is power." Here power is contemplated as a something so seated in the subject *knowledge*, that it exists together (co-exists) with it. Or considering power (as we are inclined to do here), as *con-noting* the attributes of power, these attributes are contemplated in this assertion as co-existing with *knowledge*. Again, "This man seems the leader." Here the attributes *con-noted* by the term *leader* are contemplated as *seemingly co-existing* with the subject—"the man." The predicate—modification and all—*ends* in the subject in all these cases, and hence, the subject form of the noun is used. But the complements to be considered express a something *without* and *beyond* the subject, influenced by the action of the verb. Hence, in many languages they take a form distinct from the subject form.

§ 73. (1) Are there any other modifications of verbs consisting of nouns in the same form employed as subject noun? (2) What is remarked of the pronouns? (3) What is remarked of the language from which the English is descended, and of other languages? (4) What is said of some of the complements of the predicate, formed by nouns, and yet to be considered? (5) What is now proposed?

(6) These different forms of the noun are known in grammar by the name of CASES OF THE NOUN. (7) The form used as subject noun—the real noun without addition or modification (save that of plurality), is generally counted (perhaps not with strict propriety) one of the *cases.* (8) The subject form, with which the learner may now be supposed to be familiar, is distinguished by the name of THE NOMINATIVE CASE. The singular form of the noun is called *the nominative case singular*, the plural form the *nominative case plural.* (9) If we consider *that* only a distinct case which is marked by a distinct form, we have but one other case, besides the nominative, of any of our nouns with the exception of that class called pronouns. (10) This single *case form* is called the *genitive case* by all the old grammarians. (11) Our English grammarians have very generally called it the possessive case, because the genitive most commonly denotes *possession*, on the part of the object which the modifying noun represents, in reference to the object which is represented by the *principal* noun. (12) Thus, *The merchant's store.* Here the genitive or possessive form *merchant's*, indicates that the merchant *possesses* what is denoted by the *modified* noun—*store.*

FORMATION OF THE GENITIVE OR POSSESSIVE CASE.—(13) The genitive or possessive case is formed in the *written* language by adding to the noun an *s*, preceded by an apostrophe; as *man*, genitive *man's.*

[(14) The observations in § 42, regarding the manner in which the *s* of the *plural form* is pronounced, apply with equal force to this *s* of the genitive case. (15) If the final letter of the noun to which the *s* is added is a *sharp mute*, the *s* must necessarily be pronounced with its proper *sharp* sound; as *a* SHIP'S *company*, *a* HAWK'S *flight*, *a* CAT'S *paw*, &c. (16) If on the contrary, the noun ends in a *flat mute*, a

---

(6) By what name are these different forms of the noun distinguished? (7) What is said of the form used as subject noun? (8) What *case name* is given to the *subject form*? (9) What is said of the number of *cases* marked by a distinct form in English? (10) What is the only case of nouns (excepting pronouns) answering to this description called? (11) What name has generally been given to it by English grammarians? State the reason. (12) Repeat example and illustration.

(13) How is the genitive case formed in the written language?

[(14) What observations apply to the pronunciation of this *s* of the genitive? (15) When the final letter of the noun is a sharp mute, how must the *s* be sounded? (16) How when the final letter is a flat mute?]

liquid, or a *vowel*, the *s* of the genitive is sounded like *z*; as, *a* STAG'S *horns*, *a* MAN'S *head*, *a* HERO'S *courage*.]

(17) When the *plural* form of a noun does not end in *s*, the genitive, or possessive case plural is formed, in the same manner as the genitive case singular, by adding in the written language *s*, preceded by an apostrophe to the *plural* form; as, *men*, genitive *men's*, *brethren*, genitive *brethren's*, &c. (18) But when the plural ends, as it generally does, in *s*, another *s* could not be added without giving an additional syllable to the word in pronunciation. (19) This is never done for the purpose of forming a *plural* genitive. (20) When the plural subject noun (or nominative case, as it is commonly called) ends in *s*, the genitive plural agrees with it in sound, and in the *spoken* language can be distinguished from it by the sense alone. (21) In the *written* language the genitive plural is distinguished from the nominative plural by an apostrophe (') placed after the final *s* of the nominative; as, *On* EAGLES' *wings*, *The* FRIENDS' *meeting house;* equivalent to, *On the wings of eagles*, *The meeting house of the Friends.*

[(22) The same method of distinguishing the genitive singular, is also adopted in the *written* language, when the singular form of the noun ends in *ss;* as, *For righteousness' sake.* (23) The *apostrophe* is also placed after some other words ending in an *s* sound, to indicate the genitive; as, *For conscience' sake.**

(24) In the *spoken* language, we sometimes form the genitive of singular nouns (generally proper names) ending in an *s* sound, by adding the syllable *es;* as *James' kite*, pronounced *Jamezez kite.*

* We suspect that the *s* in the next word, *sake*, has its influence here. We know no example, except this, of a genitive form of *conscience*. Peace, in the genitive, ought, we presume, to be spelled peace's, and should certainly be pronounced *peacez—For peace' or peace's sake.*

---

(17) How is the genitive plural formed, when the plural subject form does not end in *s*? (18) What would be the effect of adding an *'s* when the subject form ends in *s*? (19) Is this ever in fact done to form a plural genitive? (20) What is the genitive plural form in the spoken language when the nominative plural ends in *s*? (21) How is it distinguished from the nominative in the written language? Give the examples.

[(22) Repeat the observation in reference to singular nouns ending in *ss*. (23) Do any singular words besides those in *ss* form the genitive in the same way?

(24) What is said of some singular nouns taking the syllable *ez* in their genitive in the

(25) Perhaps such forms should be spelled, as they are pronounced, with *es* added to the nominative, or rather, with *'s*, to distinguish them from *plural* forms; as *James's*, *Thomas's*, *Douglas's*. (26) Some authors add the *'s* to such nouns—some the apostrophe alone. (27) To one noun ending in *ss*, we find the *'s* sometimes added—namely, witness; thus, *The* WITNESS'S *veracity*.]

In proper names ending in *s*, the genitive case is very generally the same with the nominative in the spoken language. This applies particularly to Greek and Latin proper names. In the written language an apostrophe is placed after the *s*, but in speaking, the genitive is not distinguished from the nominative. Examples, "Achilles' wrath; "Atreus' royal line;" "Olympus' lofty tops;" "Thetis' godlike son;" "Pirithous' fame." "Briseis' charms," &c. This form of expression is generally avoided in prose, and the Norman construction adopted; thus, *The wrath of Achilles*, &c.

We have examples of similarly formed genitives of Scripture proper names; as, "Jesus' sake;" "Moses' law." These names in the early editions of the authorised version, as well as in the versions of Tyndale, Cranmer, and that of Geneva, are printed without the apostrophe, and were undoubtedly pronounced in the same manner as the nominative; and, we believe, they are, generally, so pronounced at the present day. The use of the apostrophe, in marking genitives, was introduced, as we shall again have occasion to observe, much later than the age of the translators.

(28) REMARK.—Let the learner carefully remember, that in writing genitive or possessive cases, the mark called apostrophe (') is an essential part of the modern spelling. To omit it, is as much an error in orthography, as to omit a letter in a word.

§ 74. DECLENSION OF NOUNS AND PRONOUNS.—(1) We now propose to exhibit what is called the *declension* of nouns; that is, the regular arrangement of their cases of the singular and plural forms. (2) The declension of nouns (leaving out of view the pronouns), if we admit only the cases which possess distinct forms, would be as follows:—

	Singular	*Plural.*	*Singular.*	*Plural.*
NOMINATIVE,	Man,	Men.	Friend,	Friends.
GENITIVE,	Man's,	Men's.	Friend's,	Friends'.

---

spoken language? (25) How should such genitives perhaps be written? (26) Are authors agreed in this matter? (27) What is said of the noun witness?]

(28) Repeat the remark about spelling.

§ 74. (1) What is meant by the declension of a noun? (2) Decline the nouns *man* and *friend*, as given above, spelling them afterwards, including the apostrophe as part of the spelling.

(3) We shall, however, for reasons which will appear hereafter exhibit the declensions so as to accord with the structure of the ancient Anglo-Saxon, and the sister languages of the north of Europe, and substantially with the Greek and Latin. (4) In doing this we add two cases to those already enumerated, but which in form (save in the class of pronouns) are always the same with the nominative. (5) One of these we call, following the commonly received names, the *accusative* or *objective* case. (6) The last is the name generally given to this case by English grammarians, because its chief function is to express the passive OBJECT of an active verb. (7) The second additional case we call also by the old name, the Dative Case. This case is sometimes used to express what is called the *personal object* of a verb, the same which is more generally expressed by the noun preceded by the particle *to.*

(8) We might add a fifth case, and so conform more completely to the ancient models of declension, calling it the vocative. (9) A noun is said to be in the *vocative* or *case of address*, when it is used in calling upon that which the noun represents. (10) In the ancient languages, the noun thus employed sometimes differed in form from the nominative. (11) The subject form, when convenient, was abbreviated, as we still sometimes abbreviate the names of our familiar friends, in calling them. (12) Thus *Thomas* becomes *Tom*, *James Jem*, *William Will*, &c.

(13) But as the noun used in address does not enter into the structure of propositions, serves simply in continuous speech as the means of calling the attention of the party addressed, and gives no occupation to the student of grammatical analysis, we omit it in the model of declension.*

* Whether there are some dozen cases, or three cases, or two cases, or only one case, depends on the definition which we choose to give to the term case. This term is derived from a Latin word, which means to *fall*. *Casus*, the Latin of case, means *a falling*. The subject noun, in its singular

(3) How do we propose to exhibit the declensions? (4) What additional cases are introduced? (5) What is one of these *cases* called? (6) Why is it called the *objective* case? (7) What is the second additional case called, and what is its function?

(8) What other case might be added? (9) What is the function of a vocative case? (10) What is said of the form of this case in the ancient languages? (11) Repeat the remark in reference to the ancient forms of the vocative. (12) Give examples.

(13) What reason is given for omitting the vocative in our model of declension? (14) Decline *brother*, afterwards spelling and noting the place of the apostrophe.

FULL MODEL OF DECLENSION.

(14)	*Singular.*	*Plural.*	*Old Plural.*
NOM.	Brother,	Brothers,	Brethren.
GEN. or POSS.	Brother's,	Brothers',	Brethren's.
DATIVE.	Brother,	Brothers,	Brethren.
ACCUS. or OBJ.	Brother,	Brothers,	Brethren.

We subjoin the Declension of the Personal Pronouns. (15) It will be seen that most of these have a *form* for the accusative and dative, distinct from the form of the nominative. (16) It will

---

and plural forms, appears to have been considered (rather whimsically, perhaps) by the old grammarians as the upright or straight form—the standard form—(in Latin casus rectus) from which the other case forms were *fallings off*, or declinations. (Hence the term *declension.*) According to this view, the subject noun cannot *properly* be called a *case.* Yet a case it has been called by the ancient grammarians themselves, and we still currently call it the nominative case. If we use the term case strictly, as meaning a falling off from the form of the subject noun, or, to speak more in accordance with modern conceptions, a change of the form of the noun, we have only one case in English nouns, namely, the possessive, or genitive case. We have, however, according to this view, two cases in some of the pronouns. If we consider the noun, when used to complete a verb (as shall be shown here after), and when it is connected to another word by a preposition, as a distinct case, and call the subject noun the nominative, we shall have three cases of nouns. This is the view of the subject generally taken by English grammarians. This third case—the noun used after verbs and prepositions —they call the objective or accusative case.

Another principle on which to determine the number of cases, is to recognise every *distinct function* which a noun performs in construction, independently, without the help of other words, as a *distinct case.* On this principle, we shall have a *dative* case, at least, in addition to the three already enumerated. We have adopted this principle of determining the number of cases, so far as to admit a dative. It may be doubted whether, in consistency, we ought not to admit a case to express time, measure, &c., and a distinction between the functions of object direct of a verb, and the noun which follows a preposition. If we admit every relation in which a noun may stand to another noun, verb, or adjective, either with or without the aid of a preposition, we shall have, as we said in the beginning of this note, some dozen cases.

---

(15) What remark in reference to the accusative and dative forms of the personal pronouns? (16) Repeat remark in reference to the formation of the cases of pronouns.

also be seen that neither the possessive form nor the accusative form of these pronouns is in most cases regularly derived from the nominative.

Declension of the Personal Pronouns.

SINGULAR.

	First Person.	*Second Person.*	*Third Person.*		
			Mas.	*Fem.*	*Neut.*
Nom.	I,	Thou,	He,	She,	It.
Gen.	Mine,	Thine,	His,	Hers,	Its.*
Dat.	Me,	Thee,	Him,	Her,	It.
Accus.	Me,	Thee,	Him,	Her,	It.

PLURAL.

Nom.	We,	You, *old* ye,†	They,	In all genders.
Gen.	Ours,	Yours,	Theirs,	"
Dat.	Us,	You,	Them,	"
Accus.	Us,	You, *old* ye.	Them.	"

* Some give a double form of the genitive or possessive cases of all these pronouns except He and It. Thus, *My, or mine; thy, or thine; her, or hers; our, or ours; your, or yours; their, or theirs. My, thy, her, our, your, their,* we treat as determinative adjectives. (See Additional Observations on the Personal Pronouns, § 155.) The learner will remark, that no apostrophe is used in writing *ours, yours, hers, its, theirs.*

† *You* has not only usurped the place of *thou,* in addressing an individual, but also the place of *ye,* in addressing a number of individuals. At one period of our language, *ye* appears to have been used exclusively as the form for the nominative plural (or plural subject noun) of the second person. Many instances may be found in which *ye* is used as an *accusative,* both after verbs and prepositions: for example—"The more shame *for ye*—holy men I thought *ye.*"—Shak. This usage may have arisen from a softened or slovenly pronunciation of *you,* in conversation. It is still common enough to hear persons of good education say, *Thank ye,* instead of, Thank you; though such forms are banished from the written language.

You, was originally the proper accusative form of the second person plural, and used only for the purpose of modification, and not as subject noun. Now it performs the functions of *nominative, accusative,* and *dative,* both *singular* and *plural.* The possessives *your* and *yours,* whether we regard

(17) Decline separately each of the personal pronouns.

EXERCISE *on the Formation of the Genitive or Possessive Case.*—Write the following nouns in the Genitive Case, followed by such nouns as they can appropriately modify. Man, *singular* and *plural*. Brother Brothers. Brethren. Hero, *singular* and *plural*. William. James. Agnes. Mary. The tailor. The shoemaker. The carpenter. My father. Mother. Wisdom. Beauty. Virtue. Goodness, &c. Each of these may be applied as genitive modification of several other nouns, if this should be thought expedient.

§ 75. We now return to the enumeration of the several modifications of nouns and verbs.

(1) We direct our attention first to that modification of the noun (or complement of the subject), which consists of a noun in the *genitive* or possessive case prefixed to limit it. (2) This we may call the *Genitive or Possessive Case Modification of the Noun.* (3) Or, more briefly, the Genitive Modification (abbreviated, *Gen. Mn.*) (4) The noun in the genitive case usually expresses what stands in the relation of *possessor*, or some kindred relation to what the noun which it modifies expresses. We give a number of examples which the learner will analyze as an exercise. We mark, by using *Italics*, the words which the learner is prepared by the instructions already given to analyze. He may pass over, for the present, the words printed in Roman characters.

(5) It will be remembered that this, like other modifications, is not limited to the noun employed as *subject noun*, but may be applied to a noun whatever function it happens to perform in the construction of a proposition.

EXAMPLES TO SERVE AS AN EXERCISE IN ANALYSIS.—His *father's house stands* a *ruin.* In *God's sight, man's strength is weakness ; man's wisdom is folly ; man's hopes are vanity. Wisdom's ways are ways* of pleasantness; her *paths are peace. Prayer is* the contrite *sinner's voice. Minerva's temple stood* a *landmark* to the mariner. That *man's haste to grow* rich *became* the *cause* of his reverses

one or both as cases of *you*, or as determinative adjectives formed from *you*. have in like manner superseded the old singular forms.

§ 75. (1) Describe the modification of the noun here first presented. (2) How do we name this modification ? (3) Give a shorter name, and the abbreviation. (4) Repeat what is said of the noun in the genitive case.

(5) Repeat remark.

The *fool's prosperity becomes* his *destruction. John's escape seemed* a *miracle. William's energy secured* him an independence.

(6) The *principal* noun in this species of construction is often suppressed, when clearly indicated by the *modifying* noun in the *possessive case.* (7) Thus, *St. Paul's, St. Peter's,* &c., are used to signify the churches named in honor of the Apostles Paul and Peter; *The bookseller's, The stationer's, The grocer's,* instead of *The bookseller's shop, The stationer's shop,* &c. (8) The possessive cases *mine, thine, hers, ours, yours, theirs,* are never, in the present usage of the language, followed by the noun which they limit. (9) In other words, these possessive forms are never used except when (to avoid ungraceful repetition) we wish to suppress the *principal* noun. (10) Thus we say, *That book is* MINE, OURS, YOURS, HERS, &c., to avoid the ungraceful repetition of *book* in the predicate of the proposition which would be necessary if we employed the forms *my, our, your,* &c. *That book is* MY *book;* except we omit (as is often done) the noun of the subject, and say, That is *my book.* (11) This is the real distinction between the forms *mine, ours, thine, yours, hers, theirs,* on the one hand, and *my, our, thy, your, her, their,* on the other; the first-mentioned class are always used when the *principal* noun—the noun which they limit—is suppressed, the last mentioned when the *principal* noun is expressed.* (12) It follows that

* The word *his* is used both when the principal noun is *suppressed,* and when it is *expressed;* thus we say both, *That horse is* HIS, and *That is* HIS *horse.* In other words, the form HIS performs the double function of a possessive case of HE, and of a determinative adjective pronoun. ITS we suspect is seldom employed to perform the double function of a possessive case of ITS, namely, both to *indicate* and *limit* a suppressed noun. The grammars, which we have examined give no examples; and we cannot think of a case in which *its* could be gracefully and appropriately employed with its principal noun suppressed. If no examples can be found of this use, *its* should be degraded from the place which it occupies in our grammars as possessive case of *it,* that is, in those grammars which exclude *my, our,* &c., from this place. *Its* is a word that (even as an adjective pronoun) has no long stand-

(6) What often happens in reference to the principal noun in this construction? (7) Repeat examples. (8) What is said in reference to the possessive cases, *mine, ours,* &c.? (9) Vary the expression. (10) Repeat examples, and illustrate them. (11) State the real distinction between *mine, ours, thine, yours,* &c., on the one hand, and *my, our, thy, your,* &c., on the other. (12) What follows from what has been said of *mine, ours,* &c.? (13)

mine, *ours*, &c., (and all other possessive cases when the principal noun is suppressed), serve not only to *limit* the *principal* noun, but to *indicate* it. (13) Thus in the example, *That knife is* MINE; *mine* at once indicates *knife* and limits it=*That knife is my knife*, where *knife* is denoted by its own name, and limited by the determinative *my*. So, in the example, *I called at your* FATHER'S *this morning;* the possessive case *father's* at once indicates and limits the *principal* noun *house.*

(14) The possessive case thus indicating the *principal* noun, which it limits, often stands in the place of subject noun in a proposition, and of the noun *complementary* of the *neuter verb*, or *predicate noun*, as some call it. (15) For example: *Your horse runs fast, but* MINE *runs faster, and our* FRIEND'S *runs faster than either.* Here MINE in the second, and FRIEND'S in the third proposition, represent or stand in the place of the subject noun. *This house is* MINE, *and yonder house is your* FRIEND'S. Here MINE and FRIEND'S stand in the place of *nouns complementary* of the verb *is.*

---

ing in the language. Till the times of James I., and perhaps later, HIS served for neuter as well as masculine possessive case, and possessive adjective pronoun. It is so used in the authorized version of the Scriptures, and in the older editions of Shakspeare. "When *it* giveth *his* color in the cup."—Prov. 23 : 31. "*Its* is not found in the Bible, except by misprint."—Brown. We suspect the same might be said in respect to Shakspeare and Spenser, save where the text has been changed by the officious meddling of editors. IT was also spelled *hit* as late as the times of Shakspeare, being really a neuter form of *he*, *hit* for *het*, as *his* for *hes*—a regular genitive of *he*. But more of this in additional remarks on the personal pronouns. (§ 155.)

When we say above that the forms *my*, *our*, *your*, &c., must always be followed by the noun which they limit, an *apparent* exception may be noticed in such expressions as, *That book is* MY OWN. Here indeed the noun is suppressed, but it is indicated by *own;* or it is *own*—the last adjective (as in all similar cases), which is to be considered as employed *substantively*. *My*, therefore, does not here perform the function which distinguishes *mine* —the function of indicating the suppressed *principal* or *limited noun*, but precedes, as usual, what stands for the noun.

Repeat the illustration by an example of a possessive case of a pronoun and of a common noun.

(14) What purposes does the possessive case thus come to serve? (15) Repeat examples and illustration.

(16) In the same way the possessive case represents the noun which it is designed primarily to *limit* in other forms of modification.* (17) But in all such cases (indeed in all cases of ELLIPSIS—that is SUPPRESSION of words), the proper mode of analysis is to supply the suppressed (or omitted) word, and then analyze the proposition as filled up. At least this plan should be adopted in the commencement. (18) Thus we fill up the proposition, *This house is* MINE, by substituting the words MY HOUSE instead of mine. Then *house* is the *predicate noun*, or *noun complementary* of the verb IS, and MY *modifies* or limits *house*, and belongs to a class of modifying words to be described hereafter. (See § 91.) Again, in such examples as, *This horse is my* FRIEND'S, we supply horse after FRIEND'S, and proceed as before. (19) When familiar with this elliptical construction, the learner can say in analyzing the above example, that the verb IS is modified or completed by the complementary noun *horse* implied in the *possessive case* FRIEND'S, which at the same time *limits* and represents horse.

[(20) Of this elliptical use of the genitive, both of nouns and pronouns, there are examples in which the *suppressed* noun is not so obvious, nor so readily supplied as in those already presented. (21) Such, for instance, as "gay hope is THEIRS." We cannot here supply the ellipsis in a satisfactory manner by repeating hope. Gay hope is their hope. This does not express the poet's meaning. His meaning is, that *gay hope belongs* to them—is their possession. (22) Here *possession*, or some similar word, is to be supplied in order to complete the construction. (23) So, in the following example, "All things are *yours;*—and ye are Christ's; and Christ is God's." This is equivalent to the assertion, All things belong to you, &c. Some such word

* For instance, in the *noun and preposition* modification, as *That horse is one of my* FATHER'S=one of my *father's* horses, or one of the horses of my father.

---

(16) Does the possessive case represent its *principal* noun in other forms of modification? (17) What is recommended as the proper mode of analysis in such cases? (18) Illustrate by an example of a possessive case of a pronoun and of a noun thus employed. (19) What shorter mode of analysis may be adopted, when this construction is familiar to the learner?

[(20) Repeat the remark about this elliptical use of the genitive. (21) Give the example. (22) What word must be supplied in this example? (23) Repeat the examples, and tell what nouns are to be supplied.]

as *property*, *inheritance*, *possession*, is implied in these several genitives.]

NOTE.—We have here perhaps an example of the insensible perversion of a form of construction from its original purpose, to serve a purpose not contemplated when the form was first adopted. This is a very common occurrence in the progress of all languages, and one which has given origin to many of those puzzling idiomatic expressions which the grammarian finds most difficult to analyze. It is obvious that the suppression of the principal noun after a genitive case, was used at first only when it saved the ungraceful repetition of the *principal* noun, and when this noun, being already used in the construction, and plainly indicated by the limiting genitive, could be readily supplied; as, This *horse is mine.* But this, and similar expressions, are equivalent to saying that This horse belongs to me, and come to have this sense affixed to them. Hence they come to be used (in a manner not contemplated at first) in such propositions as that quoted above from Gray (*gay hope is theirs*), to express that something simply belongs to the party represented by the noun in the genitive, and not, as originally intended, to avoid an ungraceful or unecessary repetition. The difficulty is, that the manner in which *hope* belongs to the boys (represented by *theirs*), and in which the *horse* belongs to his owner, is not the same—the kind of possession is altogether different. And though I can complete the first example by introducing the word horse—*That horse is my horse,* I cannot, in the same way, appropriately fill up the other construction by saying, *Gay hope is their hope,* nor in the other examples by saying, *All things are your things, You are Christ's ye,* and *Christ is God's Christ.* There is in all these examples a manifest extension of this elliptical construction to cases not contemplated when the ellipsis was originally adopted. This is no solitary instance of this species of perversion, or to call it by a softer name, *extension* of a form of construction to purposes different from those which it was originally adopted to serve. The history of all such cases is somewhat like the one considered. We forget, in the progress of language, the origin and first precise purpose of a form of expression (sometimes, not always, an elliptical form), our mind seizes on the meaning which it happens generally to convey, and when we have occasion to convey this meaning, or something approaching to it, we lay hold of the form of expression, as the most convenient or first suggested to our thoughts. In this way words and phrases stray far from their original meanings, and come to be used in a way which would appear barbarous, or, in some cases, would be unintelligible to the generations which first employed them. Examples of this kind are numerous in all languages, and give much trouble to the grammarian, because they are the product of accident, caprice, sometimes ignorance, and not, like most constructions in language, founded on rational principles. As specimens in our own language, we may give the form of expression, *there is, there are,*

&c., and such passive forms as, *I was refused admittance;* in French *Il-y-a*, and the like. By the influence of the same principle, *prevent*, and several other words, have assumed new meanings. We need a name for what we have been describing. For want of a better, we may call it the *insensible extension of a construction*, or more briefly, *insensible extension*. We think that the fact described above has not been noticed as much as it deserves, in accounting for puzzling idiomatic expressions.

We subjoin some examples of this *elliptical* construction, which may be analyzed by the learner. We indicate, as before, by *italics* the parts of the construction which may be explained by reference to the instruction already given.

Examples for Analysis.—That *palace is* the *Queen's*. The mild *lustre* of the morn *is hers*, the *lustre* of the risen day *is his*. *St. Peter's is* the largest *church* in the world. This *house is* our *friend's*. That shop is the carpenter's. These *books are mine*, those *are yours*. The present *moment* alone *is ours*.

["*Be thine despair* and sceptred *care;*
To triumph and to die are *mine*."

Arrange thus: *Despair be thine*, and sceptred *care be thine*. For be see § 55, Note.]

[(24) The following observations we abridge from Crombie: When we wish to express that a single object, or set of objects, is the common property of two or more persons, only the last name takes the sign of the genitive, though in analysis all the names are to be considered as in the genitive case. Thus we say, *William and Robert's house*, *William and Robert's books*, implying that the house and the books belong to them in common. (25) But when we refer to distinct objects severally possessed by two or more persons, we must give the genitive sign to each name; as, These are William's and Robert's houses.

(26) When a name consists of more than one term, we attach the sign of the genitive only to the last term; as, John the Baptist's head. (27) When a short explanatory term (a noun in *apposition*, for example) is joined to a name, we may attach the sign of the genitive either to the name or to the explanatory term; as, "I left the parcel at Mr. Johnson's, the bookseller," or "At Mr. Johnson, the booksel

[(24) What peculiarity is noticed in the use of the genitive sign, when we have occasion to speak of two or more persons as the possessors of the same object? Repeat examples. (25) What is the usage when two or more persons are spoken of as possessing distinct objects?

(26) What is the usage when a name consists of more than one term? (27) What when

ler's. (28) But, if the explanatory term is complex, or if there are more explanatory terms than one, the sign of the genitive must be affixed to the principal noun; thus, "I left the book at Johnson's, my old friend." "This psalm is David's, the king, priest," &c.

(29) In some cases, we employ both the genitive and a preposition; as, "This is a friend of the king's," elliptically, for "This is a friend of the king's friends,"=to "This is one of the king's friends." The latter form of expression, we think, is to be preferred; the other is awkward and less perspicuous.*]

Exercises I., II., III., &c.—Form a given number of propositions, containing examples of the genitive modification, and of any of the preceding modifications of subject and predicate, varying the tenses used as much as possible.

Additional Note on the Formation and use of the Genitive.—The English genitive is derived from the Anglo-Saxon. In that language, the genitive was frequently, though not exclusively formed, by adding to the noun the syllable *es* or *s* only, when the noun ends in *e*; as, *Smith*, genitive *Smithes*; *word*, *wordes*; *ende*, *endes*, &c. This form of the genitive is found in old English, down till the time of Wiclif and Chaucer. *Is* was sometimes substituted for *es*. This may be regarded as a mere variation of the manner of writing these endings. The orthography of our language was very unfixed at that early period, and indeed till a much later time. In the absence of every thing like a standard, each author took the liberty of representing sounds as his ear directed him, regardless of the authority of others, and even, sometimes, of preserving consistency in his own orthography.

Following that propensity to curtailment so strikingly exhibited in the progress of most languages, and of ours especially, we have cut off a syllable from each of these possessive cases in pronunciation, and latterly (so late, we believe, as the end of the seventeenth century) the apostrophe

* Dr. Bullions remarks, "It is worthy of notice, that though this use of the possessive after *of*, originally and strictly implies selection, or a *part* only, it has insensibly come to be used when no such selection is, or ever can be, intended. Thus we may say, "That house of yours," "That farm of yours," without intending to imply that any other houses or farms belong to you; and when we say, "That head of yours," selection is obviously excluded by the sense."—Page 47, § 242. Another instance of that *insensible extension* described in a preceding note. Better, perhaps, not to imitate or give currency to such forms of expression.

a short explanatory term is joined to a noun? (28) What when a complex term consisting of more than one word, or several explanatory terms are attached to a name?

(29) What is said of cases in which we employ both the genitive and a preposition?]

has been introduced in the written language, to mark the place left vacant by the suppression of the *e*, and to distinguish the possessive case from the plural form of the noun.

The notion once prevalent (sanctioned by the authority of Addison, in some of his papers in the "Guardian" and in the "Spectator"), that the *s* of the possessive case stands for the pronoun *his*—*John's book*, for example, instead of John, *his* book—is now universally exploded.

We often use the preposition *of* with a noun, instead of the genitive form. This mode of expression is derived from the French, in which there is no possessive form. Here, as in many other cases, our language, being formed from two distinct sources, possesses two distinct methods of expressing one and the same thing. It would be well if we had taken full advantage of this circumstance to free ourselves from an ambiguity which sometimes occurs in those languages, which are confined by usage to the single genitive form. For example, *Amor Dei*, in the Latin language, and ἡ ἀγάπη τοῦ Θεοῦ, in Greek, may mean either God's love towards us, or our love towards God; in other words, the love of which God is the *subject* or *agent*, and the love of which God is the *object*. To express this fact, the grammarians say, that the genitive is used in an active and passive sense, or *subjectively* and *objectively*. It is only from the sense, that we can determine in which way an author, in any particular instance, intends the genitive to be understood. Though we can in *most cases*, we cannot *always* determine this point with the certainty and promptitude that is desirable. Now, if in all cases where ambiguity could occur, it were established as the invariable usage of our language to employ the possessive case to express the sense of the subjective genitive, and the noun and preposition complement, when an objective meaning is intended, it would contribute much to perspicuity. Some of our best writers avail themselves of this means of discrimination, but the majority are, apparently, guided by sound rather than by sense, in their choice between the Anglo-Saxon and Norman form of expression, even in cases where a manifest ambiguity is involved; that is to say, where the complement might make sense, but a very different sense, whether understood *subjectively* or *objectively*. Amongst those who have failed to avail themselves of the advantage presented by the double form of complement, the translators of the New Testament must be included. They use the Norman form to express both the *subjective* and *objective* genitive of the Greek. Compare Romans 8: 33; Cor. 13: 14; Tit. 3: 4; 1 John 4: 9, with Luke 11: 42; John 5: 42, &c.

We may remark here, that there is an awkwardness in modifying a genitive modification, or the Norman equivalent for a genitive modification, by another similar modification. For example, *The farmer's son's house*, and *The house of the son of the farmer*, are forms of expression avoided by writers of good taste. Say, rather, *The house of the farmer's son.*

§ 76. (1) We now proceed to consider those *modifications of the verb* or *complements of the predicate* which are formed with the *accusative* or *objective case.* (2) The most prominent of these modifications is what we may call THE OBJECTIVE MODIFICATION or OBJECTIVE COMPLEMENT, which consists of the accusative joined to active verbs to express the *passive object* of the action (see § 45 : 5); (3) that is to say, the object which is *affected directly* by the action expressed by the verb. We prefer to say, *The object to which the action is limited in the particular assertion.* (4) For example, *The smith struck the iron; The dog bit the child; The boy killed the dog.* Here the nouns *iron, child, dog*, in the several propositions, express the passive objects, and modify or complete the verbs to which they are joined; they express the direction which the action of the verb is declared in these several assertions to take, and thus *limit* it. Modern French grammarians call this modification the *Complement Direct*, to distinguish it from the *Complement Indirect*, or dative modification.

(5) This modification may be readily distinguished by the fact, that it answers, if the object is a person, to the question, *Whom?* if the object is an animal or a thing, to the question *What?* as, *James loves his father.* If we put the question, *Whom does James love?* the answer gives the *objective complement;* viz., his *father. What did* the smith strike? Answer, *the iron;* the word *iron* thus proves to be the objective complement to the verb *struck.*

[(6) It is not to be concluded that the object expressed by the noun thus joined to the verb always *suffers*, or receives some influence from the action of the verb, because it is called the *passive object.* (7) In many cases of this kind of construction, no influence whatever is asserted to pass from the subject to the object which is expressed after the verb. It is merely indicated by the grammatical structure of the proposition, that the action expressed by the verb is in the assertion limited or restricted to the *object* expressed by the subjoined noun. (8) In some cases, if any influence passes, it is in the opposite direction,

---

§ 76. (1) To what subject is it now proposed to proceed? (2) Which is the most prominent modification of the kind mentioned? (3) Repeat the explanation. Repeat the definition in the form which is preferred. (4) Repeat the examples accompanied by the illustration. What do the French grammarians call this modification?

(5) How may this form of modification be readily distinguished?

[(6) Repeat the remark under No. 6. (7) Continue the remark. (8) In what direction

viz., from the object of the verb to the subject; as, for example, *I hear the bell of St. John's; William suffers pain.* (9) Here it is surely not asserted that the *bell* and *pain* receive influence from the *hearing* or the *suffering* of the subjects. (10) These objective or accusative nouns are employed simply to limit *hearing* and *suffering* in the respective assertions to the *bell* and to *pain.*]

NOTE.—*Gramatically* considered, as contributing to the *expression* of assertion (or to the expression of thought), it is always the *objective noun* which *influences* the verb, and not the verb which influences the noun. The noun comes, as it were, to the aid of the verb, to assist in the full development of the thought. *Physically* considered, the *action expressed* by the active verb very frequently affects the *party denoted* by the objective modification, but this does not by any means always happen. *See, view, contemplate, hear*, and multitudes of other verbs, requiring an objective noun to complete them, express actions which produce no effect whatever on the so called *passive* object. *I see the sun*, for instance; what effect is here produced on the sun? Great perplexity arises in grammatical inquiries from confounding language which clothes thought, with the subject matter of thought—*words* with *that which words signify.* In the example, *The smith struck the iron, physically* considered—in relation to the *fact* expressed—the act of striking *passes over* (as the grammarians say) *upon* the *iron*—influences the iron. But when we consider the *words*—the means of *drawing out* or *expressing* the *thought*—it is the word *iron* which *limits, restricts, exercises that species of influence which one word can exercise upon another*, or, to use the terms which we have adopted, *modifies* or *completes* (not the *action*, be it observed, but) the *verb struck.*

The terms *govern* and *government*, employed time out of mind in writing on grammar, have a tendency to mislead the learner, and, we suspect, have sometimes misled authors and teachers, in reference to this matter. Certainly, if we may judge from the effect of these terms on our own mind, they have puzzled and perplexed both the teacher and the scholar. These terms have served for ages as a mysterious veil to cover much ignorance. The scholar is taught to say, that the *active verb* GOVERNS the *accusative case.* Now, to govern, surely, he thinks, means to exercise some kind of influence, what influence he cannot well imagine, but some *mysterious* influence; and so he rests satisfied that he has explained the construction. When these terms were first adopted, they were, no doubt, intended simply to import that an active verb takes after it an accusative case. The rule served (and may still serve) to direct the learner (in writing Latin, for example) that, when he has ascer-

---

does the influence in certain cases pass between the subject of the proposition and the object of the verb? Give examples. (9) Repeat the illustration. (10) For what purpose are these objective nouns simply employed?]

tained that the verb employed belongs to the class of active verbs, the directly modifying noun must be in the accusative case. But it gives no explanation of the construction; though, from the mystery hanging about the term *governs* (a term generally expressive of energetic influence), it is, we presume, generally supposed that it does give a sufficient explanation of the nature of the relation subsisting between an active verb and an accusative case. The pompous assertion, *active verbs* GOVERN *the accusative case*, when expressed in plain English, amounts to this and no more, active verbs are followed by the accusative case. But for what purpose? No response to this question can be elicited from the big word *government*. And yet the use of this word checks all farther inquiry, and settles the whole matter to most people's satisfaction by its mere ponderosity. Besides, it leads directly to the error which we have noticed above, of concluding that, in a *grammatical* point of view, some influence passes from the verb to the noun—that it *acts* upon the noun—that its action *passes over upon it*, and then comes in the appeal to the *physical* relation of the action to the object for an explanation, illogically confounding grammatical with physical, or metaphysical relations, and yet failing altogether in obtaining a solution which will apply universally. It does not apply, as we have seen, in the case of such verbs as *see*, &c., followed by an accusative.

We think it is full time to banish the term *govern* from our grammars, since it only puzzles and misleads the learner, either conveying no meaning, or a meaning different from that originally intended. There seems to be a disposition among foreign grammarians to dispense with this grammatical term.

When we say that a verb is *modified* or *completed* by an *objective noun*, we state the relation which exists between the two words, and by the very terms used refer to an explanation of the relation. When a boy says that such a noun is in the accusative case, and is governed by such a verb, and repeats the rule, "Verbs signifying actively," &c., be it observed he has said no more than that the accusative follows the active verb, without the least reference to the purpose which it serves, or the relation subsisting between these words. If the rule implies more than this, it implies what, as we have shown above, is not a fact, viz., that the verb (*as a word*) exercises an influence over the *word* in the objective, whereas the reverse is the fact.

What we have said above, applies to the use of the words *govern* and *government*, not only in the particular case before us, but generally in all cases where they are employed in grammar. The word which the grammars represent as the governing word, is the word which is *passive*, which is the recipient of whatever influence passes between the two words; it is the word which is *restricted, limited, modified, completed*, by the other word. This applies especially to the construction above considered, which we have called the *genitive case modification*. We remember no instance in which the word which the grammarians have called the governing word is not in reality the modified word, except it is when prepositions are said to govern a particular case. And here the word *govern* is so inappropriate, that grammarians and teachers are beginning to employ the less imposing and (so far as it goes) more correct forms of expression, *prepositions take after them,* or prepositions are followed by such and such a case. Even here, the preposition with the preceding word may be considered as jointly modified by the word which follows.

(11) When a pronoun has a distinct form for the accusative case, this accusative form is subjoined to the verb as *objective modification.* (12) When any other kind of noun is employed as objective modification, it is only by the order of arrangement, that it is grammatically distinguished from the noun employed as subject of the proposition. For example, let us form a proposition of the two nouns, *William, James,* and the verb *excels.* If we arrange them thus, *William excels James,* the arrangement indicates that William is the subject, and James the objective modification. If we invert the order, we entirely change the sense. James becomes the subject and William, the objective modification; thus, *James excels William.*

(13) As a general rule, the objective noun with its modifications, when it has any, should follow next after the verb. It is, for the most part, awkward in prose to allow any other modification, except the noun or pronoun expressive of the *personal* object not preceded by a preposition (or what we shall call the *dative modification*), to come between the verb and its objective modification. (See § 79.) The noun and preposition modification is sometimes placed between them.

[(14) In our language, since the Anglo-Saxon period, there exists no distinct form (except in the pronouns), for this species of modification. Even in the Anglo-Saxon period the accusative was seldom distinguished by a form different from the nominative.

---

(11) Repeat the remark in reference to pronouns. (12) How do we distinguish the objective modification when it consists of any other kind of noun, from the subject noun? Repeat example and illustration. (13) What is the usual place of the objective modification in the arrangement of the proposition?

[(14) Repeat the remark in reference to a distinct form for this modification in English since the Anglo-Saxon period. And what is said of the Anglo-Saxon period?

(15) In some languages these cases have usually distinct forms, especially in singular nouns of the masculine and feminine genders.

(16) Such languages in consequence of these distinct case forms, are not so much confined to a fixed order of arrangement of the subject noun, verb and objective modification as we are in the use of English. (17) Our usual order of arrangement is to place the *subject noun* in the proposition before the verb, and the *objective modification* after it. We follow this order generally even in the case of the personal pronouns, though in regard of these, possessing, as they do, an objective form, this arrangement is not required, as in regard of other nouns, for the purpose of securing complete perspicuity. (18) The French generally place the objective modification when it is a pronoun, before the verb, because their pronouns like ours, have a distinct objective form, though they are compelled, like us, and for the same reason, to place the objective modification when it consists of any other kind of noun, *after* the verb. (19) In the Latin and Greek languages the accusative employed in such assertions as objective modification being distinguished by a peculiar termination cannot be mistaken for the subject noun. Thus the words, *Brutus Cæsarem occidit*, in whatever order we arrange them, will always mean, Brutus killed Cæsar.

(20) The same applies to our own language when we employ a pronoun which has an accusative form as objective modification; thus *James is a worthy man, his friends esteem him.* Wherever we place the pronoun *him* in the second proposition, before or after the verb, the sense remains unchanged. (21) Whenever the predicate cannot be asserted of the passive object, we can place even a noun that has no accusative form before the verb which it limits without danger of rendering the sense obscure. Thus, *James wrote a letter.* Here we might place the objective word *letter*, before the verb without rendering the sense obscure. Thus, *James the letter wrote.* It is manifest that James is the subject, and not the letter, for the letter could not be asserted, without absurdity, to write James. (22) In prose we now rarely, as we have already hinted, take advantage of this facility of transposition.

---

(15) What is said of some other languages in reference to distinct forms for the nominative and accusative cases? (16) What advantages result to these languages from the possession of distinct forms for these cases? (17) Repeat the order of arrangement of subject, verb and objective modification. Do we follow this order when a personal pronoun serves as objective? Is the same order absolutely necessary in this latter case?

(18) Repeat what is said of the French in reference to arrangement.

(19) Repeat what is said of the Latin and Greek languages, and give the illustration.

(20) Mention a case in which *we* could without obscurity use the same arrangement. (21) Mention a second case and repeat the illustration. (22) Do we often take advantage of

(23) The pronoun, objectively employed, is sometimes for the sake of emphasis placed before the verb and subject noun, especially by our older writers. We have innumerable examples of this order of arrangement in the Bible. For example, "*Me* he restored, and *him* he hanged."—Gen. 41 : 13. "*Thee* have I seen righteous." "*Him* shall ye worship." "*Him* will I confess." "*Him* declare I unto you." "*Them* he also called—*them* he also justified," &c. (24) We may also find examples of other nouns placed before the subject noun, and the verb to which they serve as *objective modification*, though these are not so numerous as the examples of pronouns thus transposed "The *darkness* he called night."—Gen. 1: 4. "This people have I formed for myself."—Is. 43 : 21.

(25) Transpositions of this kind occur much more frequently in poetry, both where a pronoun serves as objective modification, and where other nouns perform the same function. Examples, "*Him* the Almighty power hurled headlong."—Milton. "Such *place* eternal justice had prepared," &c.—Id. "There the *companions* of his fall—he soon discerns."—Id.* (26) In some cases the

* It sometimes happens, especially in poetry, that ambiguity is produced by these transpositions, as in an example from Gray's Elegy, noticed by Grant, "And all the *air* a solemn stillness holds." Here "it is impossible to ascertain, from the mere *form* of expression, whether the *air* holds the *stillness*, or the stillness holds the air."—Grant, p. 189.

"When Pope says, Odyss., 19.

'And thus the son the fervent sire addressed.'

it may be asked, did the son address the sire; or the sire address the son? A little attention would have prevented the ambiguity. If the sire addressed the son, the line should run thus,

'And thus *his* son the fervent sire addressed.'

If the son addressed the sire—

'And thus the son his fervent sire addressed.' "—Crombie, p. 273.

Grant repeats this in the same words, and adds: "In such instances, the pronoun clearly indicates both the subject and object; as, *in sense*, it *refers* pronominally, to the former for its antecedent, and in *syntax* (construction) *associates*, definitively, with the latter."—p. 189.

We cannot altogether agree with these authors, that *all* ambiguity is re-

this facility of transposition in prose? (23) What is remarked of the pronoun objectively employed, especially in older writers and in the Bible? Illustrate by examples. (24) Are there examples to be found of common nouns so transposed? Mention those given.

(25) What is said of transpositions of this kind in poetry? Repeat the examples.

(26) Give examples of the objective modification interposed between the subject noun and the verb.

poets have placed the objective between the subject noun and the verb. We find two examples given by Mr. G. Brown. "His daring foe securely *him* defied."—Milton. "The broom its yellow *leaf* hath shed."—Langhorne.

(27) We have already remarked in treating of the passive voice, or passive form of verbs, that the *passive object* of the verb *actively* used becomes the subject of the verb *passively* employed. That is the noun which serves as the objective modification in the active form of expression, becomes the subject in the passive form of expression. We have also observed that only those verbs which take this species of modification, and consequently admit of a passive form, are recognised as active verbs. We have three additional remarks yet to make in reference to this form of modification.

(28) 1st Remark.—Many verbs classed as neuter, that is, which express an action which terminates in the subject, can take after them, as objective modification, a noun of kindred meaning; thus we say, to *sleep* the *sleep* of death. *To run a race.* The sun *runs* his annual *course.* That man *lives a life* of usefulness. *Fight* the good *fight.* Hence, too, we can say passively, *His race is run.* The battle is *fought.* Such expressions as, "The brooks ran nectar," "The trees wept gums," &c., may be referred to this usage. (See Bullions' Eng. Gram., p. 163.)

(29) 2d Remark.—Some verbs which, in their simple form are neuter, by taking a particle into combination with them so as to form a compound, or by taking a particle after them, come to admit of an objective modification, and of a passive use. Thus look is neuter in such expressions as *your friend looks well, looks tired*, &c. But to *overlook* takes an *objective modification*, and can be used passively; as, *the tower* OVERLOOKS *the* PLAIN. *The man is overlooked by his former acquaintance. To go* is neuter, expresses an action which *terminates* in the *subject*, and takes no *objective modification* (except sometimes one of kindred meaning, agreeably to the preceding remark, as, He goes a journey.) But *undergoes* and *underwent*, its past tense require an ob-

moved from the line as amended by them. We do not think that the usage of (our) language is so *completely fixed* as regards this matter, that the pronoun *his*, necessarily refers us to the subject noun, or that the determinative *the* (for this might be alleged) necessarily indicates it. We admit that the amended lines are *less likely* to be misunderstood.

(27) Repeat the substance of what is said about the passive form.
(28) Repeat the substance of 1st remark, and give the examples.
(29) Do the same in regard to the 2d remark.

jective modification like other transitive verbs, and are sometimes used passively, as, *He undergoes danger ; Danger is undergone by him.* The same may be said of *understand*, compounded of *under* and the neuter verb *stand.* So also *smiles* is *intransitive*, and *smiles on* may be considered *transitive*, since it can be used passively. *Fortune smiles on us ; We are smiled on by fortune.*

(30) 3d REMARK.—Active or transitive verbs are often used without an *objective modification* after them. Thus we say, *That boy neither reads nor writes*, *John writes well*, *The prince governed with mildness.* Here the verbs are all active, but are used *absolutely*, that is, without restriction to any particular object; though some *appropriate object* less or more definite is implied. (31) Verbs employed in this way must not be confounded with those which are sometimes employed in a neuter and sometimes in an active sense. This latter class, as we before observed § 45 : 17–23, are originally neuter, and when they become active it is in a distinct sense—often a *causative* sense, as, *To run*—neuter, *To run a horse*—active=*To make a horse run.* But transitive verbs used *absolutely*, retain the same sense as when followed by an objective modification. We call a verb transitive because it generally takes an objective modification, not because such modification is always indispensable to express complete sense.]

NOTE.—In cases like those described in the second remark, it is not always easy to determine whether we should consider the verb and particle as forming a compound transitive verb, or regard the particle and the noun as forming a *noun with preposition complement.* For example, in the propositions, *The boy went* UP *the hill ; The man came* DOWN *the hill.* Shall we call *went up* and *came down* compound *transitive verbs,* and treat the noun *hill* in both cases as an *objective case complement,* or shall we call *went* and *came intransitive verbs,* and *up the hill* and *down the hill noun with preposition complements ?* Since it is in consequence of the presence of the particle which usually serves as a preposition that the noun can be thus applied to modify verbs of this kind, it seems the most natural and the easiest way to treat the noun and particle as a *noun with preposition modification.* This, however, cannot always be done with compounds of this kind. Sometimes the *neuter verb* takes no noun after it in consequence of the combination with a particle. Thus, *to sit down* admits no complementary noun, except it be united by another connective particle; *He sat down on a stone, in a chair, upon a rock,* &c. Some verbs, taking a particle after them in this manner, are capable of being modified in certain cases by nouns alone, and in other cases de-

---

(30) Repeat 3d remark, and examples. (31) Repeat the caution, and state the distinction between active verbs used absolutely and verbs which are both *active* and *neuter.*]

mand a *noun and preposition modification.* Thus we say, *John looked down the hill. John looks down upon* the plain. Neither when the compound verb still remains neuter, nor when another particle is employed in connection with the modifying noun, nor when the compound verb is employed passively can the particle be considered as performing the function of a *preposition* in the noun and preposition complement. In all such cases we must consider the particle as directly *of itself* modifying the verb. Shall we, then, say that in the two propositions, *He is smiled on by fortune, Fortune smiles on him,* the word *on* performs different functions? We doubt whether it would be consistent with sound philosophy to do so. Perhaps, whenever a neuter verb thus combined with a particle admits of being employed passively without any change of sense, we should, when the active form is employed consider the particle as blended with the verb—forming part of the *verbal conception,* and the noun which follows as a simple objective modification to the compound thus formed. (See § 81.)

(32) In § 27 : 17, we stated that the verbal nouns ending in *ing,* and the infinitives admit the same complements as the kindred *verbs,* besides taking (especially the verbal in *ing*), the complements peculiar to nouns. The same may be said of the verbal adjective or imperfect participle in *ing.* (33) All these are transitive when the verb to which they are allied is transitive, and take after them an objective modification to complete their meaning. For example: MAKING CLOTHES *is the tailor's employment;* TO MAKE CLOTHES *is the tailor's employment; That man* MAKING CLOTHES *is a tailor.* Here the noun *clothes* is the objective modification in the first example of the *verbal noun* in ING *making,* in the second of the *infinitive to make,* and in the third of the *participle* in ING. (34) The perfect participle in combination with the verb *have,* forming the perfect tense active, is also followed by an *objective complement;* but this is perhaps to be considered rather the complement of have, than of the participle. (35) In practical analysis it may be treated as the complement of the compound verb, without determining to which of the compound elements it properly belongs. (See § 59.) (36) The perfect participle when used alone, or in the formation of the passive, does not admit the objective complement. (37) But, with this exception, all these verbals may be considered as susceptible of the modifications of their kindred

---

(32) What has been stated in reference to verbals? (33) In what are they like the verbs to which they are allied? Give example and illustration. (34) What is said of the perfect participle in combination with the verb *to have?* (35) How may we treat such combinations in practical analysis? (36) What is said of the perfect participle used alone or in forming the passive? (37) What is asserted of all verbals, with the exception stated?

verbs, whether these verbs may be of the active, or of the neuter class.

(38) This fact is not a consequence, as some of the grammarians leave us to conclude, of the formation of these words from verbs. It is not in truth *as verbs*, that is, as implying assertion, that verbs themselves admit of the several modifications which we are treating. (39) It is the *predicate* contained in the verb which receives all these modifications, and this in consequence of its peculiar meaning—a meaning which whether expressed *substantively*, *adjectively*, or *assertively*, is alike susceptible of certain peculiar modifications, of which other nouns and adjectives are not susceptible. (40) If we admit, with some of the best grammarians, that "the verb is a noun and something more," namely a *noun used assertively*, we may conclude without farther argument that even when these modifications are applied to a verb, it is to complete the noun in it, and if they modify a noun assertively used, it is perfectly natural that they should modify the same noun—the name of the same conception—*substantively* or *adjectively* employed. (41) In the example, *That man makes hats*, *making hats* is asserted of the man; *making* with an objective modification. And if *making* when asserted is susceptible of this species of modification, why not when used without assertion?

Exercises.—Analyze the following propositions. All the words in *italics* may be disposed of by the help of the instruction already given in the preceding pages. The learner may be allowed to omit the words in roman characters on first going over the book. The abbreviation *Obj. Mn.*, may be employed in written exercises to represent *objective modification.*

Exercise I.—*John's brother loves him. James wrote* a *letter. Peter*, the *farmer's boy*, *drove* the *horses.* The *Romans conquered England.* The *Greeks planted* many *colonies.* The *father received* his *son's letter. Fever produces thirst. George's farm produced* abundant *crops. Industry overcomes difficulties. Misery loves company. Telling falsehoods destroys* a *man's reputation. To relieve distress is* that virtuous *man's occupation. John finding* his *brother*, *led him* home.

Oral Analysis.—*John's brother loves him.* The subject is *John's brother*, consisting of subject noun *brother*, singular number modified

---

(38) Repeat what is asserted in the two following sentences. (39) What is it in the verb which receives modification? Repeat the inference drawn from the fact that it is the *predicate* which is susceptible of modification. (40) What conclusion may be drawn from the admission that "a verb is a noun and something more"? (41) Repeat the example and the illustration.

or limited by *John's* genitive case modification. The predicate is *loves him*, consisting of *loves*, verb active, indefinite tense, third person singular, modified by the objective pronoun *him*.

Exercise II., III., &c.—Form a given number of propositions with objective modifications attached to the verbs.

§ 77. (1) The infinitive or verbal noun is frequently used as an objective modification of verbs. (2) We have examples in *John loves to play*, *William wishes to write a letter*. Here it is plain that *to play* and *to write* with its accompaniment *a letter*, stand exactly in the same relation to the verbs *loves* and *wishes*, as any other noun used as objective complement.

(3) Many verbs which can take no other noun as an objective modification, can be completed by infinitives. (4) To this class belong several of the auxiliary verbs which, with the help of an infinitive, form the *compound tenses*. (5) When the infinitive serves as an objective modification, it may be distinguished, like other objective modifications, by answering to the question what? As in the example above, if we ask what *does John love?* The answer is *to play*—the *objective infinitive*.

[(6) Many verbs take after them infinitives to complete them, which infinitives cannot be considered as standing to the verb in the relation of objective modifications. (7) We may here notice one use of the *infinitive* after verbs, very common in our language, and very distinct from an *objective modification;* we mean the infinitive employed to express a *purpose* or an *end;* as, *He came to see you*=He came for the purpose of seeing you. *He reads to learn*=He reads for the purpose of learning. This kind of expressions cannot be translated by the infinitives of other languages, at least, without a preposition expressive of purpose prefixed to them.*

(8) Formerly the preposition *for* was often prefixed to the infinitive when employed in this manner; as, in Acts 17: 26. "And hath

---

* In French, *pour*=*for*, expressive of purpose, is prefixed; in Latin, the infinitives cannot be employed at all in this way.

---

§ 77. (1) For what purpose is the infinitive often employed? (2) Examples and illustrations.

(3) Repeat remark in reference to verbs which take only this kind of objective modification. (4) Specify verbs of this class. (5) How may the objective infinitive be distinguished?

[(6) Do all infinitives stand in the objective relation to the verbs which they complete? (7) Mention a use of infinitives distinct from the objective use, and illustrate by examples. (8) What word was often placed before this kind of infinitive in English? Give examples and remarks on this usage.

made of one blood all nations of men *for to dwell* on all the face of the earth." "What went ye out *for to see?*"—Luke 7: 26. The use of the particle *for* before these infinitives is still common in the language of the uneducated, but a regard to elegance, rather than to precision, has led the educated to stamp this form of expression as vulgar.

(9) The infinitive used as an objective modification, we may distinguish by the name of the OBJECTIVE INFINITIVE; and the infinitive used to express purpose by the name of the INFINITIVE OF PURPOSE. (10) The learner may readily distinguish the objective infinitive, by the fact that the verbal noun in *ing* without a particle prefixed, may be substituted for it without destroying the sense. Thus in the proposition, *The boy learns* TO READ, we may substitute the verbal noun *reading* for the infinitive *to read*, without materially affecting the sense (though, we admit, this would not be the most appropriate mode of expressing the assertion); *The boy learns* READING.

(11) On the other hand, in the example, *The boy reads to learn*, we cannot make this kind of substitution without entirely destroying the sense. (12) This INFINITIVE OF PURPOSE, may be distinguished by the fact that we can place the words *in order* before it, without injury to the sense, generally with advantage as regards perspicuity. *The boy reads* IN ORDER *to learn.* (13) But if we introduce these words before an objective infinitive, we either destroy, or change the sense. Thus, *The boy learns in order to read*, is either unmeaning, *ungrammatical*, or means something different from *The boy learns to read.* (14) It is generally easier to distinguish these infinitives by the fact that as the *objective infinitive* answers to the question *what?* the infinitive of purpose answers to the question, *For what purpose?* or, *In order to what?*

(15) The *infinitive of purpose* might, perhaps with more propriety, be classed with those *noun and preposition modifications*, in which the preposition is by the usage of language generally suppressed, in some cases never used.

(16) There are instances of the use of the infinitive where other

---

(9) By what names may we distinguish these two kinds of infinitives? (10) How may the learner know the objective infinitive? Illustrate by an example.

(11) If we make the substitution of the verbal in ING for the infinitive of purpose what happens? (12) How may we distinguish the infinitive of purpose? (13) Can we introduce the words *in order to* before an objective infinitive? (14) How may these two uses of infinitives be more easily distinguished in most cases?

(15) With what kind of modifications might the infinitive of purpose be classed, perhaps with greater propriety?

(16) Are infinitives used when there is a suppression of other prepositions besides *for?* Give example and illustration.

prepositions are suppressed; at least when we substitute the kindred verbal noun in *ing* which freely takes various prepositions before it, we supply other prepositions and not *for* or *in order*. Thus, *Boys delight to play*. Here when we substitute the verbal in *ing*, or gerund, we must prefix the preposition *in*; *Boys delight in playing*.

(17) These may also be classed with the *noun and preposition* modifications, in which the preposition is suppressed, both the connection and the relation of the *modifying* to the *principal word* being readily suggested to the mind without a spoken sign.

(18) Infinitives are also used after neuter verbs, especially the verb *to be*, in the same way as other nouns *complementary of neuter verbs*. (19) For example, *To be virtuous is* TO BE *happy*. Here the first *to be* is the subject noun, and the second *to be* is the *infinitive complementary* of the verb *is*. *To obey is to enjoy*. Here to obey is the subject, and *to enjoy*, infinitive complementary of the verb *is*.*

* There is a peculiar use of the infinitive (often indicating *future* action) in such expressions as "*The house is to build;*" *This house is to let*, That man is to blame, &c., which seems to have been derived from the old *gerund* or *future infinitive*, as some call it—the verbal form in the Anglo-Saxon which constantly has the particle *to* prefixed. (The ordinary infinitive in that language, as in others, was distinguished by a peculiar termination, and did not as in the present English consist of the naked root of the verb, and it never had the particle *to* prefixed to it.) This *gerund* is by some considered a *dative* of the *infinitive*. It is evidently formed by inflexion from the infinitive proper, generally by the addition of the syllable *ne* with (and sometimes without) a slight modification of the vowel of the preceding syllable; thus, infinitive, TELLAN, *to tell;* gerund or dative *to tellanne*, answering nearly to the Latin supine. So *hyran*, gerund *to hyrenne*, with the change of *a* into *e*. *Lufian* or *Lufigan;* gerund *to lufigenne*. Many of the infinitives which follow nouns and adjectives seem to have had the same origin; such as the infinitives in the following expressions: *Things* TO DO. *Trees* TO PLANT. *Hard* TO BEAR. *Fair* TO LOOK ON. *Good* TO EAT. *Easy* TO LEARN, &c. It is not unlikely that many of the examples classed under the infinitive of purpose may have originated from this *gerund*, or dative of the infinitive. For more on this subject, see R. Taylor's additional notes to the Diversions of Purley, pp. 28, 29. To the remarks of Mr. Taylor we are indebted for the matter of this note. We add an extract, bearing upon this subject, from Vernon's Guide to the Anglo-Saxon Tongue, p. 40: "The gerund, which is always preceded

(17) Where may these infinitives be classed?

(18) What is said of infinitives used with neuter verbs? (19) Give examples. Repeat illustration.

(20) We may then recognise at least four distinct uses of the infinitive after verbs, which we may call respectively, the *objective infinitive*, the *infinitive of purpose*, the *infinitive complementary of the neuter verb*, and the *infinitive complementary of the active verb* to be considered in the next section. Under these, and the class mentioned in the note, we may rank, we believe, nearly all the infinitives which follow verbs, and most of those, too, which follow other words.

It will not be necessary for the learner in passing through a first course in this book to take notice of these distinctions. He may call all complementary infinitives, that is, all infinitives not employed as subject nouns, *infinitive modifications*, or *complements* of *verbs*, *nouns*, or *adjectives*, according as they modify one or other of these classes of words. The *infinitive used in comparison* after *as* and *than*, will come under review when we treat of phrases used instead of accessory propositions for the purpose of modification, or what may be considered, if we please, as *abbreviated propositions*, or contracted accessories. (See § 142: 9–15.) What is called the *infinitive* put *absolutely*, comes under the same classification. Like the infinitive used after *as* and *than*, it is an abbreviated manner of expressing a proposition, by means of an *infinitive* of *purpose*. (See § 142: 18, 19.)]

(21) The learner will remember that some verbs take after them exclusively, the infinitive without the particle *to* prefixed. (22) Of this class are the verbs, called auxiliary, employed in forming the *compound tenses*. (23) Besides these, the following verbs generally take after them an infinitive without the particle *to*; *bid*, *dare* (=presume), *feel*, *hear*, *let*, *make*, *need*, *see*; and sometimes, *behold*, *have*, *know*, *observe*, *perceive*. (24) Examples, *I bid him tell.*

---

by *to*, and seems to be a kind of dative of the infinitive, answers to our infinitive present, active and passive, and to the Latin supines, infinitive future, active and passive, &c., as, Come thú ús tó for-spillanne? *comest thou to destroy us?* Latin, nos perditum. Hwaether is ethre tó cwethanne? *Whether is easier to say.* Latin, facilius dictu. Eart thu se the tó cumenne eart? *Art thou he that is (art) to come?* Latin, Qui venturus est. Heo byth tó lufigenne; *she is (must be, or ought) to be loved.* Latin, Amanda est." Hence the phrases, "house to let," "he is to blame," &c. We find another example of this in the expression, *to wit*, originally, *to wittanne.*

---

(20) How many distinct uses of the infinitive after verbs may be recognised, and how may they be named respectively?]

(21) What form of the infinitive do some verbs take after them?

(22) What class always takes the form without the particle *to?* (23) What other verbs take the same form of the infinitive after them? (24) Illustrate by examples.

I dare go. I feel it move. I heard him say. He lets him do it, &c.* Most of these verbs take the complementary, or factitive infinitive.

EXERCISE I.—Examples of the *objective infinitive* for analysis. *John hopes to succeed. George wishes to learn.* That *man desires to overcome* his *rivals. They sought to enter the gate. Boys expect to become men.* The *farmer's son began to plough.* The *rain ceased to fall. Justice ought to prevail. John dared* not *attempt* that *work. Seek to secure virtue's rewards. He learned to restrain his passions.* That *man pretends to be a patriot.*

EXERCISE II., III., &c.—Let the learner form a given number of propositions containing examples of this construction.

[EXERCISE IV.—Examples of the *infinitive* of *purpose. You live to eat. We eat to live. She stoops to conquer. Men came to scoff. He rose to address* the *multitude. Men labor to gain wealth. Multitudes came to see him.* EXAMPLES of verbs modified by both objective noun and infinitive of purpose. *We sent* JOHN TO BRING the *letters. James called* ME TO TELL me the *news. They invited* HIM TO SHOW him *attention. They invited* HIM TO TAKE *part* in their deliberations.

REMARK.—It may be observed that the first and last examples are different from the rest. In the other examples the infinitives express an action to be performed by the subject of the proposition, but in these the infinitive expresses an action to be performed by the person designated as object direct, or passive object of the verb. *They invited* HIM *for to take a part—in order that he might take a part*, &c. All these infinitives may be considered as abbreviated *accessory propositions;* thus, *you live* TO EAT = *you live, that* YOU MAY EAT; and so of the rest.

EXERCISE V., VI., &c.—Construct a given number of propositions containing examples of the *infinitive* of *purpose.*]

(25) What are called the perfect infinitives—that is, the infinitive of the verb HAVE, completed by perfect participles—are used exactly as the simple infinitives, chiefly, we think, as objective modifications. The learner may here be required to write a number of propositions having their verbs modified by these compound infinitives.

---

* It has been well observed by Grant (p. 193, note 2), "That, with the exception of *let*, the *to* is seldom or never omitted after the perfect participle used passively; thus, 'We are bidden *to* rest,' 'He was heard *to* say,' 'He was seen *to* move.'"

---

(25) What is said of compound infinitives?

EXAMPLES.—*John expected to have finished* his *task* before this time. *He intended to have called* upon you before his departure. This *man seems to have been wronged* on that occasion, &c.

EXERCISE.—Form a given number of propositions with verbs modified by compound infinitives, either active or passive.

§78. (1) There are some active verbs which, besides the objective modification, take after them another noun *complementary* of the action expressed by the verb.* (2) Such are the verbs *to make, to name, to call, to appoint, to elect, to constitute, to choose, to create.* (3) We have examples of this use in such expressions as, "To make *David king.*"—1 Chron. 12 : 38, and 32. *They named* HIM JOHN. *They called* HIM JOHN. *The people* ELECTED *him* PRESIDENT, &c. Here *king, John, president*, express what was *made, named, called*, in reference to the *passive object.* (4) This we may call the *noun complementary of the active verb.* (5) If we form a question, including as before, the subject and verb, and in addition the objective modification or passive object, the answer to *what* will be the *noun complementary ;* thus, *what* were they about to make David ? Ans. *King*—the *complementary noun. What did they call him? John*—the *complementary noun.*

[(6) This modification is, like the noun complementary of the neuter verb, more intimately combined with the verb, as regards *meaning*, than any other form of modification. If we speak of *meaning* (of the *thing expressed*), it is the action of the verb *modified* by *this complementary noun*, which passes over upon the passive object. If we speak exclusively of the *words*, the verb and complementary noun

* This noun usually expresses some effect or result produced on the *passive object* (the person or thing indicated by the *objective modification*) by the action expressed through the verb. The Germans have given the name *factitive* to a class of modifications including this and (what we have ventured to call) the *noun complementary of the neuter verb*, together with some other forms of modification yet to be considered. The Germans call the object expressed by nouns, thus employed, the *factitive object.* We shall have more to say of this whole class of modifications below. (See § 90.)

§ 78. (1) Repeat what is said of some active verbs. (2) Enumerate some of the verbs which are susceptible of this modification. (3) Illustrate by examples. (4) What may we call this species of modification ? (5) To what question does it answer ? Example.

[(6) Repeat what is said of this modification with the substance of the illustrations and the examples.

combined, are limited by the objective modification. In the example above, it is the action of *calling John*, or of *electing president*, that passes over on the party represented by *him*, not the bare actions of *calling* and *electing;* or, grammatically considered, the words *calling John*, and *electing president*, are limited by *him*. In other words, *calling John* and *electing president*, may be regarded as compound expressions, indicating a single action, and the objective serves to limit this action.

(7) It is because of this intimate connection with the part of the predicate expressed in the verb, that we have ventured to style this modification by way of distinction, *The noun complementary;* and yet this close connection is not indicated by the arrangement; since,]

(8) The *objective modification* is placed between the complementary noun and the verb.

[(9) The objective modification is thus embraced within the compound expression which it limits.

(10) When verbs with these two distinct modifications come to be used in the passive form, they still retain the *complementary noun* as a modification, whilst the *objective modification* becomes the *subject* of the proposition; as, *He is called John*, *He is elected president.**

* It is to be observed that, in languages which possess a form for the accusative, distinct from the nominative, or *subject form* of the noun, *the complementary noun* does not retain the accusative form when attached to the passive verb. It always accommodates its form to that of the noun affected by it. When that noun, after the active verb, takes the accusative form as *objective modification*, the complementary noun assumes the same form; and when it becomes subject noun to the verb passively employed, the complementary noun assumes the same form, and stands as nominative after the verb. It may, when thus used, be called the *noun complementary* of the *passive verb.*

In fact, it then scarcely differs from the noun complementary of neuter verbs. If, in the example, *He is called John*, we consider attentively the compound expression made up of the participle *called*, and the noun *John*, we shall find that it performs much the same grammatical function, in reference to the verb *is*, as a noun or adjective would perform. *He is what?* Ans. *Called John.*

(7) Mention the reason of the name given to this modification.]

(8) Where is it placed in reference to the verb and objective?

[(9) What is remarked in reference to the objective modification?

(10) What happens when verbs susceptible of this kind of modification come to be used in the passive form?

(11) The verbs *ask* and *teach*, take two modifying nouns after them, in the same manner as the class of verbs just considered but the *complementary noun* stands in a very different relation to the *objective* noun following these verbs. In the preceding construction, the complementary noun expresses what the passive object becomes through the action expressed by the verb. Thus, *The people elected Washington president.* Here *president* expresses what Washington became by the election of the people. But when we say, *The master taught John grammar; He asked John a question; grammar* and *question* do not express what John becomes. And hence, in languages which have an accusative form, and in which verbs of asking and teaching take two accusatives after them in the active voice, the noun expressive of what is asked or taught retains the accusative form, when the proposition is expressed passively. Thus, in the proposition, *John was taught grammar*, the word equivalent to grammar, in Latin, would be in the accusative form. (See Note.)

(12) In some of the constructions, where two modifying nouns affect the same verb, there is a suppression of the infinitive TO BE.

(13) Thus, in the proposition, *They thought him a knave*, the words *to be* may be supplied, and then the construction will come under the class about to be mentioned, in which the verb is modified by an objective noun and a *complementary infinitive*.]

NOTE.—*On the construction with* ASK *and* TEACH.—*Query?* Is it not because *ask* and *teach* are actions which may have for their *passive objects*, both persons and things, that they can take two accusatives after them? We say both to *ask* a *person*, and to *ask* a *question*. When *question* is used alone after this verb, it would be considered an objective modification, perhaps, of that class (mentioned before) made by a noun of *kindred meaning*— the only kind which some verbs admit, and perhaps the only kind expressive of a thing which this verb admits. (It admits, more frequently, a *complementary infinitive* with an objective of a person.) Now, when we have occasion to indicate the person whom we *ask*, and that what we ask is *a question*, it is natural to place both after the verb, as we should place them if singly used as objective modifications. Thus the verb comes, as it were, to

(11) Repeat the substance of what is said of the verbs *ask* and *teach*, giving illustration by examples.

(12) What is said of some of these constructions when two nouns modify the verb?

(13) Illustrate by an example.]

have a double *objective modification*, limiting it in reference to two classes of objects—the person asked and the object asked.

The same reasoning may be applied, perhaps more successfully, to the verb *teach*. This verb, in regard of objective modifications, expressive of the thing taught, is not, like *ask*, confined to nouns of *kindred meaning*. Like verbs completely transitive, it may take a great number of objective modifications of this kind. Thus we say, to teach *reading, writing, mathematics*, or any art or science; and with infinitives, *to read, to write, to draw*, &c., &c. We also say, to teach a pupil, an apprentice, &c. When only one or other of these classes of nouns is used separately after *teach*, we call it the *objective modification;* it expresses the passive object; and nouns of both kinds can be used as the subject, when we employ the passive form of this verb. We can say, *The scholar is taught*, and *grammar is taught*. (We cannot, indeed, say with propriety, *Grammar is taught the scholars*, as we can say, *The scholars are taught grammar*.) Now, when we have occasion to indicate both the party taught and the subject taught, we place both nouns, as a kind of double objective modification, after the verb. The verb teach may, in fact, be considered, as expressing two different actions, as having two distinct meanings. One, when followed by the name of a rational recipient of instruction, and another, when followed by the name of the subject taught. When we say, *He taught a boy*, and *He taught Grammar*, what is indicated as done in reference to the boy, in the first proposition, and to grammar, in the second, is manifestly altogether different.

When we say, *He taught the boy grammar*, we may be regarded as combining both uses of the verb *teach*, expressing a double meaning by a single sign, followed by the modifications appropriate to both meanings. Still, as in the verbs before considered, the action of teaching, first modified by the *subject* taught, is finally modified by the name of the person, and not in the reverse order. In the example above, *teaching* modified by *grammar*, is limited by the word *boy*, and not, we think, *teaching the boy*, by the word grammar. *Grammar*, we consider in such examples, as the more *intimate* modification of the verb, and as performing the function, for the time, of a sort of *noun complementary*, though it cannot with propriety be called the *factitive object*. It does not express what the *boy*, for example, becomes through the action of the verb (he does not become grammar), and consequently, when the passive form is used, and the person becomes the *subject noun*, the name of the subject taught does not assume the case of the person taught, but retains the accusative form in languages which have a distinct accusative form, and should be treated in our language as an *objective modification*, employed with the passive form of the verb. We shall find other instances below of an objective modification employed with passive forms. (See § 79: 25).

ADDITIONAL OBSERVATIONS ON THE NOUN COMPLEMENTARY OF THE ACTIVE VERB.—Some grammarians analyze all such propositions as, *They elected him president*, by supplying the infinitive *to be*, They elected him TO BE *president*; and then they treat the construction as a case of an *infinitive after a verb* As these grammarians class together without distinction all infinitives coming after verbs, they give themselves no farther trouble about the matter. "One verb governs another in the infinitive." This settles the question in an easy, if not in a satisfactory manner. But there are, as we have already seen, essential distinctions between the functions of infinitives following verbs, especially in our language. And this kind of infinitive performs a peculiar function, entirely distinct from the objective infinitive, if not from the infinitive of purpose. Hence we designate it, The Infinitive Complementary of the Active Verb; or, if we understand that here it expresses a purpose, *The Infinitive of Purpose Complementary of the Active Verb.* It is, however, unnecessary to distinguish the infinitives of purpose into those which follow neuter and those which follow active verbs, since, in both situations they perform the same function and stand in the same relation to the rest of the proposition, the connecting word being suppressed. Thus, in the proposition *John sent a messenger to bring a physician*, either *for* or *in order* are implied before the verb *to bring*, and it stands related to the proposition like the *infinitives* of *purpose* already considered, and like them is not capable of being rendered into other languages (Latin, for example) by a bare infinitive.

Like the noun complementary of an active verb, the infinitive *to be*, with its complementary noun, expresses what the passive object—the direct object is *made* or *becomes* in reference to the subject of the proposition. Thus, in the proposition, *They elected that senator to be president*, it is expressed that the *senator is made* or *becomes president* through the action of *electing* on the part of those represented by the subject pronoun *they*.

We may add that, in our opinion, the propositions, *They elected him president*, and *They elected him to be president*, are not exactly equivalent, and the latter, as we think, cannot always with strict propriety be substituted for the former. The first is the proper expression, when the office to which the party is elected or appointed in any mode is well known, generally recognised, definite, as, for example, King, Judge, Speaker of the House of Commons, President of the United States, Roman Consul, Dictator, &c. The form with the infinitive *to be* is more properly employed when the office has had no antecedent existence, or is not commonly recognised, or permanently established. Thus we say of a party having no previous organization, that, They chose such an one *to be* their leader in a particular enterprise, or *to be* their president or chairman for a particular occasion.

The reader will please also observe that many cases occur in which two nouns employed after a verb—the one serving as objective modification, the other as complementary in the manner described—do not admit the interposition of the infinitive *to be*. For example, *The father named his son John* or, *The father called his son John.* We cannot resolve this, by saying that 't is equivalent to, *The father named his son* TO BE *John*, or *called him* TO BE *John.*

We may remark here that the explanation given of this kind of construction by those who treat it as a case of *apposition*, considering the complementary noun as an apposition to the objective noun, is altogether unsatisfactory. This construction and apposition (as understood by the best grammarians) are totally different. What we have already said (§ 69 : 28–33) in explaining the difference between the noun complementary of a neuter verb and a noun in apposition will equally apply in this case with some slight change of terms. The noun complementary does not, as in apposition, serve merely to explain the objective noun, but completes the meaning of the verb, and it is *through the verb* that its connection with the objective noun is effected. An example in which both constructions occur will illustrate the difference between the noun in apposition and the noun complementary, to the satisfaction of all intelligent readers. *The people elected Cicero, the celebrated orator, consul.* It is manifest to every one who understands the proposition, that there is a marked difference between the functions performed in this construction by the noun *orator* and the noun *consul.*

(14) Infinitives are frequently employed as *nouns complementary* with active verbs. (15) This use of the infinitive ought to be carefully distinguished, from the uses before considered, if we would give an exact and satisfactory analysis of the language. (16) If we form a question with the subject, the verb and the passive object, the answer to the words, To BE WHAT, or To DO WHAT, will be the *infinitive complementary* of the *active verb.* Examples: *They chose him to be their secretary. They chose him to be what?* Ans. *To be their secretary—infinitive complementary* with its modifications. *He entreated* the *people to disperse.* He entreated the people *to do what?* Ans. *To disperse—infinitive complementary.**

* *Infinitives of purpose* are often employed, together with an objective modification after active verbs. These may be distinguished from the other class of infinitives by supplying an answer not only to the question, To do what? but also to the question *For what purpose?* Thus, *They sent him to announce* their *coming.* They sent him for what purpose? Ans. To announce their coming. The other infinitives will not answer appropriately to the question, *For what purpose.* This infinitive of purpose after an active verb, followed by an objective noun may be considered as at once an infinitive complementary and an infinitive of purpose, or as an infinitive of purpose used to *complete* an active verb.

(14) What remark is made in reference to infinitives? (15) Repeat the caution. (16) To what question do infinitives thus employed answer? Give examples and illustration.

(17) Care must be taken to distinguish constructions of this kind, where two accusatives follow a verb from the construction next to be considered, in which a verb is modified by a dative and accusative noun or infinitive, and also from the accusative and infinitive used as a contracted accessory. The means of distinguishing these constructions will be more readily comprehended after we have considered them both.

Examples for Analysis.—*He formed us men.* The *Romans called Cicero father* of his country. The *people elected Marius consul.* The *Senate declared Cincinnatus dictator.* The *Government appointed him envoy* to France. "*Men called him Mulciber.*" "*Crown her queen* of all the year." "*We made him* our *leader.*" The *Company appointed him manager.* "The *king created Monk Duke* of Albemarle." His *neighbors chose him delegate to represent* (inf. of purpose) them in the convention. "*God made* a *wind to pass* over the earth." "That *made* the *earth to tremble.*" "Thou *wilt make me to live.*" "The *Lord shall make men go* over dry-shod."

Exercises I., II., III., &c.—Form a given number of propositions with active verbs modified both by an objective and a noun, or infinitive complementary.*

§ 79. The Dative Modification, or Personal Object after the Verb.—(1) The *dative modification* consists of a noun or pronoun employed without an intermediary word to express the party *to* which (sometimes the party *for* which) the subject is represented in the proposition as performing the action expressed by the verb. (2) Example: *The master gave* John *a book.* Here John expresses the party *to which* the master performed the action of *giving* a book (3) Leaving *words* and referring to *things*, this modification is called by grammarians the *personal object*, as the *objective modification* is called the *passive object.* (By modern French grammarians it is called the *indirect object*, as the objective modification is called the *direct object.*) (4) These names apply not to the words, but to the

* A line of distinction might possibly be drawn between the infinitive complementary of the active verb and the infinitive of purpose after the active verb. The most marked difference is, that the infinitives after such

(17) Repeat the caution about distinguishing this from another construction.

§ 79. (1) Describe the *dative modification.* (2) Give example and illustration. (3) By what names is this modification sometimes called? (4) To what do these names apply?

things signified, and not always very appropriately to them, as we have had occasion to remark already in treating of the name passive object.

(5) This *dative modification* is not confined to active verbs; but the most striking (the best marked) examples of its use, are found in connection with this class of verbs. (6) The *dative* together with the objective modification, most frequently follows the verbs *allow, bring, buy, deny, gain, get, give, obtain, offer, pay, prepare, procure, promise, provide, refuse, sell, send, tell, yield.* (7) Perhaps it follows some others, which, like these, indicate an action having reference to a *personal object.*

(8) Both nouns and pronouns (perhaps more frequently pronouns), are used to express this *dative modification.*

We give a few examples for analysis. In each proposition the verb is modified both by a noun in the *accusative*, and a noun in the *dative.*

(9) In the order of arrangement, the *dative modification* always *precedes* the *objective modification.*

EXERCISE I.—*They allowed me credit. John brought me* a *seat. William bought* his *brother* a *farm.* The *porter denied him admittance. He gave me* a *present. They offered him* a *commission. He paid John* the *debt. Prepare us* a *place. He promised them* a *ride.* The *host provided them lodging. I refused him* my *consent.* The *farmer sold me* a *horse.* My *garden yielded me* a large *crop*, &c.

---

verbs as *make, constitute, appoint, elect, call, name,* &c., which are more strictly *factitive*, or complementary infinitives, cannot be so readily converted into accessory propositions as the infinitives which express more definitely a *purpose, end, design,* of the action expressed by the principal verb.

It is to be observed that the verb *make* sometimes takes after it a dative and accusative in our older writers. "I made *me* great works—I made *me* gardens," &c. "Riches certainly make *themselves* wings." It also sometimes takes as modifications an accusative and an infinitive of purpose: as, "Make haste *to help* me." "Their feet make haste *to shed* blood." "God made the greater light *to rule* the day," &c.

---

(5) Is this *modification* confined to active verbs? Repeat the additional remark. (6) Enumerate the verbs most frequently followed by a *dative* and *objective modification.* (7) Repeat remark after No. 7. (8) Name the classes of words employed to express the *dative modification.*

(9) What is the order of arrangement of the dative and objective modification?

In analysis of these examples, first, read off the whole subject and the whole predicate separately; next point out the verb, tell to which class it belongs, and its mode, tense, number, person; then point out the subject noun, telling class, number, gender, person, repeat rule of concord between subject noun and verb; then turn to the verb and say that it is modified by the objective (here name the word), and the dative (naming the noun in the dative).

For example, '*allowed*' in the first proposition is modified by the objective *credit*, and the dative *me*. After this, the objective and dative nouns may be classed and described.

In the analysis the words in Roman may be omitted as usual.

Exercise II., III., &c.—Let the learner write a given number of propositions formed with the verbs above given (or similar verbs, if he can find them), followed by appropriate dative and objective modifications.

(10) Some of this class of verbs admit of being modified by an infinitive and dative. (11) For example, *He allowed me to ride*, *Promised me to send*, *Told him to go*, &c.

Exercise.—Let the learner form a given number of propositions with such of the verbs in the above list as admit an infinitive and dative, accompanying the verbs in each proposition by both these modifications.

[Remark.—(12) It will be noticed that when an infinitive holds the place of an objective modification, the dative still takes precedence in the order of arrangement, though, as we shall show more fully hereafter, the objective modification has a closer relation with the verb in sense, than the dative, and though in fact it is not the verb *alone*, but the verb *modified* or *completed* by the objective noun or infinitive, that is completed by the dative. (13) If the noun or pronoun expressing the *dative modification* is placed after the objective (which is its natural place in the order of sense), it must be preceded by the preposition to. (14) This proves the kind of relation which these dative nouns hold to the verb, and that they are not to be confounded with accusatives complementary of the active verb. (15) Two circumstances distinguish the dative modification from the noun comple-

---

(10) In what manner are some of these verbs which admit a dative modified? (11) Give examples.

[(12) Repeat the substance of the remark. (13) When the noun or pronoun expressing the dative modification is placed after the objective modification, by what must it be preceded? (14) What does this prove? (15) Mention the two circumstances which distinguish the *dative modification* from the *noun complementary of the active verb*.

mentary of the active verb; first, as we have just remarked, the dative always takes precedence of the objective modification, whereas the noun complementary always follows it; and, second, when the objective modification is not an infinitive, the *dative* can be replaced without injury to the sense, by the noun or pronoun with the preposition *to* (or sometimes *for*) placed *after* the objective modification.

(16) We cannot prove the nature of this construction so directly when an infinitive follows the dative, because we cannot then replace the dative by a noun and the intermediary words *to* or *for* after the infinitive; but we ascertain the construction which the verb requires when a *noun* or *pronoun* (as objective modification) follows it, and may safely conclude, that what is a *dative* in this case, must remain a dative when an infinitive follows. (17) For example, if in the proposition, *John told him a story*, the pronoun *him* is a dative modification, we may be assured that it performs the same function in the proposition, *John told him to write.*]

NOTE.—The mode of analyzing this construction hitherto generally adopted, by saying that the noun is in the objective case, and that the *preposition* TO is suppressed, appears to us improper. If the *preposition* TO had ever been used with these datives when placed before the objective modification, this explanation of the construction might be allowed. But we believe that *to* has never, in any period of the language, been used before nouns or pronouns employed to express a *dative sense*, when placed before any kind of objective modification, whether noun, pronoun or infinitive.

This construction is in reality a remnant of the ancient Anglo-Saxon usage of a *dative modification*, which has continued in our language after the distinct *dative form* by which it was anciently indicated has entirely disappeared, except in the pronouns. What we call an accusative or objective case in the personal pronouns, has at least full as much claim to be considered a dative as an accusative. In most of the pronouns, the same form served the functions of both dative and accusative; and, as regards the pronoun masculine of the third person, HIM was in fact the ancient dative and *not* the accusative. The accusative had another form altogether distinct. *Them* also descends from the *dative* and not from the accusative plural, which in the Anglo-Saxon corresponds with the nominative plural. (See § 155.) It is therefore inconsistent with the history of this construction, to say that there is a preposition suppressed before the noun. In the ancient language the function of the word was indicated by the dative form; the same is now indicated by the place which it holds in the arrangement before the objective

---

(16) What is said of the means of ascertaining this distinction when an infinitive serves as objective modification? (17) Illustrate by example.]

modification. No complement, as far as we remember at present, except a dative of this kind, can with propriety always come between the verb and the objective modification, when it *follows* the verb. The mode in which we have ventured, in opposition to established usage, to treat this construction, is not only more consistent with the history of our language, but it prepares us better to account for the singularity, that these verbs when *passively* employed have sometimes (contrary to the general laws of language), what serves as a dative to the verb (*actively* employed) for their *subject noun.*

What we have said above might in consistency be carried much farther. Besides the fact which we shall notice presently, that many datives after what were originally *intransitive* verbs, have come to be considered objectives, and the verbs which they modify, in consequence, to be recognised as *transitive*, the nouns and pronouns which follow prepositions were originally often real datives in form and sense. For instance, in any of the above examples when we place the noun or pronoun, which serves as dative modification after the objective, and place the preposition TO before it, it is as much *historically* a dative as before. That is to say, the Anglo-Saxons employed the preposition *to* generally with the dative case, never with the accusative. Many of their prepositions, like *to*, do not take after them an accusative. But it would serve no purpose except to perplex the student to revive distinctions which in the present usage of the language are marked neither by a change of form, nor by a *particular arrangement*, and which can now serve no practical purpose.

There is one relic of the old English dative, which we must notice in order to explain a number of expressions, now obsolete, but of frequent recurrence in our older writers. (18) We allude to the following *impersonal* verbs preceded by a form of one or other of the pronouns, most generally by *me ; me seems*, *me listeth*, *me thinks*, and its past tense, *me thought*. (See § 66 : 8–14.) (19) The pronoun in all these is a dative modification. (20) *Me seems* is equivalent to *it seems to me ; me listeth*, *or me lists*, to *it listeth to me.* (21) *Me thinks* is also equivalent to *it seems to me*, and *me thought* to *it seemed to me.*

NOTE.—This verb (*think*) is now obsolete in our language. It must not be confounded with the verb *think* now in use. In many of the northern dialects, and (what is most to our purpose) especially in the Anglo-Saxon,

(18) Enumerate certain obsolete forms of expression, which are to be explained by a reference to the ancient use of a dative case. (19) What is the pronoun in all these expressions? (20) What are *me seems* and *me listeth* equivalent to? (21) What is *me thinks* equivalent to; and *me thought* its past tense?

the parent language of the English, there were two verbs nearly alike in form, the one meaning the same with our now existing verb *to think*, the other nearly what we now express by the verb *seem*.

To think.	*To seem.*
Anglo-Saxon, thencean, thencan or thincan.	Thincan.
Past T. Thohte	Thuhte,
German. Denken, *P. T.* Dachte.	Dunken. *P. T.* Dünkt.

These two verbs became confounded in form at an early period in our language, if not sometimes in the later Anglo-Saxon; but the two distinct meanings were retained and recognised as distinct down to the middle of the seventeenth century, if not later. See Mr. R. Taylor's additional notes to the Diversions of Purley, and Dr. Latham's English Language.

We add a few examples in illustration of what has been said of these forms of expression from Mr. Taylor's judicious and learned notes, p. xxxi. "Thus Shakspeare:

Prince. Where shall we sojourne till our coronation?
Glo. Where *it thinks* best unto your royal self.
Richard the Third, act 3, sc. 1.

as it stands in the first copies, though since altered to *seems.*"

"'*Me seemeth* good that with some little traine
Forthwith from Ludlow the young prince be fetcht.'
Richard the Third, act. 2, sc. 2.

'Let him do what *seemeth him* good.'—1 *Sam.* iii. 18.
'*Him ought* not to be a tiraunt.'—*Leg. Good Wom.*, 429.
'The garden that so *likid me.*'—*Chauc. R. Rose*, l. 1312.

'So *it liked the emperor* to know which of his daughters loved him best.' —*Gesta Rom.*, ed. Swan, 1. lxxii., ch. 20.

'He should ask of the emperor what *him list.*'—*Ib.* lxxxv. 41.

'Well *me quemeth*,' (pleaseth) Chauc. Conf. Am. 68. Also our common expression, 'if you please;" where *you* is evidently not the nominative to the verb, but is governed by it, (complement to it,) q. d. 'If you it please;' yet by a singular perversion of the phrase, we say, 'I do not please,' 'If she should please,' for 'It does not please me,' 'It should please her.'

'*Stanley. Please it your majestie* to give me leave
I'le muster up my friends and meete your grace.
Where and what time your majestie *shall please.*
Richard the Third, act 4, sc. 4."

It will be seen from these examples that impersonal verbs (or verbs having a proposition or phrase for their subject) without the *representative it*, were once common in our language, and took generally *a dative* complement. See another example in Par. Lost, b. II., 942.

"*Behoves him* now both oar and sail"

There are many other *latent* datives in our language now commonly regarded as objectives, and as expressing the passive object of the verbs which they modify. But as these datives have no longer a distinct form, and follow verbs which do not take a second noun (without a preposition) after them, we have no ready means of detecting them and distinguishing them from accusatives. We cannot detect them by changing the order of arrangement as when the verb takes both a dative and accusative modification. For instance, the verb *obey*, when first introduced into the language, we presume, always, like the Latin and French words from which it is derived, took after it not a *direct*, but an *indirect* object—a dative, not an objective modification. To illustrate this we may give the following examples; "*To whom* your fathers would not *obey*."—Acts 7: 39. "His servants ye are *to whom* ye *obey*." These examples prove that the translators of the Bible considered the verb *obey*, susceptible, in their time, of a dative and not of an accusative modification, since they have evidently introduced the preposition *to* in these two places, lest *whom* should be taken for an objective modification.

Wiclif in his translation often uses the preposition *to* before the noun or pronoun which follows *obey*, showing that where the preposition is omitted the case is still a dative. For example, "And thei *obeien to him*."—Mark 1: 27. In the following example we have proof that both *command* and *obey* were in Wiclif's time followed by a dative, not by an objective construction. "He comaundith *to wyndis* and *to* the *see*, and thei obeien *to him*." We still say, *approach to a place*, as well as *approach a place*, *trust to a person or thing*, or *in a person or thing*, (the latter expression is very often used in the translation of the Scriptures,) as well as *trust a person*, *escape from a danger*, as well as, *escape a danger*. This shows that when the preposition is omitted, the noun after these verbs is a *dative*, and not an objective. There are several other verbs which take after them nouns without a preposition, and which nouns we now recognise as objectives, but which, it may be fairly presumed, were originally proper datives, and the verbs instead of being active or transitive, as we now consider them, were neuter verbs, and incapable of taking after them an objective modification. Such verbs are *oppose*, *serve*, *succeed*, *succour*, from the Latin, and *answer*, *bid*, *forbid*, *follow*, *forswear*, *withstand*, from the Anglo-Saxon, which in these languages are followed by datives. If no examples can be found of a preposition employed to attach nouns to these verbs, it should not surprise us, as we find nouns with the force of datives so often attached to active verbs without a preposition. We may add to the list above the verb *profit*, which in the times of Wiclif sometimes took after it a noun with the preposition *to*, thus proving that it was not regarded as *transitive*.—"And the worde that was herd profitide not to hem" (them).

From these remarks, the learned reader will discover that our language was originally more similar than it now seems to be to the Latin and Greek languages, in reference to a certain class of verbs which, in those languages, take after them always a dative modification. The class corresponding *in meaning* in English, seem very generally to have originally taken the same form of modification. The fact has been concealed by the gradual disappearance of a distinct dative form.

It requires much greater knowledge of the sources from which our language is derived, and of its early history, than can be expected in those who are engaged in the study of grammar, to detect these datives, which have come insensibly to be regarded as accusatives. Besides, they have been long recognised as standing to their verbs in the same relation as other accusatives, and the verbs have, consequently, come to be recognised, and are now employed, in all respects, as active verbs. They generally take a passive form, having for its *subject* the noun which follows and modifies their active form; and this is usually considered the test of a transitive verb.

We do not, therefore, intend to introduce any innovation in the practical analysis of propositions in which such verbs occur, though we have thought that it would contribute to a proper understanding of the *dative form of* modification in our language, to direct the attention of the curious reader to the facts now presented.

In reference to those datives which, together with an accusative, follow *active* verbs, the case is different. These datives cannot be analyzed as objective modifications; and when we must adopt a mode of treating them distinct from the objective modification, it is best, we think, to state the facts, in accordance with the real history of our language. We may as well admit the fact, that nouns and pronouns placed between the active verb and its objective modification, have the force of datives, without any reference to the suppression of the prepositions *to* or *for*.

We have also found ourselves obliged to recognise the dative, in treating the impersonals *Me seems*, *Me thinks*, &c., because this is necessary to the correct explanation of these antiquated expressions. There are some other impersonals generally preceded by the *representative word* IT, followed by nouns which had originally a dative force. Instances are found above, among the examples quoted from Mr. Taylor's notes; *please* is one.

The remarks which we have made on the dative, afford a key to the explanation of such expressions as "Woe is me!" and "Oh, wel is him."—*Sternhold* and *Hopkins*. *Me* and *him* are simply datives, not accusatives, as is commonly supposed through inattention to the fact, that one of these forms (him) was once used exclusively in the dative sense; and the other (me) used both in the dative and accusative sense. There are likely many other expressions which may be readily explained in the same manner. Perhaps *Ah me* is to be thus explained. The expression "Wo worth the day" (Ezekiel 30: 2), is also thus explained. *Worth* is a verb (meaning *to be, to become*) current in the Anglo-Saxon, and anciently used in English, and still in German; *day* stands as dative modification to this verb. The meaning is, *Woe be to the day.*—See Bishop Lowth's note, quoted below.

We find four examples of *worth*, with its dative modifications, in the following four lines of Chaucer:

> *Wo worth the faire gemme* vertulesse;
> *Wo worth the hearbe*, also, that doth no bote (*i. e.* help, remedy),
> *Wo worth the beauty* that is routhlesse (*i. e.* without compassion),
> *Wo worth that wight* that trede ech under fote.
>
> Troilus and Cres. ii. 344.

Here *gemme, hearbe, beauty, wight*, are all *datives* to *worth*, in their respective propositions=Woe be to the fair gem, &c.

It deserves to be remarked, as a curious fact in the history of the transition of words from their original meanings and construction, that *persuade* now takes after it an accusative of the person, and what is equivalent to a dative of the thing (that is, a noun preceded by the preposition *to*), though in Latin, both *suadeo* and *persuadeo* take the dative of the person and accusative of the thing; as, *persuasit id eis=He persuaded this to them. We* say, He persuaded them to this.

(22) There is another fact in relation to datives, placed between active verbs and their objective modification, which must not be forgotten, since it is essential to the explanation and correct analysis of certain forms of expression of frequent recurrence in our language. (23) The fact to which we refer is this, that those verbs which, actively employed, admit these datives followed by accusatives, when the expression assumes the passive form, often take what served as dative modification (or indirect object) in the active form for their *subject noun.* (24) To illustrate by an example; we say in the active form, *The porter refused him admittance*, and in the passive form, *Admittance was refused to him by the porter*, or using the dative without a connective, ADMITTANCE *was refused him.* Here we employ *regularly* (in conformity with the universally recognised laws of language) *admittance*, the objective in the active form for subject in the passive form. But we also very often (perhaps more frequently) say, HE *was refused admittance by the porter*, usurping the pronoun which served as dative in the active, for subject in the passive form of expression, contrary to

(22) Repeat the remark under No. (22). (23) State the fact referred to in the last remark. (24) Illustrate what has been said by an example. (25) What will the learner here observe?

the general analogies or laws of language. (25) Here the learner will observe, that the passive verb retains after it the objective modification, as happens with the passive forms of *teach* and *ask*, and some other verbs in the ancient languages, which, like these, take two *objective modifications* in the active form.*

(26) CAUTION.—Be careful not to confound with these verbs which take two OBJECTIVE *modifications*, those which take with the objective a *noun complementary*. It will be remembered that such *noun complementary*, though used after the passive verb, stands in a very differ-

* Some grammarians contend that these passive forms of expression, in which the indirect object of the active form serves as subject, are to be rejected as altogether improper and ungrammatical. There is, no doubt, a kind of irregularity in these passive forms. We have admitted this, in saying that they are contrary to the general analogies of language. They are rare in other languages, though not exclusively confined to English. But it is too late now to proscribe these forms as bad English. They are used by our best authors, and by the best speakers.

We suspect that this construction has originated in an *insensible extension* of the same usage to these verbs, followed by a dative and accusative, which at first perhaps extended only to verbs, followed by two accusatives. We can with propriety say, both *Grammar is taught*, and *The scholar is taught.* Hence we say with propriety in the passive, The scholar is taught grammar. And from such expressions as, The scholar is taught grammar, probably an insensible transition has been made to the usage in question, where as in the passive use of *teach*, the person affected by the action becomes the subject, in forgetfulness or disregard of the fact that this person does not stand in the same relation to the active verb—is not used as in the case of teach to express its direct object.

Whatever may have been the origin of this use, there is no doubt that it has now become a settled idiom of our language; and it is vain for the grammarian to attempt to eradicate it. *His business is to exhibit the language as it is, not to attempt to make it what he fancies it should be.* When a form of expression is not yet firmly established—universally received—in the language, but apparently making its way towards general usage, the grammarian may with propriety employ his efforts to suppress it, if it does not harmonize with the general laws of language, or if it in any way offends good taste. But what is once established, he had better, like a man of modesty and good sense, admit, and spend his efforts in accounting for its reception, in contravention of general principles, rather than in the Quixotic attempt to extirpate all the apparent anomalies of speech.

(26) Repeat the caution.

ent relation to the noun which serves as *objective* of the active, and subject of the passive form of proposition, varies its case as this noun varies its function, and never holds the relation of *objective* modification to a passive verb.

We subjoin a few examples for the purpose of illustrating these peculiar passive forms of expression, and also, incidentally, the use of the dative modification. These passives which take the indirect object for their subject are confined to a few verbs (exclusively, we believe, such as we have enumerated above) which take a personal or indirect object without a preposition between them and their objective modification. Even these are not all employed passively in the manner described. We present below the two active forms of expression made with each verb, the one *with*, the other *without* a preposition before the indirect object, and the two passive forms—one *regular* with the *passive object* for its subject, the other (we may call) *idiomatic*, with the *personal object* for its subject.

Act. with Preposition,	The minister *offered* a pension *to him.*
Act. without Prep.	The minister *offered him* a pension.
Pass. Regular,	A *pension* was *offered him*, or to him, by, &c.
Pass. Idiomatic,	*He was offered a pension*, by, &c.
Act. with Prep.,	He *promised* a *present to me.*
Act. without Prep.,	He promised *me* a *present.*
Pass. Regular,	A *present was promised me*, or *to me.*
Pass. Idiomatic,	*I was promised* a *present.*

To make the learner familiar with these constructions let him write a given number of propositions after the model exhibited above (exemplifying the two active and two passive forms), with the following verbs: allow, deny, pay, refuse, tell. Let him afterwards analyze his examples, or he may, when writing the propositions, accompany them with the abbreviations used in a written analysis.

When called on to analyze the idiomatic passive form, for example, *I was promised a present*, he will say, as in the analysis of the passives of *ask* and *teach*, that the verb *was promised* is modified by the objective noun *present.* If any question is made about a passive verb taking an objective modification, the learner may reply that, *The verbs* ALLOW, DENY, OFFER, PAY, REFUSE, TELL, *&c., taking after them a dative and objective modification, sometimes, when passively employed, take the dative or personal object, instead of the passive object for their subject, and retain the same objective modification as when actively employed.*

NOTE.—The grammarians have generally classed *ask* and *teach* with those verbs which take an accusative and dative to modify them. But we think that *ask* and *teach* differ widely from this class of verbs. *Ask* and *teach* dc not naturally take after them a noun with the preposition *to*, to express the person who is *asked* or *taught*. It is not, we think, in accordance with the general usage of the language to say, I ASKED *a question* TO HIM, or, *A question was asked* TO HIM. We do not say that such expressions are never employed; but we say that they are not so consistent with ancient and well received and respectable usage as to say, *I asked* HIM *a question*, or, *He was asked a* QUESTION. *I taught grammar* TO HIM, though perhaps sometimes used, appears to us, if not absolutely ungrammatical, at least, inconsistent with ancient and established usage, as well as clumsy. In the passive we always say, *He was taught grammar*, not *Grammar was taught to him*. The form of expression, *Grammar was taught him*, is perhaps awkward, but it appears to us less objectionable, than *Grammar was taught to him*.

In a word, the two nouns which follow *ask* and *teach*, are both to be regarded as accusatives, and the employment of these two accusatives after them, is to be accounted for perhaps in the manner attempted above (§ 78, Note); and these two verbs, as we have before said, form a peculiar class by themselves.

On the contrary, the verbs *allow, deny, offer*, &c., can always take after them in both active and passive forms, their personal object preceded by the preposition *to*, without violence to the sense; and when no preposition is used, and the *personal object* is placed before the passive object in the order of arrangement, the case is always to be considered a dative, never an accusative. For example in such expressions as, *John promised* HIM *assistance; Assistance was promised* HIM *by John*, HIM is a dative, never an accusative. Even when preceded by the preposition it was in the ancient language a dative; for the preposition *to* often preceded a dative, never an accusative. But this belongs to another place.

The fact, that we have retained in so many instances the dative *use* in our language after the dative *form* had disappeared, seems to have escaped the notice of most of our grammarians, and hence their analysis of certain constructions is far from satisfactory. Bishop Lowth suggests in a note that when personal pronouns without a preposition or intermediary, are used to express the personal object after a verb, they may possibly be datives. Dr. Latham has brought the dative use of the pronouns, and the fact that the forms now called objective or accusative cases, all served anciently as datives, prominently to view. But as far as I recollect, he has not noticed that nouns under the same circumstances serve as datives, viz., when the noun expressing the personal object is placed next the verb, and before the accusative. We transcribe the chief part of Dr. Lowth's note, as it both sanctions and illustrates the view we have given of this construction. The reader will notice that we have used some of his examples already.

The note is appended to an observation, contradicted by his better judgment expressed in the note. The observation is repeated by every genera-tion of his followers, to the neglect of his valuable and well supported suggestion in the note. *The best things of Dr. Lowth are not those which have been most freely appropriated by some of his followers.* The observation is as follows: "The prepositions *to* and *for* are often understood, chiefly before the pronoun; as, 'Give me the book; get me some paper;' that is, *to me, for me.*"

NOTE.—"Or in these and the like phrases, may not *me, thee, him, her, us,* which in Saxon are the dative cases of their respective pronouns, be considered as still continuing such in the English, and including in their very form the force of the prepositions *to* and *for?* There are certainly some other phrases, which are to be resolved in this manner: 'Wo is *me!*' The phrase is pure Saxon, 'Wa is me:' me is the dative case; in English, with the preposition, *to me.* So, '*methinks:*' Saxon, '*methincth:*' ἐμοι δοκεῖ. 'As *us thoughte.*'—Sir John Maundevylle. 'The Lord do that which *seemeth him* good.'—2 Sam. x. 12. 'Well is *him,* that dwelleth with a wife of understanding.' 'Well is *him,* that hath found prudence.'—Ecclus. xxv. 8, 9. 'Wo worth the day!' Ezek. xxx. 2, that is, 'Wo be *to* the day.' The word *worth* is not the adjective, but the Saxon verb *weorthan,* or *worthan, fieri, to be, to become,* which is often used by Chaucer, and is still retained as an auxiliary verb in the German language."—Intro. to Eng. Gram., pp. 169, 170, ed. 1778.

§ 80. [ORDER OF SEQUENCE OF MODIFICATIONS OR COMPLEMENTS.—Before dismissing this subject of modifying nouns attached to verbs and nouns without the intervention of other words, it may be useful to say something about the order of *sequence* of different forms of *modifications* or *complements.* We have already touched this subject incidentally, but it is proper to invite the attention of the student more directly to a subject of such importance to a satisfactory knowledge of the structure of language.

We have noticed, as we proceeded, the *sequence in order of arrangement* of the several modifications which we have treated. (2) To recapitulate, the *noun in apposition* generally follows the *principal* noun; the *noun adjectively* employed precedes it; the *noun complementary* of the *neuter verb* follows the verb; the *genitive case modification* precedes the principal noun; the *objective modification* usually follows the verb, and comes next to it, except there is a *dative modification,* in which case this latter takes precedence; when there is an *objective* and a *noun complementary* after an active verb, the objective regularly takes precedence of the complementary noun.

---

§ 80. [(1) What is meant by the Order of Sequence of Modifications? Ans. The ***order*** in which modifications follow the *principal* word. (2) Recapitulate what has been said in reference to the order of *sequence* of the several modifications already treated.

But another question presents itself in reference to the *sequence* of modifications, or the manner in which *modifications* or *complements* follow each other—a question of the greatest importance in the investigation of the structure of language, and one to which our ordinary grammarians have unfortunately paid little or no attention. Indeed, the imperfect, clumsy, irregular, unsatisfactory mode of grammatical analysis hitherto generally adopted tends to hide this question from the student of grammar. (3) The question to which we allude is this; when two or more modifying words are attached to a *principal* word, which has the precedence *in sense* or which is most intimately connected *in sense* with the principal word? (4) Before we enter on the direct examination of this question, it is important to remark, that when two or more complements of different kinds are attached to the same principal word, they are not attached to it separately and independently of each other, with no reference to any thing but the principal word. (5) On the contrary, the complement most intimately connected in sense with the principal word, and the principal word, bound together as one compound expression, are both completed by the complement which follows in the order of *sense.* (6) Next, it will be remarked, that the question about the order of sense or meaning is not the same with that in reference to the order of arrangement. In other words, the order of arrangement in speaking and the order of *sense*—of *thought*—do not always coincide. (7) In fact, as regards the instances of two modifications of *distinct kinds* attached to the same *principal* word which we have been examining, the order of *thought* and the order of the *arrangement of the words* most commonly differ. We have already called attention to this fact in the note upon the modifications which follow the verb *teach.*

(8) To return to the original question; let us take an example first of the construction in which the active verb is followed by an *objective modification* and by a *noun complementary.* (9) *The Senate declared Cincinnatus Dictator.* (10) Here the question is, which of the two nouns, *Cincinnatus* and *Dictator*, used to modify the verb *declared*, has the more intimate connection with it, or which, taken in connection with the verb, is further modified by the other. (11) This question we already answered in giving the name *complementary*

(3) State the question which now presents itself for consideration. (4) Repeat the preliminary remark. (5) Complete the remark in reference to the most intimate complement and principal word, &c. (6) Repeat the remark about the order of *sense* and the order of arrangement. Express the remark in other words. (7) What in fact happens in the modifications already considered in reference to this matter?

(8) Of what construction do we first select an example? (9) Repeat the example. (10) What question is raised in reference to the example? (11) Where has this been already

to nouns performing functions similar to those of the word *Dictator* in the above proposition. (12) The *complementary noun* has the more intimate connection with the verb; it *completes* the expression of the action performed by the senate, which *complete action* is limited, by adding the word *Cincinnatus*, to the person bearing that name. (13) In other words, the action *declaring Dictator* is restricted to *Cincinnatus*, and not the action of *declaring* alone, *unmodified*, limited to *Cincinnatus*, nor the action of *declaring Cincinnatus* restricted by *Dictator*.

(14) Again the same question recurs, when we employ both an objective and a dative modification after a verb, which of these two modifications is most intimately, most directly, or first in *sense* connected with the verb—the *accusative* or the *dative?* For example—*The instructor gave him a book.* (15) Here it is manifest that the *objective modification*, BOOK, comes first in *sense*, though it stands last in the order of arrangement. It is not *gave* alone, but *gave a book*, that is *restricted*, *limited*, or, to use the more *general* term, *modified* by the *dative* HIM. (16) It is perfectly obvious, when the same function is performed by the word *him*, preceded by the preposition *to*, that the *objective modification* comes first in the *sequence of sense*, as it then does, also, in the order of arrangement; *The instructor gave a book* TO HIM; here *gave a book* is limited by *to him*. (17) So, also, in reference to all *noun and preposition modifications* (or adjuncts, as some call them—a name perhaps too vague, but very convenient on account of its shortness) following active verbs with objective modifications. First, as regards sense, the verb is modified by the objective, and then the compound expression, made up of the verb and the *objective noun*, is modified by the *noun with a preposition*.

(18) So far, then, as regards those forms of modification of the verb already considered, the regular *sequence* in reference to *sense* is, that the *complementary noun*, when there is one in the construction, has the closest connection with the verb, and the expression formed by the verb and it comes under the influence of the modifications superadded. The objective noun comes next in the order of *sense*, and all

---

answered? (12) Repeat the answer. (13) Repeat the latter part of the answer in other words.

(14) State the question of sequence in application to the *objective* and *dative* modifications; and furnish example. (15) Which of these modifications comes first in sense? Illustrate by example. (16) Illustrate by the case in which the dative function is performed by the pronoun preceded by the particle *to*. (17) How is it in reference to the sequence of the noun and preposition and objective modifications?

(18) Repeat what is said by way of recapitulation.

other forms of modification, such as datives and nouns with prepositions, &c., affect the expression made up of the verb and objective noun; or, in case there is present a complementary noun as well as an objective noun, affect the expression made up of the verb, the complementary noun, and the objective noun.

(19) We shall be able hereafter, without difficulty or tedious explanation, to apply these remarks in noticing the *sequence* of the several forms of modification which remain to be treated. For the same order of sense may be traced, and ought to be carefully traced, in all cases, not only when we attach modifications consisting of single words or phrases, but also when we employ *accessory* propositions to modify the *subject* or *predicate* of the *principal proposition.*

(20) Such is the mode in which the most complicated propositions are built up—such is their *structure* or CONSTRUCTION. We lay the foundation with the SUBJECT NOUN and the VERB. To each of these we add the first complements necessary to qualify them (to express more exactly our meaning); and to what we have thus constructed, still other complements, one after another, till we have completed the intended structure; just as in erecting a house, we commence with the foundation, and add stone after stone, not to the foundation alone, but to the part of the structure already raised, till the whole is finished.*

* The same order it is our wish to introduce in the ANALYSIS of language. We endeavor to follow in the resolution of every proposition the order of thought pursued in the construction of the proposition. The method we adopt is thus designed to be at once *analytic* and *synthetic*, or *constructive.* By this method, the learner is made familiar with the art of building up sentences, and not merely taught to take up the *disjecta membra*—the scattered fragments of the structure—without a proper regard to their place in the building. In other words, we examine the parts of the building regarded as a *structure* standing in all its just proportions, and not the *mass* of *unconnected* ruins which results from its violent demolition.

We think that this plan is much better calculated to guide the young student to the correct construction of sentences, to cultivate a nice perception of the defects of ill-constructed sentences, and to prepare him to amend with ease and promptitude any imperfection which he may detect. The plan pursued is intended to make him, if natural good taste is not wanting, an accomplished architect of that curious and complicated, and beautiful and most useful structure—LANGUAGE.

(19) Repeat the substance of the remark under No. 19.
(20) The same of No. 20.

(21) We must not, however, be understood as asserting that every modification is added to the whole structure already laid. (22) Often, as we shall presently see, a principal word is affected by two or more *co-ordinate* modifications or complements, sometimes with a connective indicating *co-ordination* between them; both standing in the same relation to the *principal* word, but entirely independent of each other's influence, and not, as in the examples above noticed, the modification last applied affecting the *principal* word, as already *modified* by the other.]

We have now enumerated and considered all the *modifications* (so far as we know) which consist of a noun *separately* employed, whether in its original or in its inflected forms, with the exception of a few modifications, which we purposely reserve, till in the next section we have prepared the way for their easier explanation. We next proceed to treat of a class of modifications which consist of a noun in connection with another word *essential* to the *form* of modification.*

* We mean "another word" which is not a mere modification of the *modifying* word. A word modifying a noun, used itself as a modification, is of common occurrence in the structure of language, but this word is not essential to the *form* of the modification into which it enters. It has simply a modifying word for its *principal.* Take as an example the following proposition, *John killed the shepherd's dog.* Here "*dog,*" the objective modification of "*killed,*" is itself modified by the genitive "*shepherd's.*" But this is not essential to the form of modification which we call *objective.* The learner is already prepared to treat such constructions, as he has been informed that the modifications of which nouns are susceptible, are applicable to them, not only in their function as *subjects*, but in all their functions. But when, on the contrary, we employ a *noun and preposition* to modify a word, the preposition is *essential* to the *form,* and cannot be treated as a modification of the noun. Some consider the noun a complement of the preposition. We rather consider (as will appear below) the noun following the preposition as a complement of the *principal* word, after being *first* modified by the preposition.

(21) Repeat the caution given under No 21. (22) Illustrate the caution.]

CHAPTER V.

OF PREPOSITIONS.

§ 81. (1) Our attention has been hitherto, almost exclusively, confined to the two great classes of words which form the fundamental parts of every proposition—the *verb* and the *noun*—the *noun* employed as *subject noun*, and the noun employed in the several *ministering* functions which it performs, *without the aid of other words*, in modifying both verbs and nouns.

(2) We now introduce a third class of words employed exclusively for the purpose of modification, called by grammarians PREPOSITIONS. (3) This Latin name *preposition*, indicates *what is placed before.* (4) It has been given to this class of words because, at least in one of their functions, they are *placed* (in Latin almost always, and very generally in other languages) *before* the noun which, with them, forms a *complex* modification of some *principal* word. (5) This name can scarcely be defended as *appropriate*, since it does not apply to this class of words in all the functions which they perform in language, nor even universally in a single function; but as it has obtained the sanction of long and general usage, we shall be contented to employ it.

(6) As the prepositions are comparatively few in number, we subjoin a list of the words generally recognised as belonging to this class, that the learner may have it under his eye in following our remarks. It would, perhaps, save time and labor in his future studies in *grammatical analysis* to commit this short list of words carefully to memory.

---

§ 81. (1) Repeat the substance of the introductory remark.

(2) What new class of words is now introduced? (3) What does the name preposition indicate? (4) Why has this name been given to the words of this class? (5) Can the name be defended as perfectly appropriate, and why not?

(6) What reason is assigned for giving a list of prepositions?

(7) A LIST OF THE WORDS GENERALLY CLASSED AS PREPOSITIONS.

A-bout, A-bove, A-cross, After, Against, A-long, A-mid, A-midst, A-mong, A-mongst, A-round, At, A-thwart, Be-fore, Be-hind, Be-low, Be-neath, Be-side, Be-sides, Be-tween, Be-twixt, Be-yond, By, Down, For, From, In, In-to, Of, Off, On, Over, Round, Since, Through, Through-out, Till, To, To-ward, To-wards, Under, Under-neath, Un-til, Un-to, Up, Up-on, With, With-in, With-out.

(8) We may add to these *a*, a corruption of *on*, *in*, *un*, sometimes of *of;* and *o'* still used before the noun clock (and formerly before other nouns) as equivalent to *of*, or, perhaps, sometimes *on*, and pronounced nearly like *a*, the preposition. *On* and *in* are equivalent in Anglo-Saxon, or, perhaps, rather *in* is merely a variation of *on.**

---

* We have omitted in the list above several words commonly classed with the prepositions, but which, manifestly, belong to classes of words whose functions are better defined, and more easily comprehended. The prepositions have been a source of much perplexity to the grammarians, and the inconsistencies and absurdities with which even learned and philosophical authors are chargeable in reference to them, have brought reproach on the science of grammar. We therefore adopt the principle of classing no word with them that can claim a place elsewhere. The words which we have excluded are *except* and *save*, obviously the imperatives of the verbs *except* and *save*, and capable of being always treated as such; *concerning, excepting, regarding, respecting, touching*, which are participles taking an *objective modification; during, notwithstanding*, accompanying a noun in the *case absolute*, not followed by an objective, as the grammarians erroneously represent; and *near, nigh, next*, which are adjectives taking after them, not an accusative, but a dative case, in the same manner as the adjective *like, unlike*, &c. *Round* should, perhaps, also be excluded; but as it occurs in constructions that could not be easily analyzed if *round* is simply considered as performing the functions of either an adjective or a noun, we have thought it best to retain it. *But* is also classed here as well as with the conjunctions. We doubt whether the accusatives which sometimes follow *but*, are not always really the objective modifications of a verb suppressed. If so, *but* is in such cases, as elsewhere, a conjunction. That a word not of the class of verbs takes after it an accusative (the grammarian knows not why), is ample reason to place it among the vexatious prepositions. Doing so is always, we presume, to be taken as a confession of ignorance.

---

(7) Repeat the list of prepositions; first the simple prepositions, and afterwards the compound marked by a hyphen (-).

(8) Repeat the remarks made in reference to the prepositions *a* and *o'*.

[(9) The words enumerated above perform three distinct functions in our language. (10) We do not mean that each of them severally performs these three functions, but that there are three functions performed by the class taken together; of these functions some perform perhaps but one, some two, and some, again, all three.

(11) 1st. Many of them, together with certain other words never used *separately*, and therefore called *inseparable prepositions*, are used in forming compound words. (12) They are prefixed to verbs, nouns, adjectives, and to other prepositions, and in this case generally modify the signification of these words. (13) We have examples in *down-fall*, *for-give*, *in-still*, *off-spring*, *on-set*, *over-flow*, *under-stand*, *up-hold*, *with-draw*, &c., and in several of the prepositions in the list above, of which the component parts are separated by a hyphen. (14) It will be observed that many of the above list are compounds of *a*, contracted or corrupted from *on*, and *be*, another form of *by* united with other words, generally nouns or adjectives; as, *a-cross*, *a-long*, *a-midst*, *a-round*, *be-hind*, *be-side*, &c.*

(15) 2d. Some of these prepositions are employed alone, and as separate words to modify verbs. (16) (In this case some say that the preposition is used *adverbially*.) (17) We have examples in such expressions as *Keep* OFF, equivalent to *Keep at a distance; Come* ON; *He walks or rides* ABOUT; *Cast up accounts;* "*I keep under my body.*"

NOTE.—In the last two examples, and especially in the last, it cannot be alleged that the preposition connects the nouns *accounts* and *body* with the verbs, or unites with those nouns in forming a compound modification in the manner about to be described under the next function of this class of words. *Under* is certainly not, as in the case we are about to describe, a

* In fact, when we have removed all the compounds formed by the union of a preposition with words of other classes, and by the union of two prepositions from the list presented above, the number remaining is very small. We have rendered the distinction between the simple and compound prepositions visible to the eye of the learner, by separating the component parts of those certainly known to be compound by a hyphen.

[(9) How many distinct functions do these words perform? (10) Repeat the remark in reference to their performance of these functions.

(11) What is the first-mentioned use of these words, and what other words are employed for a similar purpose? (12) To what kind of words are they prefixed to form compounds? (13) Illustrate by examples. (14) Repeat the remark about compound prepositions.

(15) Describe the second way in which these words are employed. (16) What is this use of a preposition commonly called? (17) Illustrate by examples.

modification coming in the order of *sense* between *keep* and *body;* but *body* is either the objective modification of *keep under*, regarded as a compound verb, or else the expression, *keep my body,* is farther modified by *under* = *to keep my body under.* The first is perhaps the correct view of the subject. In this case all the difference between this form of function and the first is, that in the first the preposition is placed before and unites with the verb in forming a *compound word,* in the last the preposition remains a separate word and comes after the verb. In this latter use of prepositions, our language resembles the German. This language throws much light on the subject before us, since it affords numerous examples of compounds of this kind, in which the preposition in certain constructions is connected with the verb, as in No. 1st above; in other constructions it is detached from the verb, and frequently appears after several modifications at the close of the proposition. When employed in this way after verbs, and not followed by a noun, the grammarians generally call these words *adverbs.* We think it is more consistent, more convenient, and attended with less perplexity to the learner, to give them always the same name, since in the distinct functions which they perform, they retain the same sense, and since a part of them must be recognised as prepositions, because, as we have shown elsewhere, they render the verb to which they are subjoined transitive, and capable of assuming a passive form. Thus we say, *I look upon him,* and *This man is looked* upon; *look,* which is *intransitive* without the preposition, becoming *transitive* and capable of being employed passively, when the preposition *upon* is added to it.

If we should feel inclined to deviate from the practice of calling these words invariably by the same name, it would be to distinguish those occasions when some of them perform the function of conjunctions. Even this function differs in their case little from their most conspicuous function, that which we arrange third and last in order. In the one case, they are used in connection with a noun to modify a verb, in the other with a proposition instead of a noun to serve the same purpose. It is only necessary, therefore, when we treat of conjunctions, to remark that some of the prepositions are employed to perform similar functions.

(18) 3d. We now come to the third function which these words perform; when united with a noun they serve as a modification to a verb, or to another noun, sometimes, as we shall see hereafter, to an adjective. (19) This use is common to all these words, and is that from which their name is derived, because they are most commonly *placed before* the accompanying noun. It is the use chiefly regarded in our treatises on grammar, the only use recognised in much that is taught concerning these words.

(18) What is the third function which these words perform? (19) Repeat what is said in reference to this function.

(20) A preposition and noun thus employed, we shall call the NOUN and PREPOSITION *modification* or complement.* (21) This form when applied to a noun we may call *noun and preposition* modn. of a *noun;* and when applied to a *verb*, *noun and preposition* modn. of a *verb.* (22) We believe that all the words in our list of prepositions may be employed in company with nouns in forming modifications for verbs; but some of them cannot be so employed in forming modifications of nouns.†

(23) The preposition most frequently employed in forming a modification of nouns is *of*. (24) This preposition, followed by a noun, expresses nearly the same meaning as the genitive case modification, already considered. Thus, *The hopes of man*, and *Man's hopes*, are equivalent expressions. So of *The reward of virtue*, and *Virtue's reward*, &c.

* We are strongly tempted to borrow from some of our predecessors the name *adjunct* for this species of modification, because of its brevity. The name, however, seems too vague, and equally applicable to some other complements. We suggest it as a substitute to those who may chance to prefer it to our more drawling, but more completely descriptive name—a name which conveys nearly all that has been said to the purpose about this form of modification, embracing merely facts, without leaning on any theory of the functions of these words—true or false. We regard this for the present as a *compound* modification, consisting of a preposition and a noun, and we enter not here into the controversy about the nature, origin, or use of the preposition.

† Even when apparently employed after nouns, this form of modification is supposed by some of the grammarians, perhaps not without reason, to modify not the noun directly, but a verb or adjective suppressed. Thus, in the phrases, *The house above, before, behind, below, beneath, beside,* &c., *the church, situated,* or some similar word is supposed to be suppressed. It might also be suspected that *of* is suppressed *after* these prepositions, as well as *situated before* them. If so the phrase, *The house beside the church* = *The house by the side of the church.* In this manner all the compounds beginning with *be*, as *before, below,* &c., and all the compounds beginning with *a*, might be dismissed from the list, and the number of these words about which any mystery remains, be greatly reduced. But it is not necessary to trouble the learner in the early stage of his grammatical studies with these speculations.

(20) What name do we give to this form of modification? (21) What distinction in reference to the kind of words to which this modification is applied? (22) Repeat the remark under No. (22).

(23) Which preposition is most frequently employed in forming a modification of nouns? (24) Repeat what is said of the modification made with *of*, and illustrate by an example.

(25) REMARK.—Sometimes two prepositions are employed together in forming this kind of modification, as, *He came from beyond the river; out of, from within, from without, over against, down from, down to,* &c., are employed in this way. Perhaps in *down from*, and *down to*, *down* should be considered as employed in the second function, and only *from* and *to* as employed in the third.*

(26) The preposition *a* in its separate state is chiefly employed before the *verbal nouns* in ING. Thus used it is we believe a corruption of *on*, or *in*. We have had occasion to notice this form of expression in treating of the verbs. (See § 64.)

(27) In analysis, when a preposition occurs in the first function no remark is necessary, as the compound into which it enters as a part is treated as a single word. (28) When the preposition in the second function (separate from the verb) occurs, we call it simply the *preposition modification*, and say in analysis that the verb is modified by such a preposition, naming it. Some call all prepositions thus used adverbs. It would be less objectionable, perhaps, to call them prepositions adverbially employed. (29) When the *noun* preceded by the preposition occurs, we say in analysis that the *principal noun* or *verb*, as it may chance to be, is modified by the *noun* and *preposition*, repeating the preposition and noun employed.

In written exercises the learner may employ the following abbreviations: *Prep.* for preposition, *Prep. Modn.* for preposition modification, and *N.* and *Prep. Modn.* for noun and preposition modification.]

(30) The noun which enters into this form of modification is always considered as in the accusative case. (31) When pronouns which possess a distinct accusative form enter into this modification,

* All these examples of double prepositions, may be used with good effect to prove that these words express an independent sense, and not a mere relation between other words. See additional remarks on the prepositions.

(25) Repeat the *remark* and illustrate by examples.

(26) Repeat what is said in reference to the preposition *a*.

(27) What is said in reference to the analysis when the preposition in its first function occurs? (28) How do we treat the preposition in analysis when we find it in the second function? (29) How do we conduct the analysis when it occurs in its third function—followed by a noun?]

(30) In what case is the noun which follows the preposition always considered to be?

(31) Repeat what is said of pronouns following prepositions, and illustrate by examples.

it is always their accusative form which is employed. Examples, *from me*, *to us*, *towards thee*, *beyond him*, *beside her*, *among them*, &c.*

In reference to this point the learner may, for convenience, adopt the following rule.—(32) Rule. In the *noun and preposition modification*, the noun or pronoun is in the accusative case.

[(33) As regards the order of arrangement, other forms of modification occurring in the same proposition almost invariably take the precedence of the *noun and preposition*, when the modifications follow the *principal* word. (34) Sometimes the noun and preposition, especially when they express a *circumstance* of *time*, *place*, *order*, &c., are placed in the beginning of the proposition, the *subject* standing between them and the verb which is modified. (35) When they follow the verb in company with the simple modifications, such as the

* In the ancient language (the Anglo-Saxon) other cases besides the accusative were used in connection with prepositions. Some prepositions were followed always by the accusative of their accompanying noun, others by a dative, and still others by a genitive. Sometimes the same preposition was followed by one or other of these cases, according to the nature of the assertion which it and the noun served to complete. The genitive, we believe, was never much employed after prepositions—and in the most ancient times only after a few of these words. At all events, the use of this case with prepositions has long since entirely ceased in our language. And, as we have no distinct forms for either the dative or accusative in nouns, and, as there is now but one form of the pronouns for the dative and accusative, all difference among the prepositions in reference to the case of the word which accompanies them, is completely concealed in the English of the present day. It often happens that the form of a pronoun which follows a preposition is, strictly speaking, a dative, not an accusative. But there is no practical use in compelling the learner to tell what case each preposition took after it seven centuries ago, or in requiring him to distinguish when the case which now follows them ought to be considered a dative, and when an accusative. The distinction between the two cases, even in the pronouns, has been long consigned to oblivion. And it is only as a historical fact, or when, as in reference to the dative modification, it throws light on the construction of the language, that it is useful to revive it.

(32) Repeat Rule.

[(33) Repeat what is said in reference to the order of arrangement. (34) Repeat the substance of what is said under No. 34. (35) What is said of the noun and preposition when they follow the verb?

objective or *dative modifications*, the objective and dative, being more closely connected in sense with the verb, are arranged nearer to it than the *noun and preposition*.*

(36) As regards the order of sense, the *principal* word already modified by the more *intimate* complements, is farther modified by the noun and preposition. (37) For example, *John's friend sent him a present on Tuesday*. Here the verb *sent* modified by the accusative *present*, and dative *him*, is farther modified by the noun and preposition *on Tuesday*, expressing a circumstance of time less closely connected with the action—less essential to the assertion than the objective and dative complements. The whole assertion, *sent him a present*, is modified by the words *on Tuesday*.

(38) Often a *principal word*—especially a verb—is affected by several *noun and preposition* modifications. (39) When one of these modifications is more closely connected in sense with the *principal* word than the rest, it ought to be arranged nearest to it. For example, *He dined with his friends before his departure*. (40) If we change the arrangement of the modifications in this proposition, we change the sense, or render the assertion ambiguous. (41) In many cases, modifications of this kind have a connection with the *principal* word independent of each other, and sometimes it might be difficult to decide which has the closest connection in sense. (42) In such cases there is room for the exercise of taste in arrangement. (43) In propositions where several of these modifications occur, there is often an order de-

* Another reason besides the connection in sense, might be assigned for this order of arrangement. In our language, it is only by arrangement—by placing nouns immediately after the verbs which they modify—that we can clearly indicate our intention that they shall perform the functions of objective and dative complements. On the contrary, the noun and preposition together, wherever placed, express a definite function, and therefore admit more latitude of choice in regard of arrangement. In languages, which, like the Latin, have distinct forms for the accusative and dative cases, even a greater latitude of arrangement of objective and dative modifications is allowed, than with us in respect to the *noun* with the *preposition*.

---

(36) What is said in reference to the order of sense? (37) Give examples and illustration.

(38) Repeat the remark about a principal word? (39) When more than one of these *noun and preposition modifications* are applied to the same word, how are they to be arranged? Give example. (40) What happens if we change the arrangement? (41) Repeat what is said of independent modifications of this class. (42) What remark is made in reference to the arrangement in such cases? (43) Continue the remark. (44) Repeat what is said about attention to the arrangement of this kind of modifications and of adverbs.

cidedly preferable, as bringing out more clearly the exact meaning intended by the writer or speaker; and good sense and good taste are to be employed in discovering this order in each particular case. (44) To the degree of attention paid to the arrangement of this kind of modification, and of adverbs, and accessory propositions, the chief difference between a perspicuous and a confused writer, between a good and a bad style, may generally be traced.

(45) REMARK.—When two or more nouns in connection with the same preposition are employed to modify a *principal* word, the preposition is generally expressed only with the first noun, and suppressed before the other nouns, as the mind of the reader or hearer can readily supply it. Thus we say, *A man of intelligence and integrity*, equivalent to *A man of intelligence and* OF *integrity;* the second OF being suppressed by *ellipsis*, as it is called. *That gentleman travelled through France, Germany, Switzerland, Italy and Spain;* instead of *through France,* THROUGH *Germany,* THROUGH *Switzerland,* &c. Good taste must determine when such suppressions ought, or ought not, to be admitted.]

EXAMPLES FOR ANALYSIS.—*John travelled from London to Edinburgh by railroad. I sent him letters by* the *packet on Wednesday. I gave him letters to* my *brother in* the *country.** *In* the *beginning God created* the *heavens.* The *man of benevolence receives* the *reward of* his virtuous *acts, in* this *world* and the *world to come.* (*To come*, infinitive modification of noun *world.* See § 71.) "The *fear of* the *Lord is* the *beginning of knowledge.*" "*Remember* now thy *Creator in* the *days of* thy *youth.*"

---

* The learner will please take notice that the noun and preposition *in country* are not a second modification of the verb *sent*, but modify the noun *brother.* The verb *gave* stands in the relation of *principal* to the words *him, letters, to brother;* but *brother*—itself a modifying word—stands in the relation of *principal* to *in the country.* These distinctions cannot be too carefully observed. In tracing them, the student is tracing the connection of thought, through the connection of the signs of thought. He is learning to think accurately, to develop accurately the meaning of the writing subjected to his analysis. All properly conducted analysis exhibits the sense of a passage, so far as that is determined by the *construction* of language. That analysis or *parsing* which does not effect this is mere pedantic *gibberish.*

---

(45) Repeat the remark in reference to two or more nouns preceded by the same preposition. Illustrate by examples.]

"*On eagle-pinions borne*,
(The *muse*) *Attempted through* the *summer-blaze to rise;*
Then *swept o'er autumn with* the shadowy *gale;*
And now *among* the wintry *clouds* again,
Roll'd in the doubling *storm she tries to soar;*
To swell her *note with* all the rushing *winds;*
To suit her sounding *cadence to* the *floods*."
Thom. Win., l. 20.

"Borne," 1st line, a participle modified by "on eagle-pinions;" the same remark applies to roll'd. Several infinitives occur in these lines modified by nouns and prepositions. For "eagle-pinions" and "summer-blaze," see § 70. *O'er* in the third line is a contraction for *over*.

The learner is expected to analyze, as usual, all the words in Italics.

Let the learner now form a given number of propositions, containing one or more prepositions, followed by nouns or a pronoun. Let this exercise be repeated till he becomes well acquainted with all the prepositions in the list; and let him have credit according to the dexterity shown in introducing as many as possible of the modifications already considered in each proposition which he forms.

REMARK.—Cases sometimes occur in which a preposition is manifestly suppressed; as, *Go your way*, *Speed your course*, *He travels the same road*. *On* is here suppressed. We say to *ride a horse* and to *ride on a horse*. The first is, we believe, the most usual construction. Perhaps *ride* in this case should be considered an active verb, since we can use a passive form, and say, *The horse was ridden to death*. He resides in Bond street, No. 25. It is customary to suppress the preposition *at* in such cases.

§ 82. ADDITIONAL REMARKS ON THE PREPOSITIONS.—It is now, we believe, generally admitted by those best qualified to express an opinion on the subject, that prepositions are not an originally distinct class of words. (The same may be said of the conjunctions and the adverbs.) We regard prepositions as a *collection* (rather than a class) into which grammarians *throw* such words as take after them (to form a complement) a noun in an oblique case (that is, a case used exclusively for the purpose of expressing certain modifications)—words, too, which have lost, through the lapse of time, the marks of their descent and of their original use, as primary parts of speech, but which most likely may have been, as many philologists contend, all, or nearly all, at one time verbs or nouns. The fact that they all, when a noun is united with them in forming a complement, require that it should be in an oblique case, distinguishes them from adverbs and conjunctions. This is, in fact, their great distinguishing mark. This unfortunate collection of words has suffered very harsh and unjust usage from the hands of some of the grammarians. It has been commonly said that they express no meaning without the help of another word. Mr. Harris goes farther. "A preposition," says he, "is a part of speech, devoid itself of signification; but so formed as to unite two words that are significant, and that refuse to coalesce or unite of themselves." This absurd assertion has been abundantly exposed by Horne Tooke, in his usual acrimonious manner. The common definition still given of these words is that they "serve to connect words with one another, and to show the relation between them." We doubt the correctness of both these assertions. In performing the first two functions mentioned above, they do not connect words, and cannot show a relation between them. And yet in these functions, at least in the first, all grammarians have recognised them as still prepositions. In the second, some consider them adverbs. But if in the first use they admit that they are still prepositions, we do not see how they can consistently refuse to admit their claim to be such in the second use. Though in the third use they come between the noun, which with them forms a complement, and the word modified, and may perhaps be regarded as thus forming a sort of bond of connection between them, we doubt whether they are thus placed to serve this purpose, and whether they can with propriety be called *connectives* on this account.

As to the second assertion in the common definition of prepositions, that they show the relation between the words which they connect, it cannot, as we have already said, apply to these words when employed in the first and second functions described above; and even when employed in the third function, we think it would be difficult to prove satisfactorily that they *always* or *generally* show the relation or a relation between the *principal* word and the noun which follows them. That the preposition and the noun *together*, which follow a verb, very often express the relation of its action to place, time, &c., we admit. But this is very different from saying that the preposition expresses (and only expresses, in addition to its *connective* force) a relation between the action of the verb and what is expressed by the following noun. Let us try examples: *The man stood in the house—on the house—over the house—within the house—out of the house—before the house—behind the house*, &c. *He went along the street—up the street—down the street*, &c. Now we doubt the propriety of saying that the several prepositions in these examples merely connect *house* and *stood* and *went* and *street*, and show the *relation* between the action of *standing* and the *house*, and the action of *going* and the *street*. A man ought to be able to give a reason for *doubting*, as well as for believing. We give our reason, and, though the subject is abstruse, we hope to exhibit it in an intelligible form. Let us select any one of these prepositions which happens to be used with a verb without a noun following, or with a verb or other word in forming a compound—*down*, for example. Now if this word in the example above, expresses merely a relation between the action of *going* and the *street*, we are at a loss to tell what it expresses in the phrase *come down*, or in the compound *downfall*. It has in all three cases plainly the same significance. Shall we say, that in all it expresses merely a relation? And if so, a relation of what? We know that the term *relation* is sometimes so vaguely used, that it may mean almost any thing, and thus serve conveniently to cover a large amount of ignorance, under an appearance of profound knowledge. For our part, we are willing to admit the imperfection of our knowledge of this troublesome class of words; we are willing to receive sound information in reference to them. But so far as we know, we are inclined for the present to hold that each of them is a word significant of something that cannot with propriety be called a mere *relation*.

Our impression is, that the *principal* word (whether verb or noun) is really modified by the preposition first, and then the *principal* word and *preposition together* are modified by the noun after the preposition. To illustrate, by reference to a verb used as the *principal word:* the *action* of the verb receives a particular *direction* (we know not well what to call it, so as to embrace all cases—direction suits most cases) in *reference to place, time*, &c., from the preposition, and thus modified, thus *directed*, takes a noun to complete it. For example, *The man went up the hill;* or, *The man came into the house.* Here the verb *went* is modified by *up*, which gives a *direction* to the action of *going*, or expresses the direction of the action of going; and the action thus modified, thus *directed*, is *completed* by the addition of the noun *hill.* So the action of *coming* receives a direction from *into*, and the verb thus modified is *completed* by the noun *house.* There are a few prepositions, such as *in, of, with, for*, which can scarcely be said to give direction, and we have not succeeded in finding a common *notion* and common term under which to unite them with the other prepositions. The words *give a direction*, seem to us to express well the function of nearly all the other prepositions. We have doubted whether we ought not to accommodate our analysis to this view of the function of prepositions. As there may be a doubt about the correctness of this doctrine, we follow, like the French grammarians, the plan of treating the preposition and noun together, as forming one kind of modification (though we think it not a *single* modification). If any teacher chooses, he can readily follow the course accommodated to our suggestion above.

It will be seen that, in the above remarks, we illustrate the function of prepositions, by reference exclusively to their use, in giving a direction in relation to place, in speaking of things material. But what we have said will equally apply to them when transferred to express what has relation to objects of thought, where there is, strictly speaking, no conception of place. The original use of nearly all the prepositions appears to have been to give *local direction* to the action of verbs. From this, owing to the analogies subsisting between place or space and time, some of them were naturally transferred to express similar direction of the action in relation to time. Perhaps all the prepositions which we have enumerated, are still primarily used with reference either to place or time, except *for*, which appears to have reference always to *purpose* or to *causality*. But many of them are farther employed by a sort of figurative use, in speaking of objects of mere intellect, when the mind conceives these objects as having some analogy to objects existing in space or connected with time. For example, we say, *That man's house is above, below, beyond, under, over,* &c., *your friend's house;* or, *That man lives above,* &c., *your friend.* Here all the prepositions are employed in their original literal sense. But when I say, *That man lives above, below, beyond,* &c., *his means,* there is a figurative use of the prepositions. There is a transfer of these words to express something that the mind conceives to have a resemblance to the relations of objects in place. But, as we have intimated already, this makes no change in the relation which the preposition sustains to the words with which it is connected.

If the suggestion given above in regard to the function of prepositions is followed, we may simplify the account which we have given of them in the preceding pages; for, in this case, instead of three distinct functions, the preposition may be regarded in all its uses as performing one and the same function. The only difference is, that in one case it is attached to the modified or principal word forming a compound, in another, it stands as a separate modifying sign; and in this last case it and the principal word are sometimes further modified by a noun, and sometimes not. This account would stand instead of what has been said of the three distinct functions. These would thus come to be treated as three distinct forms of expression, into which a preposition enters while performing, all the time, one and the same function in reference to the principal word.

Treating the preposition and noun, as we have done above, as a compound modification, we were compelled to treat the separate uses of the preposition as separate functions. We consider the analysis last suggested by far the most natural and most philosophical. But it involves a total change of the current definition of a preposition. We have already, however, shown, we hope to the satisfaction of every candid and intelligent reader, that the common definition of these words is, by no means, applicable to them as a class in all their various uses. We doubt whether it is *strictly* applicable to any one of them in any one use.

[§ 83. There is a distinction of modifying expressions attached to the predicates of propositions, which we have not yet noticed, and which claims our attention in this place. (1) We have hitherto considered all modifications as affecting either the subject or the predicate of propositions directly, or some word or phrase modifying the subject or the predicate. (2) But there is another case possible, viz., a modification applied to the whole assertion made by the union of

---

[§ 83. (1) Tell how we have hitherto considered all modifications. (2) What other case

subject and predicate. (3) Such modification might, perhaps, with propriety be called a modification of the predicate, since it modifies the assertion; for, as the old grammarians have said, the *force* of the *assertion* rests in the predicate or verb. (4) Still we may distinguish, and sometimes it is important to distinguish, between such modifications as affect specially the part of the predicate contained in the verb, and such as affect the whole preceding assertion—we mean preceding in order of sense.

(5) The modifications affecting the predicate, already examined, excepting the class now under consideration, may perhaps be regarded as all of the first kind; they affect that part of the predicate contained in the verb. (6) Many of the *noun and preposition* modifications are also of the same kind, as, for instance, the *noun and preposition* used to describe the manner of an *action*. (7) This noun is perhaps always accompanied with a descriptive adjective. (8) *The man acted* IN *a becoming* MANNER. Here, *in a becoming manner* is employed to modify *acted*. The predicate asserted is, *acting in a becoming manner*. The noun and preposition with the accompanying complementary words, *a becoming*, complete *acting*.

(9) The noun and preposition employed to indicate the personal object, may also be considered as directly completing the part of the predicate contained in the verb. Example: *He wrote* TO ME, *He carried a letter* FOR ME. Here *to me* and *for me*, may be regarded as completing the predicates *writing* and *carrying*, though it is not so clear as in the case above, that we may not as well regard them as modifying the whole assertion.

(10) A large portion, however, of the noun and preposition modifications, are of the second kind. They express some circumstance necessary to complete the *assertion*, but not directly descriptive or complementary of the verbal predicate. They do not express a modification inherent in the action indicated by the verb, or conceived by the mind as specially connected with it. (11) Example: IN THE BEGIN-

---

is possible? (3) How might such modifications as now described be considered? (4) Repeat what is said about the importance of distinguishing modifications which are applied to the whole proposition.

(5) Repeat the remark in reference to the modifications already considered. (6) What is said of many of the noun and preposition modifications? (7) How is the noun in the *noun and preposition* expressing manner generally accompanied? (8) Give example and illustrate.

(9) How may the noun and preposition expressing the personal object be considered? Give illustration by example.

(10) Repeat the substance of what is said in reference to a large portion of the noun and preposition modifications. (11) Illustrate by examples.

NING *God created the heaven*, &c. Here, *In the beginning*, expresses no inherent modification of the action of *creating*, but rather completes the whole assertion, *God created the heaven and the earth. The boy wrote on Saturday to his father*. Here *on Saturday* does not modify *writing*, as the words *in a beautiful manner* modify or describe *writing*, when we say, *The boy writes in a beautiful manner*.

(12) To distinguish this species of *noun and preposition* modifications, we may call them *circumstantial modifications*. The modifications of time, distance, &c., considered in the next section, as well as many of the adverbs, belong to this class. See more on this subject in what we shall have to say on the adverbs (§ 92).

It may not be necessary, perhaps, on account of this distinction, to recognise a class of modifications affecting the *whole assertion* contained in a proposition, and not the separate parts of the proposition, since some might contend that in all the examples given above it is the *predicate* which is affected. It will be sufficient, when such a case occurs, to notice that the modification is of the *circumstantial* class.

(13) It will be observed that as these circumstantial modifications affect the general assertion, it is not so necessary to indicate their connection with the verb, by the position assigned to them in the proposition. Accordingly, *nouns and prepositions*, as well as adverbs employed to express circumstances, are often arranged far from the verb, very frequently when they express *time* or *order* in the beginning of the proposition. (14) Such circumstantial modifications are often separated by interpunction from the rest of the proposition.]

§ 84. When we entered on the consideration of the prepositions, we reserved a class of modifications formed by nouns, which require some reference to the *noun* and *preposition* modification in explaining them. We now return to these, and so finish all that we have to say about nouns employed for the purpose of modifying verbs and other nouns.

THE ACCUSATIVE OF TIME, VALUE, WEIGHT, MEASURE.—(1) Nouns which express *time*, especially the *duration* of *time*, *value*, *weight*, *measure*, including all the dimensions, are employed with-

(12) How do we distinguish this species of modifications? Mention some which belong to this species.

(13) Repeat what is said in reference to the arrangement of circumstantial modifications.

(14) What is said of separating circumstantial modifications by interpunction?]

§ 84. (1) Mention the classes of nouns employed without a preposition to express what

out the help of a preposition to express a modification equivalent to the noun and preposition modification. (2) Nouns expressing a complement of this kind are commonly said to be in the accusative or objective case, and, in every such complement, most grammarians suppose that the suppression of a preposition occurs (*a*). (3) When a modification of this kind is formed, the learner may say that the verb is modified or completed by an accusative of *time*, of *value*, &c., as the case may be (*b*).

(4) We may add to these the word *home*. When this noun is used to modify a verb signifying *motion to*—no preposition is employed with it. In other words, the preposition *to* is not employed with the noun *home*. It is not correct to say, *Go to home*, *He came to home*, but *Go home*, *He came home*. In all other cases, except when *motion to* is expressed, we employ a preposition with this word, as we would with other names of place; as, *He goes from home*, *He comes from home*, *He is at home*. We do not say, *He is* IN *home*.

We give examples of this kind of modifications, accompanying them with illustrative remarks. The examples may be used by the learner as an exercise in analysis.

(5) EXAMPLES.—1st. OF THE ACCUSATIVE OF TIME. TIME HOW LONG.—*Moses dwelt* forty *years in* the *land of Midian*. That *man has resided* thirty *years in* the *United States*. *He has lived* seven *years in London*. *David reigned* seven *years in Hebron*. TIME WHEN.—*John arrived* this *morning*. That *act was passed* last *year*. *He will come to town* next *week*.

(6) When we name a particular day of the week, or of the month, we usually employ with it the preposition ON; *He arrived on Thursday*. *He went* away *on* the first *day of May*. (7) When we designate the particular year, we employ the preposition IN, thus, *In* the *year* 1851. Where 1851 may be considered as performing the function of a noun—the proper name of the year, and year a *noun in apposition* with it (*c*).

---

is equivalent to a noun and preposition modification. In what case is a noun said to be when thus employed, and what suppression is supposed to occur? (3) What may we call such modifications?

(4) Repeat what is said of the word *home*, with the examples and illustrations.

(5) Repeat a few of the examples of the accusative of time.

(6) What construction do we use when we name a particular day of the week, or of the month? Give example. (7) What when we designate the particular year?

(8) 2d. Accusative of Value.—The only *verb* after which this is used, we believe, is *cost.* This *book cost* six *shillings*, *John's knife cost* seven *shillings*, &c. (9) Besides the accusative of the price, another accusative of the quantity—*weight* or *measure*—is often used to modify the verb *cost.* For example, *Flour costs* five *dollars* a *barrel.* That *tea costs* six *shillings* a *pound.* *Wheat costs* seven *shillings* a *bushel.* That *cloth costs* twenty-five *shillings* a *yard* (*d*).

(10] 3d. Accusative of Weight.—This is used after the verb *weigh.* The *bale weighs* one hundred *pounds.* *You weigh* one hundred and eighty *pounds* (*e*).

(11) 4th. Accusative of Measure.—This is used after the verb *measure* employed intransitively and after *extends.* This *field measures* ten *acres.* The *piece of cloth measures* twenty *yards.* (12) We do not recommend these forms of expression as *pure* English, though, we believe, they are in common colloquial use. In writing we would certainly adopt another form of expression, and avoid the neuter use of the verb *measure.* (13) This *road extends* a *mile*, &c.

(14) The accusative of the *measure of distance*, or what may be more briefly called, the *accusative of distance*, is used after the numerous verbs which express the different ways of movement from place to place. Examples: (15) *I walked* five *miles* this *morning.* *He rides* fifty *miles a day.* The *ship sailed* twelve *knots* an *hour.* *They travelled* a great *distance.* *We drove* ten *miles.* In most of these examples, there is an *accusative of time* besides the accusative of distance.

Exercise I., II., III., &c.—A given number of propositions with accusatives of time, &c., as complements.

Note (*a*). It may well be doubted whether in regard to many of these accusatives of time, value, &c., it is correct to say that a preposition is suppressed. In forms of speech where a preposition is sometimes employed, and sometimes not, in expressing the same modification, whenever the preposition is omitted, we may say that a preposition is *suppressed.* But in cases where the insertion of any known preposition would appear forced and unnatural, it is surely unphilosophical, if not absurd, to say that a preposition is suppressed. Whoever asserts that a preposition in any given instance is

---

(8) After what verb is the accusative of value or price used? Give examples. (9) Tell what second accusative is used after cost, and give examples.

(10) After what verb is an accusative of weight employed? Examples.

(11) What verbs does the accusative of measure follow? Give examples of the verb *measure* with accusative of measure. (12) What is said of the form of expression, the *field measures ten acres?* (13) Give example with the verb *extends.*

(14) What is remarked in reference to the accusative of distance? (15) Give examples of the accusative of distance used with various verbs.

suppressed, ought to be able to tell without hesitation what particular preposition, and to show that, by inserting it before a noun, the same meaning can be expressed as well, if not better, and more clearly and fully. This task we would not like to undertake in reference to many of the accusatives of duration, value, &c., which are used to complete verbs and adjectives. All this difficulty arises from commencing at the wrong end of a subject. First, it is settled or taken for granted, that the noun of time, value, &c., is in the accusative case, on what grounds, we know not, except it is because such circumstances are expressed generally by an accusative in Latin; and next the search is for some word to *govern* this accusative; and what so convenient as a preposition? And yet, were the question put, why should a preposition take the noun which follows it in the accusative, it would be full as difficult to answer, as to account for a noun without a preposition being employed to indicate *time, value,* &c. Instead of this, the true method of inquiry appears to us to be, first, to ascertain the function which these nouns of *time, value,* &c., perform, next, to mark this function by a distinctive name, without giving ourselves much trouble about settling exactly—what is, in the present usage of our language, both unimportant and obscure—the case of the word, and then we may safely let the *government* go to the receptacle (it would need to be a capacious one) of grammatical *anilities.*

The truth is, that all this class of modifications now expressed in English without the help of a preposition, were expressed in Anglo-Saxon by case forms. The noun of *measure, value, age,* was put in the *genitive;* the noun expressing the *time when,* in the *genitive* or *dative;* and the *time how long* (*duration*) was indicated by the use of the accusative.

From this it will be seen that it is not, perhaps, altogether correct to call these *modifications* indiscriminately ACCUSATIVES of *time, value, measure,* &c. But this, in reference to the name and the discrimination of cases, is of small importance in the present state of our language. Since we do not *now* employ the *genitive*—the only case form which remains to us—for any of these purposes of expressing time, &c., (the old word *whiles,* now shortened into *while,* is an example of the genitive used to express the time when,) it would be useless to attempt to discriminate between *datives* and *accusatives* of *time,* &c., after distinct forms, both of dative and accusative, have, long since, become obsolete. What is important, is to distinguish the peculiar function of these nouns; or if we speak of *case,* to distinguish the *case* used in these *modifications* from the *nominative case* used as subject noun, and for other purposes already enumerated.

The method of indicating such functions of nouns as we are now considering, as well as what we have called *genitive, dative,* and *objective modifications,* by *inflexion,* seems to have existed in most languages prior to the use of prepositions for this purpose. It is the *introduction* of prepositions to help in forming this kind of modifications, as we think, that is a comparatively modern innovation, and not the suppression of prepositions, as some grammarians would leave us to conclude. The expression of complements of *time, value,* &c., without the intervention of a preposition, is more properly considered by some a remnant of the old language, which, in this instance, has undergone no change since the earliest period known, save what has arisen from the suppression of case forms. We believe that there never was a time, as far back as the date of the most ancient remains of Anglo-Saxon, when a preposition was used in the greater part of the modifications, expressive of *duration, measure, distance,* &c.

We shall soon have occasion to observe, that some adjectives are modified in the same manner by accusatives of *time, value, measure,* &c.

NOTE (*b*).—We employ the name *accusative of time,* &c., in preference to the *objective of time,* &c., lest the learner by the use of the latter name, should be led inadvertently to confound this with the *objective modification* of verbs, from which it must be carefully distinguished. These words of time, price, &c., do not express a *passive object,* such as can become the subject of the verb employed in the *passive form.* The verbs which admit this form of modification, are in fact generally neuter verbs, having no passive form.

NOTE (*c*).—We have another way of expressing *duration of time,* or the *time how long,* by employing the word *during.* Thus we say, *He will remain with us* DURING *the day, the week, the month, the year, the holidays,* &c. But this is a totally different construction. *During,* which some call a preposition, is plainly an imperfect participle, and the construction is what is called *a noun with a participle*—an abbreviated form of a proposition. In this construction the noun may be considered as in the nominative case, if we please, or in the dative, but most certainly it is not in the accusative *governed* by *during,* as many grammarians assert. (See § 143: 13.)

NOTE (*d*).—Here, some say, the preposition FOR is suppressed, and to be *understood* before the word of quantity. But it cannot be supplied without manifest awkwardness. And hence our book-keepers resort to the Latin preposition *per*—a practice which betrays more pedantry than proper regard for the purity of our language. The preposition *for* was never, we presume, currently employed in our language before words of quantity coming after either the verb *cost,* or the adjective *worth.* If any preposition is suppressed in such constructions, we suspect that it must be BY, not FOR.

QUERY.—Is it not possible that the *a* employed in this case, instead of being the (so called) article, or the numeral, as some think, is the preposition noticed in the preceding section? To this it might be objected that we can use *the* in such constructions without much variation of the sense. *That cloth costs thirty shillings* THE *yard.* This is not so natural; when we use *the,* we believe, we most commonly insert *by.* It might also be objected, hat, if *a* thus used before a noun of quantity is the preposition, there is an unnatural suppression of the article. This ellipsis would be necessary and not unnatural, as the preposition *a* could not well be followed either by the article *a* or by *the.*

We are more inclined to think that, if there is really an ellipsis in this construction, it is the ellipsis or suppression of a *proposition*, rather than of a *preposition*, or of an article. To illustrate by an example, suppose I am asked the price of a piece of cloth, I reply, *This cloth cost thirty shillings.* This is a complete proposition, but it does not contain, as I find when I come to the end of it, a sufficiently definite answer to the question. I therefore add, as it were by *after-thought*, the words *a yard*, equivalent to the additional proposition, *A yard of it costs thirty shillings*, or to the two additional propositions, *A yard of it, I mean, costs thirty shillings.* This kind of *after-thought*, we suspect, affords the true clue to the explanation of the origin of many otherwise puzzling constructions. See another case to which it applies in the next note. We might refer the learned reader to Greek constructions which, we think, most likely originated first from *after-thought*, and at last became established *idioms* in the progress of the language. Sometimes the *insensible extension* of such *idioms*, after they have been once received, has added to the difficulties which the grammarian has to encounter in explaining them. We refer to such examples as,

Ἀλλ' οὐκ Ἀτρείδῃ Ἀγαμέμνονι ἥνδανε θυμῷ.

But it did not please Agamemnon, son of Atreus—soul; equivalent to, *It did not please Agamemnon—I mean it did not please his soul.* Such datives as θυμῷ here, we think first originated from *after-thought.* And in the same manner, perhaps, we may account for the origin of the accusative employed in Greek to specify the part, circumstance, &c., often imitated by the Latin poets.

When such expressions are often repeated, they become established *idioms;* their origin is forgotten; they are recognised as a regular mode of expressing a certain sort of modification; and are, sometimes (to increase the grammarian's perplexity), *extended insensibly* to serve purposes in language very different from those for which they were primarily employed.

The grammarians have said very little on the subject of these *accusatives of time*, &c., as we have ventured to call them, because they have unhesitatingly concluded that a preposition is in all such cases suppressed—and that this ellipsis accounts completely for the construction. A more extensive knowledge of our very earliest English authors, might throw light on some of the idiomatic constructions now noticed, and might either confirm or set aside the explanations which we have suggested. We are not perfectly satisfied on some points. We wish more light. It is to be desired that those who are engaged in exploring the dark regions of our literature, would bear in mind those points in the construction of our language, which still need elucidation. And these are not a few. To do any service in this cause, those who engage in the inquiry must do so free from the trammels of all grammatical theories.

Note (*e*).—We have another way of expressing *weight*, in which the word *weight* itself occurs as an *accusative of weight*, except we consider it as employed originally by *after-thought*, to explain a proposition already completed. (See Note *d.*) For example, This *bale* is one hundred *pounds* WEIGHT. Here we might supply the words *as to*, or *in* or *by*. This would make a very clumsy as well as finical expression—such as, we suspect, our early straightforward forefathers never employed. We suppose that the word weight was added by after-thought, as we have said, to explain that pounds *by weight*, not pounds *sterling*, were meant. The difference between these two kinds of pounds is of *ancient date* in our financial history.

CHAPTER VI.

OF ADJECTIVES.

§ 85. (1) We pass now from that class of modifications which consists wholly or partly of nouns to those which are effected by words, invented and employed exclusively for the purpose of modification—of completing the noun and the verb. Here the adjectives claim our first attention.

OF ADJECTIVES.

(2) The adjectives rank next to the nouns and verbs in importance. (3) They have received the name of ADJECTIVE, because they are intended for the purpose of being ADJECTED, or *added* to a *principal* word to determine, limit, describe, or qualify it; or, to use the more general expression, which we employ as including all these purposes, to *modify* it. (4) The adjective may be considered the chief *modifier*.

(5) We divide the adjectives into two classes, which we shall call *descriptive adjectives* (*des. a.*), and *determinative adjectives* (*det. a.*). (6) The descriptive adjectives are far the most numerous class, and, besides, the easiest to explain. (7) We shall consider them first, as a knowledge of their use will prepare the way for the better understanding of the determinatives.*

* It will be observed that we have not treated the participles as a distinct class of adjectives. The reason is that, except when employed in forming compound tenses, as already described, and in performing the part of

§ 85. (1) Repeat the introductory remark.
(2) How do the adjectives rank in importance?
(3) Tell the reason assigned for giving this class of words the name ADJECTIVE. (4) How may the adjective be considered?
(5) Into what classes are the adjectives divided? (6) What is said of the descriptive adjectives? (7) What reason is assigned for considering them first?

THE DESCRIPTIVE ADJECTIVES.—(8) The name *descriptive* is given to this class of words because they *describe* an object (expressed by the noun to which they are attached as attributives, or of which they are predicated), by some quality or property either attributed to it or asserted of it. (8 *a*) These words, by some called *adjective nouns*, are, like the *abstract nouns*, the names of *qualities*, *properties*, *attributes* of *objects*, but they are not, like the abstract nouns, employed as the subjects of propositions. (9) To illustrate this by an example, *goodness* is an abstract noun, the name of a moral quality, and can be employed as the subject of a proposition, *Goodness is one of the divine attributes.* Or it can be employed in modifying other nouns with the help of a preposition, as, *A man of goodness.* But *good*, also the name of the same moral quality, can

---

predicates in *contracted accessory* propositions to be described hereafter, they differ nothing in their functions from descriptive adjectives. The difference between them and common descriptive adjectives is in meaning. The adjectives express qualities inherent in objects, the participles express actions attributively of which the noun they modify represents either the agent or the recipient or passive object. The participles of that very peculiar (peculiar as to significance) verb *to be*, may perhaps be regarded as forming an exception.

Participles in many cases become adjectives, when they are used not to express an action, but an inherent attribute. An action indefinitely continued, merges into an inherent attribute. Thus the participle loving, in such phrases as, *A loving friend*, comes to express an inherent attribute, because the action is capable of indefinite continuance, or, in other words, becomes habitual. Some actions again produce permanent effects, and hence their perfect participles expressing the completion of these effects, come to be used as common adjectives to express acquired inherent qualities. Thus in the phrase, *An educated man, a learned man*, the words *educated* and *learned* are used as common descriptive adjectives, and express permanent though acquired qualities.

What we have described above, we believe to be the true distinction between a participle and a participle adjectively used. The assertion of the old grammarians, that when a participle ceases to indicate time, it becomes an adjective, appears to us incorrect. At all events it cannot apply to English participles, which do not indicate time, but merely the state of the action as *completed* or *incomplete*—*perfect* or *imperfect.*

---

(8) Why is the name descriptive given to this class of words?

(8 *a*) In what are the descriptive adjectives *like*, and in what unlike, abstract nouns? (9)

only be used *adjectively*, in connection with a principal word to which it is *adjected*, which it describes, or modifies.*

(10) It cannot, like the noun *goodness*, be used as the subject of a proposition. We can assert nothing of it. (11) We find indeed such propositions as, *The good alone are happy*, but it is obvious that *the good* is in this proposition an abbreviated expression for *good men*, *good persons*, or *good people*. Either *men*, or *persons*, or some noun of similar meaning, is manifestly implied. (12) To assert of what we *understand* by the term *good*, considered alone, that it is happy would be absurd. (13) When considered (*formally*, *technically*, or *materialiter*) as a *mere word* without reference to its meaning, we can employ it as the subject of such propositions as the following: *Good is a word of one syllable or of four letters; Good is an adjective; Good expresses a moral quality*, &c. (14) But these assertions are made in reference to the word or sign, not in reference to what GOOD *denotes*. (15) If we wish to make any assertion about the quality expressed by *good*, we must employ the abstract noun *goodness*, as the subject of the proposition.

(16) Lest we should be misunderstood, we must call the attention

* The adjective is a more brief, compact, complete way of expressing the same thing that is expressed by the *noun and preposition*. *A good man* is equivalent to, *A man of goodness*, and generally speaking, a much more convenient phrase. When we have an adjective to express a quality, it forms the most *perfect* kind of complement. The adjectives may be regarded as a most artificial contrivance—one of the last results of the refinement of language. The want of a word of this sort to express a quality, is often felt as a serious disadvantage by those who value a compact, terse, and forcible style of writing. For example, we have no adjective to express the attribute *sensibility;* for *sensible* does not express this attribute, but one entirely distinct from it. If we wish to speak of a man possessed of this quality, we have to say, *A man of sensibility*. Such lumbering complements, especially when often repeated, enfeeble style.

Illustrate this by an example. (10) What farther is said of the adjective *good?* (11) What is said in reference to *the good* in such an assertion as *The good alone are happy?* (12) Can we assert any thing of *good* alone in its proper sense? (13) Repeat the remark in reference to *good* and similar adjectives considered (*materialiter*) as mere words. Repeat examples. (14) What is said of the assertions in the examples? (15) What word must we use, when we wish to assert any thing about the quality expressed by good?

(16) What two purposes does the same word sometimes serve? (17) Illustrate by ex-

of the learner to the fact, that the same word sometimes serves both as a noun and as an adjective. (17) Thus *cold* is used as a noun, when we say, *The* COLD *is excessive;* but as an adjective, when we say, COLD *weather often injures tender plants.* (18) In such cases, it is by the function which the word performs, that we distinguish the noun from the adjective. (19) The discrimination is easily made. (20) It may appear more difficult to draw an exact line of distinction between words which are sometimes substantives and sometimes adjectives, and those nouns which are *adjectively used.* (21) The noun adjectively used, is generally employed only in certain set forms of expression, and serves most frequently to express, in an abbreviated manner, some modification which nouns and not adjectives are employed to effect. (See § 70.) (22) If it should be doubtful, in some cases, whether we should say of a certain modification, that it consists of a noun *adjectively employed*, or that the word which forms this modification is a word of *double sense* or *double function*, sometimes noun, sometimes adjective, it is a matter of small importance, since the two kinds of modification, in many instances, and especially in such doubtful instances, are almost, if not altogether, equivalent. (23) Those words which are both nouns and adjectives, generally occur so frequently in the adjective sense, as to preclude all doubt as to the course to be pursued in regard to them. They are not very numerous in our language. (24) The adjectives expressive of color, are very often used as nouns, though we have abstract nouns formed from them. (25) Thus we say, *Green is pleasing to the sight; Red is disagreeable*, &c.; though we have the nouns *greenness*, *redness*, &c. We suppose we should say, in such cases, that the *Adjective is substantively employed*, rather than that the same word is both noun and adjective.

(26) The learner will most readily acquire a knowledge of the descriptive adjectives, by directing his attention to the different classes of qualities or properties which fall within human knowledge. The classification here is precisely the same as in respect to the abstract nouns. (See § 26.)

---

ample. (18) How do we distinguish the noun from the adjective in such cases? (19) Is the discrimination easily made? (20) What distinction may be more difficult to make? (21) Repeat the substance of what is said in reference to the noun adjectively employed. (22) What remark is made in reference to doubtful cases? (23) What is said in reference to words which are used both as nouns, and as adjectives? (24) Repeat the remark about adjectives which express color. (25) Illustrate by examples.

(26) How may the learner most readily acquire a knowledge of the descriptive adjectives?

(27) The first great division of qualities, attributes, or properties, is into those which we ascertain by our external senses, and those which we ascertain by the help of an intellectual process. The first we may call material qualities, the second mental or immaterial qualities. (28) Of the first, a subdivision may be formed in reference to the particular external sense by which we discover them. (29) Thus (A) we have adjectives expressive of qualities which we discover by sight; in other words, expressive of the different colors—*white*, *red*, *green*, *blue*, &c. (B) Adjectives expressive of qualities ascertained by the sense of hearing, or expressive of the different properties of sound—*loud*, *shrill*, *hoarse*, &c. (C) Adjectives expressive of qualities ascertained by the sense of touch; as, *rough*, *smooth*, *dry*, *moist*, *hard*, *soft*, &c. (D) Adjectives expressive of qualities ascertained by the sense of smell; as, *fragrant*, *fetid*, &c. (E) Adjectives expressive of qualities ascertained by the sense of taste; as, *sweet*, *sour*, *bitter*, &c. Some properties, as those of extension—*long*, *broad*, *thick*, *high*, &c.—are perhaps ascertained by the aid of two senses.

(30) The second great division of adjectives includes those which express all the qualities of the human mind, and what we know of the attributes of higher spiritual natures—the feelings, instincts, &c., of the lower animals. (31) As a sample of such adjectives, we may give the following: *Virtuous*, *vicious*, *mild*, *stern*, *gentle*, *froward*, *proud*, *humble*, *compassionate*, *cruel*, *good*, *bad*, *wild*, *tame*, *wise*, *foolish*, &c., &c.

[(32) It may be here observed, that a large proportion of our *abstract nouns* are derived from adjectives, and manifestly of later formation, since the adjective is often plainly the original or primary word. (33) By the addition of the termination *ness* to a large portion of the adjectives above enumerated, we form the corresponding *abstract noun.* For example—from *white* is formed *whiteness;* from *loud*, *loudness;* from *smooth*, *smoothness;* from *sweet*, *sweetness;* &c. (34) From some, nouns are formed by other *suffixes;* as, from *wise*, *wisdom;* from *long*, *length;* from *fragrant*, *fragrance;* &c. (35) In all

---

(27) What division is proposed of these adjectives founded on the nature of the qualities which they express? (28) What subdivision is proposed of the first class—the class which expresses material qualities? (29) Enumerate these subdivisions giving examples of each.

(30) What does the second great class of adjectives include? (31) Give a sample of this class of adjectives.

[(32) What is said in reference to the formation of many of the abstract nouns? (33) What termination is often added to adjectives for this purpose? Give examples. (34) Give examples of abstract nouns formed from adjectives by the addition of other suffixes. (35

these, it is evident that the adjective is the primary word, and the abstract noun the derivative. (36) The adjectives appear, therefore, at least in all the instances enumerated, and in all like cases, to be an older part of the language than the corresponding abstract nouns. (37) On the other hand, some adjectives are formed from abstract nouns; as, from *virtue* comes *virtuous*, &c.; and many adjectives are formed from *concrete* nouns; as, from *gold*, *golden*; *wood*, *wooden*; *fool*, *foolish*, and from this again the abstract *foolishness*.]

EXERCISES I., II., III., &c.—Find a given number of adjectives expressive of qualities or properties ascertainable by the several senses, arranged under each sense in order; the same also in regard to the adjectives expressive of spiritual, mental and animal qualities; placing after each adjective an appropriate noun.

We have said, perhaps, enough for the present of the nature of descriptive adjectives; we proceed next to treat of the grammatical functions which they perform in language, and after this we shall consider their modifications.

§ 86. (1) Descriptive adjectives are used for two purposes, 1st, to complete nouns, 2d, to complete verbs.

1st. THE DESCRIPTIVE ADJECTIVE USED TO COMPLETE NOUNS.—The learner has already acquired some knowledge of this use of the descriptive adjective from the preceding remarks, and from the examples introduced, and the exercises which have been prescribed. (2) We may, if we please, call this the *attributive* use of the adjective, since it expresses some attribute or property represented as inherent in the object denoted by the noun to which it is attached. (3) The adjective and noun together express not two objects, but a single object, qualified in the way expressed by the adjective. (4) The adjective may be regarded as constituting an essential part of the whole name of the object which we contemplate. (5) In the phrase, *A bay horse*, the word *bay* is as essential a part of the name of what I intend to indicate as the word *horse*. (6) Hence, descrip-

---

What is evident in regard to the adjectives in all these examples? (36) Which in these instances is the oldest part of the language—the adjectives or the abstract nouns. (37) Are adjectives ever formed from abstract nouns? Examples. Are any formed from concrete nouns? Examples.]

§ 86. (1) Mention the two great purposes for which descriptive adjectives are used. (2) What may we call the first use? and state the reason. (3) What do the adjective and noun together express? (4) How may the adjective be regarded? (5) Illustrate by an example. (6) Repeat what is said about descriptive adjectives being accounted *concrete* words.

tive adjectives are accounted *concrete* words, as *growing with* or *adhering* to a real substance, in opposition to the *abstract nouns* which denote qualities or properties *abstracted* or considered separately from the substances and other properties with which they co-exist.

(7) We may call this form of modification, THE DESCRIPTIVE ADJECTIVE MODIFICATION OF NOUNS.

(8) The noun modified or completed by a descriptive adjective may be either the subject noun of a proposition or a noun used for the purpose of modification. (9) If it be the *subject noun*, the *assertion* is made, not of what the noun alone denotes, but of what the noun and adjective together denote. (10) If it be a noun employed for *modification*, the meaning of the *principal* word is not *modified* by what the noun alone denotes, but by what the noun and adjective together denote. (11) For example, *A good conscience is an inestimable treasure.* It is not of *conscience* that the assertion in this proposition is made, but of *a good conscience.* And it is not by *treasure*, but by *inestimable treasure* that the verb *is* is completed.

(12) The usual place of the descriptive adjective in English is immediately before the noun which it completes. (13) When the adjective itself is attended by a noun and preposition modification, or by an infinitive modification, it is generally placed after the noun to avoid confusion. Thus, we say, *A man desirous of glory.* We could not, without great awkwardness and confusion, say, *A desirous of glory man.* We say, *A man addicted to falsehood;* and not *An addicted to falsehood man.*

(14) Often more than *one* adjective is employed to complete the same *noun.* (15) Sometimes two or more adjectives are applied *independently* of each other to the same word, each giving it a separate modification. Adjectives thus applied are usually connected by conjunctions. For example, *A* WISE *and* GOOD *ruler ought to be respected.* Here *wise* and *good*, independently of each other, modify the noun

---

(7) What may we call the form of modification made by applying a descriptive adjective to a noun?

(8) What remark is made in reference to the noun thus modified? (9) To what does the assertion apply when the subject noun is modified by an adjective? (10) What is said of a modifying noun accompanied by an adjective? (11) Illustrate by an example.

(12) What place does the descriptive adjective usually occupy in the arrangement of a proposition? (13) What exception to the usual arrangement? Give examples and illustration.

(14) Can several adjectives be used to complete the same noun? (15) How are two or

ruler. This species of compound modification we shall notice hereafter, when we have first considered the functions performed by the class of words called conjunctions. (16) But there is another case of the application of two adjectives in modifying the same noun, which may be considered here; viz., when one of the adjectives modifies the noun as already completed by the other adjective. (17) For example, *A pretty wooden bowl;* here *wooden* is the more intimate modification of the word *bowl*, and the adjective *pretty* does not modify *bowl* separately, but the words *wooden bowl*. (18) *Pretty* may be called the more *remote* modification. We may add that the determinative *a* is a still more remote modification applied to the noun as modified by the two descriptive adjectives. (19) The more intimate complement is placed nearest in the order of arrangement to the principal word, the most remote farthest from it; or, in other words, *each modifying word precedes that part of the phrase which it modifies.* This may be exhibited to the eye in writing, thus: a [pretty (wooden bowl)]; or, in analysis, thus: [(Bowl *n-mod. by* wooden *des. a.*) *mod. by* pretty *des. a*] *mod. by* a *det. a.;* to be read thus, the noun *bowl* is modified by the descriptive adjective *wooden*, *wooden bowl* by the descriptive adjective *pretty*, and *pretty wooden bowl* by the determinative adjective *a*.* (20) Two descriptive adjectives

* When we express the analysis of a passage in writing, it will be necessary, in order to secure perspicuity, to follow invariably the same order of arrangement. The arrangement which we recommend is, to place whatever applies to a single *principal* word immediately after it, and when a modification applies to any *combination of words*, let these words be included within *parenthetic marks*, as above, or under a *vinculum*, and let what applies to such combination be written immediately after the close of the parenthesis or termination of the vinculum. Whatever thus immediately follows parenthetic marks, is to be considered as applied to the expression which they include. Thus, in the above example, the words, *modified by* pretty *des. a.*, apply to the combination (Bowl, *n. md. by* wooden *des. a.*); and the words, *mod. by* a *det. a.*, apply to the whole combination [(Bowl, *n. md. by* wooden, *des. a.*) *md. by* pretty *des. a.*] By means of the parenthetic marks thus employed, and the abbreviations adopted to express the several forms of modification, a satisfactory analysis can be written with considerable brevity and perspicuity.

more adjectives sometimes applied to the same word? How usually connected? Illustrate by an example. (16) Mention another case of the application of two adjectives to the same word. (17) Illustrate by an example. (18) What is said of the modification *pretty* in the example? (19) What is said of the order of arrangement of such complements, or modifications? (20) What remark is made about the use of two adjectives in this way? (21)

are not very often employed in this way, but determinatives, as we shall find, are very frequently applied to nouns affected by a descriptive adjective, so as to modify or limit the united adjective and noun. (21) Nouns modified by *a noun adjectively* employed expressive of the material of which an object is made, or, as some consider them in this use, adjectives expressing the material, are often, together with their more intimate complement, modified by an additional adjective. For example, *An* [*expensive* (*gold watch.*)] *A beautiful marble statue. An elegant silver lamp*, &c. (22) Many examples might be given in which the more *intimate modification* is an adjective expressing the country in which an article is produced or manufactured. *A superb French clock; a valuable English watch; A beautiful Turkish carpet; An elegant Etruscan vase*, &c. (23) The following are examples of a different class: *A rich gilded ceiling. The beautiful blue sky.*

(24) The learner should remark that the practice of suppressing the conjunction between adjectives which are really intended as *distinct* modifications of a noun is common, especially with the poets. For example, *The deep blue sea.* This does not mean the *blue sea* which is *deep*, but the *sea* which is both *blue* and *deep*. "*The deep unclouded sky*," meaning the *sky* which is both *deep* and *unclouded.*

[(25) There is another construction often employed by the poets, which must be distinguished from those mentioned above. This is the use of an adjective *adverbially* to modify another adjective. (26) This poetic use may be illustrated by the following example: "*The deep rooted mountains*," &c. Here the word *deep* (generally employed as a *descriptive* adjective) modifies neither *mountains* taken separately nor the combined words *rooted mountains.* It is not implied by the expression that the mountains are *deep*, nor that the *rooted mountains* are *deep*, but that the mountains are *deep-rooted*, equivalent to *deeply rooted.* Consequently, *deep* performs the function of modifying an adjective—a function usually ascribed exclusively to adverbs.

(27) We may also remark, that descriptive abjectives have, in many cases, become so united with nouns as to form with them one word. Such words may be treated in analysis as nouns, or compound

---

Repeat what is said about nouns modified by a noun adjectively employed? Illustrate by an example. (22) Of what might numerous examples be given? (23) Give examples in which the more intimate modification is not expressive of country.

(24) What fact is the learner warned to remark? Illustrate by examples.

[(25) Mention another distinct purpose for which adjectives are used by the poets. (26 Illustrate this poetic use fully by an example.

(27) State what is said of compound words formed of an adjective and a noun modified by it. Illustrate by examples.]

nouns. We have examples in *smallcraft*, *blackberry*, *blackbird*, *white-lead*, *whitewash*, &c.]

(28) The functions of participles are the same as those of descriptive adjectives. We subjoin a few examples for analysis. We mark, as usual, the words which the learner should now be able to analyze.

EXERCISE I.—*Wise men profit by* the *sad experience of fools*. *Idle boys* seldom *become useful men*. The *white rose was* the *emblem of* the *house of York*. The *red rose was* the *emblem of* the *house of Lancaster*.

"Our *dying friends come o'er us* like a cloud
To damp our *brainless ardors*."—Young.
"Now *morn*, her *rosy steps in* the *eastern clime*
Advancing, *sowed* the *earth with orient pearl*.—Milt.

EXERCISES II., III., &c.—A given number of propositions containing examples of descriptive adjectives.

§ 87. (1) We have already had occasion to notice *incidentally* that adjectives are frequently employed *substantively*; we must here bring this fact more directly under the consideration of the learner. (2) The largest class of adjectives substantively employed, are those with which the noun men, or persons, &c., is implied. (3) Such are *the rich*, *the poor*, *the wise*, *the learned*, *the rude*, *the vulgar*, *the noble*, *the good*, *the virtuous*, *the vicious*, *the just*, *the pious*, &c., &c., equivalent to *rich men*, *poor men*, &c. (4) No other noun is suppressed with such words except men or persons, and hence, by conventional usage, they serve the double function of denoting objects, and, at the same time, qualifying them, or, in other words, they signify objects with an accompanying and distinguishing property. (5) In such cases the *property*, or *qualification*, is that which is most important—that which is intended to be expressed with emphasis. (6) Such terms are all *concrete*, they are used to denote *substances*, not abstract properties.

---

(28) What is said of the functions of participles, or verbal adjectives?

§ 87. (1) To what fact is the attention of the learner here called? (2) What is said o. the largest class of adjectives employed substantively? (3) Mention a number of examples. (4) What noun is always suppressed after adjectives thus employed? And what double function do these adjectives serve? (5) What is remarked of the qualification expressed by the adjective in such contracted forms of expression? (6) To which class of nouns do such terms belong?

NOTE.—In languages which have distinct inflected forms of the adjective to be applied to nouns of different genders, adjectives can be employed as *substantives* to a much greater extent than in English, without any sacrifice of perspicuity. For example, the adjective *bonus* used alone in the Latin language, clearly indicates *a good man*, *bonum*, *a good thing*; the plural *boni*, *good men*, or *the good*, and *bona*, *good things*, and hence, *goods*, *effects*. Sometimes, also, the feminine forms of certain adjectives are used to denote females possessed of the property indicated by the adjective. A great number of the Latin adjectives are thus used with the suppression of a word=*person* or *persons*, *thing* or *things*, thus representing two distinct nouns in both numbers, whilst we are necessarily confined by the nature of our language, which has no inflexion of adjectives to denote gender, to the expression of one noun, and that only in the plural. *Thing* or *things* we cannot indicate in this way. Whereas, the Latin language always indicates *thing*, singular and plural, in its most common use as employed in company with an adjective by the adjective alone. In fact, there is no word in the Latin language which answers to our word *thing*, used as above described. There is no need for such a word. The neuter forms of the adjectives supply its place. We must not omit to remark here, that numerous instances of adjectives used substantively, a *singular noun being suppressed*, may be found in the authorized version of the Scriptures. Take the following as examples: "So the *poor hath* hope." "The *wicked borroweth* and *payeth* not again; but the *righteous sheweth* mercy, and *giveth*," &c. Here the singular noun *man*, is obviously to be supplied. This employment of descriptive adjectives to represent singular, as well as plural, *concrete* nouns is rarely, if ever, to be found in modern writers. It has very properly fallen into disuse, since it would necessarily create ambiguity, especially when such adjectives happen to serve as the subject nouns of verbs in any other than the indefinite tense, and when they are employed as complementary nouns. For example, "The *righteous shall inherit* the land; The mouth *of the righteous* speaketh wisdom." It is only by the context that we ascertain that "*the righteous*" here represents an individual. Ambiguity in such cases is, however, of little importance, as there is no material difference in the sense, whether we consider the word singular or plural.

(7) There is another class of adjectives substantively employed, which, unlike those already mentioned, are *singular* nouns. They are also entitled to be classed as abstract nouns, since they do not denote *substances*, but *properties* or *attributes* contemplated separately from the objects or substances with which they co-exist. (8) We subjoin examples: *The sublime*, *the beautiful*, *the infinite*, *the finite*, *the ridiculous*, *the pathetic*, *the vast*, *the profound*, &c. (9) These are generally philosophical terms.

---

(7) In what two respects does another class of adjectives substantively employed differ from those just considered? (8) Give examples. (9) Repeat the remark under No. 9.

(10) It will be observed that with these, as with the class already considered, the determinative THE is invariably employed. (11) This is essential in the employment of all adjectives in either of these ways in English.

(12) Should the same adjective happen to be used in both these ways, as a concrete plural noun, and as an abstract singular noun, it would create ambiguity. The adjective *beautiful*, is very commonly used in the latter way, and sometimes, we think, *the beautiful* is used in the first way to mean persons possessed of beauty. This use of the word is rare, and it seldom happens that any of the adjectives used as *abstract singular* nouns are the same which are used as *concrete plurals.*

(14) In analysis the concretes may be treated as adjectives, the learner supplying the suppressed noun, or, more briefly, they may be classed as adjectives substantively used—*concrete plurals.* (15) The abstracts must be treated as adjectives used as abstract nouns, since, in their case, there is really no original suppression of a noun. They are adjectives employed to express a new *abstract conception*, which had no previous name. It would generally prove a vain search to attempt to find a suppressed noun.

(16) Both these forms of expression are often employed both as subject nouns of propositions, and to perform some of the modifying functions.

We subjoin a few examples for analysis.

EXERCISE I.—*To despise* the *poor becomes* not the *rich.* The *proud are hated by* their *fellow men.* The *vain are despised by* the *wise.* "*He taketh* the *wise in* their own *craftiness ;* the *counsel of* the *froward is carried* headlong." The *simple are* the *prey of* the *crafty.* "The *prudent are crowned with knowledge.*" "The *light of* the *righteous rejoiceth ;* the *lamp of* the *wicked shall be put out.*" There *is* but a *single step from* the *sublime to* the *ridiculous.* The *finite cannot comprehend* the *infinite.* "*To* the *sublime in building*, *greatness of dimen-*

---

(10) In what are these words like the last class? (11) And what is essential to adjectives employed in both ways?

(12) What would happen were the same adjective employed in both ways? (13) Name an adjective perhaps used both ways.

(14) How may the concrete class of these words be treated in analysis? (15) How must the abstracts be treated? and assign the reasons.

(16) How are both kinds of words employed?

sions seems requisite." "The *ideas of* the *sublime* and the *beautiful stand on foundations* so *different*," &c.

EXERCISE II., III., &c.—Form propositions having their subjects completed by descriptive adjectives. IV., V., &c. Having *objective* modifications, and other modifications, consisting of nouns completed by descriptive adjectives.

§ 88. 2d. We now proceed to consider the second general function of descriptive adjectives, namely, that of completing verbs. (1) We may call this the *predicative use* of the adjective.* (2) This

---

* It must not be inferred, from the fact that we treat this use of the *descriptive adjectives* after the *attributive use*, that we agree with the grammarians who consider this use as posterior in origin, or as in all cases resolvable into the attributive use. On the contrary, we are inclined to think that adjectives (we do not say all adjectives) were employed to complete the predicate (especially with the verb TO BE) earlier than to modify the subject. In the nascent state of human society, men would likely need adjectives for the purpose of *declaring* to one another the properties of the objects around them, before they needed them as modifications of subject nouns. We think, for example, that men would sooner need to make such assertions in their interchange of thought as, *The weather is cold, The river is deep*, or *dangerous*, &c., than they would need to make some assertion in regard to *cold weather*, or *a deep or dangerous river*. The use of attributive words to express more exactly a complex conception, we look on as a refinement in language, required only after a step had been taken towards philosophical thinking, however rude. The purpose of modifying the subject was, we think, most likely first attempted by the addition of a *proposition* to the subject noun. Indeed the *descriptive adjective modification* may be considered as a species of *latent* or *implied* predication. For example, *The good man is loved*, is equivalent to *The man who is good is loved*. Here the proposition *who is good*, expresses what is, in the present improved state of language, generally expressed in the more compressed form by the adjective applied as an attributive to the subject noun. (See § 111.)

Remember, we do not say that all adjectives were invented for the purpose of being employed to complete the predicate. If such a step as we have described has really been taken in language, it must have preceded the origin of many of the adjectives now in use. Many of these have manifestly been designed from the beginning, exclusively for the purpose of modifying nouns, and not for the purpose of completing the predicate. In this class we may include all the determinative adjectives, and many of the

---

§ 88. (1) What may the second function of adjectives be called? (2) To what is this

function of the descriptive adjective, is exactly similar to that of the *noun complementary* of the verb. (3) Like the *noun complementary*, the adjective is attached to neuter and to active and to passive verbs. (4) If the learner bears in mind what has been said of the noun complementary of the neuter and active verbs, it will assist him much in comprehending what we shall say in reference to adjectives employed to complete verbs; that is, to complete the part of the *predicate* expressed in the verbs. (5) For it will be remembered that, as in the case of all other complements of verbs, it is not the *verb as an assertive word*, but the *verb as expressing* (what it always does) *the leading part of the predicate* which is affected by the complement. (6) In other words, it is not the *copula*, but the *predicate*, which in all cases is affected by *modification*. (7) Hence, as we have before said, verbal nouns and verbal adjectives take the same complements or modifications as the verb or assertive word itself.

(8) To mark the close analogy between the *descriptive adjective*, used to complete the predicate, and the *noun* employed for the same purpose, and at the same time to assist the memory of the learner, by introducing as much simplicity and clearness as possible in *classification* and in *nomenclature*, we give *names* to these adjective modifications of the verb, exactly similar to those which we gave to nouns used to complete verbs. (9) We call them THE ADJECTIVE COMPLEMENTARY OF THE NEUTER VERB, THE ADJECTIVE

descriptive. As, for example, those which express the material of which a thing is made, such as *golden*, *brazen*, *wooden*, &c. These are not now employed to complete the predicate, and perhaps never were so employed. They have been adopted as now used, for the express purpose of modifying nouns, not verbs. But the use of determinatives must be looked on as a refinement introduced later than descriptive adjectives in the progress of language; and such descriptive adjectives as those mentioned above, have about them the indications of modern introduction.

---

function of the descriptive adjective similar? (3) In what is it like the noun complementary? (4) Repeat the suggestion to the learner. (5) What is it in the verb that is affected by this and by other *complements*? (6) Express the same thing in other words. (7) What follows from this in reference to verbal nouns and verbal adjectives?

(8) Repeat substantially the motives which have influenced us in choosing a name for this species of modification. (9) What is the name by which we distinguish this kind of modifications in reference to the classes of verbs to which they are applied?

COMPLEMENTARY OF THE ACTIVE VERB, and THE ADJECTIVE COMPLEMENTARY OF THE PASSIVE VERB.*

THE ADJECTIVE COMPLEMENTARY OF THE NEUTER VERB. (10) This complement is most extensively employed with the verb TO BE. (11) We subjoin a few examples: *The steward is faithful; The boy is industrious; The fields are green; The weather is warm; Vanity is contemptible; Pride is detestable; Industry is commendable.* (12) We need not multiply examples, since this is in fact one of the most common forms of construction in all languages. Mankind have constantly occasion to *predicate* or *assert* the *existence* of attributes, or qualities in the objects which come within their knowledge.

NOTE.—We have already, elsewhere, had occasion to observe, that the adjective thus employed with the verb *to be*, is generally thought by logicians and grammarians to contain (either alone or with its appropriate complements) the entire predicate, and the verb to perform solely the function of *copula*. We have given our reasons for thinking that this opinion, so long and so generally entertained by the philosophical world, is destitute of foundation, and for holding, as we do, that the verb *to be*, in its assertive form, includes either the *entire* predicate, or the *leading part* of the predicate, like all other verbs. The verbal noun BEING, is exactly equivalent to the predicate contained in this verb, as we have elsewhere endeavored to establish, by an appeal to the understandings of our readers. What is *asserted* or predicated in such propositions as, *The steward is faithful*, is *being faithful*, not barely the attribute *faithful*. But, for the more full examination of this matter, we refer to § 46, and note. Here it is only necessary to remind the learner of the manner in which we view this subject, and our reason for treating the adjective, in this kind of construction, as *comple-*

* We omit the term *descriptive* before the adjective, as in this case unnecessary; though it will be remembered, that rarely any other than a descriptive adjective is used in this way. If an adjective employed generally as a determinative, is sometimes used to complete the predicate, it is in this case to be considered as performing a descriptive function. For instance, in such expressions as, "The laborers are few," the word *few*—generally employed as a determinative—is, perhaps, to be considered as a descriptive adjective, expressing an attribute belonging to the "laborers," *collectively* considered, and here (with *being*) predicated of them.

(10) With what verb is the adjective complementary of neuter verbs chiefly employed? (11) Give examples. (12) Why is it unnecessary for us to multiply examples?

mentary of the verb or of the predicate; in other words, as a part only, and not the whole of the predicate.

For the same reason assigned above, we do not subjoin numerous examples for analysis. We rather leave the learner to furnish his own examples of this very plain and familiar construction, assured that this will prove no difficult task.

(13) All that is necessary to be said in analysis in *reference to the adjective* in a construction of this kind is, that the verb, for example in the proposition *The man is ignorant*, is modified or completed by the complementary adjective *ignorant*. When the learner has become familiar with these terms, he may omit *complementary*, and after having given the usual account of the subject noun and verb, simply add that the verb is *completed* by the *adjective*—naming the adjective which occurs in the particular case.

EXERCISES I. II. &c.—Supply a given number of written propositions formed with the verb *to be* in its several tenses, accompanied in each instance by a complementary adjective making a predicate, such as can rationally be asserted of the subject chosen.

(14) The neuter verb *become* is generally modified in the same manner. It is always completed either by an adjective or by a noun, and never stands as the *complete predicate.**

(15) *Examples* of Become, with an adjective complementary. *That man becomes old; The boy has become impatient; James will become learned; That nation has become powerful; John has become generous*, &c. The verb *grow* is similarly modified, as, *The field grows green; The boy grows large*, &c.

Many other neuter verbs are completed in the same manner, though not so frequently as the verbs we have just noticed. (16) Amongst those thus occasionally *completed*, we may enumerate the following:

* In this it is unlike the verb *to be*, which stands, as we have seen already, often as the complete predicate; much oftener *in reality* than in our language is apparent at the first glance. (See § 46, Note p. 81.)

(13) Repeat the substance of the direction in reference to the analysis of this species of modification.

(14) What is said in reference to the verb *become?* (15) Give examples.

(16) Enumerate some of the neuter verbs which admit of the same kind of modification

Look, *seem*, *feel*, *taste*, *smell*, *blow*, *shine*, *remove*, *stand*, *continue*, &c. Some of these words are used both as active and as neuter verbs. We have concern with them here only in their neuter signification. We subjoin examples of some of these verbs, accompanied by a complementary adjective. (17) The analysis of these examples is to be conducted as in the case of the verbs *to be*, *to become*, *to grow*, completed by an adjective.

Examples for Analysis.—*Mary looks cold. William seems disappointed. Black feels rough, white feels smooth. Honey tastes sweet. Roses smell fragrant. The wind blows soft. The moon shone bright. The work remains unfinished. The door stands open. The weather continues stormy.* We take the following examples from D'Orsey. The first is altered from the imperative to the assertive form:—

He *looks big*. "He turns pale."—Addison. "Half the women would *have fallen sick*."—Addison. "A miser *grows rich* by *seeming poor*; an extravagant man *grows poor* by *seeming rich*."—Shenstone. "Dappled horses *turn white*."—Bacon. "They all shall wax old."—Heb. 1: 11. "This horror will *grow mild*."—Milton.

"With what eyes could we
Stand in his presence *humble*, &c."—Milton.

(18) After *look* and *seem* the infinitive *to be* might be supplied without injury to the sense, and some may choose to take this mode of analyzing the propositions in which these verbs occur, followed by an adjective; saying, in such cases, that they are completed by the verb *to be* suppressed, and considering the adjective as complementary of the suppressed infinitive. We have no objection to this course. We believe the infinitive necessary to the full expression of the assertion. But when this is once understood, we consider it unnecessary on every occasion to supply the omitted infinitive.

(19) This remark will not apply to most of the other verbs enumerated. The introduction of the infinitive *to be* between the verb and adjective is inadmissible, as it would mar the sense. And yet the *existence* of the quality expressed by an adjective in connection with the subject is perhaps always implied; *i. e.* the existence of the quality in the subject in the *mode* or *manner* expressed by the verb. Thus, *Honey tastes sweet.* Here the quality *sweet* is asserted to exist in *honey* in connection with its taste, or in the mode or manner expressed by the verb *taste.*

---

(17) What remark is made about the analysis of the subjoined examples? (18) What is said in reference to the analysis of the propositions in which the verbs *look* and *seem* occur?

(19) Will the remark in regard of the verbs *look* and *seem* apply to the other verbs above enumerated? Repeat the substance of the illustration.

[(20) We must be careful to distinguish this species of modification from the adverbial modification to be considered presently. The adjective in the case before us expresses an attribute pertaining to the *subject in connection with the predicate*, or together with the verb expresses the *condition* of the *subject;* the adverb expresses only the manner of the *action* of the *verb*, or some circumstance affecting the assertion in general, as of *time*, *place*, &c. Or, in other words, an attribute of the action asserted, not of the subject itself of which it is asserted. A few examples will render this more clear: *John feels warm*, and *John feels warmly*. In the first proposition the *adjective warm* expresses an attribute of John in connection with the predicate *feeling;* or, perhaps, rather we should say, *warm* with the predicate feeling expresses a condition here asserted of John. *The wind blows soft; The wind blows softly*. The same remark will apply here. A *wind* that is not *soft* may blow SOFTLY—that is, *gently;* but none, except a wind possessing the attribute expressed by soft, can truly be said *to blow* SOFT. We may subjoin a few more examples: *William looks proud*, and *William looks proudly on the result of his persevering efforts. That lady looks cold;* and *That lady looks coldly on the gentleman by her side*. In all these cases, the difference between the adjective and adverb is plain enough.]

EXERCISE.—After the analysis of the above examples, the learner may construct a given number of propositions with the verbs enumerated above, containing examples of *the adjective complementary* appropriately employed with these verbs.

We may remark that sometimes active verbs seem to take an adjective complementary, having reference like the adjective complementary of the neuter verb to the subject noun. Examples of what we mean may be found in such expressions as, John spends his time thoughtless of the purposes of existence. There are three ways in which *thoughtless* and its modifications might here be regarded; 1st, as a descriptive adjective, modifying John the subject noun; 2d, as an adjective adverbially used, expressing manner and modifying the predicate; or, 3d, as an adjective complementary, expressing an attribute applicable to John in the mode of spending his time. This last we think the most accurate mode of analysis. Constructions of this kind are seldom used. This is altogether unlike the adjective complementary of the active verb, which affects not the subject but the objective.

§ 89. THE ADJECTIVE COMPLEMENTARY OF THE ACTIVE VERB.

[(20) Repeat the substance of the remarks in reference to the distinction between an adjective complementary modification and an adverbial modification.]

—We now pass on to consider the *adjective complementary* of the ACTIVE verb.

(1) This complement is very similar to the NOUN *complementary* of the *active verb.* (2) The difference is this: when the *noun complementary* is used, we intimate that the *passive object* becomes something *substantive* by the action expressed by the verb; on the contrary, when the adjective complementary is used, we intimate that the passive object becomes possessed of some *property* or *attribute*, by the action expressed by the verb. (3) When allowance is made for this difference, nearly all that we have said in reference to the *noun complementary* will apply to the *adjective complementary* of the active verb.

(4) It will be observed that here the adjective does not as when employed with the neuter verb express the condition of the SUBJECT as affected by the action indicated by the verb, but the condition of the *passive object* under the influence of the action indicated by the active verb. (5) It expresses the *complement* of the action which affects the passive object. For example, *Virtue renders life* HAPPY. Here *happy* expresses the condition of *life*, as influenced by the *action* of *virtue*, or a property of which *life* becomes possessed through the action asserted of virtue. *Happy* thus *completes renders.* (6) The *complete* action asserted here of virtue is *rendering happy*, and this action has for its objective modification *life*—the word expressing that to which the *complete action*, "*rendering happy*," is in this assertion *limited* or *directed.*

We submit a number of examples of the *adjective complementary* of the *active verb*, in order that this construction may be more perfectly understood.

"*We call* the *proud* HAPPY." ANALYSIS. After going through the analysis in the usual manner till we come to the modifications attached to the verb, we say the verb *call* is here modified by the *complementary adjective happy*, and the predicate (thus completed) *calling happy*

---

§ 89. (1) To what other form of complement is the *adjective complementary of the active verb* said to be similar? (2) What is the only difference between these two modifications? (3) Will what has been said of the one apply to the other?

(4) Repeat what is said of the distinction between the adjective used with the neuter and with the active verb. (5) What does the adjective used with the active verb express? Illustrate by an example. (6) Continue the illustration.

is further modified by the objective modification *proud*, which is an adjective *substantively used*.

REMARK.—The learner may follow this model as regards the construction we are considering, giving the full analysis of all the propositions, which we are about to adduce as examples.

"*All nations shall call him* BLESSED." "*Make us* GLAD." "*Oppression maketh* a *wise man* MAD." "*Hope deferred maketh* the *heart* SICK." "*Thou makest* the *earth* SOFT *with showers*." *Men call* the *prosperous* HAPPY; Oh, when *will they learn to think* the *virtuous alone* HAPPY? The *true philosopher accounts* the *good man* HAPPY. "*Leave* the *lily pale*, and *tinge* the *violet blue*." This *struck me dumb*.

(7) The usual place of the *adjective complementary* of the *active verb* is, like the *noun complementary*, after the *objective modification*, as in the examples now given. (8) But it is sometimes placed between the verb and the *objective modification*, especially when the objective is accompanied by modifications. (9) This will be seen in the following example. "The *streams* whereof *shall make* GLAD the *city of God*." Here, because the noun "*city*" is modified by the *noun and preposition* "of *God*," which a regard to perspicuity forbids to be separated from it, the *complementary adjective* "*glad*" is more conveniently placed first. (10) A *complementary adjective* is sometimes employed with the verb *make*, and the expression so formed employed in a general sense—without the limitation of an *objective modification*. For example: "*I make alive*."—Deut. 32: 39. Compare 2 Kings, 5: 7.—"The *hand of* the *diligent maketh* rich." (11) The force of the *complementary adjective* is perhaps better seen in such examples. (12) It is manifestly here a complement of the *verb*, and not a mere modification of the objective of the verb, as grammarians have very generally considered it, when in company with an objective. (13) We might multiply at pleasure examples of the use of complementary adjectives with the verb *make*. Such as, "*Make thee fruitful*." "*Make thee plenteous*." "*Make thy way prosperous*." "*Make themselves clean*." "*God made man upright*." "*Make manifest* the counsel of the heart." Here the *complementary* adjective comes before the *objective noun*, and for the same reason, as was mentioned above, viz., because the

---

(7) What is the usual place of the *adjective complementary* of the active verb in the arrangement of a proposition? (8) Where is it sometimes placed, and for what reason? (9) Illustrate by an example. (10) Repeat what is said in reference to a complementary adjective employed with the verb make; and give examples. (11) Repeat the remark on these examples. (12) What is the adjective manifestly in such examples? (13) Adduce more examples of the verb *make* thus completed.

objective "*counsel*" is accompanied by the modifying words "*of the heart.*"

(14) As in the case of the *noun complementary* of the *active verb*, so in the case of an adjective used after an active verb, the infinitive TO BE seems often to be *implied* in the construction. (15) Thus, *We thought him* WISE. *We considered him* PRUDENT. *They found him* INCAPABLE, or IGNORANT, or FOOLISH, or HONEST, &c. (16) These expressions may be considered, and may be treated in analysis, as abbreviated for, *We thought him* TO BE *wise*, &c. And then the pronoun *him* with the verb TO BE, having *wise* for its *complementary adjective*, will be *noun and infinitive contracted accessory complementary* of the verbs, *to think*, &c. (See § 142: 28.)

(17) As in the case of the *noun complementary* of the *active verb*, these *adjectives complementary* of the *active verb* are retained when the passive form of expression is employed. (18) They may then be called *adjectives complementary* of the *passive verb*. (19) Thus, *The Athenians called Aristides* JUST, becomes in the passive form, *Aristides was called* JUST *by the Athenians*. (20) The remarks made already in regard to the *noun complementary* employed with *passive verbs*, will apply, without much change, to the adjective thus employed. (See § 78.)*

It will be proper to bring all these kindred forms of the *noun* and the *adjective complementary* together, that their close similarity of character may be exhibited more clearly to the learner. The arrangement of these *complements*, which we are about to present, will also serve the purpose of fixing them more strongly in the memory of the young grammarian. (21) We have, then, *The noun complementary* of

* There is a manner of employing adjectives after verbs, especially prevalent in poetry, which perhaps has originated in an *insensible extension* of the construction we are now considering; and which we may call for the sake of distinction, *the adjective adverbially employed.* This use (or abuse) of adjectives we shall be able to explain with less trouble after we have considered the adverbs. We also reserve, till we come to the adverbs, the remarks which we have to make on the distinction between adjectives and adverbs.

(14) What word seems to be often *implied* in these constructions? (15) Illustrate by examples. (16) How may the expressions given as examples be treated in analysis?

(17) What happens when the passive form of expressing such assertions is used? (18) How may the adjective be called, when the passive form is used? (19) Illustrate by examples. (20) What remarks apply in this case?

(21) Enumerate the various species of the *noun complementary* and of the *adjective complementary*, and give an example of each from the table.

the NEUTER *verb*, *the noun complementary* of the ACTIVE *verb*, and *the noun complementary of* the PASSIVE *verb*. We have, in like manner, *the adjective complementary* of the *neuter verb*, *the adjective complementary* of the *active verb*, and *the adjective complementary* of the *passive verb*. We exhibit these symmetrically in the following table, with an example of each form of complement annexed:

	Noun Complementary.	*Adjective Complementary.*
Neut. V.	The boy becomes a *man.*	The boy becomes *manly.*
Act. V.	"Thou hast made thy servant *king.*"	"They made the king *glad.*"
Pass. V.	"The Word was made *flesh.*"	"The simple is made wise."

§ 90. GENERAL OBSERVATIONS ON THESE FORMS OF MODIFICATION.—These forms of modification have been, as we have already observed, first treated with that attention which their importance demands by the German grammarians. We exclude, of course, from this assertion the particular case of adjectives used with the verb TO BE, since much has been said of the construction of this verb with adjectives by grammarians and logicians in all ages. But from the view commonly taken of this construction, we have felt obliged by our convictions to record our dissent; the reasons for this dissent we have stated fully in another place. (See § 46, and note.) The Germans, too, so far as we know, have treated the adjectives after the verb *to be*, like all other grammarians, as forming the predicate of the propositions in which they are found, and the verb itself as being the simple *copula*, including no part of the predicate. But all these constructions exhibited in the above table, viz., the *noun* and the *adjective complementary* with all *neuter* verbs, except the verb *to be*, and the *noun* and the adjective with active and with passive verbs, the German grammarians have called the construction of the FACTITIVE OBJECT, dividing this *factitive object*, into the *factitive noun*, the *factitive infinitive*, the *factitive adjective*, and the *factitive noun and preposition*. This last we have not thought it necessary to notice, or to distinguish among the *noun* and *preposition complements*, as *in form* it differs nothing from the others. It is only distinguished by the *meaning* which it conveys—a distinction, as the logicians would call it, of *matter* not of *form*, and therefore not essential to language. We have an example of what the Germans mean by the *factitive object* expressed by a noun and a preposition in the assertion, *water was changed* INTO WINE. Here "*into wine*" expresses the *factitive object*—that into which the water was changed.

The name FACTITIVE OBJECT has been given to this species of complements by the German grammarians from the circumstance that they *often* express that which in the *neuter* and *passive* construction the *subject* is represented to be *made* or *constituted*, and in the *active* construction, that which the passive object is represented to be *made* or *constituted*, or represented to be *thought* or *imagined* to be *made* or *constituted*. The name seems to have been adopted from regarding as peculiarly conspicuous, among such constructions, examples like those given above, formed with the verb MAKE. To us the name appears to be not sufficiently comprehensive to embrace all the constructions which the Germans themselves have classed under it. This objection becomes still stronger when we bring into the same class of constructions (as *we have done*) the nouns and the very numerous adjectives which complete the verb *to be*. We regard the nouns and adjectives attached to the verb *to be*, as performing precisely the same kind of function, which nouns and adjectives attached to other neuter verbs perform. We cannot, therefore, consistently with these views follow the German grammarians in the employment of the name *factitive object*, as applicable to this whole class of complements. First, this term is not sufficiently comprehensive; and to use it might, on this account, only mislead the student. He might suppose that the term expresses a leading peculiarity *common* to this whole class of constructions—the *factitive object* implying some *effect* produced—in which he would find himself mistaken. Secondly, the term refers not to the *form* of language, but to the *matter* expressed. Now all grammatical divisions and terms should, as far as possible, refer to the proper subject of grammar, viz.: the *form* of expression, and not to the *matter* expressed. We do not deny that the grammarian may often profitably have recourse in his inquiries to the *matter* of expression—to *thought*. But his classifications and terms ought to have their foundation as much as possible in the peculiar properties of language—that is, in the peculiar properties of the *form* of *expression*. We have not been able to find a term that suits us to replace the German term. Such a term we want, as will adequately express the common properties, or some leading common property, of this whole class of complements. Till such term can be found, the kindred nature of these modifications may be indicated by the term *complementary*, common to the names which we have given to them severally, and which we have purposely confined exclusively to this particular class.

We may remark here the difficulties which grammarians have to encounter (*experto credite*), who have unthinkingly admitted that the distinction between adjectives and adverbs is, that adjectives modify or qualify *nouns*, and adverbs, on the contrary, modify *verbs, adjectives,* and other *adverbs.* They may call the adjective after the verb *to be,* the *predicate,* and say (without being able to allege a good reason, and in contradiction to all seeming likelihood) that a *noun* is always implied with such adjectives; that, for example, in the proposition, *The man is virtuous,* the noun man is implied in the predicate = The *man is a virtuous* MAN. This supposition appears to us wholly gratuitous, implying the actual existence at a remote period of an awkward form of expression in all languages, which we could not, perhaps, satisfactorily prove to have ever had customary place, at any period, in any language. Still, this manner of treating the adjective after the verb *to be* is incomparably better than to confound it, as some loose thinkers (perhaps we should not call them grammarians) have done, with the ordinary adjective modification, and make it agree with and belong to the subject noun. The same persons treat the adjective complementary of the active verb as a mere modifying adjective attached to the objective noun. According to the grammatical teachings of such persons, we could establish no distinction in analysis between propositions so diverse as, *We call the boy* GOOD, and *We call the good boy.* But, to return to the more consistent grammarians and logicians, who, to establish the assertion that adjectives never complete verbs, hold that a noun is always implied with every adjective in forming the predicate in propositions made with the verb *to be,* what will they say of the adjective in such examples as, *Honey tastes* SWEET, *The weather feels* COLD, *The fields look* GREEN? What noun can be supplied in these and in numerous similar examples? The fact appears to us incontestable—though a fact too long and too generally overlooked by grammarians—that adjectives are *very extensively* employed in all languages to complete verbs, and, consequently, that the true distinction between them and adverbs is to be sought in something else, than the untenable assumption that adjectives modify *nouns* and adverbs modify *verbs,* &c. How much confusion and waste of thought has been occasioned by yielding inconsiderately to the authority of the commonly received definitions of these two classes of modifying words!

We might, indeed, with more consistency assert that adjectives modify nouns exclusively; since *we* hold that the *predicate* included in every verb is a *noun,* and that it is the *predicate*—the noun part of the verb—not the copula or assertive force that is *completed* by the complementary adjective, as well as by every other form of modification. It may then be asked, Why not say at once, in accordance with *our* views, that the complementary adjective here, as elsewhere, modifies a noun—namely, the noun expressive of the predicate contained in the verb? We answer, because it would serve no useful purpose, and might mislead the learner. The only purpose which it could be expected to serve would be that of *simplification;* and this purpose, in our opinion, it could *not* serve, since, as will be seen from all that we have said, we look on the adjective thus employed as performing a function in reference to the predicate entirely different from that which it performs as the *descriptive* modification of an ordinary noun (To retain a *distinction* where there is no *difference* is unphilosophical, and often leads to important errors. But to get rid of a distinction where there is a real difference is equally unphilosophical, and equally calculated to mislead.) We should, therefore, be obliged to resort to some means of discriminating between this species of modification and the ordinary descriptive adjective modification; and none is more convenient than that presented to us by the usual distinction of the classes of words to which they are applied. *The descriptive adjective modification,* to ordinary *nouns,* the *adjective complementary to verbs and to verbal words.* It must not, however, be forgotten that it is not *as verbs* (in the sense in which we use this term), that is, as *assertive words,* that verbs are susceptible of this species of modification, but in consequence of the nature of the *matter* which they express, altogether independent of the fact that it is expressed in the assertive form. Hence, like other modifications applicable to verbs, these are applicable to verbal nouns, and verbal adjectives. We say, for example, *To make a man glad,* and *making glad,* as well as, *makes glad,* &c.

The difference between the *descriptive adjective modification* and the *complementary adjective modification,* may, perhaps, be briefly stated thus. The *descriptive adjective modification* expresses a quality or property contemplated, as inherent in the object expressed by the noun to which it is applied; the complementary adjective does not express a quality inherent in the conception expressed by the *verb* or *predicate* which it completes. On the contrary, when used with a neuter verb, it expresses an attribute asserted to pertain to the *subject* in the *mode* signified by the *predicate* in the neuter verb; and when used with an active verb, it expresses an attribute asserted to become the property of the *passive object,* in the mode or manner signified by the predicate contained in the active verb. To illustrate our meaning by examples: *The weather is cold, The weather grows cold, The weather feels cold.* Here the attribute *cold* is asserted to pertain to the *weather,* in the first proposition in the mode or manner expressed by *being;* in the second in the mode expressed by *growing;* and in the third in the mode expressed by *feeling.* Again, *A wise son makes his father's heart* GLAD; *The world calls the successful* GREAT. Here the quality expressed by *glad* is asserted to become the property of a *father's heart* in the mode signified by making, and the quality *great* is asserted to become the property of the *successful* in the mode signified by *calling.*

We have now finished what we have to say at present of the descriptive adjectives. We reserve what we have to say of the modifications which adjectives undergo, whether effected by *inflexion* or by the use of other words till we have considered the adverbs.

§ 91. THE DETERMINATIVE ADJECTIVES.—(1) We now proceed to make some remarks on the determinative adjectives. (2) We commence by enumerating the principal words of this kind in our language, since they are not, like the descriptive adjectives, a very numerous class. We shall enumerate them in groups, mentioning the names which grammarians have commonly given to these groups. We mentior

(3) 1st. *An*, which becomes *a* before a consonantal sound, and *the*. These two words have commonly been erected into a distinct *part of speech* by the grammarians, and called *the articles*—*an* or *a* being styled the *indefinite*, and *the* the *definite article*.

(4) 2d. The second group in our enumeration consists of the words called by the grammarians, the demonstrative pronouns, viz., *this* and *that* with their plural forms *these* and *those*, and the words *yon* and *yonder*.

(5) 3d. We may count what the grammarians have called indefinite pronouns as a third group. Among these are enumerated *all*, *any*, *both*, *few*, *many*, *much*, *no*, *none*, *other*, *another*, *several*, *some*, *such*, *whole*, and perhaps some other words.

(6) 4th. What are called distributive pronouns may be given as a fourth group. These are *each*, *every*, *either*, *neither*.

(7) 5th. The possessive pronouns form a fifth class. These are *my*, *thy*, *his*, *her*, *its*, referring to a single person or thing, and *our*, *your*, *their*, to a plurality of persons or things.

For more minute information in regard to some of these groups of determinatives, see *additional observations* on the determinatives and the pronouns. (See §§ 156, 158.)

(8) 6th. We enumerate as the sixth and last group the numerals, both the *cardinal numbers one*, *two*, *three*, *four*, &c., and the *ordinal numbers first*, *second*, *third*, *fourth*, &c.

(9) When a noun is accompanied both by a descriptive adjec-

---

§ 91. (1) What name do we give to the second class of adjectives? (2) Are the adjectives of this class numerous?

(3) Enumerate the first group of these adjectives and tell what is said of them. (4) Enumerate group second. (5) Group third. (6) Group fourth. (7) Group fifth. (8) Group sixth.

(9) Repeat the substance of what is said about the arrangement of the determinative and illustrate by examples.

tive and a determinative, the determinative is placed first, since i: applies to the noun as *described* or *modified* by the other adjective, or in other words completes the phrase made up of the noun and descriptive adjective together. Examples: A *virtuous man is esteemed;* THE *good man is loved;* THIS *upright man is prosperous;* THAT *innocent man was acquitted;* EVERY *vicious man is contemptible*, &c. Here the determinatives *a*, *the*, *this*, *that*, *every*, affect not the noun *man* alone, but man as already modified by the descriptive words *virtuous*, *good*, *upright*, &c. Hence, according to the usual mode of arrangement already described (see §§ 80 and 86: 17–19), it is placed before all that it *affects*—before both the *descriptive adjective* and the *noun.*

EXERCISES I., II., III., &c.—Let the learner form for himself a given number of propositions containing examples both of *determinative* and *descriptive adjectives.* When a determinative affects a *united descriptive adjective* and *noun*, let this be indicated by inclosing all that the determinative affects within parenthetic marks; thus, *A (spreading oak.)* (10) In analysis it will be sufficient to say in reference to a *determinative adjective*, that the noun which it affects is modified by the *determinative adjective*, or simply by the *determinative*, repeating the particular determinative.

[(11) Words of this class do not, like the *descriptive adjectives*, express a quality or property inherent in the things represented by the nouns to which they are attached. They only assist in giving a *determinate* meaning to the noun, or rather, in many cases, they merely indicate that the noun is employed *determinately;* the determining influence arising from some other accompanying modification, or something implied by the *matter*—the nature of the thought. (See *additional observations on determinatives*, § 158.) (12) In other words, *determinative adjectives* indicate the manner in which the mind of the speaker views an object, and intends to present it, not any property or attribute inherent in the object itself.

(13) It follows from the fact that the determinatives do not express properties which pertain to objects, that they are not employed in completing the *predicate*—that is, as *adjectives complementary* ot

---

(10) In analysis what is to be said in reference to determinatives? [(11) Repeat the substance of what is said in reference to the distinction between descriptive and determinative adjectives. (12) What do determinatives indicate?

(13) Are determinatives employed in completing the predicate? (14) Illustrate by examples.]

verbs—except when a noun suppressed by ellipsis is manifestly implied in them, on which the mind rests as the real *complementary* word. (14) For example, we cannot say that any thing *is*, or *becomes*, or *grows*, or *feels*, &c., *a* or *the*, or *any*, *all*, *every*, *some*, or even *this* or *that*, without something beyond implied, on which the mind rests, as the real *complement* of the predicate.]

NOTE.—The word THIS apparently serves as *complement* of the predicate in such expressions as, *The truth is* THIS, *he cannot succeed, because he is not industrious.* Here either we rest on the word truth implied again after *this; The truth is* THIS TRUTH, &c.; or, rather, the determinative *this* in such cases is employed exactly in its usual function in reference, not to a single word, indeed, but to the following compound proposition, *He cannot succeed*, &c., which here performs the grammatical function of a noun complementary of the predicate in the proposition having *truth* for subject, and *is* for verb. In corroboration of this latter view of the construction, it may be remarked that we can suppress the word *this* in the case before us, without altering, or indeed affecting the sense, save in a very slight degree, *The truth is, he cannot succeed*, &c. The only difference between the two forms of expression is, that in the first mentioned the predicated assertion is indicated as determinate—to that extent of determinateness which the sign *this* marks—that is, it is indicated as an assertion pointed out, as it were, to the eyes of the hearer. (*See additional observations on determinatives*, § 158.) There are a few words which seem to perform sometimes the part of determinative, and sometimes of descriptive adjectives, and there are perhaps words in regard of which it is not easy to decide exactly under which class they should be ranged. *Many men were present.* Here *many* is obviously determinative. It indicates nothing inherent in the men, but simply the manner in which the mind of the speaker regards them. In other words, the modification which the determinative *many* gives to the subject, is not essential to the truth of the proposition. The same assertion could be made of the men, whether regarded separately or collectively or in whatever way; *They were present.* But when I say, *Many hands make light work*, the modification given by many is essential to the truth of the assertion. *Many* thus employed, ranks amongst the descriptive adjectives, and it can be employed in the same descriptive sense (as equivalent to numerous), as a *complement* of the *predicate.* For example, *The spectators were many.* The determinative few is used in the same way in the proposition, "*The laborers are few.*" This has been already noticed.

CHAPTER VII.

OF ADVERBS.

§ 92. GENERAL REMARKS. (1) We now proceed to treat of another class of words, employed exclusively like the adjectives, for the purpose of modification. (2) This class of words has been called ADVERBS—*words attached to verbs*—because grammarians have generally entertained the notion that they perform a function in reference to verbs, similar to that which adjectives perform in reference to nouns. They have been considered, as it were, the *adjectives* of the *verb*. We shall have more to say presently of the characteristic marks of adverbs. (3) In the mean time, one fact will enable the young grammarian to distinguish them from adjectives; they are never employed alone to modify or complete a *noun* (except *verbal* nouns,) though the adjective is, as we have seen, often employed in completing *verbs*. (4) The adverbs are easily distinguished from all other classes of words, except the prepositions *adverbially* employed; and these are all included in the list given. § 81.

(5) The adverbs may be regarded as the most recently formed class of words in all languages. (6) We could, in expressing our thoughts, dispense with the use of them more easily than we could dispense with the use of any other class of words. All we express by them, can generally be expressed with equal clearness by means of other forms of modification. (7) They may be regarded as

---

§ 92. (1) For what general purpose are the adverbs exclusively employed? (2) What is said in reference to the name *adverb*? (3) By what fact may they be always distinguished from adjectives? (4) Repeat what is said about distinguishing adverbs from prepositions in one of their uses.

(5) How may the adverbs be regarded in reference to their antiquity? (6) What is said in reference to dispensing with the use of adverbs? (7) To what form of expression may they be regarded as equivalent? (8) Illustrate by examples.

abbreviated forms of expression, equivalent to a modification, consisting of two, more frequently of three or four, distinct words—a *preposition*, and a *noun* generally preceded by a *descriptive* adjective, often by both a *descriptive* and a *determinative* adjective. (8) We subjoin a few examples, for the purpose of illustration:

Wisely = *In a wise manner; or in a wise way.*
Moderately = *In a moderate manner.*
Now = *At the present time.*
Where = *In what place?*
Why = *For what reason?* &c., &c.

(9) The learner will readily discover that we could dispense with the use of the above and all similar adverbs, without any injury to the perspicuity of language; but he will, at the same time, see that they contribute greatly to compactness and brevity of expression. (10) The use of this class of words has thus an important influence on the strength of language, enabling us to avoid a multiplication of words, which, especially in the case of small words like prepositions and determinatives, tends greatly to enfeeble the expression of thought. (11) There are a few words classed with the adverbs, to which some of these remarks do not strictly apply, such as the negative particle *not*, &c. But of this in another place.

REMARKS IN REFERENCE TO THE FUNCTIONS OF ADVERBS.

(12) Adverbs are employed either to modify verbs, or to modify adjectives or other adverbs. (13) The great majority of this class of words is employed exclusively to modify verbs. (14) A few are employed exclusively to modify adjectives and adverbs, and very few to modify both verbs and adjectives. (15) Regarded in this point of view, the adverbs may be divided into three classes

(9) What may be discovered from these examples? (10) On what has the use of adverbs an important influence? (11) Are there some words classed as adverbs to which these remarks do not strictly apply?

(12) What classes of words are adverbs employed to modify? (13) What class do the great majority of adverbs modify? (14) State the manner in which a few of them are employed. (15) Enumerate the three classes into which adverbs may be divided in reference to the kind of words which they modify.

—1st, modifiers of verbs; 2d, modifiers of adjectives; 3d, modifiers both of verbs and adjectives.

[(16) We do not make a separate class of those adverbs which are employed to modify other adverbs, because the words employed for this purpose are the same which are employed to modify adjectives, and because the adverb employed to modify another adverb, virtually modifies an adjective, viz., the adjective involved in the modified adverb. In other words, it is because of the adjective contained in the modified adverb, that it admits of being affected by another adverb. For example, *That man acted* VERY WISELY. Here the adverb *wisely* is affected by another adverb, *very*. The true nature of this modification, or that which is really affected by it, will be clearly seen when we expand *wisely* into the phrase of which it is an abbreviated expression. *That man acted* IN A VERY WISE MANNER. Here we see that *very* modifies the adjective *wise;* and as the two propositions are exactly equivalent, it is manifest that, in the first proposition, what it really modifies is the same adjective involved in *wisely*. (17) The fact, therefore, that an adverb modifies another adverb, resolves itself into the fact, that an adverb modifies an adjective. This simplifies our division of the uses or functions of adverbs. In the enumeration of these functions, we may safely overlook the fact, that they modify other adverbs (as this is included in the function of modifying adjectives), and say that they modify either verbs, including verbal words, or adjectives including those contained in adverbs.

The grammarians, we think, have not sufficiently attended to the fact, that the adverbs generally employed to modify adjectives, are altogether distinct from those which modify verbs, and incapable of being applied to verbs; and the great mass of those applicable to verbs and verbal words are, on the other hand, incapable of being applied to adjectives.]

(18) The adverbs employed exclusively with adjectives, are chiefly those which indicate *intensity*, or the *degree*, in which the same *quality* or *attribute* is found to exist, or conceived to exist. (19) We may enumerate as examples, the words *very*, *too*, *much*, *extremely*, *exceedingly*, *supremely*, &c. And the words used to express

---

[(16) Repeat with illustration by examples the reason assigned for including adverbs which modify other adverbs within the class which modify adjectives. (17) Into what, in conclusion, does the fact that an adverb modifies an adverb resolve itself?]

(18) What kind of adverbs are employed exclusively with adjectives? (19) Enumerate

comparison *equally*, *more*, *most*, *less*, *least*, &c. (20) Some of these are found after verbs, but then they have the force of adjectives employed substantively, and should be treated as such in analysis. (21) Even the few adverbs which admit of being employed both with verbs and adjectives, seem generally to express a different sense with verbs from that which they express with adjectives. (22) We may illustrate this by the words *as* and *so*. These are used to modify both adjectives and verbs. *He thinks* AS *I think*. *He is* AS *wise* AS *learned*. *He thinks* SO. *He is* SO *prudent*. In these examples it is obvious that these words *as* and *so*, employed with the verb *think*, express a *manner* of thinking; but employed with the adjectives *wise* and *prudent*, express the *degree* of intensity of these qualities. (23) We do not maintain that *as* and *so*, *themselves*, have, as here employed, two different senses, but that the word *implied* with these abbreviations is different, according as they are employed to modify a verb or an adjective. (24) *Manner or way* is implied when they are used with a verb, and some such meaning as that expressed by *degree* when they are used with adjectives. (25) In a word, the adverb modifying the adjective, and the adverb modifying the verb, may be regarded as having some claim to be considered as distinct *parts of speech*, or classes of words.

EXERCISES.—Form propositions containing adjectives modified by adverbs.

[(26) We may recognise a distinction among adverbs similar to that which we have recognised among adjectives—a distinction which might be expected since adverbs are formed from adjectives, or imply the sense of adjectives of both classes. (27) As we have descriptive adjectives expressing inherent qualities or attributes of objects, and determinative adjectives expressing, not qualities of objects, but some relation to other objects, or some circumstance of place, number, &c., or, in other words, the form, or relation, in which the speaker chooses

---

a few examples. (20) What is said of some of these when found after verbs? (21) What is said of the few adverbs which are used both with verbs and adjectives? (22) Illustrate by the uses of the words *as* and *so*. (23) Do we maintain that *as* and *so* have each two different senses? (24) What word is implied when they are used with a verb, and what when used with an adjective? (25) Repeat what is said of the difference between these two classes of adverbs.

[(26) What distinction may be recognised among adverbs? (27) Illustrate further the nature of this distinction.]

to present objects; so we have *qualifying* adverbs, and adverbs ex pressive of *circumstances* of *time*, *place*, *order*, &c. This distinction may, perhaps, be traced in the adverbs employed to modify *adjectives*, but it can be much more clearly traced, and it is of more importance to mark it, in reference to those adverbs which are employed to modify verbs.]

(28) In reference to *meaning*, we may distinguish two grand classes of the adverbs which modify verbs. Those of the first class express the *manner* of the action indicated by the verb, and are generally known by the name of *adverbs of manner;* those of the second class express some *circumstance*, generally of *time*, *place*, or *order*, in reference to the assertion in the proposition in which they are found. This class we may venture to distinguish by the name of *adverbs of circumstance*, or *circumstantial adverbs.*

(29) The grammarians usually distinguish them by the names of *adverbs* of *time*, of *place*, of *order*, &c.—names which we shall apply, as others have done, to the sub-classes, whilst we give the name *circumstantial adverbs* to them all in common. We give this common name to mark that they possess common properties, as distinguished from the adverbs of *manner.*

(30) Now the *adverbs* of *manner* nearly all involve in their meaning the sense of a descriptive adjective, and like descriptive adjectives, express an *inherent* qualification of the *action* denoted by the predicate which they complete. (31) For example, *That boy acts* PRUDENTLY. Here *prudently* involves the sense of the descriptive adjective *prudent*, from which it is formed, being, in fact, equivalent to the phrase, *in a prudent manner*, and it serves as a *descriptive inherent* qualification of *acting*, as here predicated of the *boy.**

EXERCISES.—Form propositions having verbs modified by *adverbs of manner.*

---

* There are a few adverbs of manner which involve the sense of a de terminative, not of a descriptive adjective. We may take as examples, *as*

---

(28) Describe the two classes into which adverbs which modify verbs are divided, and mention the names by which we distinguish them.

(29) By what names do grammarians usually distinguish circumstantial adverbs, and how do we apply these names?

(30) What is always involved in the meaning of adverbs of *manner?* And in what do they consequently resemble descriptive adjectives? (31) Illustrate this by an example.

(32) CIRCUMSTANTIAL ADVERBS, on the contrary, do not express a qualification descriptive of the action denoted by the verb, but express a *circumstance* which rather modifies the *whole assertion* than completes the *part of the predicate contained in the verb;* and

---

and *so*, when employed to modify verbs. As, then, means *in the manner*, or *in the same*, or *a similar manner*, and so, *in such manner*. But these words, whether employed with adjectives or verbs, do not express a complete modification, but serve as *conjunctive words* of *reference* to introduce (or direct to) the real modification, the essential part of which is expressed by the subjoined proposition, or abbreviated proposition, or sometimes, in the case of *so*, by a preceding proposition referred to. For illustration let us take the example, *He thinks as I think*. Here, *I think*, is the essential, the really descriptive part of the modification—what describes the manner in which *He thinks*—and *as* performs a function similar to what we shall find presently the conjunctive pronouns perform in connecting modifying propositions. The assertion in the example may be expanded into *He thinks* IN THE MANNER IN WHICH *I think*, or *He thinks* IN WHICH MANNER *I think*. The conjunctive word *which*, together with *in the manner*, we here see, are necessary to form a complete equivalent for what is indicated by the (so called) adverb *as*. We may subjoin examples of the use of *so*. *This young man conducts himself* so, *that all his companions esteem him*=IN SUCH A MANNER, *that all his companions esteem him*. *That all his companions esteem him*, describes the *manner* in which the young man conducts himself, and so *refers* us to this description. Even after we have expanded the assertion in the example as above, there is, perhaps, still an ellipsis of another proposition. But the full expansion of such assertions is not necessary to our present purpose. We may give as a second example, *The man acted* so, *as to deserve much praise*, equivalent to *The man acted in such a manner*, viz., *the manner to deserve much praise*. *To deserve much praise*, is here the real description of the manner in which the *man acted;* and the predicate *acting* is really completed by *manner* with this description attached. This infinitive form of modification is that which most commonly follows the word *so*. But *so* is also employed to refer to a modification expressed in the preceding part of a discourse; as, *But this man could not treat his friends* so; referring to some manner of treating friends already described.

What we have said of *as* and *so* employed with verbs will equally apply to them when employed with adjectives, since, in both uses, they indicate comparison, and refer for the development of the sense, which they for a moment *represent*, to another proposition, or phrase occupying the place of a proposition.

---

(32) What is here said of the circumstantial adverbs?

the adjective implied in these *circumstantial adverbs*, when one is implied, is often a determinative.*

[(33) Let us illustrate this by a few examples: *The boy* NOW *writes to his father; The house stood* HERE. FIRST, *our friend is industrious;* SECONDLY, *he wrongs no man;* THIRDLY, *he is kind to every body.* In these examples, it will be seen that the adverbs *now*, *here*, *first*, *secondly*, *thirdly*, do not qualify the predicate or complete its sense, but modify the *whole assertion*. *Now* in the first does not express a quality of *writing*, as *beautifully* does, when we say, *The boy writes beautifully*, but a modification of the whole assertion, *The boy writes to his father*. *Here* does not express a quality of standing, as *gracefully*, for example, does, when we say, *The man stands gracefully;* but modifies the whole assertion, subject and predicate taken together, *The house stood.* In other words, it modifies not *standing* alone, but the asserted *standing of the house.* (34) Though adverbs of this description have not a connection so intimate and exclusive with the verbal predicate, as the adverbs of manner (or what we may call descriptive adverbs), still they have a close connection with it, since they modify the *whole assertion*, and *the force of every assertion is concentred in the predicate.* Hence, both classes of adverbs are considered by the grammarians as words modifying the *verb*. Still the distinction which we are tracing between *adverbs* modifying the *verbal predicate directly*, and those which affect the *assertion generally*, is of some importance when we come to a strict analysis of language as a vehicle of thought. We shall also find presently that adverbs of the latter kind—circumstantial adverbs—admit of an arrangement in reference to the verb different from that which descriptive adverbs admit. (35) We must not omit

* We say often, because we have not examined these adverbs so completely as to venture to assert in an unqualified manner, that all which imply an adjective, imply a determinative, and not a descriptive adjective. Some words usually reckoned as adverbs, and which, if so considered, must be classed among the circumstantial adverbs, imply no adjective, but simply a noun and preposition. Such are, *perhaps, perchance, peradventure,* and likely, some others.

[(33) Illustrate by examples what is said of the circumstantial adverbs modifying the whole assertion, and not the verb merely. (34) What farther is admitted in reference to the circumstantial adverbs? State the reasons for which the grammarians consider them as modifying the verb of the proposition in which they occur.

(35) What fact is noticed in reference to the circumstantial adverbs given in the examples above? (36) Illustrate.]

the fact that all the above *circumstantial* adverbs either imply or contain in them a *determinative*, not a *descriptive* word. (36) Thus *now* and *here* imply the determinative *this*. *Now* = *at this time*, *Here* = *in this place*. *First* is a determinative adjective—an *ordinal numeral*—used adverbially, and *secondly*, *thirdly*, each contain a determinative, namely, the *ordinal numerals*, *second* and *third*.]

ARRANGEMENT OF ADVERBS.—(37) The adverb which modifies an adjective or another adverb is generally placed before the word which it modifies. The adverb *enough* is an exception; it follows the adjective which it modifies; as, *He is wise enough*, *He is rich enough*.

(38) The descriptive adverb is most generally placed after the verb which it modifies; as, *This man acted wisely*. (39) But the circumstantial adverb admits of much greater freedom of arrangement.

[(40) This was to be expected from what we have said of the function of this species of adverb. Since it modifies the whole assertion and not the predicate in particular, it is not necessary that it should accompany the verb so closely as the adverb of manner, which has for its function to describe the action expressed by the verb. Example: NOW, *the boy studies; The boy* NOW *studies; The boy studies* NOW *in earnest*, or *studies in earnest* NOW. Here the adverb *now* is arranged in three different manners. But the writer of delicate taste will not employ these three forms of expression indifferently. In the first, the adverb occupying the more emphatic place has peculiar force. It implies a contrast in reference to the occupation of the boy. *Now he studies*, though formerly he did not. In the second, it implies his present occupation to the exclusion for the time of other pursuits. In the third form a contrast is implied between his present and his former *manner* of studying. The force of *now* applies to the assertion as modified by the words *in earnest*. (41) *Circumstantial* adverbs often take the first place in the proposition, especially adverbs of time, as *always*, *sometimes*, *often*, *never;* and adverbs of order, as, *first*, *secondly*, &c.

---

(37) Where is the adverb which modifies an adjective or an adverb placed? Mention the exception.

(38) What is said of the arrangement of the descriptive adverb, or adverb of manner? (39) What is said of the arrangement of the circumstantial adverb?

[(40) What reason for expecting greater freedom in the arrangement of this species of modification? Illustrate by an example. Show how the sense is affected by a change of the arrangement.

(41) What place do circumstantial adverbs often take in the proposition?

The same is true of the equivalent *noun and preposition* modifications, *at all times*, *at no time*, *in the first place*, *in the second place*, &c. (42) When *never* is placed first, the subject and verb are generally transposed; as, "Never *was* a *man* so used."

The circumstantial adverb, especially when thus placed before the verb, is also, like the noun and preposition so placed, often separated by interpunction from the other parts of the proposition, by a comma after, if it comes first in order, by a comma both before and after, when part of the proposition precedes and part follows it. (See appendix on punctuation.)

(43) As a general rule in reference to the arrangement of adverbs, those adverbs which modify a particular word in a proposition must be so placed, in order to secure perspicuity, that the reader cannot mistake the word which they are intended to modify. (44) The word *only* is peculiarly subject to be misplaced, as, for instance, in the oft-quoted and oft censured passage in one of the papers of Addison: "By greatness I do not *only* mean the bulk of any single object, but the largeness of a whole view, considered as one entire piece." Here "*only*," to avoid obscurity, should have followed "*object.*"

(45) Adverbs, when employed to connect propositions, are necessarily placed in the beginning of the modifying proposition which they unite to the principal proposition. Such adverbs we shall notice hereafter under the name of *Conjunctive Adverbs*, when we come to treat of conjunctions. Adverbs used in interrogation are also placed first in the interrogative proposition.

We may here enumerate and classify some of the principal *circumstantial adverbs*. It would be useless to attempt to enumerate the adverbs of manner, or descriptive adverbs, such is their multitude; and they seem to need no classification.

Among the circumstantial adverbs we enumerate

(46) I. Adverbs of Place.

1. *In a place.*	Here, there, where.
2. *To a place.*	Hither, thither, whither.*

* See Note at the end of this section.

(42) What inversion usually happens when a proposition commences with the adverb *never*? What is said of interpunction?

(43) Repeat the general rule in reference to the arrangement of adverbs. (44) What adverb is peculiarly subject to be misplaced, and therefore claims peculiar care?

(45) What is said of the place of conjunctive adverbs, and interrogative adverbs?

(46) Repeat the enumeration of the adverbs of place.

3. *Towards a place.* Hitherward, thitherward, whitherward.
4. *From a place.* Hence, thence, whence.

(47) II. Adverbs of Time.

1. *Present time.* Now, instantly, &c.
2. *Past time.* Heretofore, already, hitherto, lately, &c.
3. *Future time.* Afterwards, hereafter, presently, ever, never.
4. *Definite repetition.* Once, twice, thrice, again, &c.
5. *Indefinite repetition.* Often, seldom, frequently.

(48) III. Adverbs of Order.

First, secondly, thirdly, &c.

(49) We might add interrogative adverbs as a class. Some of these are circumstantial, as, *Why*, *wherefore*, *when*, *where;* some express manner interrogatively as *how*=*in what manner*.

(50) We may here remark that the verb *to be*, and some other neuter verbs expressive of *posture* or a *state of being*, such as *stand*, *sit*, *lie*, &c., are rarely modified by adverbs of manner. These same verbs are most frequently modified by adjectives; they freely admit the modification of circumstantial adverbs, and all, except *to be*, take the modification of some few adverbs of manner. Thus we say, *to stand or to sit gracefully;* but when we wish to say that a man, for instance, stands or sits in an erect or upright manner, we have recourse to the adjective modification, and say, *The man stands* ERECT, *The man sits erect.*

(51) The verb *to be*, scarcely, so far as we recollect, admits the modification of an adverb of manner, or descriptive adverb. The expression, formed by this verb with the word *well*, in such propositions as *He is well*, may seem an exception. But *well* here, we think, is plainly an adjective; just as *unwell* and *sick* are in the propositions, *He is unwell*, *He is sick.*]

Exercises I., II., &c.—Form propositions containing examples, 1st of adverbs of place; 2d, adverbs of time; 3d, adverbs of order, &c.

Note.—It has become so common to employ *here*, *there*, *where*, instead of *hither*, *thither*, *whither*, when we express motion to a place, that it would scarcely be safe to call such expressions as *Come here*, *Go there*, *Where are*

(47) The adverbs of time. (48) The adverbs of order.
(49) Repeat the remark about the interrogative adverbs.
(50) Repeat the remark about the verb *to be* and some other neuter verbs in reference to the adverbial modification. (51) Does the verb *to be* take adverbs of manner as modification.]

you going? ungrammatical. The proper old forms of expression, *Come hither*, *Go thither*, *Whither are you going?* seem likely to become altogether obsolete, especially in colloquial discourse. It is a misfortune to lose the useful distinction which the employment of *hither*, *thither*, &c., affords us; but in matters of language mankind in our day seem to regard their *ears* more than their *intellect*—*sound* more than *sense;* and the ears decide the question against these rough northern terminations in *ther*.

Hence, means *from this place; Thence, from that place*, &c., without the employment of a preposition. Most grammarians declare against *From hence*, *From whence*, &c., as improper forms of expression. Yet these forms are found in our best authors, and even in the pages of those who denounce them as ungrammatical. In colloquial discourse, they are constantly used. There is not the same apology for this abuse as for that mentioned above. *From hence* is no improvement as regards sound, compared with *hence*. And the expression introduces a grammatical anomaly—an adverb preceded by a preposition. The abuse has arisen from regarding *hence* as a noun meaning *this place*. Perhaps it really is a noun with something like a case ending, implying the same sense as the preposition *from*, and which, like other cases, has been unable to maintain itself in the conflict with the *noun and preposition* form of modification. Hence we come to employ *from* before *hence*, as before other nouns, not regarding the fact that its form already implies the force of *from*. The resistance to this abuse has not yet been relinquished by those who aim at correctness in writing and speaking, and we think should not be relinquished.

The reader will please observe the analogical formation of the above adverbs of place—a beauty not often met in the English of the present day. This uniformity will be more clearly seen under the following arrangement.

	This place.	*That place.*	*What place?*
In.	Here,	There,	Where?
From.	Hence,	Thence,	Whence?
To.	Hither,	Thither,	Whither?
Towards.	Hitherward,	Thitherward,	Whitherward?

§ 93. Derivation and Formation of Adverbs.—(1) Some of the adverbs may be regarded as *primitive* words, since they are always employed in the present use of the language as adverbs, and are not derived from any other known word. These, however, form but a small proportion of this very extensive class of words, and even these were probably at an earlier date nouns or adjectives. We give as examples, *Here*, *there*, *then*, *now*.

§ 93. (1) What is said of primitive adverbs? Give examples.

(2) A large proportion of our adverbs of manner are formed from adjectives, by adding the termination *ly*; as, from *virtuous* is formed the adverb *virtuously*; from *wise*, *wisely*, &c. (3) An adverb of this sort may be accounted an abbreviated method of expressing the adjective which it involves, together with the word *manner*, preceded by the preposition *in*. Thus, *Virtuously*=*In a virtuous manner*, *Wisely*=*In a wise manner*, &c.

(4) The adverbs of order are also formed by adding *ly* to the several ordinal numbers, *second*, *third*, *fourth*, &c. Adverbs, *secondly*, *thirdly*, *fourthly*, &c. *Firstly* has also been sometimes used, but instead of this form we now employ *first*, both as ordinal adjective and adverb of order. *Secondly*, *thirdly*, &c., are equivalent to *In the second place*, *In the third place*, &c.

[(5) The termination *ly* has come to us from the Anglo-Saxon *lice*, from which has descended our word *like*. (6) It may be observed here that the Anglo-Saxons formed many of their adjectives by adding the termination *lic* to nouns; and adverbs by adding *lice* to adjectives. (7) In our language the distinction between *lic* and *lice* has been lost, and both are represented by *ly*. (8) For example, from the nouns *God*, *man*, *ghost*, *king*, *world*, &c., we form the adjectives *godly*, *manly*, *ghostly*, *kingly*, *worldly*, &c. And from the adjectives *just*, *gracious*, *generous*, &c., the adverbs *justly*, *graciously*, *generously*, &c.; completely confounding the terminations expressive of the adjective and the adverbial meanings. We find, however, little difficulty in distinguishing these classes of words by their functions. (9) We may also generally distinguish the adverb by the fact that it is formed from an adjective; though a few words formed from nouns by the addition of *ly*, are employed both as adjectives and adverbs; as *daily*, *weekly*, *monthly*, *yearly*, &c. These may be classed with *adjectives adverbially* employed. (10) From the adjective *good* we have formed *goodly* employed as an adjective, and not as an adverb.]

(11) There are some irregularities in the formation of these adverbs

---

(2) How are many of the adverbs of manner formed? Examples. (3) How may such adverbs be considered? Example.

(4) What is said of the formation of adverbs of order? Examples.

[(5) Repeat what is said of the origin of the termination *ly*. (6) What is said of the manner in which some adjectives and adverbs were formed in Anglo-Saxon? (7) Has the distinction observed in Anglo-Saxon been retained in English? (8) Illustrate by examples. (9) How can we usually distinguish an adjective ending in *ly* from an adverb having the same termination? (10) Mention an exception.]

(11) Repeat what is said of the irregularity in the formation of adverbs from adjectives

in *ly*. From adjectives ending in *le*, adverbs are formed by omitting the final *e* and adding *y*. Thus from *able*, is formed *ably*, from *simple*, *simply*, &c. These may be regarded as contracted and softened forms, for the more uncouth words, *ablely*, *simplely*, &c. (12) When the adjective ends in *e*, the *e* is often omitted; as, *due*, *duly*, *true*, *truly*. Here the *e* is preceded by a vowel. When it is preceded by a consonant, it is generally retained; as, *sole*, *solely*, *servile*, *servilely*, &c., but *whole*, makes *wholly*. When the adjective ends in *ll*, one *l* is omitted in the adverb; as, *full*, *fully*, &c. But these are matters of spelling rather than of grammar.

Exercises.—Give examples of adverbs formed from adjectives. Adjectives from nouns.

(13) We may here notice that many words recognised as adverbs, are compounded of two or more words, which, separately taken, form some one of the species of modifications already treated. We have examples in *Therefore* = *for this; Where-with* = *with which; In-deed, Never-the-less* = *never in the less degree*, *degree* or some such word being *implied*. In *therefore* and *wherefore*, thing, or some such noun is also *implied*.

(14) Many words compounded with the abbreviated preposition *a* have been classed by the grammarians among the *adverbs;* such as, *abed*, *aloft*, *ashore*, *aground*, &c. These words, we think, are seldom, if ever, used as adverbs. If we do not analyze them as *noun and preposition modifications*, but treat them as single words, they are not *adverbs*, but *adjectives* employed, generally, as *complementary* of *neuter verbs.** (15) We may illustrate this by the example, *He lies abed.*

* All words like these which modify verbs have been thrown by the grammarians into the class of adverbs, because they have not adverted to the fact that many verbs are modified by *adjectives*, but consider all single words with the exception of objective nouns as adverbs when they are employed to modify *verbs*. It will be seen from what we have already said that this view cannot be maintained; that on the contrary there are several verbs which rarely admit an adverbial modification, but freely take a *complementary adjective*. The verb *to be* is an example, and most verbs which express the state or posture of the subject; as, *to stand*, *to lie*, *to sit*, &c.

in *le*, and give examples. (12) Repeat remarks as to those formed from adjectives ending in *e* preceded by a vowel, and in *e* preceded by a consonant. Give the examples.

(13) Repeat what is said of adverbs formed of words which separately taken constitute one of the modifications already considered. Illustrate by examples.

(14) What is said of certain words formed with the preposition *a*? Give examples (15) Illustrate the assertion that these compounds are not adverbs, using for this purpose as an example, *He lies abed.*

Here we must either say that *abed* is equivalent to *on bed—noun and preposition modification*—or that it is an *adjective* compounded of these words. Surely *abed*, taken as a single word, is as much an *adjective*, when we say, *He lies abed*, or *He is abed*, as *flat* is an adjective, when we say, *He lies flat*, or *The roof is flat*. The same reasoning will apply to *asleep*, *aloft*, *ashore*, &c., in the propositions *He is asleep*, or *He lies asleep; The ship is ashore*, or *lies ashore; The bird rises aloft*, or *sings aloft*, &c.

(16) Many adjectives are employed in our language *adverbially*—generally as *adverbs of manner*—some noun being suppressed which the mind of the hearer is expected to supply. We may give as examples of adjectives often so employed the words *better*, *best*, *worse*, *worst;* as, *He acted better*, *best*, *worse*, *worst*—expressions equivalent to *He acted in a better manner*, *in the best manner*, &c. (17) The employment of adjectives as adverbs is more common in some languages than it is in ours. In German, for instance, "all adjectives are employed as adverbs of manner, without assuming any distinctive termination like the English *ly*." (Becker's Germ. Gram. for the English, p. 162, Frank. 1845.)

(18) It often happens that an adjective preceded by a preposition is used *adverbially*. Examples: *In vain*=*In a vain manner; In short*=*In a short way, or manner; In general*=*In a general way, or manner*. In some cases the ellipsis cannot be so easily supplied. For example, *at least*, *at most*, *at all*, &c. In such expressions a whole proposition is sometimes left to be supplied by the hearer or reader; and what proposition, or what words, we must ascertain in each particular case from the connection of the discourse. The easiest (though certainly not the most satisfactory) way of treating such abbreviated expressions is to call them, as the grammarians generally have done, *adverbial phrases*.

EXERCISES.—Propositions containing what are called adverbial phrases; always supply the noun in analysis.

(19) It may be observed, once for all, that it is a lazy and unphilosophical practice to treat every word, which expresses a circumstance modifying the predicate of a proposition, and which happens to be somewhat difficult to analyze fully and correctly, as an adverb, or, if more than one word, as an adverbial phrase. (20) The proper, the only

(16) What is said of adjectives employed in our language as adverbs of manner? Illustrate by examples. (17) What is said of the practice in other languages of employing the unchanged adjective as an adverb?

(18) Repeat what is said of (the so-called) *adverbial phrases*, illustrating by examples.

(19) Describe a practice characterized as lazy and unphilosophical. (20) What is repre-

rational method of analysis, is to treat as an adverb no expression which can be readily brought under any of the other classes of modifications. (21) Adverbs are only contracted or abbreviated forms equivalent to other modifications, and every one, in order to show that he thoroughly understands the analysis of language, must be able to exhibit in every case the expression to which the adverb is equivalent, or which it represents. (22) To call any expression an *adverb*, or an *adverbial phrase*, which admits of being directly brought under one of the other forms of modification, is therefore wholly unwarrantable and improper.

(23) In consistency with these remarks we cannot admit that such words as *yesterday*, *to-day*, *to-night*, *to-morrow*, belong to the class of adverbs. Yesterday is a compound noun formed by the union of an adjective, now obsolete (save in composition), with the noun *day*. The same observation applies to the expressions *to-day*, *to-night*, *to-morrow*. Whatever may have given origin to the use of the particle *to* in this manner before the words *day*, *night*, &c., this particle, as here used, is now manifestly equivalent to the determinative *this*. Compare, *I will go to-day*, and *I will go this week*. Such expressions we analyze as nouns—nouns performing the function of the *accusative of time*. (See § 84.)

(24) There are several words commonly classed among the adverbs which do not come, as it seems to us, within any definition which has been given of this species of words. One of these is the *negative particle* NOT. This can scarcely, with propriety, be called a *modifying* word. Whether we consider it as affecting, exclusively, the assertive force of the verb, or as affecting the predicate (including the *part* of the predicate contained in the verb), it cannot, in strict propriety of language, be said to *modify* that which it serves rather completely to *reverse* or *exclude*. We prefer to call it by a name peculiar to itself, *the negative particle*.

NOTE.—It is a question among logicians, whether the negative particle in all cases affects the *copula?* whether, consequently, we are to admit two forms of the copula, viz., the *affirmative* form, employed in what are called *affirmative propositions*, and the *negative* form in negative propositions? or,

---

sented as the proper and rational method of analysis? (21) What are adverbs here said to be, and what should we be able to exhibit in analysis when an adverb occurs? (22) What mode of analysis is said to be unwarrantable and improper?

(23) Enumerate some forms of expression commonly called adverbs of time, and give the reasons for excluding them from this class.

(24) Repeat the substance of what is said in reference to the word NOT.

whether the negative particle may not, at least in some cases, be considered as affecting the predicate? Now, if we refer to what most of the *followers* of Aristotle (though not Aristotle himself) have considered as the primary form of propositions, and to which they attempt to reduce all propositions, that is, those which have some tense of the verb *to be*, for their assertive word, accompanied by a complementary adjective, we agree with those who maintain that the *negative* always affects the verb IS, which the logicians have hitherto regarded (we think, *improperly*) as the naked *copula*, and that it never affects the *adjective alone* which they have recognised as forming the complete predicate. But when we distinguish (as we have felt compelled by the results of the investigation described in another part of this treatise to do) in the verb *to be*, as in other verbs, the *predicate part* of the word from the *indication* of assertion, it may probably lead to an important modification of the manner in which logicians commonly present this subject. Though in such a proposition as *The steward is* NOT *faithful*, the negative *not* cannot be regarded with propriety, we believe, as affecting only the adjective *faithful*, yet it may be that it affects, not the assertive force of the verb *is*, but that part of the predicate contained in this verb. We are inclined to think, that it is exactly this which the negative in all cases affects; and if it affects what we have recognised as the leading part of the predicate, it really, through this, affects the entire predicate, though not *directly* or *exclusively* that which logicians have generally regarded as the predicate of propositions of this form. Thus, in the proposition, *The steward is not faithful*, though we agree with those who deny that it is logically correct to say, that NOT *faithful* is asserted of the steward, yet we think it may not be incorrect to say, that NOT BEING *faithful* is asserted of him.

It will be seen that we suspect both parties to this question—those who regard the negative as affecting what *they* call the predicate, and those who regard it as affecting the copula alone—to be in error; and that they have been led into error by adopting what we cannot but consider an incorrect analysis of propositions. In opposition to both, we expect that it will be found that the negative affects the *real predicate*—the *whole predicate*, according to our analysis, which finds in propositions of the above form the *leading part* of the predicate in what has been hitherto considered the mere copula.

We do not, however, feel prepared to assert any thing very positively on this point. Our examination of the bearing of the views we have adopted in reference to the copula, on the distinction between the affirmative and negative proposition, has not been sufficiently extensive and exact to satisfy our own mind completely, or entitle us to speak more decidedly on this subject. We leave the matter to the care of the logicians. If our analysis of propositions shall be found correct, and should be adopted, we think it must lead to some modification—we hope to a simplification—of the treatment of negative propositions.

(25) The words YES and NO are commonly, but we think very improperly, classed with the adverbs. These words are not modifying words; they are never applied either to verb or adjective for this purpose. Neither do they belong to any class of words hitherto examined by us. (26) Each of them is, in fact, equivalent to a whole proposition. YES, employed in answer to an *interrogative* proposition, is equivalent to that proposition asserted *affirmatively;* and NO employed in the same way is equivalent to the *interrogative* proposition asserted *negatively.* For example, *Is your brother at home?* Ans. YES, equivalent to *My brother is at home;* Ans. NO, equivalent to *My brother is* NOT *at home.* We may distinguish these two words by calling them THE RESPONSIVE PARTICLES.*

(27) *Surely*, *certainly*, *assuredly*, &c., are sometimes employed in answer to a question. These may be regarded as elliptical expressions, standing for propositions of which the suppressed parts are to be supplied from the preceding discourse. For example, *Will you oblige me by asking that favor for me from your friend?* Answer, *Certainly*, equivalent to *I will certainly oblige you by doing so*, or *I will certainly do so.*

(28) When *certainly*, *surely*, &c., occur as answers to a question, in attempting an analysis, we must first supply the words suppressed, and then their function in the completed proposition will appear manifest. (29) But when we meet with *yes* and *no*, we have simply to call them responsive particles, or signs of assent and denial. Since they are equivalent to whole propositions, they do not come within the range of grammatical analysis. Whenever a judgment of the mind is expressed by a single simple sign, as in this case, there is no room for the introduction of analysis. The grammarian's business is primarily with the proposition (which has been very properly called the "unit of speech," as judgment is the unit of thought; see N. Brit. Rev., No. 27, art. 2), and with this only when it consists of separable parts. If propositions were not made up of separable signs, grammar, as we have already said, would be a very different thing from what it is.

* These remarks do not apply to the *adjective* NO.

(25) Is it proper to class YES and NO with the adverbs? Are they modifying words? (26) What is each of these words in fact equivalent to? Illustrate this fact by examples.

(27) Repeat what is said in reference to the words *surely*, *certainly*, etc.

(28) How are we to act when these words occur in analysis? (29) How when *yes* and *no* occur?

(30) In reference to the use of the negative NOT, the learner will remember that in what is now recognised as the correct usage of our language, this word always *reverses the sense* of the proposition in which it is employed; or, in other words, a proposition where the negative is added is *always contrary* to the same proposition without the negative. (31) This fact is to be carefully regarded in those cases in which the negative is employed in a proposition having negative words (especially words compounded with the negative *no*, or the negative particles *un* and *in*) among the modifications of its predicate. (32) Thus: *This man is* NOT IN*fallible*, is the reverse of *This man is* IN*fallible; This man is* NOT UN*learned*, is the reverse of *This man is* UN*learned*. (33) The rule commonly given in reference to two negatives occurring in the same proposition is perhaps expressed with too little precision. It is this: "Two negatives destroy one another," or, "Two negatives make an affirmative." This would imply that such propositions as *The steward is not unfaithful*, and *The steward is faithful; The man is not unwise*, and *The man is wise*, &c., are completely equivalent, which we think is not the case. In the first forms there is simply a *negation* of *unfaithful* and *unwise*, not an *affirmation* of *faithful* and *wise*.

(34) We have violations of this rule in the following expressions, common among the uneducated: *I haven't got nothing, I haven't done nothing, I haven't seen nobody*, &c.*

(35) We have already, in treating of compound tenses, indicated the place which the negative usually takes when employed with verbs,

* In some languages two negatives are employed to strengthen negation. Double negatives often occur in the Greek language to express negation more emphatically. They were also used in Anglo-Saxon, and in old English by the most respectable authors, as late even as the times of Shakspeare. Hence the origin of the usage of the uneducated above noticed, which, though now called *vulgar*, is merely an adherence to the ancient idiom, whilst the educated have adopted the Latin usage. In this case certainly the usage borrowed from the Latin appears to us a decided improvement. It is at once more favorable to perspicuity, and more accordant with the general analogies of language.

(30) State the remark in reference to the use of the negative *not*. (31) In what cases is the fact mentioned about the negative to be especially regarded? (32) Give examples. (33) Repeat the rule commonly given about double negatives, and the remarks in reference to it.
(34) Mention the cases in which this rule is chiefly violated.
(35) What is said of the arrangement of the negative when used with verbs? When used with infinitives and nouns?

viz.: after the verb; i. e. after the auxiliary, for it is chiefly used with compound tenses; when used with simple tenses the order is the same: NOT *follows the verb.* On the contrary, NOT, when employed as it sometimes is, with infinitives or other nouns, takes precedence. For example: "*Not* a drum was heard, *not* a funeral note," &c. (Here observe *not* takes precedence of the noun and its complements.) NOT *to discountenance vice is to favor it.*

§ 94. We next proceed to consider the modifications which are applied to adjectives and to adverbs. For these modifying words are themselves affected by modifications in order to express the products of thought with greater accuracy and nicer discrimination.

(1) We have thought it best to consider these two classes of words together in reference to the modifications by which they are affected, because the few modifications of which the adverbs are susceptible are also common to adjectives, and, especially, because the adverbs are susceptible of these modifications in consequence of their near relation to adjectives—in fact, as a consequence either of their possessing a common form with the adjective, being *adjectives used adverbially*, as the grammarians say, or of their involving an adjective in their meaning, and generally also as the radical constituent of their form.

(2) As regards form, the modifications applied to adjectives, like those applied to nouns and verbs, are of two kinds; those which are effected by *inflections*, that is, by a termination added to the adjective, and those which are effected by the employment of separate words.

(3) The only inflection of which English adjectives are susceptible is that employed where we have occasion to express that a quality exists in one object compared with another object or objects in a higher degree of intensity.* (4) Grammarians have called this

* English adjectives, unlike those of many other languages, have no variation to indicate number, case, or gender, with the exception of the two

§ 94. (1) What reason is given for considering the modifications of adjectives and adverbs together?

(2) How many kinds of modifications are applied to adjectives?

(3) Describe the only purpose for which an *inflection* is attached to English adjectives. (4) What name have grammarians given to this change of the adjective? (5) What kind of adjectives are susceptible of *comparison*? (6) Illustrate by an example.

inflection *comparison* of adjectives, because when the inflected forms are used there is generally a comparison expressed or implied between the objects to which the qualities indicated by the adjectives are attributed. (5) It is only such adjectives as express qualities manifested in different degrees of intensity—generally descriptive adjectives—which are susceptible of *comparison*. (6) For example, the quality expressed by the adjective *cold* is manifested in different

---

determinative adjectives, *this* and *that*, which have for plural forms, *these* and *those*. The word *one* has sometimes a plural form, and even a possessive case; as, "I have commanded my sanctified *ones*, I have also called my mighty *ones*." (Is. xiii. 3.) "The great ones of the earth;" *one's country and one's friends are dear to every one*. This word, however, is not properly an adjective. It has all the characteristics of a noun, or pronoun, like *on* in French, and *man* in German and Anglo-Saxon, with which it has affinity in derivation, as well as in meaning, rather than with the numeral *one*.

The word *other* when used with a noun has no plural form; for example: OTHER *men have made the same mistake*. But, when employed alone substantively, it has a regular plural form; as, OTHERS *have made the same mistake*. The singular form of this word is, we believe, never used substantively, but its compound *another* serves as a singular substantive form, and has a regular possessive case; example, "The tender for *another's* pain." *Others* plural has a possessive, viz.: *others'*. These words used substantively may be thus arranged as a single declension:

	Singular.	*Plural.*
Nominative,	Another,	Others.
Genitive,	Another's,	Others'.

The young student can scarcely conceive the amount of labor saved to him by the absence of all inflection in the adjectives of our language. In learning other languages, he must be able to determine the number, case, gender, of the noun, in order to ascertain the form of the adjective which he is to employ with it. To ascertain in most languages the gender to which every noun belongs is a long and laborious task.

Yet it must not be supposed that the inflection of adjectives, to make them correspond to the number, case, gender of the noun which they modify, is a mere useless incumbrance, occasioning toil to no purpose to those who use languages possessing this peculiarity. On the contrary, it affords many facilities for abbreviating speech, without prejudice to perspicuity, and in the ancient languages, where this kind of inflection is carried to the greatest extent, it affords such liberty of arrangement as enables an ingenious writer to secure more easily both force and harmony in the expression of his

degrees of intensity; one cold day is more intensely cold than another. This higher intensity we express briefly by adding to the adjective the termination ER. *This day*, we say, *is* COLDER *than yesterday*. Again, we may wish to assert of a number of days (more than two) that some one was the most intensely cold. This we do by applying to the adjective *cold* the termination EST, and using it with this inflection to complete the noun *day*. Thus, *This is the* COLDEST *day of the week; The day before yesterday was* COLD, *yesterday was* COLDER, *but this day is the* COLDEST *of the three.* Here we have the quality *cold* expressed in three different degrees of intensity, each distinguished by a different form of the adjective, *Cold*, *colder*, *coldest.*

(7) These forms, including the original adjective, are called the *three degrees of comparison.* Grammarians have given each a distinct name. (8) The original adjective they have named the *positive degree*, the form in ER the *comparative*, and the form in EST the *superlative degree.*

(9) These modifications of the form of the adjective are generally, as in the case of the word cold, effected by adding the syllable ER to the positive (or original form of the adjective) for the *comparative degree*, and the syllable EST for the *superlative.* (10) When in the *written* language the adjective happens to end in *e* mute, *r* alone is added to form the *comparative* and *st* to form the *superlative;* as, *sure*, *surer*, *surest.* (11) In the *spoken* language, the sounds represented by ER and EST are always added to the original adjective as it is at present pronounced. In other words, a syllable is always added to the adjective to form the comparative and superlative degrees.

---

thoughts. Still we cannot hope to attain these advantages, and to use with correctness the languages which possess them, without submitting to much repulsive labor.

---

(7) What name have grammarians given to these forms intended to express qualities in different degrees of intensity? (8) What names have been given to each of these distinct forms of the adjective?

(9) How are the comparatives and superlatives of adjectives formed? (10) How are they formed in the written language when the adjective ends in *e* mute? (11) What sounds or syllables are always added in the spoken language?

(12) We may observe here that we have another way in English of expressing *comparison*, namely, employing the adverbs *more* and *most* before the adjective to express the *comparative* and *superlative degrees* respectively; as, *amiable, more amiable, most amiable.* This comes under the *adverbial modification* of the adjective already considered.

(13) Words consisting of one syllable are usually *compared* (as the grammarians call it) by adding to them the syllables *er* and *est*, by which they become words of two syllables. (14) A few words of two syllables—especially those which end in an accented syllable—are sometimes compared in the same way; as, *severe, severer, severest; divine, diviner, divinest.*

(15) With all adjectives of more than two syllables, and with most adjectives containing two syllables, we employ *more* and *most* for the purpose of expressing a higher degree of intensity. (16) *More* and *most* may be employed for this purpose with all adjectives which admit of comparison, and are to be employed whenever the use of the inflected form would produce any harshness of sound. (17) But except where harshness is to be avoided or some rhetorical purpose to be served, the inflected form of *monosyllables* is generally preferred as more brief and more forcible.

(18) When we wish to express the existence of a quality in an object in a high degree without comparison—without reference to the degree in which other objects possess the same quality—we generally employ the adverb *very* or *more than usually*, &c.; as, *A very high mountain.* (19) Sometimes we express the same thing, or nearly the same thing, by the *superlative form;* as, *The* GREATEST *difficulties are overcome by perseverance.* This differs little from VERY GREAT *difficulties are overcome*, &c. It is more spirited, but

---

(12) Describe another way of expressing comparison in English.

(13) How are words of one syllable usually *compared?*

(14) Are any words of two syllables compared in the same way? If any, what kind of words?

(15) With what classes of adjectives are *more* and *most* always employed for the purpose of expressing increased intensity? (16) When are these words to be employed with adjectives even of one syllable for the same purpose? (17) In what sort of words, and with what exceptions, is the inflected form preferred?

(18) How do we express intensity without direct comparison? (19) Is the same thing sometimes done by means of the superlative inflection? Illustrate by an example.

still implies little, if any comparison.* (20) Grammarians have called such expressions as, *A very high mountain* the *superlative absolute*, while the form employed when reference is expressed or implied to other objects possessing the same quality, is called the *superlative relative*.

(21) *Descending comparison*, or diminution of the intensity of a quality expressed by an adjective is denoted by the adverbs *less* and *least*; as, *less studious, least studious*; or sometimes by adding to the adjective the termination ISH; as, *whitish, blackish*, &c.

(22) The comparison of equality is always expressed by means of additional words; as, *That man is as learned as his brother*. (23) In this, and, indeed, in every case of comparison formally stated, there is a *modifying proposition* employed—a species of *complement* or *modification* which remains to be treated hereafter.

---

* Perhaps the use of the superlative in this way in our language may be considered as merely exaggeration, or a rhetorical contrivance adopted for the purpose of imparting force and sprightliness to style. To represent any object as possessing an attribute in the highest degree of all the objects of its class is more forcible than to represent it as simply possessing it in a very high degree. The *superlative absolute* is tame when compared with the other form. It is only however when the adjective is used attributively, or as the complement of a noun, that the *superlative comparative* can be thus substituted in English for the *superlative absolute*. We do not, as far as we know, employ the superlative comparative, (that is, the form made with *st* or its equivalent—the adjective modified by the adverb *most*,) as *complementary* of the verb except when we intend comparison.

In some languages the same form is very frequently used to express both the *superlative comparative* and the *superlative absolute*; and that when the adjective serves to complete a verb as well as when it completes a noun. Thus in Latin, *mons altissimus* means, when reference is made to other mountains, *the highest mountain*; or, when no such reference is intended, *a very high mountain*. *Mons est altissimus* may also be used to assert that *a mountain is very high*. Even the comparative form is used, though less frequently, in the same way; as, "*Si tibi quædam videbuntur obscuriora.*" "*Obscuriora*" here means obscure beyond the ordinary degree—more than commonly obscure.

---

(20) By what name have grammarians distinguished this from direct comparison?

(21) How is *descending comparison*, or diminution of intensity expressed? Give examples.

(22) What is said of the comparison of equality? (23) What is necessary in all cases when a comparison is formally stated?

(24) A few cases occur in which the different degrees of the same quality are represented by words entirely distinct in form; and a few other cases occur in which there is some irregularity in the formation of the comparative and superlative. The chief irregularities of both kinds are exhibited in the following table.

(25) TABLE OF IRREGULAR COMPARISON.

Positive.	*Comparative.*	*Superlative.*
Good	Better	Best.
Bad, evil, or ill	Worse	Worst.
Little	Less	Least.
Much / Many	More	Most.
Near	Nearer	Nearest. / Next.
Late	Later / Latter	Latest. / Last.
Old	Older / Elder	Oldest. / Eldest.
Far	Farther / Further	Farthest. / Furthest.

(26) EXPLANATION.—*Much* is used in speaking of *quantity*, *many*, in speaking of *number*; *nearest* is used in reference to *place*, *next*, in reference to *time*; the forms *later* and *latest* are used in speaking of *time*, *latter* and *last*, in speaking of *order*; *older* and *oldest* are the forms generally employed at present, *elder* and *eldest* are more ancient forms, and are now less frequently employed. *Further* and *furthest* are perhaps formed from *fore*, which we have in the word *foremost*, and not from *far*. The meanings, as well as the derivation, of these forms were likely once different—*further* meaning *more in front*; *farther*, *more distant*. But in modern usage, *farther*, on account of its softer sound, has nearly superseded the harsher word, *further*, the difference of their signification not being so great as to preclude this substitution.*

* It is a curious fact that in the best known ancient and modern languages the adjectives irregular in comparison are usually words of similar signification. Thus the words which denote the same qualities with our

(24) Repeat the remark in reference to irregular comparison.
(25) Repeat the table of irregular forms.
(26) Repeat the remarks in explanation of the use of the irregular forms.

[(27) There is a class of superlatives ending in *most;* as, for example, *foremost*, mentioned above, *hindmost*, *upmost*, *utmost*, &c., about the formation of which the grammarians are not yet agreed. The most

---

words *good* and *bad* are irregularly *compared* in Greek, Latin and all its modern progeny, Italian, Spanish, French, &c., and also in Anglo-Saxon, German (as regards *gut*, good,) and other Teutonic dialects. These irregularities have generally come down from the remotest periods to which languages can be traced, and have been transmitted from the ancient languages to the dialects derived from them. Thus, from the comparative *melior* (better) in Latin are derived the words of similar signification in all the modern languages descended from the Latin, in Italian, French, &c. The irregularity of *good*, *better*, *best* comes to us from the Anglo-Saxon, and to this and the other Teutonic dialects, likely, from some remote common parent-language.

That the adjectives expressive of these particular qualities are irregular in so many apparently independent languages, is, perhaps, to be accounted for from the fact that these are the very words of the class of comparatives and superlatives which must have been earliest employed and most frequently employed in the dialects to which they respectively belong. Words to express the qualities *good* and *bad* in different degrees of intensity becoming very early necessary in the everyday intercourse of life, may have been received into current use and have obtained fixed and immovable possession as articulate signs, long before any general law for the formation of comparatives and superlatives came to be recognised in language. In other words, terms expressive of the meaning of *better* and *worse* may have been established immovably in many languages anterior to the use of inflection to express *comparison*.

Again, words very frequently used in the intercourse of life, especially words used much by the illiterate, (and all men were illiterate when their languages were yet in the early period of their formation,) suffer greater *wear and tear*, than words more rarely employed and current chiefly among the learned. In the progress of a language such words undergo greater and more rapid changes. These considerations may account for the anomalies and contractions which occur in some of the forms enumerated in the above table of irregular comparison, and in the adjectives of similar meaning in other languages.

It will be seen that these remarks are not restricted in their application to adjectives, but may be employed to explain the general fact that the chief irregularities of inflection fall in all languages upon words which express similar meaning and perform similar functions. The verbs, for instance, which express a meaning equivalent to our verb *to be* are irregularly inflect-

---

[(27) Repeat the substance of what is said of a class of superlatives ending in *most*.

common opinion is, that these and similar words are compounds of *fore*, *upper*, *out*, &c., with the adverb *most*. This view is adopted by Rask. (See Rask's Ang. Sax. Gram. § 133.) Grimm, on the contrary, thinks the *st* in these words to be the superlative termination, added by *excess of expression* to the Anglo-Saxon superlatives, *forma*, first, *ufema*, upmost, *utema*, outmost, &c., as if from *worst*, forgetting that it is already a superlative, we should form *worstest*, or as from *chief*, which is a word superlative in meaning, we sometimes find the form *chiefest*. (See Latham's Gram. p. 79, and Eng. Lang. 2 ed. p. 270.) Dr. Latham seems inclined to adopt the views of Grimm.

(28) There is another small class of superlatives in which the word *most* is added to comparative forms. We may enumerate those of most common occurrence. *Hind-er-most*, *inn-er-most*, *neth-er-most*, *out-er-most*, *upp-er-most*, *utt-er-most*. We have so divided these words by *hyphens* as to exhibit their composition to the eye. We might, like Dr. Latham, have divided *most* in each case into its constituents m-ost, (or perhaps mo-st, for more and most are formed from the old English *mo* or *moe*,) and have written *hind-er-m-ost*, *inn-er-m-ost*, as he has done, or, perhaps still more correctly, we might have represented their elements thus: *hind-er-mo-st*, *inn-er-mo-st*, &c.]

§ 95. Comparison of Adverbs.—(1) Some adverbs admit of inflectional comparison like adjectives; as, *soon*, *sooner*, *soonest*; *oft* or *often*, *oftener*, *oftenest*. (2) Such adverbs, however, are very few in number. We know of none besides *soon* and *often*, except those which are originally adjectives, and come under the class of adjectives *adverbially* employed. (3) The comparatives and superlatives of some adjectives are used *adverbially*, though the *positive* form of these adjectives is not so employed. (4) For example, *better* and *best* are

---

ed in all the languages enumerated above; and in how many more we know not. The assertion of *being* or *existence* is often expressed in the different tenses and even in the different persons and numbers by words entirely distinct. The reasoning above used applies, if possible, with greater force to this verb than to the irregular adjectives. The forms employed in the most ancient languages to express its different tenses were, likely, immovably fixed in common use, long before any regular law of tense-formation was recognised in those languages.

---

(28) Repeat what is said of another class ending also in *most*.]

§ 95. (1) Do any adverbs admit of inflectional comparison? Give examples. (2) What is said of the number of such adverbs? (3) What is said of the adverbial use of the comparatives and superlatives of some adjectives? (4) Illustrate by examples.

used adverbially, and when so used, serve as the comparative and superlative of the adverb *well;* but good is never used adverbially by those who speak correctly.* In the same manner, *worse* and *worst* are employed adverbially, but not the adjective *bad. Badly* or *ill* may be considered the positive form of *worse* and *worst,* when used *adverbially.* The comparatives and superlatives *more* and *most* and *less* and *least* are, as we have already seen, employed to modify adjectives. The positive *much* sometimes modifies comparatives, as, *much wiser,* &c. *Little* rarely modifies other adjectives.

(6) Adverbs of manner very often admit of comparison, because the quality denoted by the adjective involved in the meaning, and generally in the form of these adverbs has different degrees of intensity. Thus, *wisely* admits of comparison for the same reason that the adjective *wise* involved in it admits of comparison. (7) But these adverbs, when regularly formed from adjectives (except the adjective itself, as in the case of *better* and *best,* is usurped as an adverb) have a form too unwieldy to admit of inflectional comparison. (8) They are, therefore, compared by using the modifying words *more* and *most;* as, *wisely, more wisely, most wisely; justly, more justly, most justly.*

(9) In the analysis of such adverbs, we may as well take the two words separately, and consider *more* and *most* as *adverbial modifications* of other adverbs.

(10) The comparative and superlative of adjectives when formed by the help of *more* and *most* may as well be treated in the same way in

---

* (5) The adjective *good* is often used (by careless speakers in the United States and perhaps in some other places) instead of the adverb *well.* For example, we may hear persons who have received an imperfect education say: *The boy writes good, the fire burns good, I did that good,* &c. Such expressions are grossly ungrammatical and vulgar, and when children catch them from uneducated persons around them, it requires much labor and watchfulness to unlearn them. This may be regarded as an improper *extension* of the adjective complementary modification.

---

(5) Repeat the substance of tne note.

(6) What remarks are made in reference to adverbs of manner? (7) Are adverbs of manner inflected? (8) How are they compared? Illustrate by examples.

(9) How may we proceed in the analysis of adverbs accompanied by *more* and *most?*

(10) How in the analysis of the comparatives and superlatives of adjectives made by more

analysis; the words more and most being regarded simply like other adverbial modifications of adjectives. (11) They differ in no respect, as regards grammatical form or grammatical function, from other adverbial modifications. There is no necessity for mentioning the names *comparative* and *superlative degree*, except when these degrees **are** formed by inflection. (12) Then it will be necessary, when the comparative or superlative form occurs, to say that the adjective is an adjective in the comparative or superlative degree, or that it is an adjective with the comparative or superlative inflectional modification. In writing we may express this by the abbreviations, *Des. A. Comp. and Des. A. Sup.*—Descriptive adjective of the comparative degree, and descriptive adjective of the superlative degree.

(13) We may notice, before we leave this subject, that a *superlative adverb* is sometimes accompanied by the determinative *the*; as, *This boy writes* THE BEST; *John acted the* MOST PRUDENTLY. Some seem to treat the determinative in this case as belonging to the form of the superlative, and attempt no further analysis. We think it belongs to the noun (generally the noun *manner*) implied in the adverb. For example, the expressions above may be resolved thus: *This boy writes in the best manner; John acted in the most prudent manner.* Here it is obvious that the determinative affects *manner*. (14) Sometimes, especially in colloquial usage, a descriptive adjective as well as a determinative, is used in connection with a superlative adverb, and this too must be regarded as modifying the noun implied in the adverb; as, *The boy behaved the best possible under the circumstances;* equivalent to, *The boy behaved in the best* MANNER *possible*, &c. This use of a descriptive adjective with an adverb is not, in our opinion, an elegant form of expression, but rather one to be avoided. It is much better in such cases to employ the full form with the word *manner* expressed, than to resort to the abbreviated adverbial form.

[(15) The same may be said of such expressions as, *This boy behaves the best of all.* The analysis of this form of expression presents a difficulty. What word does the *noun and preposition modification* OF ALL affect? (For *all* is here evidently an adjective employed as a noun, or implying a noun.) What does it modify? Does it affect the

---

and most. (11) Assign the reasons for pursuing this course. (12) In what manner do we treat the inflectional forms in analysis?

(13) What is said of a superlative adverb accompanied by the determinative *the?* Give example and explanation. (14) What is said in reference to the use of a descriptive adjective with such superlatives?

[(15) Repeat the substance of what is said about such forms of expression as, *This boy behaves the best of all.*

subject noun *boy*, and are we consequently to supply with it the word *boys?* The expression will then be equivalent to *This boy of all the boys behaved in the best manner.* We incline to adopt this as the best mode of analyzing this class of expressions, and to think that there is here an awkward separation of the complement *of all* from the word which it modifies, or that *of all* is introduced, as it were, by after thought. Other modes of analysis of such expressions might be suggested, such as considering *of all*, like the determinative *the*, and the descriptive adjective in the forms above considered, as modifying the word *manner* implied in *best;* but all these modes seem to us to present greater difficulties, and to involve longer and more awkward suppressions. We think that it is better in all such cases to forego the use of the adverb, and adopt the circuitous mode of expression.]

We give no exercises for the present on the above modifications of adjectives and adverbs, because an *accessory proposition* is necessary to make full sense.

§ 96. Having considered the modification of adjectives by inflection, we proceed to consider the various ways in which they are modified by separate words. (1) We shall not need to spend much time on this subject, since all the modifications of this kind applied to adjectives correspond exactly either to those which are applied to nouns, or to those which are applied to verbs, and these we have already explained. We shall give notice as we pass along, when any of these modifications are applicable to adverbs.

MODIFICATIONS OF ADJECTIVES AND ADVERBS CONSISTING OF SEPARATE WORDS.—(2) 1st. Some adjectives admit of a *dative* modification, like verbs. (3) The adjectives most frequently so modified are *like, near, nearer, nearest, next.* We subjoin a number of examples which may be used as an exercise in analysis.

(4) "He cometh forth like a *flower*." "Who teacheth like *him?*" "He shall be like *a tree*," &c. "Lest I become like *them*," &c. "The righteous shall flourish like *the palm-tree*, he shall grow like the *cedar* in Lebanon." "There was none like *thee* before thee."

---

§ 96. (1) What remark is made in reference to the modifications consisting of separate words applied to adjectives and adverbs?

(2) What is the first modification of this kind here mentioned? (3) Enumerate the adjectives most frequently modified by a dative.

(4) Repeat some of the examples, and point out the adjective and the modifying dative [in] all the examples.

"The men near Micah's *house*." "They knew not that evil was near *them*." The mouth of the foolish is near destruction." John sat near his *brother*. His sister sits next *him*.

[(5) All these adjectives instead of the dative are frequently followed by a *noun and preposition modification*, the preposition *to* or often *unto* being interposed between them and the completing noun. (6) Hence most grammarians in the analysis of the above examples would supply the preposition *to* before the nouns which follow *like*, *near*, &c., and say that these nouns are in the accusative or objective case after *to*. (7) We think that there is really no ellipsis in these examples, but that they exhibit another remnant of the ancient dative, not yet altogether superseded by the noun and preposition, but employed interchangeably with it. (8) We are obliged to recognise a dative in English (see § 79,) in order to explain satisfactorily several forms of expression still used in our language. We may therefore, as well recognise the dative in cases like those before us, and in all similar cases, where we have a manifest remnant of the old dative usage.

(9) Some grammarians have ventured to call *near* a preposition whenever it is followed by a noun or pronoun, without the intervention of a preposition. The noun, according to their analysis, is in the objective case after the preposition *near*. This mode of analysis is altogether unwarrantable, and no recent grammarian of acknowledged high standing, we believe, has adopted it. To supply the preposition *to* is far preferable to this, though we think the recognition of a dative use of the noun in such expressions is the proper course to adopt.]

EXERCISE.—To form propositions containing examples of adjectives modified by a dative.

(10) 2d. Some adjectives are modified by an *accusative or objective of price, time, measure or dimension*, like verbs. (See § 84.) We subjoin examples, which may serve, like those in the last paragraph, for an exercise in analysis.

[(5) By what kind of modification are these adjectives often accompanied instead of a dative? (6) How do grammarians generally explain the dative in the above kind of propositions? (7) Is there really an ellipsis or suppression of a preposition in the above examples? (8) Repeat the remark about the English dative.

(9) What have some grammarians considered *near* when followed by a noun, and what is said of their mode of analysis?]

(10) What is the second form of modification of adjectives by separate words?

[(11) This house is worth *four thousand pounds.* The book is worth *ten shillings.* That work is worth *all the labor* expended upon it. It is worth *while* to consider a subject, &c. (*while* is here a noun in the accusative). William departed this life, aged *thirty-five years.* That man is *sixty years* old. This table is *five feet* long and *three feet* wide. The house is *four stories* high. The wall is *eighteen inches* thick, *ten feet* high, and *two hundred feet* long. The river, in this place, is *fifteen feet* deep.

(12) It will be noticed that the adjective *old* and the adjectives of dimension take the accusative of time and measure before them.]

Exercise.—Form a given number of propositions containing examples of adjectives modified by *an accusative of time, measure,* &c.

Note.—Those who class the word *ago* among the adverbs, must assign it a place with those which take an accusative of time before them. For example, *That event happened* TWENTY YEARS *ago.* We cannot admit this explanation of the modification of the word *ago*, and consequently, must decline classing it among the adverbs. *Ago* or *agone*, or *agon* (for so the word was often spelled in our old authors—we have an instance in 1 Sam. 30 : 13, "Three days *agone* I fell sick;" and in Archbishop Tillotson, as quoted by H. Tooke, "Thirty years *agone*") was once in common use as the perfect participle of the verb *go.* See H. Tooke, pp. 254–257, Mr. R. Taylor's edition, 1840. We select a few of the examples adduced by Mr. Tocke, enough, we think, to settle this matter beyond the reach of all cavil.

"Her love is after soone AGO."—Gower.

"The remenant was all AGO."—Idem.

"For after that he was AGO."—Idem.

"God wotte, worldely joye is soone AGO."—Chaucer.

"AGO was every sorowe and every fere."—Idem.

"Of any thinge of suche a time AGONE.—Idem.

"May sigh, that thei were AGONE."—Gower.

"Whan that the mysty vapoure was AGONE."—Chaucer.

"For I loved one, ful longe sythe AGONE."—Idem.

"But sothe is said, GONE sithen many a day."—Idem.

It is, we think, perfectly manifest from these examples, that our old authors used AGO interchangeably with GONE, as the participle of GO. This fact affords us the best guidance to the true analysis of the forms of expression in which AGO occurs. In the proposition, *He lived thirty years* AGO,

---

[(11) Repeat some of the examples, and in all the propositions given point out the adjective and the accusative of *price, time,* &c.

(12) Repeat the remark in reference to the adjective *old* and the adjectives of dimension.]

we might consider the noun *years* as the accusative of time to the verb *lived*, and itself modified by the participle AGO. Or, what we think better, we may consider *years* as subject noun to the verb *are* suppressed and modified by the participle AGO. In accordance with this view the above expression may be completed thus, *He lived thirty years* ARE (*since*) *ago or gone.* That this is the true way of supplying the ellipsis, we are the more confirmed in thinking, by such examples as the last two given above: "Ful longe sythe (= since) agone;" "Gone sithen (= since) many a day." Mr. Tyrwhitt, Moxon's edition, 1843, gives this line, we know not on what authority, "Gone sithen *is* many a day." This would be more to our purpose, if we could confide in Mr. Tyrwhitt's readings. But we cannot.

Another mode of analysis, not essentially different from the last, is to treat the noun of time as in the *case absolute* with the participle AGO.

(13) 3d. Many adjectives are modified or completed by infinitives in the same manner as verbs. We subjoin a few examples for exercise in analysis.

[(14) Your friend is very ambitious *to excel* his neighbors. The young man is desirous *to learn.* He is anxious *to succeed* in his enterprise. That action is worthy *to be imitated.* This boy is prone *to do* mischief. That boy is prompt *to perform* his duty. John is now ready *to go* home.*

(15) Participles or adjectives formed from verbs which take an

* The following examples may be regarded as somewhat different in character. He is too lazy *to learn.* He is wise enough *to take* care of himself. Such infinitives assist, together with the adverbs *enough* and *too*, in indicating the degree of intensity which the adjective is made to express in these particular cases. They serve a purpose similar to that served by accessory propositions which indicate degrees of intensity. (*See* §§ 120–122.)

Some adverbs take also a modifying infinitive; as, *He does not know* HOW TO ACT; *He does not understand* WHEN TO BE SILENT, *when to speak.* "The Son of Man hath not *where to lay* his head." When we resolve the adverbs, these become identical with the infinitive which modifies a noun. *How* = *in what manner; when* = *at what time,* and *where* = *at what place.* The nouns *manner, time, place,* are what the infinitives above really modify.—These infinitives, with their accompaniments, may be considered as contracted accessory propositions (*see* § 142).

(13) What is the third modification of adjectives?

[(14) Repeat some examples, and point out the adjective and infinitive modification in all the examples.

(15) Repeat the remark about participles.]

infinitive modification of course take the same modification. Such adjectives, for example, as *accustomed*, *habituated*, *inclined*, *addicted*, *disposed*, &c., come within this description.]

EXERCISE.—Form a number of propositions containing examples of this construction.

(16) 4th. Many adjectives are modified by a *noun with a preposition*, like nouns and verbs. (17) A few of the adverbs, formed from adjectives which take this modification, are sometimes completed in the same way. (18) We have examples in the following propositions: *The man acted conformably* TO *your* ORDERS; *John acted consistently* WITH *his* CHARACTER. When we resolve the adverbs *conformably* and *consistently*, as in the equivalent propositions, *The man acted* IN A MANNER CONFORMABLE *to your orders*, *John acted* IN A MANNER CONSISTENT *with his character*, we shall see that they are modified by a *noun and preposition*, because the adjective involved in them is so modified.

[(19) Different adjectives take after them different prepositions with a modifying noun, and the same adjective always takes the same preposition, or the same set of prepositions after it. Most adjectives taking after them a preposition are confined exclusively to a single preposition; a few take two or more, but generally with some change of meaning. It may be useful to enumerate the prepositions which are most frequently employed in modifying adjectives.

(20) The greatest number of adjectives susceptible of this form of modification take the preposition *to* exclusively; as, *adequate to*, *agreeable to*, *convenient to*, &c.

(21) Many adjectives take the preposition *of* exclusively; as, *desirous of*, *capable of*, *full of*, *worthy* or *unworthy of*, *careful of*, &c. The *of* before the noun is sometimes omitted after *worthy* and *unworthy*. *Careful* sometimes takes after it the preposition *in*, but with a different sense.

(22) Some adjectives take the preposition *for*; as, *fit for*, *useful for*, *thankful for*, &c.

---

(16) Mention the fourth form of modification applied to adjectives. (17) Are adverbs ever modified in the same way? (18) Illustrate by example, and explain why the adverb is susceptible of this modification.

[(19) Repeat the substance of what is said in reference to different adjectives taking different prepositions after them.

(20) What preposition do the greatest number of adjectives take after them?

(21) Mention some that take after them *of*. (22) Some that take *for*; some *from*. (23.

Some take *from*; as, *distant from*, *remote from*, *far from*, &c.

(23) Some take the preposition *with*; as, *replete with*, *level with*, &c.

(24) Some take the preposition *in*; as, *fruitful in*, *abundant in*, *rich in*, *poor in*, &c.

(25) Some few take *on* or *upon*; as, *intent on* or *upon*, *dependent on* or *upon*.

(26) A few take the preposition *at*; as, *expert at*, or *expert in*.

Some few adjectives perhaps take other prepositions.

(27) Adjectives, especially those derived from verbs, are sometimes modified (like verbs) by a preposition alone without a noun. (*See* § 81 : 28.)

(28) We have already had occasion to notice that adjectives are often modified by adverbs, and sometimes adverbs by other adverbs. (*See* § 92.) It seems unnecessary here to add any thing more on this subject.

(29) We have now finished the course of instruction which we deem necessary for the analysis of simple *assertive* propositions. We shall follow this up in the next chapter by a brief account of the construction of *Interrogative* and *Imperative* propositions.]

Examples for Analysis.—Virtuous actions are agreeable *to* the *will* of our Creator. That boy's capacity is fully equal *to* the *task* imposed upon him. This unfortunate man is bereft *of* all his *property*. That man is careful *of* his *money*. The member is absent *from* his *place*. His life is conformable *to* his *principles*. That man's life is not consistent *with* his *professions*. Men are generally too fond *of pleasure*. Fear is inseparable *from* the *consciousness* of guilt. I am thankful *for* your kind *advice*. That physician is very successful *in* his *practice*. All men do not live conformably *to* their *resolutions*. Many act inconsistently *with* their *professions*. To live a virtuous life is to live agreeably *to reason*. That stranger is far *from* his own *country*.

Exercises.—Form a given number of propositions containing examples of adjectives accompanied with this species of modification.

Some that take *with*. (24) Some that take *in*. (25) Some that take *on* or *upon*. (26) Some that take *at*.

(27) In what way are adjectives, especially verbals sometimes modified ?

(28) Repeat remark about adjectives modified by adverbs.

(29) What have we now finished, and what do we next proceed to consider ?]

CHAPTER VIII.

OF INTERROGATIVE AND IMPERATIVE PROPOSITIONS.

§ 97. INTERROGATIVE PROPOSITIONS.—(1) As regards *matter*, the *interrogative* proposition is that employed in asking a question. (2) As to its form, the *interrogative* proposition differs from the *assertive* proposition only in the arrangement of the subject noun and the verb, and not always even in this. (3) Some interrogative propositions commence with an interrogative word which serves to mark their character. (4) When the *interrogative* word is the subject of the proposition, or a modification of the subject, the order of arrangement is exactly the same as in the assertive proposition. That is to say, the subject noun precedes, the verb follows. (5) But when the *interrogative* word is not the subject of the proposition, nor a modification of the subject;* or when an interrogative proposition is formed without an interrogative word, the order of arrangement is reversed, and the verb precedes the subject noun. (6) It will here be remembered that in the *compound tenses*, it is the auxiliary which is the verb—which possesses the assertive force—and that it is this

* We have no word in our language to indicate interrogation exclusively. All our interrogative words perform another function in the proposition besides indicating that it is interrogative. In other languages there are words which perhaps indicate interrogation exclusively. The Latin *ne enclitic* may be given as an example.

§ 97. (1) What is said in reference to the matter of the interrogative proposition? (2) In what does its form differ from the form of the assertive proposition ? (3) How is the character of some interrogative propositions marked ? (4) What is the order of arrangement in the proposition, when the interrogative word is the subject noun, or completes the subject? (5) What is the general order when the interrogative word is not the subject noun, or when there is no interrogative word used in forming an interrogative proposition. (6) Repeat the remark about the compound tenses.

alone which in interrogative propositions comes before the subject noun.

(7) It must also be noticed, that in all interrogative propositions which require the subject noun to be placed after the verb, we use the tenses formed by combining the verb *do* with the infinitive of the several verbs (i. e., the *progressive forms*), instead of using the simple indefinite and simple past tenses of those verbs. (8) The verbs *to be* and *to have* are exceptions, since they have no tenses formed by the verb *do*. (See § 60.) (9) In our older authors, and in poetry, the simple tenses are often employed in interrogations, when the order of subject and verb is inverted, but scarcely ever in prose composition or in conversation, as the language is now used.

(10) We may express the rule at present followed in our language in the arrangement of interrogative propositions briefly thus: When an interrogative proposition has an interrogative word for its *subject noun*, or accompanying and completing its subject, it is arranged in the same order as the assertive proposition; but when it has not an interrogative word for *subject noun*, or complement of its subject, the order of arrangement is inverted, and the subject noun placed after the verb. (11) The learner will observe that in the written language all interrogative propositions are indicated by the interrogative mark (?). (12) In the spoken language, all interrogations—all questions—which do not commence with an interrogative word are distinguished, by good speakers, from assertive propositions, by a strongly marked rising inflection of the voice at their close.

We give examples of the different forms of the interrogative proposition, and, to render the distinction between it and the assertive proposition more clear, when this distinction is effected by arrangement and without an interrogative word, we shall place the *assertive* opposite to the *interrogative form.*

---

(7) What else is to be noticed in regard of the formation of interrogative propositions? (8) Repeat the remark in reference to the verbs *to be* and *to have.* (9) What is said of the practice of our older authors, and of the poets?

(10) Repeat the rule for the arrangement of interrogative propositions. (11) How are interrogative propositions indicated in the written language? (12) How are those which do not commence with an interrogative word distinguished in speaking?

(13) 1st. Interrogative propositions having the interrogative word for their subject noun, or to complete the subject. These do not differ in arrangement from assertive propositions. The interrogative word alone distinguishes them. Examples: Who is at the door? Who went to the post-office? Who has read that poem? Who will lend me a knife? Which boy is the best scholar? What lies on the table? What broke the glass? What has happened? &c.

(14) 2d. Interrogative propositions in which the interrogative word is not the subject noun, but completes the predicate. Here the order of the subject noun and verb are inverted. Examples: Whom do you see? What have you done? Where have you been? Why do you complain? When did he arrive? Whither (where) will he go? How does he succeed? &c.

(15) It will be observed that in all cases the interrogative word begins the proposition.

(16) 3d. Interrogative propositions (or questions) formed without an interrogative word, contrasted with the corresponding assertive proposition.

Assertive Form.	*Interrogative Form.*
I am right.	Am I right?
I have time.	Have I time?
We were right.	Were we right?
They had horses.	Had they horses?
He goes to town.	Does he go to town?
He went to town.	Did he go to town?
You gave him money.	Did you give him money?
I have seen.	Have I seen?
He had arrived.	Had he arrived?
They will come.	Will they come?

(17) Here the subject noun is invariably placed after the verb; when a compound tense is used, after the auxiliary verb, as it is called.

It will be noticed that with all verbs, except TO BE and TO HAVE, the *emphatic indefinite and past tense made with* the verb TO DO, is employed in the interrogative form, in all cases where the subject noun

(13) Give examples of the first class of interrogative propositions, viz.: those which have an interrogative word for their subject noun.

(14) Of the second class. (15) Where does the interrogative word always stand?

(16) Give examples of the third class, contrasting the assertive with the interrogative form.

(17) Repeat over again the observations about the place of the subject noun when a compound tense is used, and about the use of the *emphatic* tenses.

and verb are inverted, or when the subject is not an interrogative word, or completed by an interrogative word.

(18) We may give some examples from the antiquated and poetical language of the simple indefinite and past tenses employed interrogatively, when the order of arrangement is inverted: "*Despisest thou* the riches of his goodness?" "*Know ye* what I have done to you?" "Having eyes, *see ye* not?" "Through breaking the law, *dishonorest thou* God?" "Thinkest thou this right, &c.?" "Believest thou this?" "Believest thou the prophets?" "But what *meant you* of fugitives herein?"—Spencer's State of Ireland. "How *commeth it* then to passe?"—Idem. "What hear I?"—Idem.

We subjoin some examples from the poets:—

"What *fear we* then?"—Milton.

"What now *avails* that noble *thirst* of fame?"—Thomson.

"Now *blame we* most the nurslings or the nurse?"—Cowper.

"Where *finds philosophy* her eagle eye?"—Idem.

"And *chase we* still the phantom through the fire?"
"And *toil we* still for sublunary pay?"—Young.

"*Seest thou* thy lover lowly laid?
Hearest thou the groans that pierce his breast?"—Burns.

"*Breathes* there the *man* with soul so dead?"—Scott.

"And *said I* that my blood was cold?"—Idem.

The reader will find on examination that in all these propositions, if expressed in the current prose of the present day, we would introduce the tenses formed with the auxiliary DO instead of the simple tenses.

There is a rule in reference to the answer made to an interrogative proposition, which we may give in this place. It is an important rule, and one often violated by uneducated and careless persons in conversation.

(19) RULE.—The pronoun in the answer must be in the same case with the interrogative word in the question.

EXAMPLES.—*Who is in the room?* Ans. *I*= *I am in the room.* To such questions the uneducated often answer *me.* The impropriety of this answer is manifest when we supply the words suppressed and exhibit the complete proposition implied; thus, ME *is in the room.* Even

---

(18) Repeat a number of the antiquated and poetical examples which differ from the present order of English prose composition.

(19) Repeat the rule and illustrate by examples.

the least educated person perceives the impropriety of this. *Whom do they blame?* Ans. *Him* = *They blame him. Whose hat is this?* Ans. *John's* or *mine* = *This hat is John's, or mine.*

§ 98. Remarks on the Interrogative Words.—(1) The interrogative words used as subjects of interrogative propositions are *who, what, which,* and formerly *whether*=which of the two. (2) These are commonly called the *interrogative pronouns.* (3) The word *who* has an undoubted claim to this appellation. It always performs alone the function of a noun. It cannot take a noun with it; we cannot, for example, say *who man* did so? It cannot, therefore, be alleged that a noun is understood with it or implied in it. Who is used exclusively to represent persons, and not the lower animals or inanimate things.

(4) *What* interrogative, when used *alone*, always represents a thing. It appears in Anglo-Saxon grammars as the neuter form of *who*, which is masculine and feminine. In the language as now used *what* differs from *who* in this, that it is employed as an adjective, and thus employed, sometimes accompanies nouns which denote persons. For example, "What man is there of you?" Matt. 7 : 9. "What man knoweth the things of a man?" 1 Cor. 2 : 11. This is more emphatic than to say, Who is there of you? and Who knoweth the things of a man?

(5) *Which* is perhaps to be considered an adjective, and, when used alone, as having a noun implied, like any other adjective employed substantively. (6) Used interrogatively, this word may accompany nouns significant either of persons or the lower animals and things, and when used substantively, may represent objects of both these classes. Thus we say, *which boy did that? which is to blame?* speaking of persons—as well as, *which road leads to the village?* and *which is the best bound?* speaking of books. (7) *Which* has been improperly represented as the neuter of *who.* Instead of

---

§ 98. (1) Enumerate the interrogative words used as subjects of propositions. (2) What are these words commonly called? (3) Repeat what is said of the word *who.*

(4) Repeat the remarks in reference to *what;* and give examples of *what* employed as an adjective.

(5) How may *which* be considered? (6) What kind of nouns does it accompany when used as an interrogative? Give examples. (7) How has *which* been improperly represented? And in what light is it considered by the most recent grammarians?

this the modern grammarians have assigned plausible reasons for considering it a compound of the interrogative root *wh* and *lic*, the Scotch *whilk* being a step in its progress to its present English form. (See Latham, Eng. Lang. p. 253, 2d Ed. and Grimm Deutsche Gram. vol. iii. pp. 47, 48.)

(8) *Whether* appears, also, to be a compound of *wh* and *either*. It is now scarcely in use as an interrogative. Instead of it we use *which of the two*. We have examples of the ancient usage in the questions, "*Whether* of them did the will of his father?" "*Whether* is greater, the gold or the temple?"

(9) The interrogative *who* may be employed plurally as well as singularly. For example, "*Who* are these that fly as a cloud?" &c. "*Who* are happiest among men?" This word has also a possessive or genitive form, *whose*, and another form, *whom*, which was anciently used as a dative, but now is employed as an accusative. (10) *What* and *which* have no possessive *form*, and are indifferently employed as *nominatives* or *accusatives*; that is, as *subject nouns* or *objectives*, or *noun with preposition* modifications.

(10) Some of the other interrogatives, which serve only as modifying words and not as subject nouns, and are therefore called adverbs, seem to have been originally cases or derivatives of *who*. At least, they generally contain what may be considered the interrogative sign in our language, viz.: the consonantal sound *wh*. (11) *Where* = *in what place* seems to have been an old feminine dative with a noun implied, *why* = *for what cause*, an ablative, *when* = *at what time*, an accusative. *Whither* = *towards what place*, is manifestly a derivative or compound from the same root. (12) *How* = *in what manner*, is supposed to come from the same source, the *w* of the *wh* having been suppressed, possibly because the combination of *wh* with the vowel sound represented by *ow* was unpleasant to pronounce and disagreeable to the ear.

---

(8) Repeat the remarks in reference to *whether*; and give examples of it used interrogatively.

(9) Is *who* ever used plurally? And what cases has it? (10) Repeat the remarks in reference to case forms of *what* and *which*.

(10) What do some of the interrogative words not used as subject nouns seem to have been originally? (11) Tell what is said of *where*, *why*, *when*, and *whither*. (12) What is said of *how*?

We shall have more to say of these forms elsewhere, especially when we come to treat of the *relative* or *conjunctive* pronouns, and in *additional remarks on the determinatives and the pronouns*, §§ 158, 159.

EXERCISE I.—Form a given number of interrogative propositions with interrogative words for their subject nouns.

EXERCISE II.—A given number commencing with an interrogative pronoun which does not serve as subject noun.

EXERCISE III.—A given number commencing with an interrogative adverb.

EXERCISES IV., V., &c.—A given number of interrogative propositions formed without interrogative words.

§ 99. OF IMPERATIVE PROPOSITIONS.—(1) As regards *matter*, the imperative proposition is distinguished by the fact that it is employed in expressing commands, requests, entreaties, &c. (2) As regards *form*, it is distinguished by the following peculiarities—1st. The imperative form, or mode of the verb, consisting in our language of the root without inflection, is employed in this class of propositions. 2d. The subject of such propositions in the prose language of the present day, is always of the second person; that is, always a party or parties addressed. 3d. The subject noun, being always the pronoun of the second person singular or the second person plural, and capable of being readily supplied, is most commonly suppressed. 4th. When the pronoun is expressed, it is placed after the verb. (3) The suppression in the one case, and the arrangement after the verb in the other case, equally serve to distinguish the *imperative* from the *assertive* form. (4) When the pronoun is placed after the verb the plural *imperative* proposition does not differ in form from the plural *interrogative* proposition in the indefinite tense, so far as the words and arrangement are concerned. Thus, *resist you, or ye, evil*, may form either a question or a command—an interrogative or an imperative proposition. (5) In speaking, the tone of command or entreaty is clearly distinct from the tone or inflection of inquiry. This fact prevents all mistake of the one form for the other in

§ 99. (1) What is said of the *matter* of the imperative proposition? (2) Repeat separately the four peculiarities which distinguish the *imperative* proposition. (3) What two circumstances distinguish the imperative from the assertive proposition? (4) With what other kind of proposition does the plural imperative sometimes agree in form, and in what case? Give an example. (5) In this case how are these two kinds of propositions distinguished in spoken discourse? How in written discourse?

spoken discourse. The mark of interrogation serves to distinguish the interrogative form in written discourse.

(6) Some imperative propositions, having a subject of the third person, occur in our older writers and in the poets. In these the subject noun is expressed, and generally placed after the verb. For examples of these antiquated and poetical imperative propositions, see § 55, p. 112.

We subjoin a few examples of imperative propositions for an exercise in analysis.

(7) "Fret not thyself because of evil men." "Honor thy father and thy mother." "Hear the instruction of thy father." "Forsake not the law of thy mother." "Drink waters out of thine own cistern." "Buy the truth; sell it not." "Get wisdom, get understanding." Show me your exercise. Be courteous to all. "Reveal none of the secrets of thy friend. Be faithful to his interests. Forsake him not in danger. Abhor the thought of acquiring any advantage by his prejudice."

(8) Examples with the Pronoun expressed.—"Despise not thou the chastening of the Almighty." "Blessed be thou," &c. "Be thou an example," &c. "Be not thou ashamed of the testimony," &c. "Go ye therefore," &c.

Exercise.—Form a given number of imperative propositions.

(9) We may here remark that the *vocative*, or *noun of address*, is very often used in connection with this form of proposition. For examples of the *vocative* in this connection, we may take the following propositions: "Go to the ant, *thou sluggard;* consider her ways." "*My son*, forget not my law."

> "Daughter of Faith, awake! arise! illume
> The dread unknown, the chaos of the tomb."—Campbell.

(10) These vocatives, or nouns, employed in addressing or calling on the party to which our discourse is directed, do not form any part of a proposition, though they stand alongside, or sometimes in the middle of it, and therefore they admit of no grammatical analysis. It is the mere utterance of a name for the sake of indicating the party whom we address, or for the purpose of arresting his attention. It is often

---

(6) Repeat the remark about imperatives having a subject of the third person.
(7) Give examples of imperative propositions in which the subject pronoun is suppressed
(8) Give a few examples having the pronoun expressed.
(9) Repeat what is said of the use of the vocative or case of address; and give examples.
(10) Repeat the remarks in reference to the function which vocatives serve in discourse.

used, as in the quotation from Campbell, in solemn and emphatic invocation. (11) The noun or pronoun thus employed is often accompanied, as in the examples above, by the usual modifications of nouns, by *adjectives*, by *nouns in apposition*, by *noun and preposition modifications*. (12) In the example above, "Thou sluggard," and in similar cases, it may be doubted whether *sluggard* is to be considered a noun *apposed* to *thou*, or *thou* as a sort of *determinative* giving greater emphatic force to *sluggard*.

(13) The *vocative* is also often used before interrogative propositions to arrest the attention of the party whom we interrogate. For example:

"*Vain man!* is grandeur given to gay attire?"—Beattie.

It is also employed for the same purpose before assertive propositions. For example: "Son, thou art ever with me," &c.

(14) The *vocative*, having no grammatical dependence on the accompanying proposition, is usually in printed books separated from the rest of the discourse by commas. (15) In analysis all that the grammarian has to do with these *vocatives* is to assign them their name, keeping them separate from the proposition, and to describe the manner in which they happen to be modified.

We have now finished what we have to say on the construction and analysis of propositions, whose subject noun and verb are only modified by single words—not by other propositions. It is possible that the learner may meet with forms of expression in simple propositions which the preceding pages will not enable him to analyze satisfactorily. Such expressions, we think, will rarely occur in pure and dignified composition. He who has made himself completely master of the system of analysis here taught, will generally be able to discover for himself a method of explaining any construction which we may have overlooked. We believe that by the help of this method of analysis the learner may explain, in a rational manner, all the constructions accounted for in the syntax of other grammars (except those involving *relative* pronouns), and a number of constructions besides which these grammarians do not satisfactorily explain.

The student of grammar should bear in mind that the first—the most important—step in attempting the analysis of difficult constructions, is to supply correctly all words omitted by ellipsis, and complete the structure

---

(11) What is said of the modifications of which vocatives are susceptible? Illustrate this by the examples above. (12) What remark is made in reference to the example, "Thou sluggard?"

(13) Is the vocative introduced before other kinds of propositions, and if so, for what purpose? (14) What is the rule of punctuation in reference to vocatives? Tell the reason of the rule. (15) What is to be done when we meet with vocatives in analysis?

of the proposition. The whole difficulty in analysis often arises from abbreviated forms of expression. In such cases, when the construction is filled up, the difficulty vanishes.

Another class of difficulties may be traced to what we have called the *insensible extension* of a usage in construction. This often gives rise to idiomatic expressions which cannot be satisfactorily explained without reference to the history of the language. Cases of this kind do not come within the scope of an elementary treatise on grammar. It is well to advert to the most important and the most current of these idiomatic expressions; but as the grammarian cannot reach them by laying down general principles, he must discuss each separately, and since they are numerous, he cannot hope to explain them all. Much here, as well as in the case of abbreviated expressions, must be left to the ingenuity of the learner. Good sense and a careful study of the grammatical contrivances of language, will enable him to surmount most difficulties. Continual practice in analysis will secure facility and readiness in supplying ellipses and developing abbreviated expressions.

It must not be thought that by this species of exercise the student is merely learning words, as is vulgarly supposed; he is, on the contrary, learning the art of interpreting and expressing thought. He is learning to think accurately, whilst he is learning to express thought accurately. It is not with that part of grammar which relates to the construction of language to serve as a convenient vehicle of thought, as with the learning of the mere forms and inflections of words. This latter is commonly thought a very barren and unprofitable study; and so it is, if we confine our grammatical learning to mere forms and inflections. But the construction of language, to which these forms and inflections are subservient, is one of the noblest arts of which we are possessed, and, if the work of man's intellect, one of its greatest, if not its very greatest achievement. It claims the highest admiration as a display of human ingenuity, and the highest estimation as the most valuable of all contrivances. It is worthy of the most careful study, as connected with all the operations of thought—with the acquisition, the retention, and the communication of all the varied products of man's intellectual energies.

§ 100. In closing what we have to say upon modifications consisting of single words, it may be useful to present a synoptical table of all the forms of modification, which we have separately considered, classing them in reference to the kind of words they are used to *complete.*

The several kinds of words susceptible of modification are: 1st, nouns, including pronouns and verbal nouns; 2d, verbs; 3d, adjectives, including verbal adjectives or participles; and 4th, adverbs. In regard to verbal nouns and verbal adjectives, it has been already observed that they are susceptible of some of the peculiar modifications both of nouns and of verbs. To avoid unnecessary repetition, we form our table irrespective of this peculiarity of the verbals. We exclude them from our consideration in the mean time, that we may not be compelled to repeat (to the confusion of the learner) nearly all the peculiar *complements* of the verbs under the head of nouns; and at the close the student may be reminded that these verbal words, because of their serving the *function* of nouns on the one hand, and expressing a common *meaning* with predicates on the other, take part at least of the modifications of both classes of words.

In the following table, it will be observed that we pursue a different order of arrangement, from that adopted in the preceding pages. We now present the several modifications in the order of their importance, determined chiefly by the comparative frequency of their recurrence in discourse. We do not however pledge ourselves to any very scrupulous examination of the question of relative importance where there might be a doubt which of two modifications has the preponderance, since such nice discrimination is altogether unnecessary to our purposes. Our only aim is to give precedence to those forms of modification which recur so often, and are so indispensable to complete certain kinds of words, that they claim the special regard of the learner.

We prefix a number to each modification of each class, which, together with the letters, *N.*, *V.*, *A.*, and *Adv.* for noun, verb, adjective, and adverb, may serve to denote them in written analyses, or references for any other purpose. We also annex to each modification the number of the section in which it is explained.

This tabular view, it will be observed, is intended to exhibit those modifications only which consist of separate words, and not those which are effected by means of a change of the form of the modified word, such as *plural* forms, *case* forms, *tense* forms, and comparison expressed by *inflection*, &c.

I. Forms of Modification of Nouns.

1. Determinative Adjective,	§ 91.
2. Descriptive Adjective,	§ 86.
3. Genitive Case,	§ 75.
4. Noun and Preposition,	§ 81.
5. Noun in Apposition,	§ 69.
6. Infinitive,	§ 71.
7. Noun Adjectively employed,	§ 70.

II. Forms of Modification of Verbs.

1.	Adjective Complementary of Neuter Verbs,	§ 88.
2.	Adverb,	§ 92.
3.	Objective after Act. and sometimes Pass. V.	§ 76.
4.	Objective Infinitive,	§ 77.
5.	Noun and Preposition,	§ 81.
6.	Accusative of Time, &c.	§ 84.
7.	Dative,	§ 79.
8.	Infinitive of Purpose,	§ 77.
9.	Noun Complementary of Act. and Pass. Verb,	§ 78.
10.	Infinitive Complementary of do.	§ 78.
11.	Noun Complementary of Neuter Verbs,	§ 72.
12.	Adj. Complementary of Act. and Pass. Verb,	§ 89.
13.	Preposition without Noun,	§ 81 : 28.

III. Forms of Modification of Adjectives.

1.	Adverb,	§ 92.
2.	Noun and Preposition,	§ 96.
3.	Infinitive,	§ 96.
4.	Dative,	§ 96.
5.	Accusative of time, value, &c.	§ 96.
6.	Preposition without Noun,	§ 96 : 27.

IV. Forms of Modification of Adverbs.

1.	Adverbial,	§ 92.
2.	Noun and Preposition,	§ 96.

Remark.—We might, perhaps, present a fifth class of modifications affecting the *assertion generally* both subject and predicate. (See § 83.) These would consist of noun and preposition modifications, accusatives of time, and circumstantial adverbial modifications. But it is perhaps unnecessary to make a distinct class of this kind, since it might, after all, be questioned whether it is not equally correct in analysis, for example of such a proposition as, "In the beginning God created the heaven," to say that what is asserted of the subject "*God*" is, that *he* "*created the heaven*" "*in the beginning*," as it is to say that the whole assertion is modified by the circumstance "*In the beginning*."

SUMMARY DESCRIPTION OF THE PURPOSES SERVED BY THE SEVERAL MODIFICATIONS EXHIBITED ABOVE.—It may be serviceable to the learner to present a *summary description* of the chief uses of the forms of modification treated in detail in the preceding pages. In describing these uses, we must express their character in the fewest words possible. Cases will, no doubt, occur in which our description will not apply to every particular use of a modification. For minute information, reference must be had to the formal explanation of each modification in the section indicated in the table. It cannot be expected that in this summary we shall mention any but the most prominent use.

I. MODIFICATIONS OF NOUNS.—(1) The *determinative adjective* either indicates that the noun is employed in a sense determined by other means, or serves itself to determine the extent in which the noun or name is employed. (See § 158.)

(2) The *descriptive adjective* limits a noun or name by a description —by expressing some quality or property of the object which the noun represents.

(3) The *genitive case* limits a noun by expressing the person or thing to which it (in some sense) belongs.

(4) The *noun and preposition modification* (attached to a noun) most generally expresses the same modification as the genitive case. Sometimes it indicates other relations besides that of possession.

(5) The *noun in apposition* limits the *principal* noun to an object to which both may serve in common as names.

(6) The *infinitive* limits a noun by expressing some purpose to which it has relation.

(7) A *noun adjectively employed*, as the name indicates, limits the noun nearly in the same manner as a descriptive adjective.

II. MODIFICATIONS OF THE VERB.—(1) The *adjective complementary of the neuter verb*, as the name indicates, *completes* the signification of the verb by adjoining a quality or property pertaining to the subject of the proposition in the mode asserted by the verb. The same may be said of the adjective complementary of the passive verb.

(2) The *adverb* limits the verb by a description of the manner of the action, or by a circumstance of place, time, &c., attendant on the action which it expresses.

(3) The *objective* limits the action of the verb to some object which it directly regards.

(4) The *objective infinitive* limits in the same manner the action of the verb to some other action which it directly regards.

(5) The *noun and preposition modification* limits the action of the

verb, usually, by giving it a particular *direction* in reference to some person or object.

(6) *Accusatives of time, value, measure*, &c., express a limitation to a *precise time, value*, &c.

(7) The *dative* limits or modifies the verb by expressing the *person* in reference to whom or for whom the action is performed, or what is called the *personal object.*

(8) The *infinitive of purpose* limits by expressing the *purpose* or design of the action of the verb.

(9) The *noun complementary of the active and passive verb* limits or completes it by expressing what the passive or direct object (in the active form of assertion) is *made* or *becomes*, or is conceived to be made or become, through the action of the verb.

(10) The *infinitive complementary of the active and passive verb* expresses what the passive or direct object (in the active form of assertion) is made to do through the action of the verb.

(11) The *noun complementary of the neuter verb* expresses what the subject of the proposition *is, becomes*, &c., in the manner expressed by the verb.*

(12) The *adjective complementary of active and passive verbs* expresses a quality or property of which the *passive object* becomes possessed in the manner expressed by the verb.

(13) The *preposition* (used alone without a noun) gives some direction to the action of the verb, generally in reference to place.

III. MODIFICATIONS OF THE ADJECTIVES.—(1) The *adverb* limits the meaning of the adjective usually by indicating the degree of intensity of the quality expressed.

(2) The *noun and preposition modification*, as in the case of verbs, usually gives a particular direction of the quality expressed by the adjective in reference to the person or object indicated by the noun accompanying the preposition.

---

* This might also stand for a summary description of the noun complementary of the passive verb, which we have included with the *noun complementary of the active verb.* We have done the same with the *adjective complementary of the passive verb.* These modifications of the passive verb may be brought within the description of the modification of the active verb by adverting to the fact that the *passive object* becomes the *subject* of the passive form. They come within the description of the modifications of the neuter verb by simply treating the *passive* as a *compound form* of the verb, without any further accommodation.

(3) The *infinitive* limits the adjective by expressing some action to which it has reference.

(4) The *dative* limits the meaning of the adjective by expressing the person or object to which in the particular case it has reference.

(5) The *accusative of time, value*, &c., limits a few adjectives, which express time, value, dimension, &c., by indicating the precise time, value, measure, &c.

(6) The preposition (without a noun) is employed, especially with verbal adjectives, to give a particular direction to their meaning, as in the case of verbs.

MODIFICATIONS OF ADVERBS.—(1) The *adverb* usually modifies adverbs, as it modifies adjectives, by indicating the degree of intensity of the quality which they express in common with the adjective from which they are formed.

(2) The *noun and preposition modification*, as in the case of adjectives, gives a particular direction of what the adverb expresses in reference to the person or object expressed by the noun.

That the learner may have the whole apparatus necessary for the analysis of propositions (such as we have hitherto considered, involving only modifications consisting of simple words without accessory propositions), presented in a summary and connected manner, we subjoin the following rules already presented in the preceding pages.

RULES I. AND II.—We may call the first and second, Rules of Concord. We shall add others, when we come to treat of the connection of propositions.

RULE I.—The verb in a proposition must always agree in number and person with the subject noun.

RULE II.—Collective nouns, when the collection of individuals which they represent is regarded simply as a collective unity—"as a whole" —have verbs of the singular form; but when reference is made in the assertion to plurality in the subject — "when the collective expresses many as individuals"—the verb is generally of the plural form. This may be regarded as an exception to Rule I. For examples, &c. see § 56 : (7 *a*).

RULE.—In the *noun and preposition modification*, the noun or pronoun is in the accusative case. See § 81 : 32.

We here subjoin a statement of the order which we recommend to be pursued in the analysis of propositions.

ORDER OF ANALYSIS OF PROPOSITIONS.—1. Point out the verb—the assertive word—telling of what kind it is, whether *neuter* or *active*, and if active, whether of the *active* or *passive* form; then *mode*, *tense*, *number*, *person*.

2. Point out the *subject noun* telling of what kind it is, and its *number*, *gender*, *person*; and repeat the rule of concord between verb and subject noun. These form the foundation or basis of the proposition.

3. We turn next to the modifications; and first to those of the *subject noun*, if it has any. Designate each by name in the order of their connection in thought, telling to how much of the subject they apply, whether to the bare subject noun alone, or to the subject noun accompanied by more intimate modifications. The *determinatives* often apply to the subject noun as already modified by a *descriptive adjective*, a *genitive case*, a *noun and preposition* or *an infinitive*. Care must be taken throughout to distinguish between modifications which apply directly to the *principal* word (which in this case is the subject noun) either alone or after being partially modified, and those which apply directly to other modifying words, and only *indirectly* (through their influence on them) to the principal word.

4. Having shown how the subject is completed, turn lastly to the modifications of that part of the predicate expressed by the verb. These are to be designated in the same manner in the order of their connection with the verb, and with the same discrimination between those which directly modify the verb, and those which apply to another modification; and those which apply to the verb alone, and those which apply to it as already affected by other more intimate modifications. The learner will remember that the adjective complementary and the noun complementary both of verbs neuter and active (and passive too, if we consider the auxiliary and participle together as a compound form) have (when they occur) the precedence, on account of their close connection, of all other complements. The preposition used alone has also the nearest connection with the verbs which admit it. Next come objective modifications (whether common names or infinitives), and next datives, when the verb has such; next adverbs of manner. Nouns with prepositions and accusatives of time, &c. come last. These give little trouble, as in our language they are generally arranged when they come after the verb, in the order of their connection, and usually apply to so much of the predicate as precedes them. Sometimes, as we have seen, circumstantial modifications are placed in the beginning of the proposition before both subject noun and verb. Such modifications may usually be treated last, as most remote in order of sense from the verb, and generally applying to all

the predicate (exclusive of themselves), if not to the whole proposition.

All this will be best understood by attention to the models already presented.

There is not much to be said in reference to the punctuation of single propositions having only one subject noun and one verb. Since the great purpose of punctuation (or interpunction) is to separate propositions from one another for the purpose of securing greater perspicuity, a point is seldom employed within such propositions, and what point shall come at the close of a proposition depends on its connection with the rest of the discourse, and cannot with propriety be settled at this stage of our inquiries.

The only instance in which *commas* are introduced in the course of a simple proposition has been already considered (see § 92 : 42), viz.: that in which an adverb, or a noun and preposition expressing a circumstance, that might be separated from the proposition without destroying its general sense, is distinguished by interpunction. The circumstantial expression thus separated from the proposition by punctuation (or rather in this case *interpunction*), is to be regarded as *parenthetic*—as *thrown* into the proposition to express something additional to that which is absolutely essential to the communication of the thought. Commas, here and on many other occasions, serve nearly the same purpose as parenthetic marks. (See Appendix on Punctuation.)

The pupil can now be exercised in analyzing the propositions in any piece of discourse, omitting, in all compound and connected propositions, the conjunctive and connecting words.

The teacher may ask the pupil to tell the principal use of each modification in order, to repeat the rules, and then to describe fully the order of analysis. This description ought to be given after some practice on the examples.

CHAPTER IX.

OF COMPOUND PROPOSITIONS.

§ 101. (1) We pass now from propositions of which all the parts and all the modifications consist of *words*, not of *propositions*—as regards matter, consist of the *names of conceptions*, not of *assertions*—to those which involve in their structure a *proposition*, either as subject of the principal proposition, or as a modification of one of its members.

(2) To express this distinction among propositions with greater brevity, we may call that species which we have hitherto considered, having words only for their members and modifications, *simple propositions*, and those which we are now about to consider, involving a proposition as a member of the main assertion, or one or more propositions as modifications of subject or predicate, *compound propositions*.

NOTE.—We use the term *compound* here as it is used by the grammarians in speaking of words. A *compound* word means a word formed of two or more words united to constitute a single sign; so a compound proposition, as we use the expression, means two or more propositions united to express a single assertion. When two or more propositions which express assertions independent of each other are connected together, we do not consider such connected propositions as *compound propositions*. We may, for distinction's sake, call these when we afterwards come to consider them *connected* or *combined propositions*.

By using the term *simple*, we do not mean to imply that the *forms of modification* in simple propositions are more simple than those in compound propositions. We do not mean to say that the use of single words to modify nouns, verbs, &c. is more ancient than the use of propositions for the same purpose; nor that modification by means of propositions is an extension and

---

§ 101. (1) To what subject do we next pass?

(2) State the distinction between simple and compound propositions.

refinement of grammatical construction. On the contrary, we believe that some, at least, of the modifications of simple propositions already considered are a refinement on the employment of propositions for the same purpose. This will be seen when we come to treat of certain kinds of accessory propositions, especially of the adjective accessory proposition. Again, we do not consider that these two classes of propositions are separated by any very exact line of demarcation. By abbreviating the accessory proposition, a compound proposition often assumes the form of a simple proposition, so that the two forms pass into one another by an easy transition. As regards sense, it is often optional with the writer or speaker to employ either a simple proposition with modifications, such as we have treated in the preceding pages, or a compound proposition involving an accessory proposition as its subject or as a modification. The use of the compound proposition having an accessory for modification, may sometimes be more consistent with simplicity of expression than the more abbreviated and often more artificial mode of adopting single-word complements. The distinction then between *simple* and *compound* propositions regards chiefly the *forms* of modification employed in each respectively. When all the complements consist of single words or phrases, we call the proposition *simple;* when some of the complements are accessory propositions, we call the whole proposition *compound,* as consisting of more than one proposition and more than one verb, though expressing only one direct assertion of the speaker.

(3) In the analysis of compound propositions, we shall, in conformity with the mode of expression employed in treating of the complements in simple propositions, call the proposition which contains the direct assertion of the speaker, the *principal proposition*, and that which performs a *subordinate* part (constituting the subject of the *principal*, or a complement of some part of it), we shall call the *accessory* or subordinate proposition.

(4) REMARK.—The learner will please bear in mind that, when we speak of a *principal* and a *subordinate* or *accessory proposition*, we refer to the *form* of language—to the grammatical arrangement of propositions—not to the relative *logical* importance of the *matter* which they express. The proposition, which, *grammatically* considered, holds the rank of subordinate or accessory (as we shall generally hereafter call it), may be, and often really is, the most important part of the compound proposition, as regards *matter*. To illustrate by

---

(3) State the distinction between a principal and an accessory proposition.
(4) Repeat the substance of the remark, and illustrate it by an example.

examples: *They say our foes are coming; The servant announced that the house was on fire.* In both these compound propositions the first proposition is *grammatically* considered the *principal* containing the *direct* assertion of the speaker, but the latter proposition in both cases undoubtedly contains the most important part of the matter, and is therefore, logically considered, the most important.

§ 102. Accessory Propositions. — (1) A knowledge of the several kinds of accessory propositions and of their functions is indispensable to the satisfactory analysis of compound propositions. To aid the learner in acquiring this important knowledge is the task which we now propose.

Note.—If we should perform it imperfectly, we might plead as our apology the intrinsic difficulty of the undertaking, and the small degree of assistance which we can derive from the labors of our predecessors, especially from those who have written on English grammar. We do not mean to say that all parts of the subject before us have been entirely neglected by writers on universal grammar; but so little has been done by our more philosophical grammarians to simplify and to give systematic arrangement to the doctrine of the connection of propositions in discourse, so little to render it readily intelligible and capable of being used in popular elementary education, that the authors of our English school grammars, left without authoritative guidance, have evaded all regular discussion of this subject, and contented themselves with giving instruction, which, with the exception of a few particulars, applies exclusively to simple propositions. It would be much easier for us to follow their example, if we could do so in consistency with our plan of analysis. But if we were, in pursuing our method, to neglect altogether the consideration, especially of accessory propositions and their functions in language, the deficiency would be so conspicuous as to awaken the attention of even the least observant inquirer. We are in treating this subject much more indebted to the German than to our own grammarians, as regards *matter*. Our *method* is essentially different from theirs.

Classification of Accessory Propositions.—(2) Some of the German grammarians have arranged accessory propositions under three classes, viz.: *substantive accessory propositions, adjective accessory propositions*, and *adverbial accessory propositions*, because they perform functions in discourse resembling one or other of these

---

§ 102. (1) What is indispensable to the analysis of compound propositions?

(2) Name the three classes in which the German grammarians have arranged accessory propositions; and tell the reason of this arrangement,

three classes of words, substantives, adjectives, or adverbs. In our treatment of accessory propositions, we shall find it convenient to follow the order of this ingenious classification. We shall have abundant opportunity as we proceed, of perceiving that it is a well-founded and natural (not a mere capricious) classification.

(3) We may here remark that there is also a striking resemblance between the functions performed by those words which connect accessory with principal propositions and the prepositions which serve as *intermediary* words between a *completing* and a *principal* word. Indeed several of the prepositions in our list, § 81 : 7, are used before accessory propositions, as well as before nouns, and with exactly the same significance, and to perform the same function; the difference being that in the one case they give what is expressed by the *principal* word a *direction*, &c., in reference to what is expressed by a single word (a *noun*), in the other, in reference to what is expressed by an accessory proposition. For example, in the assertions, *James arrived* BEFORE *me*, and *James arrived* BEFORE *I returned*, the word *before* has obviously the same meaning and performs the same function, only in the first example it is the *intermediate* of *arrived* and the pronoun *me*, in the last, it is the *intermediate* of *arrived* and the accessory proposition *I returned*.

OF CONJUNCTIONS.—(4) The words employed to connect *subordinate* with *principal* propositions, and also those employed for the purpose of connecting *co-ordinate* or independent propositions (afterwards to be considered) are called, from the function which they perform, *conjunctions*. They *conjoin* or connect propositions. (5) Of the words employed to connect propositions, some are used exclusively for this purpose; some, on the contrary, like *before* used in the example above, are employed for other purposes, and only occasionally as conjunctions. (6) The first class, for the sake of distinction, we may call *conjunctions*, the latter, *conjunctive words*, or we may connect the term conjunctive with the original class name of these latter words, and call them *conjunctive pronouns*, *conjunctive adverbs*, and *conjunctive prepositions:* for conjunctive

---

(3) Repeat the substance of the remark about the words used in connecting accessory propositions; and illustrate by examples.

(4) What name is given to the class of words employed in connecting propositions? State the reason for giving them this name. (5) Show how words used for this purpose of connection differ. (6) Mention the means by which this difference may be marked. (7)

words of all these kinds occur. (7) Again, besides this, there is a difference in the functions which these words perform when conjunctively used. Some serve exclusively a *conjunctive* purpose, that is, to connect propositions and to indicate some relation subsisting between them. Others, besides this conjunctive function, perform, at the same time, the usual function of the class of words to which they properly belong, generally in the accessory proposition, sometimes both in the accessory and principal proposition. Of these facts we shall find abundant examples as the different forms of accessory propositions come under review. What we have now said may suffice to bring the CONJUNCTIONS—(8) one of the great classes into which grammarians divide words—directly under the student's notice. (9) Along with the form of each *accessory*, we shall consider the conjunction or conjunctive word, or the class of these words which serve to connect it with the principal proposition. (Sometimes we shall find that no conjunctive sign is needed.) In the same way we shall present the different classes of conjunctions which connect *co-ordinate* propositions, when we come to consider the different purposes for which such propositions are connected. This we think the most useful mode of treating this class of words.

§ 103. SUBSTANTIVE ACCESSORY PROPOSITIONS.—(1) We now return to the accessory propositions, and direct our attention first to the class which we have designated as *substantive accessory propositions*, because they perform some of the peculiar functions of substantives.

ACCESSORY PROPOSITION USED AS SUBJECT.—(2) The purpose first in importance for which a substantive accessory proposition is employed, is one to which we have already adverted in the preceding pages (see § 20 : 6–7), namely, to serve as SUBJECT of the *principal* proposition. (3) This species of accessory proposition is very generally preceded by the determinative word *that.* (4) *That*, when thus em-

---

Describe a further difference in their functions when conjunctively used. (8) What do the conjunctions form? (9) In what mode do we propose to treat conjunctions and conjunctive words?

§ 103. (1) What is the name of the class of accessories which we first proceed to consider? And why is this name given to them?

(2) What purpose does the first mentioned species of substantive accessory proposition serve? (3) By what word is this species of accessory generally preceded? (4) What is

ployed, is called by grammarians a conjunction, though in fact it performs precisely the same function as when they call it a demonstrative pronoun (determinative adjective according to our nomenclature); only it is placed in the one case before a noun, and in the other (which we are now considering) before a proposition performing for the time the function usually performed by a noun. (5) We subjoin examples for the purpose of illustration. *That the government of our desires is essential to the enjoyment of true liberty, is a truth never to be forgotten by the citizens of free states.* Here if we put the question (as suggested in § 15: 3) what "is a truth never to be forgotten?" the answer will exhibit the true subject of the proposition; namely, "The government of our desires is essential to the enjoyment of true liberty." Second example, *That industrious habits are essential to success in life, ought to be continually inculcated on the young.* What "ought to be continually inculcated on the young?" Answer, the proposition, the judgment of the mind, the truth:—"Industrious habits are essential to success in life." This truth, for the sake of greater emphasis, is marked by the determinative *that.* Third example, *That Julius Cæsar invaded Britain, is a well known historical fact.*

[(6) In the analysis of any piece of discourse consisting (as almost always happens) of an intermixture of simple, compound, and combined propositions, the first question for the learner to settle is, how many distinct propositions are contained in the portion proposed at one time for consideration. (This portion should always contain at least one complete assertion. Usually, it consists of what is called a sentence.) If the portion proposed contains more than one proposition, the next question is, are the propositions combined co-ordinate, or are they compound propositions? If they are only combined propositions, they are to be treated, and the nature of their connection explained, according to the instructions to be given hereafter for the analysis of such propositions. (See § 145: 25; § 147: 12.) If the sentence contains one or more compound propositions, the next step in analysis is to point out the verb, or assertive word in the principal proposition,

---

said in reference to *that* thus employed? (5) Illustrate the use of the accessory employed as subject of the principal proposition by examples.

[(6) Repeat the substance of the directions given how to conduct the analysis of a piece of discourse.]

and then the subject, as in treating a simple proposition. In the present instance this subject is the *accessory* proposition; and in this case we proceed next to the separate analysis of the subject proposition, treating the word *that* as a determinative applied to the whole proposition considered as a single compound subject. Or, if we please, we may call it here a conjunctive determinative, since it (as now understood) indicates the *conjunction* of the propositions, at the same time that it exercises its usual determinative force. Then we proceed to the analysis of the verb and other parts of the predicate of the principal proposition.

When the accessory proposition serves as a modification of the subject or predicate of the principal proposition, or of one of the complements of the subject or predicate, it is to be treated, like the modifications already described in the order which it occupies in the sense, and it may itself either be analyzed in its place, or its function and class only may be mentioned, and the analysis postponed till the principal proposition is finished. If, like a circumstantial modification, it seems to affect rather the whole *principal* proposition, than any one of its members in particular, it may be considered last, after the analysis of the principal proposition is completed.]

(7) Compound propositions of this kind are often expressed in our language in a somewhat different form. For example, the compound propositions above introduced may be presented in the following form: IT *is a truth never to be forgotten by the citizens of free states, that the government of our desires*, &c. IT *ought to be constantly inculcated on the young, that industrious habits are essential to success in life.* IT *is a well known historical fact, that Julius Cæsar invaded Britain.* In the compound propositions thus presented, the real subjects are still, as before, the accessory propositions commencing with THAT. (8) The word IT serves as a *substitute subject* to the principal proposition, till the real subject is developed in the accessory proposition. (9) This contrivance enables us to arrange the predicate—the important part—of the principal proposition first, and thus give emphasis to the assertion by presenting it before we exhibit the subject to which it applies. (10) This arrangement serves to draw the hearer's attention more powerfully to what we assert, by keeping him in suspense as to the subject to which it applies. (11) The latter form of this class of com-

(7) What fact is stated in No. 7? Illustrate by examples. (8) What is said of the function performed by *it* in the compound proposition when arranged as in these examples? (9) What are we enabled to effect by this substitution of *it* for the real subject? (10) What effect has this arrangement on the hearer? (11) Which form of the compound proposition is usually preferred by writers?

pound propositions—we mean the form commencing with *it* for *substitute subject* of the principal proposition—is generally preferred by writers, and occurs much more frequently than the other form in our language.

NOTE.—The word *it* is often employed in the same representative manner when the subject of the main proposition is an infinitive serving as a contracted accessory. (See § 142.) We subjoin a few examples of this construction, which, like the preceding, very often occurs in our language. "It is good for us to think, that this man too was our brother." What is good for us? Answer, "To think that this man too was our brother," = That we should think, that this man too was our brother, is good for us. "It is for you to decide, whether this freedom shall yet survive, or be covered with a funeral pall," &c. "To decide," &c. "is for you" = That you should decide, is for you — is your part or province. "It is not necessary to await your determination." To await your determination is not necessary = That we should await your determination is not necessary. In all such constructions *it* serves to represent for the moment the infinitive with its accompaniments, which is the real subject.

We subjoin the following examples for exercise in analysis.

"It is through inward health that we enjoy all outward things." "It was an especial precaution that none but sweet-scented evergreens and flowers should be employed." "It is greatly to be regretted that a custom so truly elegant and touching has disappeared from general use."

(12) In the analysis of compound propositions of this form, the principal proposition may be first analyzed, and, when we come to mention the representative or substitute subject IT, we must tell what purpose it serves, and refer to the accessory which it represents. (13) Some regard the accessory proposition in compounds of this form as a proposition in apposition with the pronoun *it*. But this method does not lead to an explanation of the construction so full and clear; besides, it is not, as we think, perfectly correct to say that either a proposition or a word is in apposition with that which really serves as its representative. Such extension of the term *apposition* is not to be defended.

(14) It is only as subject—never as predicate—that a proposition can become a constituent member of another proposition. (15) We

---

(12) Repeat what is said of the analysis of this form of compound proposition? (13) How do some grammarians regard the accessory in this form of proposition? State objections.

(14) Is an accessory ever employed as predicate of a proposition? (15) Assign the reason

see the reason that an accessory cannot serve as predicate in the fact, that it cannot represent the assertive word, which always, according to our views, forms an essential, indeed, the leading part of every predicate. (See §§ 13, 46.) A verb alone, not any other word, or combination of words, can perform the peculiar function of expressing the leading part of the predicate assertively. The verb of the accessory proposition, having its own subject, cannot serve at the same time as verb of the principal proposition.

(16) PUNCTUATION.—In this construction, the principal and accessory are usually separated by a comma.

EXERCISES I., II., &c.—A given number of compound propositions of the first of the above described forms. A given number of the second form.

§ 104. (1) We next come to treat of substantive accessory propositions employed for the purpose of modification. (2) We thus pass again to the subject of modification; for all the accessories which we have now to consider—the *adjective* and *adverbial*, as well as the *substantive*, serve to modify either the subject or predicate, or a modification of the subject or predicate of the *principal* proposition, or, like circumstantial adverbs, and circumstantial nouns with prepositions, to modify the whole principal proposition.

(3) These *modifying* accessories constitute an important part of the structure of language; and yet, with the exception of what regards the adjective accessory, they have received very little attention, so far as we know, from our English grammarians.

(4) In treating this part of our subject, we derive great advantage (and the student will participate largely with us in this advantage) from the method pursued in the treatment of the complements or modifications of simple propositions; for the complements or modifications which consist of accessory propositions have generally a close analogy to those which consist of separate words.

(5) In passing under review these modifying accessory propositions we shall pursue an order suggested by the classification of

(16) What is said of punctuation in reference to this kind of compound propositions?

§ 104. (1) Mention the subject to be next considered. (2) Repeat the remark in reference to all the accessory propositions which remain to be treated.

(3) What are the modifying accessories said to constitute, and how have they been regarded by English grammarians?

(4) From what do we derive advantage in treating these modifying accessories?

(5) What is said of the order to be pursued in treating the modifying accessories?

accessories already given, and this will correspond nearly with the order observed in treating the complements of simple propositions.

(6) 1st. We shall notice the accessory propositions of which the functions bear an analogy to the functions of nouns employed in modification.

2d. Those which bear an analogy to the adjective modifications.

3d. Those which bear an analogy to adverbial or noun with preposition modifications.

4th. And lastly, we shall consider certain accessory propositions which perform peculiar functions which cannot be performed by single words or phrases.

(7) This order of arrangement, and constant reference to the complements already treated, which each accessory most resembles in function, and with which it in some cases interchanges place, will much assist the learner in following our observations on *modifying accessory propositions.*

SUBSTANTIVE ACCESSORY PROPOSITIONS EMPLOYED FOR THE PURPOSE OF MODIFICATION.

§ 105. (1) Here we shall mention first the substantive accessory proposition employed in *apposition* with a noun for the same purpose as the noun in apposition complement. We have already noticed this kind of modifying accessory in treating of the noun in apposition, § 69, and have given an example. (2) We subjoin additional examples. "For the promise, *that he should be the heir of the world*, was not to Abraham." "And they made proclamation throughout Judah and Jerusalem unto all the children of the captivity, *that they should gather themselves together unto Jerusalem.*" In the first example, the accessory proposition "That he should be the heir of the world" stands in apposition with the noun "promise," serving to explain or expand the conception which it expresses; and, in like manner in the second example, the accessory "That they should gather themselves together," &c. stands in apposition with the noun "proclamation."

---

(6) State at length the order to be pursued.

(7) What will assist the learner in following our observations on these accessories?

§ 105. (1) Describe the modifying accessory first considered. (2) Illustrate the use of this accessory by examples.

(3) Nouns, which imply what may be expressed more specially in the form of a proposition, generally admit of *this* proposition in apposition to explain or expand them. (4) Such nouns are, *apology, bargain, belief, conclusion, commandment, contract, conviction, decision, declaration, design, doctrine, injunction, judgment, opinion, precept, proclamation, promise, proposition, purpose, resolution, sentence, threat, truth*, &c. For example, *The opinion, belief, conviction*, &c., THAT THE SOUL IS IMMORTAL, *has been almost universally entertained. The command, precept*, &c. *of Christ addressed to his immediate disciples*, THAT THEY SHOULD LOVE ONE ANOTHER, *is binding on all his professed followers.* This form of modification, we think, is not very often employed.

(5) PUNCTUATION.—This accessory, like the noun in apposition, is separated from the rest of the compound proposition by *commas.*

EXERCISE I., II., &c.—Form compound propositions similar to those now given, using the words above enumerated for subject nouns.

§ 106. ACCESSORY PROPOSITION COMPLEMENTARY OF THE VERB TO BE.—(1) An accessory proposition is often used like a noun complementary of a verb. In this way it is used, we believe, exclusively with the verb *to be.* (2) Example, "Another cause is, *that the grave is more immediately in sight of the survivors.*" Here, "That the grave is more immediately in sight of the survivors," serves to complete the verb IS. Compare with the example the following form of expression : *Another cause is the frequent visitation of the grave by the survivors.* It is plain that the function performed in the example by the accessory proposition is the same as that here performed by the noun *visitation*, and its accompanying modifications.

(3) We may readily form principal propositions having the nouns enumerated in the preceding section for their subjects, which principal propositions will take accessories of this description to modify the verb IS. We subjoin examples which may be used as an exercise in analysis. "My sentence is, that we trouble not them," &c. *The proclamation is,*

---

(3) State the description of nouns which take such modifying propositions. (4) Enumerate some of these nouns.

§ 106. (1) Name the accessory next mentioned, and tell with what verb it is used. (2) Illustrate by an example, and mention the form of expression with which the example is compared.

(3) Describe the mode of forming propositions to illustrate the use of this accessory

that they should gather themselves together. Our opinion, belief, conclusion, judgment, &c. is, that different forms of government suit different stages of civilization. His sentence, decision, command, threat, injunction, &c. was, that the culprit should be punished. Your contract, bargain, &c. was, that you would supply us with materials. Our intention, design, purpose, resolution, &c. is, that the work shall be soon accomplished. The precept of Christ is, that his followers should love one another. The truth is, that different forms of polity suit nations in different stages of civilization. (4) In many of these examples, the more usual construction would, no doubt, be to employ, instead of an accessory proposition, the infinitive verbal noun. (5) The infinitive with its accompaniments may be considered in such cases an abbreviated method of expressing an accessory proposition. (See § 142.) *Thus, His sentence, decision, design, command, &c. is to punish the culprits. Our intention, design, purpose, &c. is to finish the work. The precept of Christ is to love one another.*

(6) Remark.—These compound propositions may all, without much change of sense, be *converted* into the form (considered above § 103) which has the *accessory for subject* of the principal proposition. Thus, *It is my sentence, that we trouble not them among the Gentiles, &c. It is our opinion, belief, &c. that different forms of government, &c. It was his sentence, that the culprit should be punished. It is our intention, design,* &c. *that the work should be finished speedily.**

(7) Punctuation.—This accessory proposition is separated by a comma from the principal.

---

* Those who consider the verb *to be* as performing solely the function of *copula*—the assertive function, without expressing any part of the predicate—would say, in consistency with their views, that what we call the complementary accessory proposition, is the *predicate* of the compound proposition. For example, in the compound proposition, *The decision of the besieging general* WAS, *that the citizens must surrender at discretion;* if WAS is regarded as simply and solely *copula*, the accessory *That the citizens must surrender at discretion* is manifestly the predicate, or that which is asserted. But we, on the contrary, holding that WAS *itself* predicates *Being* (in a past time), consider that the complete predicate here is *Being* (in a past time) *that the citizens must surrender at discretion*, making *That the citizens must*

---

(4) Mention a form of construction more usual in some cases than that in the examples.
(5) How may the infinitive here be regarded? Repeat examples.
(6) Give the substance of the remark; and illustrate it by examples.
(7) What is said of the punctuation of this construction?

EXERCISES, I., II., &c.—Construct compound propositions with complementary accessories; exhibiting at the same time the variations of form of which they may be susceptible without material change of meaning—infinitives instead of accessory propositions, and compound propositions with an accessory for subject. The construction of assertions in the three forms, when all are accordant with propriety of expression, will improve the pupil's facilities in composition, by making him better acquainted with the resources which such variations of construction afford us, for the purpose of selecting appropriate and harmonious expression.

§ 107. SUBSTANTIVE ACCESSORY PROPOSITION USED AS OBJECTIVE MODIFICATION. — (1) Perhaps the most common use of what we call substantive accessory propositions is to serve as objective modification, or complement direct of active verbs. (2) The accessory used in this way is sometimes preceded by the conjunctive determinative *that*, but it often stands without any conjunctive word.

(3) This construction occurs so frequently in our language (and indeed in all languages), that we might multiply examples at pleasure. (4) But as the use of this kind of accessory is so like the use of the objective modification, and so easily understood, a few examples will be sufficient for our purpose. (5) *I told him that a courier had arrived;* or *I told him a courier had arrived.* The learner will observe that "*him*" is here the dative modification (see § 79), and "*A courier had arrived,*" either with or without the determinative *that*, is the objective modification. Put the question, *what did I tell?* The answer given will be the objective modification—"A courier had arrived." (See § 76: 5.) *He said John was wise*, or *he said* THAT *John was wise. I know he has sent*, or *that he has sent it.*

(6) Sometimes instead of an accessory proposition we substitute the infinitive as an abbreviation. (7) This infinitive takes before it

surrender at discretion a complement of *being.* To this view we make our analysis conform. (See §§ 13 and 46.)

§ 107. (1) Which is perhaps the most common use of the substantive accessory? (2) By what conjunctive word is this accessory sometimes preceded?

(3) Repeat remark about the frequent recurrence of this construction. (4) What reasons are assigned for exhibiting few examples? (5) Illustrate by examples. (6) What is sometimes substituted for this form of accessory? (7) What do such infinitives take before

the accusative of the noun or pronoun which is the subject in the equivalent accessory proposition. (8) For example, instead of *I know that he is wise*, we can say *I know him to be wise;* instead of *I believe that he is learned*, we may say *I believe him to be learned.* (9) A small number of verbs in our language admits this infinitive preceded by an accusative instead of an objective accessory. This is a favorite construction in Latin, and the infinitives with accusatives before them of that language can most generally be expressed in our language only by accessory propositions.

(10) Sometimes the accessory in this kind of compound proposition is interrogative and commences with an interrogative word. Example, *I do not know whether it is true.* Many persons say, but with less propriety, *I do not know* IF *it is true. Do you know whether it is true?* (11) In this example, the whole compound proposition is of the interrogative form. In the preceding examples the accessory alone is interrogative, and the principal proposition, and, therefore, the compound proposition as a whole is assertive. *I do not know who it is. I cannot tell what you mean. Can you tell what he means? I cannot tell who it is.* * *I have ascertained where he is. Have they ascertained where I am? John knows well how many there are.*

---

* Instances of the false construction of such compound interrogative propositions occur frequently, even among learned authors; especially in translations from Latin and Greek. We may illustrate this and thus guard the learner against such mistakes by the following example from the translation of the New Testament. "But whom say ye that I am?" Matt. 16:15; Mark 8:29; Luke 9:20. An adherence to the universally acknowledged principles of construction demands instead of this, *But* WHO *say ye that I am?* Who belongs strictly in the construction to the accessory proposition, and should be the nominative after the verb, the same case as the subject noun *I*, since it serves as a noun complementary to the verb. In the usual language of the grammarians the verb *to be* has the same case after it which goes before it. This rule is violated in the example above, in all the three gospels, by our translators. Tyndale and Cranmer have given the correct grammatical construction in Luke, but the false English occurs in their translations of Matthew and Mark. The versions of Geneva and Rheims, like the authorized, employ the false construction in all the gospels. All these learned men were misled, no doubt, by the use of the infinitive and accusative in the original Greek, not adverting to the fact that they had, very

---

them? (8) Illustrate by examples. (9) Is this a common construction in our language? And what remark is made in reference to the Latin language?

(10) Repeat what is said of interrogative accessories, and illustrate by examples. (11)

(12) *Verbals* are of course susceptible of this species of modification as well as their kindred verbs. (See § 76: 32–41.) Examples, *Hearing that you had obtained news of that matter*, I have called upon you. *Knowing that he is a good man*, I have recommended him to you. "The world would then have the means of *knowing how many they are; who they are;* and of what value their opinions may be," &c.—Burke.

(13) PUNCTUATION.—The objective accessory is not usually separated by interpunction; though the usage in this matter is not, we believe, perfectly consistent, when the word *that* precedes the accessory. When *that* is not introduced, the comma, we think, is never used.

EXERCISES I. II. &c.—Construct compound propositions with objective accessory modifications. Construct a number of propositions in two forms, first with an accessory for objective, and second with an infinitive and accusative preceding it. The following among other verbs admit this latter construction and may be employed in constructing these propositions of double form. *Acknowledge, admit, believe, know, prove, suppose, suspect, think, warrant.*

§ 108. SUBSTANTIVE ACCESSORY PROPOSITION EXPRESSIVE OF PURPOSE.—A proposition is often employed to modify a verb in the same way as we employ the *infinitive of purpose.* (See § 77.) (2) This species of accessory proposition is preceded by the conjunctive THAT, which cannot here be omitted, as in the case of the objective accessory proposition. (3) We can express the connection of such accessories with the principal proposition more emphatically by using the words *in order that* before them, instead of the simple *that.* (4) Examples, *I eat,* THAT *I may live; or, I eat,* IN ORDER THAT

properly, in accommodation to the English idiom, adopted the accessory proposition instead of the infinitive in the Greek construction. In translating the passage in Matthew, Wiclif has followed closely the Greek and Latin idiom "*Whom* seien ye me to be?" Here "*whom*" is correctly used, as the accusative *me* precedes *to be;* but in translating the same words in the other gospels, he falls into the same mistake with the other translators.

Repeat the remarks in reference to the preceding example. (12) Repeat the remark about verbals.

(13) What is said of punctuation?

§ 108. (1) What accessory is next considered? (2) By what word is it always preceded? (3) In what other more emphatic way is this accessory sometimes connected? (4) Give examples.

I may live. James labors, that he may obtain bread ; or, James labors, in order that he may obtain bread. This boy studies diligently, that he may become learned and useful=in order that he may become &c.

(5) The *infinitive of purpose* is often employed instead of this species of accessory; thus, *He labors* TO OBTAIN *bread.* This is a less formal and less emphatic mode of expressing the thought. (6) The infinitive of purpose may be considered as a substitute, or an abbreviated form of the accessory of purpose. (7) We must take care not to confound this species of accessory proposition with the objective accessory, from which it is entirely distinct. (8) In this modification the determinative THAT is indispensable, and is always more emphatic, since it stands instead of, and represents IN ORDER THAT; and this circumstance may serve to distinguish it from the objective accessory.

(9) The remark made in the preceding section in reference to verbals, applies equally here.

(10) PUNCTUATION.—This accessory is generally separated by a comma, but usage in this case is not perfectly settled.

§ 109. SUBSTANTIVE ACCESSORY MODIFICATION OF ADJECTIVES. —(1) A substantive accessory, or rather an accessory analogous to the noun with a preposition, is frequently used to modify a certain description of adjectives. For example, "I am not worthy that thou shouldest come under my roof."

(2) The adjectives susceptible of this species of modification are generally such as express a condition of mental feeling, and the accessory preceded by *that* conjunctive indicates the object which this condition of mind regards. (3) We may enumerate among these adjectives *conscious, unconscious, heedful, heedless, ignorant, mindful, unmindful, thoughtful, unthoughtful, unthinking.* Examples, *This man,* CONSCIOUS *that he has acted shamefully, avoids his former companions. The other, unconscious that he has done wrong, exhibits the aspect of innocence.* (5) In constructing compound propositions of this kind, the adjective and its modifying accessory are very often first

---

(5) What modification is often employed instead of this accessory? (6) Repeat the remark about the infinitive of purpose. (7) Repeat the caution. (8) How may it be distinguished from the objective accessory? (9) What is said about verbals? (10) Punctuation?

§ 109. (1) Describe the accessory which modifies adjectives.

(2) Describe the adjectives which are susceptible of this modification. (3) Enumerate some of them. (4) Illustrate by examples. (5) Repeat the remark in reference to the con-

disposed of in the arrangement; then follows the principal proposition, the adjective modified by the accessory serving to complete its subject noun. (6) Examples: *Mindful that the duration of life is uncertain, this good man studies to be always prepared for death. Heedful that dangers surrounded him, he pursued his march with redoubled caution. Ignorant that we were his best friends, he treated us as his worst foes.* (7) This kind of substantive accessory proposition is, as we have already intimated, analogous to the noun and preposition used in modifying adjectives. (8) In fact, when the adjectives enumerated above take *word-modifications* (as opposed to accessory proposition-modifications), it is a noun and preposition which they take. For example *conscious of innocence, mindful of favors, heedless of danger,* &c.

(9) There are some other similar adjectives which take after them an accessory of the same form to indicate, not the object which the condition of mind expressed by them regards, but the occasion or cause of this condition of mind. (10) Such are *anxious, grateful, ungrateful, thankful, ashamed,* &c. Thus, *Anxious that his friend should not fail in his efforts, he devoted much of his time to his service.* "The humblest peasant is anxious that some little respect may be paid to his remains." *Grateful, or thankful that he was now rescued from danger, he resolved to recompense his deliverer.* (11) With most of these last adjectives *because* may be used as the conjunctive word, and the accessories which modify them come perhaps rather within the class which we call adverbial accessories, since they express the circumstance of *causality.*

(12) PUNCTUATION.—This accessory, together with the adjective which it modifies, is separated from the principal proposition by interpunction.

EXERCISES I., II., &c.—Construct compound propositions containing adjectives modified by accessories of the kind described.

We need add nothing here to what has been already said about the order in which the pupil should proceed in the analysis of compound propositions embracing modifying accessories, save to remind him that the accessory should be analyzed in immediate connection with the principal word which it modifies.

---

struction of this kind of compound propositions. (6) Illustrate by examples. (7) To which of the forms of modification already treated is this modifying accessory analogous? (8) What fact is stated as a proof of this? Give examples.

(9) State what is said of a similar class of adjectives. (10) Enumerate some of this class. And illustrate by examples. (11) Repeat the remark made in reference to this last class of adjectives and their accessories.

(12) Punctuation?

§ 110. OF ADJECTIVE ACCESSORY PROPOSITIONS.—(1) We next proceed to consider the *adjective accessory proposition.* (2) This kind of accessory is generally connected with the word which it modifies by what are commonly called the *relative*, but by some with greater propriety, the *conjunctive pronouns.* (3) These words perform some of the ordinary functions of a noun in the accessory proposition, and, at the same time, indicate the connection or *conjunction* between it and the word in the principal proposition which it serves to complete. (4) The name *relative* has been given to these pronouns because they *relate* or have *reference* to another word which they represent.* (5) This word is usually called the *antecedent*, because it *goes before.* (6) This antecedent word which the conjunctive pronoun represents, is the word which the *adjective accessory* proposition modifies or completes. Sometimes a *proposition* is represented by a conjunctive pronoun, or, in other words, serves as antecedent. "The bill was rejected by the Lords, *which* excited no small degree of jealousy," &c.

(7) The words chiefly employed as simple conjunctive pronouns are *who*, *which*, and *that.* (8) *Who* has case forms exactly as the interrogative who; namely, a genitive case *whose*, and dative and accusative *whom.* (9) The declension of this word may be exhibited as follows:

Nominative,	Who.
Genitive,	Whose.

* The circumstance that they relate, or have reference to a noun, is not peculiar to this class of pronouns; but is equally characteristic of other pronouns, especially of those of the third person. The name *relative* pronouns is not therefore so appropriate, so well adapted to distinguish these words, as the name *conjunctive pronouns* given to them by some of the French grammarians. This latter name fully indicates the double function of this class of words, viz.: that of pronoun, or representative of a noun, and that of connection or conjunction.

§ 110. (1) What kind of accessory is next considered? (2) What name is given to the words which connect this accessory with the word which it modifies? (3) Describe the functions of conjunctive pronouns. (4) Why have these words been called relative pronouns? (5) What is the word which the conjunctive pronoun represents called? (6) What is said of the antecedent? Is it always a noun?

(7) Enumerate the simple conjunctive pronouns. (8) What forms has *who*? (9) Re-

Dative, Whom.
Accusative, Whom.

(10) These forms are used to represent both singular and plural nouns, in the same manner as the case forms of the interrogative *who*. (See § 98.)

(11) *Which* has no variation for either case or number. *Whose* is sometimes employed as its genitive, borrowed from *who*. Or perhaps we should say that the distinction between *who* and *which* is not maintained in the genitive. (12) It is scarcely correct to say that *whose* is the genitive of *which* as well as of *who*. It is manifestly formed from *who*, not from *which*. (13) *That* is also invariable, performing the function of nominative, dative, and accusative, and having no genitive form. (14) The only genitive form among the three simple conjunctive pronouns is *whose*, and the use of this as a genitive of which—that is, the use of it when any other than a rational being or *person* is referred to, seems to be rather avoided by fastidious writers. (15) We have, however, the most respectable authority for using it in referring to things not *personal*, that is, not capable of taking part in discourse. We have a well known example in the commencement of the Paradise Lost.

"Of man's first disobedience, and the fruit
Of that forbidden *tree*, *whose* mortal taste," &c.

"Nebuchadnezzar, the king, made an *image* of gold, *whose* height was threescore cubits," &c. Dan. 3: 1.

Leaving *whose* out of the account, the distinction observed in the present use of these pronouns may be described as follows: (16) *Who* and its accusative *whom* are employed as conjunctive pronouns to represent persons—those who being endowed with reason and speech can take a part in human discourse—individually and plurally (but not collectively) considered. (17) They are also employed to represent the names of animals when personified, as in fables; and sometimes per-

---

peat the declension of *who*. (10) Repeat what is said of the singular and plural use of the forms of *who*.

(11) What is said of *which* in reference to case forms? (12) Is it correct to call *whose* the genitive of which? (13) Has *that* case forms? (14) Repeat the remark about *whose*. (15) Have we authority for using *whose* in speaking of things not personal? Give examples.

(16) What is said of the employment of *who* and *whom*? (17) Do they ever represent

sonified things and abstractions. (18) *Which* is *now* used only to represent *nonpersonals*, that is, irrational animals and things inanimate.

(19) It is also used to represent *collective* nouns (though signifying assemblages of *persons*), when they imply unity. The collective body, considered as a unit, though made up of persons, is not regarded as *a person*. Examples: *The* PARTY WHICH *first elevated him to power has since denounced him. The* ARMY, WHICH *he led to victory, was strongly attached to him.* (20) Which is also used to represent nouns signifying persons, when only the word, or name, or character is referred to, not the person. Examples: *You call him an* OPPRESSOR *of the poor and the weak,* WHICH *is the worst name you could give him.* "That was the work of *Herod*, which is but another name for cruelty."

(21) In the earlier usage of our language, *which* was employed to represent persons as well as *nonpersonals*. (22) Thus it is employed in the Lord's Prayer in the authorized version, and in the versions of Tyndale and Cranmer, and in those published at Geneva and at Rheims. Our *father which* art in heaven. (23) The distinction established in the present usage of our language between *who* and *which* contributes to perspicuity. *Who* and *whom* always by their very form indicate that the reference is to the names of *persons*, and *which* that the reference is to *nonpersonals*—to animals or inanimate things.

(24) *That* is used to represent the names both of persons and things. It may be considered as the *universal relative or conjunctive pronoun*, filling the place of both *who* and *which*. (25) But as the use of *who* or *which* gives greater clearness to the reference, the one limiting it to *persons*, the other to *nonpersonals*, the employment of these words is to be preferred, except where their frequent recurrence, or some awkwardness of expression connected with their use renders the employment of the less definite *that* preferable. (*See additional observations on the pronouns* WHO, WHICH, THAT, § 159.)

[The grammarians have enumerated certain cases in which the use of *that* is to be preferred to the use of *who* or *which*. We give the substance of what they have said, partly in the language of Dr. Crombie and Dr. Bullions.

---

the names of animals or things? (18) How is *which now* used? (19) Does *which* ever represent *nouns* signifying *persons?* Give examples. (20) In what other case is it so used? Give examples.

(21) What is said of the use of *who* and *which* in the earlier period of our language? (22) Mention the example. (23) Is the distinction now observed between *who* and which useful?

(24) What is said of *that?* (25) What reason for preferring the use of *who* or *which* in general to the use of *that* as a conjunctive pronoun?

(26) 1st. *That* is used after *who* or *which* (either conjunctive or interrogative) has been already employed in the sentence to avoid a disagreeable repetition of the same sound. But this change from *who* or *which* to *that* ought not to be admitted in a series of accessory propositions modifying the same noun; the same antecedent ought to be always represented in such a series by the same pronoun. Thus it would be improper to say, *The man* THAT *fears God, and* WHO *loves his neighbor.* We ought to employ either *who* in both cases, or *that* in both cases.

2d. *That* is usually employed to represent nouns modified by adjectives in the superlative degree; as, "He is the *wisest* man *that* ever lived." Also to represent nouns modified by the words *same, all, very;* and generally to represent those modified by the determinative adjectives *any, no, some.*

3d. When the conjunctive is to represent two antecedent nouns, the one signifying persons and the other *nonpersonals, that* is employed; as "the *man* and the *horse that* passed us."

4th. *That* is sometimes employed, when it is doubtful whether *who* or *which* is the proper word; as, The little *child that* was placed in the midst.]

§ 111. We now return to the consideration of the adjective accessory proposition, and the various functions, besides that of *connecting*, which the conjunctive words perform in it. It will be more convenient, after illustrating the use of these chief conjunctive pronouns, to consider the other words which serve purposes somewhat similar.

(1) Adjective accessory propositions perform functions similar both to descriptive and determinative adjectives. (2) That is to say, in other words, propositions of this kind are employed either to *describe* the object expressed by the noun which they modify, or to render the object more *determinate*—or, still in other words, either to express an attribute belonging to the object, or to indicate the manner in which the speaker chooses to limit the modified name (*See* § 91 : 11, *et seq.*)

(3) We subjoin examples of both kinds of accessories for the purpose

[(26) Mention the first case in which the use of *that* conjunctive is to be preferred. The second case, &c.]

§ 111. (1) What two kinds of functions do adjective accessories perform? (2) Express these functions in different ways. (3) Illustrate these functions by examples.

of illustration. *The man* WHO IS ALWAYS IDLE *is a burden to himself, and useless to the community.* The accessory proposition "*who is always idle*" is here descriptive of "*the man.*" *The boy* WHO STANDS FOREMOST *is the son of our friend.* Here *who stands foremost* is an accessory employed not to *describe*, but to *determine*. It expresses no attribute belonging to the boy, but simply indicates to the hearer what boy the speaker intends.

[(4) We might divide *descriptive* accessory propositions into two classes, one including those which describe an object by predicating one of its inherent qualities, another, those which describe the object by predicating of it a particular action. (5) The first class corresponds with the *descriptive* adjective, the latter with the participle employed to modify nouns. (6) The first class is formed by the employment of the verb *to be* with a *descriptive adjective*, the second by the use of the other verbs, or of the verb *to be* with a participle. (7) *The man* WHO IS IDLE *is a burden to himself*, is an example of the first class; *The man* WHO CONSTANTLY LABORS TO DO GOOD *deserves universal approbation*, is an example of the second. (8) But it is scarcely necessary in grammatical analysis to attend to a distinction like this, which has reference to the subject *matter* rather than to the *form* of the accessory proposition. (9) We notice it here merely to show the close analogy subsisting between this whole class of accessories and the different kinds of adjective modifications.*]

* That the function which this kind of accessory performs is the same with that which the adjective performs, may be shown more directly by selecting cases in which an accessory proposition and a corresponding adjective form equivalent, or nearly equivalent modifications. For example: *The steward* WHO IS FAITHFUL *deserves commendation*, and, *The* FAITHFUL *steward deserves commendation* are nearly equivalent expressions. The first of these modes of expression is more formal, more stiff, and, when it is wished to call special attention to the *description*, more emphatic. This species of modification (by an accessory) likely had place in language before adjectives were employed attributively. We suspect that the *adjective* modification is a refinement on the *adjective accessory* modification—a mere abbreviation of the accessory, always implying a suppressed predication. In the present usage of language, when we have a descriptive adjective to express an attribute, we generally employ it attributively—without the formality of predication; except when it is necessary for some reason to give peculiar force to the

[(4) Into what classes might adjective accessories be divided? (5) Tell with what each class corresponds. (6) Tell how each class is formed. (7) Illustrate by examples. (8) Is it necessary to give attention to this distinction in grammatical analysis? (9) Why have we noticed it in this place?]

We have given examples of accessories with the *conjunctive who* for subject; we now subjoin examples of the use of *which* and *that* for the same purpose. (10) "That landscape *which fills the traveller with rapture*, is regarded with indifference by him *who* sees it every day from his window." "The sweetest sounds *that art can combine*, lose much of their effect upon an ear *that* (which) is perpetually listening to melody." "The most costly luxuries *that can load the board of opulence*, are but bread to him *who* makes them his daily meal." "The brilliant lustres *that* (better *which*) *illuminate the house of public entertainment*, are no more than sober daylight to him *who* passes all his evenings there." (11) The accessory propositions intended for illustration we have marked by the use of *italics*.

(12) Remark.—The learner may observe that the author has employed *that* on two occasions, with great propriety, to represent an antecedent modified by a superlative; "The *sweetest* sounds *that*," and "The *most costly* luxuries *that*." In other places he has employed *that* where *which* was perhaps to be preferred.

(13) The accessory propositions, which we have *marked* above, all serve to modify the subject noun of the principal proposition. (14) But an accessory of this kind may be used to modify a noun which is itself employed in a subordinate function, as a *complement* of the subject or predicate of the principal proposition. (15) Of this we have examples in the passages introduced above as examples. The accessories, "Who sees it every day from his window," "That is perpetually listening to melody," "Who makes them his daily meal," and, "Who passes all his evenings there," all modify *noun with preposition* complements; namely, the first, third and fourth *him* preceded by a preposition, and the second *an ear* preceded also by a preposition. (17) In a word, the adjective accessory proposition, like the adjective, may be employed to modify a noun, in whatever function that noun may be employed, whether in a principal or in an accessory proposition. (18) It

---

modification, and then we can employ the accessory. But when we have to describe a person, or any object by an *action*, we are generally obliged to have recourse to an adjective accessory proposition.

---

(10) Give examples of accessories with *which* and *that* for their subject nouns. (11) How is the part of each passage above intended for illustration marked? (12) Repeat the substance of the remark.

(13) For what purpose do the accessories in *italics* serve? (14) Are accessories of this kind used for other purposes? And what purposes? (15) Illustrate by examples from the passages quoted already. (17) Sum up the purposes for which the adjective accessory may be employed. (18) Repeat the substance of the caution.

is, however, contrary to the principles of good taste—destructive both of perspicuity and harmony—to employ these accessories too lavishly in the modification of nouns used in accessory propositions ; especially in accessory propositions connected themselves to their principal by a conjunctive pronoun.

EXERCISES I., II., &c.—Write compound propositions of the above form.

§ 112. ACCESSORIES IN WHICH THE CONJUNCTIVE PRONOUN PERFORMS A MODIFYING FUNCTION.—(1) Hitherto we have called attention only to the cases in which the *conjunctive pronoun* serves as *subject noun* of the accessory proposition. (2) We have now to observe that conjunctive pronouns perform not only the function o subject noun, but also most of the other functions of nouns in the accessory adjective proposition. (3) They perform the several functions of *objective modification*, of *genitive or possessive modification*, of *noun and preposition modification*, and sometimes, perhaps, of *dative modification.*

We call attention first to examples of the conjunctive or relative pronoun (as it is most commonly called) employed as objective modification to the verb in the accessory proposition. (4) *I am much pleased with the gentleman* WHOM *you introduced. The book* WHICH *you bought is superior to mine.* Or, *The book* THAT *you bought is superior to mine.* "They follow an adventurer *whom* they fear, and obey a power *which* they hate;—we serve a monarch *whom* we love,"—(*we serve*) "a God *whom* we adore."

REMARK.—(5) In this form of the adjective accessory proposition, the *objective* conjunctive pronoun is often suppressed, especially in colloquial discourse. (This suppression is more common in our language than in any other which we know.) (6) Thus we may say, *The book you bought yesterday is beautiful*, *The man we saw this morning*, instead of *The book* WHICH *you bought*, and *The man* WHOM *we saw*, &c. (7) In proceeding to the analysis of such accessory propositions, it is proper that the suppressed conjunctive accusative should be first supplied. (8) The suppression of a conjunctive pronoun, when it serves

§ 112. (1) To what use of the conjunctive pronoun has our attention been confined? (2) Does the pronoun perform other functions in accessory propositions? (3) Enumerate the modifying functions which it performs.

(4) Illustrate the objective use of the pronoun by examples.

(5) Repeat the substance of the remark. (6) Illustrate the fact stated in the remark by examples. (7) What is recommended in the analysis of accessory propositions? (8) What is

any other function, except that of objective, is, we believe, very rare, and not to be imitated.*

(9) The suppression of the objective pronoun, ought to be very cautiously used, even in familiar style. This suppression is still more rarely proper in elevated style. It can never, with propriety, take place, except when the word which the pronoun represents—the antecedent—comes immediately before the accessory proposition. (10) If modifying words follow the *antecedent* and disconnect it from the accessory proposition, the conjunctive pronoun must be expressed. (11) Thus, we could not, without gross impropriety, suppress the conjunctive *whom* in a compound proposition like the following: *The* MAN *distinguished by his foppish dress and swaggering manner* WHOM *we met last night is Mr. A.* Nor would it be consistent with perspicuity to drop *which* in the following assertion : The *pictures* of the great masters *which* we saw yesterday, have been purchased by Mr. B——. The same remark applies to the conjunctive *whom* in the two following examples: "Which is Christ in you the hope of glory ; *whom* we preach," &c. "I speak here of such as retain the feelings of humanity; *whom* misfortunes have softened," &c. See below § 117, the observations respecting the collocation of the adjective accessory proposition.

EXERCISES I., II., &c.—Form compound propositions with accessories having the conjunctive pronoun as objective modification.

(12) Next, we give examples of the conjunctive pronoun employed as genitive case modification in the accessory proposition. We have six examples in the following lines:—

"Happy and worthiest of esteem are those
Whose words are bonds, *whose* oaths are oracles,
Whose love sincere, *whose* thoughts immaculate,
Whose tears pure messengers, sent from the heart,
Whose heart as far from fraud as heaven from earth."

* Mr. G. Brown has adduced the following examples of the omission of the conjunctive pronoun as subject of the accessory: "This is the worst thing—could happen."

"In this 'tis God—directs, in that 'tis man."—Pope.

The place of the pronoun is marked by a dash (—). Mr. Brown justly remarks that "the omission of the relative in the nominative case, is inelegant."

said of the suppression of conjunctive pronouns performing other functions? (9) What farther remark about the suppression of pronouns? (10) Mention a case in which the conjunctive pronoun must be expressed. (11) Illustrate this by examples.

(12) Give examples of the conjunctive pronoun serving as *genitive modification.*

"A religion *whose* origin is divine." "For there stood by me this night the angel of God, *whose* I am, and whom I serve." (13) There is in this last example a peculiar suppression of the noun complementary of the verb *am*—the word to which *whose* serves as genitive modification. The word *servant* is *implied* in *whose*, and to be *supplied*, when we analyze the accessory proposition.

Exercises I., II., &c.—Give a number of compound propositions with accessories in which the conjunctive pronoun serves as genitive modification.

(14) The conjunctive pronoun is employed with a preposition as noun and preposition modification, sometimes of nouns and adjectives, and very often of verbs. (15) Examples: *The adventurers* OF WHOM *he was chief, were surprised. The party* OF WHICH *he is leader, cannot succeed.* In these examples "*of whom*" modifies the noun "*chief*" and "*of which*" the noun "*leader*." (16) It is usual to employ the pronoun and preposition, not the genitive case modification, when the noun modified is separated from the pronoun by other parts of the accessory proposition. Thus the nouns *chief* and *leader* above, being nouns *complementary* of the verbs in the respective accessory propositions, take their place naturally after the verb, and so are separated from the pronoun which occupies the first place in the accessory. (17) But when the modified noun comes immediately after the conjunctive pronoun, as, for instance, when it is subject noun of the accessory proposition, the genitive *whose* is used, not the pronoun and preposition, especially when the pronoun represents a person. This is exemplified above under the conjunctive pronoun employed as genitive modification.

Exercise.—Similar to the last.

(18) We give the following as examples of the conjunctive pronoun and preposition employed to modify an adjective in the accessory proposition. "Withhold not good from them *to whom* it is *due*." "*Of whom* the world was not *worthy*." "That which is luxury to him *to whom* it is *new*, is none to those *to whom* it is *familiar*."

Exercise.—Furnish propositions of this form.

(19) Examples of conjunctive pronouns and prepositions modifying

---

(13) Repeat the remark in reference to the last example.

(14) What is said of the employment of the conjunctive pronoun with a preposition? (15) Give examples of the pronoun and preposition modifying a noun. (16) When is it usual to employ the pronoun and preposition? Illustrate by the examples given above. (17) When do we employ the genitive *whose?*

(18) Give examples of the pronoun and preposition used to modify adjectives.

(19) Give examples of the pronoun and preposition modifying the verb of the accessory.

the verb in the accessory proposition occur in such numbers that it is almost superfluous to present any in this place. "They *for whom* we *labor*," &c. *The world* IN WHICH *we* SOJOURN *is not our home. The Being* BY WHOM *we* ARE PROTECTED, IN WHOM *we* LIVE, *is eternal.*

(20) *That* as a relative is, we believe, never used with a preposition *before* it; perhaps, because it might be confounded with *that*, the determinative substantively employed with a preposition preceding When a preposition is to precede, we must employ whom to represent *persons* and which to represent *nonpersonals.* When the arrangement is changed so that the preposition is separated from the pronoun, we can employ *that*, as, "He is the man, *that* you were acquainted *with.* That alone without a preposition sometimes serves the purpose of a noun and preposition complement, in other words, is equivalent to which with a preposition; thus, *He cannot behave in the way* THAT *you behave,*=*He cannot behave in the way* IN WHICH *you behave.*

EXERCISES.—A given number of compound propositions to be constructed having accessories in which the verb is modified by the conjunctive pronoun and a preposition.

(21) Of the conjunctive pronoun employed as a dative modification in the accessory proposition it is more difficult to find satisfactory examples. We can readily find examples in which the pronoun is, we believe, really a dative, as, *The master* WHOM *you serve; the laws* WHICH *we obey.* But the pronoun thus used is now recognised as an accusative and the verbs as active verbs; though this recognition cannot well be reconciled with the *history* of the use of these verbs in our language. (*See* § 79, *note pp.* 219, 220.) We have an example in *Ezekiel* 31: 2 of the interrogative *whom* used as dative modification of the adjective *like:* "*whom* art thou like in thy greatness?" In the eighteenth verse of the same chapter we find "to whom art thou like in thy glory?" &c. Such expressions as *the man* WHOM *we refused admittance*, are perhaps unsanctioned by good usage. We scarcely venture to use a dative except immediately after the verb, and the conjunctive pronoun cannot occupy that place in an accessory proposition, as we shall see when we come to treat of the collocation of the conjunctive word.

§ 113. OF EXPLICATIVE, OR EPITHETIC ADJECTIVE ACCESSORY PROPOSITIONS.—(1) The adjective accessory propositions presented in our

---

(20) Repeat the substance of what is said of the conjunctive *that* employed as noun and preposition modification.

(21) Repeat the substance of what is said of the conjunctive pronoun employed as dative modification in the accessory.

§ 113. (1) Repeat the introductory remark. (2) Illustrate it by an example.

examples so far serve as essential modifications of the antecedent noun. They all express something indispensably necessary to the enunciation of the thought declared in the main assertion of the compound proposition. (2) Thus, when we say *The youth* WHO STUDIES DILIGENTLY *deserves praise*, the accessory proposition, *who studies diligently*, is an essential part of the subject of the principal proposition. It is not *youth*, but *the youth* described in the accessory, that deserves praise.

(3) But an accessory proposition is sometimes employed as merely *explicative* of the antecedent, similarly to an adjective employed as a *mere epithet* and not essential to the assertion in which it is used. We may first, for the sake of perspicuity, and because we have not alluded to this matter in treating of the *descriptive adjective modification*, give an example of the adjective employed as a mere *epithet*. (4) *Socrates* THE WISE, THE GOOD, *fell a victim to the prejudices of his fellow-citizens;* or, *The* WISE *and* GOOD *Socrates fell a victim;* or, WISE *and* GOOD *Socrates fell*, &c. Here *wise* and *good* are not essential to render the subject capable of having the predicate in the proposition asserted of it: they merely serve as *epithets*. (5) In fact, an adjective thus employed serves to add something as an appendage to a thought beyond what is mainly expressed in the proposition. Thus *wise* and *good* serve in the example above to express, in an abridged form, two thoughts in reference to the subject Socrates, distinct from that formally asserted; yet these thoughts are so thrown in as to modify in some manner the principal assertion, though not essential to it. They may aggravate the guilt of putting Socrates to death, or they may heighten the regret felt that such a character should have perished as he did, according to the purpose of the speaker or writer, as exhibited in the general tenor of the discourse. (6) Adjectives thus employed to indicate something without which the proposition would stand grammatically complete and logically true, are called EPITHETS, that is, (attributes) superadded or *put to*, because they express something beyond what is absolutely requisite to the completion of the assertion. (7) All these epithets may be regarded as expressing a kind of parenthetic thoughts—thoughts introduced within a construction intended mainly and formally to express another and distinct thought. (8) So of what has been named the explicative accessory proposition; (it might with

---

(3) In what other way are adjective accessories sometimes employed? (4) Give an example of an adjective used as an epithet. (5) What purpose does an adjective thus employed serve? Illustrate by the example already given. (6) Tell what is said in reference to the name given to adjectives thus used. (7) How may all these epithets be regarded? (8) Apply what has been said to the *explicative* or epithetic accessory. (9) What would

great propriety be called the *epithetic* accessory ;) it is thrown parenthetically within another proposition in the form, but without the force, of a modifying accessory. (9) In fact, if regarded strictly as a completing accessory, it would often change, or injure, or destroy the sense of the compound proposition. (10) Let us illustrate this by an example, "Man, *that is born of a woman*, is of few days." Here the accessory, "That is born of a woman," is merely *explicative* or *epithetic.* It expresses a thought of the subject *man*, having connection with the general train or drift of the discourse, that is to say, with the representation of man's frailty and transiency. But it does not express an essential complement of the word *man* as *subject* of the proposition "Man is of few days." In this assertion the word *man* is used unmodified in its unlimited sense, as including all mankind. It is not limited or restricted by the words "That is born of a woman," as by a true *modifying* accessory proposition essential to the sense of the principal proposition. To limit the word *man* by this accessory we must place before it the sign which in our language indicates limitation or determinativeness, and thus we change, or, rather, we destroy the sense. In fact, by treating this as an essential modifying accessory, we obtain a compound proposition which implies an absurdity. Both THE *man that is born of a woman is of few days ;* and THE *men that are born of women are of few days*, are absurd assertions; since they imply, according to the laws of our language, that only some men are so born, and only such are of few days. This is manifestly not the meaning of the words as they stand in the original quotation. There a well-known truth is expressed in a manner perfectly accordant with the established laws of language.

(11) We may here remark that in the written language this kind of *explicative* or *epithetic* proposition is distinguished by the punctuation. The ordinary *modifying* accessory proposition connected with the antecedent by a conjunctive pronoun, being essential to complete it, is not separated from the principal proposition by commas in the generality of modern printed books, whereas the explicative accessory proposition is, or, *ought to be*, separated by commas from the principal proposition. (See Appendix on Punctuation, § 160.)

(12) In a case like the example above given, the accessory is also indicated, as we have incidentally noticed, by the fact that no

often be the consequence if the *explicative* accessory should be considered as a *completing* accessory? (10) Repeat the example, and the substance of the illustration.

(11) Describe the manner in which the completing and explicative accessory are distinguished by punctuation in written discourse.

(12) Repeat the substance of what is said of another way of distinguishing these two

determinative is placed before the word *man*, which ought to be done if man were limited or restricted by the accessory proposition. A determinative — generally either *a* or *the*, sometimes, for greater emphasis, *that*, is placed before all nouns which admit of a determinative in accordance with the usage of language, when these nouns are *strictly limited* by an adjective accessory proposition. This circumstance, however, will not serve to distinguish the essentially modifying accessory from the explicative accessory. When a *common concrete* noun (the class chiefly susceptible of determinative modification) is not preceded by a determinative, we may safely consider the accessory as merely explicative or epithetic, but when such nouns are preceded by a determinative, we cannot conclude that the accessory is *not* merely explicative, because the noun may be rendered determinate by something else, though not by the accessory, and may on this account be accompanied by the determinative sign. This mode of indication would also fail us whenever the word to which the accessory is attached happens to be one of that class which does not take a determinative, (because, naturally and necessarily, always determinate,) for example, *proper names*, generally in our language *abstract nouns*, and *personal pronouns*. (13) The nature of the accessory must therefore be determined by the sense. No rule for doing this, founded on the form of language, is of universal application. (14) If fixed rules of punctuation were adopted and consistently followed, these two kinds of accessories might always be distinguished in written language.

We subjoin some examples of the *explicative accessory* for the purpose of clearer illustration.

(15) "My lord of Hereford here, *whom you call king*,
Is a foul traitor to proud Hereford's king.

"Whom you call king," is in this place to be regarded as a *parenthetic explicative* proposition. The sense of the principal proposition is not dependent on it. It was not alone "as called king" by his followers, that Hereford was a traitor. His treason was not limited to this circumstance, nor is it as displayed or indicated by this circumstance that the speaker here asserts his treason. He rather asserts him to be a traitor in despite of this circumstance. (16) In the following compound proposition, "God, who sitteth above, and presides in high authority over all worlds, is mindful of man,"

---

kinds of accessories. (13) How must the nature of the accessory be determined? (14) What is said of a means of determining it in written language?

(15) Repeat the example here given and the remarks made upon it. (16) Illustrate the distinction between completing and explicative accessories by a second example.

the two adjective accessory propositions, "who sitteth above, and presides in high authority over all worlds," may be considered, if we please, as merely explicative or epithetic. But in the proposition written as Dr. Chalmers has in fact written it, "The God who sitteth above," &c. these accessories become essential parts of the complete subject of the principal proposition.*

(17) It must be admitted that the lines of demarcation between the completing and the epithetic *accessory* (and the same, we believe, may be said of the completing and epithetic *adjective*) are not always perfectly clear. To illustrate, by an example:—

> "O pity, great Father of Light! (then I cried)
> Thy creature, who fain would not wander from Thee!"

It might, perhaps, be a question here to which class of accessories we should refer the proposition, "Who fain would not wander from Thee!" It seems to us, that it is rather to be referred to the class of epithetic accessories. The same remark may be made of the accessories in the following compound proposition:—

> "'Twas thus by the glare of false science betrayed,
> *That leads, to bewilder;* and *dazzles, to blind,*" &c.

(18) The distinction which we have been considering may be thought *logical* rather than *grammatical*, since in both kinds of accessory the *form* is exactly the same. We admit that, except in the use or omission of the determinatives, when the antecedent is a word susceptible of that limitation which a determinative indicates, the distinction is not exhibited by any thing in the structure of our language. But the distinction *deserves* the notice of the grammarian on account of the important variation of meaning sometimes involved, and it *demands* his notice in strict grammatical analysis, as frequently giving occasion either for the employment or the suppression of determinatives. A similar distinction may be traced in other accessories besides the adjective accessories.

It may be prescribed as an exercise to advanced students to furnish

* Whether Dr. Chalmers' mode of expression here is *theologically* and *philosophically* correct is another question. The form of the proposition would seem to imply that there may be *a God* to whom these accessories cannot be attributed; whereas the term God, in its highest sense and Christian acceptation, applies *only* to the *One* Great Being who "sitteth above," &c

(17) Repeat the remark in reference to the lines of demarcation between these two kinds of accessories and illustrate by examples.

(18) Repeat the substance of the remark in reference to this distinction of accessories.

examples of compound propositions containing an *epithetic* accessory. This exercise may prove more difficult than some heretofore prescribed. Let the learner select examples from older writers, as examples of the explicative accessory are more frequent in them. The relative is often used by them to introduce even a new sentence, as it is employed in Latin. Abundance of accessories of this kind may be found in the epistle to the Hebrews. See ch. 7 : 27 ; 8 : 5 ; 9 : 2, 3, 4, 5, 9, &c.

§ 114. WHAT EMPLOYED AS A RELATIVE OR CONJUNCTIVE PRONOUN. —(1) WHAT (really the neuter form of *who*, and originally, like it, *interrogative*) is also employed as a conjunctive pronoun, but with this peculiarity, that it performs the functions of a noun both in the accessory, and in the principal proposition, or, in the usual language of grammarians, *includes both the relative and the antecedent.* (2) It is thus equivalent to the determinative *that* employed substantively in the principal proposition, and *which* in the accessory. (3) In analysis some resolve every *what* of this kind into the words *that which* as the first step, and then substitute the analysis of *that which* for the analysis of *what.* (4) This mode of proceeding is, at least, unnecessary. It seems to us improper as well as unnecessary, since it implies that *what* is a substitute for these two words, or used instead of them, and therefore that the use of it is secondary and later in origin. This substitution is not proved, perhaps cannot be proved.

We submit a few examples for the purpose of illustrating the use of *what.* Keeping these in view, the learner will more readily comprehend our remarks on the form of accessory in which *what* is employed.

(*a*) " WHAT the weak head with strongest bias rules,
Is pride, the never-failing vice of fools."

(*b*) " WHAT obeys reason is free."

(*c*) " WHAT wounds his virtue wounds his peace."

(*d*) " WHAT thou biddest unargued I obey."

(*e*) " What He admired and loved, his vital smile unfolded into being."

(*f*) " What you call wisdom they esteem madness."

(*g*) " In what I have done I have consulted your interest."

(5) In examples (*a*) (*b*) (*c*), *what* serves as subject of both principal

---

§ 114. (1) State the peculiar manner in which *what* is employed as a conjunctive pronoun. (2) To what two words is it equivalent? (3) Mention the mode in which some analyze *what* thus employed. (4) State the objections to this mode of analysis.

(5) State the purposes which *what* serves in Example *a*, in Example *b*, &c.

and accessory proposition; in (*d*) (*e*) (*f*), as objective modification of the verbs in both propositions (or rather, perhaps, in (*d*) as objective in the accessory and dative in the principal); and in (*g*) it forms with *in* a noun and preposition modification of the *principal* and objective modification of the *accessory* proposition.

(6) There is another and, we think, a better—a more philosophical, as well as an easier way of treating compound propositions of this kind; namely, to consider *what* as connected with the accessory alone, and then to regard the accessory including *what* as a *substantive* accessory proposition, or, if you please, an adjective accessory proposition employed *substantively* (in a manner analogous to the adjective employed substantively), the accessory performing some function of a noun to the principal proposition. (7) By way of illustration, let us give a succinct analysis of the above examples. In example (*a*) the accessory, "What the weak head with strongest bias rules," constitutes the subject of "*is*" (the verb of the principal proposition). In the same manner, "What obeys reason," and "What wounds his virtue," are subjects in the compound propositions in which they occur. In example (*d*) "What thou biddest," modified by "unargued," is the objective (we think, more properly, the *dative*) modification to "obey" (the verb of the principal proposition). In (*e*) "What he admired and loved," is objective modification to the verb "*unfolded*;" and in (*f*) "What you call wisdom," is objective modification to "esteem." In example (*g*) "In what I have done," is noun and preposition modification to "have consulted your interest."

(8) If the reader will attentively consider these and similar examples, and especially the last, in which *what* is preceded by a preposition, he will, perhaps, find reason for agreeing with us that this last is the preferable method of analysis. It is manifest that the preposition *in* influences the whole accessory and serves as *intermediate* between it and "have consulted your interest," and that the whole thought expressed in the accessory stands precisely in the same relation to the principal proposition as a single noun coming after *in* would stand in a simple proposition. (9) The analysis of this kind of compound propositions is, if we adopt this mode, to be conducted exactly according to the rules given for conducting the analysis of compound propositions having *substantive* accessories. (10) If the accessory is subject of the

---

(6) Repeat what is said of another way of treating propositions in which *what* relative occurs. (7) Illustrate this mode of treatment by a succinct analysis of the above examples.

(8) Repeat the substance of what is said in favor of this mode of analysis. (9) What is said of the order of conducting the analysis? (10) State the order to be observed.

principal proposition, analyze it when the subject comes in regular order to be considered; if the accessory is objective or noun and preposition modification, let it be analyzed in its proper place when it comes under consideration as a part of the predicate of the principal proposition.

§ 115. COMPOUND RELATIVES AND THE ACCESSORIES FORMED BY THEIR HELP.—(1] The following compounds of *who*, *which* and *what*, are formed by adding to them the words *ever* or *so*, or both *so* and *ever*, *whoever*, *whoso*, *whosoever*; *whichever*, *whichsoever*; *whatever*, *whatsoever*. (2) When *substantively* employed, these words perform functions similar to *what*, and the accessory in which they occur may be treated in the same manner in analysis, as the examples which we have considered in the last section. (3) *Whoever*, *whoso* and *whosoever*, like the primitive *who*, are always employed as nouns; *whichever*, *whichsoever*, *whatever* and *whatsoever*, are frequently used as adjectives accompanied by the noun which they modify, and may sometimes, not always, like *which* used in the same way, be treated as determinative adjectives. (4) We subjoin some examples of the manner in which these compound conjunctive pronouns are employed in accessory propositions. *Whoever told you this is mistaken* = any one who told you this is mistaken. Here the accessory, "WHOEVER *told you this*," may be regarded as subject of the verb *is*, or that of which *being mistaken* (the predicate) is asserted. "*Whoso* removeth stones shall be hurt therewith." WHOEVER *is always idle is useless and contemptible.* "*Whosoever* committeth sin is the servant of sin." In all these, as in the first example, the accessory may be regarded as the subject of the compound proposition. "And giveth it to *whomsoever* He will." Here the accessory, "to whomsoever He will," serves as noun and preposition modification to the verb "giveth" in the principal proposition. *Whichever of these books you prefer is at your service. Whichever of these books you prefer you may take.* "Whichever of these books you prefer," is subject in the first, and objective modification of the verb of the main assertion in the second example. Whichever and whichsoever are seldom used, except as determinatives accompanying a noun which they modify. But even in this case the accessory into which they enter may often be most conveniently considered as *substantive*. Thus, *Which-*

---

§ 115. (1) Enumerate the compounds of *who*, *which*, and *what*, telling how they are formed. (2) State what is said of these compounds substantively employed, and of the accessories into which they enter. (3) What is said of the manner in which these pronouns are respectively employed? (4) Illustrate the use of the compounds of *who* by examples The compounds of *which* in like manner. The compounds of *what*.

ever course suits you will suit me. Here "*Whichever course suits you,*" may be considered the subject of "*will suit me.*" "Whatever purifies fortifies also the heart." Here "Whatever purifies" (the heart) is subject of the assertion "fortifies also the heart."

"Whate'er adorns
The princely dome," &c.
"His tuneful breast enjoys."

Here "whate'er adorns," &c. is objective modification to the verb "*enjoys.*" "I will do whatsoever thou sayest to me." The verb "*do*" has for objective modification the accessory "whatsoever thou sayest to me," as may be perceived by asking the question, *what will I do?* Ans. "Whatsoever thou sayest to me."

(5) All these compound pronouns may be regarded as having an indefinite antecedent.

(6) Of these compound conjunctive pronouns *whoever* and *whatever* are in frequent use. Whichever is less used at present, and when used generally accompanies its noun, like other adjectives, as we have already noticed. The other forms, *whoso*, *whosoever*, *whichsoever*, *whatsoever*, may be regarded as antiquated, or, at least, they "are chiefly found in poetry or legal documents."—*D' Orsey.*

We shall hereafter have to notice another use of some of these compound pronouns in the formation of a different description of accessories. (See § 138 : 25, et seq.)

(7) Before we dismiss this subject, it must be observed that we find frequent examples of *who* employed *indefinitely* (without an antecedent expressed), like *what* and the compound relatives. These examples are found chiefly in poetry and in the prose of our older writers, particularly in the authorized version of the Scriptures. (8) Examples:

"Who lives to nature rarely can be poor;
Who lives to fancy never can be rich."

"Whom the Lord loveth He chasteneth." "Whom he would he slew, and whom he would he kept alive, and whom he would he set up, and whom he would he put down." "Who steals my purse steals trash." In these examples *who* is equivalent to *he who*, and *whom* to *him whom*. "Whom the gods love die young."—Byron. *Whom* is here = to *those whom;* but the form of expression is not to be imitated.

---

(5) How may all these compound pronouns be regarded?
(6) Tell which of them are in frequent use, and which antiquated.
(7) Is *who* ever employed in a manner similar to *what?* (8) Illustrate by examples.

It is shockingly awkward, if not absolutely contrary to the usage of our language. (9) Such expressions as, "I know WHO wrote that letter," may be referred to the same class: *who* being here = *him who*, perhaps *who* should be considered in such expressions as the interrogative, and the accessory classed as an *interrogative objective accessory proposition*, or as an *insensible extension* of this form of accessory.

(10) It is not necessary to treat the accessories in which *who* is thus employed as we treat those formed with *what* and the compound pronouns, though it is obvious that they might readily be so treated; namely as substantive accessories. (11) The reason that we would not treat these as the accessory with *what* is that they are exceptional cases of the use of *who*. This is not its ordinary function in construction. The antecedent may always be readily supplied either in the form of a noun or pronoun, in which case *who* performs its usual part. But not so with *what*. You cannot supply an antecedent to it, but must, if you attempt to change the form of expression, reject *what* altogether and substitute *that which* for it, and then, instead of giving an account of *what* in the analysis, you only give an account of an equivalent expression. The same remark applies to the compound pronouns.

(12) We may remark here, for the warning of the student, that it is not uncommon to find writers of high reputation and undoubted learning commit errors in the use of conjunctive pronouns. Thus "Men WHOM they supposed could be rendered subservient to their schemes of spoliation." What is the subject of "*could be rendered*," &c., in this ill-constructed proposition? It is not *men*, for that word has its function in connection with a part of the sentence here omitted. The writer did not mean to say that *men whom they* (referring to some other party) *supposed*, that is *men* modified by the expression "*whom they supposed*," "could be rendered," &c., but that *men* should be modified by all that we have quoted of the sentence. The sense would be correctly expressed by saying *men* WHO *they supposed could be*, &c. We have already noticed a similar error in an expression repeatedly employed by several translators of the gospels. (*See* § 107. *note*.)

---

(9) What other kind of expressions might be referred to the same class? And to what other class may they perhaps be more properly referred?

(10) Is it required that we should treat these accessories formed with *who indefinite* as we treat those formed with *what?* (11) State the reason assigned for this difference in the mode of analysis.

(12) Repeat the remark about the improper use of relatives.

(13) The learner will notice that, though the conjunctive pronoun generally refers to a noun as its antecedent—as that which the accessory proposition modifies—it sometimes refers to a proposition, or rather to the predicate or part of the predicate of a proposition. (14) When this is the case, we employ the conjunctive *which*, not *who*, nor *that*. Example, *He tells the truth, which you do not.* Here *which* refers to the predicate of the preceding proposition, namely, *telling the truth.* This is what *you do not.* The accessory may here be regarded as employed instead of the co-ordinate proposition, AND *that is what you do not.* This latter is the more natural and the preferable form of expression. The other may be considered as an *extension* of the adjective accessory beyond its original purpose. *He is faithful, which that man is not* = *and that man is not so.* Here the antecedent is the adjective *faithful*—part of the predicate of the preceding proposition.

(15) The antecedent is sometimes found involved in an adjective pronoun—in other words, it is the noun which the adjective pronoun represents. We might propose as examples, THEIR *motives are unknown* WHO *performed this act;* HIS *is the crown* WHO *gains the victory.* These forms of expression are not perhaps consistent with good taste in prose composition; but they are sometimes met in poetry; for example:

"How beauteous are THEIR feet,
Who stand on Zion's hill!"

"The prison of HIS tyranny *who* reigns
By our delay."

"To know
Of things above his world, and of THEIR being
Who dwell in heaven, *whose* excellence he saw
Transcend his own so far; *whose* radiant forms,
Divine effulgence, *whose* high power, so far
Exceeded human," &c.

EXERCISES I., II., &c.—Form compound propositions involving the use of the compound relatives *whoever*, *whatever*, &c.

§ 116. PECULIAR USE OF THE WORD THERE IN THE COMMENCEMENT OF PROPOSITIONS.—(1) We may here notice an *idiomatic* form of expression,

---

(13) What is said of the conjunctive representing a predicate? (14) Which of the conjunctive pronouns is employed for this purpose? Illustrate by examples. How may this accessory be regarded?

(15) Repeat what is said of the antecedent being found in an adjective pronoun; and illustrate by examples.

§ 116. (1) State what is said of an idiomatic use of the word THERE. (2) What connec-

common in our language, in which the word THERE is employed in a peculiar manner to introduce the predicate of a proposition, before the subject is announced. This happens chiefly when the verb *to be* is employed to express the whole predicate. *

(2) Our reason for noticing this particular form of propositions in this place is, that the subject noun of such propositions is very often, though not always, modified by an adjective accessory proposition. The form commencing with the word THERE is well suited to have this kind of modification attached to it, and we thus avoid the awkwardness of first announcing a subject with a long modification, and then following it up by such a disproportioned predicate (we mean as to weight of sound) as the naked verb To Be. (3) The following examples will illustrate our meaning; THERE *are many men who seem to be the mere slaves of their appetites and passions.* THERE *are some men who appear wholly unfit to be their own masters.* These assertions are equivalent to *many men who seem to be the mere slaves of their appetites and passions* ARE ; *some men who appear wholly unfit to be their own masters* ARE. (4) The verb *are* used in this last way appears so unsupported and awkward, so ill matched with the many-worded subject with which it is connected, that it offends our sense of proportion and harmony. This is, no doubt, partly the reason of adopting the construction commencing with THERE. (5) It may be doubted whether this use of THERE is to be considered as only an *insensible extension* of its common adverbial use from cases in which the objects whose *existence* is predicated are within the view of the speaker, and the hearer's attention directed to them, to cases in which the objects are not *literally* THERE, but indicated with something of the determinateness of objects to which we point by a gesture of the hand or head. (6) But whatever may be the history of this form of construction, or at whatever period it may have been introduced in our language, THERE now performs in such cases a function similar to that of the representative words called pronouns—a function very similar to that which IT performs when we employ it as a substitute for a subject reserved to be fully presented after the predicate has first

* The general use of this mode of expression, when the verb *to be without modification* expresses the predicate, conceals the fact that this verb so *often* forms the whole predicate of propositions. (See § 46. Note, p. 82.)

---

tion has this with the adjective accessory? (3) Illustrate this idiomatic use by examples. (4) What is remarked of the equivalent propositions without *there*, and of a reason for adopting this construction? (5) What is said of the origin of this construction? (6) What

been expressed. (See § 103.) (7) The difference between the use of *it* and *there* is that *it* is the substitute for a subject expressed afterwards in the form of a substantive accessory proposition, *there* merely serves the purpose of enabling us to throw the subject after the verb, which subject may or may not be modified by an adjective accessory. (8) Both words enable us to change the order and bring the most ponderous part of the compound proposition last, and thus obtain a stronger and more harmonious arrangement.

(9) This word *there*, as we have hinted above, is often employed in the same manner when no accessory is to be introduced to modify the subject noun, but when for some reason it is desirable to throw the subject after the verb; as, THERE *were many ladies at the assembly.* (10) It is worthy of remark in this connection that *there* is often employed in interrogative propositions; and particularly that when so employed, it is placed, like the subject noun in other interrogative expressions, after the verb. This looks like serving as a *substitute* (for the moment) or *representative* of the subject noun. (11) For example: *Is* THERE *another human being that would act in the same manner? Is* THERE *any person there?* The use of such expressions as this last seems difficult to reconcile with the admission that *there* employed in the manner we are now describing was originally simply the adverb of place. In this case, we should have expected it to exclude the use of the second *there* to denote place. (12) We are at a loss for a name by which to distinguish this use of the word *there*. It ought to be distinguished in analysis. We may venture to adopt (for the sake of distinction) the name *there subjective* for this peculiar employment of *there* in connection with the subject of a proposition, without intending to give sanction to any particular explanation of this idiom. *There* was perhaps originally used *only* to modify a predicate, but in this idiom its function is transferred to the subject, and rather with the purpose of effecting a modification of the arrangement than of the sense. This much must be admitted, even though it should be contended that it still, as to *form*, modifies the predicate—that is to say, the verb *to be.*

EXERCISES.—Form compound propositions exemplifying the usage of *there is*, *there are*, *there was*, &c.

---

is said of the function which *there* thus used now performs in the language? (7) What is said of the difference between THERE used in this manner and IT *substitutive?* (8) What is common to both words?

(9) Is THERE thus used *only* when the subject is completed by an adjective accessory? (10) Repeat the remark about *there* in interrogative propositions? (11) Furnish examples and repeat the observation which follows them. (12) What is said of a name to distinguish this use of the word THERE?

NOTE.—We may notice that the word *there* is sometimes employed in the same manner with other verbs, besides the verb *to be.* For example: "But if all prophesy, and THERE *come* in," &c. "If THERE *come* into your assembly a man with a gold ring," &c. "THERE shall no man *see* me and *live.*" "THERE *remaineth* therefore a rest to the people of God." "There remaineth no more sacrifice for sins." "THERE *went* with him a band of men."

"*Breathes* THERE the man with soul so dead?"

It must not be forgotten in this connection that THERE, now recognised as an adverb of place, is originally a determinative word, and that there is but a step from the determinative to the pronominal or representative function, as is abundantly exemplified in the history of the conjunctive pronouns in our own and in other languages. (*See additional observations on the pronouns who, which, that,* § 159.) To explain the manner in which *there* came to be used to indicate place is perfectly easy. There is simply, when it is so used, a suppression of the word *place. There,* being the dative of *that,* and place being implied, means *in that place.* But the fact that *there* is a dative case seems to stand in the way of explaining the particular usage which we are considering in any other manner than as an extension of the adverbial use. This *subjective* use of *there,* has not, so far as we know, been satisfactorily explained either by grammarians or philologists. We recommend the history of the introduction of this idiom to the attention of those who have access to the fragments of the old language which approach in age the Anglo-Saxon period. We find some examples of this idiom in Wiclif, such as "And there ben many that entren bi it." But he uses it much less than the later translators; indeed, he seems generally to avoid it, and to adopt another form of expression. Some of the examples found in his translation are different from those in modern use, and might perhaps help to account for this idiomatic use. Thus, "And there weren in Jerusalem," &c. "In Jerusalem" may here be regarded as an expansion of *there* in apposition with it, both being in the same case = And in *that place,* namely, *in Jerusalem,* were, &c. May we not here have an example of the way in which the transition was made from the common adverbial use to that which we are considering?

We think, upon the whole, that this subjective use of *there* has most likely originated from an imitation of the *French idiom,* or an *insensible extension* of the adverbial use—perhaps partly from both. The French *il-y-a* is not precisely analogous to our expression, since the *il*—the pronominal word—is retained; the verb too is different in meaning, and besides, is always singular like the *unipersonal* verbs. And yet it may have suggested the use of our form *there is, there are,* at a time when our language received many other modifications from the influence of the Norman Conquest. The word *there,* as thus employed, seems to retain the determinative force originally belonging to it, as a case of *that*—whilst the indication of place—implied in its purely adverbial use is almost lost, or at least greatly obscured. Like *that*, it indicates something aloof from the speaker pointed out to the notice of the hearer, but, now at least, no longer by a reference to mere locality.

§ 117. We come next to treat of the arrangement of this kind of modification; and, separately, of the arrangement of the whole adjective accessory proposition in reference to the compound proposition, and of the arrangement of the conjunctive pronoun in the accessory proposition.

1st. ARRANGEMENT OF THE ADJECTIVE ACCESSORY IN THE COMPOUND PROPOSITION.—(1) The most appropriate place for the introduction of the adjective accessory is immediately after the word which it modifies. (2) In this case we suspend the progress of the main assertion till the modification expressed by the accessory is applied. Thus in the example, *The man* WHO ACTS VIRTUOUSLY *deserves the approbation of his fellow-men*, at MAN, the *antecedent*—the word to be modified—we suspend the progress of the main assertion, till the modification *who acts virtuously* is introduced.

(3) This order is perfectly natural, since the accessory proposition, like an adjective in similar circumstances, constitutes part of the complete subject, and is therefore closely attached to the subject noun. It is not asserted in the example that what is expressed by the subject noun *man*, that is, any or every man, or man merely as *man*, *deserves approbation*, but man described by the following accessory—namely, *The man who acts virtuously.*

(4) In the English language, however, we do not adhere rigorously—not so rigorously, for example, as in French—to the practice of introducing the accessory in immediate connection with the antecedent, or modified noun. (5) We often allow other modifications which customarily follow the noun, as, for example, the noun and preposition, to take precedence of the accessory and separate it from the antecedent; thus, *The paintings of the old masters which we saw yesterday.* Here the noun and preposition *of the old masters* comes between the antecedent *paintings* and the accessory *which we saw yesterday.* (6) The

§ 117. (1) Which is the most appropriate place for the introduction of the adjective accessory? (2) Describe what is done to introduce the accessory. Illustrate by examples. (3) What is said of the order of arrangement described?

(4) Do we always adhere to this order in English? (5) What kind of modification is sometimes allowed to take precedence of the adjective accessory? Illustrate by an example. (6) What helps sometimes to secure perspicuity to compound propositions thus ar-

distinction between who and which observed in the modern language secures perspicuity to expressions like the preceding, when the antecedent and noun with preposition, like *paintings* and *masters*, are the names the one of persons and the other of things. Thus we know above that *which* is intended to represent *paintings*, not masters. (7) But if in a compound sentence thus arranged two nouns preceding are both the names of persons or both the names of things, the pronoun should always represent only the last noun, otherwise we cannot, by the *form* of the expression, determine which is intended to be modified by the accessory. The *sense* indeed often determines this completely, and constructions are sometimes formed in which there is no obscurity though neither the collocation nor the pronoun used determines the intention of the author. (8) But compound propositions of this kind should be avoided as much as possible. Even when the sense determines the intention of the writer or speaker, the interposition of words, especially of nouns, between the antecedent and the accessory proposition, is generally awkward and betrays want of skill in arrangement. (9) We may observe, that in writing our language we are not as particular in the arrangement of these adjective accessories as is desirable for the purpose of securing a perfectly transparent and elegant style.

2d. Arrangement of the Conjunctive Pronoun in the Accessory Proposition.—(10) The general rule for the collocation of the conjunctive pronoun in the accessory proposition is perfectly clear and easy, and the reason in which it originates obvious. (11) Since the pronoun in this case is not only *representative*, but *conjunctive*, serving to indicate the junction of the accessory with a word in the principal proposition, it is naturally placed between the things which it serves to *conjoin*; namely, the modified word and the modifying accessory: hence it obtains the first place in the accessory. (12) There is one very common exception to this general rule, when the conjunctive pronoun with a preposition serves the function of noun and preposition modification. In all such forms

---

ranged? Illustrate by an example. (7) What is said in reference to the case in which both preceding nouns express persons or both things? (8) Repeat the remarks regarding compound propositions where the sense alone and neither the collocation nor pronoun determines the reference of the accessory. (9) Repeat observation in reference to negligence in arrangement.

(10) What is said in reference to the general rule for the collocation of the conjunctive pronoun? (11) State the rule giving the reason of it. (12) Describe an exception; and illustrate by an example.

of modification the preposition almost universally takes the precedence in our language, and, in the case before us, it does not yield it even to the conjunctive word. Example, *The man* TO WHOM *he wrote did not receive his letter.* Here the preposition *to* retains its usual place before the pronoun, and so comes between the conjunctive word and the antecedent.

(13) In some instances, other words beside the preposition precede the conjunctive pronoun in the adjective accessory proposition. (14) These exceptions, which it might be well to avoid as much as possible, occur chiefly, if not exclusively, when *which* with the preposition *of* is the modification of a noun in the accessory proposition. For example: *The proposition*, THE TRUTH OF WHICH *we have been considering, is important.* "A multitnde of evils beset us, *for the source of which* we must look to another quarter." (15) This mode of expression seems to be used to avoid the employment of *whose* in reference to *things*, or, in other words, as the genitive of *which.* (16) If we employ *whose* in the above propositions instead *of which*, the conjunctive resumes its natural place first, or next to the preposition in the accessory. Thus, *The proposition whose truth we have been considering*, &c. "A multitude of evils beset us, for" *whose* "source we we must look," &c. (17) We think that both these forms of expression are inelegant, and not to be imitated, except when the attempt to avoid them would occasion ambiguity or obscurity, or greatly enfeeble the expression.

OBSERVATION.—When the conjunctive pronoun happens to be the subject noun of the accessory proposition, or when the genitive *whose* is employed to modify the subject noun, the arrangement occasions no difficulty in analysis, because it corresponds with the usual order of the members of propositions—the subject first, the predicate last. But when the conjunctive pronoun serves as a modification of the predicate, the construction sometimes occasions considerable difficulty to the young grammarian in his first attempts at analysis, because the order of arrangement is completely inverted, the pronoun which forms part of the predicate taking precedence of the subject. When from this cause any difficulty occurs in apprehending the relation which the conjunctive pronoun holds to the proposition, the student may be taught to replace, for a moment, the conjunctive pronoun by its antecedent, or by a personal pronoun, or by the determinative *this* or *that* substantively used, and then the modification will fall naturally into its usual

---

(13) Do other words sometimes take precedence of the pronoun conjunctive? (14) Describe these exceptions, and give examples. (15) For what purpose is this form of expression employed? (16) What happens when *whose* is substituted for *of which?* Example (17) Repeat the remark.

position. By a momentary substitution of this kind, we may readily catch the relation of the conjunctive pronoun to the rest of the proposition. Thus the accessory in the compound proposition, *The man whom we saw this morning*, will, by the substitution above described, become *we saw him this morning;* or *we saw the man this morning.* Here the relation of *him* and *man* to the verb *saw* is manifest; and the relation of *whom* in the regularly constructed accessory must be the same.

§ 118. We may here subjoin a few directions in regard to the use of the relative or conjunctive pronouns, and condense them into the form of a rule. This rule is the same in substance as that commonly given in our English grammars.

(1) The conjunctive pronouns, as we have had occasion to observe, have no plural form; they do not indicate whether that which they represent is singular or plural; nor do they indicate *person.** (2) But when a conjunctive pronoun serves as the *subject noun* in an accessory proposition, it must be regarded as of the same person and number as the antecedent or antecedents which it represents, because the verb to which it is subject is of that number and person. Thus we say, *I who* READ, *thou who* READEST, *he who* READS, *we who* READ, &c.—the verb to which *who* is subject invariably agreeing in number and person with the antecedent. Hence the convenience of the following condensed formula for the guidance of the learner, which may be referred to as

(3) RULE III.—The relative or conjunctive pronoun is of the same number and person with the antecedent, and a verb to which it is subject must also be of the number and person of the antecedent.

(4) OBS. 1. The learner will also remember that the rule which we shall have occasion to give in relation to subjects of different persons connected by copulative conjunctions, and embraced in the same assertion made by a verb standing in a relation common to these

* The only rule to be observed in regard to the use of these words *themselves* in construction is that *who* is now used exclusively to represent persons, or beings personified, *which* to represent *animals* and inanimate things, and *that* to represent either persons, or *nonpersonals.* This we have shown at length above.

§ 118. (1) What remark is here repeated in reference to the conjunctive pronouns (2) How must the conjunctive, notwithstanding, be regarded when subject of the accessory (3) Repeat the rule.
(4) Repeat the substance of Observation I

subjects, applies to the case in which antecedents of different persons have a common representative conjunctive pronoun, which forms the subject of an accessory proposition. If a conjunctive pronoun represents an antecedent of the first person together with an antecedent of the second person or of the third person, the conjunctive pronoun is to be considered as of the first person plural, and of course the verb to which it may be subject in the accessory must be of the same person and number; again, if the conjunctive represents an antecedent of the second person together with an antecedent of the third, it is to be considered as of the second person, and the verb accordingly will be of the second person plural. It will be remarked that in such cases all that is indicated in our language is that when two or more singular antecedents are represented by a single conjunctive pronoun, the verb to which such conjunctive pronoun serves as subject must be of the *plural* form. As there is no distinction of persons plural marked by the form of our verbs, the person is not indicated. (See § 52.)

(5) OBS. II. It sometimes happens that the same individual is represented by words of different persons in the subject and predicate of the same proposition. Thus, *I am a friend; you are an actor; we are men.* The subjects of the first and last propositions are of the first person, the complementary nouns of the third person; the subject of the second proposition is of the second person, the complementary noun of the third person, though the subject and complementary nouns in the three propositions represent the same party in each respectively. Now such a proposition may be followed by a conjunctive pronoun and accessory, the one referring to, the other describing the individual represented by the subject noun and noun complementary of the principal proposition. Thus, *I am a friend who* TELL *you this*, or, *I am a friend who* FEELS *for your misfortunes.* The question has arisen, with which antecedent, representing the same individual, should the conjunctive pronoun and the verb in the accessory proposition agree in person; for instance in the example before us, with *I* or with *friend?* To answer this we have only to consider whether the accessory proposition is intended to modify the subject noun or the complementary noun in the predicate of the principal proposition. If it is designed by the speaker or writer to modify the subject, as for example the subject in the proposition, *I am a friend who* TELL *you this*, the verb must be, as here, in the first person; and a better arrangement in such cases will be, in conformity with the general rule laid down above, to place the accessory immediately after the subject, and suspend the progress of

(5) Repeat the substance of Observation II.

the main assertion till our subject is completed; thus, *I who* TELL *you this am a friend.* If, on the contrary, the accessory is designed to modify the noun in the predicate, the verb in the accessory must agree with that noun in person, and the proper arrangement is that exhibited above; *I am a friend who* FEELS *for your misfortunes*=*I am such a* FRIEND *as feels*, &c. the accessory describing *friend.* In the form, *I am a friend who feel for your misfortunes*, or, more properly arranged, *I who feel for your misfortunes am a friend*, it is *I* the subject that is described by the accessory, and not *friend.* The person *I* described by the accessory is asserted to be a *friend*, not the person *I* asserted to be the kind of friend described by the accessory.

In closing our remarks on the conjunctive pronouns, we must not omit to notice certain compound words formed of a conjunctive pronoun combined with a preposition. Compounds of this kind were much used by our old authors—by the translators, for example, of the Bible—instead of the simple pronoun and preposition. Such words are, *whereat*, *whereby*, *wherefore*, *wherein*, *whereof*, *whereto*, *whereunto*, *wherewith*, &c. There are some other similar compounds, which, like some of these, may be considered as belonging to other classes of accessories, such as *whereabout* to those of place, *whereas* to causals, and *wherewithal* to the interrogative pronouns. The word *where* in all these compounds is the *dative* or *ablative* of *what*—the case employed in Anglo-Saxon with the prepositions attached. As these words do not often occur in the modern language, it will be best, when we meet them, to resolve them into their component parts and treat them as nouns with a preposition, or rather as adjectives *substantively* employed with a preposition, the noun being *implied.* The noun ought in each instance to be *supplied* by the learner in analysis. Thus, *whereby* = *by what* or *by which*, referring to something easily discovered, and supplied, as being the antecedent to which *what* or *which* refers. This is a decidedly more useful and more satisfactory mode of analysis than to call such words *adverbs*, as they are usually called in dictionaries and grammars.

PROMISCUOUS EXAMPLES OF ADJECTIVE ACCESSORY PROPOSITIONS.—We subjoin examples of compound propositions containing adjective accessories, for the purpose of exercising the learner in analysis.

"The fixed and unchanging features of the country also perpetuate the memory of the friend with *whom* we enjoyed them; *who* was the companion of our most retired walks, and (who) gave animation to every lonely scene. His idea is associated with every charm of nature; we hear his voice in the echo *which* he once delighted to awaken; his spirit haunts the grove *which* he once frequented," &c.

"Satisfy yourselves with *what* is rational and attainable." "The time *which* they suffer to pass away in the midst of confusion, bitter repentance seeks afterwards in vain to recall. *What* was omitted to be done at its proper moment, arises to be the torment of some future season." "But he *who* is orderly in the distribution of his time takes the proper method of escaping those manifold evils." "Miserable is the man *who* has no resources within himself, *who* cannot enjoy his own company, *who* depends for happiness upon the next amusement, or the news of the day." "The leaf quivers on the branch *which* supports it. A breath of wind tears it from its stem, and it lights on the stream of water *which* passes underneath. In a moment of time, the life *which* we know by the microscope it teems with, is extinguished." "The enjoyments to *which* he looks up are not superior to his own. *There* are those *whose* appetites are courted by more costly provision than his; *whose* senses are excited by more stimulating entertainments, and soothed by smoother accommodations; *whose* days are spent in more expensive amusements, and *whose* nights are passed upon softer pillows: but he *who* fares sumptuously every day, sits down to no sweeter feast than he; he *whose* delight is daily stirred by more pungent excitements, is no more animated by them than he is by his cheaper and soberer pastime; and he *whose* love of ease is lulled in a downier lap, *whose* situation is covered in every part of it with cushion, and lined all over with pillow, enjoys not a more delicious recumbence," &c. "Those persons *who* know not how to distinguish between liberality and luxury, are under a great error. Abundance of men know how to squander *that* do not know how to give." "They who are ignorant of *what* happened before their birth, will remain children all their lives." "He *who* imagines he can do without the world" (*substantive accessory objective*), "deceives himself much; he *who* fancies the world can do without him, is under a far greater delusion." "He *that* hath no rule over his own spirit is like a city *that* is broken down and without walls." "The veil *that* covers from our sight the events of succeeding years, is a veil woven by the hand of mercy." "He *that* trusts his own wisdom proclaims his own folly." "He *that* rejoices at the prosperity of another man, is a partaker thereof." (We mark the suppression of the conjunctive pronoun in some of the following examples by a dash, thus —) "It is the spot — I came to seek." "The throne — we honor is the people's choice; the laws — we reverence are our brave fathers' legacy; the faith — we follow teaches us to live in bonds of charity with all mankind," &c. *Whoever* shows a man his mistakes in a kind manner is his friend. "*Whatever* is, is right." They saw *whatever* could be seen. "At once came forth *whatever* creeps." "*Whosoever* hath Christ for his friend will be sure of counsel; *whoever* is his own friend will be sure to obey it."

"He is the freeman *whom* the truth makes free."

"The duke yet lives *that* Henry shall depose."

Show the intentional ambiguity in this line, and express the two senses which it bears in such a way that the one cannot be confounded with the other.

"*Who* never fasts, no banquets e'er enjoys;
Who never toils or watches, never sleeps."

"And fools *who* came to scoff remained to pray."

"Let me take a horse *who* is to bear me." "Like mountain cat, *who* guards her young." "A score of vagabond dogs, *who* served his purpose." "Wine is like a strong serpent, *who* will creep unperceivedly into your empty head." (Observe the *personification* in the four preceding examples.)

"*Whatever* nature has in worth denied,
She gives in large recruits of needful pride!
For, as in bodies, thus in souls, we find
What wants in blood and spirits, swelled with wind."

"Just as absurd to mourn the tasks or pains,
— The great directing MIND OF ALL ordains."

"Call imperfection *what* thou fanciest such."

"That something still *which* prompts the eternal sigh,
For *which* we bear to live, or dare to die;
Which still so near us, yet beyond us lies."

"Couldst thou divine
To *what* would one day dwindle that *which* made
Thee more than mortal?"

What is here interrogative, and the compound proposition, *To what would one day dwindle that which*, &c., is an interrogative substantive accessory, forming the objective modification of the verb *divine*.

"I hear a voice — you cannot hear,
Which says, I must not stay;
I see a hand — you cannot see,
Which beckons me away."

Observe, *I must not stay*, is substantive accessory objective modification to the verb *says*.

§ 119. OF ADVERBIAL ACCESSORY PROPOSITIONS IN GENERAL.—We now come to treat of *adverbial accessory propositions*. (1) In entering on this subject, the learner will do well to revert to what we have said of adverbs (§ 92), namely that they are an abbreviated method of expressing the same kind of complement which is more formally expressed by a modified noun and preposition. Otherwise, when a single word expresses what is expressed by a noun and preposition modification, we call that word an *adverb.* (2) Now we here call all those accessories which express modifications similar either to those expressed by adverbs or by that of which an adverb is an abbreviation (a noun completed by a descriptive adjective and preceded by a preposition) *adverbial accessories*, since in them, as in the adverb, the preposition is *generally* suppressed. (3) It is not always suppressed; for some accessory propositions are connected, as we shall see, to their principal proposition by the intervention of a preposition exactly as a single noun is connected by a preposition with the modified word. We might have arranged these among the substantive accessories, and formed of them a class of *substantive accessories connected with their principals by a preposition.* (4) The learner will then remember that we do not separate into distinct classes the accessories which retain the *form* of *noun and preposition*, and the *adverbial* which do not retain this form; but consider them promiscuously, since, like the *noun and preposition modification* and the *adverb* they differ rather in mere form than in the purpose for which they are employed. We shall, however, carefully notice the cases, as they pass in review, in which a preposition serves to connect accessories of this class.

(5) Obs.—We shall treat these adverbial accessories with more brevity (considering their number), than the preceding class; not because a knowledge of them is unimportant, but because what has been already said, especially in reference to the adjective accessories connected by the conjunctive pronouns, prepares the learner to understand us without entering so minutely into details, which must consist in a great measure of the mere repetition, with slight change, of matter which has been introduced in treating the classes of accessories already considered. A hint or a reference to the preceding pages will, we hope, be sufficient to bring before the student's mind facts and illustrations which it would consume much time to repeat again at full length.

---

§ 119. (1) To what is the learner requested to revert in entering on the consideration of adverbial accessories? (2) Mention what accessories we include in the class of adverbial accessories. (3) What is said of accessories connected by a preposition, and of the mode in which they might be classed? (4) What is the learner here to remember?

(5) Repeat the substance of the observation in reference to brevity.

(6) We are not certain that we may not be found to have omitted important classes of the adverbial accessories; but we trust that, by the help of the illustrations about to be given, the cases, which may not come clearly within our classifications, will present no insuperable obstacle to the student. Let him try his own skill in explaining any forms of construction which we may have overlooked, and in devising formulæ by which they may be readily recognised and subjected to a rational analysis.

(7) There is another thing of which it may be well at this step of our progress to caution the learner. It has reference to our use of the terms *principal* and *accessory* applied to propositions. When we speak of a *principal* and of an *accessory* proposition, the student will please notice that we use these terms *relatively*, not *absolutely*. By a *principal proposition* we mean one which is principal *relatively* to a particular *accessory* by which, at least as regards grammatical form, it is modified. But this *principal*, in relation to the accessory in question, may itself, perchance, be only an *accessory* to some other proposition, which it modifies. In other words, we do not restrict the appellation *principal proposition* to the *main* proposition in a whole sentence or *compound* proposition, but of two propositions to that *one* which is modified or completed in some way by the *other*. As it is important that we should have a common understanding with our readers in reference to this matter, we illustrate our meaning by examples. And, since what we have now noticed applies to the use of these terms in speaking of the parts of compound propositions with substantive and adjective, as well as adverbial accessories, we shall choose an example in which the accessories are of the form already familiar to the learner. "Do you imagine that *all* are happy, *who* have attained to those *summits* of distinction, towards *which* your wishes aspire?" Here the *main* proposition "*Do you imagine*" is modified by the substantive accessory "*that* ALL *are happy*;" and this in its turn is *principal* to the accessory "*who have attained to those summits*," &c., which completes the word *all*. Again, the accessory proposition "*who have attained to those summits of distinction*" is principal in reference to the accessory "*towards which your wishes aspire*," which completes the words "summits of distinction." Here we see that a proposition may serve as accessory to an accessory of an accessory of another proposition; or to view the facts in another point of view, a word in a principal proposition may be modified by a compound proposition.

---

(6) What is said in reference to classes of these accessories which may be overlooked?
(7) State the substance of the caution, and illustrate it by examples.

The verb "*imagine*" in the main proposition above is modified by the whole doubly compounded proposition which follows to the end of the example; "*all*," in the first accessory, is modified in like manner by the whole compound proposition which succeeds it. We subjoin another example which the learner may examine, and apply for the purpose o. illustration. "Philosophers *teach* us, that the mind creates the *beauty* which it admires in nature."

CLASSIFICATION OF ADVERBIAL ACCESSORIES.—(8) We shall classify the adverbial accessory propositions in a manner similar to that in which we classified the adverbs. It will conduce to the ease of the learner to adopt this classification already familiar to him, and to pursue, as far as convenient, the same order in explaining *adverbial accessories* which we have employed in explaining *adverbial modifications.*

(9) We divide these accessories agreeably to this method into two classes:

I. Adverbial accessories which modify *adjectives.*

II. Adverbial accessories which modify *verbs*, or sometimes perhaps the entire *principal proposition.*

For an account of the distinction between those which, like the adverbial propositions of *manner*, obviously modify verbs, and those which may, perhaps with greater propriety, be considered as modifying the whole principal assertion, we refer the reader to what we have said on this subject in reference to noun and preposition and adverbial modifications. (*See* § 83.)

§ 120. 1. ADVERBIAL ACCESSORIES WHICH MODIFY ADJECTIVES.—(1) The adverbial accessories which modify adjectives, like the adverbs which modify adjectives, usually express degrees of intensity. They do this generally by the introduction of a comparison.

(2) We express an *equal* degree of intensity comparatively by a form of accessory connected with the principal proposition by the word AS. We use *as* both before the adjective to be modified and after it to connect the accessory.

(3) The *as* before the adjective (whatever may be the origin of

---

(8) Repeat the remark in reference to the classification of adverbial accessories.
(9) Mention the classes into which we divide adverbial accessories.
§ 120. (1) What is said generally of the adverbial accessories which modify adjectives?
(2) Describe the manner in which we express equality of intensity. (3) What is said of

the word whether *pronominal* or *determinative*) is now *adverbially* used to help in modifying the adjective; the second *as* may be considered a *conjunctive* adverb, since it performs the function of conjunction in joining the two propositions, and at the same time the function of adverb in the accessory. (4) Some call the word *as* a conjunctive pronoun. (5) We admit that it performs nearly the same function as a conjunctive pronoun, but so do many other adverbs (or words universally acknowledged to be adverbs), as we shall see presently. We need not dispute about names, where no gross error lurks under them. We subjoin an example of this construction. (6) *That man is* AS *wise* AS *you are* = *That man is as wise as you are wise.* Some call this the *comparison* of *equality.* (7) Generally both the verb and the adjective are omitted in the accessory proposition; but in such cases the verb, at least (if not both verb and adjective), is clearly *implied*, and should always be *supplied* in a formal analysis. On this account we do not class this form of expression with the *abbreviations* used for accessory propositions. (See § 140: 3, 4.) These are merely cases of obvious ellipsis or suppression.

(8) In the example which we have presented, the equal intensity of the same (adjective) quality in two different subjects is expressed, but the same form of accessory is also employed to express the same degree of intensity of different qualities in the same subject. For example, *That man is* AS *good* AS *he is great.*

(9) These adverbial accessories may readily be resolved into adjective accessories. By doing this we may more clearly comprehend their structure and their use. Thus, *That man is wise in the same degree in which you are wise*, or simply, *wise in the degree that you are wise.* And *that man is good in the* (*same*) *degree in which he is great.* (10) Here we may discover that the first *as* is an abbreviation, like all other adverbs, for a noun and preposition modification, and the latter *as*, in like manner, an abbreviation for a conjunctive pronoun and preposition.

(11) In analysis the learner may call the proposition commencing

---

the double use of the word AS in this kind of modification? (4) What have some called *as* when employed to connect an accessory? (5) What remark is made in reference to the name given to this word? (6) Repeat the example. (7) What generally happens in accessories of this kind?

(8) Mention another purpose for which this form of accessory is employed.

(9) Mention another form into which this kind of accessory may be resolved. Illustrate by examples. (10) What may be discovered after this resolution is effected?

(11) Tell the name given to distinguish these accessories, and describe the method of treating them in analysis.

with the second AS *The adverbial accessory expressive of equal intensity*, telling the adjective which it modifies. Then *as* may be treated as an adverb in both the *principal* and the *accessory* proposition. (*a*)

Before we dismiss this subject, we may remark that adverbs, as might be expected, are susceptible of modification from the same kind of accessories attached to the principal proposition, in which the adverb occurs, and in exactly the same manner. Thus, *That man labors as diligently as his neighbor. This man acts as wisely as his father acted.* (*b*)

(12) PUNCTUATION.—This accessory is not usually separated by interpunction; though in this, as in other cases, usage is perhaps not altogether settled.

EXERCISES I., II., &c.—Form compound propositions with *accessories* expressing equality of intensity for the purpose of limiting an adjective in the *principal* proposition.

NOTE.—(*a*) This kind of accessory may be regarded as expressing the identity of the degree of intensity, either of the same quality in different subjects, or of two distinct qualities in the same subject, in the same way as some accessories of *time, place, manner*, express identity of *time, place, manner*. As, for example, *He came* WHEN *I came; He was arriving* WHILE *his brother was departing; You think* AS *I think*. The only difference is that the connecting words *when, while, as*, are not twice used as in the former case, though they really perform a function in the principal as well as in the accessory proposition. This is seen when we complete these compound propositions; thus, *He came* AT THE TIME WHEN *I came*, or *He came* AT THE TIME AT WHICH *I came*. Here it is manifest that when performs the function both of a complement in the principal and in the accessory; because in the case under consideration the adverbial word *as* is repeated in both propositions, and because this does not happen in other cases the construction is regarded as singular, and as occasioning difficulty in the analysis of such compound propositions. But, in truth, the construction before us is more simple, less artifical, less elliptical than the accessories of *time, place*, and *manner* introduced above. There is in the one case a suppression which does not exist in the other. The suppression takes place perhaps for two reasons, namely, that such words as *when* (if not interrogative) and *while* have always a conjunctive force, and cannot therefore stand in a principal proposition; and that if used in such principal propositions as they succeed, they would naturally come last, and coming last in the principal and first in the accessory a disagreeable repetition of the same word would occur. Neither reason applies to *as*. It is not always used conjunctively, but often as a simple adverb; and its natural place is not last in a principal proposition

---

(12) Punctuation?

followed by an accessory expression of equal intensity, but before the adjective which it modifies. Had it come after the adjective it would, no doubt, have been suppressed, as other words are in similar circumstances; or as happens with *as* itself when used to express manner, as in the example, *You think* AS *I think* = *you think* IN THE MANNER IN WHICH *I think.*

NOTE.—(*b*) Some accessories of this kind have been gradually, by *insensible extension,* diverted from their original purpose; as, for example, the phrase *as well as.* In the compound proposition, *This musician sings as well as he plays;* "*as he plays*" is manifestly an ordinary example of the *adverbial accessory of equal intensity* applied to the adverb *well,* and the assertion is equivalent to *He sings in a manner equally good with the manner in which he plays.* But when we say *This musician sings as well as plays,* the meaning is altogether different, though the difference in form consists merely in the suppression of the subject pronoun *he* before plays. This last proposition only expresses that the musician, besides being able to play (which both parties to the discourse are supposed to know already), can also sing. It is equivalent to saying *You know that the musician plays, in addition to this I inform you that he also sings.* The two propositions thus stand to each other nearly in the relation of *co-ordinate propositions. As well as plays* may be considered rather as an addition to the preceding assertion, than as a modification of it. It stands in no closer relation to the other than co-ordinate propositions often stand to one another. If it is to be regarded as an accessory, and as modifying any thing in the preceding proposition, it cannot be *well,* nor even *sings well* (for the manner of singing is not in this case indicated), but it is simply the verb *sings* which it affects. At all events, the words *as well as plays* have here a very different effect from the words *as well as he plays* in the first example, and a very different effect from the ordinary adverbial accessory of equal intensity.

§ 121. ACCESSORY OF GREATER OR LESSER INTENSITY.—(1) The adjectives of the comparative degree, whether of superiority or inferiority (that is, adjectives modified by the termination *er*, or the adverbs *more* or *less*, and thus indicating greater or lesser intensity), are generally completed or limited by an adverbial accessory proposition connected with the principal proposition by the conjunction *than.* (2) Examples: *He is taller than his brother is. He was more prudent than the preceding sovereign was. That boy is less studious than his cousin is.* (3) Here the adjective is never repeated in the accessory proposition. The verb too, as in the *comparison of equality,*

---

§ 121. (1) What form of adjectives is modified or restricted by the *accessory of greater or lesser intensity?* (2) Illustrate by examples. (3) Mention the parts usually suppressed in accessories of this kind.

is generally suppressed, and the compound proposition reads thus, *He is taller than his brother. That boy is less studious than his cousin.* But in all cases both the verb and the adjective are *implied* in the accessory.

(4) In the examples given, there is a comparison between two distinct subjects in reference to the degree, in which they possess the *same quality.* We use a similar form to express the comparison of the degrees in which two different qualities are possessed by the *same subject.* (5) Thus, *He is braver than he is wise,* or, suppressing the verb of the accessory, *He is braver than wise.* As this accessory helps to express a greater or lesser degree of intensity, we call it *the accessory of greater or lesser intensity;* or *of the comparative degree.*

(6) The learner will remark that this form of accessory, like the one last considered, is employed to complete the modification of comparative *adverbs* as well as comparative *adjectives.* For example, *He acts more wisely than his brother.* For the reasons that *adverbs of manner* are susceptible of this and other modifications in common with adjectives, see § 94.*

EXERCISE.—Form examples of this construction.

(7) Related to this in regard to the purpose which it serves,

* Than (in old English *thanne,* in later English often *then,* in Anglo-Saxon *thonne,* or *thanne,* &c.) is undoubtedly the accusative of the Anglo-Saxon determinative or article, used also in that language as a *conjunctive* pronoun. The appropriation of *quam* in Latin to connect the accessory of the comparative degree seems precisely analogous to what has happened in our language. In both languages there is likely the suppression of a preposition before, perhaps of a noun after, *quam* and *than*; or there is a peculiar employment of the accusative equivalent to the suppression of a preposition, as in the accusatives of *time, value,* &c. We suspect that *ofer* (*over*) was the preposition suppressed in the Anglo-Saxon, since this preposition succeeded by an accusative is found after the comparative degree. For example, *gif thonne strengra ofer hine cymth* = If then (one) stronger *over* him come. If we supply the suppressions in one of the above examples according to this conjecture, it will run thus, *he is taller* OVER THAT (*degree*) *his brother is tall.*

(4) Mention another purpose for which this form of accessory is employed. (5) Give examples.

(6) What is said in reference to the modification of comparative adverbs?

(7) Describe another similar purpose for which an accessory is employed. (8) Illustrate

though dissimilar in form, is the accessory employed in expressing *similarly increasing intensities*, or that the intensity of one quality is as the intensity of another, or, again, that the intensities of the two qualities vary in opposite directions, the one increasing as the other decreases. (8) We commence with examples: *The* HIGHER *that man's elevation is, the* GREATER *will be his fall.* (9) In this kind of construction the verb is very generally suppressed both in the principal and in the accessory proposition. Thus, *the higher the elevation, the greater the fall; the more, the merrier; the fewer, the better cheer.* In speaking of property employed for good purposes, we say, *The more, the better*=*The more a man has, the better it is for himself and those around him.* If, on the contrary, employed for bad purposes, we say, *The less, the better.* Of some things we say, *The warmer, the better;* of others, *the colder, the better; the less warm, the better; the less cold, the better.*

(10) In this construction there occurs a very peculiar use of the word *the*, which claims a moment's notice. (11) The learner will observe, before we proceed, that in this construction the accessory stands first, and the principal proposition last. (12) It will help to render this fact manifest, and to further our purpose of explaining the use of *the* in both propositions, to substitute a construction equivalent in sense to that presented in the above examples. Thus, *The fall is greater* IN THAT (or IN THE) DEGREE, IN WHICH (DEGREE) *the elevation is higher.* This is manifestly equivalent to the construction in the example; or rather is the same construction expanded, and having the suppressed words supplied. (13) Here, then, we see that *the* in the principal proposition is employed in its usual determinative function, but *adverbially*, both a noun and preposition being implied, as in adverbs, or adjectives adverbially used; and that in the accessory it performs the function, as it formerly did in the Anglo-Saxon, of a conjunctive pronoun used in the same manner, preposition and noun being suppressed. In other words, *the* in the principal proposition = *in the* (or *that*) *degree;* and in the accessory = *in which* (*degree*). We give another example for illustration: THE *more intelligent*, THE *more libe-*

---

by an example. (9) What suppression generally occurs in this construction? Illustrate by several examples.

(10) What peculiarity occurs in this construction? (11) Which stands first, the accessory or the principal, in the examples above? (12) What reasons are assigned for presenting a substitute for the above construction? Mention the substitute, and illustrate the use of *the* by it. (13) How is *the* employed in each proposition?

ral. Speaking of men = *Men are more liberal* IN THE DEGREE (or *in the proportion*) IN WHICH *they are more intelligent.**

(14) Since this accessory has some connection with the science of quantity, we venture to borrow a name from the mathematicians. We call it *The accessory used in expressing intensities equally varying directly or indirectly;* or, more briefly, ACCESSORY OF EQUALLY VARYING INTENSITIES.

EXERCISE.—Furnish a number of examples of this construction.

(15) There is another form of accessory applied to adjectives for the purpose of indicating the degree of intensity designed to be expressed in a particular case. This accessory describes the *intensity* by an example of the effect produced by it. Thus, *The weather is* SO COLD, *that the water freezes in the ponds; The weather has become* SO WARM, *that the snow on the mountains begins to dissolve.* Here the intensity of the cold in the one case, and of the heat in the other, is indicated by the effect produced. *One man is* SO RICH, *that it gives him trouble to expend his wealth. Another is* SO POOR, *that he can scarcely get bread to eat.*

(16) In this construction, the adjective is first modified in the *principal* proposition by the adverb *so*, and as thus modified is further completed by the accessory proposition introduced by the conjunctive determinative *that.* (17) The same construction is employed in modifying the *determinative* SUCH as well as descriptive adjectives preceded by *so.* Thus, That man's character is *such*, that nobody can confide in

* This construction may be compared with the Latin construction in which *quo* and *eo* or *hoc* serve the same purpose as *the* serves in the case before us. For example, *Quo difficilius, hoc praeclarius* = The more difficult, the more glorious. *Eo minor est arcus, quo altior est sol* = The higher the sun is, the less is the rainbow. *Homines quo plura habent, eo ampliora cupiunt* = *The* more men have, *the* more they desire. *The* here performs the functions both of *eo* and *quo,* as it very frequently does in Anglo-Saxon. In this construction we have a remarkable relic of the conjunctive use of *the*, perhaps the only remnant of this use in the language. (See §§ 158, 159).

(14) What is said of naming this accessory? Repeat the name.

(15) Describe another form of accessory used to express the degree of intensity; and illustrate by examples.

(16) Describe the manner in which the adjective is modified in this construction.

(17) Repeat what is said of the modification of *such* and illustrate by examples.

him. *Such* here seems to be equivalent to *so bad—so suspicious*, or the like; in other words, *such* = *so*, with an adjective. Hence it is not strange that *such* should be modified by the same form of accessory that an adjective preceded by *so* takes to complete it.

(18) This kind of accessory we may designate by the name of *The adverbial accessory indicating the degree of intensity by example or by effect.* More briefly, *The accessory indicating intensity by effect.*

(19) We may remark here, that when, instead of a complete accessory of this kind, we adopt the infinitive form of *contracted accessory* (see § 142: 9, 10) we employ *as*, not *that*, to connect this *contracted accessory* with the *principal* proposition. Examples: *This weather is* SO WARM AS TO DISSOLVE *the snow on the mountains. He is so wise as not to confide in men whom he does not know. He is so poor as to beg—so mean as to steal. That man's character* IS SUCH AS TO DESTROY *all confidence in his promises.*

EXERCISES I., II., &c.—Furnish examples of these forms of construction.

(20) We next notice a form of accessory which expresses an *indefinite* or *unbounded degree of intensity*. (21) The conjunctive adverb used to introduce this is *however*. (22) We give as an example, HOWEVER *powerful that man may be, he is not likely to succeed in that enterprise.* = Though that man may have *any* or *every degree of power*, he is not likely to succeed, &c. (23) This accessory is exactly similar to the concessive accessory to be considered below (see § 138: 27, and note), only that the force of the adverb *however* here falls upon the *adjective.*

REMARK.—(24) The adjective and the adverb *however* are sometimes used alone in accessories of this kind, the rest of the proposition being *implied;* as, "No examples, *however awful*, sink into the heart" = No examples, however awful they may be, &c.

§ 122. (1) We may here notice another form of compound proposition, which may be regarded as standing related both to the class we have been considering and to the class to which we are presently to direct our attention. (2) We shall first present examples, and

---

(18) What name is given to this form of accessory?

(19) Repeat the substance of the remark, and illustrate by examples.

(20) What form of accessory is next noticed? (21) What conjunctive word is employed to introduce it? (22) Illustrate the use of this accessory by an example. (23) To what other accessory is this exactly similar?

(24) Repeat the substance of the remark.

§ 122. (1) What is said of the compound proposition about to be noticed? (2) Give examples.

then proceed to examine them. *As Aristides was conspicuous among the Athenians for integrity, so Themistocles was conspicuous for political sagacity and adroit management. As John is loved for his benevolence, so Peter is despised on account of his unfeeling selfishness. As his elevation was great, so his fall is humiliating.*

(3) These propositions somewhat resemble the compound propositions which express the *comparison of equality.* (4) In some cases of this construction it may not be clear, at first sight, which is the accessory proposition, or whether the two propositions are not to be regarded as *co-ordinate*, the writer designing to express two distinct assertions, and to add to the effect of both by placing them together. (5) Upon changing slightly the construction, we shall, in most cases, readily discover which is, at least in form, the accessory, and which the principal proposition. (6) For illustration let us take the second example above, *As John is loved for his benevolence, so Peter is despised on account of his selfishness.* This is equivalent to, *Peter is despised on account of his selfishness* IN SO GREAT DEGREE *as John is loved*, &c. (7) It is evident that the proposition which comes last in the original example and first in the substituted construction, " *Peter is despised*, &c. is the principal proposition. (8) We can even omit the adverb *so* in the principal proposition, and by placing it first express the same meaning, though perhaps not so forcibly; thus, *Peter is despised for his selfishness, as John is loved for his benevolence.* (9) It is really so (=*in so great degree*) in the principal proposition which is modified by the accessory. When not expressed, so or its equivalent *in such* or *so great degree* is implied, and modified by the accessory. (10) The accessory is connected by the conjunctive adverb *as.* This word *as* may also serve to indicate to the learner which is really the accessory proposition.

(11) This construction differs in two things from that into which the

---

(3) What other class of compound propositions do these resemble? (4) Tell what it may be sometimes difficult to determine in constructions of this kind. (5) Describe a mode of discovering which is the principal and which the accessory proposition. (6) Illustrate by an example. (7) Which in the example is evidently the principal proposition? (8) What is said of the suppression of the word *so?* (9) Which is the word really modified by the accessory? (10) By what word is the accessory in this construction connected? And what may the connecting word serve to indicate to the learner?

(11) Mention the two things in which this construction differs from that with an acces-

accessory of equal intensity enters. It does not express *strictly equal* intensity, but rather *similarity* of intensity, and even that in a loose way. And, in the second place, this kind of accessory does not affect exclusively (as the one referred to does) the adjective in the principal proposition, but the whole predicate. ((12) Of this predicate, it generally happens, that the adjective is the most prominent part; and therefore the adjective appears as if it were peculiarly affected by the accessory.) (13) Thus, when I say, using the accessory of equal intensity, *Your brother is as cold as you are*, I indicate simply the equal intensity of the quality cold in the case of your brother and you. But when I say, *As John is loved for his benevolence, so Peter*, &c. I indicate some sort of equality in a loose manner, or rather of *similarity*, between Peter's *being despised for his selfishness* and John's *being loved for his benevolence.*

(14) This accessory may perhaps be considered as expressing the *manner* of Peter's being despised rather than the *degree* of intensity of the despite. If so, it approaches in character (if it belongs not entirely) to the class of accessories which we are next about to consider, and thus affords a natural transition from the one class to the other.

(15) We may designate this by the name of *The Accessory indicating Similar Intensity*—more briefly, *The Accessory of Similar Intensity.* It stands, as we have just intimated, between two classes of accessories—those which modify adjectives and those which modify verbs, but has stronger claims to be arranged with the latter class.

EXERCISE.—Furnish examples of this construction.

§ 123. (1) We next proceed to consider those adverbial accessory propositions which manifestly modify the *verbs* or *predicates* of the principal propositions, or sometimes the whole principal assertion.

(2) Here we shall first direct our attention to that class of accessories in which the *manner* of the action predicated by the verb is expressed.

---

sory of equal intensity. (12) Mention the remark about the adjective in the predicate of this accessory. (13) Illustrate by examples.

(14) Mention the remark about the class to which this accessory belongs. (15) How may this accessory be designated? And where is it represented as standing?

§ 123. (1) Describe the kind of accessories next to be considered.

These are exactly analogous to the adverbs of *manner* already considered. (*See* § 92.)

(3) There are different forms of this species of adverbial accessory. One form describes the manner of the action predicated in the principal proposition by *comparison*—by reference to another action of the same subject, or to the same or sometimes to a different action of another subject. This accessory follows the principal proposition, and is connected with it by the conjunctive adverb *as*. (4) For example, *That man died* AS *he lived. He acts in this affair* AS *he has acted on other occasions. William thinks as I think. That man grows in the esteem of his friends*, AS *his neighbor sinks into infamy*. Here the man's *manner of living* is employed to indicate his *manner of dying*. His *manner of acting on other occasions* to indicate his *manner of acting in this affair*, &c.

(5) We can invert the order of these propositions, and place the accessory first; but then we must supply the word *so* before the principal proposition. Thus, *As that man lived, so he died; As I think, so William thinks.*

(6) In this form of compound propositions the word *as*, like *what* in adjective accessories, performs the function of an adverb both in the *principal* and *accessory* proposition, at the same time serving to indicate their connection. (7) As regards the *thought*, the real bond of connection is *sameness* or *identity of manner*. (8) That *as* performs the double function which we have ascribed to it, is obvious when we invert the compound proposition and are obliged to call in the services of *so*.

(9) We may call this *The Adverbial Accessory denoting Manner by Comparison;* or, more briefly, *The Accessory of Manner by Comparison.*

(10) In such expressions as, *He acted as chairman of the meeting*, we have perhaps an elliptical construction=*He acted to the meeting* AS

---

(2) Which class of these do we first notice? (3) Describe one of the different forms of this species of accessories. (4) Illustrate by examples.

(5) What is said of inverting the order of these propositions? Illustrate by examples.

(6) What is said of the functions of *as* in such compound propositions? (7) What is said of the bond of connection in *thought*? (8) How is it shown that *as* performs the double function attributed to it?

(9) How may we name this accessory?

(10) What is said of an elliptical construction? Example for illustration.

a chairman of a meeting acts. Some call *as chairman*, &c. in such constructions, a *noun in apposition;* but improperly, as we think.

We may here notice that there is an extension of this kind of construction to express sameness of time. This will be considered when we come to treat adverbial accessories of *time*.

(11) REMARK.—This form of accessory, like most of the adverbial accessories, may be replaced, when the construction is fully expanded by an adjective accessory. In order to this we must supply in the principal proposition that for which *as* may be regarded as a substitute, namely, the noun and preposition modification *in the manner*, or *in the same manner*, and then add an adjective accessory. Thus, *That man died* IN THE SAME MANNER IN WHICH *he lived*, &c.*

(12) Another form of this species of accessory describes the manner of the action (like the similar accessory which is applied to adjectives) by its effect. Thus, *This man acts so, that all his friends are proud of him*. Here we use *so* in the principal proposition, and *that* conjunctive to connect the accessory. (13) This form, when expanded, becomes identical with one of the forms of the accessories which modify adjectives. *So* expanded=*in such manner*. Then the above example runs thus, *This man acts* IN SUCH MANNER, *that all his friends are proud*

* Sometimes an accessory denoting manner by comparison is apparently connected by two conjunctive words, *as* and *if*. For example, *That boy acts* AS IF *he were insane*. *He moaned* AS IF *he were in great pain*. In constructions of this kind there is a suppression of a proposition between *as* and *if*. When we supply this suppression, the whole construction is clear. Thus, *That boy acts as* HE WOULD ACT, or AS ONE WOULD ACT, *if he were insane*. *He moaned as* HE WOULD MOAN *if he were in great pain*. The accessory proposition here connected by *as*, when thus fully developed, is itself a *compound proposition* of the *hypothetical* form (*see* § 137), and the connection between the principal proposition and this compound accessory is exactly the same which we have been describing. In such cases, AS may be considered as representing the accessory proposition which is itself modified by the hypothetical accessory commencing with the *conditional* conjunction *if*.

Instead of *as if*, *as though* is sometimes employed in the same manner, and with the same force. Examples, "He made *as though* he would have gone further." "It was *as though* it budded." "I will shoot three arrows on the side thereof, *as though* I shot at a mark." This form of expression may perhaps be regarded as antiquated.

(11) Repeat the substance of the remark, and illustrate by examples.

(12) Describe another form of the accessory of manner. Give example. (13) With what other form of accessory does this become identified when expanded? Illustrate by an example.

of him. Or, *This man acts* IN A MANNER SUCH, *that all his friends are proud of him.* Here, *that all his friends are proud of him* is obviously an adverbial accessory modifying the *determinative* SUCH.

(14) We may distinguish this form by calling it the accessory denoting the manner of action by its effect or consequence; or more briefly, *The Accessory describing an Action by its Effect.*

(15) REMARK.—When we employ the infinitive abbreviation for an accessory proposition of this kind, we use (as in the accessory of like form which modifies adjectives) AS instead of THAT for *conjunctive* word; thus, *This man behaved so,* AS *to gain the applause*, or, *so* AS *to be applauded by all his friends.*

EXERCISE.—Furnish examples of these constructions.

§ 124. ADVERBIAL ACCESSORIES EMPLOYED TO INDICATE THE CIRCUMSTANCE OF PLACE.

(1) This class of accessories is usually connected with the principal proposition by the adverbs of place, *where*, *whence*, *whither*, and their compounds formed with *ever* and *so*, *wherever*, *wheresoever*, *whencesoever*, *whithersoever*. (2) When so employed we call these words *conjunctive adverbs.* (3) They are all of the family of the *conjunctive* (originally *interrogative*) pronouns *who* and *what.* (4) Used to introduce accessory propositions, they are all equivalent to a conjunctive pronoun and the noun *place* preceded by a preposition. In this respect they resemble the other adverbs. (5) Like *what,* they generally, though not always, perform the function of adverb, or of noun and preposition modification both for the *principal* and the accessory proposition, besides serving to indicate the relation between the two propositions. The conjunctive adverb marks as the *accessory* that proposition to which it is attached and which it introduces.

We next proceed to class the accessory propositions of *place,* and to show briefly the purposes which they serve in discourse.

---

(14) By what name may we distinguish this accessory?

(15) Repeat the substance of the remark, and illustrate by an example.

§ 124. (1) By what words are adverbial accessories of place connected with the principal proposition? (2) What do we call these words when so used? (3) What is said of the family and origin of these words? (4) To what are they in this use of them equivalent? (5) Mention the several functions which they serve in compound propositions.

(6) 1st. We give as a first class of the adverbial accessories of place, those which serve to determine the place *in which* or *at which* what is predicated in the principal proposition exists; in other words, its local position; or, to use a colloquial expression, the *whereabouts* of the main assertion. (7) We may call this *The Adverbial Accessory of Locality.*

(8) The conjunctive word employed to connect these accessories is WHERE, when a *definite* place is indicated, WHEREVER and WHERESOEVER when *whatever* place is designated. (9) Example, *I live* WHERE *your friend lives.* Here *where your friend lives* determines the place where *I live*=*I live* IN THE PLACE IN WHICH *your friend lives.* (10) It is obvious from inspecting the expanded form of the construction here presented, that WHERE represents and performs the functions of the noun and preposition complement *in the place* in the *principal*, and of the conjunctive pronoun and preposition *in which* in the *accessory* proposition. (11) When the construction is thus expanded, the accessory becomes an adjective accessory proposition, modifying the word *place* in the principal proposition. (12) WHERE here performs functions precisely similar to those performed by WHAT (of which it is in fact merely the dative form); namely, those of a complement both in the principal and in the accessory, besides serving to indicate the connection and relation of the two propositions.

(13) We give examples of the less definite form of this class of accessories. *I will lodge* WHEREVER *my friend determines to lodge. He will abide* WHERESOEVER *you may choose to command.* Here the particular place is not *absolutely specified*, but it is, as in the preceding case, determined so far as the description in the accessory can limit it. (14) The place described in the accessory in the first case is supposed to be fixed, and known to the speaker; but the place described in the *indefinite* accessory is supposed to be yet unsettled, or, at least, yet unknown to the speaker. The accessory determines it to the extent of his ability.

---

(6) Describe the first class of accessories of place. (7) What name is given to this class?

(8) What conjunctive words serve to connect accessories of locality? (9) Illustrate by an example. (10) Show what functions WHERE performs in such constructions. (11) What does this accessory become when the construction is expanded? (12) With what are the functions performed by WHERE compared?

(13) Furnish examples of the indefinite form of this class of accessories, and tell what is

REMARK.—(15) In all classes of these adverbial accessories of place, those which are to follow, as well as that which we have considered—IDENTITY OF PLACE, is the *real bond* of connection (in *thought*) between the principal and the accessory proposition. It is this *identity* which adapts the accessory to modify or complete the principal in reference to the circumstance of *locality*—local position—or of direction towards, or direction from a place.

(16) Sometimes *where* is employed in an accessory proposition to represent a noun of place expressed in the principal proposition. (17) In such cases *where* performs precisely the function of the pronoun conjunctive and preposition *in which;* and the accessory might with propriety be classed with the adjective accessory, since it simply serves to modify or *determine* the noun of *place* in the principal proposition. Example: *He lives in the same place* WHERE *his brother lives*=*He lives in the place* IN WHICH *his brother lives.* Here *where his brother lives* may be considered, and may be treated if we please, as an adjective accessory proposition. (18) That these two kinds of accessories—the *adjective* and the *adverbial*—are sometimes (or perhaps we should say very generally) resolvable into one another, or blended together, is not surprising, when we remember the intimate relation subsisting between the functions of adverbs and adjectives,—all adverbs involving, as part of their function, *the function*, and often, as part of their form, *the form* of an adjective.

(19) When the principal proposition is placed after the accessory, which often happens, the adverb *there* is sometimes employed in the principal proposition to represent the place determined by the accessory. "That *where* I am, *there* ye may be also."

The other accessories of place do not express *local position* but local *direction*, either towards, or from a place. We include in our

(20) 2d class those which describe the place towards which the action predicated in the principal proposition is directed. (21) The conjunctive adverb *distinctly* appropriated to connect this class of accessories, when a definite known place is to be indicated, is

---

said of the effect of the accessories in the examples. (14) State the difference between the two forms of accessory.

(15) Repeat the substance of the remark.

(16) How is *where* sometimes employed in accessories? (17) What function does *where* thus used perform? And how might the accessory be treated? (18) What is said in reference to the fact that these two kinds of accessory are resolvable into one another?

(19) What word is introduced in the principal proposition, when it follows the accessory?

(20) Describe the second class of accessories of place. (21) By what conjunctive word

WHITHER. (22) We have said in speaking of *where* and *whither* in their original function of interrogatives (*see* § 92, *note p.* 291), that *where* has usurped the function of *whither* in addition to its own peculiar function. The same remark applies to *where* conjunctively used. It is now almost universally employed in this as well as in the preceding form of accessory, and *whither*, which our forefathers employed exclusively to express *to* or *towards a place*, is nearly obsolete.

(23) The same remark applies to the compound word *whithersoever*, which was formerly used to express direction towards *whatever* place; as, "I will follow thee *whithersoever* thou goest." We would now say, WHEREVER *thou goest. Wheresoever* is also rarely used in the current language of the present times.

(24) 3d. We introduce, as a third class of the accessories of place, those which describe the place *from which* the action predicated in the principal proposition is *directed*. (25) These accessories, like those just considered, refer sometimes to a determinate known place, sometimes to one determined only by the accessory, but otherwise unlimited.

(26) The conjunctive word employed for the first purpose (when a fixed locality is to be designated) is WHENCE. Example: "*This deliverance comes* WHENCE *every blessing flows.*" Here the accessory, *whence every blessing flows*, determines the place from which *the deliverance comes.*

(27) The remarks which we made (*see* § 92, *note p.* 291) in reference to the use of the preposition *from* before *whence interrogative* apply also to *whence* used as a *conjunctive adverb. From* is very generally employed superfluously before the conjunctive *whence*. (28) The same objections apply to the use of the preposition before this word in both cases. (29) In the authorized version of the Bible, there are abundant examples of *whence* conjunctive preceded by *from*, and a considerable number in which the more correct construction, without a preposition, is employed.

---

were these accessories originally preceded? (22) What is said of another word having usurped the place of *whither?*

(23) To what other word does the same remark apply?

(24) Describe a third class of accessories of place. (25) What division of this class?

(26) What conjunctive word is employed with the first division? Example.

(27) What is said of remarks which apply to *whence?* (28) What is said of objections to the expression *from whence?* (29) Where may examples of this usage be found?

(30) To indicate *any place you plense from which* we would now employ the words *from whatever place.* Example: *He will come from* WHATEVER *place his friend comes. Whencever* and *whencesoever* may be regarded as obsolete. They may be found in our more ancient authors, and, perhaps, sometimes employed in accessories of this description.

(31) We have already said that *where* is used as equivalent to *in which* to represent an *antecedent noun. Whence* equivalent to *from which* is employed for the same purpose. Examples: "Look to the rock whence ye are hewn." "I will return to my house whence I came."

(32) The accessory propositions commencing with *where* and *whither* are often placed before the principal proposition. In the older authors, we think, the accessory is most frequently placed first. Examples: "Whither I go, ye cannot come." "Whither I go, thou canst not follow me now." "Whither thou goest, I will go; and where thou lodgest, I will lodge."——"Where thou diest, will I die."

REMARK.—The observations made in reference to accessories commencing with *what* conjunctive (*see* § 114: 6, *et seq.*) apply to many of the accessories of place of the first and second classes. (33) When these accessories come after certain transitive verbs, which take an accessory proposition for their objective modification, they might be treated as *substantive* accessories serving as objectives of these verbs, and analyzed in the manner recommended in treating the accessories connected by *what.* (34) We present examples: *I know where you have been.* "Let no man know *where* ye be." "*Whither* I go ye know." "We know not *whither* thou goest." In all these compound propositions the accessory may be regarded as a *substantive accessory* serving as *objective modification* of the verb in the principal proposition. (35) If we choose to supply the ellipsis it becomes an adjective accessory modification of the noun *place*—the *implied* objective modification of the verb in the principal proposition. (36) As this mode of analysis will not suit when the verb in the principal proposition is

---

(30) How do we describe an *indefinite* place *from which?* Example.

(31) What is said of *whence* = *from which?* Examples.

(32) Repeat the remark about the accessories commencing with *where* and *whither.* Examples.

(33) How might the accessories of place of the first and second classes be treated, when they follow *transitive* verbs? (34) Give examples, and apply the remark to them. (35) What other form do these assume when the ellipses are supplied? (36) State the reason for treating them as adverbial accessories.

neuter or *intransitive* (as it is in most of the examples given above), it will be more convenient to treat all these *accessories of place* as *adverbial*, though it may be good to know the other forms into which some of them may be readily resolved.

(37) Punctuation.—As may be seen from some of the examples introduced above, in which we have followed the original punctuation, accessories of locality are sometimes separated by interpunction from the principal proposition, and sometimes not. The accessory, when it precedes the principal proposition, is perhaps generally followed by a comma; as, "Whither I go, ye cannot come." When the accessory follows the principal proposition, we believe the comma is seldom inserted. Here, as in other instances, the punctuation is not settled on fixed and consistent principles. If we would maintain consistency, we ought either to insert a comma *always* between the principal and the accessory, or we should never insert it. *See Appendix on Punctuation.*

Exercises I., II., III., &c.—Form compound propositions with accessories expressing the place *where*, the place *whither*, the place *whence;* also with the conjunctive words *wherever*, *whithersoever*, &c.

§ 125. Adverbial Accessory Propositions Indicating the Circumstance of Time.—(1) We next proceed to consider that class of compound propositions in which the circumstance of time is the *real* bond of connection between the principal and its accessory.

(2) Some of the accessories employed in this class of propositions have a close analogy with those in which the circumstance of place is the bond of connection. We proceed to classify the accessories used to express the circumstance of time.

1st. (3) We shall consider first those accessories which limit or modify the principal proposition, by the predication of some occurrence falling within the same point of time with the matter of the principal assertion. (4) Examples: *I will go with you to the exhibition* WHEN *I shall have finished my work.* "Thou shalt talk of them *when* thou sittest in thine house," &c. "They linger about it

---

(37) State the substance of the remarks in reference to the punctuation of this description of compound propositions.

§ 125. (1) What class of propositions is now to be considered?

(2) To what other class are these analogous?

(3) Describe the first class of these accessories. (4) Furnish examples. (5) What

on the Sabbath, when the mind is disengaged from worldly cares." (5) The conjunctive adverb WHEN is used to introduce such accessories. (6) It indicates coincidence of time—the point in which the principal and accessory agree. This point of time, assumed as fixed in the accessory, serves to determine the time of what is asserted in the principal proposition. Thus, in the examples, *when I shall have finished my work*, determines the time when *I will go to the exhibition*; and "*when* thou sittest in the house," determines a time when the Israelites were to talk of those things which God had commanded through Moses. (7) We may call this the ACCESSORY OF COINCIDENT TIME.

(8) WHEN, like *where*, is of the family of *who*, neuter *what*. It seems to us to be merely an inflection of *who*. The Anglo-Saxon accusative of *hwa* (*who*) is *hwone* or *hwaene*; and *hwaene* is employed adverbially, like *when* in modern English. It may, perhaps, be regarded as originally an *accusative of time*, the word *time* being suppressed, but at first clearly implied — *in* or *at what* (time). In modern use it has come by *insensible extension*, to be considered as *directly expressing* time. (9) *When*, like *where*, usually performs an adverbial function both in the principal and in the accessory propositions, besides serving as a conjunctive word to indicate their connection and relation. Because it performs this last function, we call it a *conjunctive adverb*, as we have, for the same reason, named *where*, *whither*, &c., *conjunctive adverbs*. (10) When is therefore equivalent to the words *in* or *at the time in* or *at which* (time), as may be found by expanding the above compound propositions; thus, *I will go with you at the time, at which (time) I shall have finished my work.* "Thou shalt talk of them" *at* or *in the time in which* "thou sittest," &c.

(11) As in assertions modified by an *accessory of place*, the place is sometimes expressed in the principal proposition (see § 124: 16, 18), so in the compound propositions under consideration, the word of *time* is often in the principal proposition, and *when* retained as the conjunctive word and adverbial modification of the accessory. Example: *This event happened* AT A TIME *when men least expected it. When* is here equi-

conjunctive word is employed? (6) Describe its function in such cases, and illustrate by examples. (7) What name may be given to this accessory?

(8) Repeat what is said of the derivation of WHEN. (9) Describe the functions which it performs; and tell the name given to it in consequence of these functions. (10) To what is it said to be equivalent? Illustrate by example.

(11) What is said about a word of *time* being introduced? Illustrate by example.

valent to *in which*, and when thus expanded, the accessory coincides with the adjective accessory.*

(12) This kind of accessory also often takes precedence, in order of arrangement, of the principal proposition, so that here, as in the case of the accessories of place, the speaker or writer is at liberty to choose the most striking or the most harmonious arrangement, as his own taste may direct. Example: "*When* the morning calls again to toil, begin anew thy journey and thy life." Here, too, when the principal proposition comes after the accessory, the word *then* is sometimes employed in the principal to represent the time determined by the accessory. Thus, "*When* my father and my mother forsake me, *then* the LORD will take me up."

(13) In this form of compound proposition, that takes place which occurs sometimes in other forms of compound propositions; namely, the thought which *logically* is the principal, is expressed under the accessory form, and that which is logically subordinate usurps the form of principal proposition. This is a matter which properly lies within the sphere of the logician and the rhetorician, rather than within the province of the grammarian, whose business is with the *form* not the *matter* of discourse. Whatever has the *form* of an accessory, is to be considered an accessory with the grammarian, without weighing nicely the comparative importance of the thought which it expresses, or the purpose for which a writer or speaker may on occasion choose to employ it. (14) Still, it may prevent misconception to advert to this fact in reference to the use of accessories, and to present examples. "He was one evening sitting thus at his supper, when the landlord of a little inn in the village came into the parlor," &c. =When "he was one evening," &c., for "*the landlord*," &c., is logically the principal proposition, and the first proposition serves only to determine the

* As we use *wherever* to introduce an accessory indicating an unsettled place—*whatever place*—so we employ *whenever*, when we intend to express coincidence with *whatever time;* as, WHENEVER *you choose to walk in the park I will accompany you.* The coincident time in such cases is contingent or unsettled as regards the speaker, except so far forth as the accessory proposition limits it. *Whensoever* was sometimes used for the same purpose by our old authors. Simple *when* is now often employed in expressing coinci dence with *whatever time.*

(12) What is said in reference to the arrangement of this form of compound propositions?

(13) Repeat the remark in reference to the logical importance of the principal and accessory in this form of compound proposition. (14) Illustrate what has been said by examples.

time of the landlord's coming into the parlor. "I was hearing this account," 'continued the corporal,' "*when* the youth came into the kitchen," &c. = When "I was hearing this account," &c.

(15) Before leaving this particular form of accessory, we must observe that it has by *insensible extension* (as we suppose) come to be used when there is either none or only a very slight reference to time. For example: "When we contemplate the close of life,——who can avoid being touched with sensations at once awful and tender?" = the assertion, *nobody* can avoid being touched, &c. We can express nearly the same sense by substituting for *when* the conjunctive word *if*, which has no reference whatever to time; thus, if we contemplate the close of life, &c., or we might express the same sentiment, perhaps somewhat awkwardly, by saying simply, contemplating the close of life, &c. The meaning obviously is, that what is asserted in the principal proposition is a consequence of what is asserted in the accessory. The consequence, or result of contemplating the close of life is, that we cannot avoid, &c. (16) This kind of accessory might, perhaps, with propriety be classed with the accessories of causality which we are soon to consider. Still it has evidently arisen from an insensible extension of the accessory expressive of coincident time, and may be considered as indicating the connection of a cause and its effect by declaring their co-existence in time. (17) In such examples as, *When the sun rises, darkness vanishes*, we may possibly discover the origin of this *insensible extension.* The rising of the sun, which is *coincident* in time with the vanishing of darkness, is also *the cause* of its vanishing. So in other cases the cause of an effect is coincident in point of time with the appearance of the effect, and perhaps from this circumstance the relation of coincidence of time is used to indicate the relation of causality, which is found to accompany it.

(18) We sometimes employ the conjunctive word AS when we intend to express a still closer coincidence or limitation to a point of time. For example, *John arrived* AS *his brother departed.* (19) Sometimes we employ the word *just* with *as* to express more markedly limitation to the same point of time, as *John arrived* JUST AS *his brother departed.* (20) That this form expresses closer limitation to the same

---

(15) Repeat the substance of what is said about the *extension* of this form of accessory to other purposes, and illustrate by an example. (16) What further is said of the classification of the accessory thus used? (17) Repeat the substance of the explanation given of the probable origin of this *extension.*

(18) What other word is sometimes employed to connect this kind of accessory? Give example. (19) What word is added to express more close coincidence? (20) Illustrate the fact that *as* expresses closer coincidence than *when.*

moment than the form with the conjunctive *when* will appear, if we substitute *when* for *as* in the above example. Thus *John arrived when his brother departed*, might mean that John arrived about the time of his brother's departure—perhaps a little after, perhaps a little before; but the form with *as* expresses the exact coincidence of the arrival and departure, and that with *just as* the same thing still more emphatically.

(21) Another form of accessory, related to this as expressing coincidence of time, is that used to indicate that an event succeeded immediately on the completion of another. The conjunctive words used for this purpose are, *as soon as;* thus, *He came to see me*, AS SOON AS *he arrived*. This is more properly classed with the accessory expressive of *equal intensity* employed with adverbs as well as adjectives. Thus, we say, *as quickly as, as rapidly as, as suddenly as*, &c., (see § 120.)

(22) The accessory of coincident *time* is often separated from the principal by a comma, but the punctuation is unsettled.

EXERCISE.—Furnish examples of compound propositions having accessories expressing the limitation of coincident time.

§ 126. 2d. (1) We give, as a second class of accessories of time, those which limit or modify the principal proposition, by predicating something falling *within* the same *period* of time—a period regarded as having duration in opposition to a point or moment of time. (2) We may call this the accessory of coincident duration. (3) The conjunctive words employed for this purpose are *while* and *whilst*. (4) *While* was originally a noun and meant much the same as the word *time;* but never being employed as *subject noun* in the language of the present day, it has come to be classed with the adverbs. This word is really, however, the case of a noun, and is still often employed to express the *accusative of time;* as, *We remained* A WHILE *with them*, or, *We remained* A LONG WHILE *with them*. Here the determinative and descriptive adjectives applied to this word indicate plainly to what class it belongs. The genitive of this word *whiles* was formerly used as we now use *while*, and whilst to express duration of time.

---

(21) What is said of another form of accessory used for nearly the same purpose? (22) Punctuation?

§ 126. (1) Describe the second class of accessories of time. (2) By what name may we call them? (3) What conjunctive words are employed in this case? (4) Give the substance of what is said of *while*.

(5) *Whilst* (or whilest as it is often found written in old authors) appears to be a corruption of the old genitive *whiles*. *Whiles* is stil. found in the language down till the seventeenth century. It is now obsolete, and even whilst is seldom used in modern writings.

(6) We subjoin examples of compound propositions involving this species of accessory. "Seek ye the LORD *while* He may be found." "Agree with thine adversary quickly *whiles* thou art in the way with him." "*While* his humble grave is preparing, * * * * * * it is good for us to think that this man too was our brother."

> "*Whilst* all the stars that round her burn,
> And all the planets, in their turn,
> Confirm the tidings as they roll," &c.

(7) In ancient times the determinative THE was occasionally prefixed to whilst.

> "The whilst in ocean Phœbus dips his wain."

(8) *While*, like *what*, performs a function both for the principal and the accessory in a compound proposition. (9) A word of time, which is sometimes employed in the principal proposition of the preceding class, and referred to by *when*, is rarely, if ever, introduced in this class of compound propositions. (10) The reason of this difference perhaps is that *when* is originally only an adjective having the word *time* implied, but *while* (itself a substantive) originally meant time. Were we to say, as in the case of *when*, *at* or *in the time*, *while*, there would be an awkward repetition of a word of equivalent meaning. And let us remember that to our forefathers this awkwardness would have appeared much greater than to us, since the original meaning of *while* was more familiar to them.

(11) *During the time* is an equivalent expression for *while*. Example: *He was writing* DURING THE TIME *his brother was reading*. *During the time*, we consider here an instance of the *case absolute*—a form of contracted accessory to come under our notice below. In the example we have really three propositions. *He was writing while the time dured (lasted) that his brother was reading.*

(12) The word *while* may also be expanded into the phrase, *and*

---

(5) Repeat what is said of *whilst* and *whiles*.

(6) Furnish examples of compound propositions having this kind of accessories.

(7) Describe an ancient usage in regard of *whilst*.

(8) What functions does *while* perform? (9) Is a word of time used along with it as with *when?* (10) Exp'ain the reason for not using a word of *time* with *while*.

(11) Mention an equivalent expression for *while*, and give an example, and explain the construction.

(12) What other phrase may be substituted for *while?*

at the same time. Thus, "He can live to God and his own sou., *and at the same time* attend to all the lawful interests of the present world." Here a co-ordinate proposition serves the purpose of an accessory. (See § 146: 5, et seq.)

(13) We believe that this form of accessory is sometimes *extended* to express, like the preceding class, the relation of *causality*; but after what we have said already of such *insensible extension*, this need not perplex the learner.

(14) The punctuation here again is unsettled.

EXERCISES I., II., &c.—Furnish examples of this kind of compound propositions.

§ 127. 3d. (1) We may rank as a third class of the accessories of time those which determine the time of the action or event expressed in the principal proposition by reference to something which *succeeded* it, or, in other words, by some action or event which that asserted in the principal proposition *preceded*. (2) This kind of accessory is united to the principal proposition by the preposition BEFORE. (3) Some call *before*, when thus employed, an adverb; but it is used in this case with exactly the same force, as when the grammarians agree in calling it a preposition. (4) The only difference is that in the one case it is followed by a noun, in the other by a proposition, which (when considered apart from the preposition) is substantively used. (5) Hence this, and some of the accessories of time which follow, might with propriety be treated as *substantive accessory propositions with a preposition*, in a manner analogous to the *noun and preposition modification*. (6) We shall call *before*, and other prepositions below, when they precede an accessory, *prepositions* conjunctively employed.

(7) We propose the following as examples of compound propositions involving this species of accessory. *They set out on their journey* BEFORE *the sun rose. I must finish my work* BEFORE *I can go.* "Doth our law judge any man *before* it hear him?" Sometimes the *accessory*, as in many other forms of compound propositions, precedes the

---

(13) Repeat the remark about the extension of this form of accessory.

(14) What is said of punctuation?

§ 127. (1) Describe a third class of accessories of time. (2) What word is employed to connect these? (3) What is said of calling *before* in such cases an adverb? (4) What is the difference between *before* thus employed and *before preposition?* (5) How might this accessory be treated? (6) What shall we call BEFORE thus used?

principal; as, "*Before* I was afflicted I went astray." (8) These compound propositions are equivalent to, *They set out on their journey before* THE TIME IN WHICH *the sun rose.* "*Before* THE TIME IN WHICH *I was afflicted I went astray,*" &c. Here we find the original accessory resolved into the noun *time*, modified by an adjective accessory proposition, and preceded by the preposition *before.* (9) The words, *Before the sun rose* are thus grammatically considered a contracted form for a preposition and a noun modified by an adjective (in this case an adjective accessory); and this is precisely what most *adverbs* are equivalent to. (See § 92: 7.) Hence we have classed this and other forms similarly resolvable as *adverbial accessories.*

(10) The connection of these forms of construction, with the *noun and preposition modification*, or, rather, the fact that the word *before* is in such constructions really a preposition, may be illustrated by introducing a slight change in the form of the first example, without affecting the sense; thus, *They set out on their journey* BEFORE THE RISING *of the sun.* Here we express the same thing by a noun and preposition modification, which is expressed above by an accessory proposition. Now we ask what is the difference between the use of the word *before* here and in the example first given? Does it belong to a distinct class of words in the one use from that to which it belongs in the other?

(11) We may call the accessory now considered, *The adverbial accessory, indicating the precedence in time of the fact asserted in the principal proposition.* More briefly, THE ACCESSORY OF PRECEDENCE IN TIME.

(12) This accessory is not generally separated by a comma from the principal.

EXERCISE.—Furnish compound propositions of this form.

§ 128. 4th. (1) There is a fourth class of these accessories of time exactly similar in form to the preceding class, but indicating subsequence or posteriority in point of time. (2) In these accessories the prepositions *after* and *since* serve *conjunctively.* (3) Examples: *John arrived* AFTER *his brother departed. John arrived* SINCE *his brother departed.* Both accessories express the *subsequence* of the fact asserted in the principal proposition. (4) When we use *after*

---

(7) Produce the examples. (8) Illustrate the manner of resolving these compound propositions into compounds of another form. (9) What is shown by this resolution?

(10) Illustrate the fact that the word *before* performs the same function before accessories as it does before nouns.

(11) Give a name to this accessory. (12) Punctuation?

§ 128. (1) What is said of the fourth class of accessories of *time?* (2) What conjunctive words are used to connect them? (3) Furnish examples. (4) State the distinction drawn between the accessory connected by *after*, and the accessory connected by *since?*

we indicate subsequence to another event *near* in point of time (subsequence to a proximate event) predicated by the accessory. When, on the contrary, we use *since*, we have reference to the portion of time which has elapsed from the event predicated by the accessory; and we assert that at any point in this period, near to or distant from the time indicated by the accessory, the principal event may have happened.

(5) Sometimes the accessory with *since* seems to indicate a reference, not to a *point* in the period elapsed as above, but to the whole continuous period from the moment of the event indicated by the accessory till that of making the principal assertion. (This seeming reference to the whole intervening time depends, perhaps, rather on the nature of the principal proposition than on the form of the accessory.) Thus, *John has been successful* SINCE *he commenced business for himself. That man has been faithful* SINCE *he has been in my service.*

(6) *Since* is sometimes employed in a way in which it is *apparently* equivalent to the word *ago*; thus, *It is five years* SINCE *I saw that man.* This is nearly, but not precisely equivalent to, *I saw that man five years* AGO. In the form given in the example, we dwell on the consideration of the *length of time* passed from the period at which we saw the man. In the other this is not brought under consideration. The example first given is equivalent to, *Five whole years have passed from the time in which I saw that man.*

(7) *After* is sometimes followed by *that*; as, "After *that* I have spoken, mock on." This form of expression is now antiquated. The words *the time* are perhaps here suppressed between *after* and *that.*

(8) PUNCTUATION.—The same as in the preceding construction. In neither completely settled. In both, when the accessory precedes, a comma is usually inserted.

EXERCISE.—Furnish compound propositions constructed according to the model presented in the examples.

§ 129. 5th. (1) There is a fifth form of these accessories of time which limits the principal assertion by expressing an anticipated

---

(5) What further is said of the use of *since*?
(6) What is said of *since* used nearly in the sense of *ago*?
(7) By what word is *after* sometimes followed? And what is said of this construction?
(8) Punctuation?
§ 129. (1) Describe a fifth class of accessories of *time*. (2) What words connect these,

event to which it has reference and in which it terminates. (2) The words used to connect and indicate this species of accessory are the prepositions *till* and *until*. When thus used, we may call them *prepositions conjunctively employed*.

(3) Examples: *You will remain here* TILL, *or* UNTIL *I return. He must not depart* TILL *the courier arrives.* "All the days of my appointed time will I wait, *till* my change come." "Go thou thy way *till* the end be." "The people will not eat *until* he come." (4) Here the anticipated event (expressed in the accessory) which the principal assertion regards, and in which it terminates, is future at the time of speaking, because the main assertion itself has reference to the future. (5) But when the main assertion has reference to the past, the anticipated event expressed in the accessory, though future at the time to which the assertion refers, may be past when the assertion is uttered. Example: "I was wandering in a beautiful and romantic country, *till* curiosity began to give way to weariness," &c. (6) We may call this *The accessory limiting by an event in anticipation;* or, for the sake of brevity, THE ACCESSORY OF ANTICIPATION.

(7) PUNCTUATION.—When the accessory is strictly limiting, a comma is not inserted; when, as in the last example and the third above, it does *not* limit strictly, a comma is used.

(8) We need not repeat the observations made in reference to the accessory indicating precedence of time. The observations were intended to apply to all those accessories which are connected with the principal assertion by means of prepositions.

EXERCISE.—Furnish examples of this form of compound propositions.

REMARKS.—(9) Before passing from the consideration of the adverbial accessories of *time*, we may notice that co-existence and immediate subsequence in point of time are sometimes indicated by the co-ordinate construction of propositions. Example:

"Up rose the sonne, and up rose Emilie."—Chauc.

This is equivalent to *Emily rose, when the sun rose*, or *as the sun rose*, or immediately after the sun rose. But more of this hereafter when we come to treat of co-ordinate construction. (See § 146.)

---

and what is said of these words? (3) Give examples. (4) Repeat the remark in reference to these examples. (5) What is said of the case when the main assertion refers to the past? Illustrate by an example. (6) What may we call this class of accessories? (7) Punctuation?

(8) What observations apply to this class of accessories, and others preceded by prepositions?

:* what is said of another way of expressing coincidence of time.

(10) We may also notice here, what we shall have occasion to notice at more length presently, that accessories of time are sometimes apparently introduced by two separate conjunctive words. We have an example in the following lines of Milton;

"*As when* Alcides from Œchalia crowned
With conquest, felt the envenomed robe," &c.

(11) The two conjunctive words *as* and *when* here perform separate and distinct functions, that is they connect, not the same, but different pairs of propositions. *As* indicates a comparison with the preceding facts, and connects a compound accessory of manner, of which the principal proposition being clearly implied is suppressed, and only the accessory part of this compound accessory proposition of manner is expressed. If we supply the words *it happened* or some similar proposition after *as*, we shall see clearly the nature of the construction and the distinct functions of the conjunctive words; thus, AS *it happened*, or, as happened, WHEN *Alcides*, &c.

§ 130. (1) We next proceed to consider a numerous class of accessory propositions which have been called by some of the German grammarians *accessories of causality*. (2) The leading accessories of this general class assign a cause or reason for the assertion in the principal proposition; and hence the name given to them. Some of the accessories thus classed come properly within this designation, others we think it better to arrange under more distinctive names.*

* This class of accessories, and all the classes generally which follow, affect the whole proposition to which they are attached, not the subject or predicate separately, or any single word in them. In this they are distinct from the preceding classes, which usually modify some word either expressed or implied in the principal proposition. We shall find too that their grammatical connection with the principal proposition is, at least in some cases, much more loose. Some of them as we shall presently see, though, perhaps, entitled to the name of accessory propositions, are scarcely to be considered as *dependent, subordinate,* or *modifying* propositions. They are, indeed, subjoined to other propositions, and may on this account be called accessories, but they express an independent thought. They may be considered perhaps as forming an intermediate class between subordinate and co-ordinate, or modifying and completely independent propositions.

(10) What other remark is made about accessories of time? Illustrate by example. (11) Explain the distinct uses of the two conjunctive words.

§ 130. (1) What general name is given to the class of accessories next to be considered? (2) What remarks are made in reference to this general class?

1st. (3) We shall consider first those which are more strictly accessories of *causality*, which express literally *a cause* for what is asserted in the principal proposition. (4) These we shall distinguish by the name of CAUSAL ADVERBIAL ACCESSORIES, or ADVERBIAL ACCESSORIES OF CAUSALITY. (5) The conjunctive word most generally employed in introducing these and expressing their peculiar relation to the principal proposition is BECAUSE.

(6) We proceed to illustrate the form and use of this accessory by examples. *I cannot go with you*, BECAUSE *I have not time.* The accessory *I have not time* is here evidently introduced for the purpose of expressing the cause for which *I cannot go with you.* (7) This kind of accessory is often arranged by our more ancient authors before the principal proposition which it completes. Examples: "Because thou hast done this, thou art cursed," &c. "Because I live, ye shall live also." It is most usual in modern English to place the accessory after the principal in such compound propositions.

(8) The word *because* may be regarded as a noun and preposition (= *by cause*) modifying the verb in the principal proposition. (9) When *because* is thus regarded, the accessory which follows it is properly speaking *an apposition complement* to the noun *cause.* We may illustrate this by reference to the first example; thus, *I cannot go* BY *(a or the)* CAUSE *expressed in the accessory;* namely, *I have not time* = *I cannot go, I have not time is the cause.* (10) *That* is sometimes (though rarely, we think, by correct speakers or writers) introduced after because; thus, *I cannot go,* BECAUSE THAT *I have not time.* (11) When this rather clumsy form of expression occurs, *that* is to be regarded as a determinative placed before the accessory used substantively *in apposition* with *cause.*

(12) For *because* we can substitute *for the or this reason that;* thus, *I cannot go with you,* FOR THIS REASON, THAT *I have not time.* Here the accessory preceded by the determinative is to be regarded as an apposition modification to the noun *reason.*

(13) Other words besides *because* are sometimes used to introduce

---

(3) Describe the subdivision first to be considered. (4) By what name do we distinguish them? (5) What is the conjunctive word most frequently employed?

(6) Give examples. (7) What is said of arrangement? Example.

(8) What is said of the word *because?* (9) What does the accessory become, when *because* is thus regarded? Illustrate. (10) What word is sometimes introduced after *because?* (11) How is *that*, when thus introduced, to be regarded?

(12) What phrase can be substituted for *because?*

(13) What other words, besides *because*, are used to indicate *causality?* Illustrate.

a causal accessory. Among these we may enumerate *since*, *seeing that*, *as*, *whereas*. We might substitute any of these conjunctive expressions for *because* in the above examples without much change of the sense, though some of them would give an antiquated appearance to the *form* of the language. Thus, *I cannot go*, SINCE *I have not time. I cannot go*, SEEING *or* SEEING THAT *I have not time.**

(14) These conjunctive words differ from *because* in this, that they intimate that the cause assigned in the accessory is manifest—apparent to the party addressed. (15) Thus, *I cannot go*, SINCE *or* SEEING THAT *I have not time*, is equivalent to *I cannot go*, *the reason is apparent to yourself*, viz.; *I have not time*, or *I cannot go*, *you see I have not time.* Using *as* we say, *I cannot go*, AS *I have not time.* (16) This may be regarded as a less formal, less forcible way of alleging a cause for not going. (17) With the conjunctive *whereas*, we say WHEREAS *I have not time*, *I cannot go.* When this word is used, the accessory comes first. But *whereas* is now seldom employed except in contracts and formal papers.

(18) PUNCTUATION.—Here a comma is inserted between principal and accessory.

EXERCISES.—Furnish examples of this construction.

§ 131. 2d. (1) There is a species of accessory very similar to the last, sometimes interchanging place with it, in which the preposition FOR serves chiefly as the conjunctive word. (2) The proper use of this species of accessory seems to be to express a *reason*—an *argument* to enforce the assertion in the principal proposition; in other words, to express a *logical cause.* (3) We do not think that *for conjunctive* (that is employed before an accessory) is entirely restricted to cases in which the *cause* is of a *logical nature*,

* *Since* in this sense and *seeing* may be regarded as different forms of the same word. It is not so certain that *since*, which we have had occasion to notice in treating of accessories of time, and which means from a *definite time onward* or *down* is exactly the same word, though agreeing now in form. (See Diversions of Purley on these words. R. Taylor's Ed. p. 144.)

---

(14) How do these conjunctive words differ from *because?* (15) Illustrate by examples. (16) How may this mode of expression be regarded? (17) What is said of the use of the word *whereas?* (18) What is the usage as to punctuation?

§ 131. (1) Describe another form of accessory similar to the preceding, and tell the conjunctive word. (2) What is the proper use of this accessory? (3) What is said in reference to its restriction to this use?

or what is properly called a *reason*. Our older authors, we think, sometimes use it where *modern* usage would demand *because*.*

(4) Upon the whole, we think that FOR *conjunctive* is now seldom employed for any other purpose except that of *assigning a reason*. We select a few examples for the purpose of illustration. (5) We can find the most abundant examples of this use of *for* in the writings of the apostle Paul as rendered in our authorized translation. (6) In the translation, we find conjunctive *for* used only, as far as we recollect, to introduce an *argument*—a *reason* for some preceding assertion, or statement of doctrine embracing perhaps numerous propositions. (7) It is often used in the commencement of a new sentence to indicate the connection between it and the preceding discourse. (8) "In all these things we are more than conquerors, through him that loved us. FOR I am persuaded that neither death, nor life, &c., shall be able to separate us from the love of God." Here FOR introduces the apostle's reason, or argument to corroborate the assertion, "*In all these things we are more than conquerors.*" (9) We extract another short passage from the Epistle to the Romans, in which there are five examples of this species of accessory. "*For* with the heart man believeth unto righteousness; and with the mouth confession is made unto salvation. *For* the scripture saith, Whosoever believeth on him shall not be ashamed. *For* there is no difference between the Jew and the Greek; *for* the same Lord over all is rich unto all that call upon him. *For* whosoever shall call upon the name of the Lord shall be saved." (10) The first *for* indicates the purpose of the first proposition quoted; namely, that of an accessory to corroborate the sentiments uttered in the preceding verses. The purpose served by

* *For* is sometimes employed as a simple preposition (that is, before a single noun as opposed to an accessory proposition), in assigning a physical cause, though this is only one purpose for which it is employed, and perhaps the purpose for which it is now most rarely employed. Thus, *He acts so* FOR *fear; He cannot do so* FOR *shame*, FOR *pride*, &c. It is now more common to use another form of expression in such cases; thus, *He acts so* BECAUSE *of fear*, THROUGH *fear*, or, *On account of fear*, according to the particular manner in which the word *fear* may be modified.

---

(4) Repeat the opinion given in reference to the use of FOR conjunctive. (5) Where may we find abundant examples of this use of FOR to connect an accessory? (6) What is said of the use of FOR in the authorized translation? (7) For what purpose is it said to be often employed? (8) Adduce examples for illustration. (9) Present a written copy of the passage from Romans in which FOR occurs five times. (10) Show the use of each of these

for in other parts of the extract can be discovered without reference to any thing beyond what it contains. (11) "*For*, *for* this cause pay ye tribute also." Here the first *for* is *conjunctive*, the second a *preposition*. When the passage is arranged in a different order, the construction is perfectly clear. *For* ye pay tribute for this cause. (12) Though the word *cause* occurs in this accessory, the proposition as a whole expresses a *reason*, not a *cause* as distinguished from a reason.

(13) For is often followed by other *conjunctive* words. When this occurs, the student will take notice that the two *conjunctive* words introduce (except they form a compound conjunction) two distinct accessories. (14) We often find *for* followed by *if*, sometimes by *when*. Examples, "*For*, *if* Abraham were justified by works, he hath whereof to glory." Let us change the arrangement, and it will become manifest that the two conjunctive words belong to, and introduce distinct propositions. Thus, FOR *Abraham hath whereof to glory*, IF *he were (was) justified by works.* "*For*, *when* ye were the servants of sin, ye were free from righteousness," = FOR *ye were free from righteousness*, WHEN *ye were the servants of sin.* (15) We find sometimes three conjunctive words together, each introducing a distinct accessory. Example: "*For*, *if*, *when* we were enemies, we were reconciled to God by the death of his Son; much more, being reconciled, we shall be saved by his life." Here *for* introduces the whole compound accessory, having connection especially with the main or leading proposition in this compound accessory, "much more, being reconciled, we shall be saved by his life." *If* introduces the proposition "we were reconciled by the death of his Son"—an accessory to the main proposition just mentioned; and *when* introduces the proposition before which it immediately stands, "we were enemies," which is an accessory to "if we were reconciled to God," &c. So that this last is the accessory of a compound accessory of a main compound accessory. If we arrange the passage in the following order, the student will readily see the functions which the several conjunctive words perform. FOR, *being reconciled to God, we shall much more be saved by the life of his Son*, IF *we were reconciled by his death*, WHEN *we were enemies.* (16) The

---

conjunctive FORS, viz., the propositions which they connect. (11) Give an example with two consecutive FORS. Explain it. (12) Repeat the remark about the word cause.

(13) What is said of cases in which FOR is followed by other conjunctions? (14) By what *conjunctions* is *for* often followed? Write the two examples, and, with them before you, explain the connection. (15) Write out the example commencing with three conjunctions, and explain the connection of the passage. (16) Repeat the substance of the remarks which follow

reader will observe how vastly inferior this arrangement is to that of the translators in energy, and even in perspicuity. This may teach us to appreciate the skill of the translators (Wiclif is the leader, followed by Tyndale, Cranmer, &c.), and the importance and difficulty of the art of arranging language, so as to express our thoughts with clearness and with force. It will be seen that it was not without reason that three conjunctive words are huddled together in this construction. Still this huddling together of conjunctive words, though here employed for good purpose, is not to be imitated, without the most urgent reasons.*

(17) We may call this species of accessory, THE ARGUMENTATIVE ACCESSORY. By *argumentative* in this case we mean that which assigns a *reason* or *argument*.

(18) PUNCTUATION.—Such accessories are usually separated from their principal by a comma, if not, as in many of the above examples, by a greater point.

We may notice some compounds of *for*, which are used, especially in older writers, to serve nearly similar purposes with *for* conjunctive. (19) We may enumerate *forasmuch as*, *for that*, *for why*, among these. (20) The accessory which originally followed *forasmuch as*, was, no doubt, a sort of Accessory of the Comparison of Equality, indicating that the principal assertion had an equal extent with the assertion in the accessory. But this form of expression has now come *insensibly* to indicate a *reason*, perhaps sometimes a *cause*, in the same way as the accessory with *since* or *seeing that* has come to do the same thing. This accessory, with *forasmuch as*, has the same form with the *Accessory of Equal Intensity* (*much* being the adjective compared), only that *for* is introduced before the *as* which precedes the adjective.†

* It would form a useful grammatical exercise to select a number of passages similar to those above, and then ascertain which proposition each conjunctive word serves to introduce. Abundant examples can be found in the same treasury from which we have selected the above specimens.

† If we admit that *much* is here *substantively* employed (that is, has a noun *implied*, which it certainly has), the form exactly coincides with the following, in which the accessory is evidently of the class to which we have

(17) By what name may we call this accessory?

(18) Remark on punctuation.

(19) Enumerate some compounds of FOR used by old writers for similar purposes. (20) Repeat the substance of what is said about the accessory which follows *forasmuch as*, illustrating by examples. Write the examples.

Examples: "*Forasmuch as* I know that thou hast been of many years a judge unto this nation, I do the more cheerfully answer for myself," = *Since*, or *seeing that* I know, &c. The accessory, "Forasmuch as I know," &c., expresses the apostle's *reason* for more cheerfully answering for himself; or, if you please, the *cause* that he more cheerfully answered for himself, but a *logical*, not a *physical cause*. "Be ye steadfast, unmovable, always abounding in the work of the Lord, *forasmuch as* ye know that your labor is not in vain in the Lord," = *Since ye know*, &c., in the Greek simply *knowing that*. Here the accessory follows the principal proposition; in the former example it preceded it.

(21) We also meet with *Forasmuch then as* = *therefore since*, or *therefore if*. For example, "*Forasmuch then as* we are the offspring of God, we ought not to think that the Godhead is like unto gold," &c. = THEREFORE SINCE *we are the offspring*, &c. Both *then* in the example and *therefore* in our substitute belong to, and connect the second proposition, or rather the whole compound proposition, "we ought not," &c., with the preceding discourse. "Forasmuch as we are the offspring of God" is the accessory in this compound proposition.

(22) These accessories which commence with *forasmuch as*, are represented in some of the other versions by accessories commencing with *because*, *since*, and in Wiclif (Luke xix. 9), by *for that*.

(23) *Inasmuch as* is also employed nearly in the same way, but retaining more similarity to the accessory of Equal Intensity. (See Ex. Heb. vii. 20.)

(24) In Wiclif's translation, as above noticed, we have *for that* = *since* or *because*, and in James iv. 15, our translators have employed *for that* as equivalent to *therefore*. "*For that* ye ought to say," &c. = THEREFORE *ye ought to say*. The word *therefore* in fact is *for that* inverted; since *there* is simply the dative feminine corresponding to *that*, now used as of all genders. The dative *there* is used because

given the name of accessories of equal intensity. *It is outrageous* FOR AS RICH A MAN AS *you are to oppress the poor;* or, *for a man as rich*, &c. We believe this is English, though *so* would be more proper before the adjective than *as;* at all events, the example will serve the purpose of illustration.

---

(21) Repeat in substance what is said of *forasmuch then as*. Illustrate by examples.

(22) Repeat the remark about accessories with *forasmuch as*.

(23) Remark in reference to *inasmuch as?*

(24) Repeat the remarks in reference to *for that*, and *therefore*, and show the relation between these expressions.

in the Anglo-Saxon, the preposition *for* takes a dative or accusative with it. *Therefore*, more properly written *therefor* = *for there* = modern *for that*.

(25) *In that* is used to connect accessories of similar import. Examples: "Thou hast shamed this day the faces of all thy servants * * * *in that* thou lovest thine enemies," &c. = BECAUSE *thou lovest thine enemies*, &c. "And was heard *in that* he feared." This is intended, we presume, to mean *because he feared*. (Marginal reading "For his pietie;" Wiclif, "and was herd for his reverence;" Tyndale, "was also hearde because of his godliness.")

(26) *For that* and *in that* may be considered obsolete as conjunctions. The accessories in which they occur may be treated as substantive accessories preceded by *that* determinative, having the prepositions *for* and *in* prefixed with the same force as when they are prefixed to nouns. (27) This is the ultimate result of a thorough analysis of this sort of accessories, and it is best and perhaps easiest to come to this at once, especially in cases which are rare of occurrence or not to be found except in ancient authors. Accessories which are of frequent recurrence we may class, and bring under a formula and a denomination, to which we may refer without the trouble of having recourse in every case to complete analysis.

EXAMPLE.—Furnish examples of compound propositions with argumentative accessories.

§ 132. There is a kind of accessories which it may be useful to consider in connection with the causal and argumentative accessories, because by contrast they may serve to illustrate each other. (1) Instead of expressing a *cause* or a *reason* the class we are about to consider express an *effect* or a consequence. (2) Like the causal, they are of two species. (3) One species exhibits the *effects* which proceed from *physical causes*, the other the *conclusions* or *inferences* deduced from arguments or reasonings. (4) The word *therefore* is much used in introducing both these species of accessories. (5) We may call the first *The Accessory of Effect*, the second *The Accessory of Inference*.

---

(25) What is said of the use of *in that?* Illustrate by example.

(26) How may *for that* and *in that* be considered? How may the accessories which they connect be treated when they occur? (27) Repeat the remark.

§ 132. (1) Describe, generally, another class of accessories. (2) How many species of these? (3) Distinguish those two species. (4) What word is employed to connect them. (5) By what names may we call them?

(6) We submit examples of the accessory of effect. *This farm is carefully cultivated*, THEREFORE *it is productive. The soil in this place is good, therefore the trees grow large.* (7) The first proposition in both examples expresses a *physical cause* to which that expressed in the subjoined propositions (which for the time we call accessories) is ascribed. *Cause*—the soil is good; *effect*—the trees grow large. "I believed, *therefore* have I spoken." Here again is a physical though immaterial cause—a cause acting through the medium of the human mind.

(8) We can in all such cases employ the causal form of accessory to express nearly the same meaning, by making what we have here regarded for the time being as the *accessory* the principal in a new compound proposition, and giving the *principal*, or what we have been above regarding as *principal*, the form and accompaniment of an accessory of cause. Thus, *This farm is productive*, BECAUSE *it is carefully cultivated. The trees grow large in this place*, BECAUSE *the soil is good. I have spoken*, BECAUSE *I believed.*

(9) Again, we have many examples in which the one proposition assumes the form of the accessory of cause, and the other the form of what we have been calling the accessory of effect. (10) Thus, "*Because* sentence against an evil work is not executed speedily, *therefore* the heart of the sons of men is fully set in them to do evil." The question here presents itself, which of these propositions shall we consider accessory? Both have accessory forms, or, at least, the form which a proposition assumes when it is to be connected with another. We think that the proposition which expresses the effect is to be considered the principal one. It is so *logically*, and grammar and logic should be exhibited as accordant, when it is possible to do so, without straining the construction of language or the laws of thought.

(11) It seems to follow from what we have now said, that what we call the *accessory of effect* is not properly a *subordinate* or merely *modifying* proposition; but either, as in the last example, the principal proposition, or a second independent proposition referring back by the medium of the word *therefore* to the preceding proposition as expressing something which stands to what it expresses in the relation of *cause* to *effect*. The relation in which the two propositions, in such

---

(6) Give examples. (7) Repeat the substance of the illustration.

(8) What form of expression can be substituted for that above? Describe the substitution, and illustrate by examples.

(9) Describe another form in which such compound propositions are presented. (10) Write the example, and holding this, answer the question discussed; namely, which proposition shall we in such cases consider as the accessory?

(11) Repeat the substance of what is said in reference to the accessory of effect.

compound propositions as we have given above as examples, stand, may be regarded as intermediate between the relation of principal and subordinate, and of co-ordinate propositions united in the manner which we shall consider presently. That their relation is very nearly the same as that of co-ordinate propositions, is rendered evident by the fact, that we can unite them by the copulative *and* without injury to their relation to one another or any change of the sense which they convey. Thus, *This farm is carefully cultivated*, AND *therefore it is productive.* These remarks apply with equal force to the *accessory of inference*, which we are about to consider.

(12) We have more formal methods of introducing an accessory of effect —such as, *for this cause*, or, *for that cause*, *because of this*, *on this account.* (13) We would treat propositions commencing in this way as independent, save that by these forms of expression they refer back to a cause involved in the preceding discourse. (14) *Therefore*, when employed in what we call the accessory of effect, may be regarded as an abbreviated method of expressing *for this* or *that cause. There*, as we have already had occasion to remark, is equivalent to *that* in the dative case, and joined with *for* (in the inverted order common in the earlier stages of our language) forms *therefore*=*for that* or *this*, and when it precedes the accessory of effect=*for this* or *that cause*, the word *cause* being *implied.*

(15) PUNCTUATION.—A comma is always inserted between the propositions in this kind of construction.

EXERCISE.—Produce examples of the form of construction described.

§ 133. ACCESSORY OF INFERENCE.—(1) The conjunctive adverb *therefore* is also employed to connect the accessory of inference, which is a proposition expressing a conclusion or inference drawn from an argument contained in the preceding proposition, or, as often happens, in a larger portion of the preceding discourse.

(2) Examples: *This farm is productive*, THEREFORE *it is carefully cultivated.* That is, *for the reason* that the farm is productive *I conclude*, or *infer* that it is carefully cultivated. *The trees in this place are large*, THEREFORE *the soil must be good.* That is, from the fact that

---

(12) Mention more formal methods of introducing an accessory of effect. (13) How may propositions commencing in this way be treated? (14) Repeat remarks on *therefore*. (15) Punctuation?

§ 133. (1) Describe the *accessory of inference*, and tell the word which connects it.

(2) Illustrate by examples.

the trees are large, stated in the first proposition, I *conclude* that the soil must be good.

(3) This accessory must be carefully distinguished from that which expresses a physical effect. The meanings expressed by these two accessories, though apparently so like in form, are altogether dissimilar. It is by no means intended to assert above that the goodness of the soil is the *effect* of the largeness of the trees, or that the careful cultivation is the effect of the productiveness of the farm. It may perhaps be regarded as a defect in our language that the same word THEREFORE is employed for these two purposes so dissimilar, and, in many cases, so apparently inconsistent. We must guard against being misled by this double use of *therefore*. We might distinguish these uses by naming *therefore* employed for the first purpose *therefore causal*, that is, *therefore* introducing an effect and referring back to its cause, and naming *therefore* employed for the second purpose, as it has been named by the logicians already, *therefore illative*, that is, *therefore* introducing an *inference* or *conclusion* of the understanding from a preceding argument. (4) The learner will perhaps understand the matter better, if we tell him plainly that the difference of meaning arises from the different words *implied* with the determinative part of *therefore* in the two cases. These words we have already seen are *cause* and *reason*. In the first use *therefore* is equivalent to *for this* or *that* CAUSE, as we have shown above; in the second it is equivalent to *for this* or *that* REASON.

(5) We have already taken occasion to say that the remarks in reference to the relation between the accessory of effect and the principal proposition, apply to the relation of the accessory of inference to the principal proposition. The accessory of inference, like the accessory of effect, is not properly an accessory in the sense which implies *subordination*, or *subservience* to the mere *completion* of a principal proposition. Here, too, we can introduce the *copulative conjunction* before the accessory—indicating *co-ordination* or *independence* to a certain extent. Thus, *The trees in this place are large*, AND *therefore the soil must be good.*

(6) This kind of connection of the *inference* with the *argument* is often more formally indicated by such expressions as *from this I infer*,

---

(3) Repeat the caution against confounding the accessory of effect and the accessory of inference. Illustrate the difference. (4) Give an explanation that will appear more clear to those not conversant with logical distinctions.

(5) Repeat substance of remark as to the true nature of this so-called accessory.

(6) Mention more formal methods of indicating the connection of *inference* with *argument*.

or *conclude that*, *for this reason I infer that*, *hence I conclude that*, &c. Here we see that *therefore*, like many other *conjunctive* words, serves the purpose of a distinct proposition to assert the relation between two other propositions.

(7) *Then* and *now*, both originally adverbs of *time*, are frequently employed between propositions with a slightly *illative* or *inferential* force, sometimes with a merely *continuative* force. In other words, they are sometimes employed to introduce less formally—less emphatically, a proposition which expresses an inference or conclusion, and sometimes one which is only a continuation of the same train of thought —a continuation of the same argument. (8) We illustrate by examples: "We *then* that are strong ought to bear the infirmities of the weak." This is obviously an inference drawn from the preceding reasoning, and we might substitute *therefore* for *then* without any other effect, save giving stronger indication of *inference*. "Tell me *now* what thou hast done." "*Now*, as soon as it was day, there was no small stir among the soldiers," &c. "Now that which decayeth and waxeth old is ready to vanish away." In these examples *now* is slightly illative. Sometimes the translators of the Bible employ both *then* and *now* together; as, "Now then, it is no more I that do it," &c. (9) *So* expressive of manner often precedes both *then* and *now conjunctively* employed. In the same way it sometimes, but perhaps more rarely, precedes *because* and *since*. *So* in such cases is to be treated as an *adverb* of *manner*=*in such manner*, referring to *a manner* already expressed—*a manner common* to the proposition or some part of the discourse which precedes and the proposition which follows.

(10) The employment of both *then* and *now* for the purpose described above, has, no doubt, arisen from an *insensible extension* of their proper adverbial use. A transition has been (naturally enough) made from using *then* to indicate a definite, distinct *time* to indicate a definite, distinct *juncture* of circumstances; from using *now* to indicate a present *time* to indicate a present *juncture* of circumstances, described in the preceding discourse. (11) *Then* is a formation from *the* or *that*, an accusative most likely, and still means *that* with the word *time* implied=*at* or *in that time*. Now the transition from *in that time* to *in that case* or *in that juncture of circumstances*, is both natural and easy. The same has happened to *when*, perhaps (as we have

(7) State the substance of what is said of the conjunctive use of *then* and *now*. (8) Illustrate this use of these words by examples. (9) State the substance of what is said of the use of *so* in connection with *then* and *now*.

(10) What explanation is given of the inferential use of *then* and *now*? (11) Repeat

already observed) originally like *then* an accusative of *time*, the word *time* being in both cases *implied*. (12) We illustrate this by examples, in some of which we may find these words in the state of transition from the expression of time to the expression of a case or conjuncture of circumstances. "*Then* shall I not be ashamed, *when* I have respect unto all thy commandments." *Then—when* might here be taken in their original sense=*at that time—in which time*, and give some sort of approximation to the sense; but it is evident that they rather indicate the *same case*, the *same conjuncture of circumstances*, than the *same time*. "If our youngest brother be with us, *then* will we go down." "For now should I have lain still and been quiet, I should have slept: *then* had I been at rest with kings and counsellors of the earth." "He seeth wickedness also; will he not *then* consider?" In these examples, if we substitute the words *in that case* for *then*, we shall express the sense intended. (13) In the same manner we might illustrate the use of *now*=*in this case* by examples. We shall content ourselves with one as a sample. "There is therefore *now* no condemnation," &c.=There is therefore *in this case* — *in the conjuncture* described in the preceding discourse, no condemnation, &c. *

(14) We shall presently notice that *then* is employed in the principal proposition of hypotheticals in the same way—as equivalent to *in this case*.

(15) Punctuation.—A comma is inserted between the principal and accessory.

Exercise.—Furnish examples of compound propositions containing *Accessories of Inference*.

---

* It is worthy of remark that in translating the passage partially quoted above (Rom. viii. 1), Wiclif, the Rheims, and the authorized version, employ *now;* Tyndale, Cranmer, and the Geneva version, *then;* all evidently intending to express the same sense. This shows that there is little difference between *then* and *now* in this use. It proves also that they have, when thus employed, been diverted from their more common acceptation; for, where time is distinctly implied, it is impossible to make such an interchange between these words, without a marked change of the sense. They refer to opposed points of *time*. "*Then* I was happy, but *now* I am miserable."

---

what is said of the origin of the word *then*. (12) Illustrate the transition in the case of *then* and *when* from their original to this secondary use. Write out examples.

(13) Illustrate the *illative* use of now by an example.

(14) Repeat the remark about *then* used in hypotheticals.

(15) Punctuation?

§ 134. (1) The next kind of accessory which we shall consider is that which expresses the purpose of what is asserted in the *principal proposition.* (2) This we may call THE ACCESSORY OF PURPOSE. (3) This accessory is generally introduced by THAT *conjunctive.* (4) Example: *I have come that I may assist you*=*I have come* TO *assist you*, or, *I have come* TO *your assistance.*

(5) This accessory may perhaps fairly be regarded as a substantive accessory in the dative case. This appears plainly enough when, as in the example above, we can substitute a noun for the proposition. *I have come* TO *your assistance.* Here *to your assistance*=a dative, since the preposition *to* expresses the *dative* relation. (6) This accessory is very often contracted into the corresponding *infinitive* or verbal noun, and then becomes what we have already, in treating of the complements in simple propositions, called the *infinitive of purpose.**

(7) *That* serves, as we have seen, to introduce several kinds of accessory propositions. We may easily ascertain whether the accessory is an accessory of purpose by trying to substitute *in order that* for simple *that.* If we can do so without injury to the sense, we have the accessory of purpose.

(8) PUNCTUATION.—A comma generally separates the principal and accessory propositions.

EXERCISE.—Furnish examples of compound propositions containing an accessory of purpose.

§ 135. There is another form of proposition which may be brought within the class of accessories of purpose. (1) The *purpose* in the form to which we refer is *negative*, or, perhaps, we should rather say, *preventive.* (2) This accessory is introduced and connected with the principal proposition by the *conjunctive* word *lest,*

* Those acquainted with Anglo-Saxon will observe that all these forms of expression commence with prepositions which, in that language, take after them a *dative.* This justifies the assertion that this species of accessory may be considered as a substantive accessory in the *dative* relation.

---

§ 134. (1) Describe the accessory next to be considered. (2) Name? (3) *Conjunctive word?* (4) Illustrate by example. (5) How may this accessory be regarded? (6) Into what is it frequently contracted?

(7) What is remarked of *that*, and how may we distinguish *that* thus employed?

(8) Punctuation?

§ 135. (1) Describe another species of accessory of purpose. (2) *Conjunctive word?*

which is nearly equivalent to *that not.* (3) We may call this, for distinction's sake, *the accessory of purpose preventive.*

(4) Example: *I make my visit short,* LEST *I may interfere with your occupations* = *I make my visit short,* THAT *I may* NOT *interfere,* or IN ORDER THAT *I may* NOT *interfere,* &c. (5) We sometimes employ the *hypothetical* form of the verb instead of the *conditional* in this kind of accessories; thus, *I make my visit short,* LEST *I* SHOULD *interfere,* &c. The *conditional* form is proper, when we know that the party addressed has definite business on hand, which we do not wish to interrupt; the *hypothetical* when we know nothing definite, but wish to intimate our desire not to interfere with occupations which the party addressed may *possibly* have on hand. (6) This form of accessory is very common in our language. Examples: "Love not sleep, *lest* thou come to poverty." "Make no friendship with an angry man, and with a furious man thou shalt not go; *lest* thou learn his ways," &c. "Give me neither poverty nor riches; feed me with food convenient for me; *lest* I be full, and deny thee, and say, Who is the Lord? or *lest* I be poor, and steal, and take the name of my God in vain."

(7) PUNCTUATION.—Separate by a point.

EXERCISE.—Furnish examples involving the accessory of purpose preventive.

§ 136. EXCEPTIVE ACCESSORY PROPOSITION.—(1) We may next mention what we shall call the exceptive accessory, which is generally introduced by the exceptive conjunction UNLESS. (2) Example: *I cannot succeed,* UNLESS *my friends assist me.*

(3) We supply an example from Hooker, "Seeing then no man can plead eloquently *unless* he be able first to speak; it followeth, that ability of speech is in this case a thing most necessary."—Hooker, B. I. ch. 14. This affords a good example for practice in analysis. The whole compound proposition expresses a conclusion or inference introduced by the illative or continuative conjunctive word *then,* which neither claims precedence, as would be natural, nor is united to its own proposition, "it followeth," which is the leading one of the whole

---

(3) Name? (4) Example? (5) What form of the verb is sometimes employed instead of the *conditional?* When is the one form proper, and when the other? (6) What is said of the frequency with which this kind of accessory recurs in language? Give more examples. (7) Punctuation?

§ 136. (1) What accessory is next considered, and what is the conjunctive word? (2) Example? (3) Bring a written copy of the example from Hooker, and, with this before the eyes, repeat the analysis given above.

passage. If *therefore* had been used, it would have claimed the first place, but the slightly illative *then* is often thus thrust out of its regular place into a secondary position. *Seeing* introduces "No man can plead eloquently;" *unless* introduces the proposition before which it stands, "he be able," &c. And the last proposition, "That ability of speech is in this case," &c. is a substantive accessory and the real subject of the leading proposition, the verb "*followeth*" taking *it* as a *representative* and *temporary* subject till the *real* one is developed.

(4) The *accessory* of this kind often precedes the *principal.* "*Unless* the LORD had been my help, my soul had almost dwelt in silence."

(5) *Except*, and *except that*, and sometimes *save* are used for the same purpose. (6) These are all imperatives, and the proposition following them is really a substantive accessory used as objective complement to these imperatives. Horne Tooke maintains that *unless* is also an imperative of the Anglo-Saxon verb *onlesan*, which means to *unlease* or *unloose.*

(7) PUNCTUATION.—Separate by a comma.

EXERCISE.—Furnish compound propositions involving examples of the exceptive accessory.

§ 137.—(1) Those accessories which follow may perhaps be regarded as a fourth class having no analogy with the modifications of simple propositions.

CONDITIONAL AND HYPOTHETICAL PROPOSITIONS. — (2) We come now to consider a very peculiar and important class of compound propositions—we mean *important* in a *grammatical* point of view—namely, *conditional propositions.**

(3) These and hypothetical propositions (which it will be convenient to consider in connection with them) differ from other forms

* The learner will please study carefully, in connection with what we say upon conditional and hypothetical propositions, the remarks on the use of the auxiliaries *will, shall, may, can,* and their past forms *would, should,* &c., and on the past tense employed *hypothetically.* (*See* § 63.)

(4) Repeat remark, and give example.

(5) Enumerate other words used to introduce this kind of accessory. (6) Repeat what is said in reference to these words.

(7) Punctuation?

§ 137. (1) What is said in reference to the accessories which follow?

(2) What is said of the class next considered, and what is the name given to them?

(3) In what do conditional and hypothetical propositions differ from other forms of com-

of compound propositions in this respect, that they convey no *absolute* assertion. (4) In the conditional proposition the assertion depends upon the *condition* (hence the name *conditional*) expressed in the accessory. If this condition is granted the assertion holds, but if not it is void. (5) In the hypothetical proposition the assertion is based upon a mere *hypothesis* (hence the name *hypothetical*), upon a supposed case, which (it is generally implied by the nature of the expression) has no real existence, but on the supposition that this case had existed in the past, the assertion (now admitted void) would have been valid. Hence the past tense is employed, as we shall see, both in the principal and in the accessory of the hypothetical compound proposition. (*See* § 63.)

(6) The word employed both in the conditional and in the hypothetical proposition to connect the accessory is generally IF. This word is commonly supposed to be the imperative of the Anglo-Saxon verb *gifan, to give.* (7) The form *gif* for *if* is found in older writers, and in the Scottish dialect of the last century.

"*Gif* I could fancy aught's sae sweet or fair."
"Gif I cou'd find blae-berries ripe for thee."—Ramsay.

(8) In the *conditional* the verb of the principal proposition is either of the *future* form or of the *conditional* form made with the help of the auxiliaries *can* and *may.* (9) When the *future* form is employed, the *futurity* of the event expressed in the principal proposition is asserted, subject to the *condition* or *contingency* expressed in the accessory. When the conditional form with *can* or *may* is employed, only the *power* or *liberty* to do the action—in other words, only the possibility of the event—expressed in the principal proposition is asserted, subject, as before, to the *condition* or *contingency* expressed in the accessory.

(10) Examples: "*I shall go*, IF *circumstances compel me. He will*

---

pound propositions? (4) On what does the assertion in conditionals depend? (5) Describe the hypothetical proposition.

(6) What word is employed to connect conditional and hypothetical accessories? (7) Examples of *gif* for *if.*

(8) What is said of the form of the verb in the *principal* of conditionals? (9) What is asserted when the *future* tense is employed in the principal proposition? What when the conditional with *can* or *may* is employed? (10) Illustrate by examples. (11) What is said about the arrangement?

go, IF *you are willing to go with him. I can go*, IF *my friends permit me. I may go*, IF *the weather shall prove favorable.* (11) Here we have arranged the principal propositions first; but the accessory in all these examples may be arranged first without any impropriety as regards order, or any change of sense. In all cases we are at liberty in using conditional propositions to place that first to which we wish to secure the greatest emphasis, or to accommodate the arrangement to our notions of harmony. The same remark applies equally to hypothetical propositions.

(12) There are other words besides *if* sometimes employed to connect conditional accessories. Such are, *provided* or *providing that*, *suppose that* or *supposing that*, *in case that*, *put case that*, *set case that*, &c. Examples of all these may be found in our older writers, but they are now seldom used, with the exception of *provided* or *providing that*, and *in case that.* (13) We give examples of the propositions connected by *provided that*, *providing that*, and *in case that. I will remain* PROVIDED THAT *you remain with me.* (14) Here we may regard the accessory proposition as a substantive accessory preceded, as usual, by *that* determinative, and as forming with the participle, *provided*, the construction called a *substantive with a participle in the case absolute.* (See § 143: 13, et seq.) (15) PROVIDING THAT *I have your assistance. I will attempt the business.* Here *I have your assistance* may also be regarded as a substantive accessory preceded by *that*, and forming the *objective* modification of the participle *providing;* the whole being a participial construction used instead of the compound accessory proposition, *If you*, or *somebody provide*, or, *if it be provided that I have your assistance.* IN CASE—or, IN CASE THAT—*you cannot go, I will not go*, = IF *you cannot go, I will not go.*

(16) An *imperative* proposition is sometimes employed with the same force as a conditional accessory. Examples: *Be good, and you shall be happy. Be industrious, frugal, and honest, and you cannot fail of success.* These are manifestly equivalent to, IF *you are good, you shall be happy.* IF *you will be industrious, frugal, and honest, you cannot fail of success.* In some cases, by using the imperative proposition, we render the expression more animated.

---

(12) Mention other words employed to connect conditionals; and repeat the remark in reference to their use. (13) Give examples of the use of such of these connecting words as occur in modern writers. (14) How may such accessories be regarded? (15) Transcribe the example, "*providing that*," &c., and explain it, with the copy in hand.

(16) Repeat the remark about the use of imperative propositions; and illustrate by examples.

(17) It will be observed that in such constructions the imperative proposition and the principal proposition are simply united as *co-ordinate* propositions by the copulative *and*. The real relation of the propositions here, as in many other cases, is left to be discovered from the *matter*, rather than the form of the expression. (See § 146.)

EXERCISE.—Furnish examples of conditional propositions.

We next give examples of *hypothetical propositions*. (18) These differ in form from conditional propositions only in one circumstance, that either the *hypothetical* or a *past tense* is employed in them. Indeed, both as to *form* and *purpose*, the hypothetical may be regarded as a subdivision of conditional propositions; namely, that class of conditionals in which the condition is not *contingent* or *doubtful*, but imagined to exist that we may have the opportunity of asserting *hypothetically* what we would assert *absolutely*, on the supposition that this condition really existed. (19) Hypothetical propositions are generally, like conditional propositions, constructed with IF preceding and introducing the hypothetical accessory. (20) Examples: *I would go*, IF *I could;* implying that I cannot now go, but that it is supposable that I had the power at a past time, and if so, that I had the will to go. *He could write more frequently* IF *he had the inclination to write;* implying that he has not the inclination, but that it is supposable that he possessed it. IF *I had the book I would give it to your friend.* More examples may be found in the remarks on the Conditional and Hypothetical Forms of the verb. (See § 63.)

(21) Hypothetical accessories can be introduced by means of the other words or phrases which introduce conditional accessories. Thus, *I would certainly go*, PROVIDED THAT or IN CASE THAT, &c., *I could leave my business.*

(22) In hypothetical accessories, the *conjunctive* word is often omitted, especially when in the arrangement the accessory takes precedence of the principal proposition. Thus, *Had I the book, I would give it to you*, = *If I had the book, I would give it to you.* (See § 63.)

(23) In the hypothetical accessory the *conjunctive* past tense of the verb *to be* is employed, and not, as in other verbs, the indicative

---

(17) Repeat the observation about these constructions with imperatives.

(18) Explain the difference between hypothetical and conditional propositions. (19) What connective word is chiefly employed in hypotheticals? (20) Illustrate by examples.

(21) What is said of introducing hypotheticals by other words and phrases? Examples?

(22) Repeat what is said of the omission of the *conjunctive* word. Give example.

(23) What form of the verb *to be* is employed in hypotheticals? Example. (24) When *if* is suppressed, what arrangement is preferable?

past. Example: *I would do that for you*, IF *I were able*, or, *were I able*. (24) When we suppress *if*, it is best to place the accessory first. *Were I able, I would do that for you.*

(25) Conditional and hypothetical propositions are used in the *Interrogative* form; as, *Will he not assist me*, IF *he can? Would I not assist you*, IF *I could?*

(26) *Then* illative (*indicating a consequence or inference*), is sometimes employed to introduce the principal proposition in conditionals and hypothteicals. In this case the principal proposition comes after the accessory. Examples: *If I can help you*, THEN *I will. If I could help you*, THEN *I would.* "If I knew, *then* would not I tell?" *Then* used in this manner appears rather stiff, and is, we believe, seldom introduced in the modern written language.

(27) It has been noticed already, in the remarks on the hypothetical form of the verbs, that the *negative* hypothetical accessory, exactly the reverse of all other negative propositions, implies that the supposed condition actually exists. This might have been anticipated from the fact already known, that the accessory of the *affirmative* form implies the present *non-existence* of what it expresses. The negative being the counterpart in *form* of the affirmative accessory, should also be its counterpart in *sense*. Examples: IF *that man could* NOT *pay his debts, he would not be so blame-worthy.* This implies that the man is actually able to pay his debts, and therefore worthy of greater blame. IF *he were* NOT *a worthy man, we would not defend him so zealously.* This implies that we take him for a worthy man.

(28) We must observe here that the hypothetical form of compound proposition is sometimes used, when we do not intend to express a *foregone conclusion;* in other words, when it is not implied that the condition expressed in the accessory no longer exists. Such cases may, perhaps, be regarded as an *extension* of the use of this form to express an assertion in a softened manner under the cloak of a hypothesis. Example: *If your friend would come to me to-morrow, I could, or might, or would explain to him the difficulty which perplexes him.* This is a promise less absolute than when I say, *If your friend* WILL *come*, I CAN, or MAY, or WILL, &c. In the latter case my ability, power, will to explain the difficulty is *absolutely* asserted, but in the former case it is

---

(25) Repeat the remark about the interrogative form. Give examples.

(26) What is said of the use of *then* illative in conditionals and hypotheticals? Illustrate by examples.

(27) Repeat in substance what is said of the negative hypothetical proposition; and illustrate the statement by examples.

(28) Repeat the substance of the observation, and illustrate by examples.

only asserted as dependent, at least, on your friend's will to come, and perhaps on other casualties.

(29) PUNCTUATION.—In conditionals and hypotheticals a comma separates the principal and accessory.

EXERCISE.—Furnish examples of hypothetical propositions.

§ 138. (1) In the conditional and hypothetical proposition the accessory might be represented as expressing a concession asked by the speaker, on which concession the validity of the main assertion depends. (2) There is another kind of compound proposition, in which the accessory also expresses a concession, but a concession *granted* or *admitted* by the speaker, and, notwithstanding which, the assertion is made, and made *absolutely*, not *conditionally*. (3) This kind of accessory has been called by some of the Germans the *concessive accessory;* and this name we adopt for want of a better, though not perfectly satisfied of its appropriateness.*

(4) In this class of propositions, the accessory is most generally introduced in the English of the present day by the words THOUGH and ALTHOUGH, sometimes in ancient writers and in imitations of the antiquated style by ALBEIT. (5) The force of the conjunctive *though* is often supported by the introduction of the adverb YET in the principal proposition; perhaps sometimes by STILL. *Yet* is only introduced when the principal proposition follows the accessory. The *yet* thus introduced may be regarded as equivalent to *after all, notwithstanding the objection.*

(6) We present examples both with and without *yet.* "*Though* thou detain me, I will not eat of thy bread." "*Though* hand join in

* We are not sure that this name sufficiently distinguishes this accessory from the conditional accessory. Nor do we think that it exactly expresses the purpose of the accessory. The name applies, perhaps, better to the *compound* proposition taken as a whole, which expresses an assertion, and, connected with it, a *concession* of something apparently adverse to it, but held not to invalidate it.

(29) Punctuation?

§ 138. (1) Remark about the conditional and hypothetical proposition. (2) Describe another kind of compound proposition. (3) What has the accessory in this kind of proposition been called?

(4) What words are most generally employed to introduce the accessory in these compound propositions? (5) What is said of the use of *yet* in concessive propositions? (6) Adduce examples for illustration. (7) What is said of the verbs in these examples?

hand, the wicked shall not be unpunished." "*Though* he slay me, yet will I trust in him." "*Though* the Lord be high, yet hath he respect unto the lowly." That is to say, admitting—conceding—that the Lord is high, and that this admitted fact might appear an objection to his acting in the manner to be asserted, *still*, *setting this aside*, *this notwithstanding*, it is asserted, that "*He hath respect unto the lowly.*" It may here be observed that our translators generally employ the conjunctive form of the verb *To Be* after though, even when a matter of fact, as in the last example, is expressed by the proposition. (7) The verbs in the other examples, and in that which we are about to give, may be regarded as contracted future conditional, or hypothetical forms. (See § 55, p. 111.)

"*Yet*, *though* destruction sweep those lovely plains,
Rise, fellow-men! your country yet remains."

The first *yet* is here to suit the versification, separated from its proposition. Its proper place is before the verb "*rise.*"

(8) We give examples of *Although*, the first two as found in Richardson's Dictionary.

"ALL THOUGH a man be wise hym selve,
YET is the wisdom more of twelve."—Gower.

"In which ALTHOUGH good fortune me befall,
YET shall it not by none be testifyde."—Spencer.

"ALTHOUGH all should be offended, YET will not I."

(9) We give the following as examples of the now antiquated ALBEIT:

"Who are you, tell me for more certainty.
ALBEIT I'll swear that I do know your tongue."
"One whose subdued eyes,
ALBEIT unused to the melting mood,
Drop tears," &c.—Shak.

"ALBEIT betwixt them roared the ocean grim,
YET so the sage had hight to play his part."—Scott.

This example from Scott is an imitation of the antiquated style. (10) It will be seen from these examples that *although* and *albeit* are employed exactly like though, and for the same purpose. The composition of these two words is obvious. *All-though; All-be-it.*

---

(8) Give examples with *although* for conjunction.
(9) Examples of *albeit*? (10) Repeat remark about *although* and *albeit*.

(11) The words NOTWITHSTANDING and NEVERTHELESS are used in a principal proposition to set aside an objection, which might be drawn from the preceding part of a discourse. They may be regarded as equivalent to *though this is so, yet.* (12) The use of *notwithstanding* may be thus explained: The preceding proposition, or a portion of the preceding discourse is taken with the participle *withstanding* and the negative, in the manner of the *case absolute.* = *This* (what precedes) *not standing against, the assertion which follows holds true.* (13) *Nevertheless*, when resolved into the words which constitute it, explains itself. *Never the less on account of what precedes*, the assertion still holds true. (14) Examples: "Notwithstanding I have a few things against thee." That is the character given in the context, *not withstanding—not opposing—not forming* a *valid* though *apparent objection.* (15) The word notwithstanding refers thus to an objection arising from the concessions in the preceding discourse, which objection it serves to set aside.*

Examples of the use of *nevertheless.* (16) *He acted imprudently on that occasion;* NEVERTHELESS *he is not a fool* = *never the less*, or *not the less* (anciently *natheless*) *on this account, he is not a fool.* "Wisdom is better than strength; *nevertheless* the poor man's wisdom is despised."

---

* The determinatives *this* or *that* (referring to the apparent objection contained in the preceding discourse), may be regarded as implied after *notwithstanding. That* is often in fact expressed after it; and sometimes even the objection in the preceding passage is summed up, in a word or phrase, and placed alongside the participle *notwithstanding.* We quote the two following apposite examples from Dr. Webster's Dictionary, together with a part of his illustration. "'It is a rainy day, but *notwithstanding that*, the troops must be reviewed;' that is, the rainy day not opposing or preventing. *That*, in this case, is a substitute for the whole first clause of the sentence. It is to that clause what a relative is to an antecedent noun, and *which* may be used in the place of it; *notwithstanding which*, that is, the rainy day.

"'Christ enjoined on his followers not to publish the cures he wrought; but *notwithstanding his injunctions*, they proclaimed them.' Here, *notwithstanding his injunctions*, is the case independent or absolute; the injunctions of Christ not opposing or preventing. This word answers precisely to the Latin *non obstante*," &c.

---

(11) Repeat what is said of *notwithstanding* and *nevertheless.* (12) Explain the use of notwithstanding. (13) Repeat the remark about *nevertheless.* (14) Illustrate by examples. (15) To what does the word notwithstanding refer?

(16) Illustrate the use of *nevertheless* by examples.

(17) The word *howbeit* is employed in older writers for much the same purpose. We have an example in the book of Ruth. "I am thy near kinsman; *howbeit* there is a kinsman nearer than I." This is nearly equivalent to *notwithstanding*, or *nevertheless* "there is a kinsman nearer than I."

(18) *Still* is also sometimes used for a similar purpose. Example:

"*Still*, as you rise, the state, exalted too,
Finds no distemper while 'tis changed by you."—Waller.

EXERCISE.—Furnish examples of concessive propositions.

(19) There is a kind of concessive proposition, in which an objection proposed in the form of an alternative is set aside. The accessory in this kind of proposition is introduced by the word *whether* = *which of two*, and the *alternative* by *or*. (20) We give examples: WHETHER *you go, or do not go, I shall certainly go.* Or, with the principal proposition first in order, *I shall certainly go*, WHETHER *you go or do not go;* (more commonly expressed in an abbreviated form, *Whether you go, or not, I shall certainly go.*) Here it is implied, that there is something adverse, something opposed to *my going* either in *your going*, or *not going* (most generally in the last alternative, but this would be manifest in an *actual* conversation from the connection of the discourse), and this something is set aside by this form of expression as unavailing in reference to what is asserted in the main proposition. Your going or not going cannot avail to prevent my going. In other words, after conceding the alternative that you go, or do not go, the assertion stands, that I go. "Every man who had to live by his wit wrote plays, whether he had any internal vocation to write plays or not."

(21) This form of compound proposition is equivalent to a conditional proposition with an alternative accessory; *If you go, or if you do not go, still I shall go.* Or (what is the same thing) it is equivalent to two conditional propositions having the same main assertion, *I shall go, if you go;* and *I shall go, if you do not go.* (22) It may admit a doubt whether this form should be classed under the concessive or the conditional. As it contains an absolute assertion, notwithstanding the conceded objection, we have classed it with concessive propo-

---

(17) What is said of the employment of *howbeit?* Illustrate by examples.

(18) Give an example of *still* employed for a similar purpose.

(19) Describe another species of concessive proposition; and tell the word by which it is introduced. (20) Illustrate by examples.

(21) To what is this kind of compound proposition equivalent? (22) What doubt is suggested about classifying it?

sitions. (23) We venture to call it *The Concessive Compound Proposition with Alternative Accessory.*

(24) PUNCTUATION OF CONCESSIVES.—A comma between the principal and the accessory.

EXERCISES.—Furnish examples of this form of compound proposition.

(25) There is still another form of concessive proposition, in which the objection conceded and set aside is of an indefinite, unlimited, all comprehensive description. (26) We may call this *The Concessive with Indefinite Accessory.* (27) These *concessives* have for their conjunctive words the compound conjunctive pronoun *whoever* serving as the *subject* of the accessory, or the conjunctive *whatever*, serving as *subject*, or as *objective modification* of the predicate, or the adverb *however*, performing its adverbial function, besides that of conjunctive word.* (28) Examples: WHOEVER *may oppose that man, he will succeed*, or *that man will succeed*, WHOEVER *may oppose him* = *Though any or all men should oppose him, that man will succeed.* WHATEVER *obstacles lie in his way, he readily surmounts* = *Though obstacles of any or all descriptions lie in his way*, or *though he meets any or all descriptions of obstacles, he readily surmounts them. However he is baffled, he always persists in what he undertakes* = *Though he is baffled in any, or all ways, he always persists*, &c. (29) PUNCTUATION the same as in the last case.

---

* It is to be noticed that *however* is often used in such a manner as to represent itself alone a sort of concessive proposition. It is then equivalent to *however this may be*, referring to the preceding discourse for the matter conceded. We give an example, and, in order to render it satisfactory, we are obliged to quote a portion of the preceding sentence. "I served three campaigns with him in Flanders, and remember him; but 'tis most likely, as I had not the honor of any acquaintance with him, that he knows nothing of me. You will tell him, *however*, that the person his good nature has laid under obligations to him, is one Le Fevre," &c. "You will tell him, HOWEVER" *this may be*, (that is, *conceding* the likelihood that he knows nothing of me, or, in other words, setting aside the objection that he may know nothing of me), "that the person," &c. (*See* § 121: 20–24.)

---

(23) What name is given to it?

(24) Punctuation?

(25) Describe another form of concessive propositions. (26) By what name may we call this form? (27) By what conjunctive words is the accessory in these introduced? (28) Illustrate by examples.

(29) Punctuation?

EXERCISE.—Furnish examples of this kind of concessive proposition.

§ 139. (1) There is a form of accessory, which we may call *The Accessory of Reference*, commencing with the conjunctive *what* preceded by the words *as to*, or *as for*, to indicate its connection and show its relation to the principal proposition.

(2) Examples: AS TO WHAT *we have been talking of, my opinion is already fixed.* AS FOR WHAT *that man says, I have no confidence in it.* More tersely, *I have no confidence in what that man says.* (3) In these examples *as* is equivalent to the words *in reference*, and is manifestly an *adverbial modification* of the principal proposition. (4) We shall see the nature of the construction more clearly by substituting for *what* the equivalent words *that which.* (5) *In reference to* THAT WHICH *you say, my opinion is fixed*, or *my opinion is fixed in reference to that which you say. What you say*, may be regarded as a *substantive accessory* with *to* forming a *noun and preposition* modification of the adverb *as*, or what is implied in it, namely, the conception expressed by the word *reference.* (6) *As*, we may here observe, is sometimes modified in the same manner by a noun as well as by substantive accessories; thus, AS TO THE QUESTION *in hand, my opinion is fixed.*

(7) Though this form of construction admits, as we have seen, of being reduced by analysis under the class of *substantive*, or ultimately of *adjective accessories*, still it is convenient to treat it as a separate form, if it were only for the purpose of explaining the method of effecting this analysis.

(8) PUNCTUATION.—Comma between the principal and accessory.

We may have omitted some forms of accessory propositions; and several compound constructions may possibly be found, of which no description is given in the preceding observations. But after studying carefully what we have set forth in the above pages, the learner will, we hope, be able himself to devise means of analyzing any ordinary construction of this kind, which we may have overlooked.

Those who are best qualified to form an opinion of the subject now

---

§ 139. (1) Describe the accessory of reference. (2) Illustrate the use of this by examples. (3) Repeat the remark in reference to the word *as* in these examples. (4) By what substitution shall we be enabled to see the nature of the construction more clearly? (5) Illustrate by example. (6) Repeat the remark about the manner in which *as* may be modified.

(7) Repeat remark about the grammatical treatment of this construction.

(8) Punctuation?

treated, and who know how little assistance we have been able to draw from the works of our predecessors, will be most ready to excuse any omission which may be discovered. We hope that nothing important to a general knowledge of the structure of our language has been altogether overlooked.

§ 140. CONTRACTED ACCESSORIES. GENERAL REMARKS.—One subject still remains to be treated in order to complete our account of the construction of compound propositions; (1) namely, certain forms of expression, which, though devoid of the grand characteristic of propositions, since they have in them no assertive word, yet perform functions equivalent to those of accessories. (2) These we may call *contracted accessory propositions.* (3) We do not include in this class those propositions in which some important part, though suppressed, is plainly *implied.* (4) Such cases come under the head of Ellipsis, and the first thing to be done, as we have already said, in attempting to analyze such elliptical propositions, is to supply the suppressed part, or parts, and then proceed as in treating complete propositions. (5) But what we here intend to treat under the name of *contracted or transformed accessories*, differ from all propositions in having the word which serves as predicate in the *substantive* or *adjective*, not in the *assertive* form.

(6) These forms of expression are constructed by the help of the verbal nouns and the verbal adjectives. (7) Some of them serve the purposes of *substantive*, some of *adjective*, and some of *adverbial* accessories. (8) Consequently we might treat them in the same order, in which we have treated the accessories; but it will be more conducive both to brevity and to perspicuity to consider together the chief *contracted accessories* formed by the help of each of the verbal nouns and the verbal adjectives or participles.

NOTE.—It is not our intention here to introduce all the modifying forms of expression which might legitimately be considered contracted accessory propositions. A large proportion of those which we have treated as complements of the subjects and predicates of simple propositions may, as we

---

§ 140. (1) Describe certain forms of expression yet to be treated under the head of compound propositions. (2) How may we name these forms? (3) What do we exclude from this class of forms? (4) How are these excluded forms of expression to be treated? (5) In what do contracted accessories differ from propositions?

(6) By the help of what words are these contracted accessories formed? (7) What purposes do contracted accessories serve? (8) What is said of the order in which they might be treated, and the order in which we actually treat them?

have had frequent occasion to hint, be regarded as abbreviations of what was perhaps first expressed by an accessory proposition, and of what *can* still be expressed in the same manner. Perhaps all the modifications of nouns and adjectives, and many of the modifications of verbs are abbreviations of what can be (though less conveniently) expressed by *predication*, and what was once so expressed. Even the descriptive adjective modification may perhaps be regarded as originally a contracted accessory, or an abbreviated way of expressing a modifying predication. We have already said that we suspect that the modification by a proposition is of older date than that by a descriptive adjective, and that every descriptive adjective modification may be regarded as implying a suppressed predication. (*See* § 88, *note* p. 266.) We think, for example, that *The river which is swift* is a more simple, less artificial, and likely more primitive form of expression than *The swift river*, and that this last form of expression is a refinement of language.

Some grammarians, on the contrary, seem to regard the accessory as an *expansion* of the *participial* and *verbal-noun forms*, which we call contracted accessories; and this, because these latter forms are found to abound most in the earliest stages of the languages with which we are best acquainted. The persons to whom we allude conceive that as refinement advances these forms are expanded into accessory propositions. We do not think that there is any sufficient reason alleged to support this opinion. We admit that in the progress of *modern languages* a very general tendency has been displayed to abandon all complicated constructions, such as the *case absolute*, &c., as well as case terminations and tense terminations. But this does not prove that these latter are not more artificial forms of expression than those which have superseded them, nor that they are not the fruit of long cultivation and of a progressive development of language. Some of the modes of expression used in common by the Greeks and Romans, and our own remote Northern ancestors, may have been more refined, more artificial than ours, though our less remote ancestors may have abandoned them. This admission is not inconsistent even with the opinion that our modern languages have been improved by laying aside altogether, or only sparingly employing, refinements which were the fruit of long and slow development. But however this may be, we believe that the disuse of the ingenious contrivances of our earlier ancestors, is attributable to the advent of times more barbarous than those in which these contrivances originated, and to the confusion arising from the mingling of dialects—Norman with Anglo-Saxon—rather than to any design entertained of improving and simplifying language. The present English was formed and the chief of the innovations to which we have alluded introduced in an age, perhaps, much ruder and less learned than that of Alfred, when the Anglo-Saxon reached its full development and is found in greatest purity.

§ 141. CONTRACTED ACCESSORIES FORMED BY THE HELP OF THE VERBAL NOUNS IN ING.—(1) Contracted accessory propositions are sometimes formed with the verbal nouns in *ing*, either alone, or accompanied by verbal adjectives (*participles*) forming what are usually (but improperly) considered *compound participles substantively employed*. (*a*) (2) Contracted accessories of this kind are employed instead of substantive accessory propositions, serving as subject noun, or as objective modification, or as noun and preposition, or adverbial modification to the verb of the *principal* proposition.

REMARK.—(3) Every verbal noun which has a subject expressed or plainly implied in the construction—that is, what would be the subject noun, when the assertive form of expression is used—may be considered as a contracted accessory. This remark may be extended to the other verbals; viz.: the infinitives and participles.

(4) We subjoin a few examples of this class of contracted accessories. "*Their neglecting* this was ruinous"=That they neglected this was ruinous. In this last the learner will recognise a substantive accessory employed as subject of the verb *was*. The word *their* expresses or includes what becomes the subject of the complete accessory. *They will call before* LEAVING *the city*=They will call before *they leave the city*. Here the subject of the action is plainly implied, since it is manifestly *their leaving the city* which is indicated. The accessory here is adverbial, expressing time, or equivalent to a noun and preposition modification. The word *before* performs the function both of preposition and conjunction. "*Your having been* so humble as to take notice of the epistles of other animals, emboldens me," &c.=That you have been so humble, &c. emboldens me. (Substantive acc. subject of the principal verb.) "*His being smitten* with the love of Orestilla was the cause," &c. (The same analysis applies to this example.) "He recollected *his being undressed*" = *He recollected that he was undressed*. (Objective accessory proposition.) "After *turning* from the main road—we came in sight of the cottage" = After we turned from the main road, &c. (Adverbial accessory of time, = noun and preposition modification.) SINCE WRITING *that let-*

---

§ 141. (1) Describe the class of contracted accessories first considered. (2) Mention the various purposes for which this class of contracted accessories is employed.

(3) Repeat the substance of the remark. To what may the remark be extended?

(4) Illustrate by examples. The best mode is, perhaps, for the learner to provide a written copy of the examples, make himself master of the explanations, and repeat them with the help of his copy.

ter, he has changed his mind = Since he wrote that letter, he has changed his mind. (Analysis the same as of the last example.)

(5) The verbal in *ing* is very often accompanied by a preposition. When it follows those prepositions which are used before accessories, such as the words *before*, *after*, *since*, it is always very easy to exchange the *contracted* form of accessory for the *complete* accessory, as may be seen in the examples above in which these words are employed before the verbal. But when the *verbal noun* is preceded by prepositions which are not used to connect accessories, it is not always easy, perhaps not always possible, to make this kind of exchange. Sometimes it can be readily done. For example: *That man told me the news* IN RIDING *out of town* = *That man told me the news as we were riding out of town.* It is not, however, absolutely necessary in analysis to change these abbreviated forms into complete accessories. They may be regarded as a distinct method of expressing what can in many cases be more fully expressed by accessories, and what in some cases cannot now be so conveniently, if at all, expressed in this way; and they may always be treated simply as nouns (but nouns susceptible of peculiar modifications in common with verbs), used as the subjects of propositions, or performing some other function of nouns. We do not, therefore, prescribe any new mode of analysis for these forms of expression. We have brought the consideration of them before the reader, because it is often useful in writing to be able readily to substitute an accessory for these forms when the employment of them would involve, as it sometimes does, some awkwardness or ambiguity.(*b*)

(6) PUNCTUATION.—The same as in simple propositions.

NOTE (*a*).—The ultimate analysis of these verbal nouns in *ing*, accompanied by participles, is exactly similar to that of the compound tenses of their kindred verbs. In the case of the verbal *being*, as in the passive tenses, the accompanying participle is really an *adjective complementary.* In the example, "His being smitten," &c., the word *smitten* is really an *adjective complementary;* of which form of modification the verbal *being*, like its kindred verb, is susceptible. The same remark applies to all those combinations called passive participles, as well as to all the compound passive tenses, except those into which the verb *have* enters as a component part. The three kinds of words, *verbs*, *verbal nouns*, and *verbal adjectives*, as we have already said, take modifications in common. This arises from their common nature as words expressing predicates, and not merely in the case of the verbal nouns and adjectives, from their connection with verbs. The susceptibility

---

(5) Repeat the substance of the remarks about *verbal nouns* used after certain prepositions, and the mode of treating this class of verbals.

(6) Punctuation?

of (what we may call) *verbal* complements has no connection with the assertive function. It is the *matter* of the expression, not the *form, derivation,* or *grammatical functions* of verbal words (whether verbs, nouns, or participles), which renders them susceptible of certain modifications in common.

The explanation, which we have given of the use of *have*, with perfect participles in forming compound tenses, applies to the verbal noun *having* modified by participles, and also to the compound participles formed by the help of this word. There is no difficulty in resorting in every case, if we please, to the ultimate analysis of the verbal nouns and adjectives formed with the word *being*. The participle attached to them may always be considered as an adjective complementary of the *verbal*. But it is more difficult to resort to the ultimate analysis of verbal nouns and adjectives formed with the word *having*, especially when the participle which follows is of a neuter signification. The difficulty, as we have already said, seems to have been caused by an *insensible extension* of a usage appropriate only to active predicates to neuter predicates. Owing to this difficulty, it will be convenient tc treat verbals, whether nouns or adjectives, accompanied by participles as *compound verbals*, in the same manner as we treat verbs, with exactly similar participial modifications as compound forms, or tenses.

Note (*b*).—There has arisen much controversy among the grammarians about some of the constructions formed with verbal nouns in *ing*. Many are disposed to reject forms which are sanctioned by reputable and very general usage, because they do not conform with their notions of what is, or rather what ought to be, pure grammatical English. We have, with the valuable assistance of Mr. R. Taylor, attempted to establish two points which will enable us to reconcile most of these rejected or suspected forms with the general laws of language. These are, that the verbal noun in *ing* is distinct in origin from the participle—that is, it is not the participle *substantively* employed; and that this verbal, as well as the participle, from its own nature—owing to the *matter* which it expresses, as described in the preceding note—is susceptible of the modifications which belong to verbs, as well as of those which belong to nouns. The full admission of these two points, which are settled, at least to our satisfaction, will set aside the objections to many of the constructions referred to. Mr. Grant seems to us to have laid down the correct view of this matter in the passage which we subjoin, though he was not, so far as we can see, acquainted with the fact that the verbal noun in *ing* had an origin independent of the participle. His remarks are not the less valuable on this account. "Notwithstanding the objections of Lowth, L. Murray, &c., it may be safely affirmed that the several phraseologies, 'by sending them,' 'by sending of them,' 'by the sending them,' 'by the sending of them,' in all which the word in *ing* is evidently nothing but a verbal noun, are sanctioned by the usage of our best writers, and are perfectly accordant with the genius of the language."—Grant's English Grammar, p. 196 Lond. 1813.

Mr. Grant adds in a note, "I certainly prefer, *as forms*, 'by sending them,' and 'by the sending of them;' and allow that, when the verbal is preceded by the article, the *of* is very rarely omitted." With this, too, we agree; but we would rather say that when *of* is placed before the noun which modifies the verbal, the article is always properly employed; but omitted when the verbal is followed by an objective modification. The presence of the preposition and noun renders the article necessary, not the reverse. When a noun is rendered determinate by a noun and preposition modification, the article, or some other determinative, is used to indicate its determinateness. But the article is not used before a verbal modified by an adjective (since the two words together express a conception which may be regarded as single—*see note in next section*), except when the verbal and its objective modification are farther modified by another complement; as, for example, *The sending such a message* AT THAT PARTICULAR CRISIS, *was improper.* The article in such forms of expression, should, no doubt, be employed, in conformity with the laws of language, to indicate that *sending such a message* is rendered determinate by the words *at that particular crisis.* (*See Additional Observations on Determinatives*, § 158.)

"But there is a manifest difference," says Mr. Grant in the same note, "*in sense*, between 'hearing the philosopher,' or 'the hearing the philosopher,' and 'the hearing *of* the philosopher;' between 'preaching Christ,' or 'the preaching Christ,' and 'the preaching *of* Christ.' In the forms which do not contain *of*, the nouns *philosopher* and *Christ* are passive; in the forms containing *of*, these words would generally be considered as *active.* Still, however, in this sense, the substitution of the Saxon for the Norman genitive would render the meaning clearer; thus, 'the philosopher's hearing,' 'Christ's preaching.' In the course of a trial, Lord Ellenborough used the following words; 'I think the plea does not justify *the killing of the gamekeeper.*' Now, I do allow that here the gamekeeper *may be supposed* to be either active or passive. According to the meaning intended, he was active, the trial being for 'a gamekeeper's killing a gentleman's dog;' which last phraseology evidently removes the ambiguity."

The ambiguity in such expressions does not arise from the verbal, but from the double use of what Mr. Grant calls the "Norman genitive." This is employed both *subjectively* and *objectively.* Thus, *The love of God*, may mean either the love of which God is the *subject*, or that of which God is the *object*—God's love towards us, or our love towards God. It would be good perhaps always, when there is danger of ambiguity, to employ the English or Saxon genitive *subjectively;* and the Norman genitive, or modification with *of*, *objectively.*

We have given place to these observations, because some of the grammarians have mixed up these ambiguities with the consideration of the verbal noun or *gerund*, which in most of its uses they treat as a participle, and have thus increased the confusion in which they have involved themselves and their readers.

Confusion arises we believe in some instances from the fact that nouns in *ing* are often used with meanings distinct from their *gerundive* and proper verbal meaning. We have already noticed that some words in *ing*, agreeing exactly in form with the *gerunds*, have become *concrete* nouns. Thus, *writing* is used to signify a *something written*, as well as the *act of writing*. There is little danger of confounding meanings so distinct as these. But there are other variations more slight than this, which overlooked might lead to error—to the attributing of that which arises from a variation of the meaning of a word to a distinct grammatical function. Thus when I say, Your son's *writing* is admirable, I mean by *writing* either *manner of writing*, or some definite *specimen of your son's writing*, not the *action of writing*, or that which the *gerund* strictly taken indicates. "Your horse's running," may mean either the *manner* of his *running*, or his *act of running*. Dr. Priestley, in a much *vexed* passage, having confounded these two senses of *running* (which are both in common every day use, the first especially in speaking of the performance of horses), has fallen into the error of either making a distinction where there is no difference, or of stating the difference incorrectly, and has hence been led, with some who have followed him, to contradict his own carefully established principles.

We would caution the young student in English composition to guard against employing verbals in any way which might occasion awkwardness or ambiguity. Better in all such cases to resort to the use of the complete accessory. Many even of our good writers might have improved their style, by attention to such counsel.

We might here notice that the participle or verbal adjective is sometimes used for the verbal noun—the participial for the gerund form. For example, *Catiline* BEING SMITTEN *with the love of Orestilla was the cause*, instead of *Catiline's being smitten*, &c. This is a Latin rather than an English idiom, and an idiom scarcely worth the trouble of transplanting. The English expression is more logical. Catiline, however modified, is not logically the subject of the main verb *was*, but the FACT *of his being smitten with the love of Orestilla*. This participial Latin form has, however, been used by reputable authors; and though we would not like, by precept or example, to encourage the employment of it to supersede the genuine English idiom, we must be contented to restrict ourselves to the proper function of the grammarian—viz., to exhibit the usages of the language, and account for them so far as he is able, without denouncing such of them as have obtained a reception among good society.

§ 142. CONTRACTED ACCESSORIES FORMED WITH INFINITIVES.—(1) Nearly all the constructions into which the infinitive enters, except when it is employed as the objective modification of an active

§ 142. (1) What is said of constructions into which infinitives enter? Note the excep-

verb,* may be more formally expressed by accessory propositions. (2) We have already had occasion, in treating of the various forms of infinitive modification, and in examining the various kinds of accessory propositions, to notice several of these contracted modes of expression, in which the infinitive alone or with accompanying complements fills the place of a regular proposition.

We may here recapitulate a few of these forms. (3) Infinitives sometimes serve instead of accessories as the subjects of propositions. Thus, "*To obey* is better than sacrifice" = *That men should obey* is better than sacrifice. "*To do* justice and judgment is more acceptable to the Lord than sacrifice" = *That men, or that we should do justice*, &c. We have noticed already that infinitives thus employed instead of accessories are sometimes placed after the verb and represented by the pronoun *it*. (*See* § 103.)

(4) The *infinitive of purpose* is a contracted form of the *accessory of purpose*. (*See* §§ 77, 108.)

(5) The infinitives which modify nouns and adjectives may also generally be regarded as contracted accessories. Thus, *The boy has a desire* TO LEARN = *The boy has a desire* THAT HE MAY LEARN. *That*

* The objective modification, whether it consists of an infinitive or of a noun of some other kind, is of all modifications that which is least capable of being resolved or expanded into an accessory.

There is scarcely any modification of nouns which cannot be expanded into an accessory, as we have already had occasion to notice. A *descriptive adjective* may be so expanded, a *genitive case*, a *noun in apposition*, a *noun and preposition*. But many of the modifications of the predicate are less capable of this kind of resolution—above all, the objective modification, whether infinitive or other kind of noun, admits not of this expansion or substitution of an accessory. The verb and this modification, as we have already remarked, form only one complete conception. The relation between them is more close and inseparable, than that between any other principal word and its modification, excepting perhaps that between the verb and the *noun complementary*. In fact, the active verb, without this kind of complement *expressed* or *implied*, is *incomplete* or *imperfect;* it conveys only part of a conception, or, at most, a very indefinite conception.

tion. (2) Repeat the substance of the remark about the notice given already to such constructions.

(3) Give examples of infinitives used, instead of accessories, as subjects of propositions; and suggest the equivalent accessory.

(4) What infinitive is next mentioned, and for what accessory is it used?

(5) Mention the next class of infinitives; and illustrate by examples, substituting the construction with an accessory.

he may learn is here an accessory in apposition. (*See* § 105.) *The boy is desirous* THAT HE MAY LEARN. Here, *That he may learn* is a substantive accessory modifying an adjective. (*See* § 109.)

(6) In the same manner those infinitives which are attached to adverbs (*see* § 96, foot note) may be regarded as contracted accessories. Example: *He does not know* HOW TO ACT *in this case* = *He does not know* IN WHAT MANNER TO ACT *in this case* = *He does not know* HOW HE SHOULD ACT *in this case;* or IN WHAT MANNER *he should act;* or THE MANNER IN WHICH HE SHOULD ACT, &c. In the first and second forms of the accessory, we may consider *How he should act*, or *In what manner he should act*, or *is to act*, as substantive accessories—objectives to the verb *know*; in the third and more fully developed form, *In which he should act* is an adjective accessory modifying the noun *manner*. In a similar way, the expressions, *He does not understand* WHEN TO BE *silent*, *He cannot find* WHERE TO REST, may be resolved into *He does not understand* WHEN or AT WHAT TIME HE SHOULD BE SILENT, *He cannot find* WHERE HE MAY REST, or A PLACE IN WHICH HE MAY OR CAN REST.

(7) All the preceding forms of construction may be treated in analysis as *Infinitives*, either the *subjects* of propositions, like other nouns, or as *Infinitive modifications* of the several words to which they are attached, agreeably to the instructions given in treating simple propositions, not forgetting the fact that they may be expanded into complete accessories. (8) But in the analysis of the contracted accessories which follow it will be expedient to treat them always as the representatives of accessories, and the proposition with which they are connected as a compound proposition.

(9) We have already noticed (§ 121 : 19) that the *accessory indicating Equal Intensity by Example*, or by the *effect* produced, is often contracted into an infinitive form. Example: *The weather is* SO WARM, AS TO DISSOLVE *the snow on the mountains* = *The weather is* SO WARM, THAT IT DISSOLVES *the snow on the mountains.* This must be analyzed by reference to the accessory which it represents. (10) We may call it the *Contracted Accessory indicating Equal Intensity by Effect.*

---

(6) What is said of infinitives attached to adverbs? Illustrate fully by examples, making the required substitution of accessories for infinitives.

(7) What is said in reference to the treatment of the preceding forms of construction? (8) What remark is made about the contracted accessories which follow?

(9) Mention an accessory which is often changed into an infinitive, and illustrate by an example. (10) How may this contracted accessory be named?

(11) PUNCTUATION.—Unsettled. Best perhaps to insert a comma.

EXERCISE.—The learner may furnish a few examples of this construction.

(12) There is another of these infinitives used to modify adjectives, which it is the more necessary to notice here, because there is no corresponding complete accessory in common use; and because, on the other hand, it is manifestly a contracted form of accessory, and cannot well be explained as a simple infinitive modification. We have examples of the construction to which we allude in the following propositions. *Henry was* WISER THAN TO ACT *in that way. That man is* MORE BRAVE THAN TO DO *such a cowardly action. He is* MORE LEARNED THAN TO COMMIT *such a blunder*, &c. The conjunctive word *than* indicates clearly that this form of expression is to be regarded as a contracted, or, perhaps, rather an elliptical accessory.*

(13) This infinitive may be regarded as representing an accessory indicating greater intensity by example. (14) This kind of modification is rarely made in our language by a complete accessory; but we may suppose the construction when fully developed to be something like the following: *This man is wiser than to act in this manner is wise*, or *would be wise;* or *This man is wiser than that he should act in this manner.* This last is similar to the Latin construction, though in our language it seems a little awkward. We might expand the construction into *He is wiser than it would be wise to act in this manner.* We might expand it perhaps in other ways; but none of them appears exactly agreeable to our idiom. When the learner meets with such constructions, it will be necessary to refer to this account of them. (15) They can be called CONTRACTED ACCESSORIES INDICATING GREATER INTENSITY BY EXAMPLE.

(16) PUNCTUATION.—Unsettled. Comma not generally inserted.

* Owing to the presence of *than*, we cannot treat this as a simple infinitive modification of an adjective, or an infinitive of purpose, as we can treat the infinitive in such expressions as, *He is* WISE ENOUGH, *or* TOO WISE TO LEARN.

---

(11) Punctuation?

(12) Repeat the substance of what is said of another contracted accessory formed by an infinitive. Adduce examples for illustration. (13) How may this contracted accessory be regarded? (14) Illustrate by examples. (15) Give a name to the contracted accessory.

(16) Punctuation?

EXERCISE.—Furnish a number of examples of this construction.

(17) Besides these there are two other uses of the infinitive, which it will be necessary to treat always as contracted accessories, and not as mere infinitive modifications in simple propositions. In the analysis of the constructions in which these occur, we should always produce the accessory to which they are equivalent, or which they represent. In treating the preceding contracted accessory, this course is not recommended, because the complete accessory is not always found in common use, or readily exhibited.

(18) One of these uses of the infinitive has been called the *Infinitive Absolute*, because it (with its complements) stands grammatically independent of the rest of the construction. (19) We have examples in the following propositions; "*To confess* the truth, I was to blame;" To PROCEED *with the story ;* To CONCLUDE *this narrative ;* To BEGIN *with the first*, &c. All these may be regarded as contracted accessories of purpose = *In order that I may confess the truth ; In order that I may proceed in my story ;* &c.

(20) In such constructions as these, there is besides the employment of a contracted accessory, a suppression of the leading proposition, which this accessory is designed to modify. (21) The full construction in the first example is, *I admit or declare, in order that I may confess the truth, that I was to blame.* (22) In the contracted and elliptical form of construction, the proposition *That I was to blame*, which in the full construction is an objective accessory proposition modifying the principal verb, assumes the appearance and form of the principal proposition. (23) In analysis, such constructions should be expanded, and the suppressed parts supplied. We may call the infinitive with its complements thus employed, *The Contracted Accessory of Purpose.*

(24) Infinitives, apparently absolute or independent, are employed sometimes instead of other accessories. Examples: "For every object

---

(17) Repeat the remarks made concerning two other infinitives used in forming contracted accessories.

(18) What is the first of these infinitives called? (19) Illustrate by examples.

(20) What suppression occurs in constructions of this kind? (21) Supply the full construction. (22) What remark is made in reference to the proposition *I was to blame* in the example? (23) How should such constructions be treated in analysis?

(24) Give examples of infinitives absolute used for other forms of accessories.

has several faces, *so to speak*, by which it may be presented to us." *So to speak* is here equivalent to, *If I may so speak*, or, *If you allow me so to speak*, which are conditional accessories.

'Ah, fool! *to exult* in a glory so vain."

This is equivalent to *Fool that he* (man) *is!* BECAUSE HE EXULTS, or *that he exults* "in a glory so vain!" That is, the infinitive here serves as an accessory of cause. Possibly infinitives may be found placed independently to serve the functions of other kinds of accessories.

(25) Such constructions as, "*To be*, or *not to be*, that is the question," we do not consider as belonging to this class of examples. It may be questioned whether a revery, such as this is selected from, is to be subjected to strict grammatical analysis. Hamlet's language, true to the condition of his mind, is incoherent, as presented by the poet. But if it is to be subjected to grammatical analysis, *To be*, or *not to be*—the choice between existence and non-existence—is the real subject to *is*, that which it is asserted *is the question*. There is a repetition of the subject in the determinative *that*. (26) In such examples, as in the expressions, "Your *fathers*, where are *they?* and the *prophets*, do *they* live for ever?" and "That the soul be without knowledge, *it* is not good," &c., there is what we may call in reference to grammar an emphatic repetition of the subject—a repetition intended for rhetorical effect. By this contrivance, the prominent conception in the proposition is presented first and alone; the speaker pauses upon it, and leaves the hearer's mind to pause for a moment upon it, and in proceeding to finish his assertion assumes a representative of the subject, which receiving emphatic force gives still greater prominence to the principal conception. (27) How much would be detracted from the force of these expressions by reducing them within the limits of the usual construction? *To be or not to be is the question*, *Where are your fathers? Do the prophets live for ever?* are forms of construction manifestly *flat* when compared with the original examples.

The second construction, which must be treated in the same way, and not as a *simple* infinitive modification, is one already noticed in treating of the substantive accessory employed as an objective

---

(25) Repeat what is said about such constructions as, "*To be*, or *not to be*, that is the question." (26) What explanation is given of the repetition of the subject in this and in such examples as, "your fathers, where are they"? (27) What would be the effect of reducing such expressions within the limits of the usual form of construction? Illustrate by example.

modification. (§ 107 : 6—9.) (28) It consists of a noun or pronoun in the accusative case and an infinitive, together forming the objective modification of a verb. (29) We submit the following as examples of this construction.

"I know *thee to be* expert in all customs," &c. = *I know that thou art expert*, &c., which is a substantive accessory employed as an objective modification. "And saw no *harm come* to him" = *And saw* THAT NO HARM CAME *to him.* The verb *to see* is, we believe, rarely followed by an infinitive. It is often followed by a substantive accessory with conjunctive *that*, sometimes by an interrogative substantive accessory with *whether* or *if.* *He wishes his* SON TO LEARN *grammar* = *He wishes* THAT HIS SON SHALL LEARN *grammar.* *I expected* HIM TO COME = *I expected* THAT HE WOULD COME. "I feel the *table to be* hard" = *I feel* THAT THE TABLE IS HARD. *I find* HIM TO BE *a good workman.* "I found his opinions to accord with mine' = I found *that his opinions* accorded, &c. "I commanded the *people to be* numbered" = *I commanded* THAT THE PEOPLE SHOULD BE *numbered.* "His Lord commanded *him to be* sold" = *Commanded* THAT HE SHOULD BE *sold* [(30) Here the party to whom the command is given is suppressed; namely, in the first example, the officers of government, and, in the second, the other servants of the Lord. This party, if expressed after *commanded*, would according to the original use of this verb be the dative modification. Sometimes the party to whom the command is given and the party which would form the subject, when the full accessory follows the verb *command* are identical; as in the example "Jonadab commanded his *sons* not *to drink* wine" = *Jonadab commanded his sons, that they should not drink wine.* *His sons* may be regarded in the original example either as the dative after *commanded*, or the accusative before *to drink;* or perhaps as fulfilling both functions (partly by implication). If we regard the verb *command* as taking the name of the person to whom the command is addressed as its *objective modification*, as, we believe, it is now commonly regarded, all these infinitives after it, especially that in the last example, must be considered as infinitives expressing the purpose, or end for which the command is given. This way of viewing the construction is less accordant with the original use of the verb *command*, less consistent with the old English idiom, and in other respects objectionable. (*See* § 79. *Note p.* 219.)]

---

(28) Describe the second construction above alluded to. (29) Adduce examples, and transform the infinitive construction in each into an accessory. Repeat the remark in reference to the verb *see.* [(30) Repeat the substance of the remarks on the verb *command.*]

(31) There are several other verbs, besides those employed in the examples, such as *imagine*, *suppose*, *consider*, *believe*, *deem*, &c., which occasionally take after them a contracted accessory of this kind. But this construction is far from being so common in English, as it is in the Latin and some other languages.

(32) This construction may be distinguished from others, in which infinitives perform a part, by the fact, that it can be exchanged for an objective accessory, having the same word which as accusative precedes the infinitive, for its subject noun. In this manner it can be readily distinguished from the infinitive which indicates the *purpose*, or end of the verb's action. This latter sort of infinitive cannot be exchanged for an accessory having the accusative which precedes the infinitive for subject, without a change of sense. The difference between these two kinds of construction may be best seen by trying examples of the infinitive indicating *purpose*, or *end* employed after some of the verbs in the examples given above. (For some of these verbs admit of both constructions after them, but with results, as regards meaning, markedly different.) Thus, "That we may *find grace to help* in time of need." If, as in the examples adduced above, we substitute for this, *That we may find* THAT GRACE WILL, CAN, &c., HELP US *in time of need*, we totally change the meaning. To retain the same meaning, we must *retain* the word grace, which is the true objective modification, in the principal proposition, and supply a subject in the accessory proposition; thus, *That we may find* GRACE, THAT IT MAY HELP US, &c. "They *found nothing to answer*" (Neh. v. 8), in like manner must be changed, not into *They found that nothing would answer*, which changes the sense; but into *They found nothing, in order that they might answer*, or *nothing they could answer*. In these examples the accessory is added *after* the real *objective modification*, and shows the *purpose* or *end* of the action of *finding* "*grace*," and *finding* "*nothing*." Besides, the accessory is of an entirely distinct class; it is not as in the former examples an *objective substantive accessory*, but an adverbial accessory of purpose.

(33) In analysis, we may recognise this construction by the name of the *accusative and infinitive contracted objective accessory*; or we may call it, for the sake of greater brevity, by the name

---

(31) Enumerate other verbs which occasionally take after them a contracted accessory of this kind. Is this construction very common in our language?

(32) Repeat the substance of the directions given to enable the learner to distinguish this use of the infinitive from other uses, illustrating by examples. Write the examples.

(33) What is the name given to this construction? (34) Repeat the caution.

familiar to Latin grammarians, *The Infinitive with the Accusative be fore it*, (34) taking care to distinguish it from the infinitive of purpose, and bearing in mind that the whole construction—accusa tive and infinitive with their complements, if they have any—forms the Objective Modification of the principal verb.

(35) This construction may be distinguished by the fact that, like the simple objective modification, it answers to the question formed by WHAT with the principal verb. Thus, taking the example, "I feel the table to be hard," the answer to *What do I feel?* is, "*The table to be hard.*" "I know thee to be expert." *What do I know?* Answer, "THEE TO BE EXPERT." On the contrary, it requires the two questions made with WHAT and TO or FOR WHAT PURPOSE to elicit in answer both accusative and infinitive, when an accusative and infinitive of *purpose* follow a verb. To illustrate by examples: *That gentleman has found, or procured, or engaged an able tutor* TO INSTRUCT *his son.* What has the gentleman found, or procured, or engaged? Answer: *An able tutor.* For what purpose has he found, &c., an able tutor? Answer: *To instruct his son. The Christian finds grace* TO HELP *in time of need.* What does the Christian find? Answer: *Grace.* For what purpose does he find grace? To help in time of need.* If we propose these two questions in the case of an accusative and infinitive contracted objective accessory, we shall find that the answer to the first question exhausts the *matter;* and that the second question is irrelevant. To illustrate by an example; "I found his opinions to accord with mine." What did I find? His opinions? No; but "his opinions to accord with mine" = *That his opinions accorded with mine.* For what purpose, or end, or in order to what did I find *that*

* Perhaps such propositions might be employed or understood so that the infinitive would be equivalent, not to an accessory of purpose, but an adjective accessory. The Christian finds grace that will help him in the time of need. The gentleman has procured a tutor, who will instruct his son. Explained in this way, *grace* and the accompanying accessory form an objective modification—an answer only to the question, *What does the Christian find?* But this is a different sense from that contemplated above, and from that intended in the passage which we have slightly altered—Καὶ χάριν εὕρωμεν, ΕΙΣ εὔκαιρον βοήθειαν. Heb. 4 : 16.

(35) Describe a way of detecting this construction by a form of question. Illustrate this by examples; and show that the question will not apply to other infinitives preceded by accusatives. (36) Punctuation? Answer. No interpunction.

his opinions accorded with mine? There is no response to this in the example. The question is irrelevant. Compound infinitives are also used in this kind of construction. Luke ii. 44.

Exercises I. II. &c.—Furnish examples of this construction.

§ 143. Contracted Accessories formed by the help of Participles.—(1) Participles being a species of descriptive adjectives—adjectives which describe an object by the attribution of action progressive or completed*—the remark already made, that, perhaps, all adjectives might be regarded as contracted accessories, applies to this class of words. (2) We shall, however, in this place notice only the uses of the participle, in which it *manifestly* performs the part of a verb, and the construction in which it stands serves instead of an accessory proposition. (3) All other participles we leave to be treated as simple descriptive adjectives.†

(4) We here distinguish two modes in which a participle is employed. (5) First, a participle is employed as the modification of a noun performing a function in a proposition, either as subject, or as a modifying word; (6) and, secondly, a participle is employed with a noun which performs *no function* in a complete proposition, but stands *grammatically* independent of the *principal* proposition, to which the construction formed by said noun and participle, with, or without accompanying modifications, serves *logically* as an accessory.

(7) The participle in the first case can be treated in the same

* Even the participle *being*, may be regarded as implying action in some sense—*activity* in opposition to mere *passivity*. The perfect participles express, of course, action completed.

† The reader will remember that whenever a verbal in *ing* performs *any* function of a noun, *we* do not class it with the participles, but treat it as belonging to a distinct species of words. Some grammarians have caused much confusion, both to themselves and their readers, by regarding the verbal in *ing* as always a participle when it takes after it an *objective*, or *adverbial* modification; though often in such cases it performs as clearly some function of a noun, as when they admit it to be a substantive—viz., when it is accompanied only by the modifications appropriate to other classes of nouns.

§ 143. (1) Repeat the remark about participles. (2) To what uses of the participle do we restrict our notice here? (3) How are participles to be treated in other cases? (4) How many modes of using participles may be distinguished? (5) Describe the first mode. (6) Describe the second mode.

(7) How may the participle be treated, when employed in the first mode?

manner with other adjective modifications. (8) When employed in the second way, the noun and participle must be treated as a peculiar construction which does not come within the reach of any of the modes of analysis yet considered. They must of necessity be treated as a contracted accessory. The participle cannot be treated as a simple adjective modification.

(9) We furnish some examples of the first kind of construction, and place over against the propositions of a simple *form* in which they occur equivalent compound propositions, with complete accessories, instead of the participial construction. "The neighbors *hearing* what was going forward, came flocking about us"=WHEN THE NEIGHBORS HEARD, &c., *Accessory of Coincident Time.* "*So saying*, he dismissed them"=*As he so said, he dismissed them.*" Same species of accessory.

"Aspiring to be gods, if angels fell,
Aspiring to be angels, men rebel"

=*If angels fell when they aspired, or because they aspired*, &c.; *men rebel, when or because they aspire*, &c.—Accessory of Causality. (*See* § 125: 15, 16.) *Embarrassed by vulgar cares, he cannot spend his time in making himself wiser*, &c.=*Because he is embarrassed*, &c.—*Accessory of Causality.* "The two ladies, having heard reports of us from some malicious person, were that day set out for London." (10) The construction with this compound participle can be expanded most conveniently into a CO-ORDINATE proposition, preceding that which is *logically* the *principal* proposition, and which is really modified by it, though the construction is co-ordinate, and not of the accessory form. Thus, *The two ladies had heard reports, &c., and had set out for London that* morning. We shall take farther notice of co-ordinate propositions employed with a modifying effect, when we come to treat of *co-ordinate* construction. (See § 146.)

"All the tumult of a guilty world,
Tost by ungenerous possions, sinks away"

=*Which is tost by ungenerous passions.* An adjective accessory. "*Received us falling*"=*Received us when, or as we fell*—Accessory of Coincident Time.

---

(8) How must the participle be treated, when employed in the second mode?

(9) Copy examples, and transform the participial construction into an equivalent accessory in each case, naming the accessory. (10) Repeat what is said of constructions with the compounds formed with *having*.

(11) When, as in these last examples, the participle modifies a substantive which performs a function different from that of subject noun, it is not always so easy to change the participial construction into an accessory, because the participial construction is sometimes the only mode of expression in use. When this is the case, the participle may be treated like a descriptive adjective modification. Even when it can be readily exchanged for an accessory, it may, as we said above, be treated in ordinary analysis as a *simple* modification. But we advise the learner to exercise himself in trying to supply the equivalent construction; not so much for the purpose of obtaining a satisfactory analysis of the language, as for the important purpose of increasing his facilities for writing with elegance and harmony. Sometimes, the full construction, with a complete accessory, will be found preferable in reference to style; at other times, the participial construction will be found more compact and forcible. It is highly advantageous, for the purpose of speaking and writing with fluency and smoothness, to be able to avail ourselves *readily* of all the resources which language affords for varying or improving our modes of expression.

(12) Punctuation.—When a participial construction is separated from the noun which it modifies, it is cut off from the rest of the construction by a comma, or commas, in the same manner as a circumstantial adverb, or adverbial phrase. This construction falls under the same rules, as to interpunction, with the circumstantial modification.

We add a few poetical examples of the participial construction, which the learner may transform into accessory propositions.

"He sung, Darius, great and good
By too severe a fate,
Fallen! fallen! fallen! fallen!
Fallen from his high estate,
And *weltering* in his blood!"

"War, he sung, is toil and trouble;
Honor, but an empty bubble;
Never *ending*, still *beginning*,
Fighting still, and still *destroying*."

"The Passions oft, to hear her shell,
Throng'd around her magic cell,
Exulting, *trembling*, *raging*, *fainting*,
Possessed beyond the Muses' painting."

---

(11) What is said of constructions in which the participle modifies a noun which **is not** the subject of a proposition?

(12) Punctuation?

"And *dashing* soft from rocks around,
Bubbling runnels join'd the sound,
Through glades and glooms the mingled measure stole;
Or o'er some haunted stream, with fond delay—
Round a holy calm *diffusing*,
Love of peace and lovely *musing*—
In hollow murmurs died away."

"Vital spark of heavenly flame!
Quit, oh quit this mortal frame:
Trembling, hoping, lingering, flying," &c.

"*Defeating* oft the labors of the year,
The sultry *south* collects a potent blast."

"*Strained* to the root, the stooping *forest* pours
A rustling shower of yet untimely leaves."

Exercises I. II., &c., furnish examples of this construction, accompanied by equivalent compound propositions with complete accessories.

Noun and Participle Contracted Accessory, or Noun and Participle Absolute. (13) We next proceed to give examples of the participial construction, consisting of a participle attached to a noun which performs no grammatical function in the *principal* proposition.

"The *command devolving* upon Eustace St. Pierre, he offered to capitulate with Edward." "*This being resolved*, my wife undertook to manage the business herself." "*The door being opened*, the child addressed him." See an example in Heb. xi: 39, 40.—"The *sea* and the *waves roaring ;* men's *hearts failing* them for fear," &c.

"Where rapture burns with rapture, every *line*
With rising frenzy *fired*."

"Thus, *darkness aiding* intellectual light,
And sacred *silence whispering* truths divine,
And *truths* divine *converting* pain to peace,
My song the midnight raven has outwinged," &c.

"*This said*, he sat" = *When this was said*," &c.

"The *service past*, around the pious man,
With ready zeal each honest rustic ran."

"But see the fading many-colored woods,

(13) Give a few examples of participial construction of which the noun and participle are independent. These may be written.

Shade deepening over shade, the country round
Imbrown."

"*Shade*, unperceived, so *softening* into shade;
And *all* so *forming* an harmonious whole."

The learner having transcribed these examples, may, after studying the following remarks, be exercised in transforming the substantives and participles into equivalent coustructions, whether compound or co-ordinate propositions.

(14) We may call this construction THE NOUN AND PARTICIPLE ABSOLUTE, or NOUN AND PARTICIPLE CONTRACTED ACCESSORY. (15) It is most commonly resolvable into an Accessory of Coincident Time, preceded by the conjunctive adverbs *when* or *while;* as in the example above, "*This being* resolved," is equivalent to *When this was resolved*, "my wife," &c. Some of these participial constructions are equivalent to an accessory of causality, for instance that referred to in Heb. xi. 39 : 40, "God having provided some better thing for us," &c. — *For*, or *because God had provided*, &c.*

* This construction is commonly called by the grammarians *The Nominative Absolute.* Like the accusative and infinitive contracted accessory, to which it is in some respects analogous, this is a very common construction in the Greek and Latin languages; but it is a construction uncongenial to modern English—an exotic derived from a different soil. For, though a similar form of construction was not uncommon in Anglo-Saxon, it seems to have disappeared in the early English of the old chroniclers, and to have been reintroduced, as at present used, by the learned in imitation of Latin models. It is known in Latin by the name of the *Ablative Absolute,* in Greek by the name of the *Genitive Absolute;* the *ablative* and *genitive cases* being employed in these languages respectively in the formation of this construction. In Anglo-Saxon the dative (which performs the functions both of the Latin dative and ablative) is the case employed in this construction. We may still find examples of the employment of the *dative* form (now commonly, but improperly, recognised as exclusively an *accusative* form) in some respectable English authors. Milton uses the expression, "Him destroyed, or won." And Archbishop Tillotson, "Him only excepted." These expressions must be rejected as solecisms, except we choose to defend them as remains of the Anglo-Saxon construction, or admit the use of *him* for the nominative case, as, on some occasions, legitimate. The compound *himself* is often so employed. We cannot, we think, defend these constructions as remains of the Anglo-Saxon idiom, since this mode of expression seems to

(14) How may we name this construction? (15) Into what kind of accessory is it most commonly resolvable? Illustrate by examples.

(16) It is, in many (perhaps in most) instances where this participial construction could be introduced, more congenial to our idiom instead of either noun and participle or accessory, to employ a *Co-ordinate Proposition.* This co-ordinate proposition is placed before the principal, proposition which it *logically* modifies, though this is not decidedly indicated by the form of the construction. The coincidence, or (what is nearly the same) immediate subsequence in time, or whatever happens to be the relation between the two propositions, is to be gathered only from mere juxtaposition, and order of arrangement. (*See* § 146.)

(17) When a *noun and participle* absolute occur in analysis, we give the name of the construction, and furnish the equivalent accessory, or equivalent co-ordinate construction, if this happens to be more agreeable to our idiom.

(18) REMARK I.—Constructions of this kind are found consisting of a participle without a noun expressed. Examples: *This conduct,* VIEWING *it in the most favorable light, reflects discredit on his character* = *This conduct,* WE VIEWING *it,* &c., or, with an accessory, *This conduct,* IF WE VIEW *it,* &c. "His conduct, *generally speaking,* is honorable" = WE, or I *speaking generally;* or IF WE SPEAK *in a general way,* &c. *The boy is far advanced in learning,* CONSIDERING HIS AGE = *If we consider his age.* This may be distinguished by the name of the *Participle Absolute.* In all the examples above given, it seems equivalent to a conditional accessory.

(19) REM. II. Sometimes, on the contrary, the participle is suppressed in this kind of construction, especially by the poets. But in such cases it is easily supplied, and ought to be supplied as the first step in the analysis of such elliptical forms of expression. Examples:

" The *bow* well bent, and smart the *spring,*
Vice seems already slain," &c.

= *The bow* BEING *well bent, and the spring* BEING *smart.*

---

have become obsolete in our language long before the times of Milton and Tillotson; and if we should make allowance for the use of *him* as a nominative in these and similar instances, it must be with the caution, that the practice is not to be imitated. (*See* § 155 : 14, 15.)

---

(16) What other construction for the same purpose is more congenial to our idiom?

(17) How are we to treat this construction in analysis?

(18) Repeat the substance of the remark on the participle absolute, and illustrate by examples.

(19) Repeat substance of Remark II. and illustrate by examples.

"Whilst thou, more happy power, fair Charity,
Triumphant sister, greatest of the three,
Thy *office* and thy *nature* still the same,
Lasting thy *lamp*, and unconsumed the *flame*,
Shalt still survive," &c.

The participle *being* is here *implied* with the nouns *office*, *nature*, *lamp* and *flame;* and must be *supplied* in analysis.

(20) PUNCTUATION.—The noun and participle absolute must always be separated from the rest of the discourse by a comma, or by commas, when it does not stand first in the sentence.

EXERCISES I., II., &c.—Furnish examples of constructions containing the noun and participle absolute; and present in contrast with them equivalent forms of expression containing either an accessory, or in suitable cases, a co-ordinate proposition, instead of the *participial*, or *independent* form of construction.

---

(20) Punctuation?

CHAPTER X.

COMBINATION OF INDEPENDENT PROPOSITIONS.

§ 144. (1) We have now finished the important part of our proposed task—the analysis of the structure of propositions. We have considered the *subject* and the *predicate*—the parts essential to every proposition; the *subject noun* and *verb*, which are the principal, the prominent or central constituents of these essential members of propositions; and the various modifications which nouns and verbs receive from *inflection*, from *single words* employed to complete them, and from *propositions* employed to complete them. (2) It now remains to consider the connection of propositions (simple or compound) *grammatically independent* of each other, in order to form *discourse;* and with this the connection of independent members of propositions, and independent complements or modifications which enter into the structure of propositions. The connection or combination of independent propositions will chiefly engage our attention, but the combination of independent members under the form of a single assertion, and of independent complements modifying the same principal word must not be forgotten.* (3) Propositions *grammatically* independent are, when connected together, sometimes called *co-ordinate propositions* to distinguish them from *subordinate* or accessory propositions, used to modify other propositions, to which, on this account, they are regarded as *subservient* or *subordinate.* Independent members and complements may also be called *co-ordinate members* and *co-ordinate complements.*

* It must be remembered that we here speak of propositions, members of propositions, and complements as *grammatically* independent—of independence as regards construction, not of absolute *logical* independence.

§ 144. (1) Recapitulate progress made. (2) State what remains to be done. (3) What name is given to independent propositions when combined? To independent members and complements combined? And what name to the connecting or combining of such propositions?

The connecting or combining of independent propositions may be called *co-ordinate construction*, or the *construction of discourse*, as distinguished from the construction of propositions.

General Remarks.—(4) It may be proper here to remark that independent propositions, uttered in succession, and without coherence, do not form what we call discourse. Speech is a representation of thought, discourse a representation of a *process* of thought. Now, in thinking, what passes in a sane man's mind is not an endless succession of scattered incoherent thoughts, but thoughts connected together, each thought suggesting the succeeding thought, in accordance with certain laws of association. Even in the most desultory conversation of a man of sound mind, there is a regular succession of thought communicated to those whom he addresses; and if he expresses a thought which seems manifestly foreign to the general purport of his discourse, the hearer is disappointed, and feels ready to ask, what connection has this with the subject under discussion. Much more do we expect this kind of coherence—this connection of the thoughts and of the propositions which express them—in a regular and carefully prepared discourse, whether spoken or written.

(5) When the train of thought in a discourse is natural and coherent, and the words chosen to express it appropriate, and well arranged, the mere *juxtaposition* of the propositions often serves to indicate sufficiently the nature of their connection. Hence it often happens that no word or sign is employed to unite consecutive independent propositions. But because no *connective word* is used, we must not conclude that there is no connection. On the contrary, propositions most closely connected by the train of thought which they express, often least need the aid of connectives.

(6) If only connection—mere joining together of Independent Propositions were to be effected, a single connective would be sufficient for this purpose. Indeed, we might in this case dispense altogether with connective words, and indicate connection by mere *juxtaposition*. But there are other relations, besides that of being linked together in expressing a train of thought, subsisting between co-ordinate propositions, though these relations are not those of *grammatical dependence*. Some of these relations are shown by the contrivances adopted in co-ordinate construction. The words used for the purpose of combining such propositions often, if not always, imply more than mere con-

(4) State the substance of this paragraph.

(5) State the substance of what is said about the omission of connective words.

(6) Explain the reason that we have more than one connective for independent proposi-

nection. (7) The words thus employed are called *Conjunctions*, though they ought to be carefully distinguished from those *conjunctions* and *conjunctive words* which serve to connect accessory with principal propositions. When we wish to distinguish these conjunctions from those employed with accessories we may call them *Conjunctions*, or *Connectives* of *Co-ordination*, or simply *Connectives*.

(8) All these connectives serve one purpose in common, viz.: they indicate that the construction is co-ordinate, as distinct from the connection of principal and accessory in compound propositions.

(9) But besides this common purpose, these words serve peculiar and distinct purposes. This fact, that distinct purposes are served by co-ordinate construction, implies the possibility of dividing such construction into separate species, according to the several purposes which it effects. (10) We shall call attention to three well marked species of *Co-ordinate Construction*, each serving a distinct purpose, besides the common purpose of indicating *co-ordination*. We shall treat each of these three species briefly, noticing varieties under them, and illustrating each by examples. We shall also subjoin some additional observations on this kind of construction, and on some of the words which are chiefly employed as connectives.

§ 145. I. (1) The first species of Co-ordinate Construction which invites our attention is that which we may call COPULATIVE CO-ORDINATION, or *Simple Connection*. (2) This is the most simple and the most frequently employed of all the forms of co-ordinate construction. It indicates less beyond simple connection in the same train of thought than any other species of co-ordinate construction, perhaps, sometimes nothing beyond this. Hence this comes to be used in all cases where there is nothing in the relation of propositions to one another calling for the other forms of construction. All that is, in any case, implied by this species of co-ordination, beyond mere conjunction, is that the connected propositions have the same relation to the general drift or bearing of the *discourse*.

(3) The word chiefly employed to indicate this species of co-or-

---

tions. (7) What are the connectives used for this purpose called? From what words must they be distinguished, and how?

(8) What common purpose does this class of connectives serve? (9) Do they serve any other besides this common purpose? (10) How many species of co-ordinate construction may be distinguished?

§ 145. (1) What name is given to the first species of co-ordinate construction? (2) State the substance of what is said of this kind of connection of propositions.

(3) What is the word chiefly employed to indicate this species of connection? (4) Men-

dination is AND. This word is the *grand copulative.* (4) The adverbs *also*, *moreover*, *too*, are sometimes employed with a copulative force, and the adverbial phrases, *besides this*, *in addition to this*, &c. (*Eke* may be regarded as obsolete.) *And*, however, is often employed along with these, and when it is not, it is perhaps always *implied.* It may perhaps be admitted as the correct statement of fact, that when these adverbs or phrases are employed, the suppression of *and* is more readily admitted. We shall say something more of these adverbial conjunctives after we have first treated *and.* (5) We subjoin an example or two of propositions connected by AND.

"Length of days is in her right hand; *and* in her left hand are riches and honor." "Her ways are ways of pleasantness, *and* all her paths are peace." Here *and* connects *simple* grammatically independent propositions. In the following example it unites two compound propositions. "She is a tree of life to them that lay hold of her; *and* happy is every one that retaineth her." Again in the following it connects two accessory propositions, which in relation to one another are independent, or what we may call co-ordinate accessories. "When wisdom entereth into thine heart, *and* (*when*) knowledge is pleasant unto thy soul, discretion shall preserve thee," &c. We need not multiply examples; the form of construction is so very common and familiar. We can scarcely write a line without the employment of an *and.*

(6) The word *and* may be considered as performing alone the function of a proposition—perhaps, an imperative proposition. It is pretty generally agreed, even by those who differ most widely about the derivation of this word, that *and* means *add*, or something equivalent. (7) By substituting the imperative proposition *add*, or *add to this*, in the examples above adduced, the meaning will remain unchanged, though the *junction* will naturally appear more clumsy from the exclusion of the customary form of expression, and the introduction of an unusual one. Thus, "Length of days is in her right hand;" *add*, or *add to this*, "in her left hand (*are*) riches and honor." (8) If *and* is thus recognised as an imperative, and equivalent to an imperative pro-

---

tion some other *subsidiary* words, and tell how they are used. (5) Give examples of the connection of simple independent propositions, of compound propositions, and of accessory propositions independently used to modify the same principal proposition.

(6) What is said of the function which AND performs, and of its original sense? (7) What word may be substituted for it, without destroying the sense? Illustrate by examples. (8) What results if AND is recognised as an imperative?

position, the proposition which follows it becomes an objective accessory to it. Add to this "in her left hand"=*that* "in her left hand" (*are*) "riches and honor," will then be a *compound proposition*, and *co-ordinate* with the preceding simple proposition.

(9) There is perhaps still another proposition implied in this kind of juncture; for it indicates, agreeably to the usage of language, that the assertion which follows the connective is *simply additional* or *continuative* of the same train of thought in the same direction, not opposed to the preceding assertion, or expressing an exception to it. (10) From this it follows that *and* (and the remark applies to other conjunctions) serves as the abbreviated form of a proposition, or propositions employed for the purpose of uniting other propositions, besides indicating that a certain relation exists between these connected propositions.

(11) All this, however, may be overlooked in practical analysis. *And* may be called the simple Copulative Conjunction, and the propositions between which it stands may be regarded as *co-ordinate* and connected by its means.

(12) The words *also*, *moreover*, *besides*, *besides this*, *in addition to this*, &c., employed, sometimes with, and sometimes without *and*, in the junction of *co-ordinate* propositions continuative of the same train of thought, are to be regarded as performing their usual functions, but not in the proposition which follows them, and which they help to connect. If we thrust them upon this following proposition, we create confusion. They are to be regarded as complementary of (what we may be allowed to call) the conjunctional or connecting proposition. In other words, they modify the conjunction *and*, expressed or implied, or some other implied verb. Example: "Moreover, by them is thy servant warned." = *Add* or *join moreover*, or *beyond this*, or *I say more beyond this*, "by them," &c. If we bring moreover as a modifying adverb into the subjoined proposition we spoil the meaning. *Also* is perhaps rarely to be included in the *connective proposition;* but *besides this*, or *besides* alone, with *this* implied, and *in addition to this*, are often a part of the *juncture*. They are when alone equivalent to *add*, or, *I say besides this; I say in addition to this*, &c. In analysis, they may be treated when thus employed as copulative phrases or expressions.

---

(9) What more is implied in this kind of *juncture* of propositions? (10) Repeat the remark in reference to AND and other co-ordinate conjunctions.

(11) How may *and* be treated in analysis?

(12) Repeat the substance of what is said about the subsidiary words used with or without AND. Illustrate by example.

(13) We have already said that words are not always indispensably necessary to connect a train of propositions. In connecting *periods*, or *sentences*, consisting often of several co-ordinate propositions, and closing with a rest, or momentary suspension in the progress of the discourse, conjunctions are very generally dispensed with in our language. And co-ordinate propositions in the same period, when there is no danger of ambiguity or misapprehension arising from the suppression of connective words, are often placed together without the intervention of the copulative. We may give as an example, Cæsar's celebrated dispatch, "Veni, vidi, vici," *I came*, *I saw*, *I conquered*. The suppression of the conjunction in such cases may be regarded rather as a *rhetorical* contrivance, than as an ordinary *grammatical* construction. (14) But when more than two similar propositions follow each other in succession, it is customary to omit the copulative between all but the last proposition and that which precedes it. For example: "The hill appeared more steep, the fruits seemed harsh, their sight grew dim, *and* their feet tripped at every little obstruction." Here are four propositions all connected in co-ordinate construction, and the copulative employed only between the last two. This may be regarded as the regular grammatical mode of connecting co-ordinate propositions, co-ordinate members of propositions, and co-ordinate complements of propositions.

(15) Sometimes, for rhetorical effect, the copulative is placed between each co-ordinate proposition, or co-ordinate member, &c., and that which is connected with it. We select an example from Dr. Chalmers, who seems to have had a strong partiality for this rhetorical contrivance. "We scarcely recognise them as men and women, who can rejoice *and* weep, *and* pine with disease, *and* taste the sufferings of mortality, *and* be oppressed with anguish, *and* love with tenderness," &c.

"Vapors *and* clouds *and* storms."—Thomson.

(16) This repetition of the copulative is sometimes employed with good effect to cause the hearer's mind to dwell on each of a series of important propositions by retarding the enunciation. On the contrary, the total omission of the conjunction indicates the rapid move-

---

(13) Repeat what is said of the occasional connection of propositions without conjunctions.

(14) Tell when the suppression of conjunctions is customary, and illustrate by an example.

(15) Repeat what is said of the repetition of the copulative between each pair of co-ordinates. (16) What is the effect of this repetition? And what the effect of the total suppression of the copulative?

ment of the mind from thought to thought, imitating, as in the example above, the rapidity with which the events expressed succeeded each other.*

(17) When the same assertion is to be made of two or more distinct subjects, for the sake of brevity and compactness of expression we unite the subjects together by the copulative, and employ the verb only once for all the united subjects. For example, William and James are industrious. (18) When two subjects are thus united they are sometimes preceded by the determinative *both ;* as, *Both William and James are industrious.* This unites the subjects more *emphatically.* Both is also sometimes employed in the same way before two united complements. It seems scarcely proper to place *both* in this way before more than two members, or complements, since it implies *duality.*

(19) It will be observed that in this construction the verb is in the plural form. We shall express this fact in one of the rules to be given at the end of this chapter. Propositions of this kind we may distinguish by the name of *Plural Propositions.*

(20) When we employ the *plural* form of a single noun as subject of a proposition, we have what may be regarded as one species of *plural propositions;* for every proposition with a plural form for subject noun has really two or more, sometimes innumerable subjects, but all of the same class of objects, and indicated by the same common name, or general term.

(21) On the other hand, it often happens that two or more predicates are asserted of a single subject. In this case, too, the verbs are connected by the copulative. Thus, "The leaves *fade away, and leave the parent stem desolate,*" = *The leaves fade away, and the*

* The rhetoricians call the suppression of the copula the *figure asyndeton,* = *construction without connectives ;* and the introduction of it between all the propositions, members, &c., when there are more than two, *polysyndeton,* = *construction with many connectives.*

(17) Repeat what is said of the union of several subjects under the same assertion. Example. (18) What is said of the use of the word *both* in uniting two subjects? Example.

(19) What form of the verb is employed in such constructions?

(20) Repeat the remark about the plural form of nouns.

(21) What is said of the use of more than one predicate to the same subject? Example.

leaves leave the parent stem desolate. (22) Sometimes several subjects are united with several predicates in the same construction. "In that season of the year, when the *serenity* of the sky, the various *fruits* which cover the ground, the discolored *foliage* of the trees, *and* all the sweet, but fading *graces* of inspiring autumn, *open* the mind to benevolence, *and dispose* it for contemplation," &c.

(23) Lastly we give examples of the connection of simple modifications of the *same class* used to complete the same principal word. *The dishonest* AND *unfaithful steward has been dismissed. And* here unites two *Descriptive Adjective Modifications*, both affecting the noun *steward. George studies grammar, geometry,* AND *chemistry.* "And leaves the world *to darkness,* AND *to me.*" It is unnecessary to multiply examples of this kind, as they are to be found abundantly in every page we read.*

(24) To recapitulate, we connect by the copulative AND independent propositions, similar accessories modifying the same word independently of each other, subjects having a common predicate or common predicates, predicates having a common subject or subjects, and similar modifications completing the same word in simple propositions, when these propositions, members, modifications con-

* Complements which are not of the same class or kind are seldom united together in this manner, and, when they are so united, we believe they are always ungraceful. We have an example of dissimilar complements connected by *and* in the following: "Hear now this, O foolish people, *and* without understanding." Here we have a noun and preposition complement connected in co-ordinate construction with a descriptive adjective modification; except we shall say that there is an ellipsis of the word *people* after "and." This could have been avoided by translating the passage, O people, foolish and void of understanding. This would be an equally close translation of the original which is literally, O foolish people, and no heart or no intelligence. It might be said that "without understanding" is equivalent in *sense* to an adjective modification. Admitted; but we think that only complements of similar *form* can be gracefully united by the copulative. We would caution the student, if the caution should appear necessary against the imitation of such forms of expression.

(22) Illustrate the union of several subjects with several predicates by an example.
(23) Adduce examples of co-ordinate complements connected by the copulative.
(24) Recapitulate what has been said on the use of the copulative.

cur in carrying forward a train of thought uninterrupted by objections or exceptions.

(25) In analysis, when co-ordinate propositions, members, &c. occur, we must say that they are connected in simple copulative co-ordination by the conjunction *and* alone or modified by *moreover*, *besides*, &c., as the case may be. When the copulative is omitted, the omission must be noticed and accounted for in the manner already stated.

PUNCTUATION (*or rather* INTERPUNCTION) OF CO-ORDINATES CONNECTED BY AND.—(26) Between propositions, whether absolutely independent or accessory, connected in co-ordinate construction, a comma is always placed, whether the copulative is employed or omitted.

In regard of co-ordinate members of propositions, subjects or predicates, and in regard of co-ordinate modifications, the rule is somewhat different. When there are only two *members* or modifications connected by *and*, no comma is employed. The copulative sufficiently indicates the construction. When no copulative is used, a comma must always be placed between co-ordinate members and co-ordinate modifications. So far all are agreed. But when more than two co-ordinate members or modifications are connected, some place a comma between each member or modification and that which succeeds it, even between the last two, though connected by *and*. Others, in the connection of members and modifications, invariably omit the comma where the copulative is employed. This seems to us the simplest and the most consistent rule. Those who place a comma between all the co-ordinates, when there are three or more, in the case of connected subjects, place also a comma after the last before their common verb. Example: John, James, *and* Thomas, are good men. When only two subjects are united by *and* a comma is *not* placed after them by these authors, thus, John and James are good. The distinction established by those who adopt this mode of punctuation between the case of two and three or more subjects appears to us capricious. (27) If we dismiss this distinction, the rule for pointing this whole class of constructions is very simple; viz., place a comma *always* between co-ordinate propositions; and a comma between co-ordinate members and co-ordinate

---

(25) Repeat the directions given in reference to the analysis of copulative constructions.

(26) Repeat the substance of the remarks on the punctuation, or interpunction of co-ordinates connected by AND. (27) Repeat the simplest form of the rule for the interpunction of this class of constructions, dismissing certain capricious distinctions.

modifications whenever the copulative is omitted. When co-ordinate modifications are themselves attended with modifications, a comma is sometimes used in connection with the copulative.

(28) There is a variety of this kind of construction in which the co-ordinate members are connected in pairs, and a comma placed between each pair. Example: "Interest and ambition, honor and shame, friendship and enmity, gratitude and revenge(,) are the prime movers in public transactions." Here the last comma seems to us improper.

EXERCISES I., II., &c.—Furnish examples of co-ordinate propositions, members, &c.

§ 146. (1) This is, perhaps, the proper place to make some remarks on the occasional employment of the co-ordinate form of construction instead of a compound construction; in other words, of a proposition independent in *form* and connected by the *copulative*, yet, *in use*, having the *force* of an accessory, and serving the purpose of an accessory. We have already adverted to this matter in the end of the section on accessories of time, and in treating of participial constructions. (*See* §§ 129 : 9, and 143 : 16.)

We shall notice only two distinct cases of this employment of the construction with the copulative. (2) The first is to serve instead of an accessory or an infinitive of purpose. We may give as examples, *Will you not come, and dine with us? Why does he not go, and tell his father? Come and see us. He came yesterday and visited us. We shall go to-morrow, and see the exhibition.* These are equivalent to *Will you not come to dine with us?* or, *Will you not come that you may dine with us*, &c. The *coming* is for the purpose of *dining*; the *going* for the purpose of *telling*, &c. (3) Such forms of expression are colloquial, perhaps they might be called vulgar. They are more commonly employed in the interrogative and imperative, than in the assertive form of propositions. We suspect that they are used imperatively and interrogatively in the colloquial intercourse even of good and well-educated society, still they lack precision and elegance. Examples may be found in our standard authors; but few educated men of the present day would be willing to introduce such forms in any kind of dignified discourse. We give an example from Shakspeare:

---

(28) Describe a variety of this kind of construction, and the mode of interpunction, illustrating by an example.

§ 146. (1) Tell what is said of the use of co-ordinate instead of compound construction.

(2) Describe the first case of this use, illustrating by examples. (3) Repeat the substance of the remarks on this use; give example from Shakspeare.

"Could you on this fair mountain leave to feed,
And batten on this moor?"

= *That you might batten*, or *to batten on this moor*.

(4) In this case it is the last of the two connected propositions that serves the purpose of an accessory.

(5) The second case of the employment of co-ordinate for compound construction is that in which one of the two connected propositions—always, we believe, the first one—serves instead of an *accessory of time*, or instead of the *participial construction* which serves the same purpose. (6) This employment of the co-ordinate form of construction is sanctioned by far more general and more respectable usage. It may be regarded as a settled idiom of our language. We use this kind of construction very generally, when, in the ancient languages, a participial construction is employed. (7) Let us illustrate this usage by a few examples. "He opened his mouth, and taught them." The original expresses what is contained in the first of these propositions by a participial construction—a participle modifying the subject noun of the second proposition. The literal translation is, *Having opened his mouth*, or, perhaps, rather, *Opening his mouth, he taught them.* The latter form expresses the intended connection of the thought more exactly than the authorized version. But the translation, as it stands, is more *consonant* to the English *idiom*, especially to the idiom of the period when the translation was made, before the complicated, exotic constructions fashionable in the times of the Commonwealth were forced upon our language. Even to this day, it is less stiff than the *Participial* form of expression. We have similar examples in the following passages: "The same day went Jesus out of the house, and sat by the sea side" = *The same day Jesus, having come out of the house, sat*, &c. or, with full construction, *The same day, when Jesus had come out of the house, he sat*, &c. "He came to the first, and said." (Greek, *Having come*, or *coming to the first, he said.*) "And he answered, and said." "And he came to the second, and said," &c. In all these cases a participial construction is employed in the original Greek. (*See Acts* 18: 1, 2, *and the New Testament, passim.*) (*a*)

(8) In the following example from Shakspeare the latter of two

---

(4) Which proposition in this case serves the purpose of an accessory?

(5) Describe the second case of this employment of co-ordinate construction. (6) **Repeat** the remarks made on this use. (7) Illustrate by examples.

(8) Repeat what is said of the example from Shakspeare.

propositions in the co-ordinate form of construction is equivalent to a conditional or concessive accessory.

"Can one be pardoned, and retain the offence?"

Here the conjunctive words, *though* or *if* or *whilst*, would, perhaps, more precisely indicate the relation between the two propositions. It would be still more *explicit*, though *awkward* and *flat* beside the original, to say, *May one who retains the offence be pardoned?*

(9) In all cases two propositions connected by AND may be considered, as regards *form* of language, *co-ordinate* or independent. Their true relation, as regards *sense* in such exceptional cases as we have presented above, is to be ascertained from the nature of the thought. This relation is indicated by no distinct grammatical contrivance, except we consider *juxtaposition* in this light.

NOTE. (a)—We may be allowed to observe, in connection with this subject, that the translator of the Book of Acts has improperly introduced the copulative in a great number of passages where the employment of it cannot be justified by a reference to idiomatic usage, and when it injures or perverts, to a certain degree, the sense of the original. We refer to Acts 1 : 16; 2 : 29, 37, and 13 : 15, &c., in which we find the expression, "Men *and* brethren." The translator has indeed in all these examples placed *and* in *italics*, indicating that it is not in the original. But this does not help the reader to ascertain the exact sense of the original. The word "brethren" is in the original a noun in apposition in all these passages. The English reader would never find this out from the present translation, even with the help of the *italics*, because *men brethren* is not a usual form of apposition in our language. With the Greeks it was. They employed currently such expressions as *men soldiers*, *men Romans*, *men Athenians*, &c., in which the latter noun serves to designate the employment, the nation, &c., of the men. These expressions we uniformly translate *soldiers*, *Romans*, *Greeks*, &c., suppressing the word *men*, in accommodation to the English idiom. The translator ought to have done the same in the passages above referred to, and in several others, which the reader can readily find by the help of a concordance. In Acts 7 : 2 and 22 : 1, we find the expression "Men, brethren, and fathers," making the hearers addressed in these passages by Stephen and the Apostle Paul to consist of three distinct classes, viz., men, brethren, and fathers—a very illogical division; but it is the division of the translator, not of Stephen or the Apostle Paul. The expression rendered into correct idiomatic English is, simply, *Brethren and Fathers.* Wiclif renders these passages correctly, "Britheren and fadris," and Acts 1 : 16 and 2 : 29, 37, &c.,

---

(9) Repeat the remark in reference to the manner in which we may always regard propositions connected by AND.

"Britheren." This makes it appear the more strange that the translators in the authorized version, and the translators of the 16th century, Tyndale, Cranmer, &c., should have overlooked the Greek idiom to which we have referred.

§ 147. II. ADVERSATIVE OR EXCEPTIVE CONNECTION.—(1) The form of expression, "John arrived in the morning, *and* went away at noon," is that which we would employ, if it were our purpose to give another person simply an account of John's movements. But suppose a friend calls at our house expecting to meet John, and tells us that he has come, because he heard that John arrived this morning, we would naturally say in reply, "John arrived indeed this morning, BUT he went away at noon." Here we are not to give simply an account of John's movements, but to inform our friend why he does not find John at our house, though he did arrive in the morning. That he arrived is in favor of our friend's purpose, but that he went away is adverse to it. This opposition of the added assertion, in reference to the purpose in view, is indicated by the *connective* or *conjunction* BUT.

(2) AND and BUT agree, then, in so far, that they both indicate a connection between propositions; but they differ in this, that *and* connects propositions expressing consentaneous assertions concurring to the same purpose, *but*, on the contrary, connects propositions expressing assertions opposed in reference to their bearing on the point under discussion. (3) We might perhaps say more simply, BUT serves the purpose which AND serves; namely, to *connect propositions*, &c.; and, besides, serves a purpose which *and* cannot serve; namely, to indicate some contrariety in the propositions connected. We may consider AND as by way of pre-eminence the simple connective, and BUT as the *adversative* (sometimes the exceptive) *connective*. (4) We shall call the connection effected by *but adversative* (and sometimes *exceptive*) connection.

(5) The most marked case of adversative connection is that in which BUT is employed between an affirmative and a negative propo-

---

§ 147. (1) Repeat the illustration of the distinction between the connection effected by AND and by BUT.

(2) State the distinction between the uses of BUT and AND. (3) State it more simply.

(4) What name is given to the connection effected by BUT?

sition; thus, *Your father will go to the exhibition to-morrow,* BUT *he will not take you with him.* (6) That *but* is used in such cases is not attributable to the change from affirmative to negative, but to the fact that such change very generally arises from some change or variation in the train of thought. A negative proposition is not necessarily connected with an affirmative one by *but*, and *but* is very often employed to connect two affirmative, and, perhaps, sometimes two negative propositions. Examples: "Fear thou the Lord and the king; *and* meddle *not* with them that are given to change." "Righteousness exalteth a nation, *but* sin is a reproach to any people."

(7) *But* is sometimes employed like *and*, though less frequently than *and*, in connecting members of propositions and complementary words, especially when such words represent a proposition. Examples: *Not John, but James is wrong.* "I shall not die, but live," &c. *John has learnt all his lessons* BUT *one.* "None of them is lost, BUT the son of perdition" = *John has learnt all his lessons, but one he has not learnt;* and, "None of them is lost, but the son of perdition" *is lost.* (8) BUT in such cases expresses an exception, and may generally be represented by the imperative EXCEPT. Thus, John has learnt all his lessons, except one.

NOTE.—This is perhaps a use to which *but* was applied, before it came to be used merely as an adversative—the manner in which it is now most commonly employed. *But,* at least the *but* thus used, is supposed to have been originally an imperative or participle in the Anglo-Saxon language, signifying *be out, except, save,* or *being out, excepting, saving.* We regard the use of this word first mentioned above, viz., to indicate the addition of a proposition in a lesser or greater degree opposed to the previous current of thought, as a secondary use to be traced perhaps to the effect of *insensible extension.* The opposition expressed by *but* in the present use of the language, is in many cases so slight that *and* may be substituted for it without much change of sense. If, indeed, there is no opposition whatever, no variation of the train of thought, *but* cannot with propriety be used. When there is but a trifling variation of the thought we may use *but* to indicate such variation, or we may employ the simple *copulative and,* leaving the hearer or reader to detect and appreciate for himself the opposition between the propositions. If, on the contrary, we think the opposition worthy to be marked, we must do it by the employment of *but.*

---

(5) Mention the most marked case of adversative connection. (6) Repeat the remark about the connection between the change from affirmative to negative assertion, and the employment of adversative construction. Illustrate by examples.

(7) What is said of the use of BUT to connect members of propositions and complementary words? Illustrate by examples.

(8) What does BUT in such cases express? How may it be represented? Example?

If we look into versions made by different translators from the same passage in a foreign tongue, we shall find that, when the opposition between two co-ordinate propositions is slight, one translator will employ *and*, another *but* as the connective word. For example, turning, in *Bagster's Hexapla*, to Luke 21 : 9, we find in the authorized version "BUT when ye shall hear of wars," &c.; in Wiclif, "AND whanne ge schulen here," &c.; in Tyndale and Cranmer, "BUT," &c., and in the versions of Geneva and Rheims "AND," &c. On the contrary, these all agree in using BUT in the commencement of the twelfth verse of the same chapter, perhaps, because there is, if not a more marked *opposition*, at least a more marked *transition* of thought. It is to be observed that in the original Greek, the conjunction employed in both passages is the same, a conjunction performing without discrimination the functions of both AND and BUT, (that is, *but* in the first-mentioned sense as a weaker adversative, but not *but* when decidedly *exceptive*,) and which Greek conjunction (δέ) we translate by one or other of these words, according as the sense of the author, and the genius of our own language demand.

(9) We must not forget a very peculiar use of the conjunction *but*, in which it is nearly equivalent to the adverb *only*. Examples: "Our light affliction, which is BUT for a moment." "If I may touch BUT his clothes." "We shall BUT die." These are nearly equivalent to "which is ONLY for a moment." "If I may touch ONLY his clothes." "We shall only die," *no more*. This use of *but* is apparently of more recent origin than either of the two already mentioned. (10) In propositions of the above form, the negative, it is supposed, was anciently employed; and this use of *but*, so unlike, as it now seems, to the two above mentioned, is thought to have arisen from the habitual suppression of the negative in such expressions. If we insert the negative in the examples above given, *but* will have the force which it has in the second mentioned, and now less prevalent, though, we believe, older use (viz., the *exceptive*) and the sense will remain unchanged. Thus, "Our light affliction, which is" *not* "but for a moment." "If I may" *not* "but touch his clothes." "We shall" *not* "but die." When the *not* is inserted *but*, as in what we have called the older usage, can take *except* or *save* for its substitute. Thus, "Our light affliction, which is" not, except or save "for a moment," &c.*

* When *not* was employed in such expressions as the above, it would naturally receive very little force in pronunciation: thus, which *isn't* but for a moment. This fact may perhaps help to account for the gradual sup-

(9) Describe a peculiar use of *but*, and illustrate by examples. (10) Repeat what is said in reference to a supposed suppression in such cases. Illustrate by examples.

(11) As in the case of simple connection by the copulative, so in the case of adversative connection certain other words besides *but* are sometimes employed in company with it, as subsidiary to it, and often where *but* is suppressed, to express more emphatically the adversative nature of the connection. We notice among these the expressions, *On the contrary*, *on the other hand*, &c. *But* is also sometimes followed, like *and*, by the word *besides*, or *besides this*, *in addition to this*, &c. Examples: *Many think this man a patriot*, ON THE CONTRARY, or BUT ON THE CONTRARY, *we think him a mere time-serving*, *selfish politician. This man is industrious and enterprising*, ON THE OTHER HAND, or BUT ON THE OTHER HAND, *he is very extravagant. This lady is very beautiful*, BUT BESIDES THIS, or BUT IN ADDITION TO THIS, *she is very haughty*. As we remarked in treating of simple connection, it is, perhaps, most proper—most correct—to treat all such words as forming part of the connecting or conjunctive proposition; as modifications, if we please, of BUT (which may be regarded as implied when not expressed), or of some other suppressed verb—such verbs as *add*, *join*, *say*, &c., as I add, say, &c., or *but I add*, *or say on the other hand*, &c. This will save us from thrusting them as modifications on the following proposition, in which they will often appear misplaced and unmeaning.*

pression of the negative. (*See more on this use of* BUT *in Additional Observations*, § 150.)

* It may be remarked that the proposition joined to another by *but exceptive* (and consequently that joined by *but* = *only*) stands often more in the relation of a *subordinate* than of a co-ordinate proposition. It may sometimes be regarded as an *accessory proposition*, designed to modify that to which it is attached by expressing a necessary exception, rather than as an independent proposition. In fact it serves often nearly the same purpose as the *exceptive accessory* already considered.

Propositions in *adversative* construction, are more generally strictly coordinate. This is proved by the fact that in such propositions we can sometimes substitute the *copulative* AND for the *adversative* BUT without material change of the sense. But, as we have seen, even AND, the great connective of co-ordinate propositions, is sometimes employed to join propositions which in sense are really accessory or modifying; and BUT adversative (as well as BUT exceptive) is perhaps much oftener employed in the same way. Yet both AND and BUT are chiefly used to connect propositions essentially independent in *sense*, as well as in *form*. The real criterion of the independence of pro-

(11) Enumerate other subsidiary words employed in adversative construction. Repeat the remarks on their uses, and illustrate by examples.

(12) In the analysis the manner of procedure is the same as in the case of simple connection. The nature of the connection must be stated, whether *adversative* or *exceptive*, distinguishing these from each other, and adverting to the explanation given of the use of *but=only*, when this word occurs in this peculiar use.

(13) As to the punctuation, when *but* joins complete propositions, a comma is always inserted before *but*. (14) When other adversative words, as *on the other hand*, &c., are inserted, for the more full expression of adversative connection, we place a comma also after the whole *connective* phrase, separating it from both the propositions connected. Besides this, it is most usual, we think, to place a comma between *but* and the accompanying words, when both *but* and an adversative phrase are used. This is proper, if we suppose a verb suppressed, and that the connective is really made up of two contracted propositions. Thus, *but on the other hand* may be considered equivalent to *be out* or *except this, that I add or say on the other hand.* (15) When BUT exceptive is employed to connect a single word serving as a member or complement of an incompletely expressed proposition, it is not generally preceded by a comma, except when the connected word draws lengthened accompaniments after it. Thus, in the assertion, *John has learnt all his lessons but one*, a comma is not generally inserted before *but*. In "None of them is lost, *but* the son of perdition;" and "Neither was I taught it, *but* by the revelation of Jesus Christ," the comma is inserted. But in this matter usage is not consistent. Perhaps the comma should in all these cases be inserted. Before BUT for *only* the comma is not employed, as may be seen in the examples given already. When *but* adversative is separated from the proposition which it really connects by another proposition, or an adverbial phrase which requires interpunction, such proposition or phrase, of course, is separated from *but* and its proposition by commas.

---

positions is the *sense* of the discourse, not invariably the *form* of the expression, or, in other words, the conjunction which is employed to connect them. The relation of propositions to one another is not always precisely indicated by the construction of discourse. It is not always necessary that their relation should be so indicated, because it is often rendered sufficiently clear by the train of thought. Neither AND nor BUT can be regarded as ever used for *the express purpose of indicating subordination.*

---

(12) What is said of the mode of analysis?

(13) What is the punctuation when *but* separates complete propositions? (14) What when other adversative words are introduced? (15) What when *but* exceptive is employed to connect a single word? Illustrate by examples.

EXERCISES I., II., &c.—Furnish examples of propositions connected adversatively by *but* and other adversative phrases.

Examples of Exceptive Connection. Examples of *but=only*.

§ 148. III. ALTERNATIVE CONNECTION.—(1) In discourse we often find occasion to introduce two distinct, independent propositions, with the intention of asserting one or the other, but not both. In many cases, we may not know which is to be asserted as true, while we are assured that one of them must be true: in other cases, we may not wish to express decisively which we think true, though we have perhaps formed a decided opinion. We therefore submit to the party addressed a choice between two or more alternatives, expressed by two or more independent propositions. (2) The word chiefly employed as a *connective* for this purpose is OR. (3) As this word serves to conjoin *alternative* assertions, we may call it the *Alternative Connective*, or the *Alternative Conjunction.*

We may illustrate this form of construction (of *discourse*) by the following examples. (4) *These men will govern their passions*, OR *their passions will soon govern them. He will act honorably in this matter*, OR *I shall be greatly disappointed.* (5) In such forms of expression an *alternative* is proposed; neither both propositions, nor one or other by itself is asserted absolutely, but some one of the two. If the first is admitted, the last is abandoned; and, if the first is abandoned, the last is admitted. If it is true, that *the men will govern their passions*, then I abandon the assertion that *their passions will govern them;* but if it is not true that *they will govern their passions*, it is positively asserted that their passions will govern them.*

* It will be noticed that there is some kind of analogy between alternative propositions and conditional propositions. We can sometimes substitute the alternative form of construction for the conditional; or, in other words, we can express the same thought by the conditional and by the alternative form. In the one case we use negative, in the other affirmative propositions. Example: *If the boy does not study, I shall certainly not countenance his negligence. The boy will study*, OR *I will not countenance*, &c. The alternative is a softened and weaker form (a hope is indicated in the example, that the boy will study); and here, as perhaps in all cases of the use of *co-*

§ 148. (1) State the circumstances under which alternative construction is resorted to. (2) What word is used chiefly as connective? (3) How do we name it? (4) Give examples of this construction. (5) Illustrate with reference to the examples.

(6) What frequently happens in alternative construction? Give examples of common

(6) It happens most frequently that assertions connected alternatively have either a *common predicate*, or have a *common subject*. Thus, with common predicates, we have propositions of this form, *William* OR *Robert will accompany us*= *William will accompany us*, OR *Robert will accompany us*. With common subjects, of this form, *Riches may become a blessing* OR *prove a curse to their possessors*. Sometimes also OR is used to connect alternative *complements;* thus, *I see a cloud* OR *a mountain dimly in the distant horizon*. Such expressions can generally be readily resolved into two separate and complete propositions connected by the alternative conjunction. (7) But they cannot in all cases be so resolved. For example, *Riches become a blessing* OR *a curse to their possessors, according to the use which they make of them*, cannot, without a change of the modifications of the predicate, be resolved into separate complete propositions. (8) The grammarians, we think, may safely admit that all *co-ordinate conjunctions* may be used to connect *co-ordinate propositions, co-ordinate subjects*, and *predicates* of propositions and *co-ordinate complements*. See more of this in the additional observations on the co-ordinate conjunctions.

(9) There is another distinct use of the conjunction OR, in which it is always placed between words and not between propositions, and performs a function which has exclusive reference to words. In this use it indicates what we may call *verbal* alternation, or the proposal of a choice of *terms* or *signs* of the same conception, not a choice of *assertions* or of *conceptions*. (10) Thus we say *Alexander*, OR *Paris*, referring to the Trojan prince known by both names. *Logic*, OR *the art of reasoning*. (11) Here OR plainly connects words, and these *mere* words, not words expressive of separate and distinct conceptions, but alternative names for the same conception. This use of OR is so distinct from the preceding that some languages (Latin for example) have a word or sign for this peculiar purpose, altogether different from that employed to perform the first mentioned and more general function of OR.

---

ordinate for *accessory* construction, the former effects *indirectly*, by the aid of inference, that which the modifying construction effects *directly* and indicates explicitly.

---

predicates, &c. (7) Can such constructions be always resolved into separate propositions? (8) What may grammarians safely admit in reference to the connection of co-ordinates?

(9) Describe a distinct use of the conjunction OR. (10) Illustrate by examples. (11) What does *or* plainly connect in this case? What is said of the equivalent for *or* thus employed in other languages?

(12) When we wish to express alternation, or propose a choice of assertions with *greater emphasis*, we employ the word EITHER before the propositions, besides using *or* to connect them. Thus, EITHER *John* OR *William is mistaken*. (13) Some call EITHER, when thus employed, a conjunction; but it is here, as elsewhere, a determinative word, meaning one of two, and serves a purpose similar to that which BOTH serves before co-ordinate propositions, members of propositions, &c., connected by *and*. The expression in the above example is equivalent to, ONE OF TWO *things is asserted*, *John is mistaken*, OR *William is mistaken*.

(14) If what we believe to be the proper sense of EITHER were strictly attended to, it should be used only when a choice of two co-ordinates is proposed; but the use of this word has been *insensibly* extended to cases where there are more than *two alternatives* proposed.* Thus, "*Either* he is talking, *or* he is pursuing, *or* he is in a journey," &c.

(15) The word ELSE is sometimes employed with *or*, sometimes without *or* for the purpose of connecting alternatives. Thus, *William must go with us*, ELSE *I will not go* = OR *I will not go*.

(16) The word *otherwise* is also employed in the same way to connect alternatives. Example: *We must govern our passions*, OTHERWISE *we shall become the worst of slaves*. This is a more emphatic, but also a more stiff manner of indicating *alternation*. *Or* might be used before OTHERWISE, and consequently both *else* and *otherwise* may be regarded as modifications of *or*, just as we may regard *besides*, *on the contrary*, &c., as modifications of *and* and *but*.

(17) In like manner the phrase, *in other words*, is used, sometimes alone, sometimes preceded by *or* to indicate *alternation* between two modes of expressing the same assertion, in the same manner as *or* is employed to indicate alternation of single terms or signs. This may be regarded as a species of *verbal alternative connection*, viz.: the

* The word alternative also means properly *one of two*, and in strictness ought not to be extended to a greater number; but we have ventured to depart, for the sake of convenience, from the strict usage.

(12) What word is used where alternation is to be expressed with emphasis? Example? (13) What do some call EITHER when thus employed? State objection.

(14) What is said of the strict use of either? Give example of its use when there are more than two co-ordinates.

(15) What is said of the use of the word *else* in connecting alternatives? Example?

(16) What of *otherwise?* Example? Is *or* used with *otherwise?*

(17) Repeat what is said of the use of the phrase, *in other words*. Example?

species in which there is a choice presented of different modes of expressing the same *assertion*, or a choice of equivalent propositions. Example: *That man has succeeded in the world*, OR, IN OTHER WORDS, *he has made a fortune;* or simply, IN OTHER WORDS, *he has made a fortune.*

(18) OR may be regarded as the *great sign* of the alternative combination of propositions, members of propositions and complements. The other forms of expression are only subsidiary.

(19) OR has a negative form NOR, and EITHER a negative form NEITHER. We must make a remark or two on the use of these negative forms.

(20) NOR is sometimes employed as a connective when we couple one negative proposition to another. In this case it is equivalent to AND NOT. Thus, *John is* NOT *at home*, NOR *is his brother* = *John is not at home*, AND *his brother is* NOT *at home. That man has* NOT *got money*, NOR *has he got credit.* In such constructions it will be observed that we place the subject after the verb. The poets do not restrict themselves to this mode of arrrangement.

> "What though his bowl
> Flames *not* with costly juice; *nor* sunk in beds,
> Oft of gay care, he tosses out the night," &c.

(21) Neither is sometimes used in the same way. "They toil not, *neither* do they spin," &c.

(22) The more common and emphatic way of connecting two or more members of propositions or complements, in *negative alternation*, is to place NEITHER before the first, and NOR before the second, third, &c., if there are more than two. Examples: NEITHER *John* NOR *his brother is at home. That boy* NEITHER *reads* NOR *writes.* "Give me *neither* poverty *nor* riches." "I am persuaded that *neither* death, *nor* life, *nor* angels, *nor* principalities, *nor* powers, &c., shall be able to separate us from the love of God."

(23) It will be observed that NOR and NEITHER——*nor* express the negation of that which OR and EITHER——OR indicate; that is, they *exclude* an *alternative.*

---

(18) How may OR be regarded? How other forms employed in expressing alternation?

(19) What are the negative forms of OR and EITHER?

(20) How is NOR sometimes employed? Examples? What is remarked about the arrangement? What is said of the poets? Example? (21) What is said of NEITHER?

(22) What is the more common and emphatic mode of connecting *members* of propositions and complements in negative alternation? Illustrate by an example.

(23) What observation is made in reference to *nor* and *neither—nor*?

(24) *Observations on the poetical use of* OR and NOR.—The poets often employ OR instead of EITHER, and NOR instead of NEITHER before the first of two alternative propositions.* OR is most frequently found employed instead of EITHER, and NOR instead of NEITHER in connecting *complements.* Examples:

"Whose greater power
OR bids you roar, OR bids your roaring cease."

"OR other worlds they seemed, OR happy isles."

"OR floating loose, OR stiff with mazy gold."

In prose this would be expressed thus, EITHER *bids you roar*, OR, &c. EITHER *other worlds they seemed*, OR *happy isles.* EITHER *floating loose*, OR *stiff*, &c.

"NOR wife, NOR children more shall he behold,
NOR friends, nor sacred home."

In prose this would be expressed thus, NEITHER *wife*, NOR *children*, &c.

(25) In the poets NOR for *and not*, not only often follows an *affirmative* proposition, but commences a new sentence or section.

"NOR less the palm of peace inwreathes thy brow."

"NOR art thou skilled in awful schemes alone."

"NOR purpose gay,
Amusement, dance, or song, he sternly scorns."

"NOR less at hand the loosened tempest reigns."

In all these examples NOR commences a new sentence, as well as follows affirmative propositions.

"For who * * * * * *
Left the warm precincts of the cheerful day,
NOR cast one longing, lingering look behind?"

---

* This may perhaps be regarded as an imitation of the Latin usage. This language expresses emphatic *alternative connection*, by employing the same *alternative conjunction* before both propositions, or members of propositions or complements. We may remark that it also expresses emphatic simple connection or combination, by a similar repetition of the copulative. Thus, in Latin *Vel—vel* = *Either—or*, *Nec—nec* = *Neither—nor*, *Et—et* = *Both—and.*

---

(24) Mention a usage of OR and NOR peculiar to the poets. Give examples.

(25) Describe a poetical use of *nor*, and illustrate by examples.

Milton has employed NOR as equivalent to *not even:*

"For Heaven hides nothing from thy view,
NOR the deep tract of Hell."

(26) The same mode of punctuation is adopted generally in *alternative* connection of discourse as in *simple* connection. Propositions completely expressed are separated by a comma. When members of propositions or complements take OR or NOR between them the comma is *generally* omitted; though in this matter usage is far from uniform, as will be seen in some of the examples above in which we have followed the punctuation of the copies from which we have quoted. When several co-ordinate complements or members of propositions are connected and the conjunction suppressed, a comma is always inserted. When alternative *names* are connected by *or*, the comma is usually interposed, as, *Alexander, or Paris.*

EXERCISES I., II., &c.—Furnish examples of propositions connected by OR and by EITHER—OR; of the members of propositions—subjects and predicates so connected; and of complements so connected.

(27) YET appears to be sometimes employed in connecting co-ordinate propositions either alone or in connection with *and, but, nor,* &c. We believe, that, generally, in such cases it indicates the suppression of a *concessive* proposition. (*See* § 138: 5.) For example, "I have smitten thee with blasting and mildew, &c., YET have ye not returned unto me" = *And* THOUGH *I have done this, ye have not returned unto me.*

A similar remark might, perhaps, be made in reference to the word *still*, when it apparently serves as the connective of co-ordinates. But most generally this latter when placed thus between co-ordinates modifies some word in the latter proposition.

(28) There are certain forms of expression employed to introduce explanatory matter, such as TO WIT, VIDELICET, usually expressed in writing by the contraction VIZ.; and NAMELY. These may all be regarded as a species of *conjunctive contracted propositions.* In analysis they may be designated conjunctive phrases used to introduce an explanation or enumeration of particulars. They are equivalent to such propositions as the following; *I state particulars to help you to know*, or *that you may see for yourself, I give you names*, or *the names are*, or *by name they are*, or the like. To these we may add *et cœtera*, commonly written, &c., which indicates the connection or addition of unnamed particulars similar to those just enumerated.

---

(26) Tell what is said of the interpunction of alternatives.

(27) What is said of the use of YET in connecting co-ordinate propositions?

(28) What is said of TO WIT, VIDELICET, NAMELY, and &c.?

§ 149. (1) We have already, in treating of simple propositions. given the rule of agreement, or of *concord*, as the grammarians call it, between verbs and subject nouns of the singular and plural forms and of different persons; namely that the verb and subject must be of the same number and person. (2) Some further rules of *concord* become necessary in certain cases of *combined* construction, when two or more subject nouns having common predicates are, for the sake of abbreviation, connected by conjunctions and the predicate expressed *once* for them all together. (3) When two or more subjects are embraced in this manner under one common predicate, they are generally such as are connected by the copulative AND or the alternatives OR or NOR. (4) In rare cases, indeed, BUT is employed between two subjects, but then the verb manifestly applies only to the last subject, and is suppressed after the first. The same rule may be given for such cases of adversative construction as for alternative construction. The facts, so far as regards the form of the verb agree, though we should rather, in the cases of adversative connection, explain the construction, as we have just said, by saying that there is a suppression or ellipsis of the verb after the first subject. The following example will serve as a model of the kind of construction which we mean; *Not interest*, BUT *duty* HAS *determined his choice.*

Leaving out these rare cases of adversative construction to be treated as cases of the ellipsis or suppression of a verb, or, if the reader chooses, to be brought under the rule for alternative subjects, we proceed to lay down rules applying to the case of subjects united by the copulative and of subjects united by the alternative conjunction. (5) The subjects may be all singular, or second, they may be all plural, or third, they may be some singular, and some plural. (6) Omitting the case when all the subjects are plural, because this manifestly comes under Rule I., given in reference to the agreement of verbs and subjects in simple propositions, we have only to do with the cases where all the subjects are singular, or some singular and some plural. (7) These cases need not be considered distinctly in giving a rule for subjects connected by the copulative, as it

---

§ 149. (1) Repeat the reference to a rule of concord already given. (2) In reference to what cases do farther rules become necessary? (3) How are several subjects embraced under one assertion usually connected? (4) Tell what is said of constructions with *but* employed between two subjects. Give an example.

(5) Enumerate three distinct cases of the combination of subjects. (6) Which of these cases may be left out of consideration, and why? (7) Is it necessary to consider these cases distinctly in giving a rule for the concord of verbs with subjects connected by the copulative? Give a reason.

makes no difference whether these subjects are all singular, or partly singular, partly plural. Two subjects, though both singular, when coupled together and both embraced under the same assertion, form a plural and require a plural verb. This fact may be expressed thus as a rule of concord.

RULE IV.—(8) When an assertion is made by a single verb in reference to two or more subjects *conjointly*, the plural form of the verb is employed ; as, *Integrity and industry* DESERVE *success. Pride and poverty* ARE *ill assorted companions.* (*a*)

This rule of course applies whether the *copulative* is employed or suppressed. Example of suppression :

"Love, wonder, joy alternately *alarm*."

(9) We need not give a rule in English for the case in which subjects connected by the copulative are of different persons, since the plural form of all our verbs is always the same for all three persons. (*b*)

EXERCISES I., II., &c.—The learner will furnish examples of propositions having a plurality of subjects in simple connection.

NOTE (*a*).—It is only when the assertion is made of the singular subjects *conjointly* that this rule applies. There are cases in which AND (as well as BUT) is employed between two subjects, and yet the assertion does not apply to both but only to one of the subjects. Thus, *John,* AND *not James,* IS *to blame.*

Sometimes two nouns connected by the *copulative,* express but one single subject, in which case the verb is of the singular number; as, *This great philosopher* AND *good man* LIVES *in poverty.*

Similar to this is the case when an author employs two nouns of kindred meaning, to express more fully a single conception; as, "Their safety and welfare *is* most concerned."

Some writers seem to have imitated the Latin and Greek authors, who often make the verb accord in number and person with the last subject, and leave it to be *supplied* with the others. We do not condemn this practice as inconsistent with any general fixed principle or law of language. If it were a usage universally adopted in such cases, to make the verb, when there are two or more subjects, agree invariably with the last, and leave it to the party addressed to supply it in its proper form with the rest, the grammarian would have no reason to object. But general *good* usage does *not* in our language sanction this mode of expression. The employment of the plural form of the verb, in all cases where the assertion embraces two

(8) Repeat RULE IV.

(9) Why is no rule necessary when the subjects are of different persons?

distinct subjects, is so completely established that every tyro in grammar is ready to detect and condemn as blunders all aberrations from this fixed usage. We recommend in such cases conformity to the general custom of the language. But when men of education have chosen, on some occasions, to adopt a mode of construction not uncommon in the most respectable Greek and Latin classics, we think it improper to regard such variations from the ordinary construction as *blunders.* The grammarian steps out of his place, as we have had occasion before to observe, when he attempts to *legislate* in regard of language. His business is to investigate and describe the usages of language, and to account for them, if he can; but not to dictate what they ought to be. He may with propriety distinguish anomalous and clumsy, or otherwise objectionable forms of expression, and caution the learner against imitating them, though they may be found in writers of the highest celebrity; but he ought not to *stigmatize* as *blunders* forms which have obtained the sanction of reputable usage.

Some examples may be found in respectable authors, of a *singular* noun connected with others by the preposition *with* taking the plural form of the verb; as if, for example, we were to say, *John with his brothers* ARE *going to the country.* We would not imitate this model of construction.

Tenses connected together should be all of the same *form,* whether *simple, emphatic,* or *progressive.* Thus, *The man* EATS *and* DRINKS, or *The man is* EATING *and* (is) DRINKING. DOES *he* EAT *and* (does he) DRINK, or *Is he eating and drinking.* Verbs of different *times,* however, are often connected by the copulative in the same construction; *John* ARRIVED *this morning, and* WILL GO AWAY *this evening.* The tense to be used must be determined by the sense, and a knowledge of the functions which each tense performs; not by the connection.

NOTE (*b*).—In languages which have distinct forms for the several plural persons, the rule is the same as when individuals of different persons are united under the same plural pronoun. If óne of two or more individuals performs the part of the first person, (namely, that of *speaker,*) the plural pronoun is the first person, and the plural verb is, of course, the same person. Again, if of two or more individuals one performs the part of the second person, (the party *addressed,*) and the rest the part of third persons, (that is, of parties only *spoken of,*) the plural pronoun is the second person, and the verb, of course, is of the same person. The pronouns and verbs are of the third person plural, when all the individual subjects represented by the pronouns are only spoken of—that is, in other words, when both the speaker and the party addressed are excluded.

RULE V.—(10) When two or more singular subjects are connected by the alternative conjunction OR, the verb employed is of

(10) Repeat RULE V.

the singular form; as, *James or William* IS *going to accompany me.* That the verb should be singular follows from the fact that the assertion applies only to one of the subjects, not to both.

RULE VI.—(11) When two or more singular subjects are connected by the negative alternative *nor*, the verb employed is of the singular form, as, *Neither James nor William* IS *about to accompany me.*

(12) In this case, though the verb is of the singular form, the negation applies to both subjects. It is denied that either one or other is about to accompany me. The assertion is to be regarded as made of the two subjects separately viewed, or as suppressed in the first, and to be supplied from the second proposition.

There are exceptions found to these two rules; but they are rare in English, and not to be imitated.

RULE VII.—(13) When two subjects, the one singular, the other plural, are connected in the same assertion by OR or by NOR, if the latter is plural, the plural form of the verb is employed; if the latter, on the contrary, is singular, the verb is singular. This is when the verb follows the subjects, which is generally the case; if not it agrees with the nearest subject.

In other words, when two subjects, the one singular, the other plural, are connected in the same assertion by the conjunctions *or* or *nor*, the verb is of the number of the nearest subject. For example, *Either the master or his servants* ARE *to blame. Either the servants or the master* IS *to blame. Neither the master nor the servants* ARE *to blame. Neither the servants nor the master* IS *to blame.*

(14) We are not certain that as regards this last rule examples of a contrary usage may not be found in reputable authors, but we believe that it may be followed with safety in all cases.

(15) When subjects of different persons are connected by OR or NOR it is more difficult to settle the usage. Most of the grammarians agree

---

(11) Repeat RULE VI., with example.

(12) Repeat the remark about the extent of the negation in this case. Any exceptions to the two preceding rules?

(13) Repeat RULE VII., particularly the second form of it with examples.

(14) What is said of exceptions?

(15) What is the opinion of most grammarians in reference to the concord of verbs witl

that the verb should be of the same person with the nearest subject, that is, with the last, except in some few instances in which the verb precedes the subject nouns. (16) Others contend that all constructions with a single verb applied to subjects alternatively connected of variant persons or variant numbers should be avoided. (17) But the fact is, they have not been avoided, but have been used by good authors. (18) Generally speaking the practice is the same in regard of variant persons as variant numbers; namely, the verb is made to agree with the nearest. (19) The employment of singular and plural alternative subjects to the same verb, it seems to us may be always practised with propriety according to RULE VII.; but the use of different persons in this kind of elliptical construction is sometimes excessively awkward. (20) Whenever this happens it is advisable to repeat the verb with each subject, and complete both propositions. Thus, instead of *Either the boy or I* AM *wrong*, we may better complete the construction and say, *Either the boy* IS *wrong, or I am wrong.* With this explanation we may give as,

RULE VIII.—(21) When subjects of different persons are connected alternatively in the same assertion, the verb agrees in person with the nearest subject.

EXERCISES I., II., &c.—Furnish examples to illustrate RULES V., VI., VII., VIII.

§ 150. We here add some additional explanation of the use of BUT equivalent to *only*, drawn partly from Mr. H. Tooke. We commence by selecting two examples (furnished by Mr. Tooke) from Chaucer, of the *full* construction with the *negative expressed.*

"For myn entent is NOT BUT to play."

"That I may have NAT (not) BUT my meate and drinke."

"We should now say *my intent is* BUT *to play*," &c. We add two more examples from Chaucer.

"All N' IS BUT conseil to virginitee."

"For gentillesse N' IS BUT the renommee
Of their auncestres, for hir (their) high bountee," &c.

---

subjects of different persons connected by OR or NOR? (16) What do others think? (17) What has in fact happened already in the use of language? (18) Repeat what has been the general practice as to concord. (19) What opinion is asserted by the author? (20) What advice is given, when the connection of subjects of different persons leads to awkward forms of expression?

(21) Repeat RULE VIII.

We should now say, "*All is* BUT *counsel to virginity*; and *Gentillesse is* BUT *the renown*, &c. N' is = Ne is = is not.

"The omission of the negative before BUT," says H. Tooke, "though now very common, is one of the most blamable and corrupt abbreviations of construction which is used in our language," &c.

Dr. Noah Webster says, "This use of *but* is a modern innovation." The term "modern" is rather vague. We shall not therefore venture to contradict Dr. Webster's assertion. We state the fact, that BUT was employed in the manner described above, the manner to which Dr. Webster refers, before the middle of the sixteenth century. We find *but* thus employed in Tyndale's version, 1534; Cranmer's, 1539, and in the Geneva version, 1557. We give Tyndale's translation of Mark 5: 28, already quoted, as an example from the authorized version. "For she thought: yf I maye *but* touche his clothes," &c. We find examples of this use even as early as the fourteenth century. "But that ligt thing of oure tribulacioun that lastith now BUT as it were bi a momente," &c., Wiclif, 1380. The following are from Wiclif's cotemporary, Chaucer:

"Now, sire, quod she, BUT o (one) word er I go."
Cant. Tales, line 7433.

We have noted another example, but have lost the reference:

——— "Which that am BUT lorne,"

= am BUT lost = *only* lost.

Dr. Webster may well say that this use is "perhaps too firmly established to be corrected." He adds, "The common people in America retain the original correct phrase, usually employing a negative. They do not say, I have but one. On the other hand, they say, I have *not but* one," (pronounced I haven't but one); "that is, I have not except one—except one, and I have none." *Webst. Dict., art. But.*

It might possibly be objected to this explanation of the use of *but* equivalent to *only*, that, if we introduce the negative before *but* thus used, the sense is in some cases entirely changed. Thus, we say, *He can* BUT *fail in his attempt*, and *He can*NOT BUT *fail in his attempt.* The first expression is equivalent to, *He can* ONLY *fail, nothing more;* the last to, *He can do nothing else but must fail* (so far as the opinion of the speaker is concerned), *in his attempt.*

The objection drawn from such examples as this is not, we think, insuperable. We can readily imagine that, after the suppression of the negative, originally used, had become idiomatic, and had been forgotten, it was found convenient to give some of these idiomatic expressions a negative form. This seems to us the probable history of the usage on which the supposed objection rests. To illustrate by an example, when the proposition, *He can* BUT *fail in the attempt*, had become idiomatic—the received formula to express, *He can* ONLY *fail in the attempt*, there would appear no objection to affix the particle *not* to *can* for the purpose of expressing, *He cannot* (*do any thing*), *or he can do nothing* ONLY *fail.* Both forms of expression may be regarded as idiomatic and elliptical, and as expressing a sense which could scarcely be ascertained by a mere reference to the ordinary laws of language. We must in addition have recourse to the history of the language, if we would trace such usages successfully. In such cases, the *whole expression* has come, by *conventional usage,* to bear a meaning which is not to be discovered by ascertaining the proper *import* of the several words and their *construction.* This seems to us the proper description of *idiomatic* expressions. In forming all such, the laws of language—the fixed principles which have generally guided its development—have been held in abeyance, and a conventional sanction has been given to the products of accident, or of the caprice of fashion.

We see no reason, because of such examples as that now considered, for refusing to acquiesce in the account of this singular use of the word BUT given by Mr. Tooke, and sanctioned by Dr. Webster and other lexicographers and grammarians. We cannot give the same ready acquiescence, as will be seen presently, to some other opinions advanced by Mr. Tooke in reference to this word.

§ 151. The word BUT performs such important and various and apparently dissimilar functions in our language, that it has given occasion to much speculation among grammarians and philologists. For these reasons, we subjoin a few additional observations, in which we shall attempt to trace the steps by which it has made the transition from the earliest use, with which we are acquainted, to that which is apparently its latest, and, certainly, its most common use at the present time. We are the more induced to do this, because the accounts commonly given of the origin of the adversative and exceptive uses of BUT do not appear to us completely satisfactory. We cannot acquiesce in some of the rash conclusions which Mr. H. Tooke defends in his usual dictatorial manner. We shall subject his reasonings to a brief examination, reject what appears to us inconclusive, and endeavor to trace the probable history of the transition from the *exceptive* to the *adversative* use of this very important word.

The word *but* was employed in the earliest times in a sense distinct from any in which it is now employed. It seems to have been nearly equivalent to *without,* and to have had a just claim to be considered a preposition.

Mr. Tooke, in his attempt to establish a distinction between *but* and *bot,* has furnished a host of examples of this apparently original use of *but* from Gawin Douglas's Translation of the Eneid. We give a few of these examples in the briefest manner consistent with our purpose, and refer the inquisitive reader to the Diversions of Purley (article on the word *but*), for the passages in connection with these examples.

"Thare is gret substance ordanit the BUT dout."

In modern English, *There is great substance* (wealth, fortune) *ordained* (de creed) *to thee* WITHOUT *doubt.*

"And als mony nychtes BUT sterneys leme."

= *And as many nights* WITHOUT *star-light.*

"Before Eneas feite stude, BUT delay."

= *Before Æneas' feet stood* WITHOUT *delay.*"

"Bot of the bargane maid end, BUT delay."

We have followed the pointing of Mr. Taylor's edition of the Diversions of Purley. We see no reason, however, for using the comma in the last two examples, if it is unnecessary in the first two.

In all these passages BUT is employed, like a preposition, before single nouns. It connects a *word-complement,* not a *proposition-complement.* Mr. Tooke draws no distinction between this use of *but* and its still current use, to express *exception.* No doubt, the two uses are allied, and we believe the present exceptive use has originated from the more ancient use exhibited above. Still there is a marked transition from the one to the other. In not one of these passages could *except* or *save* be substituted for BUT, as they can generally, if not universally for *but* exceptive. Compare with these examples, *John has learnt all his lessons* BUT *one.* "All *but* the wakeful nightingale." Here *but* is manifestly equivalent to *except, save.*

Examples of the use of BUT similar to those above from Gawin Douglas are, we believe, to be found chiefly in Scotch authors. This use is rarely found in the writers of South Britain, of even the earliest date.

Mr. Tooke has attempted to prove that BUT adversative, employed to connect a proposition in some respect opposed to the tenor of the preceding discourse, is a word entirely distinct from BUT employed for the other pur poses above mentioned; and his conclusions in reference to this matter have been followed by many since his time, apparently without much examination. This adversative *but* is, according to Mr. Tooke's view, the imperative of an Anglo-Saxon verb *botan* to *boot,* and was spelled *bot;* whereas *but* is the imperative of *be-utan, to be out.* In reference to Mr. Locke, he remarks, "It was the corrupt use of this *one* word (BUT) in modern English, for *two* words (BOT and BUT) originally (in the Anglo-Saxon) very different in signification, though (by repeated abbreviation and corruption) approaching in sound, which chiefly misled him." By this passage we might be led to conclude that *bot,* distinct from *but,* is found employed as a conjunction in the Anglo-Saxon language. The word *bot* or *bote* meaning *boot, advantage, remedy,* is indeed found in Anglo-Saxon employed as a *noun.* But we doubt whether this word was ever used alone in Anglo-Saxon or old English, as a *connective.* (*To bote,* is sometimes used to mean *moreover.*) As to the verb *botan,* and its imperative *bot* or *bote,* we can find no reason to believe that they ever existed, except in the imaginations of Mr. Tooke and some of his followers.

We suspect that *bot* in Gawin Douglas is only a variation in spelling, the orthography of those times being, as Mr. Tooke himself admits, very unsettled. Mr. Richardson in his dictionary has given examples of *bot* and *bote* from Robert of Gloucester and others; but in these examples there is no distinction maintained between *but* and *bot* or *bote*. *Bot* and *bote* are used on several occasions, when the sense is plainly *butan*, *except*. As, for example,

"Ne that *no* man ys wurthe to be ycluped (called) Kyng.
Bote the heye king of heuene," &c.
"That in all the lond suld be *no* king *bot* he."

Bote and *bot* are plainly here employed for *but* = except, and not for the adversative *but*. Such examples show that the authors, to whom Mr. Tooke and Mr. Richardson appeal, are not to be relied on to establish the different origin of the adversative *but*, and *but* = *without* and *except*, since they spell the word in all these senses indifferently *bot* or *bote* or *but*. Mr. Richardson himself, as well as the authors whom he quotes, seems to confound these meanings of *but*, which he meant to separate. He has arranged one, if not two, examples under *but* or *bot*, which should have been, on his principles, placed under *but*. We refer to the citations from *Holland*, *Plinie*, &c., and from *Feltham*. The last is perhaps doubtful. *See Richardson's Dict. Art. But.*

Examples of *butan* or *buton* used in the *adversative* sense of our modern *but* are not, we suspect, to be found in Anglo-Saxon. The connection which we express by *but* adversative seems to have been expressed invariably in that language by *ac*; never by *bot*, as an incautious reader of the Diversions of Purley might be led to suppose. No trace of *ac* thus used (except it is in *eke*) remains in our language. Its place seems to have been supplied not by *bot* from *botan*—the invention of Mr. Tooke—but by an *insensible extension* of the exceptive *but*. The transition from the exceptive use of *but* to *but* adversative, in cases where it has the greatest force, does not appear to us so violent as Mr. Tooke represents it. Let us take for example that passage in the 115th Psalm; "They have mouths, *but* they speak not, eyes have they, *but* they see not," &c. The transition from the *exceptive* to the use here found does not seem to us much wider than from the use equivalent to the preposition *without* to the *exceptive* sense. And yet Mr. Tooke thinks these so much alike that he does not recognise them as distinct. By *but* exceptive we except a complementary word, by *but* adversative a proposition. The first, in other words, indicates an exception *from a proposition*, the latter an exception from the discourse—*from the train of thought*. Mr. Tooke seems to us to have been led, by his attempt to support a foregone conclusion, to rob *but* adversative of an essential part of its significance. It fits his purpose to make it mean only *add*, and in this way he has entirely destroyed ll distinction between this word and AND.

It may be added that Mr. Tooke admits that ancient authors have not consistently observed the distinction between *bot* and *but*. He confesses that no trace of it can be found in Chaucer, and we can find none in Wiclif's New Testament, printed by Bagster from a good manuscript.

We certainly see no necessity for the high-handed course pursued by Mr. Tooke in order to account for the distinction between *but* adversative and *but* exceptive. But we do not presume to pronounce a positive opinion. We leave the question to be settled by those who possess sufficient acquaintance with Anglo-Saxon, and old English literature, in which we do not pretend to be versed. We regard Mr. Tooke's rash and confident *ipse dixit* as of no weight in the case before us, and consider the question open for discussion.

In the mean time we have traced the transition of *but* from one meaning to another, so far as we have been able to do it by the helps accessible to us. To sum up the results we have,

1st. BUT = WITHOUT. This is likely the primary use of this word, and likely enough, as H. Tooke and others allege, both the Anglo-Saxon *butan* or *buton* and this are the imperative *be-utan* of *beon-utan*. It is now found almost exclusively in the older Scotch writers, and is, perhaps, the same word still used *adverbially* in the colloquial Scotch in the expression *gang* BUT = go *out*.

2d. BUT = EXCEPT. This meaning, like the last, is usually traced to the original sense of the compound *be-utan, be out = except*. Both these meanings are expressed in the Anglo-Saxon by *butan* or *buton*.

3d. BUT = ONLY. This is the same as the last when the negative is supplied. So far we accept the account given by Mr. Tooke & Co.

4th. BUT *Adversative*. This indicates, as we have already shown, the addition or connection of something variant from what precedes; or perhaps we may venture to say an *exception* in reference to the train of the discourse, whereas *but* in the second sense indicates an exception in reference to the proposition in which it is employed.

There remains a point yet to be settled. With what class of words shall we arrange BUT *Exceptive?* When employed in the first-mentioned manner as equivalent to *without*, the Anglo-Saxon grammarians call it a preposition. and class it with those which take after them a dative case; with this use we have nothing to do in this place, as it is long since entirely obselete.

BUT *exceptive* has also been recognised by many of our late grammarians, and by some lexicographers as a preposition. But if *but* exceptive is a preposition, it should, according to the definition which these same grammarians give of a preposition, take the noun which it connects always in the accusative case. This we think it never does, according to the most reputable usage of the language, except when the accusative which follows is plainly the objective modification of a verb suppressed. For example, we consider, *There is nobody here* BUT *I*, the true construction, and not, *There is nobody here* BUT

ME. When this expression is fully developed, it would be, *There is nobody here* BUT *I am here* = *except I am here.* When the verb suppressed is an active verb, and the noun after *but* would, if the verb were supplied, stand to it in the relation of objective modification, we place this noun in the accusative thus, *I saw nobody* BUT HIM = *I saw nobody but,* or, *except I saw him.* That is, *I saw nobody* BE OUT *I saw him.* In this form *I saw him* is subject to the *conjunctive* verb BE OUT.

We believe that examples may be found in reputable authors of the use of an accusative dependent on *but* alone; but we think they are not to be imitated. We subjoin a few examples of what we consider the correct usage of the language in this matter, as well as the general usage of educated speakers and writers. The intelligent reader will readily perceive that the older these examples are the more weight they have in determining the question before us. If old, they prove that the present usage is not a modern refinement of the educated classes, or based on grammatical theories, but the effect of spontaneous development. We adduce first a line already quoted from one of our oldest English authors.

"That in alle the lond suld be no king *but* HE."

"There is none other *but he.*" Mark 12: 32. He hath not grieved me *but* in part." "Neither was I taught it *but* by the revelation of Jesus Christ." In all these examples, whether we say that *but* connects a complementary proposition, or that it only connects a complementary word, it is obvious that it has not the characteristic of a preposition. In the first two examples it is followed by a nominative case, in the last two by a preposition.

It is not perhaps uncommon to hear persons use *me* after *but* where *me* cannot be the objective modification of any other word. Perhaps the same persons might be found to say, *there is* nobody in the house *but he,* and yet say, there is nobody here *but me.* This may be attributable to the fact to be noticed in another place (See § 155: 12), that in the language of the uneducated *me* is used as nominative in all cases where it is not manifestly the immediate subject-noun to a verb. Thus, the answer of the uneducated classes to the question, *Who is there?* is universally ME. In the same manner the accusative (or rather in this case we should say the dative) is still used by the uneducated after *comparatives* and *than,* as *He is taller* THAN ME. We may place these expressions on a level with, *There is nobody here* BUT ME, as regards purity of language. The dative after *than* has perhaps stronger claims to be recognised as English than the accusative after *but;* and consequently *than* has as great if not greater claims than *but* to be considered *sometimes* a preposition. We may cite Milton as authority for the use of a dative or accusative after *than.*

"Belial came last, THAN WHOM a spirit more lewd
Fell not from Heaven," &c.

The present usage of correct writers and speakers, we believe, is to avoid all constructions alike, in which either BUT or THAN take after them an oblique case, which is not the modification of some other word expressed or implied in the discourse.

In a word then, we consider *but* as now employed in our language a *conjunctive word,* (a conjunctive *proposition,* if you please), not a *preposition;* though the old *but* = *without* was rightly considered a preposition, that is, a word used in connection with a single word employed to modify a principal word, as distinguished from a word used to connect either two propositions, or two independent modifications of the same proposition or the same principal word. In the following passage from Ælfric's Colloquium, we have beautiful examples of *buton* conjunction and *butan* preposition. Whether the distinction here observable in the spelling is intentional or not, we are not able to determine. "Ne canst thee huntian BUTON mid nettum?" *Canst thou not* (or *knowest thou not how to*) *hunt* EXCEPT *with nets?* = EXCEPT *to hunt with nets.* This usage exactly agrees with that of *but* exceptive in the language of the present day. Buton here connects either two propositions or two independent modifications of *canst* (or perhaps *huntian*), according as we choose to supply the construction. The answer to the above question is, "Gea, BUTAN nettum huntian ic maeg." *Yes, I can hunt* WITHOUT *nets.* Here *butan* is a preposition and with the dative *nettum* forms a noun and preposition modification of the infinitive *huntian.*

ON THE DISTINCTION BETWEEN PREPOSITIONS AND CONJUNCTIONS.

§ 152. We may here submit a few remarks on a subject which has caused some controversy among grammarians; we mean the distinction which separates the two classes of words called prepositions and conjunctions.

The more ancient grammarians have generally represented prepositions and conjunctions as having the common property of serving as connectives, and as distinguished by the sole fact, that prepositions connect only words, and conjunctions connect only propositions. Many of the modern grammarians contend, on the contrary, that conjunctions sometimes connect words, as well as propositions. All admit that two or more subjects, two or more predicates, and two or more similar and independent complements may be united by a conjunction; but the first-mentioned class, including some recent grammarians, as well as the more ancient, contend that in all such cases the discourse may be resolved into as many propositions, as there are similar members of a proposition connected by conjunctions. Thus, *John* AND *James are studious,* may be resolved into the two independent propositions, *John is studious,* and *James is studious. John reads* AND *writes,* may be resolved into the propositions, *John reads,* and *John writes. William studies Greek* AND *mathematics,* into *William studies Greek,* and *William studies mathematics.*

The other class of grammarians contend that words are *sometimes* con nected together by conjunctions, when no such resolution into separate propositions can be effected. They present in confirmation of this fact such examples as the following: "A man of wisdom and virtue is a perfect character." "Three and three make six." "The sides AB, BC, and CA form a triangle." "John and Mary are a handsome couple." "John and Thomas carry a sack to the market." "Here (to use the language of Dr. Crombie) it is not implied that a man of wisdom is a perfect character; but a man of wisdom combined with virtue." It is not implied that *John is a handsome couple*, or that *Mary is a handsome couple;* that *John carries a sack to the market*, or that *Thomas carries a sack to the market*, but that they jointly carry the sack. Dr. Latham (First Outlines, p. 21), as quoted by Sir John Stoddart, says, "The answer to this lies in giving the proper limitation to the predicates. It is not true that John and Thomas each carry *a sack;* but it is true that they each of them *carry.* It is not true that each three makes *six;* but it is true that each three *makes* (i. e. contributes to the making). As far then as the essential parts of the predicate are concerned, there are two propositions; and it is upon the essential parts only that a grammarian rests his definition of a conjunction." We are astonished at the authoritative air with which Dr. Latham propounds this argument, and at the readiness with which Sir John Stoddart approves it, and avails himself of it. Suppose we propose as an example, *John and Mary are a couple whom all their neighbors admire*, how will Dr. Latham give us a "*proper limitation*," so as to exclude the word *couple?* And how will he apply his *arbitrary* method of limitation to the following proposition, *Two and three are five?* Will he say that *are*, which he represents, in common with other grammarians, as performing *solely the function of copula*, is the essential part of the *predicate?* Dr. Latham's argument appears to us wholly unsatisfactory, and Sir John's commentary does not seem to help it. If the definitions of prepositions and conjunctions given by the old grammarians were worth defending, (which we think they are not,) it seems to us the best mode of defence to maintain boldly, that a *plurality of subjects* constitutes a *plurality of propositions*, and that in the words, *John and Mary are a happy couple*, two propositions are found, because there are two distinct subjects.

In the whole of this controversy it has been taken for granted by one party, (and not explicitly denied by some of their opponents,) that there is little *functional* distinction between conjunctions and prepositions, save as regards the classes of expression which they come between. So far as concerns the conjunctions which connect co-ordinate propositions, and it is in reference to these exclusively that the controversy has originated, we think this a great mistake. The functions of this class of conjunctions are essentially distinct both from those of prepositions and from those of the conjunctions and conjunctive words which connect accessories with principal propositions. Both prepositions and this last-named class of conjunctives are employed as we have before intimated in forming *modifications*, the prepositions with a noun, the conjunctives with a proposition. Sometimes the same word is employed for both these purposes. When employed in the first way the grammarians choose to call it a preposition, when in the latter way a conjunction. Between these two classes of words as defined by the grammarians, we admit freely, that the distinction, often the sole distinction is, that the one class performs a function between words, the other between propositions.

But the class of conjunctions which we are now considering, and the only class involved in the controversy, serve a purpose totally distinct from prepositions and the conjunctives of accessories. They are not employed to indicate the connection of *modifications*, but the connection of *co-ordinate* or *independent expressions.* Now, as modifying expressions sometimes consist of single words or phrases, sometimes of propositions; so, co-ordinate expressions, that is, expressions which we have occasion to connect in *co-ordinate construction*, may sometimes happen to be single words or phrases, as well as propositions. We have occasion in fact, as we have already seen, to connect independent propositions having no modifying influence on each other, to connect independent members of propositions, and to connect independent modifications. We mean, of course, independent of each other. As this *co-ordinate connection* is a very simple function, it is altogether unnecessary to employ different words to unite these several classes of co-ordinates. Another reason for employing the same words to connect these different classes of co-ordinates is, that co-ordinate members, and co-ordinate modifications can *very generally* be readily expanded into complete independent propositions. But cases occur, in which this is perhaps impossible, and attempts to effect it are fruitless, and lead, as we have seen, to *absurdities.* If the distinct functions of the two great classes of conjunctive words had been properly exhibited, the grammarians would likely have kept clear of this controversy. At least, so we think.

CHAPTER XI.

OF INTERJECTIONS AND EXCLAMATORY WORDS AND PHRASES.

§ 153. INTERJECTIONS.—(1) In the introduction we distinguished two species of language or great classes of signs used as means of intercommunication between different minds, namely, the *natural* and the *artificial;* and we remarked, that (what are called) interjections belong to the first of these classes. (2) This class of words does not, as we may suppose, claim a large share of attention from the grammarian, whose proper province is to investigate the structure of artificial or articulate language. (3) Yet as interjections enter into the structure of discourse, and even, as we shall see, sometimes of compound propositions, we must not pass them over with entire neglect.

(4) The name interjection, meaning something *thrown between*, has been given to this class of signs, because they are *thrown between* the parts of *discourse;* not between the parts of speech or parts of propositions, as some have inconsiderately asserted. (5) As we have said already, they may be regarded as portions of *natural language* superadded to *artificial language.* (6) When naturally introduced, they spring spontaneously from the emotion of the speaker or writer, serving to give animation to discourse, or to express feelings more briefly and more impressively than can be done by artificial speech.

(7) One distinguishing circumstance to be remarked in reference to this class of signs is, that each of them expresses a particular feeling or emotion completely, and so is equivalent to a proposition.

---

§ 153. (1) What is referred to as mentioned in the introduction? (2) Do interjections claim much attention from the grammarian? Reason? (3) Why may they not be altogether overlooked?

(4) What is the meaning of the name interjection? (5) How may these words be regarded? (6) From what do they spring, when naturally introduced, and what purposes do they serve?

(7) Mention an important circumstance in reference to this class of words.

(8) Since in this case propositions are expressed by single signs, there is no *structure*, so far as a solitary interjection is concerned; and, therefore, no work for the grammarian—no analysis of a simple proposition. (9) Thus *O*, often spelled oh, is equivalent to *I wish*, *de sire*, &c., in a weaker or stronger degree, according to the force given to the sound in utterance. *Oh* (*Scotice* and more expressively *och*) = *I feel pain*, or *anguish*. *Ah* = *I am filled with wonder*, *surprise*, &c. *Alas* = *I feel grief*, *sorrow*, *pity*, &c. *Lo* = the imperatives *look*, *behold*, *see*, &c. These are the only interjections which find a place often in dignified discourse. (10) In writings of a dramatic character, exhibiting colloquial discourse, and in ordinary conversation many other words of this class enter.*

(11) We have one more (and an important) remark to make in reference to this class of words. Interjections being, as we have said, equivalent to propositions, like other propositions, some of them admit of modification by accessory propositions. (12) This fact is perhaps most remarkable in the case of O, or oh, the interjection expressive of *wishing*. This word frequently takes after it a *substantive accessory* as *objective modification* to the verb which is implied in it. (13) Examples: "*Oh* that I had wings like a dove." = *I* WISH *that I had wings like a dove.* "*Oh* that I were as in months past," &c. "*Oh* that I

---

* We subjoin the following classified list of the principal words generally recognised by grammarians as interjections, borrowed chiefly from Dr Crombie, with some suppressions, additions and modifications:

1. Interjections expressive of joy, as *hey*, *io*, &c. 2. Of grief: *oh*, *ah*, *alas*, *alack*. 3. Of wonder: *ah! hah! aha! hah!* 4. Of wishing: *O*, *oh*. *O* is often used with the vocative or case of address. 5. Aversion or contempt: *tush*, *pshaw*, *fie*, *poh*, *pugh*. 6. Laughter: *ha ha*. 7. Desire of attention: *lo*, *halloo*, *hem*. 8. Languor: *heigh ho*. 9. Desire of silence: *hush*, *hist*, *mum*. 10. Deliberation: *hum*. 11. Exultation: *huzza*, *hurrah*, &c. 12. Pain: *oh*. It will be observed here that the same word, that is, a word represented by the same characters *in writing*, is used to express very different emotions; but then the word is very differently uttered, with a sound and intonation in each case accommodated to the emotion, so that in the spoken language these words may be regarded as in fact different signs, or distinct utterances. The above list might be greatly enlarged, without introducing into it, after the example of the grammarians, exclamatory words and phrases.

---

(8) What follows from this circumstance? (9) Give examples of the use of the principal interjections. (10) In what kind of writings do interjections chiefly occur?

(11) What other important circumstance is mentioned in reference to interjections? (12) In what case is the fact mentioned most remarkable? (13) Give examples.

knew where I might find him." "*Oh* that there were such an heart in them."

"*Oh*, that this too, too solid flesh would melt."

(14) The proposition which follows *lo* might, perhaps, be regarded in the same way as accessory to it; for example, in expressions of this form, "Lo the winter is past," &c. We are rather inclined to consider *lo*, in such expressions as equivalent to a simple imperative proposition, like the exclamatory words, *behold*, *see*, employed for the purpose of calling the attention of the party addressed, and the following proposition as independent. (15) What is here said may be extended to many imperatives used in exclamation. (16) The vocative or case of address is used also for the purpose of arresting attention, and like these imperatives stands independent, and does not mingle in the construction of the neighboring proposition. It may be said to be used in an interjectional way.

§ 154. Exclamatory Words and Phrases.—(1) Exclamatory words and phrases often serve a purpose very similar to that which interjections serve. (2) The distinction is that interjections serve *only* the purpose mentioned, but the exclamatory words are signs of *articulate* language, and are most commonly employed like other words in forming regular propositions. (3) Indeed these exclamatory words and phrases should, perhaps, always be treated as *contracted propositions*, and in analysis, the learner should be taught to supply the ellipsis, when there is a suppression of the parts essential to a complete proposition. This is the only method of obtaining a satisfactory explanation of this kind of expressions; and when this is done, they are brought within the reach of the ordinary rules for the analysis of propositions.

We need not include among exclamatory words and phrases expressions which are manifestly complete propositions. Yet some forms of expression which have been enumerated even among the interjections ought to be considered as propositions. (4) Such are the imperatives, *behold*, *begone*, *hail*, *hold*, *look*, *mark*, &c. When these occur there is perhaps seldom any necessity of supplying a word. (5) They are the imperative in its usual form, with the subject implied. Such of these verbs as are active either have an objective modification

---

(14) What is said of *lo* in reference to taking an accessory? (15) To what class of words does this remark extend? (16) What is said of the case of address?

§ 154. (1) What kind of purpose do exclamatory words and phrases serve? (2) What is the distinction between them and interjections? (3) How should they, perhaps, be treated?

(4) Mention some forms of expression improperly classed as exclamatory or as interjections. (5) What is said of these words?

implied, or take the following proposition, or sometimes a larger portion of the following discourse as their objective modification or limitation.

(6) In the use of many other exclamatory expressions there is an obvious ellipsis. (7) For example: *Welcome* = *(you are) well-come; it is well, I am glad, that you have come. Adieu* = *To God (I commend you.) Me miserable*, perhaps = *It is* MISERABLE *in reference* to *me*, or, *It is* MISERABLE *for* ME. ME in all such cases is likely a remnant of the Anglo-Saxon dative. (8) *Ah me! Alas for him!* and similar exclamations may, perhaps, be regarded as exhibiting a mixture of natural and articulate or organized language. *Me* and *for him* are either dative and noun and preposition complements to the verbal conception included in *ah* and *alas* respectively, or they are used elliptically instead of accessories to these verbal conceptions. *Ah me* = *I feel sorrow for me*, or, *I feel sorrow, as regards me* (myself).

(9) *Would God*, and *Would to God* are also sometimes used in the exclamatory way without a subject. We have examples both with the subject suppressed and with the subject expressed. "*Would* God it were morning!" "*Would* to God ye could bear with me." "*I would* to God ye did reign." "*I would* to God, that not only thou," &c. Acts 26: 29. A comparison of these passages affords a satisfactory explanation of the ellipsis.

(10) The true way of explaining all such exclamatory expressions is to expand them into propositions. If the grammarian thinks this business lies out of his path, he will content himself with calling them exclamatory expressions. The learner must not hope in all cases to succeed by this process of expansion or development in obtaining propositions which will express the intended meaning with the same spirit and energy as the exclamatory word; but if we can succeed in transforming such expressions into a proposition, giving the sense even in a homely and flat manner, it affords a test, and perhaps the only satisfactory test, that we thoroughly understand them.

NOTE—The learner must not be surprised if he should sometimes find it peculiarly difficult to unravel exclamatory language. The difficulty is not attributable to the perplexity of grammatical principles, but to the fact that such expressions are the language of passion, and that passion disregards grammatical laws, as it often does all other laws. Grammar and

---

(6) What occurs in some other exclamatory expressions? (7) Explain a number of these. (8) Repeat what is said of *ah me!* and *alas for him!* &c.

(9) Repeat what is said of the exclamation *would God*, or *would to God*. Give examples.

(10) What is the true way of explaining exclamatory expressions?

grammatical principles are the product of human reason; they regulate the *rational* interchange of thought; they have no certain application to the *reveries* of deep emotion. The man overpowered by strong emotion, especially in his reveries addressed to himself, does not take the trouble to express himself fully, or with reference to the usual laws of language. Hurried on by passion, he utters fragments of the train which occupies his mind, perhaps only the main conceptions, in a disjointed manner. If grammar should fail to reduce such language under law, it is what is to be expected. We may illustrate this by a reference to some of the celebrated soliloquies given by dramatic writers, which soliloquies often consist wholly of exclamatory words and disjointed conceptions. In these the speaker often shows a disregard of all laws alike of regular thought and regular language. It would be equally improper on the one hand to subject such outbursts of emotion to grammatical animadversion, and, on the other, to demand that the grammarian shall explain them in conformity with the general laws of language.

It is unnecessary, in closing our investigation of the different forms of compound construction, to submit examples for the exercise of the student in analysis, since he is now supposed to be competent to analyze any piece of discourse, and no longer to require that passages involving only certain classes of constructions, should be selected for his use.

When the student is once perfectly familiar with the structure of simple propositions, we would recommend the separate exercise of the *analysis of discourse*—the examination of the relations of the *propositions* which constitute a sentence, omitting the examination of the structure of individual propositions. In this way a large portion of discourse may be analyzed very rapidly and with great profit to those who wish to make progress in the correct knowledge of construction. This part of analysis should indeed always be conducted separately from the analysis of single propositions by the advanced student; and, when both kinds of analysis are to be applied to the same passage, the *general analysis* of the structure of the discourse—separating the several propositions which constitute this structure, and describing their connection whether of *co-ordination*, or as *principal* and *accessory* in compound assertions—should always precede the analysis of the individual propositions. It will not be necessary in the case of those who are proficients, to accompany the general analysis always by the particular analysis of each proposition, nor that the particular analysis should when introduced be extended over all the passage embraced by the general analysis. A good method is to call the student's attention, when engaged in the general analysis, to whatever is most important, most difficult, most necessary to be inculcated by frequent repetition. In this way a due regard to the economy of time and labor may be combined with thorough training. The economy recommended appears the more important in the case before us, when we remember that grammatical analysis is an exercise in which the minds of students cannot be long employed at one time with profit. As much as possible should be effected before the attention flags, whilst the intellectual powers are fresh and vigorous.

§ 155. We have some additional observations to make on the personal and conjunctive pronouns, and on the determinative adjectives, which we have purposely reserved till the present time, because some of them can be better understood, as well as more briefly expressed, after the reader is already acquainted with the structure of the language.

ADDITIONAL OBSERVATIONS ON THE PERSONAL PRONOUNS.

For convenience in reference, we head these observations with a tabular view of the declension of Anglo-Saxon personal pronouns.

Declension of the First Person.

	Singular.		*Plural.*	
NOM.	Ic	*I.*	We	*we.*
GEN.	Min	*of me.*	Ure	*of us.*
DAT.	Me	*to, for, with me.*	Us	*to, for, with us.*
ACC.	Me	*me.*	Us	*us.*

Declension of the Second Person.

NOM.	Thu	*thou.*	Ge	*ye or you.*
GEN.	Thin	*of thee.*	Eower	*of you.*
DAT.	The	*to, for, with thee.*	Eow	*to, for, &c., you.*
ACC.	The	*thee.*	Eow	*you.*

These two pronouns have a dual form, which we have omitted in the above table as irrelevant to our purpose.

Declension of the Third Person.

SINGULAR.

	Masc.	*Fem.*	*Neut.*	
NOM.	He	Heo = (He-e)	Hit = (He-t)	*he, she, it.*
GEN.	His = (He-es)	Hire = (He-e-re)	His = (He-es)	*of him.*
DAT.	Him = (He-um)	Hire "	Him	*to, &c., him.*
ACC.	Hine.	Hi	Hit	*him, her, it.*

PLURAL.

NOM.	Hi	*in all the genders*	*they.*
GEN.	Hira	"	*of them.*
DAT.	Him	"	*to, &c., them*
ACC	Hi	"	*them.*

(1) The nominative *I* and accusative *me* of the first person are forms which appear to have no etymological connection. The same remark applies to the corresponding pronouns in the northern dialects and in the Greek and Latin and its descendants. In all these languages the equivalent pronouns appear to have descended from the same two distinct roots from which our *I* and *me* have descended. It is likely that these two roots may have been in use, to express the functions of the pronoun of the first person, before the introduction of *inflection* to distinguish the functions of nouns and pronouns. We suspect that many irregularities in all languages are to be accounted for in the same way. See what has been said on this subject in speaking of the comparison of adjectives. (§ 94, p. 305, note.

(2) A connection between *we* and *us*, as some grammarians think, may be traced through the possessive form *our* by the help of the other northern dialects. *See Latham's Eng. Language.*

(3) The second persons *thou* and *thee* are evidently only different forms of the same word. The same may be said of the plurals *ye* and *you;* (4) but between the singular and plural forms of the pronouns both of the first and second persons, there seems to be no etymological connection now traceable.

(5) *He*, *she*, *it* (Anglo-Saxon He, Heo, Hit, see table above) appears to have been originally a determinative adjective with the usual inflections to indicate gender, number and case (*a*). (6) *Hit* instead of *Het* was simply the neuter form of *He*, *t* being the regular inflection to denote the neuter gender. *Hit*, losing the aspirate in pronunciation, has in the modern language become *It;* but the ancient form *Hit* is found in our old writers down till the age of Shakspeare. (See Diversions of Purley, pp. 339—341. T. Tegg. Lond. 1840.) (7) From *It* there has been formed, within a comparatively recent period, a new *genitive* or *possessive pronoun* ITS instead of the old *possessive* HIS (= *He-es* regular genitive of *He*,) which as we have already remarked (§ 75, p. 188 note), was used in Anglo-Saxon and in English, both as *masculine* and *neuter*, as late as the times of James the First of England. To the examples in proof of this, given in the place above referred to, we may add the following from Bacon's Essays, cited by Dr. Lowth: "Learning hath *his* infancy, when *it* is but beginning and

§ 155. (1) What is said of the forms *I* and *me?*

(2) What of the connection between *we* and *us?*

(3) What is said in reference to the *singular* pronouns of the second person? (4) What of the plural pronouns of both first and second persons?

(5) Repeat the remark in reference to *he, she, it.* (6) Repeat what is said of the origin of *it* and the changes of inflection, &c., which it has undergone. (7) What is said of the

almost childish; then *his* youth, when *it* is luxuriant and juvenile; then *his* strength of years, when *it* is solid and reduced; and lastly *his* old age, when it waxeth dry and exhaust." Essay 58. "Put up again thy sword into *his* place." Matt. 26: 52.

NOTE (*a*).—It is worthy of remark, that the words which serve as pronouns of the third person in Greek and Latin, were originally determinative adjectives. One of the words which served this purpose in Latin (*ille, illa, illud,*) is still, though with some change of form, employed as the pronoun of the third person in the languages of the South of Europe derived from the Latin. The Italian *egli*, feminine *ella;* French *il, elle;* Spanish, *el, ella;* and Portuguese, *elle, ella*, are all forms (corrupted forms, if you please) of the Latin pronoun *ille.* The (so called) definite articles of the three first-named languages are also manifestly derived from the same *ille.*

(8) *Hit* occurs in the older editions of Shakspeare, and still more frequently in English of earlier dates. (See Div. of Purley as cited above.)

(9) The *dative* common to *He* and *Hit*, as will be observed in the *paradigm* above, was *Him*, which our grammarians now recognise as an accusative form, but which still, like *me, us, thee, you,* &c., often performs a *dative* function. In Anglo-Saxon it performed always a dative or ablative, never an *accusative*, function. The use of *datives* in the English of the present day has been sufficiently explained. § 79, p. 220, note.

(10) Instead of *Heo*, the old feminine form of *He*, we have adopted the word SHE in modern English. Some suppose this a corruption of the feminine form of the *determinative Se*, SEO, *Thaet*, used in Anglo-Saxon for the same purpose as our article *the*, and also as a demonstrative and relative pronoun. (Quære: May it not have been formed by the coalescence of *Se*, or *Seo* and *Heo* = *the she?* Douglas spells the word *sche.*)

(11) The plural form of *He, Heo, Hit* in the Anglo-Saxon, as will be seen above, was nominative and accusative *Hi*, genitive *Hira*, dative *Him*, for all genders. In the progress of the language the present forms *they, their, them* have been substituted, though not all at once,

---

formation of the word *its*, and what was the old neuter genitive or possessive? Repeat part of the examples.

(8) Repeat the observation about *hit.*

(9) What was the old dative form of *he* and *hit*, and what is the present use of this form? Does it still serve sometimes as a *dative?*

(10) What is said of the origin of the form SHE?

(11) Repeat the substance of what is said of the plural of the third person.

for these old forms. We find *they* in Chaucer and Wiclif. In the latter (Translation of the New Testament), this word is uniformly written *thei*. See Bagster's Hexapla, in which we have an edition from an ancient manuscript. Most likely the early manuscripts of Chaucer have the same orthography. Our modern editors are justly censured for having taken improper liberties with the orthography of our old writers, and having thus rendered their editions much less serviceable to the philological inquirer. Neither Wiclif nor Chaucer (so far as we know) appears to have used *their* or *them*. Instead of these they retain the older English forms *hir* and *hem*, which are the Anglo-Saxon forms with a slight change of orthography. Wiclif seems to prefer the use of *hem* with the preposition *of* to *hir*. (*Of hem* instead of *hir* = the modern *their*.) (*b*)

NOTE (*b*).—The old forms *hi*, *hir*, *hem*, were all in use in the age of Robert of Gloucester. Our philologists have not satisfactorily accounted for the introduction of *they*, *their*, *them*, to supersede these forms. "It is very difficult to say from whence, or why, the pronouns *they*, *them*, *their*, were introduced into our language. The Saxon pronouns, *hi*, *hem*, and *hir*, seem to have been in constant use in the time of Robert of Gloucester." (*Tyrwhitt's Essay on the Lang. and Vers. of Chaucer, note* 28.) Dr. Latham (*Eng. Lang.*, *p.* 243, 2*d Ed.*) says, "The plural forms *they*, *them*, in the present English, are the plural forms of the root of *that*." His account of the matter seems to us very unsatisfactory. He answers one of the queries suggested by Mr. Tyrwhitt only by his bare assertion, and does not, as it appears to us, give a sufficient response to the other.

Query. Is not *they* (uniformly written by Wiclif, as has been already observed, THEI) a word formed from the coalescence of the *determinative the* with the old form *hi*; *the hi* being contracted into *thei* equivalent to *the they* in the modern language? Compare with this the Greek *οὗτος*, and the French *celui* = *ce-lui*, and *celle* = *ce-elle*, &c. Are not *their* (= *the-hir*) and *them* (= *the-hem*) formed in the same manner by a coalescence of the determinative with the old pronoun?

We invite the attention of those who have access to writings, especially to manuscripts of the age preceding Chaucer, to this conjecture. If the conjecture is well founded, we may expect to find traces of the use of the determinative with the old forms previous to their complete coalescence, or, at least, evidence that the form with the determinative was used at first in cases where the pronoun is emphatically or determinately employed. If such traces should be discovered, they would leave scarcely a doubt in regard of the true origin of *they*, *their*, *them*, and both queries suggested by Mr. Tyrwhitt might be satisfactorily answered.

Since writing what precedes, we have found a passage in an old version of parts of the Evangelists made before the times of Wiclif, which seems favorable to our conjecture. The manuscript of this version is described, and the passage to which we refer cited in the "Historical Account of the English Versions of the Scriptures," prefixed to Bagster's Hexapla, p. 8. The writer of the translation in the portion given in the Hexapla, uses *hem* for *them;* and *hii* invariably for *they,* except in the following sentence: "And *hii* that were sent *thei* were of Phariseus." Is not the *thei* here substituted for *hii* because the pronoun is used determinately?

Anomalies in the Use of Me, Us, Him, &c.—(12) In vulgar usage *me* is treated as a sort of "indifferent form" (to use the term adopted by Dr. Latham), like *moi* in French. Like *moi*, it is employed by the *uneducated*, whenever they have occasion to use the pronoun of the first person singular in any other way, except as immediately accompanied by the verb to which it serves as subject. It is used in the predicate in such expressions as these: *Who is there?* The answer of the uneducated class to this is invariably, Me, or *It is me*, like the French, *C'est moi. Who did that? It was* me. It is also by the same class used as subject, when its verb is suppressed, as in comparisons: *He is wiser than* me, instead of the form of expression recognised as good English by the educated class; namely, He is wiser than I.

(13) *Us*, *him*, *her*, *them* are also employed in similar forms of expression, where the educated employ the *nominative* form of these words. This is, and has been for ages the current usage of the unlearned, wherever our language is spoken; and, had it not been for the general study of the Latin language, it would long since, we suspect, have been the current usage of all classes.

(14) There are some forms of expression still retained in what is considered pure grammatical English, which may be regarded as remains of this unlearned colloquial usage, not yet eradicated from the written language by the prevalence of classical constructions, or, perhaps, because of a casual coincidence with the classical forms of expression. Such are the exclamations, *Ah me! Me miserable*, &c. Some of these may have been real accusatives or datives completing some word now suppressed, or they may be in some instances forms introduced by the learned in imitation of Latin idioms; but some of them, we think, can be most readily accounted for, by considering

---

(12) Repeat what is said of the employment of *me* by the uneducated classes.

(13) What of the words *us*, *him*, &c., and of the extent of this usage?

(14) Repeat what is said in reference to the supposed retention of some vestiges of the colloquial usage of the uneducated.

them remains of the dialect of the uneducated, in which *me* is regarded as an "indifferent form."

(15) We have already observed (§ 143, p. 455, note), that in Anglo-Saxon, when a substantive and participle are used absolutely, the substantive is of the dative form; and that some might be disposed to explain such expressions, as "us dispossessed," in the following lines of Milton by reference to this Anglo-Saxon construction.

"This inaccessible high strength, the seat
Of Deity Supreme, *us dispossessed*,
He trusted to have seized."

We need scarcely repeat the caution, that such constructions (however accounted for) are not to be imitated, since there is no tendency in the present age towards such imitation.

(16) The word *self* plural *selves* is combined with some of the personal, perhaps with some of the possessive pronouns, for the purpose of giving them greater emphasis. (17) The compound pronouns thus formed are *myself*, *thyself*, *himself*, *herself*, *itself*, and the plural forms, *ourselves*, *yourselves*, *themselves*. These words serve the functions both of nominatives and accusatives. (18) In the function of accusatives they are generally used in a *reflexive* sense, referring back to the subject of the proposition; as, *I hurt myself*. *Myself* here refers back to the pronoun of the same person used as the subject. In such cases the agent and the recipient of the action expressed by the verb are the same individual. *Cato killed himself; The man brought that calamity on himself*. In the last example *himself* is used to form a *noun with a preposition complement* to the verb *brought*. Still it refers reflexively to the name of the agent, to "*the man*," which is subject of the proposition.*

* The use of the plural form of the pronoun of the first person where only an individual is intended to be indicated, is common in our language, especially in royal proclamations, in periodicals of all kinds when the editor speaks of himself, and in public speaking. This usage has arisen partly from the desire of writers and speakers to give more authority to what they say by representing it as a declaration emanating from the united wisdom of numbers, as in a royal proclamation from the sovereign aided by his council; or from a real or affected modesty, which shrinks from individual responsibility, or from giving offence by appearance of egotism. This latter

(15) Repeat the remarks in reference to a construction found in Milton.

(16) What is said in reference to the word SELF? (17) Enumerate the compound pronouns formed with this word, and tell what functions these compounds serve. (18) What is said of their use in the function of accusatives?

(19) We have said that these compound pronouns of the first person perform the functions both of nominatives and accusatives. But we do not think that it is accordant with good or with general usage to employ them as subject noun of a proposition. We think they are rarely employed in any other way as nominatives save in connection with another pronoun or noun which is the direct nominative of the verb and to which they serve to give emphasis, being appended to it as a sort of apposition. Such expressions as "Myself did it," "Them selves brought their misfortunes on them," &c., though sometimes used, appear to us not merely inelegant, but unsanctioned by current usage either of the educated or uneducated classes.

(20) Some grammarians have considered the word *self*, when added to the genitive case of the personal pronouns (or to the possessive pronouns, if we choose so to call them), a noun, and when added to the accusative case of the pronouns of the third person, HIM, HER, IT, THEM, as an adjective. (21) SELF or SYLF seems to have been regarded by our Anglo-Saxon ancestors as performing, in all these compounds, the function of a noun in apposition; or, at any rate, the same function in them all, whether that of a noun in apposition or of an adjective. (22) They attached this word to all the cases of the several personal pronouns, and inflected it to suit the case to which it was attached. For example, they used ICSYLF = *Iself;* genitive, MINSYLFES = *of myself;* plural, WESYLFE = *weselves;* genitive, URESYLFRA = *of ourselves.* (23) In modern English we have retained only a part of these forms. All the nominatives compounded with SELF have fallen into disuse, except *itself* for *hitself*, either nominative or accu-

purpose is often more effectually secured by resorting to the third person and presenting the author's own sentiments, as the sentiments entertained by those around him, using such forms of expression as, "It is thought;" "Some think;" "Many here think," &c. But these are all rhetorical contrivances, and the explanation of them scarcely belongs to the department of the grammarian. As we employ *We* for *I*, and *You* for *Thou*, we substitute also *Ourself* and *Yourself* for *Myself* and *Thyself*. (*Ourself* has almost fallen into disuse.) Here whilst the pronoun of the first and second person assumes the plural form, the word *Self* remains singular, indicating that a single individual is represented by the compound sign.

(19) What is said of the employment of these compound pronouns as subject nouns?

(20) How do some grammarians consider the word *self?* (21) How does it seem to have been regarded in Anglo-Saxon usage? (22) How did they attach this word to pronouns, and to what cases? (23) What forms used in the Anglo-Saxon have fallen into disuse, and what is said in reference to those which have been retained?

sative. The forms retained with the exception of *ourselves* (*ourself*), and *yourselves* (*yourself*), were, in our opinion, either datives or accusatives; namely, *myself*, in Anglo-Saxon *mesylf*, dative or accusative; *thyself*, Anglo-Saxon *thesylf*, dative or accusative; *himself*, Anglo-Saxon *himsylf*, dative; *herself*, Anglo-Saxon *hiresylf*, a dative. *Themselves* is also, obviously, a dative or accusative, though the word *them* is not Anglo-Saxon. *Our* and *your* in the words *ourselves* and *yourselves* seem to be either *genitives* or possessive pronouns.

(24) The fact that *himself* and *themselves* (obviously formed by the union of a dative or accusative of the pronoun of the third person with the word *self*) are employed as nominatives for all purposes, except the great purpose of serving as the direct subject of a verb, may, perhaps, be accounted for in the same way, as we account for the use of *me* and *us*, *him* and *them* among the uneducated for similar purposes. The only difference in the two cases is perhaps this, that, in regard of the compounds of *self*, the usage of the uneducated has become the *universal* usage, while, in reference to the simple pronouns, this common usage has been opposed and rejected by the educated.

QUERIES.—Has the Norman use of *moi*, *toi*, *lui*, as "indifferent forms," led to the use of *me*, *us*, *you*, as indifferent forms; and has this use afterwards extended to *him* and *them*, *himself* and *themselves*, though so distinctly marked by form as oblique cases? Are there any traces of this "indifferent" usage of any of these forms before the Norman times?

(25) We may add here a remark on the pronoun ONE which we have already noticed in § 30 : 17.

This word is entirely distinct from the *numeral one*. Though the two words are identical in sound, and are represented by the same letters in the written language, they are totally dissimilar in every thing else—in meaning, in *etymology*, and as to the source from which we have received them. ONE, the *numeral* is of Anglo-Saxon origin; the other ONE, whether we call it noun or pronoun, is apparently of Norman origin, and the same with the present French indefinite pronoun *on*. If it has connection with any Anglo-Saxon word in our language, it is with MAN, not with the numeral ONE. The French *on* is generally admitted to be a corruption of *homme* from the Latin *homo hOMINis*, which is again generally admitted to be a form made from

---

(24) How may we, perhaps, account for the use of *himself* and *themselves* to perform certain functions of the nominative case?

(25) Repeat the substance of what is said of the pronoun ONE.

the *root* MAN. The root is more clearly exhibited in the word *huMANus* formed from *homo*. The Germans still use the word *man* for the same purpose for which the French employ *on*, and for which we (less frequently) employ ONE.

(26) Let the learner observe that this word *one* has both a plural form, and a genitive form regularly made. "I have commanded my sanctified *ones*, I have also called my mighty *ones*." We also say, ONE'S *reputation;* ONE'S *interest*, &c.

§ 156. (1) Each of the personal pronouns has, according to most of our grammarians, a genitive or possessive case, both of the singular and of the plural forms. (2) In the case of all these pronouns, except *it* and *he*, there are two forms which have been thought to possess claims to the distinction of serving as their genitives. The two forms, connected with *I* (at least in significance), are MY and MINE, both evidently formed from *me;* with WE, OUR and OURS; with THOU, THY and THINE; with YE or YOU (but evidently sprung from YOU), YOUR and YOURS; with SHE, HER and HERS; and with THEY, THEIR and THEIRS. HE has only one genitive or possessive form HIS, and IT only one form, ITS.

(3) Where two forms occur, some grammarians recognise only one of them as genitive of the personal pronoun, and call the other forms possessive pronouns. (4) But those who agree in making this distinction are not agreed, as to which are genitives of the personal or substantive pronouns, and which are the possessive or adjective pronouns. (5) The older grammarians generally considered *mine*, *ours*, *thine*, *yours*, *hers*, *theirs*, as exclusively genitives, and, consequently, *substantives;* and *my*, *our*, *thy*, *your*, *her* (except when used as an accusative), *their*, as *pronominal adjectives*. *His* and *its* they regarded as performing both functions. (6) Some of the more modern grammarians reverse this arrangement. (7) Exceptions might, perhaps, be taken to the reasons assigned by both parties for the course pursued by them in this matter. (8) We regard the subject of dispute as of very small importance, since every *genitive* performs nearly the same function as an adjective. This is plainly seen, when we happen to

---

(26) Of what modifications of form is this pronoun ONE susceptible? Examples?

§ 156. (1) What is said in reference to *genitives* of the personal pronouns? (2) What of the forms connected with each claiming this distinction?

(3) What course is pursued by some grammarians, where double forms occur? (4) Are the grammarians agreed which form is genitive, &c.? (5) Describe the course pursued generally by the older grammarians. (6) Do all the modern grammarians acquiesce? (7) What remark is made in reference to the course pursued by both parties? (8) Repeat the substance of the reasons assigned for considering this dispute or difference between the

possess an adjective formed from a noun, or an adjective of similar meaning, though not of the same derivation. Thus, in Latin, *hominis natura*, and *natura humana;* in English, *a parent's fondness*, and *parental fondness.* Here the *genitives* and the *adjectives* formed from common *roots* perform functions scarcely distinguishable, at least, in many cases. To the same purpose we might adduce such examples as the following: *his father's mansion, his paternal mansion; a brother's love, brotherly love;* "Agamemnoniæ phalanges," *Agamemnonis phalanges;* Ἑκτόρεος χιτών, Ἕκτορος χιτών. We do not allege that these double forms of expression are always *exactly* of the same import, or always interchangeable, though some of them are in some cases manifestly interchangeable. We mean only to show the identity, or, at least, close similarity of the functions of genitives of nouns and of adjectives. (9) To distinguish the genitive case of a personal pronoun from a possessive adjective formed from that pronoun, by its function in language, is therefore both a difficult and an unprofitable task.

Dr. N. Webster (as quoted in Well's Eng. Gram., p. 74) makes the following observation in reference to this subject. "That *mine, thine, yours,* &c., do not constitute a possessive case, is demonstrable; for they are constantly used as the nominatives to verbs, and as objectives after verbs and prepositions." "Constantly used," we presume is only a dashing way of saying *can be used.* But even making this allowance, Dr. Webster's argument proves too much, as may be seen by comparing the following forms of expression, which are all equally in accordance with the settled usages of speech. *My friend and I bought each a pair of horses; his are bays,* MINE *are grays; his surpass* MINE *in beauty,* MINE *surpass his in speed; he gave a larger price for his, than I gave for* MINE. Compare with this the following: *My friend and I bought,* &c., as before; *my* FRIEND'S are bays, &c.; *mine surpass my* FRIEND'S; *I would give a larger price for mine, than for my* FRIEND'S. If it is "demonstrable" from the fact, that they can be used "as the nominatives to verbs, and as objectives after verbs and prepositions," "that *mine, thine,* &c., do not constitute a possessive case," what shall we say of the word *friend's* in the above forms of expression? (*See* § 75: 14, *et seq.*) The argument from the FUNCTIONS of *mine, ours,* &c., is, we think, decidedly more favorable to the arrangement of the old grammarians, than to that adopted by Drs. Webster, Latham, &c.

To prove from their *form,* that any of these sets of pronouns are genitives or not genitives of the pronouns which correspond with them in person and

---

grammarians of little importance. (9) What is said of the attempt to distinguish the *genitive case* of the personal pronoun from a *possessive pronoun?*

number, is equally difficult, since none of them have the regular inflection of the genitive case. *Ours, yours, hers, theirs,* have the appearance of genitives; but, if they are genitives, they cannot be proved from their *form* to be the genitives of *we, ye* or *you, she* and *they.* They are, manifestly, not formed from these words; but from the genitives or possessive adjectives (whichever we may choose to call them) *our, your, her* and *their.* If we have recourse to the Anglo-Saxon, it will not extricate us completely from the difficulty. It will, however, show that the forms *min, thin, ure,* &c., which are given in the grammars as the genitive cases of *ic, thu, we,* &c., are susceptible of all the variations of gender, case, and number, like other adjectives.

We think, that the best way to treat these pronouns is to class them all of both forms as determinative adjectives formed from the personal pronouns (as the words which answer to them are classed in the grammars of all the languages of Southern Europe, derived from the Latin), and then indicate the distinct purposes for which they are employed, or distinct occasions on which the different forms are used. This we have done already (*See* § 75.)

We may notice here that in ancient times, and, perhaps, sometimes at present in the *solemn* style, *mine* and *thine* are used instead of *my* and *thy* before a noun commencing with a vowel sound; "Mine iniquity," "Mine hour," "Mine eye," "Thine eye," &c.

The possessive pronouns, especially those of the first order (as we may call *my, our, thy, your, her,* &c., for the sake of distinction), are often accompanied by the adjective OWN, for the purpose of greater emphasis; thus, "Mine own life," "Thine own person" (in these examples *mine* and *thine* are used for *my* and *thy,* because *own* commences with a vowel sound; see preceding remark), "Our own power," "Your own nation," "His own head," "Their own things," &c.

We may notice here the fact that in the English language the possessive pronouns of the *third person* singular agree in gender with the *noun which they represent,* not with the *noun which they modify,* as in Latin and the modern languages of the South of Europe. This may be, otherwise, expressed as follows; the possessive pronouns of the third person agree in gender with the name of the possessor, not with the name of that which is possessed. Thus in French *son père* means either his father or her father; *sa mère,* either his mother or her mother. In this particular case our language has the advantage as regards perspicuity. *His* or *her* carries our mind directly to the person represented, and in some cases prevents ambiguity; and even where there is no danger of this the construction is more clear and lucid. The change of form, as in French, &c. according to the gender and number of the modified noun secures no advantage, where (as in that language, as well as in our own) the possessive is placed always immediately before the modified noun.

§ 157. Additional Remarks on the Genders.—This classification of nouns is a very important matter in the grammar of some languages—a subject which demands much attention and much study, on the part of all who wish to speak or write these languages with propriety. But, as regards English grammar, it is a matter of very little importance. In the Greek and Latin, and also in all the languages of the South of Europe derived from the Latin (and in most of the Teutonic dialects), adjectives assume a different termination according to the gender as well as the number of the noun which they complete. And, besides, where the nouns, as in Greek, Latin, German, have terminations for different cases the adjectives have case terminations also. That the adjective must agree with the substantive which it qualifies, or renders determinate, in gender, number and case, is an expression full of meaning in those languages. But in English we have no change of termination in our adjectives for such purposes. Were it not for the three forms of the personal pronoun of the third person, *he, she, it,* their possessive forms and their compounds with *self* (see § 155: 16. *et seq.*), even the mention of the genders would be superfluous in teaching English grammar. In this pronoun we have, as we have seen, a distinct singular form for the male sex, for the female sex, and for things without sex, or of which the sex is not intended to be discriminated. And to use these pronouns correctly, we must have regard to the classification in reference to sex; that is, to the genders of nouns.

In the Latin, Greek and German languages, there are *three genders* or *classes of nouns*, but the arrangement of the nouns under these classes is not precisely the same as in English. In the *masculine gender* or *class* in these languages all the *males* are arranged, and from this circumstance the class takes its name, *masculine gender*, that is, *class of males.* But with the *males* many names of things without *sex* are arranged in the same *gender*, that is in the same *class.* In making this arrangement, or, in other words, in applying adjectives of the *masculine* rather than of the *feminine* or *neuter* form to nouns, those who used these languages were guided either by some notion that the things represented by these nouns *participated of masculine qualities*, or by the mere *similarity of termination.* In the feminine gender or class, were arranged in like manner the names of all *females;* from which circumstance the appellation *feminine ;* and together with these many other names of objects neither male nor female. In the third class called the neuter gender (that is the class of *neither* males nor females), were arranged the names of the residue of things without sex. In the languages derived from the Latin, the neuter gender is omitted (in other words, adjectives have no *neuter form*) and all nouns are arranged under the *masculine*, or *feminine* gender. In all these languages, these classes of nouns have received their appellation (not because they include the *masculine class*, *males* exclusively, and the *feminine class*, *females* exclusively, but) from the noblest and most distinguished portion of the objects represented by the nouns arranged under these classes respectively. The masculine is so called from containing all the names of males (that is of all animals *discriminated* as males), the feminine from containing all the names of females.

It may here be observed that many grammarians have perplexed themselves and their readers by insensibly confounding *gender* with *sex*, or at least, attaching to the term gender, ideas which belong only to *sex*. Some have even thought it necessary to make an apology for the impropriety supposed to be implied in the expression *neuter gender;* though there is really no impropriety whatever in the form of expression, correctly interpreted, consequently, no need of an apology. Those who introduced in Latin grammar the term *genus*, meaning sort or kind (from which we have in French, *genre*, meaning also sort or kind, and in English, *gender*), attached no conception to the word inconsistent with the notion of a *genus neutrum*, a *neuter class* or class of neuters, that is, of names of objects which are neither masculine nor feminine,—neither male nor female. The same may be said of the *common gender*, (recognised in some of the grammars of the ancient languages), which includes those names sometimes applied to a male, sometimes to a female, as for example, the nouns parent, cousin, friend, &c. in English.

The expression *common gender* has been ignorantly and presumptuously called a solecism. If we have a clear conception of what the ancient grammarians meant by gender, we can easily perceive the perfect propriety of the expression *common gender*—that is, a class of names *common* to males and females—as well as of the expression *neuter gender*. But with the following definitions laid down (and, apparently, tacitly assented to, when not expressed in words), "Gender is the distinction of nouns with regard to sex," and "Gender is the distinction of sex," it is not strange that the notion of a neuter and of a common gender should present insuperable difficulties and incongruities. This definition, if closely examined, will be found to involve not only a total misconception of the meaning of the term *gender*, as employed by the old grammarians, but an absurd (not to say ridiculous) assertion, whatever we may understand by the word *gender*. Of what could it be asserted with propriety, that it is the *distinction of sex!* If we could find such a thing, what business has it among the terms of grammar? From this absurd definition, what could be expected to follow but confusion and inconsistency in every matter of detail founded upon it? No wonder that it was thought necessary to censure the old grammarians, or to apologize for them, when they were supposed to talk of a *neuter* "*distinction of sex!*" and a *common* "*distinction of sex!*" The old gentlemen knew, we think, much better what they said, and whereof they affirmed, than their inconsiderate critics.

Many other definitions of gender, though not chargeable with the same absurdity as those already noticed, yet afford evidence that their authors labored, less or more, under the influence of a similar misconception of the sense of this very simple term; simple, we mean as it was evidently understood by those who first introduced it into grammar. "Grammatical gender points out the sex, or the absence of sex." This assertion might with more propriety be made of the masculine, feminine, and neuter *terminations* of adjectives in Latin, Greek, and most of the modern languages, or of such terminations appended to a noun as distinguish the female occupant of an office, station, &c., from the male occupant: the termination *ess*, for example, in English, as *abbot*, a male head of an abbey; *abbess*, a female head of an abbey; *prince*, *princess*, &c. The same may be said of the following: "Gender, in grammar, is an alteration generally in the endings of words, to mark distinction of sex." "Gender in *grammar*, a difference in words to express distinction of sex."—Webster's Dict. The two following definitions are still more faulty: "Genders are modifications that *distinguish objects* in regard to sex." "Gender is the *distinction of objects* in regard to sex." Whatever gender may be, whilst it is recognised as a term of grammar, it has reference to *words*, to the *signs* of objects, and not to *objects* themselves. To say that gender is a modification of *objects*, or a *distinction* of *objects*, is therefore altogether irrelevant. This is the old and very common error of confounding *words* and *objects*—*things* and the *names of things*.

Most modern writers on grammar have taken care not to commit themselves by giving a direct definition of gender. They have *dodged* the question, what is gender? This was perhaps a prudent course, especially if these writers labored in any degree under the apparently very general misconception of this matter, originating, as we think, in confounding the meaning of the terms *sex* and *gender*. No rational definition could be expected till this misconception was completely cleared away.

Another subject has generally, in our English grammars, been treated under the head of Gender, though it has connection rather with the original structure of *single words* than with the changes which they undergo in order to perform their grammatical functions, and might, without impropriety, be wholly omitted in this place. In the case of some offices or stations, which may be held both by men and women, and in the case of the more conspicuous animals, there is a separate name for the separate sexes. These names are sometimes formed, the feminine from the masculine, by the addition of a syllable or some change of the termination, generally by the syllable *ess*; as, *priest*, *priestess* or *female priest*; *prince*, *princess*, &c. Sometimes the words which indicate the female are less clearly connected with the male form, and sometimes altogether distinct. According to the custom of the grammarians, we subjoin a list of some of the masculine and feminine forms which most frequently recur.

List of Masculine Names which have a Feminine Form in ESS.

Abbot,	Abbess.	Baron,	Baroness.
Actor,	Actress.	Benefactor,	Benefactress.

Count,	Countess.	Master,	Mistress.
Duke,	Duchess.	Peer,	Peeress.
Emperor,	Empress.	Priest,	Priestess.
Heir,	Heiress.	Prince,	Princess.
Host,	Hostess.	Prophet,	Prophetess.
Jew,	Jewess.	Shepherd,	Shepherdess.
Lion,	Lioness.	Songster,	Songstress.
Marquis,	Marchioness.	Viscount,	Viscountess.

Some names have a feminine form in *ix;* as,

Administrator,	Administratrix.	Testator,	Testatrix.
Executor,	Executrix.	Director,	Directrix.

We give no list of those names for males and females which are entirely distinct in form; as, *husband, wife; father, mother; brother, sister; horse, mare,* &c., since the fact that these different names are given to animals of different sexes has nothing to do with the structure of language, nothing to do with grammar. All this is to be learnt from dictionaries or vocabularies, not from treatises on *construction.*

§ 158. The Articles.—The two determinative adjectives an or a, and the have been called very generally by English grammarians the *definite* and the *indefinite article.* Under this name these two words have been raised to the dignity of forming a separate class by themselves, and have been placed in the foremost rank among the *parts of speech.* Yet, so far are these words from being entitled to so much consideration from the indispensable importance of the functions which they perform in speech, that there are many highly polished languages—amongst these the Greek—which possess no separate distinct word equivalent to our *an* or *a*—the (so styled) *indefinite article;* and the Latin has no word exclusively used to perform the functions either of the *definite* or of the *indefinite* article.

To the mere English scholar the term *article* applied to the words *an* and *the* conveys no meaning whatever. When we have traced it to *articulus* in Latin, and ascertained that this was employed to translate ἄρθρον—the name applied by the Greek grammarians to a word nearly equivalent to what our grammarians have called the *definite article*, and learned that these Latin and Greek words mean a *joint*, we are still far from unravelling the mystery which hangs about this strange term. Why *a* and *the* should be called *joints* or *hinges*, and joints or hinges in contradistinction to all other words in the language, remains still to be explained.

The application of this name to the Greek determinative ὁ, ἡ, τὸ, is accounted for in the following manner: The Greek grammarians originally gave the appellation ἄρθρα (*joints*) to two words in connection, which they afterwards distinguished by the names of the *prepositive* and *postpositive articles* or *joints*. These two words *taken together* serve indeed as *joints* or *hinges* of language, and have been named by the Greeks not inappropriately. One of these is the word above mentioned, the *prepositive* article ὁ, ἡ, τὸ, which alone retains this name, though it has no claim to it, save what it obtained through its alliance with the *postpositive*. This latter (the postpositive article) is what has been commonly called the *relative pronoun*, equivalent to our *who*, *which* and *that*. To this the name joint was appropriately given. Some modern grammarians (whom in this we willingly follow) still call it by a name of nearly the same import—the *Conjunctive* Pronoun. We may readily comprehend the reason of giving the name *joint* to the relative or conjunctive pronoun and the determinative equivalent to THE, if we consider attentively the Compound Proposition with Adjective Accessory already described (§ 111). For example: THE *man* WHO *promised to assist us disappointed our hopes*. Here the word *who* serves as a *joint* to connect the adjective accessory, *promised to assist us*, with the word *man*, which it modifies or completes. In performing this function it is assisted by the determinative sign *the* used before the noun modified.

The intimate relation of the article and conjunctive pronoun in Greek served to render the reference of the latter with its accessory to the former and its noun more striking. The article and relative in that language resemble each other in sound, are of the same family, or rather varieties of the same word, and seem to have been used indiscriminately, in ancient times, as conjunctive pronouns. Ὁ ἄνθρωπος ὅς, *The man who*, was a form almost like *Which man who*, or *The man the*. If this kind of expression were now admissible with us, it would evidently serve to establish the closest relation between the noun *man* and the accessory introduced by *who*. This is no imaginary case, as regards the use of the article *the* in our language. *The*, like the Greek article, was currently used both as article and relative in the Anglo-Saxon. The determinative use, we suspect, as we shall have occasion to say in another place, was in both languages the earliest and the original use out of which grew the relative or conjunctive use. In other words, we suppose all relatives to be determinatives used in a peculiar mode. But be this as it may, the mode of writing accessory adjective propositions in Anglo-Saxon was to introduce the accessory by the word *the*, whilst the noun modified by the accessory was preceded by the proper case of the determinative *se*, *seo*, *thaet*, which seems to be the same word, at least the same root subjected to flection. The only forms which are exceptions are *se*, and *seo*. All the other forms of all genders, numbers and cases, appear to be formed from the root THE.

Thus viewed these words might well be compared to a double joint—a *prepositive* and *postpositive article* to connect or lock the word which the one preceded and the other followed with the clause in which the latter performed some prominent function.

In many cases the explanatory proposition and postpositive article came to be suppressed, because readily suggested to the mind of the hearer or reader by the drift of the discourse. In such cases the article may be considered as indicating such suppression—as warning us of the Ellipsis. Let us take as an example the following words from the first chapter of Genesis: "God said, Let there be light; and there was light. And God saw THE light, that it was good." Here the word light is twice used without any determinative, and the third time with one. "God saw THE light," that is *the light which has been just mentioned—the light which he had called into existence*. Some accessory proposition is evidently implied, and the determinative sign *the* indicates (to all who understand the usage of our language) that the light referred to is the same that has been already mentioned.

What we have said accounts sufficiently for the ancient Greek grammarians calling this determinative and the conjunctive pronoun taken in connection articles or joints. But it can scarcely vindicate the conduct of their successors, when, having given a distinct name to the form of the determinative which, in time, came to be used exclusively to perform the conjunctive function, they gave the name of *joint* to that form which no longer served alone as a *joint*, but only occasionally lent its aid to the *jointing* or conjunctive word. Much less can these historical facts serve as a just excuse for continuing to call the determinative THE, without any allusion to its co-operation or original connection with the conjunctive pronoun, by this inappropriate and (to the mere English scholar) unintelligible name; less still can they justify the application of this name to the word *an* and its equivalents in the modern languages. This practice, we believe, is confined at present to our own language. The grammars of most modern languages recognise only one article. Yet, if, as originally, the connection with the conjunctive pronoun were recognised in applying the name *article*, AN might set up an equal claim with THE to the appellation of prepositive article. In the assertions, A *man who always does to others, as he would wish others to do to him, is a good citizen*, and, THE *man who always*, &c., A and THE in connection with the conjunctive WHO perform functions of a similar nature. But this function seems to be merely to indicate a lesser (in the case of *a*) or greater (in the case of *the*) degree of *determinateness*, or, in the language of the common grammars, to *point out* the word to which the conjunctive refers and to which it *joints* the accessory proposition. But THIS and THAT, ANY, SUCH, ALL, in fact most determinatives perform the very same function.

There seems not a shadow of apology for considering these two little words as forming a distinct part of speech, or division of the signs of our language, and then entering on the vain search for some function pertaining exclusively to them, by which they may be discriminated from all other classes of words. Such a course presents strong temptation to the exercise of ingenuity in finding grounds of distinction where none actually exist, and, thus, to pervert as well as perplex the grammar of the language. Injudicious classification—the application, especially, of distinctive names to things which are not in fact different (in the aspect in which they are regarded in classifying them), naturally leads to false speculation. It is not a sufficient apology in such cases to allege that the classification can do no harm, because the things classified remain unchanged by the classification. The establishment of a class is the implied assertion of a *distinctive* difference—a difference worthy too of the attention of an inquirer. Where such difference does not exist, the implication that it exists is an error, and may, like other errors, which in themselves appear trivial, lead in the end to more important errors.

If we wish to account for the fact that the articles have been placed foremost in the list of the *parts of speech*, we must look for the explanation, as before, to the Greek grammarians. These grammarians very properly placed the nouns at the head of their classification of words, and finding it convenient to indicate the *genders* of these nouns by prefixing the article which accorded with them in gender, they were led to give the declension of the article ὁ, ἡ, το, the first place in their treatises on language. The article is still used in our Greek lexicons to indicate the genders of nouns, instead of using, as we do in Latin dictionaries and those of the modern languages, abbreviations for *masculine*, *feminine* and *neuter*.

The most intelligent of our modern grammarians are unanimous in the decision, that it is improper to consider the articles a distinct class of words, or part of speech. See Dr. Robinson's Translation of Buttman's Greek Grammar, pp. 120, 121, note, &c., &c.

THE DETERMINATIVE AN OR A.—Contrary to what is asserted, or

implied in most of our grammars, the original form of this word is *an*, and *a* is a contraction. It is not strictly correct to say that "*a becomes an* before a vowel and a silent *h*." We should rather say that *an* becomes *a* before a syllable beginning with a consonantal sound.

A is employed *before* words commencing with a consonantal sound; that is, 1st, before all words commencing with the sounds represented by the letters called consonants, in the written language; 2d, before words commencing with an aspirated *h*, as, *a hand*, *a hammer*, &c.; 3d, before all words commencing with what is called the long sound of *u*—equivalent to the sound given to the combination of the semivowel *y* with the vowels *ou* in the word *you*, or in the word *youth*, as, *a union*, *a university*, &c. On the contrary, before *u* short, or purely *vocal*, as well as before the other vowels, and before silent *h*, *an* is employed; as, *an uncle*, *an animal*, *an hour*, &c.

An is perhaps the weakest of the determinative adjectives—of all the *determinatives* the *least determinative*.*

When used with a noun it indicates that a single individual of the species, of which the noun is a general sign, is intended to be designated. Thus the word *man* used alone means the whole species, or race of men, as in the words of the poet, "*The proper study of mankind is* MAN." But A *man* indicates a single individual of the race. The *a* prefixed shows, 1st, that we do not intend to include a whole class; nor 2d, a number of the class, but a single individual of a class, and "farther it saith not." What particular individual is meant is left wholly undetermined.

The word *an* with its contract form *a* descends to us from the Anglo-Saxon *an*, or *ane*, the word expressive of *unity* in that language, and from which we have, with a little variation of sound and orthography, our modern sign of unity, the numeral *one*. *Ane* or *ae* to express unity is a form still extant in the Scottish dialect, little differing in orthography and pronunciation from the Anglo-Saxon sign of unity, on the one hand, and our modern English determinative, on the other. Indeed, *an* more nearly resembles the Anglo-Saxon numeral in *form* than *one*, which corresponds exactly with the parent word in sense.

In the present usage of our language, AN and ONE *agree* in this, that both imply individuality. But they *differ* in this, that *an* implies, as we have already said, that an individual of a class is indicated, as dis-

* Hence many of our grammarians have been led to commit the solecism of classing *an* among the *definitives*, and then calling it the *indefinite* article—the *indefinite definitive* !

tinguished from the whole class of which the noun is the common appellation; whereas *one* implies that a single individual is meant, as distinguished from a *number* of individuals of the same class. The force of the two words and their distinct functions can be most clearly exhibited by the aid of examples. For this purpose we present the following questions, with suitable answers: *Can* A *man perform that piece of work? No; but* A HORSE *can perform it. Can* ONE *man perform that piece of work? No; but* TWO MEN *can perform it?* In the first question the emphasis is on the word *man*, in the second on the determinative word *one*. The inquiry in the first case is, whether man (a human being) can do the work; in the latter, whether *one* man or *more than one* are necessary to perform it.

It will be seen from this that the employment of the determinative *an* (differing in form from the numeral *one*) introduces a convenient distinction in our language. Yet, in languages which employ the numeral for both purposes, no peculiar inconvenience is experienced, since a variation of emphasis is sufficient (in spoken language) to mark the discrimination of meaning. For example, the words *un homme* (in French), by laying a slight stress of voice on *un*, imply *one man;* without this stress, and giving preponderant force to *homme, a man.*

We may here notice a use of the word ONE resembling that of the indefinite (more properly, *less definite*) article, in such expressions as "*One* Simon, a tanner," "*One* Mnason of Cyprus," &c. This use, certainly, more nearly resembles that of the article *an*, than the common use of the numeral. It may be doubted whether this word ONE is not the indeterminate pronoun described in § 155: 25. It strongly indicates *indeterminateness*, and hence is often employed contemptuously to insinuate a reproach of obscurity, want of notoriety and social importance. The word is, we believe, in this use employed only with the names of persons. Thus used it is equivalent to the Greek indefinite pronoun τις, and the Latin *quidam.*

The word *any* is of kindred meaning as well as of kindred origin with *an*. It is formed from the Anglo-Saxon numeral *ane* or *aen*, with the addition of the affix *ig*, and was originally written *aenig*, meaning *one like*. This word may be regarded perhaps as more loosely determinative than *an*. Though originally implying unity, it is, unlike *an*, often employed before plural nouns. We can say *any men*, as well as *any man*. We may observe the distinction between *an* or *a*, *any* and *some* in the following examples: *Can* A *boy do that? No; but* A *man can. Can* ANY *boy do that? No; but* SOME *boys can. Some* is commonly in present usage employed with plurals, anciently it was used with nouns of the singular form with the force of the Latin *aliquis;* as

"Some man will say," &c. We have examples of this usage in the compound words *somebody*, *something*.

All three words *an*, *any*, *some*, agree in this that they indicate the partition of the class of objects represented by the nouns to which they are applied, and that only a part (in the case of *an* only an individual) is embraced under the expression. If the noun is accompanied by a limiting or descriptive complement, they indicate that only a part (an individual in the case of *an*) of the objects represented by the noun so limited is embraced: for example, *a wise man*, means an individual of the class indicated by the words *wise man*. It is always implied that there are more individuals of the same kind not embraced by the expression.

In this respect *an* and the other determinatives now mentioned are markedly different from those which we are about to consider.

Before passing from *an* or *a*, we may remark an apparent exception to the assertion that it indicates individuality in the fact that it is placed before plural nouns modified by numerals. Thus we say, *a dozen men*, or *a dozen; a thousand men*, *a hundred men;* &c. In all such cases the word dozen, or hundred, or thousand is regarded as expressing a *collective* unit. The proof is at hand. We can equally say, *one dozen*, *one hundred*, *one thousand*, &c.

The Determinative THE.—This word is used before both singular and plural nouns to indicate that they are to be taken in a strictly determinate sense. It indicates that the object or objects represented by the noun, as limited either by an expressed or implied modification, are embraced in their complete totality. Thus, *the man of integrity*, indicates the class *man*, as limited by the words *of integrity*, in its complete totality. If we make any assertion about *the man of integrity*, it ought to apply to every individual of this whole class. The phrase, *a man of integrity*, agreeably to what we have said in considering *an*, implies the partition of the class, and that only an individual is embraced in the expression. There are numerous instances in which these two forms of expression may be employed indifferently in expressing the same truth. Thus, A *man of integrity would not do such an action;* and, The *man of integrity would not do such an action*. These two assertions are nearly equivalent, for, if an individual of integrity taken at random would not do a certain action, it is obvious to infer that the whole class (included under the expression, *the man of integrity*) would not do it. But this is not explicitly declared in the assertion. Something is left for the exercise of the hearer's judgment—something to be inferred.

That the two expressions are not in themselves (without the assistance of *inference*) exactly equivalent may be readily discovered by attending to *similar forms* of expression in which the *subject matter* is different. For example, A *man whom we saw yesterday came to my house this morning*, and THE *man whom we saw yesterday came*, &c. In the first of these forms it is indicated, that the man whom we saw yesterday is only one of a class—an indefinite individual of a number whom we saw; but, in the latter form, a definite man, about whom we have an understanding—whom we both know, as *the* man whom we saw yesterday, is indicated.

We must, if we wish to understand this subject, guard carefully against confounding the function performed by the determinatives with the function performed by the more intimate limiting words. We believe that the determinative *the* is never employed in our language except with a noun that is otherwise limited either expressly or by implication. The determinative THE indicates the fact of such limitation, the mutual recognition of such limitation by the speaker and the party addressed, and further that the object or class of objects represented by the noun so limited is embraced in its totality by the expression. When some grammarians say that the article *the* "limits a noun and shows how far its signification extends," they seem to confound together the function performed by the determinative and the functions performed by the more intimate modifications, expressed or implied, which together with the noun taken as a whole compound conception come within the determinative influence of the article. It is, perhaps, more correct to say that the article is placed before a noun because it is already limited, than to say that it is placed before the noun for the purpose of limiting it. It rather refers to a limitation expressed or implied than expresses one itself, and it thus exercises a force similar to that of the *relative* pronouns. In fact the closest relation in origin and function exists in most languages between determinatives and relatives. In some cases the same word, like our *that*, performs both functions.

We reiterate, at the hazard of being charged with repetition, that the noun, which is the name of a class, is first limited by what we have called its more intimate modifications (descriptive adjectives, genitives, &c.), expressed or understood and coming, as is taken for granted, within the cognizance of the party addressed; thus generally forming a subclass by means of the limitations, which subclass, it is further indicated by the article, is to be taken in its totality. A subclass, we say, is *generally* formed, but sometimes the determinate expression embraces only an individual object limited as above described; that is, the limitation itself implies individuality; for example, *the key of my desk*, *the virtue of temperance*, *the sun*, *the earth*. Here the expressed or implied (as in the case of *the sun* and *the earth*) modification limits the noun to an individual object.

For the purposes above described, the determinative THE is employed before nouns limited by most of the forms of modification of which they are susceptible—before nouns modified by a descriptive adjective, by a genitive case complement, by noun and preposition complement, by an infinitive, and by an adjective accessory proposition. All common nouns—nouns universally employed as names of classes, whether always reckoned and used as *common* or not—if restricted by the complements enumerated, when of the singular form take either *an* or *the*, except they are preceded by some other determinative. Plural forms stand without a determinative, when the singular form would take *an*. Whether a singular noun modified as above shall take *an* or *the*, and whether a plural noun shall take *the*, or stand without a determinative, is to be decided by reference to what we have already said.

We have had occasion to notice that adjectives employed substantively are always preceded by the determinative *the*. Such forms of expression as *the wise*, *the virtuous*, &c., are equivalent to the noun *men* or the noun *persons* restricted by the adjectives *wise*, *virtuous*, &c. Hence they come within the class of limited nouns mentioned above, namely those limited by a descriptive adjective; and because in such expressions a whole class in its *totality* is indicated, the determinative employed is always THE, never AN.

It may be noticed that when a noun is restricted by a genitive case, the determinative is used only before the genitive noun, or, perhaps, it would be more proper to say, before the whole expression, including the modification; for example, *the Queen's palace*, *the President's house*. If we substitute for these the Norman forms of expression with a noun and preposition instead of the genitive, the determinative is expressed before both nouns, because both are in fact determinately used. Thus, *the* palace of *the* Queen, *the* house of *the* President. Here *palace* and *house* are limited *expressly* by the accompanying complements, and Queen and President by implication in a manner to be now described.

It must be remembered that nouns a e often employed determinately without being accompanied by any *expressed* limitation or restriction. Such nouns equally with those which are *expressly* limited take before them the determinative *the*. Hence we employ *the* before the names of objects of eminence, and of objects which stand alone, the only individuals of their kind in which we are interested; as, *the President*, *the King*, *the Queen*, *the Sun*, *the Moon*, *the Earth*, &c. Some limiting complement may here be regarded as suppressed, because it naturally suggests itself to the mind of the party addressed. This complement may be any one of those above enumerated. Sometimes several different complements may equally serve the purpose. In such cases the noun is not less determinate, because one or more determinative or limiting circumstances are so well understood by speaker and hearer mutually, that it is unnecessary to express them in the form of an accessory proposition, or by any other form of complement. We employ the determinative also in such expressions as, *the sciences*, *the mathematics*, and before the names of many important mechanical inventions, as *the press*, *the steam engine*, *the lever*, *the wedge*, &c., because all these names are employed determinately. For similar reasons we use the determinative before the singular class names of animals when we intend to designate the species in its totality; for example, *the horse*, *the dog*, *the ox*, *the lion*, &c., meaning the whole kind. *The horse is a noble and useful animal; the dog is faithful to his master*, &c.

A noun often becomes determinate by the fact that it has been already employed by the speaker with reference to some individual person or thing. Hence when a noun under these circumstances is repeated, the determinative is used. Here it indicates that the noun which it precedes is employed in reference to the same object already mentioned, and by this circumstance rendered determinate to the hearer. For example, "Two men went up into the temple to pray; the one *a* Pharisee, and the other *a* publican. *The* Pharisee stood and prayed," &c. "And *the* publican, standing afar off, would not lift up so much as his eyes unto heaven," &c. Here we have first "*a Pharisee*," and "*a publican*"—individuals of certain classes, but no farther determinate. Next we have "*the Pharisee*," and "*the publican*," because now determinate individuals—the same already introduced to the hearer's notice, who went up to the temple to pray. As John was taking a walk in the park *a boy* came up to him and entered into conversation with him. They soon after passed near a number of boys, who were endeavoring to raise a kite. As they were passing *the boy* exclaimed, &c. Here *the boy* refers the hearer to the boy who joined John in the walk. If we substitute *a* for *the*, the reference will be to some other boy—an indeterminate individual of the group engaged in raising the kite.

Nouns modified by a noun in apposition never, we think, take the determinative THE, at least, in consequence of this species of modification. The noun placed in apposition, on the contrary, very generally takes the determinative. The nouns which most commonly take after them a noun in apposition are proper names; for example: *Plato, the philosopher; Cicero, the orator.* In such forms of expression the noun in apposition is always preceded by the determinative. When the noun appended or *apposed* is a personal or official title, no determinative is employed; for example: *George Washington,* PRESIDENT *of the United States,* COMMANDER *in chief,* &c. *Victoria,* QUEEN *of Great Britain,* &c. When the noun expressing an official title is placed before the proper name, the article is also generally omitted; as, *General Washington, President Adams, Queen Victoria,* &c. But it may be doubted whether these are properly examples of apposition. The words appended have by general usage become part of the appellation of the individuals to whom they are applied, as much so almost as a cognomen in the case of private individuals. To the following forms of expression, apparently little differing from the last mentioned, we customarily prefix the article. *The emperor Constantine, The emperor Trajan,* &c. *The frigate Constitution. The ship Albion. The steamer Europa,* &c. Here *frigate, ship, steamer,* seem to partake more of the nature of apposition, although, contrary to the most usual arrangement of the noun in apposition, they are placed before the noun which they serve to complete.

When *a noun in apposition complement* is appended to an abstract noun, the usage is the same as when it is appended to a proper name. The noun that is completed takes no determinative, at least none on account of the complement, and the complement, if of the singular form, takes either the determinative *an,* or *the;* and if of the plural form it either takes *the* or takes no determinative, according as it is more or less determinately used. Example: *Justice, a virtue indispensable to the stability of every form of government, should be strenuously inculcated and scrupulously practised by all true patriots. Justice, the virtue most indispensable to the stability of every form of government,* &c. Examples of a noun of the plural form used in apposition. *Justice and humanity, the virtues most indispensable,* &c. *Justice and humanity, virtues which highly promote the welfare of states,* &c.

With common or general nouns (as distinct from abstract nouns and proper names) we still more rarely employ the *noun* in apposition complement, and when we do, the usage, so far as we are aware, is the same in regard of the determinatives. Example: *Man, the only animal endowed with reason, is, at the same time, the only animal endowed with speech.*

A noun modified by an *explicative* or *epithetic* accessory proposition never takes the determinative in consequence of this complement.

This fact has already come under our notice (§ 113). There is a close analogy between the noun in apposition and the *epithetic* modification, as we have already shown that there is an analogy between the latter and the adjective employed as a mere *epithet*. These modifications do not, as we have already said, limit or restrict the noun, or render it more determinate. They are not, in fact, a necessary or essential part of the proposition in which they are inserted, but something superadded for illustration, or, sometimes, merely for ornament.

The noun in apposition may be expanded into an explicative accessory: *Cicero, the great orator, was both a statesman and philosopher*, may be expressed more fully, thus, *Cicero, who was a great orator, was both a statesman*, &c. The noun in apposition may, perhaps, be regarded as an abbreviated form of the explicative accessory.

The same kind of analogy may be traced between the restrictive accessory and the other complements which restrict or limit nouns; namely, the genitive case complement, noun in apposition, and limiting descriptive adjective complement. These latter, as in the case of the noun in apposition, seem to be only more compendious methods of expressing what is more formally expressed by the restrictive adjective accessory. For example: *The mansion which belongs to his father*, is more compendiously expressed by the words, *The mansion of his father;* more compendiously still by the words, *His father's mansion;* and perhaps yet more compactly by the words, *His paternal mansion.*

The determinative *the*, as we have seen, is prefixed only to nouns which are employed in a limited or determinate sense; but we must not conclude from this that it is prefixed to all nouns which are so employed. On the contrary, nouns are often, from the nature of the objects which they designate, so clearly and so invariably determinate, that they need no indication of determinateness. To nouns of this kind we do not generally prefix determinatives in our language.

1. Of this class of nouns are proper names, which, being appropriated to individuals, admit of no further determination or restriction. We might connect with these the personal pronouns, especially of the first and second person. The pronouns of the third person and the relative or conjunctive pronouns may themselves be regarded as a sort of determinatives, or as involving the *force*, if not sometimes the form of a determinative word.

2. Common nouns, when employed in the whole extent of their signification, are completely determinate, and in English generally take no article; as, for example, *Man is mortal; Tea is brought from China; Cotton is cultivated in the United States;* &c. We have already noticed what appears an exception to this usage, in

the case of the names of animals, as, *the horse*, *the ox*, &c. In these last examples possibly *animal* or some such word is implied, which is rendered determinate by the name of the species, and so takes the article.

3. Abstract nouns, when employed in the whole extent of their signification, are not in our language accompanied by the determinative *the;* for example: *Virtue is immortal; Vice always, sooner or later, produces misery;* &c. But, when we employ abstract nouns in a limited sense, or, in other words, restricted by complements, especially by the noun and preposition, or the adjective accessory, we prefix the determinative sign; as, for example, *The virtue of temperance; The faith which overcomes the world;* "The wisdom that is from above is first pure," &c.

4. The determinative *the* is, of course, seldom used when any other determinative is prefixed to a noun. It would be manifestly absurd to employ it in company with *an* or *a*, which are used for the express purpose of indicating a different and weaker degree of determinateness, or with *this* and *that*, which are more emphatic determinatives than itself. The article *the* is never in our language employed in company with possessive pronouns, whether placed before the nouns which they modify, or employed separately from the noun to which they refer. We can neither say, *The my book*, nor that book is *The mine.* (For the usage of other languages in such cases see the remarks in the next note.) Again the article *the* is not employed, when such words as *any*, *many*, *every*, *such*, &c., are placed before nouns.

On the contrary, the determinative *the* is employed before the de terminative *same*, and after the determinative *all*, and sometimes after *both;* as, for example, *The same man; All the world; All the men in the house;* "*Both the* men, between whom the controversy is, shall stand before the Lord."

The determinative *the* s also frequently prefixed to words limited by a *numeral;* as, *The two men.* This means two definite men about whom the speaker and hearer have a mutual understanding; whereas the words *two men* imply any two men indeterminate except as to number.

The presence or absence of the determinative *the* affects very materially the sense of some words in our language. For example, what a difference between the meanings conveyed by the expressions, *Earth* and *The earth; Faith* and *The Faith; Thou art man*, *Thou art a man*, and *Thou art the man?*

The same remark applies to the determinative *an* or *a*. For ex ample: *Few* and *A few*; *Little* and *A little*. *A few* implies a positive, though small number; *A little*, a positive, though small quantity; but *Few* and *Little* verge towards the very borders of absolute negation of number and quantity respectively.

"Ah! *little* think the gay licentious proud."

This almost amounts to saying, that they do not think at all.

NOTE.—In those languages which have a determinative adjective equivalent to our determinative *the*, great diversity prevails as to the extent of its application. In English, it is *generally* omitted whenever the noun is of itself determinate without any complement; as in the case of proper names, and of abstract nouns used in the whole extent of their signification. In the Greek language, on the contrary, the article is often employed with proper names, with abstract nouns employed in the whole extent of their signification, especially when subjects of propositions, and even with the infinitives of verbs. By prefixing the different forms of the article (which has case terminations like nouns and adjectives), the Greeks are enabled to use their infinitives in all the various cases which belong to other nouns in their language. Hence the infinitive with them performs functions which in other languages it cannot conveniently perform. In Latin and English, and most other languages, infinitives are rarely employed except as subjects of propositions and complements of other verbs—in other words, only in the nominative and accusative (or objective) cases. (We have noticed some cases in which the infinitive is used in English with the force of a dative or of a noun and preposition—the *infinitive of purpose*, for example.) In Greek, by the help of the case forms of the article, infinitives are employed to perform the functions of *genitive* and *dative* (as well as nominative and accusative cases) functions in Latin generally performed by the gerund, and in English also by the gerund or verbal in ING.

In French and many other modern languages the article is prefixed to common nouns taken in their *general* or most extensive sense, as *l'homme est faible, man is weak;* to the names of countries, as *la France, France;* to abstract nouns employed in the whole extent of their signification, as *la vertu est aimable, virtue is amiable;* and to possessive pronouns, when employed separately from the nouns to which they refer, as *le mien, le nôtre,* &c., (in which case it may be regarded as indicating the suppressed noun.) In Italian, the article is employed even with the possessive pronouns prefixed to nouns, *il mio libro, my book,* literally, *the my book.*

The omission of the article in English, and the employment of the article in other languages, does not render the noun in the one case less, or in the other case more determinate. The article adds nothing to the definiteness of the expression. The French, &c., prefix it, because the noun is definitely used; we omit it, because the noun is in its nature invariably definite. The use and omission is an idiomatic peculiarity of the respective languages

The remark, that the article adds nothing to the definiteness of the expression, is apparently applicable, when it is prefixed in our own and in other languages, to the names of rivers, mountains, &c., as, *the Hudson, the Thames, the Tiber, the Seine; the Alps, the Pyrenees, the Alleghanies*, &c. But these forms of expression seem to have arisen from the suppression of the words *river*, and *mountains* respectively. The full expression would be, *the river Hudson; the Pyrenees mountains*, &c. Here the determinative is appropriately joined with the *common* nouns, "*river*" and "*mountains*," because they are used determinately, being limited by the addition of the words *Hudson* and *Pyrenees*.

Perhaps, the use of the determinative with other proper names; as, for instance, the names of countries, or even its use with the proper names of individual persons in the Greek language, might be accounted for in a similar way. Ὁ Ξενοφῶν, the Xenophon, may have arisen from an abbreviation of Ὁ ἀνὴρ Ξενοφῶν, *the man Xenophon.* In support of this explanation it might be alleged that the Greeks were accustomed to employ the word Ἀνήρ, and its plural form Ἄνδρες, in a manner which appears to the moderns redundant; as in the phrases Ἄνδρες στρατιῶται, *soldiers;* literally *men soldiers;* Ἄνδρες, ἀδελφοὶ κὰι πατέρες, *brethren and fathers;* literally *men brethren and (men) fathers.* (*See* § 146. *Note*, p. 469.)

When several nouns are connected in the same construction, the determinative is often, in English, suppressed before all but the first noun; as, for example, *The men, women and children whom he met gazed upon him with wonder;* instead of *The men, the women and the children*, &c. (The same remark applies to the determinative *an.*) When emphasis is intended, the determinative is repeated; and when special discrimination is required it must be repeated before each noun; for example, "Cincinnatus, the dictator, and *the* master of the horse marched against the Æqui." If, in this sentence, the determinative were omitted before "master of the horse," it would, to a person guided by the mere form of the expression without other knowledge of the fact, appear that the appellations "dictator" and "master of the horse" were both intended to apply to Cincinnatus, whereas the master of the horse was a distinct person. The article before an adjective employed substantively should never be suppressed. It would be improper to say, *the wise and good*, for the wise, and the good, if we intend to indicate two distinct classes of men. If we mean one class of men possessed of the two qualities expressed by *wise* and *good*, only one article should be employed, since only one noun is suppressed. The article is often improperly suppressed by careless writers, so as to injure sometimes the perspicuity and sometimes the force of discourse. In French and some other modern languages, the determinative is repeated before each individual noun far more generally than in English. This practice conduces to render the language both more clear and more forcible. The repetition of the article would in some cases appear stiff in our language. It is better, however to repeat it unnecessarily, than to omit it where its presence is requisite to prevent ambiguity.

THIS AND THAT.—We have already observed one marked peculiarity of these two determinatives, viz; that, unlike our other adjectives, they both possess a plural form. (*See* § 94. *note p.* 300)

These words are much more determinate (that is, used with nouns much more determinately employed) than the (so called) definite article *the*. Their primary use is to accompany nouns intended to designate objects present to the view of the speaker, and determined by some look or gesture, or intimation borrowed from the signs of natural language, to which natural sign they call the attention of the hearer. Hence they have been called *demonstratives* by the grammarians, because, as they allege, they point out (*demonstrate*) the particular objects designated.

This is prefixed to nouns representing objects relatively near to the speaker, *that* to objects more remote, *the* differs from these words in being, though less determinative, of far more general application. It is employed in speaking of objects absent, as well as present, and indicates a limitation given to its noun by *artificial*, or *articulate language*, without the aid of natural signs. In these respects it differs from *this* and *that*. Another difference worthy of observation is that we often employ *this* and *that* substantively, suppressing the noun which they designate, but we never so employ either of the determinatives *the* or *an*.

A secondary use of the determinatives *this* and *that* is to indicate in written discourse, and, sometimes, in formal addresses—*this*, something proximate in the *order* of the discourse, *that*, something relatively more remote.

" Some place the bliss in action, some in ease;
Those call it pleasure, and contentment *these*."—Pope.

" The palaces and lofty domes arose—
These for devotion, and for pleasure *those*."—Idem.

Here relative proximity in the arrangement of the words serves the same purpose of rendering the reference determinate, as proximity in place does in the case of the speaker, who has the objects to which he refers under his eye, and employs a natural gesture to assist artificial language in fixing on them the attention of the hearer. The determinative words *former* and *latter* are more frequently used for this purpose, and perform this function generally in a more natural and graceful manner—with much less stiffness and formality than *this* and *that*.

With *this* and *that* may be classed *yonder* and *yon*. These words, though at present in less common use, have been employed by many of our best authors. They are used to designate objects in sight but distant from the speaker. Ex. "*Yon* flowery arbors, *yonder* alleys green." —Milton. "Save that from *yonder* ivy-mantled tower."—Gray.

NOTE.—We have had occasion to speak elsewhere of the several functions performed by *that* as a conjunctive pronoun and as a conjunction. We may here declare unreservedly our agreement with the opinion of those who hold that THAT in all these diverse functions, is one and the same word; and that, in all the uses which it serves, it still retains its original force, namely, that of a determinative adjective. We believe that all its functions may be traced to its original determinative function.

The and *that* with *then*, *there*, *than* are all forms, as we believe of one original word. *Thence* and *thither* are derivatives from these, and we suspect that *thou* (Ang.-Sax. *thu*) and *thee* (Ang.-Sax. *the*) are of the same family. We exhibit the declension of the Anglo-Saxon article, and mark the words by italics, which have been retained in modern English.

	Singular.			Plural.	
	Masc.	Fem.	Neut.	All Genders.	
N.	Se,	Seo,	*Thaet.*	Tha,	*The.*
G.	Thaes,	Thaere,	Thaes.	Thara,	*Of the.*
D.	Tham,	*Thaere,*	Tham.	Tham,	*To the.*
A.	*Thone,*	Tha,	*Thaet.*	Tha,	*The.*

Se is most likely only a corruption of the sound of *the*, and *seo* of *theo*. From *thaet* we have our English *that;* from the dative *thaere* our adverb *there*, as explained elsewhere; and from the accusative *thone*, *thaene*, *thaenne* or *thanne* we have *then* and *than*, written in Anglo-Saxon *thonne* or *thaenne*.

ORDER OF ARRANGEMENT OF THE DETERMINATIVES.—We have already observed elsewhere that, when nouns are preceded both by *descriptive* and *determinative* adjectives, the determinatives take the precedence because they affect the noun as limited or restricted by the descriptive adjectives. Examples: *many wise men ; all degrading vices ; your black horse ; two important truths ; a beautiful landscape ; the setting sun ;* &c. Here *many*, *all*, *your*, *two*, *a*, and *the*, being determinatives, and embracing within their influence the nouns together with their more *intimate* modifications (or, in other words, the nouns as already modified by the descriptive adjectives), naturally take the precedence, or, perhaps, we should rather say, the more remote place from the noun, since they are the more remote complements.

When more than one determinative precedes the same noun, the determinatives *an* and *the* usually take the precedence of all other determinatives. We have already had occasion to observe that many determinative words exclude the *articles;* such are the possessive pronouns; the demonstratives *this*, *that*, *yon*, *yonder*, already noticed; of the class which the grammarians have called indefinite pronouns, *any*, *much*, *no*, *none*, *some;* and all the distributives *each*, *every*, *either*, *neither*. Those which admit the use of the articles before them are the whole class of numerals, together with *few*, *other*, *same*, *several*, *whole*, *former*, *latter*, *last*.

We have had occasion to notice that *all* and *both* take precedence of *the;* in the same manner *many* and *such* and the interrogative *what* precede *an* or *a*, as, "Full many *a gem* of purest ray serene," &c. *Such a man; what a monster!* In the same manner *an* or *a* is placed after descriptive adjectives modified by the adverbs *as*, *how*, *so*, *too*. Examples: *You have as* LARGE A *house; How* WISE AN *answer that man gave; So* FINE A *landscape is rarely found; Too* FOOLISH AN *action for a sane man to perform;* &c.

Some have attempted to account for such expressions as *all the world*, by alleging that there is a suppression of the preposition *of* in cases of this kind; that *all the world* is a contraction of the expression *all of the world*. We believe that all these forms of expression are to be explained by reference to the same principle which regulates the sequence of descriptive and determinative adjectives; namely that the more intimate modification is placed in closest contact with the noun and the more remote which modifies the noun as already modified by the more intimate complement stands at the greatest distance. For example, in the expressions *all the men*, *both the men*, it is *men* under all the restriction or limitation (a limitation of which the parties to the discourse are supposed to have mutual cognizance) indicated by *the* to which the force of the determinative *all* is applied. The same explanation we presume may be given of the expressions in which *an* or *a* is preceded by another determinative. An object after being *individualized* (if we may be allowed the expression) comes under the modification of the other determinative. For example, in *Full many a gem*, the gem is regarded first as an individual, and as thus regarded it is affected by the word *many* = Many individual gems.

§ 159. We take the opportunity of presenting in this place some observations on the CONJUNCTIVE PRONOUNS, which, though not suitable to be introduced as a part of the elementary instruction intended for younger students, are yet necessary to the full description, as well as to the full history of this important class of words; nor less necessary to place us in a proper position for obtaining correct views of some of the uses which they serve. These observations may be perused with advantage, after the student has become familiar with the common purposes which Conjunctive Pronouns serve in the current language of the day.

It may be useful to remember that *who* was not originally employed as a Conjunctive Pronoun. This word, and all the family to which it belongs commencing with the consonantal modification of sound represented by the letters *wh*, were originally only *interrogative*. They were used only as interrogatives in the Anglo-Saxon, and not as conjunctive or relative words. In Anglo-Saxon this function of Conjunctives is performed by the words *se*, with feminine form *seo* and neuter *thaet*, and *the*, which we have been considering above. These words also performed the function of determinatives, as *thaet* = *that*, and *the* do still in the modern language. This circumstance exhibits in a strong light the connection in Anglo-Saxon, as in other languages, of the determinatives and the conjunctive pronouns. In fact conjunctive pronouns seem to have originated from a peculiar usage of determinatives, contrary to the views of those grammarians who have taken so much pains to trace the article (in the Greek language, for example) to the relative pronoun. If they had spent the same labor in tracing the *relative* to the determinative, we think they would have been more successful. The conjunctive use or function appears to us to have originated in a peculiar employment of determinative words; namely, in the repetition of the determinative which modifies the antecedent before the accessory proposition to mark that it applies to the same word (the antecedent) to which the preceding determinative is attached. Or, perhaps rather, the determinative before the accessory is to be considered as implying the *repetition* of the antecedent noun to be modified by the accessory, which noun was most likely *repeated* with the determinative in the accessory proposition. The following form of expression will exhibit what we mean: *The* MAN, THE MAN *met us in our travels last year, is dead.* This, we think, was likely the form in which the first attempt at using an adjective accessory proposition was made. The transition from this to the abbreviation, *The man,* THE *met us,* &c., is perfectly natural. And this is precisely the form of the adjective accessory proposition in Anglo-Saxon.

We find, in confirmation of this view, examples, in the classical languages and in the most classical authors, of the oldest form of the adjective accessory proposition—that in which the antecedent is repeated with the relative. For example, we find in Cæsar, "Diem dicunt, *qua die* ad ripam Rhodani omnes conveniant," and "Erant omnino itinera duo, *quibus itineribus* domo exire possent."

Those who are acquainted with German know that the article *der die, das* is still often employed as a conjunctive pronoun to introduce an adjective accessory proposition. This usage presents a clear illustration of our views.

From what has been said of the use of the article in Anglo-Saxon as a representative word in forming accessory propositions, it will appear that the word THAT (in Anglo-Saxon written *thaet*), which is the neuter form of the Anglo-Saxon article = to our THE, has claim to be considered the oldest conjunctive pronoun in our language. Originally, indeed, it represented only neuter nouns, but for this purpose was employed in accessory propositions long antecedent to the use of *who* or *which* for the same purpose. We present an example of this use which will further illustrate the remarks which we made above. *Ic geendode* THAET WEORC THAET *thu me sealdest to donne.* I have finished *the work which* thou gavest me to do. John 17: 4. This is exactly equivalent to "*the work the.*"

Mr. Addison showed such strong preference for *that* as a conjunctive pronoun, that (by the influence of his example) he seemed at one time likely to render the use of *who* and *which* as relatives altogether unfashionable. Had he known the history of these words he might have justified his preference for *that*, by saying that he was only endeavoring to restore this unfortunate word to the possession of its ancient rights in the language. This word is however still perhaps more than enough employed in the language, and this is a good argument with others against imitating Mr. Addison in the unnecessary frequency of introducing it as a relative. In one respect, we have extended its use in the modern language by employing it, though originally a neuter form, as the Anglo-Saxons employed THE, to represent nouns of all genders. But, on the other hand, we give it only a divided empire with *who* and *which* the interrogative words, that have usurped a large part of the domain which once belonged exclusively to the determinatives *se, seo, thaet,* and *the.*

We are not in a position to explore fully the history of this usurpation. It seems to have been begun in the second period of our language—the *old English* period. We know not what light might possibly be cast on this history by a careful examination of the remains of the earlier old English, and the later Anglo-Saxon. Possibly the innovation took place at a period of which the written remains are most scanty, and perhaps its commencement cannot be satisfactorily traced. We beg leave to commend the inquiry to those who are conversant with these scanty remains of early documents of various kinds—we could scarcely with propriety say, remains of our early *literature.* We may remark that the word THAT appears to have been much more used as a relative in the times even of Wiclif and Chaucer, than at the present day. We suspect, on a cursory examination, that *who* and *whom* are seldom used as relatives by these authors. Chaucer often uses *which* and *that* together in reference both to *persons* and *non-personals.* Examples: "Unto the cure of hem (them) *which that* they han (have) in hir (their) governaunce," speaking of physicians. "Than shuln (then shall) ye examine the second condition, *which that* the same Tullius addeth in this matere. For Tullius putteth a thing, *which that* he clepeth (calleth) consenting."—(Tale of Melibeus.) In the first of these examples *which that,* refers to persons—the patients of the physicians; in the two last to *non-personals.* In all these examples—and there are three more similar examples besides these within a few pages—*which* is evidently used adjectively with *that,* which serves as the true *representative* word. It may be that here we have a step in the introduction of *which* to its present relative function. We have, at all events, a satisfactory proof of the priority of *that,* which we have asserted above.

We may remark, that a similar usurpation of the relative function by the interrogatives seems to have occurred in the Latin language. We presume that *qui* or *quis* (different forms of the same word) was originally exclusively interrogative in Latin, or the language from which Latin sprung. The sound represented by *k* and sounds akin to it, as *qu* and *h* hard, seem to have characterized the interrogative words in the *Indo-Germanic* (or *Arian,* as some modern philologists choose to call it) family of languages generally. (See Latham Eng. Lang. p. 250, 2d edit., and Grimm, vol. iii., pp. 1–3.) We have a numerous family of these *interrogative* words commencing in modern written English with the letters *wh* (in Anglo-Saxon with *hw,* which lettters still represent more exactly the present pronunciation), and in Scottish with *quh,* which exhibits the connection with the Latin *qu.* We may enumerate among these *who* and its neuter *what, when, where* (both originally only cases of *who*), *whence, whether, which* (supposed to be a compound of *who* and *lic, Scotice quhilk,* see Grimm as above), *whither, why,* and their numerous derivatives. To these we may add *how,* which retains the characteristic hard sound of *h,* but has lost the *w,* perhaps, through a regard to euphony. (*See* § 98.) All the primitive words of this class were originally (and originally perhaps exclusively) employed interrogatively. Some of their derivatives, having been formed after the primitives had been usurped in a *determinative* sense (for the conjunctive pronouns may all be regarded as essentially determinatives—determinatives used substantively, and with an implication of connection or conjunction), were possibly never employed as interrogatives. We mean such derivatives, for example, as *whosoever, whensoever,* &c.

We may here also notice a similar uniformity in the leading and principal consonantal articulation of the original determinatives. This characteristic articulation in the Indo-Germanic languages seems to have been that represented by the letters *t, th,* or *d*—all kindred sounds. In our language the characteristic sound of this class is that of *th.* With the articulation which these letters represent, the determinatives *the, that,* and *there, then, than* (all three cases of the article), *thence, thither,* commence—all apparently from the same root; and perhaps *thou, thee, thine,* as well as *they, their, them,* involve the same radicle.

We have in English still another class of words kindred in sound, like the above-mentioned classes, and kindred in meaning, commencing with the hard aspiration represented by the letter *h,* as *he, him, her, here, hither,* &c. It is likely that these classes of words had each their origin in a single sound, a single utterance from which each respective kindred family sprung. Shall we say that *who, the,* and *he* are the patriarchal ancestors of these kindred families? It will be noticed that the two last-mentioned families of words afford answers to the interrogatives; thus,

Who?	Ans.	The, or that man,	or He.
What?	"	That,	or This.
Where?	"	There,	Here.
Whither?	"	Thither,	Hither.

This seems to have migrated from its own family, as the interrogatives have done; or some change may have happened to its form, as has happened to *they, their, them.* (See § 155.) The words commencing with the *h* sound seem to have indicated proximity to the speaker, the words in *th* distance from the speaker, or rather perhaps proximity to the hearer. This distinction is best and most manifestly retained between the words *here* and *there, hither* and *thither.*

We have already remarked (§ 98), that *who* interrogative is a *substantive pronoun*—always performing the function of a *noun.* The same may be said of it when employed *conjunctively.* We never connect this word with a noun, and say, for example, *who man,* or *who woman. Which,* on the contrary, *conjunctively,* as well as *interrogatively* employed, is properly an adjective. It is still employed as an adjective, even, when necessary, with words signifying *persons,* since *who* disclaims this servile function and abandons it to its derivative *which.* We give examples: "By the *which* will we are sanctified." WHICH *person, it happens, that I have never seen.* A determinative (article) is sometimes employed before which, namely, the article that belongs to the noun suppressed after *which.* This *article* indicates clearly the suppression of the noun. Examples: "In *the which* I will appear unto thee." In *the which* ye also walked." "That worthy name by *the which* ye are called." *Which,* we think, is always to be considered an adjective; and when employed as it usually is, to represent a noun, as an adjective employed *substantively.* (When the noun is expressed with it, *which* should be treated in analysis as a determinative.) The same is to be said of the determinative *that,* when employed as a conjunctive pronoun. It is really an *adjective;* but in its determinative function it is *often,* in its conjunctive function, we believe, *always,* employed *substantively.* The only real *substantive* conjunctive pronouns in our language, are *who* and its compounds *whoever, whosoever,* &c. The facts now stated are important to the right understanding of the uses of *who* and *which.*

The above observations, it will be seen, apply to *who* and *which* interrogative, as well as conjunctive.

APPENDIX ON PUNCTUATION.

§ 160. (1) In spoken language pauses are necessarily introduced that the speaker may have opportunity to draw his breath. (2) But at the same time that pauses *directly* serve this indispensable purpose, a part, at least, of these necessary rests of the voice are so managed by good speakers as to mark *incidentally* the grammatical and logical divisions of discourse; and besides this pauses are often introduced for rhetorical purposes. (3) The pauses which mark grammatical divisions of discourse may be arranged in two classes; namely, those which consist of a mere rest or suspension of the voice, and those which consist of a rest preceded by a full *cadence*, or closing fall of the voice. (4) In continued narration, regular cadences and full pauses are used to close the enunciation of portions of discourse which, forming each complete sense, stand grammatically independent of what precedes and what follows. (5) Such portions of discourse are commonly called sentences.* (6) Rests or pauses without a full cadence of the voice are used in speaking to mark the grammatical and logical divisions which occur within the limits of a single sentence, exclusive of the final pause.†

(7) In *written* language a number of *diacritical* marks called *points* (often improperly named *pauses*, we object even to calling them signs of pauses) are employed for the same purpose of marking the gramma-

*See note (*a*) at the end of this appendix.
†See note (*b*) at the end of this appendix.

---

§ 160. (1) What is the *direct* purpose of pauses in spoken language? (2) For what other purposes are pauses employed incidentally in speech? (3) In what classes are pauses which mark the divisions of sense arranged? (4) For what purpose is the pause preceded by a full cadence employed? (5) What name is given to a portion of discourse closed by a full cadence? (6) For what purpose are pauses without a full cadence employed in speech? (7) What contrivance has been adopted in written language for the purpose of marking

tical and logical divisions of discourse not to *represent* pauses. (8) This contrivance of written language is called PUNCTUATION, by others, perhaps more properly in some of its applications, INTERPUNCTION. (9) It is manifest that this contrivance has a close connection with grammar; and that a knowledge of its principles, founded as they are upon grammar, is important to every one who has occasion to commit his own thoughts to writing, or to peruse understandingly the writings of others, since a judicious use of punctuation contributes greatly to the perspicuity of written discourse.*

THE FULL POINT OR PERIOD.—(10) The point employed to indicate the end of a sentence—the completion of a construction independent in sense and in grammatical structure—is called a *full point* (.), or *period.* (11) It is necessary to observe here that the same point, or mark is used to indicate contractions as, Mr. = *master* (pronounced *mister*); M. P. = *member of parliament;* i. e. = *id est* (in English *that is*); &c. = *et cætera.* (12) When a point indicating *contraction* occurs at the end of a sentence, another point is not added, but the same point serves both to indicate contraction and for the purpose of punctuation. This happens most frequently with the phrase &c., as no contraction is so likely as this to occur often at the close of a sentence. For example: *His brother sent him his clothes, books, papers,* &c. Here the point after &c. supersedes the use of the full point required to close the sentence. (13) In correct orthography every new sentence commences with a capital, or large letter, which serves (except when the first word for other cause has a large letter) to mark the division of sentences, and enables us the more readily to dispense with the repetition of the point to mark the punctuation. (14) The learner may be warned that the occurrence of a point as a mark of contraction does not supersede the use of any other, except the full point. The *comma*, semicolon and other points follow &c. and other contractions, when the sense and construction require their use. (15) In interro-

*See note (*c*) at the end of this appendix.

the divisions of sense which are marked by pauses in spoken language? (8) What is this contrivance called? (9) Repeat the remarks made in reference to the importance of punctuation.

(10) What is the point employed to indicate the termination of a sentence called? Describe the form of this point inclosed above in parenthetic marks. (11) For what other purpose is this same point or mark employed? (12) What is done, when a point used to indicate contraction occurs at the end of a sentence? Illustrate by an example. (13) What circumstance enables us the more easily to dispense with the second point on such occasions? (14) Does the occurrence of a point indicating contraction supersede the use of any point except the period? (15) By what other marks is the use of the period or full point superseded?

gative and passionate forms of expression the use of the full point at the end of a sentence is superseded by the marks of interrogation and of exclamation.

(16) Three distinct signs are employed to indicate the more or less marked divisions which may occur within a sentence. These signs or marks are called *the comma* (,), *the semicolon* (;) and *the colon* (:). (17) The *comma*, which marks the lesser intersections, or *cuttings* (the term *comma* means a *cutting*) of discourse, or rather of a sentence, is the point of this class which comes into most general use; especially with our modern authors, who generally strive to avoid the long and complicated constructions freely employed by the writers of the seventeenth century.

USE OF THE COMMA. — (18) We may distinguish three purposes for which the comma is employed: 1st.—To separate the propositions which follow one another, or are intermixed in compound constructions; or to separate the several co-ordinate propositions, or members or modifications of propositions which an author chooses to connect in the same sentence: 2d.—To inclose something (which is, at least, grammatically independent) within a construction: and 3d.—To indicate an ellipsis or suppression of a word.

(19) Of the first two uses (the principal uses, and closely allied to each other) we have furnished abundant exemplification in the consideration of compound and of combined or connected propositions. We have in treating of these classes of propositions exhausted all that we have to say, whilst we are confined to the mode of punctuation now in use. We consider it the most judicious way of teaching the use of the comma especially, to point out where it is usually introduced in compound and complicated constructions, when we are engaged in the analysis of such constructions, and when the pupil is called upon to furnish examples of these constructions. By requiring him to point all his examples, he comes without labor to learn the principles of punctuation (so far as our present system has any principles), and to apply them practically. We confine ourselves at present to a partial recapitulation of what we have already taught in illustration of the first two uses of the comma.

---

(16) How many distinct signs are employed to mark the divisions within a sentence? Name these signs, and describe their form. (17) Which of these three points is in most general use with modern writers? What is the original meaning of the word *comma*?

(18) For how many distinct purposes is the comma employed in written language? Mention the 1st purpose; the 2d purpose; the 3d purpose.

(19) Where has abundant exemplification of the first two uses of the comma been furnished already? Repeat the substance of the remarks in reference to the best manner of teaching the application of the comma,

1st. (20) As to the first purpose; the comma is often employed in separating accessory from their principal propositions. (21) The employment of the comma (as we have already had more than one occasion to observe) is not in all cases of this kind determined by fixed usage; and neither the customary interposition, nor the customary omission of this sign can be always explained by an appeal to clear and well settled principles. (See note (*c*) at the end of this appendix.)

(22) Generally speaking, the comma is not interposed between *substantive* or *adjective accessories* and the *principal* propositions to which they are attached. (The substantive accessory used as subject is generally separated by a comma, § 103.) (23) On the contrary, most of the *adverbial accessories* are either uniformly separated from their principal propositions, or the usage in reference to them is not uniform. (24) The accessories used in comparison of the intensities of qualities with the conjunctions *as* and *than* are not generally separated from the principal proposition by a comma, nor the adverbial accessories of time preceded by the prepositions *before*, *after*, *since*, when these accessories follow the principal proposition. (25) When the construction is inverted, and such accessories precede the principal proposition, they are generally separated by interpunction.

(26) When independent, or co-ordinate propositions are connected, a comma is always interposed; and when co-ordinate members of propositions, or co-ordinate complements are arranged together, a comma should be interposed, except when a conjunction is placed between such co-ordinate members and such complements. (27) A conjunction interposed sufficiently indicates the separation of words thus employed and the nature of the construction. For further details we refer back to the remarks on punctuation which follow the discussion of the different forms of compound propositions, and of the different modes of connecting co-ordinate propositions together in the same construction.

---

(20) What kind of propositions is the comma often used to separate? (21) Repeat the observation in reference to the separation of accessory from principal propositions by a comma.

(22) What classes of accessories are generally not separated by a comma? (23) What class is most generally separated? (24) Enumerate some adverbial accessories which are not generally separated by interpunction. (25) What happens when the construction is inverted, and the accessory precedes the principal?

(26) What is said of the punctuation of co-ordinate propositions? What of co-ordinate members of propositions, and of co-ordinate modifications? (27) Mention the cases in which the comma is omitted between co-ordinate words and the reason

2d. (28) We have already observed on several occasions the use of the comma for the second purpose, that of inclosing a word, phrase or proposition within a construction. We have examples in the case of such adverbs and adverbial phrases as *perhaps*, *possibly*, *generally*, *indeed*, *therefore*, *then*, *without doubt*, *on the contrary*, *in the first place*, *beyond dispute*, &c. &c., which are generally separated from the rest of the discourse by commas. We have examples also in the case of *noun and-preposition* modifications expressing circumstances, when these are placed before and at a distance from the part of the predicate which they modify; and especially when they modify the proposition *generally* rather than the predicate *particularly*. (29) This use of the comma, to separate, or *insulate* single words or complements, should perhaps be confined to cases in which these words or complements suggest other additional propositions distinct from those in which they are interpolated, or before which they are placed.

(30) We may notice again that the words by which we address persons to call their attention, &c., whether their own names or pronouns or appellations of respect and honor as *Mr.*, *Sir*, *My Lord* (in a word, what are known by the name *vocatives*), are usually separated by a comma from the adjoining proposition. (31) The noun in apposition, especially when followed by a train of modifying words, is generally separated by commas (and perhaps should in consistency be always separated, *when it follows the principal noun*) from the proposition in which it occurs. (32) The explicative, or epithetic proposition (which, as we have had occasion elsewhere to observe, bears a strong analogy to the noun in apposition) should always be inclosed, or *cut* off from the rest of the construction by commas.

3d. The third use of the comma to indicate ellipsis is altogether peculiar, arbitrary, as it seems to us, in its application, and little, if at all, connected with the other uses of this mark. (33) In this use, it indicates the suppression of a verb which belongs in common to two or more successive propositions, but which is expressed only in the first. (34) Examples: "Homer was the greater genius; Virgil, the better artist." The comma after "Virgil" indicates the suppression

---

(28) What examples are referred to of the second use of the comma? (29) To what cases should this use of the comma in *insulating* single words and complements, perhaps, be confined?

(30) Mention another class of words usually separated by interpunction. (31) What is said of the noun in apposition? (32) To what kind of accessory proposition is reference made as the last example of this use of the comma?

(33) Describe the third use of the comma. (34) Illustrate this use by examples.

of the verb "was." "In one we most admire the man; in the other, the work." Here the comma after "other" indicates the suppression of the verb "admire." Sentences constructed in this artifical manner are rare, and the comma is not invariably employed in such cases.

REMARK.—This use of the comma seems to have originated from the attempt to indicate all the pauses of speech by points in written language. It is certainly natural to indicate the suppression in propositions, like those now quoted as examples, by a suspension of the voice in speaking. But we doubt much whether the use of a diacritical point as above, separating the parts of a proposition most closely connected grammatically and logically, can contribute much to perspicuity. We can conceive cases in which it would confuse the reader. It is vain to hope that we shall be able to represent by diacritical marks to the eye, all the delicate distinctions which the human voice can convey to the ear by pauses, suspensions, tones, &c. Confusion, it seems to us (instead of greater clearness), has resulted from endeavoring to represent all pauses by points, instead of contenting ourselves with the use of these marks to distinguish the important divisions of discourse.

USE OF THE SEMICOLON.—(35) When a sentence arranges itself into two or more larger and less closely connected divisions, containing (one or more of them) subdivisions which demand the use of the comma, a semicolon is employed to mark the separation of the larger divisions. Example: "We then relax our vigor, and resolve no longer to be terrified with crimes at a distance; but rely upon our own constancy, and venture to approach what we resolve never to touch." (36) Such greater divisions as are separated by semicolons are generally co-ordinate and independent in sense, though the subsequent divisions often borrow words or whole members, sometimes both subject and verb from a preceding division of the sentence. Thus, in the example, the verbs *rely* and *venture*, which follow the semicolon, borrow their subject *we* from the propositions which precede the semicolon. An example will be adduced presently in which a series of propositions, separated by semicolons, borrow both subject and verb from the first in the series. All is suppressed in the subsequent propositions of the series except the modifications of the predicate. (37) Members between which the semicolon is used, being *co-ordinate*, are very generally, *though not invariably*, connected by *co-ordinate* conjunctions.*

* Some writers make the whole distinction between the use of the semi-

(35) Describe the chief purpose for which the semicolon is employed. Illustrate by an example. (36) State what is said of the relation between members separated by semicolons. (37) How are such members generally connected?

(38) Sometimes propositions enunciating independent facts, which might, if the writer chose, be separated by periods as distinct sentences, are comprehended within the same construction, and separated only

---

colon and the colon to consist in this, that the semicolon is properly placed only between members connected by a conjunction, and the colon between members which are not so connected. In this case it would be very important to determine what conjunctions are intended; whether all conjunctions and conjunctive words in general, or only the co-ordinate conjunctions. The rule seems to us to lead to strange inconsistency in the use of points. Those who advocate it admit that the colon is employed to mark a greater division in sense and construction than the semicolon. The very names given to these two points imply this fact. Yet the rule, as laid down in some treatises, would lead us in many cases to employ the colon where, not even the semicolon, but the comma only can with propriety be introduced. Members (whether consisting of single propositions or of groups of propositions separated by commas) unconnected by a conjunction, sometimes stand in closer relation, both in sense and grammatical construction, than members connected by conjunctions. The rule would often require the introduction of a colon between a noun and the noun which stands in apposition with it. An advocate of this rule gives the following sentence as affording examples of the improper use of the colon: "He first lost by his misconduct the flourishing provinces of France, the ancient patrimony of the family: he subjected his kingdom to a shameful vassalage under the see of Rome: he saw the prerogatives of his crown diminished by law, and still more reduced by faction: and he died at last," &c. We agree with our friend that the colons are here unnecessarily used: for in this case semicolons are sufficient. But our reason for rejecting the colons is not simply because the members are connected by *and* expressed between the last two members and implied between the other members. We cannot, however, agree with him, when he remarks, speaking of the passage quoted above, "At *France*, we have perfect sense: consequently the comma should be displaced by the colon: *which were*, the connective and the verb, being suppressed." Why; it may be alleged that *who* or *which* and some tense of the verb *to be* is suppressed in any and every case of apposition; therefore, if such apposition occurs where the preceding words happen to form complete sense, a colon must be introduced between the noun and the apposition, notwithstanding their close connection as *principal* and *complement*. Such punctuation, it seems to us, frustrates the great design of punctuation, which is to contribute to perspicuity. The confounding of *points* with *pauses*, is the original source of trouble in this matter. A longer pause is used (perhaps) between members, when a conjunction is suppressed. Therefore a higher point should mark

---

(38) Describe another purpose for which the semicolon is employed, furnish examples, and repeat the substance of the remarks.

by semicolons, though no one of these propositions admits of subdivision by a comma. Example: "True gentleness teaches us to bear one another's burdens; to rejoice with those who rejoice; to weep with those who weep; to please every one his neighbor for his good; to be kind and tender-hearted; to be pitiful and courteous; to support the weak; and to be patient towards all men." These propositions by the way in which they are here gathered together are rendered constructionally, though not logically dependent. We adverted to this sentence above as an example of a construction in which succeeding propositions borrow both subject and verb from the first in the series. The following example presents a series of independent propositions similarly comprehended in the same sentence, but in this case all the parts of each proposition are fully expressed. "The pride of wealth is contemptible; the pride of learning is pitiable; the pride of dignity is ridiculous; but the pride of bigotry is insupportable." Some writers would employ only a comma in the punctuation of such sentences as we have exhibited in these two examples; and certainly a comma would in constructions of this kind answer all the usual purposes attained by punctuation. A semicolon indicates more clearly the writer's sense of the marked distinctness of the assertions comprehended together, and gives greater emphasis to this fact. There are again writers who would place a period after each of these propositions, and exhibit them as forming separate sentences.

USE OF THE COLON.—(39) In the punctuation of the last and of preceding centuries, the colon seems to have borne the same relation to the semicolon which the semicolon bears to the comma. When a sentence was so constructed that it contained two larger members, themselves, or at least one of them, subdivided by semicolons, and these subdivisions of course again subdivided by commas, the colon became necessary to distinguish the larger subdivisions.* (40) In

it. That is, the point is to represent the pause, and not merely to discriminate the sense. This reasoning would necessarily lead to the use of the colon in instances, when the conjunction is (as usually happens) suppressed between all the members of a series except the last two. Consequently no colon, except the last, in the above quoted passage should be exchanged for a semicolon, contrary to the author's views in which we have acquiesced.

* We do not mean to imply, by what is here said, that the colon itself was of later invention than the semicolon. The point on a level with the lower part of the letter, and the point on a level with the upper part thus˙,

(39) What is said of the use of the colon in earlier writers? (40) Tell why it is that the

modern composition we generally contrive to avoid the construction of sentences so long and so complicated as to involve *subdivisions of subdivisions*. Hence the colon is now much less frequently used in writing than in former times. (41) It is still occasionally introduced principally for the following purposes: To separate a member added to a complete construction in order to express some remark or short explanatory observation; before a formal enumeration of particulars; and before examples, quotations and speeches, when formally introduced. The sentence just finished affords an example of the second use. We subjoin additional examples.

Colon before an additional remark.—"There is no greater monster in being than a very bad man of great talents: he lives like a man in a palsy, with one side of him dead." "We labor to eat, and we eat to live, and we live to do good, and the good which we do is as seed sown with reference to a future harvest: but we must come at length to some pause." *Hooker's Eccles. Pol.* I. 11. *Oxford*, 1843. "A family connected with a common parent, resembles a tree, the trunk and branches of which are connected with a common root: but let us suppose that a family is figured, not barely to be like a tree, but to be a tree; and then the simile will be converted into a metaphor, in the following manner:

"Edward's seven sons, whereof thyself art one," &c.—*Kames El.* xx. 4. This last passage might he given as an example of the old use of the colon, as the member which follows it is divided by a semicolon. In this passage we have also an instance of a colon preceding the introduction of an example. The colon is more liberally employed in the "Elements of Criticism" than in most books of equally modern date. We refer, in making this remark, to a London edition, 1805. It may be noticed that both in the example from Hooker and Kames the colon precedes a member commencing with a conjunction.

Colon before an enumeration of particulars.—"Man doth seek a triple perfection: first, a sensual, consisting &c.; then an intellectual, consisting &c.; lastly, a spiritual and divine, consisting" &c.

Colon before quotation.—"When a Persian soldier was reviling Alexander the Great, his officer reprimanded him by saying: 'Sir, you were paid to fight Alexander, and not to rail at him.'"

---

and the two points now called the colon were in use, we believe, long before either comma or semicolon. The present use of the points is of modern invention, though diacritical marks of some kind seem to have been employed, at least by more careful writers, in very remote times.

---

colon is seldom introduced in modern composition. (41) State the several purposes for which it is occasionally employed, and illustrate by examples.

NOTE OR MARK OF INTERROGATION.—(42) We have already had occasion to notice the use of the interrogation mark (?) in treating of interrogative propositions. This mark is employed after each separate proposition, when employed for the direct purpose of asking a question. Sometimes an interrogative proposition is included in a construction which is assertive or imperative; thus, *I asked the man where he was going; Ask that man where he is going.* In such cases the mark of interrogation is not employed, because the interrogative proposition is not here used for the purpose of *inquiry*. The same remark applies to propositions of the interrogative form employed figuratively to express a thought in a more striking or moving manner, when no answer is expected. Such propositions are usually classed with exclamations, and followed by the same mark, which we are about to describe. Examples:

"How jocund did they drive their team afield!"

"O, how canst thou renounce the boundless store
Of charms which Nature to her votary yields!"

It must be admitted, however, that there is little consistency observed in the punctuation of these passionate interrogations. Sometimes the interrogation mark is used, and sometimes the exclamation mark.

NOTE OR MARK OF EXCLAMATION.—(43) The mark of exclamation is used after impassioned exclamations, and generally after all interjections, except O. Both the note of interrogation and the note of admiration, though rhetorical rather than diacritical marks, supersede the use of the period, comma, &c., whenever they are introduced after sentences or members of sentences.

USE OF THE DASH.—(44) The dash (—) is perhaps most properly employed in impassioned discourse to indicate a sudden transition of thought. It is used sometimes to indicate merely a rhetorical pause often between words closely united in construction, to call special attention to the part of the discourse which follows the pause. Examples:

"When I do see the very book indeed
Where all my sins are writ, and that's—myself."

The *dash* has come within the last twenty or thirty years to be much used to indicate a certain class of parenthetic remarks, viz.: those which present a thought in a new dress, or in a new point of view to exhibit it with greater clearness. Such expressions may be regarded as substitutes offered for that

---

(42) Repeat what is said of the mark of interrogation.
(43) What is said of the use of the *mark of exclamation*?
(44) What of the use of the *dash*?

which precedes the dash. Sometimes a comma is used before the *dash* thus employed, sometimes not. Usage in this respect is unsettled. In such cases the construction of the member which follows the dash must be carefully adjusted to the construction of that which precedes. When the dash alone is used, if the parenthetic or substituted or amended expression does not close the construction (or, at least, affect, equally with what precedes the whole construction following), another dash must be used after it. We give examples: "Neither should writing be disfigured by the contrary practice,—by omitting capitals, when, in all propriety, they ought to be introduced." In pointing this we should prefer to omit the comma before the dash, and substitute a dash for the comma after "capitals." "I may be censured—perhaps I may be laughed at, for having said so much against the colon and semicolon." The writer in the last example, as it were, amends his expression, or introduces a substitute. A dash is not repeated after the substituted expression, because the following part of the sentence affects or modifies the substituted and the original expression alike. "In 1746, he published 'The Castle of Indolence'—the most highly finished of all his compositions," &c. "The view from this remarkable group of mountains—the most remarkable by far in the island—differs much from any other with which I am acquainted." In this example the words between the dashes are explanatory.

Upon the whole, we must agree with those who have asserted that the dash has been too unsparingly and too recklessly employed by many English authors. Yet we do not condemn the use of this mark judiciously employed for the purpose last mentioned. This use may be regarded as a legitimate extension of its original use to denote a *break* in the *sense*. This is a break in the *construction*—a sudden turn in the form of the expression. It often happens that what is thus separated by a dash might be separated by parenthetic marks. Parenthetic marks are used when a new, often an extraneous thought is thrown between the parts of a construction, and they can be used in multitudes of cases when neither commas nor dashes can with propriety be employed. We would use the parenthetic marks to indicate an interpolated thought (without confining them exclusively to this function, for they may with propriety be used to separate an explanatory expression), and the dash or dashes to indicate the introduction of another mode of expressing a preceding thought, a repetition of the same thought in a different form, or an equivalent substituted for it. The usage described, we think, agrees with the practice of the best writers of the present day.

(45) The dash is sometimes used to indicate the place of an omitted word, or, more generally, some letters of a word; thus, The M——rs, for The Ministers. Omitted words and letters are also represented by

---

(45) Describe another purpose for which the *dash* is sometimes employed, and tell what other marks are used occasionally for the same purpose.

asterisks; thus, * * * * Omitted letters are often represented by hyphens, or by dots or points; a hyphen or point being usually substituted for each letter omitted; thus, P........t, for Parliament.

PARENTHETIC MARKS.—(46) The use of parenthetic marks, or *crotchets*, has been incidentally explained in treating of the dash. They are employed to introduce a sentence, a phrase, or sometimes a single word within a sentence. Sometimes a thought having a very remote (if any) connection with the general tenor of the discourse is introduced in this way. Neither commas nor dashes can with propriety be employed in such cases. In reading, such parentheses are usually marked by a suppression of the voice. *Brackets* [ ] are sometimes employed for similar purposes, most frequently, we think, to inclose interpolated words. When a parenthesis occurs within a parenthesis (an occurrence which should be avoided), *brackets* are employed to indicate the greater parenthesis, and crotchets to indicate the parenthesis included within the greater.

We may here describe some other marks used for certain purposes in written discourse.

(47) THE APOSTROPHE (') is used to mark the omission of a letter; thus, *e'er* for *ever*, *'tis* for *it is*, &c. We have already noticed the manner in which the apostrophe is used to indicate the English genitive case. In this case, too, it marks the omission of the *e* or *i* which anciently belonged to the genitive termination.

(48) THE HYPHEN (-) is used to indicate compounded words; as, *printing-press*, &c. The hyphen is used when part of a word is carried to the next line. In doing this, care must be taken never to divide a syllable.

(49) QUOTATION MARKS (" ") are used at the beginning and end of a passage to indicate that it is quoted or borrowed from some other writer. Sometimes these marks are repeated at the commencement of every line of a quotation. These marks are called by the French "Guillemets," we believe, from the name of the inventor of this contrivance. We have no appropriate name for them in English.

(50) THE DIÆRESIS consists of two points placed over the last of two vowels, to indicate that they are to be pronounced in separate syllables—not as a diphthong. They are unnecessary except over vowels which generally coalesce into a diphthong, and not even then in words which are in familiar use. We have examples in the proper names Laocoön, Boötes, &c.

---

(46) Describe the use of *parenthetic marks*, or *crotchets* and *brackets*.
(47) Describe the use of the *apostrophe*.
(48) Describe the two uses of the *hyphen*.
(49) Describe the use of *quotation marks*.
(50) Describe the use of *diæresis*.

(51) THE BRACE is employed to connect two or more lines, for the purpose of indicating that the words on the opposite side of the brace have a common relation to what these lines severally contain. Example:

"Future, { I shall / I will } write."

Here we have two braces; the second indicates that the word *write* belongs in common to *I shall* and *I will*—that, in fact, it is to be repeated with both; and the first brace indicates that all which follows and is *embraced* by it, has a common relation to the word *future*. More examples of the use of this mark may be found in the Synoptical Table of English Verbs, pp. 152, 153. This mark is now seldom employed, except in the construction of tables. Formerly it was often used in poetry to connect *triplets* (*see Appendix on Versification*): but both *triplets* and *braces* are out of fashion at present.

(52) THE ACCENT (′) is used (chiefly in dictionaries) to mark that syllable of a word on which the chief stress of the voice is laid in pronunciation.

(53) THE SECTION (§) is used to mark the divisions of discourse. Formerly THE PARAGRAPH (¶) was used to indicate the transition to a new subject; but it is now seldom employed for this purpose, except in some editions of the Sacred Scriptures.

(54) THE CARET having the form of an inverted v is placed, in manuscript, under the line to indicate the accidental omission of words. The words omitted are placed above the line, and the caret shows the place at which they are to be inserted. This mark is not used in printed books.

(55) The following marks are employed in referring to notes placed at the bottom of the page, and generally in the order of precedence in which we here arrange them: viz., for the first note THE ASTERISK (*) is employed to indicate the place to which the note belongs, and to designate the note; for the second, when more than one note occurs on the same page, THE OBELISK (†): for the third, THE DOUBLE OBELISK (‡); and so in succession THE SECTION (§); THE PARALLELS (‖); THE PARAGRAPH (¶); THE INDEX (☞). Sometimes, when these marks are all exhausted, we commence again from the beginning, doubling each mark; thus (**), (††), &c. Letters and figures are often used for the same purpose.

(56) CAPITAL LETTERS.—These are employed at the beginning of words.

1st. To mark the commencement of every sentence; of every line of poetry, and of every quotation and every example formally introduced.

---

(51) Describe the use of the *brace*.
(52) Describe the use of the *accent*.
(53) Describe the use of the *section*.
(54) Describe the use of the *caret*.
(55) Enumerate in order the several marks used for reference.
(56) Mention the several purposes for which capital letters are employed in the beginning of words.

2d. To distinguish every proper name, including the appropriate designations of persons, countries or regions, states, mountains, rivers, cities, ships, and all adjectives formed from such proper names; the names of months, and days of the week; titles of honor, or office, which have become a part of the appellation of the individual to whom they are applied; and names of personified objects; as, for example:

"Hail, sacred Polity, by Freedom reared!
Hail, sacred Freedom, when by Law restrained!"

3d. The pronoun I, and the interjection O are always written with a capital letter.

4th. Writers often commence with a capital the word which expresses the subject of present discussion, or any word to which they wish to draw particular attention.

(57) ITALICS are often employed in printing words or passages to which the author wishes to call the special attention of the reader, or which he wishes to distinguish for any purpose. SMALL CAPITALS are introduced, generally as a more emphatic indication of the same purpose; and CAPITALS for a still more emphatic. *Italics* are represented in manuscript by a single line under the word or passage, small capitals by two lines, and capitals by three.

NOTE (*a*).—The word *sentence* is most loosely employed by grammarians. Sometimes it is used to express what we have thought it expedient to call in the course of the preceding treatise a PROPOSITION, avoiding the term *sentence* on account of the vague manner in which it is applied by most writers. Most generally the word sentence is used to signify so much of discourse as forming *complete sense* is closed by a full cadence in speaking, and by a period or full point in writing. Of such a sentence no good definition has been given, nor, we believe, can be given. It is essential to such an assemblage of words that they should be fit to stand logically as well as grammatically independent, or form a *sense*. *Sentence* (*sententia*) from its etymology implies this. But whilst this condition is satisfied, authors and speakers are left at full liberty, especially in constructions consisting of an agglomeration of independent propositions, to include less or more matter in a sentence according to their own judgment or their caprice. Some divide that matter into several separate sentences separated by full points, which others separate only by semicolons—sometimes only by commas.

There are strong objections to excessively long sentences, and to an unvaried succession of very long or very short sentences. But whilst a lucid grammatical structure is secured, the whole subject of long and short sentences comes under the supervision, not of the grammarian, but of the rheto-

---

(57) Describe the purposes for which *italics*, *small capitals*, and *capitals*, are occasionally introduced in printing.

rician. It is not generally the mere length of a sentence, but the complication and clumsy arrangement of its modifying members which produces obscurity, and renders it faulty as a grammatical structure. Very long sentences are sometimes so carefully constructed as to be perfectly clear, and entirely unobjectionable in a grammatical point of view; and, on the contrary, short sentences do not always escape the charge of obscurity from faulty grammatical construction.

NOTE (*b*).—It is important here to observe that pauses in discourse are employed for other purposes, besides that of indicating the grammatical divisions of discourse, whilst *diacritical points* are employed nearly exclusively for this last purpose. Pauses are often employed for rhetorical purposes, and for purposes connected with versification, where no pause is required to indicate any grammatical division. A suspension of the voice for the purpose of drawing breath may take place where there is no grammatical division in the construction, for example, between the subject and the predicate; and *rhetorical* pauses are often made for effect (to draw attention) between words which are in the closest grammatical union. This fact has been apparently overlooked by our writers on punctuation. You would suppose from their language that the points are used to represent the pauses in spoken discourse, instead of helping to exhibit the grammatical structure of discourse more clearly. So far as pauses in speech are used for the same purpose, points and pauses will naturally correspond with each other, being intended to mark the same distinctions, though the former are not to be regarded as the representatives of the latter. But when it is attempted, forgetting the direct purpose of punctuation, to make it agree with the pauses throughout, we immediately involve ourselves, as was to be expected, in difficulties, and subject our rules and practice to a charge of inconsistency, by attempting to accommodate our system to two sets of laws which do not always coincide; namely, the laws of grammatical construction, and the laws which regulate the pauses in human speech. We have an example of this inconsistency in the rule given by some grammarians for placing a comma between the subject and predicate of a simple proposition, when the proposition happens to be long and the subject noun is accompanied with inseparable adjuncts. For instance, those who give this rule would place a comma before the verb *is* in the following proposition; thus, "To be totally indifferent to praise and censure, is a real defect in character." This makes punctuation depend not on grammatical structure, but on the length of a proposition. Such punctuation capriciously separating the subject of a proposition from its predicate, is certainly not well calculated to assist the reader in readily ascertaining the sense of an author; which is the great purpose of punctuation. We may in this manner indicate where a pause or suspension of the voice may be made within a simple proposition with least injury to the expression of the sense; but this is aside from the proper purpose aimed at by the punctuation used in our books. To indicate the places in discourse, where pauses may be admitted, or perhaps required in order to a just elocution, would demand a distinct system of notation and various marks to represent pauses of different degrees of duration. It follows from this that the rules given in reference to the length of time, or the proportional time that we may pause at each of the several points, are utterly useless and unfounded. A speaker who would attempt to follow these rules, would render himself ridiculous. All this matter of pauses must be left to be regulated by the taste of good speakers and the laws of elocution. In order to maintain consistency in punctuation, we must regard the sense and grammatical structure, and these only, and guard against considering points as the mere representatives of pauses. We have had occasion to notice that the dash is sometimes used to represent a pause where there is no break in the sense. We here submit another example of this use.

"Is it like? like whom?
The things that mount the rostrum with a skip,
And then—skip down again."

NOTE (*c*).—The system of punctuation, it seems to us, is not yet satisfactorily settled. Perhaps, a deeper knowledge of the structure of language, than can be acquired from the grammars hitherto in use, is necessary before this can be effected. In the preceding note we have adverted to the confusion which has arisen from regarding *diacritical marks* as the direct signs of pauses, and consequently assuming that a *point* may be placed wherever a *pause* is proper or allowable in speaking. We have also noticed, in treating of the punctuation of compound propositions, that, in many cases, it is not settled by unvarying usage whether a *comma* should, or should not be introduced between a *principal* proposition and its *accessory*. We have not proposed to ourselves to give a *complete* or *improved* system of punctuation in this appendix. The attempt to introduce such a system would, as we think, oblige us to propose important innovations—innovations which we have no hope that we could influence the public generally to adopt. And this is one of those things in which universal agreement is of more importance, than that the method on which we agree should be the best conceivable. All we have aimed to accomplish is to put the student in possession of the rules at present followed by authors and printers, as well as we can within a narrow space.

We believe that the most effective method of teaching the use of the comma (and this is both the most important, and the most difficult part of punctuation), is that which we have adopted; viz., by pointing out to the learner, in the construction of the several classes of compound and combined propositions, in the connection of contracted accessories, of co-ordinate members of propositions and of co-ordinate complements, where a comma is commonly used, where it is not used, and where the usage is unsettled.

We may be allowed to suggest, as the first and most important step towards the formation of a complete and consistent method of punctuation, the introduction of a point to be employed exclusively in separating principal and accessory propositions in compound constructions. If we had a sign always used for this and for no other purpose, the rules of punctuation might be greatly simplified, whilst the use of points would, we think, contribute much more than under the present system (or systems, for universal agreement is wanting) to the perspicuity of discourse. Every proposition of every kind could then be separated from all other propositions, contracted propositions and words which do not perform a function in propositions or in connecting propositions. The separation between accessory and principal propositions could be indicated by a new mark (say by a mark like an accent, such as the Germans use for a comma, thus (ˏ), and the separation between independent propositions, members, &c., as at present, by commas. The use of the other points, the semicolon, colon, &c., would require little change or modification.

There are, as it appears to us, only two principles on which a consistent method of punctuation can be based; namely, the principle that every proposition of every kind is to be distinguished from all other propositions, &c., or the principle that only independent assertions with all their modifications, however numerous, and whether consisting of single words or of propositions, are to be separated from one another by punctuation. To adopt this last principle would greatly abridge the use of punctuation in complicated constructions—the very case in which its service seems most necessary. If the principle last mentioned cannot, for the reason now indicated, be admitted, we must choose between making the effort necessary to introduce the system sketched above, and following the present inconsistent and perplexed method, equally difficult for the teacher to explain, and the scholar to understand and apply in actual practice.

APPENDIX ON VERSIFICATION.

§ 161. (1) English verse is distinguished from prose by a fixed order of succession of strong and weak syllables, by the recurrence of pauses at measured distances, and the recurrence of sounds chiming with each other at some of these pauses. (2) In other words, the elements of English verse, as distinguished from prose, are—1st. METRE; 2d. PAUSES AT MEASURED DISTANCES; 3d. RHYME. (3) The first and second of these elements are *essential*, the third is not essential: it does not accompany all our verse, though it is a constituent of a large proportion of English poetry.

(4) Such a portion as forms a complete specimen of the law of succession of *weak* and *strong* syllables in any species of verse is called a METRE or MEASURE or FOOT, because it is employed to *measure* the particular kind of verse which consists of a repetition of this *foot* or *measure*. (5) By these two circumstances, viz. the *nature of the measure*, and the *number of times* it is repeated in a *single verse*, together with the fact of the *presence* or *absence of rhyme*, the various species of English verse are distinguished from each other.

(6) We shall indicate the *strong* syllables, which enter into metres, by the symbol (¯) placed over them, and the *weak* syllables by the symbol (˘); thus, *ăspēct*, *rĕpēat*, &c.

NOTE.—We have assumed the same names to distinguish *measures* or *feet* which are employed by writers on Greek and Latin versification, and the same marks to indicate the different kinds of syllables which enter into the several measures. But these names and these marks do not indicate the

§ 161. (1) Mention the circumstances by which English verse is distinguished from prose. (2) Repeat the names of the three elements of English verse. (3) Which of these elements are essential to verse?

(4) Describe a *metre*, *measure* or *foot* in verse. (5) How are the various species of English verse distinguished?

(6) By what symbols are *strong* and *weak* syllables distinguished?

same things in treating of English versification or other modern species of versification and in treating of ancient Greek and Latin versification. *Measures*, and, consequently verse, in these ancient languages consist of *long* and *short* syllables, and in treating of the versification of these languages the symbol (‒) is used to indicate a *long* (not a *strong*) syllable, and the symbol (⏑) to indicate a *short* (not a *weak*) syllable. The melody of ancient verse is founded mainly on the metrical succession of syllables distinguished by the time which they occupy in pronunciation; or what, in treatises on prosody, is called QUANTITY (i. e. the relative *length* of syllables). (7) The melody of English verse is founded mainly on a succession of *strong* and *weak* syllables; or on what is sometimes called BEAT, or, perhaps not altogether correctly, ACCENT; in other words, *on the relative force of syllables or sounds.*

(8) It may as well be observed here, that good measure or the perfect *beat* of verse does not depend upon the absolute force of the individual syllables employed, but on their force relatively to the syllables with which they are matched in the same *measure* or *foot.* Hence it often occurs, in the connection of monosyllabic words in one metre, that the same word (according as it is matched with a *weaker* or a stronger syllable, that is with a word that demands greater or lesser force in pronunciation) occupies sometimes the place of a *strong*, sometimes the place of a *weak* syllable.

(9) Versification is perfect, so far as concerns measure, when the arrangement of the words in a verse is such that, regarded as mere prose, the relative force which the syllables demand for correct pronunciation corresponds with the demands of the measure of the verse; in other words, when good pronunciation of a passage naturally produces metrical melody. To this we may add that the perfection of verse, as regards pauses, consists in so arranging the words that the metrical pauses demanded by the laws of the verse shall occur at places where a pause is allowable without injury to the sense. When in both these respects the demands of the particular measure and form of verse are complied with, without greater departure from the ordinary grammatical arrangement of language than is allowable and becoming in poetical compositions, the versification is good, so far as regards all but rhyme (if rhyme is present). The demands of rhyme we shall consider presently.

1st. MEASURE.—(10) There occur in our language four principal kinds of *metre* or *measure*, and these are distinguished by the names

---

(7) On what is the melody of English verse mainly founded?

(8) Repeat the observation in reference to what good measure depends upon.

(9) State the substance of what is said in reference to the constituents of good versification.

(10) How many distinct species of measure occur in the English language? What are their names? (11) Repeat the names given to the single measures.

IAMBIC MEASURE, TROCHAIC MEASURE, ANAPAESTIC MEASURE and DACTYLIC MEASURE. (11) A single Iambic measure is usually called an *Iambus;* a single Trochaic measure, a *Trochee;* a single Anapaestic measure, an *Anapaest;* and a single Dactylic measure, a *Dactyle.*

(12) An IAMBIC MEASURE OF FOOT consists of a *weak* syllable followed by a *strong* syllable whether in the same or in different words. We may give as examples the words, *rĕpēat*, *rĕspōnd*, and the combinations, *thĕ wīnd*, *ă gēm*, *ăn hōur*, *ăt hōme*, &c. (13) A single iambic measure is represented by the symbols (⏑–).

(14) *Remark.*—Any two successive syllables of which the second is sufficiently distinguished from the first by the relative degree of force which it requires in pronunciation may be regarded as forming an *iambus.*

(15) A TROCHAIC FOOT OF MEASURE consists of a *strong* syllable followed by a *weak* one, as in the words, *strāngĕr*, *vīctŏr*, *nātŭre.* A trochee may be formed of two monosyllables, or of any two successive syllables of a word of more than two syllables, when the first of these syllables must, in accordance with the sense of the passage and the proper accentuation of the words, be pronounced with considerably greater force than the second. The symbols which represent the *trochee* are (–⏑).

(16) A single ANAPAESTIC MEASURE OF ANAPAEST consists of two *weak* syllables followed by one *strong* syllable. There are few single words in our language which serve as good examples of an *anapaest.* *Cŏlŏnāde* and *Lĕbănōn*, have been used by the poets as *anapaests.* Generally anapaests are constituted in the English language of syllables from more than one word. This measure is represented by the symbols (⏑ ⏑–).

(17) A DACTYLE consists of one *strong* syllable followed by two *weak* syllables. We may give as examples the words *sēnsĭblĕ*, *crūcĭblĕ*, &c. It is represented thus (–⏑⏑).

(18) We may exhibit along with these two other feet, which, though they do not *alone* (indeed *cannot*) form, or give name to any species of Eng-

---

(12) Of what does an iambic foot consist? Give an example. (13) What symbol represents it?

(14) Repeat the remark about the formation of an iambus.

(15) Describe a trochaic foot; give examples; repeat remark; tell how it is represented by symbols.

(16) How is the *anapaestic* measure constituted? Adduce examples; tell how this measure is generally formed in English, and how represented by symbols.

(17) Describe the *dactyle;* give examples; tell how it is represented.

(18) State the substance of what is said about two other feet.

lish verse, are often used as occasional substitutes for some of the feet already described. These are called the *spondee* (‒ ‒), consisting of two strong syllables; and the *pyrrhic* (⏑ ⏑), consisting of two weak syllables. Some call these secondary feet.

We exhibit all these feet together in the following table:

Iambus ⏑ ‒	Trochee ‒ ⏑
Anapaest ⏑ ⏑ ‒	Dactyle ‒ ⏑ ⏑
Pyrrhic ⏑ ⏑	Spondee ‒ ‒

NOTE.—Some introduce a third trisyllabic foot, the *amphibrach* ⏑ ‒ ⏑, consisting of a strong syllable flanked by two weak ones. We think it unnecessary to introduce this either as a *primary* or a secondary measure. Most of the examples adduced of its use come under the class of mere double rhymes at the end of iambic verses. Such verses as the first and third in the following four from Burns ought, if we have regard to rhyme, to be written each as two verses, consisting of a single iambus with an additional weak syllable, and having, as all iambics ending with a weak syllable must have, double rhymes.

" It warms me, it charms me,
To mention but her name;
It heats me, it beats me,
And sets me a' on flame."

To exhibit the rhymes we must write thus:

" It warms me,
It charms me,
To mention but her name:" &c.

The examples of measure consisting of amphibrachs selected by Dr. Latham (*Eng. gram.* pp. 204–206) we should regard as anapaests having an iambus substituted for the first foot. This substitution is common, even in the purest specimens of anapaestic measure. (*See Beattie's Hermit.*) The movements in such verses as,

" I'vĕ foūnd | oŭt ă gīft | fŏr my fāir;
I've found where the wood pigeons breed:" &c.

is surely undistinguishable from the anapaestic movement. The lines, we think, are more properly printed thus,

" I hăve foūnd | oŭt ă gīft | fŏr my fāir;" &c.

in which form they appear to be what they really are—pure anapaests. Dr. Latham seems to have presented the lines in a form to suit his purpose.

That the anapaest and iambic admit readily of interchange we shall have occasion again to observe.

(19) Verses formed of iambic measures may be said to have *iam-*

---

(19) Repeat what is said of the different species of *movement*, or *rhythm* of verse.

bic movement, or *iambic rhythm;* verses formed of *trochees*, of *anapaests*, of *dactyles*, *trochaic*, *anapaestic* and *dactylic movement* respectively.

REMARKS.—(20) These different *movements* or species of *rhythm* affect the ear and mind very differently, and are consequently, suited to different classes of subjects. The *anapaestic* and *dactylic* measures having two *weak* (or *light*) syllables to each *strong* (or *heavy*) syllable, may be regarded as less adapted to grave and solemn subjects than the other measures. The iambic seems of all our English measures the one best adapted to solemn subjects. The poets in choosing measures have not always attended sufficiently to these facts.

2d. PAUSES.—(21) A *pause* or *rest* of the voice determines the end of a verse. This is usually called the *final pause* of a verse. (22) The place of this pause is marked in written verse by turning to a new line, each separate verse being contained in a separate line.

NOTE.—The name VERSE has originated from this fact: *Verse* (in Latin *versus*) means *a turning*, so called because the end of it is indicated by *turning* back to a new line.

(23) But, besides the pause in reading which marks the termination of a verse, other pauses occur in the course of each verse, of considerable length. These (at least the chief pauses of this kind in each verse), are called *cæsural* pauses, because they *cut* the verse. We shall have more to say of these pauses, when we come to treat of the number of measures, or feet contained in a verse.

NOTE.—The word *verse* is often employed in ordinary language as the name of what is more definitely called a *stanza*. At the end of a stanza, as at the end of a *verse* properly so called, there is *a turning*, but, in this case, *a turning* not only to another line, but to the recommencement of a form of poetical composition consisting of a number of verses arranged in a fixed order.

Verse is also employed as the name of a well-known division of the Sacred Scriptures, adopted in modern times for the purpose of securing easy reference to any particular passage. These divisions are called *verses*, because in most printed editions each of them begins on a new line, and consequently there is a *turning* (*versus*) at their termination.

3d. RHYME.—(24) *Rhyme* consists in a certain correspondence of sounds, or the chiming of the last syllables of two or more verses with one another. For example:

---

(20) Repeat the substance of the remark in reference to different species of rhythm.
(21) What is said of the *final* pause? (22) How is its place indicated in written poetry?
(23) Repeat what is said of the *cæsural* pause.
(24) What constitutes rhyme? Illustrate by an example.

"As some tall cliff that lifts its awful *form*,
Swells from the vale, and midway leaves the *storm*,
Though round its breast the rolling clouds are *spread*,
Eternal sunshine settles on its *head*."

At the close of these verses the words "form" and "storm" rhyme with each other; and in like manner "spread" and "head." Endings like these are called rhymes.

(25) Three things are essential to *perfect* rhymes: the syllables which constitute such rhymes must be strong (heavy), or, generally speaking, what are called accented syllables; the vowel sounds of these syllables and the modifying consonantal sounds which follow them, when these syllables are closed by consonants, must be the *same;* and, lastly, the consonantal modifications which precede the vowel sounds must be *different.* Thus, in the rhymes closing the first two lines of the above example, the vowel sound in *form* is the same as in *storm;* the consonantal modification which follows is the same in both cases, namely, the modification represented by the consonants *rm;* and the modifications which precede the vowel sound are different, being the modification represented by the letter *f* in one verse, and that represented by *st* in the other. In other words, syllables, to form perfect rhymes, must end with the same vowel sound, closing (if modified in the close) with similar modifications, and must be unlike in their commencement. The last mentioned circumstance is indispensable to a good rhyme. Every one will discover the awkwardness in the rhymes of the following verses from Spenser:

"Dan Chaucer, well of English unde*fyled*,
On fame's eternall beadroll worthie to be *fyled*."

NOTE.—It is to be observed that many of the rhymes employed in verse do not conform perfectly to these conditions. The poets feel themselves often compelled to have recourse to *imperfect rhymes*, that is, rhymes formed with syllables in which the vowel sounds and the following consonants are not precisely the same, but more or less similar. But the more perfect the rhymes, the more pleasing the versification, so far as rhyme is concerned. The frequent recurrence of *imperfect rhymes*, especially of rhymes *very* imperfect (for the imperfection of rhyme admits of various degrees), is a great blemish in poetical compositions. Rhyme may be regarded as an ornament; and every thing intended as an ornament, if not excellent of its kind, utterly fails of its purpose.

---

(25) Mention three things essential to perfect *rhymes*, and illustrate by reference to the example given above.

It ought to be remarked that rhymes which, when written, seem perfect to the eye, are not always perfect to the ear. If we would form good rhymes, we must attend exclusively to *sound* and not to orthography. Examples: *head* and *bead* are not perfect rhymes, while *head* and *bed* (though unlike in writing), are perfect rhymes.

(26) "An accented syllable followed by an unaccented one, and coming under the condition given above" (namely, that the accented vowel sound and all that follows it shall be the *same*, and what precedes *diverse*), "constitutes a *double* rhyme."—Latham's Eng. Gram. p. 187. Examples:

"So she strove against her *weakness*,"
"Shaped her heart with woman's *meekness!*"
"When the praise thou *meetest*
To thine ear is *sweetest*,
Oh! then remember me."

See other examples in the verses quoted from Burns in a preceding note: "It *warms me*," &c.

(27) In the same manner, a strong syllable followed by two weak syllables, coming under the same condition, constitutes a *triple* rhyme. Such rhymes rarely occur in serious poetry. Mr. Moore has introduced a whimsical assortment of them in some of his satirical pieces. For example:

"I suspect the word 'crucified' must be made '*crucible*,'
Before this fine image of mine is pro*ducible*."
"Who lived just to witness the Deluge—was *gratified*
Much by the sight, and has since been found *stratified*."

It now remains to exhibit some of the principal kinds of English verse formed by the combination of the three elements considered; namely, the several species of *measure* variously repeated, *pauses* and *rhyme*.

1st. Iambic Measures.—(28) By far the largest proportion of our English poetry consists of *iambic measures;* and of English *iambic* poetry far the largest proportion consists of verses containing each five measures; in other words, verses containing ten syllables alternately weak and strong, commencing with a *weak* and ending with a *strong* syllable. This verse may be called Iambic Pentameter —

(26) Describe *double* rhymes, and repeat examples.
(27) Describe *triple* rhymes, and repeat examples.
(28) Repeat the remark about the prevalence of iambic measure in English poetry.

Iambic *five metre* VERSE. It is often called HEROIC VERSE, because *Heroic or Epic Poetry* is written in this verse.

(29) The following scale represents this species of verse so far as regards the measures or feet:

⏑ – | ⏑ – | ⏑ – | ⏑ – | ⏑ –

(30) Nearly all the verse without rhyme in our language is of this form. Such verse for the sake of distinction is called BLANK VERSE. Much of our *rhyme* verse is of the same form. To distinguish this from *blank verse*, it is sometimes called *rhyme.*

(31) A perfectly regular verse of this kind, besides admitting a *final* pause without violence to the grammatical arrangement and sense of the language, should also admit a pause either after the second or third measure or between the syllables of the third measure. That is, one or other of these places should coincide with the ending of a word which can, without impropriety, be separated from the following word by a moderate pause. When a pause is not only *allowable*, but *demanded* by the sense, the *beauty* of the verse is enhanced.

NOTE.—This *cæsural* or principal pause is sometimes deferred, both in rhyme and blank verse, till we come to the middle of the fourth foot; sometimes again it occurs (all that is allowed for it), so early as the middle of the second foot. These pauses have a less pleasing effect—are less melodious than the three legitimate pauses first mentioned. This failure of melody is more perceptible in *rhyme*, especially in heroic couplets, than in blank verse. In blank verse the only cæsural pause occurs sometimes even so early as after the first, and again, so late as after the fourth measure. Such unequal division of the verse injures the melody, and if too frequently repeated, detracts greatly from the pleasure which good versification yields. A *little* harshness when it does not recur too often, may contribute to variety. When the *cæsural* pause falls so near the beginning or the end of the verse, the final pause in reading sometimes becomes scarcely perceptible, so that the hearer cannot always distinguish where a verse ends; especially when the reader takes care not to sacrifice the sense to the melody. All really good readers and reciters of blank verse follow the sense in the employment of pauses, leaving the poet himself to look out for the melody.

(32) Besides the cæsural pause each verse of this form usually admits of one—generally of more than one secondary pause. Much of the

---

(29) Write a copy of the scale and explain it.
(30) Repeat what is said about verse without rhyme. How is it named?
(31) Repeat the substance of the remarks on the pauses of this kind of verse.
(32) What is said of *secondary* pauses?

melody both of blank verse and rhyme depends upon the proper adjustment of the pauses of the versification so as to accord with the pauses which the sense requires, or, at least, readily admits. (33) We submit a few examples of *blank* verse, marking the chief (cæsural) pause by two perpendicular lines. We give also a scale over these verses.

Yĕ nō|blĕ fēw ! ‖ whō hēre | ŭnbĕnd|ĭng stānd
Bĕnēath | līfe's prēs|sūre, ‖ yēt | bēar ūp | ă whīle,
And whăt | yōur bōund|ĕd vīew, ‖ whĭch ōn|lȳ sāw
A līt|tlĕ pārt, ‖ dēemed ēv|īl īs | nŏ mōre:
Thĕ stōrms | ŏf wīn|trȳ Tīme ‖ wĭll qūick|ly pāss,
And ōne | ŭnbōund|ĕd Sprīng ‖ ĕncīr|clĕ āll.

The melody of the verse depends greatly on the degree in which a marked contrast between the weak and strong syllables is attained by the arrangement. Observe as an illustration the superior melody and beauty of the fifth line, "The storms," &c. The strong syllables are all *decidedly* strong (not merely allowed through courtesy to the poet to pass as such), in contrast with the weak ones. In these lines we have three examples of the substitution of a *spondee* (– –) for the *iambus*. The second and fourth measures of the second verse, and the third measure of the fourth verse ought to be read as spondees, if we pay regard to the proper force of the syllables.

(34) Besides the spondee, blank verse freely admits the trochee (an *equivalent* measure, but with contrary movement), especially in the first place. Examples:

"*Thīck ăs* | aūtŭm|năl leāves ‖ thăt strēw | thĕ brōoks."

"*Swēet ĭs* | the breath of morn, ‖ her rising sweet."

A pyrrhic (⏑ ⏑) is also found in the first and sometimes in other places, and often followed by a spondee as *compensation*, the two together being equal to two iambic measures = two weak and two strong syllables. Example:

Wĭth thĕ | *fīxed stārs*, ‖ fīxed ĭn | thĕir ōrb | thăt flīes."

The anapæst (⏑ ⏑ –) is also freely admitted (we believe in all places) in blank verse, and imparts what some consider a pleasing variety to the measure. The anapæst, though differing in measure, resembles

---

(33) Copy the verses given as examples with scale, and repeat the remarks made upon them.

(34) Tell what other measures may be substituted for the *iambus*, and illustrate by examples.

the iambus in movement, as it commences with weak, and terminates in a strong syllable. When the anapæst is introduced the number of syllables in the line is increased beyond ten. The introduction of other feet as substitutes for the iambus does not increase the number of syllables. In the following verses we have examples of anapæsts substituted for iambic measures.

"Nŏw mōrn | hĕr rōs|y stēps ‖ *ĭn thĕ ēas*|tĕrn clīme."

"Hĕ scārce | hăd cēased, ‖ whĕn thĕ | sŭpēr|*ĭŏr fīend*
Wăs mōv|ĭng tōward | thĕ shōre: ‖ hĭs pōn|*dĕrŏus shīeld*," &c.

"Tŏ slāv|*ĕry prōne*, ‖ ănd bāde | thĕe rīse | ăgāin."

"By līk|ĕnĭng spīr|ĭtŭal ‖ tō | cŏrpōr|ĕăl fōrms."

NOTE.—In the last verse, if we pronounce "likening" and "spiritual" as words of three syllables, and "corporeal" as a word of four syllables, we shall have three anapæsts; which we think two more than enough in one verse. If we pronounce "spiritual" as a word of four syllables, as it is pronounced in prose, we shall have four weak syllables (for "to" in that case ought to be reckoned weak) instead of an iambus. Perhaps the best way of pronouncing the verse is according to the scale which we have placed over it, though "to," we admit, does not well support the dignity of a strong syllable. In some of the examples, it will be observed that there is a *hiatus*, or concurrence of vowels between the weak syllables of the anapæst: that is, the first weak syllable terminates in a vowel, and the second commences with a vowel. These vowels might be allowed to coalesce into a single syllable, in which case the anapæst becomes an iambus. Thus, if in the first verse above we allow the *e* of the word "the" to coalesce in pronunciation with the sound of *ea* in "eastern," "ĭn th' ēastĕrn clīme" will form two regular iambic measures. In a similar way, if in the next verse we pronounce "superior" as a word of three syllables (*superyor*), the anapæst disappears. It is much best in all such cases to pronounce all the syllables (perhaps a little more slightly and quickly than in prose) and class the measure as a substituted anapæst, or secondary foot. By this course, instead of detracting from the beauty of the versification, we improve it by introducing greater variety. The poet would not thank us for any effort made to reduce his verses in recitation to uniform iambic measures. For similar reasons, we would pronounce as well as write such words as *slavery, ponderous, dangerous*, always as three syllables, sounding lightly the middle syllable. In some editions we find the last two printed "pond'rous," "dang'rous" in situations like that in which ponderous occurs in one of the above verses. This mode of printing is wholly *unnecessary*, in whatever way we may choose to pronounce the words. It is altogether improper, if the views above stated are correct; and they accord, we believe, with those of the best poets, prosodians, and readers of poetry. It is the common error of careless and inexperienced readers of verse to yield themselves to the prevalent measure and movement, and thus force all the syllables, in violation of the rules of correct pronunciation and correct emphasis, into strict accordance with this prevalent measure, obliterating every trace of the secondary or substituted measures.

The chief poems written in blank verse are Milton's Paradise Lost, Thomson's Seasons, Akenside's Pleasures of the Imagination, Young's Night Thoughts, and Cowper's Task. Milton, Thomson, and Akenside appear to be the great masters of this species of verse.

(35) The analysis or dividing of verse into the separate feet or measures of which it is composed is called *scanning* or *scansion* of verse. In performing this exercise the learner pronounces the syllables which form each single measure separately, at the same time naming the measure; thus, "Sweet is" *trochee*, "the breath" *iambus*, "of morn" *iambus*, cæsural pause, "her ris-" *iambus*, "ing sweet," *iambus*.

The best form of exercise is to copy a number of verses from some interesting piece of poetry, and apply a scale to each verse (as we have done in the examples given above), exhibiting all the measures and pauses.

The method which we would advise to be pursued in order to obtain a correct knowledge of versification with the least expenditure of time and labor, is to continue the analysis of one kind of verse, say of the iambic pentameter, till the learner becomes perfectly acquainted with it. After this, the other varieties of verse will present very little difficulty.

It is shameful that the subject of English versification is so much neglected in our schools. It is a curious and interesting subject. Some knowledge of it is important to all who read poetry aloud, if it were only to guard them from being led into a *sing song* mode of recitation by servilely yielding to the general movement of the measures, and overlooking the secondary or substituted measures. Only a few hours' study are required to obtain a satisfactory knowledge of this curious art, through which so much has been contributed to the higher and more refined pleasures of mankind in all ages.

IAMBIC PENTAMETERS WITH RHYME.—(36) As *Iambic Pentameters with rhyme* do not differ essentially either as to pauses or measures from *blank* verse, it is necessary to do little more in treating this subject than to exhibit specimens of the several divisions of this kind of verse in reference to the order of the rhymes.

HEROIC COUPLETS.—(37) The most common species of *rhymed* pen-

---

(35) What is said of the analysis or *scanning* of verse? What form of exercise is recommended? And what method of studying versification?

(36) What remark is made in reference to *iambic pentameters* with *rhyme*?

(37) Repeat what is said of *heroic couplets*.

tameters in the English language is what is commonly called the *Heroic Couplet.* This *couplet* consists of two verses rhyming with each other. In poems composed of these couplets the first verse and second rhyme with each other; the third and fourth, with each other; and so on of all the rest in succession. (38) Sometimes three verses rhyme together. Such verses are called *Triplets*, and are sometimes indicated by a *brace* uniting them.

Verses of this kind are written and printed in unbroken succession.

(39) We have already given a specimen of Heroic Couplets in treating of Rhyme: "As some tall rock," &c. We submit others.

"Of all | thĕ cău|sĕs, ‖ thăt | cŏnspīre | tŏ *blīnd*
Măn's ĕr|ring judgment ‖ and misguide the *mind*,
Whăt thĕ | wēak hēad ‖ with strongest bias *rules*,
Is pride, ‖ the never-failing vice of *fools*."
"Sō, plēased | ăt fīrst, ‖ thĕ tōw|ĕrĭng Alps | wĕ *try*,
Moūnt o'ĕr | thĕ vāles, ‖ and seem to tread the *sky*;
Thĕ ĕtēr|năl snōws ‖ appear already *past*,
And thĕ | fīrst clōuds ‖ and mountains seem the *last*:
But those attained, ‖ we tremble to *survey*,
The growing labors ‖ of the lengthened *way*;
Thĕ ĭncrēas|ing prospect ‖ tires our wond|ĕrĭng *ēyes*,
Hīlls pēep | o'er hills, ‖ and Alps on Alps *arise*."

NOTE.—If we examine these verses, we shall find that a similar liberty of introducing other than iambic measures is allowed here as in blank verse; but it is not allowed in so great a degree. Good poets generally arrange verses of this kind so that each couplet expresses (as in the last extract) a complete thought.

Much of the beauty of this species of verse depends upon the skilful management of the cæsural pauses. These should rarely fall at any other places, except those which we have pointed out as the regular places; viz., the end of the second, the middle of the third, and the end of the third measure. It will be found by comparing the verses above, that the melody is sensibly affected by the place of the pause. For fuller information on this subject, the reader is referred to the acute and judicious observations of Lord Kames on English Heroic Verse. (See Kames' Elements of Criticism, ch. xviii., sect. 4.)

Lord Kames has examined with care the question as to what words do

(38) Repeat what is said of triplets. What is said of the manner in which couplets are written?

(39) With a written copy of these verses in his hand, let the student point out the pauses, secondary measures, &c.

not gracefully and without violence to sense and grammar admit a *cæsura* pause between them. The result of his inquiry on this matter is that pauses cannot, without manifest detraction from the perfection of the verse, occur between words used exclusively for the purpose of *modification* (adjectives and adverbs) and their *principal* word, when the *modifying* word precedes the *principal*. The reason is that such modifying words express no complete conception of themselves, and a pause or rest of the voice cannot with propriety take place except where a *complete conception* at least, if not a *complete proposition*, is presented for the hearer's mind to repose on. For the same reason a pause should not come between a preposition and the noun which it precedes, or between a conjunction and that which follows it. On the contrary there is not the same objection to the intervention of a pause, when the principal word precedes the modifying word. A pause is allowable between subject and verb; and even between the verb and its objective modification, though it is less proper here. These principles are often violated by the poets, *not without detriment to the verse*. We refer for details to the place above cited. We add here an example of a Triplet, and examples of verses with double rhymes. Verses of this last description contain, as a matter of course, an additional syllable. They are rare in iambic pentameters.

"Thou paint'st as we describe, ‖ improving *still*,
When on wild nature ‖ we ingraft our *skill*;
But not creating beauties at our *will*."
"To draw fresh colors from the vernal *flowers*;
To steal from rainbows, ere they drop their *showers*."
"The meeting points the sacred hair dis*sever*
From her fair head for ever and for *ever*."

(40) The Elegiac Stanza.—The *Elegiac Stanza*, so called, because it is generally employed for mournful subjects, consists of *iambic pentameters* with alternate rhymes, the first verse rhyming with the third and the second with the fourth. The stanzas are separated in printing by spaces. We have a beautiful and well known specimen of Elegiac verse in Gray's Elegy written in a country church-yard. We present a single stanza as an example.

"Can storied urn, ‖ or animated *bust*,
Back to its mansion ‖ call the fleeting *breath?*
Can honor's voice ‖ provoke the silent *dust*,
Or flăt|tĕry sōothe ‖ the dull cold ear of *death?*"

(41) The Spenserian Stanza.—This beautiful stanza consists of

(40) Describe the elegiac stanza, and point out the syllables which rhyme with each other in the example.

(41) Describe the *Spenserian stanza*; tell the origin of the name; mention some of

eight iambic pentameter verses, and a closing iambic *hexameter* or *Alexandrine* verse containing six iambic measures. The rhymes of the eight pentameters are alternate, and the ninth or Alexandrine verse rhymes with the eighth and sixth verses. We present an example from Spenser, from whom the verse receives its name, and another from Thomson. Some of the most beautiful poetry in our language is written in this stanza, including Spenser's Faerie Queene, Thomson's Castle of Indolence, Beattie's Minstrel, and Lord Byron's Childe Harold. The same rules apply to the measures and pauses as to other iambic pentameters.

"How oft do they their silver bowers *leave*
To come to succour us that succour *want!*
How oft do they with golden pineons *cleave*
The flitting skyes, like flying pursui*vant*,
Against fowle feendes to ayd us mili*tant!*
They for us fight, they watch and dewly *ward*,
And their bright squadrons round about us *plant;*
And all for love and nothing for re*ward:*
O, why should hevenly God to men have such re*gard!*"
Faerie Queene, B. II. Cant. 8 : 2.

"I care not, Fortune, what you me deny:
You cannot rob me of free nature's grace;
You cannot shut the windows of the sky,
Through which Aurora shows her brightening face;
You cannot bar my constant feet to trace
The woods and lawns, by living stream at eve:
Let health my nerves and finer fibres brace,
And I their toys to the great children leave:
Of fancy, reason, virtue, naught can me bereave."
Castle of Indolence, Cant. II. 3.

(42) The Sonnet.—The *sonnet* consists of fourteen iambic pentameters. As generally written by Petrarch, the great master of this species of poetical composition, the first verse rhymes with the fourth; the second with the third; the fifth with the eighth; and the sixth with the seventh.

Note.—In many modern English sonnets these eight verses are constructed with alternate rhymes; and this is certainly an improvement as regards melody, if any thing can improve this stiff, pedantic, exotic form of

---

the chief poems written in this stanza; analyze the examples, marking pauses and measures and noting secondary and faulty rhymes if such can be found.

(42) Describe the *sonnet*, and repeat the substance of what is said of it.

poetical composition. In verses arranged in the first way, so that between a pair of rhymes designed to correspond two rhyming verses shall intervene, the labor of seeking rhymes, at least, so far as regards the first and fourth verses, appears to us something worse than thrown away. Such rhymes, we think, detract from the melody of the measure and are much less pleasing to the ear than mere blank verse. We believe this to be the main cause of the unpopularity of the sonnet. We think it strange that Mr. Tennyson should have adopted a stanza with this most unmusical arrangement of rhymes in his "In Memoriam."

The six remaining verses of the sonnet have generally alternate rhymes. Often in Petrarch the ninth, eleventh, and thirteenth accord with each other in rhyme, and the tenth, twelfth, and fourteenth in like manner. Sometimes the ninth is made to rhyme with the twelfth; the tenth, with the thirteenth; and the eleventh, with the fourteenth: with the sole design, one would be tempted to think, of rendering the rhymes as little perceptible and as little agreeable to the ear as possible, after the poet has taken all the pains necessary to find them. There is however great variety in the mode of arranging the rhymes of the concluding six verses of the sonnet; but all varieties are inferior to the arrangement first mentioned; each seems to vie with the others in the trial which shall be least melodious. We select a sonnet as an example from Wordsworth:

" MUTABILITY."

" From low to high doth dissolution climb,
And sinks from high to low, along a scale
Of awful notes, whose concord shall not fail;
A musical but melancholy chime,
Which they can hear who meddle not with crime,
Nor avarice, nor over-anxious care.
Truth fails not; but her outward forms that bear
The longest date do melt like frosty rime,
That in the morning whitened hill and plain
And is no more; drop like the tower sublime
Of yesterday, which royally did wear
Its crown of weeds, but could not even sustain
Some casual shout that broke the silent air,
Or the unimaginable touch of Time."

The rhymes in the last six verses of this sonnet are in some respects worse than those which we have described above as most prevalent in Petrarch. What ear can appreciate any chime between "sublime" in the tenth verse, and "Time" in the fourteenth, at the distance of four verses?

The sonnet appears to us a most capriciously contrived unnatural poetical structure, with nothing to recommend it, save the unprofitable labor which it costs the poet. To increase this labor each sonnet, according to the law of the composition, should contain a complete subject, and only one subject. Few of our English poets have succeeded in the difficult cultivation of this exotic. Even when sonnets are good, the repetition of them soon becomes monotonous to the reader. It is not so with the truly beautiful native Spenserian stanza.

It now remains that we submit examples of the other more important kinds of iambic verse, and of anapæstic and trochaic verse. It is unnecessary for our purpose, in a brief sketch like this, to accompany these examples with many remarks. If the student has completely mastered what precedes and applied himself faithfully to the analysis of iambic pentameters, other species of versification will give him little trouble.

Iambic verse of four measures.—After the form of verse which we have been considering, iambic verse of four measures or feet is by far the most prevalent in our language. Some call this *Iambic Tetrameter.* (43) This is always accompanied with rhyme. Sometimes the rhymes are consecutive, like those of the heroic couplets, sometimes alternate, like the elegiac stanza. In the first case, as in the heroic couplets, the verses are written consecutively, in the second, as in elegiac verse, in stanzas. We submit examples.

" Thĕ wīld | rŏse, ‖ ĕg|lantīne|, ănd *brōom,*
Wăstĕd ărōund ‖ their rich per*fume ;*
The birch trees wept ‖ in fragrant *balm,*
The aspen slept ‖ beneath the *calm ;*
The silver light, ‖ wĭth qūi|vĕrĭng *glance,*
Plăyed ŏn | the water's ‖ still ex*panse,*—
Wīld wĕre | the heart whose passion's *sway*
Could rage beneath the sober *ray !*"

It will be observed that the cæsural pause usually occurs in the middle of the verse, between the second and third foot. It will also be seen from this example, that this species of verse admits the same secondary or substituted feet, as the species which we have been considering. This kind of verse also admits occasional double rhymes, and, of course, an additional weak syllable. Example:

"Exūl|tĭng, trēmb|lĭng, răg|ĭng, *fāint|ĭng,*
Possessed beyond the Muse's *painting.*"

(43) Describe the Iambic tetrameters with consecutive and with alternate rhymes. Copy the examples and apply a scale of scansion to each verse.

The following stanzas afford examples of this kind of measure with alternate rhymes.

" With listless look ‖ along the *plain*,
I see Tweed's silver current *glide*,
And coldly mark ‖ the holy *fane*
Of Melrose rise ‖ in ruined *pride*.
The quiet lake, ‖ the balmy *air*,
The hill, the stream, ‖ the tower, the *tree*,—
Are they still such ‖ as once they *were*,
Or is the dreary ‖ change in *me*?"

" When coldness wraps this suffĕrĭng *clāy*,
Ah, whither strays thĕ ĭmmōrtal *mind*?
It cannot die, it cannot *stay*,
But leaves its darkened dust be*hind*.

Above or Love, Hope, Hate, or *Fear*,
It lives all passionless and *pure*:
An age shall fleet like earthly *year*,
Its years as moments shall en*dure*."

(44) This verse is often alternated with an IAMBIC VERSE OF THREE MEASURES, which some, regardless of the frowns of classical prosodians, who have given the name to an iambic verse of six measures, have ventured to call *Iambic Trimeter*. We give an example:

" How lightly mounts ‖ the muse's *wing*,
Whose theme ‖ is in the *skies*—
Like morning larks, ‖ that sweeter *sing*
The nearer Heaven ‖ they *rise*."

(45) There is another stanza which in the third verse only has four measures, and in the first, second and fourth, three measures. Example:

" Behold the Sun, how *bright*
From yonder East he *springs*,
As if the soul of life and *light*
Were breathing from his *wings*."

NOTE.—In psalmody stanzas of four tetrameters (eight syllables) are com

---

(44) Describe a stanza formed of four and three measure iambics.
(45) Describe another similarly formed. Exhibit the scansion of both in writing.

monly called *long metre.* The rhymes are sometimes alternate, sometimes consecutive, and sometimes there is no rhyme.

Stanzas consisting of alternate tetrameters and trimeters are called *common metre.* In these the rhymes are often confined to the second and fourth verse, in which case the verses are sometimes printed as consecutive verses of seven measures each.

Stanzas consisting of three trimeters, with a tetrameter for the third verse, are called *short metre.*

We have already noticed the *Alexandrine* verse, consisting of six iambic measures. This is now only used in connection with other verses, as in the Spenserian stanza. Iambic verses of two measures, and even of a single measure with an additional weak syllable (and consequently double rhyme), are sometimes found connected with longer verses in odes formed of verses of varying length.

(46) ANAPÆSTIC VERSE.—We give specimens of the two kinds of anapæstic verse which occur most frequently in our poetry. It will be observed that as iambic verse freely admits the anapæst, so anapæstic verse admits the iambus, especially in the first measure of the verse. The following may be called *Anapæstic Tetrameter.*

"At thĕ clōse | ŏf thĕ dāy, ‖ whĕn thĕ hăm|lĕt ĭs *stĭll*
And mōr|tals the sweets ‖ of forget|fulness *prove,*
Whĕn naught | but the tor|rent ‖ is heard | on the *hill,*
And naught | but the night|ingale's ‖ song | in the *grove;*
'Twās thūs! | by the cave ‖ of the moun|tain a*far,*
Whĭle hĭs hărp | rung symphon|ious, ‖ a her|mit be*gan;*
No more | with himself, ‖ or with na|ture at *war,*
He thought as a sage, ‖ though he felt as a *man.*"

The following is an example of *Anapæstic Trimeter:*

"I ăm mōn|ărch ŏf āll | I sŭr*vēy,*
Mȳ rīght | thĕre ĭs nōne | tŏ dĭs*pūte;*
From the centre ‖ all round to the *sea,*
I am lord of the fowl and the *brute.*"

Iambuses and anapæsts are often intermingled in the same verse with pleasing effect. Example:

"Thĕ sŭm|mĕr ĭs cōm|ĭng, ‖ ŏn sōft | wĭnds bōrne,
Yĕ măy prēss | thĕ grāpe, ‖ yĕ māy bīnd | thĕ cōrn.
Fŏr mē | I dĕpārt ‖ tŏ ă brīght|ĕr shōre,
Yĕ arĕ mārked | bȳ cāre, ‖ yĕ arĕ mīne | nŏ mōre.

(46) Write out the specimens of anapæstic measure, and give an analysis of the feet. The same with the mixed *tetrameter.*

I gō | whĕre thĕ lōved ‖ whŏ hăve lēft | yŏu dwēll,
And thĕ flōwers | arĕ nŏt Dēath's— ‖ făre yĕ wēll, | făre-wĕll."

There are many sweet specimens of these mixed tetrameters in the poems of Mrs. Hemans.

TROCHAIC VERSE.—(47) It will be noticed that a verse consisting of complete *trochaic* measures must end in a weak syllable. A verse thus ending admits of none but a double rhyme, since every rhyme must, as we have seen, rest on a strong syllable. Hence in the trochaic verses which most frequently occur in our poetry, the last trochee is curtailed, or, if you please, a strong syllable is added. Some complete measures occur with double rhymes. We submit specimens of the forms which are most common in our poetry. Trochaic measure is almost exclusively confined to lyrical poetry—songs, odes, &c. We give only such forms as occur as continuous verses, not those short verses of two measures or less which occur in longer odes consisting of verses of various lengths. Example of Trochaic verse of three measures with double rhymes, and two measures with additional strong syllable.

"Thēn shŏuld | mūsĭc, | *stēalĭng*
All thĕ | soūl ŏf | *fēelĭng*,
Tō thў | heārt ăp|*pēalĭng*,
Drāw onĕ | teār frŏm | *thēe;*
Thēn lĕt | mēmŏrў | *brĭng thēe*,
Strāins I | ūsed tŏ | *sĭng thēe*,
Oh! thēn | rĕmēm|bĕr *mē*."

The last verse here is *iambic*, the fourth a trochaic dimeter (two-measure line) with an additional strong syllable, or a trimeter wanting a syllable, the other verses are trimeter trochaics with double rhymes.

We next give an example of Trochaic verses consisting of four measures (Trochaic Tetrameters), having of course double rhymes, with alternate verses of three measures, and an additional strong syllable to sustain the single rhyme.

"Everў | sēasŏn | hăth ĭts | *plēasūres;*
Sprĭng măy | bōast hĕr | flōwĕrў | *prīme*,
Yēt thĕ | vīneyărd's | rūbў | *trēasūres*
Brīghtĕn | aūtŭmn's | sōbĕrĕr | *tīme*."

"They by | parks and | lodges *going*,
See the lordly castles *stand:*

(47) Write the several specimens of Trochaic verse; describe and analyze them.

Summer woods, about them *blowing*,
Made a murmur in the *land*."

It may be noticed in the second and fourth lines above, that the trochee admits the dactyle in its place, as the iambus interchanges with the anapæst. The interchange in both cases is easy and natural, being between measures of similar *movement*. Some would read the feet which we have marked *dactyles* as *trochees*, making "flowery" and "soberer" words of two syllables. Such coarse pronounciation is far from improving the rhythm of the verse, and we think offends good taste.

See more examples of this species of verse, in Pope's beautiful ode, commencing thus:

"Vital spark of hĕavĕnlȳ | *flāme*,
Quit, oh quit, this mortal *frame*:
Trembling, hoping, lĭngĕrĭng, | *flying*—
Oh, the pain, the bliss of *dying*!"

And in Tennyson's "Lord of Burleigh."

Example of four *trochaic* measures with an additional strong syllable, and of five trochaic measures with double rhymes:

"Thĕn mĕ|thoūght I | heard ă | hŏllŏw | *soūnd*,
Gāthĕrĭng | up from all the lower *ground*.
Nărrŏwĭng | in to where they sat *assembled*,
Lōw vŏ|lūptŭoŭs | music winding *trembled*," &c.

Verses of this and the following forms are rare in our poetry.

Example of six measures:

"On ă | moūntaĭn, | strĕtched bĕ|nēath ă | hōarȳ | *wĭllŏw*,
Lay a shepherd swain, and viewed the rolling *billow*."

There are examples in Mr. Tennyson's poems of trochaic verses of seven measures, and his "Locksley Hall" is written in verse of seven trochaic measures with an additional strong syllable. Example:

"Yĕt I | dōubt nŏt | thrŏugh thĕ | āgĕs | ōne ĭn|crēasĭng | pūrpŏse | *rūns*,
And the thoughts of men are widened with the process of the *suns*."

Dactylic measures.—(48) Dactylic measures are very rare in our language; so much so that we doubt the propriety of giving them the rank of a separate class. Single dactyles are often substituted with good effect for trochaic, and also for iambic measures; but there are few specimens of English verse in which this measure so predominates as to render the name dactylic appropriate. In the following example

---

(48) Repeat what is said of dactylic measures, and write and give the analysis of the examples.

we have three *dactylic* measures with an additional strong syllable to support the rhyme:

"Erĭn, thĕ | teār ănd thĕ | smīle ĭn thīne | *ēyes*,
Blend like the rainbow that hangs in thy *skīes!*"

The first and the third verses in the following stanza consist each of three dactyles with an additional strong and weak syllable, or of four dactyles wanting one syllable in the fourth measure.

"Whēre arĕ thĕ | jōys I hăve ‖ mēt ĭn thĕ | mōrnĭng,
Thăt dānced | tŏ thĕ lārk's | ēarlў *sōng?*
Whēre ĭs thĕ | peāce thăt ă|waītĕd mў | wāndĕrĭng,
At evening the wild woods among?"

"Is it that summer's forsaken our valley,
And grim surly winter is *near?*
No, no! the bees' humming round the gay roses,
Proclaim it the pride of the *year*."

These verses ought to have double rhymes. Burns has substituted single rhymes. Could he have found double rhymes, in accordance with the general law of rhymes, it would have added much to the melody of the verse. The single rhymes falling on weak syllables, it will be seen by contrasting them with the rhymes in the alternate anapæstic verses, are almost imperceptible. The poet seems to have felt this, for in all the stanzas, except the first, he has left the dactylic verses without rhyme.

We may subjoin the following examples for analysis:

"Merrily, merrily shall I live now,
Under the blossom that hangs on the bough."

"Warriors or chiefs, should the shaft or the sword
Pierce me in leading the host of the Lord,
Heed not the corpse, though a king's in your path,
Bury your steel in the bosoms of Gath."—BYRON.

"Hail to the chief who in triumph ad*vances!*
Honored and blessed be the ever green *pine!*
Long may the tree in his banner that *glances*
Flourish, the shelter and grace of our *line!*"

THE END.

Elements of Astronomy.

ACCOMPANIED WITH NUMEROUS ILLUSTRATIONS, AND ARAGO'S CELESTIAL CHARTS OF THE NORTHERN AND THE SOUTHERN HEMISPHERE.

By J. NORMAN LOCKYER.

AMERICAN EDITION,

Revised, enlarged, and specially adapted to the wants of American Schools.

1 vol., 12mo, 320 pages.

In issuing this text-book by one of the greatest living astronomers, revised and adapted to our schools by an eminent American teacher, the Publishers feel that they have done a service to the cause of science in this country. Too often, when scientific knowledge characterizes a text-book of this character, the style is heavy, and the mode of presentation unintelligible; and, on the other hand, when the treatment is unobjectionable, there is sometimes a lack of scientific knowledge. In this text-book both these essentials are united in the happiest manner.

Astronomy has made great strides within a few years past; and Lockyer, who has himself been the pioneer in many important researches, has incorporated in the present volume all recent discoveries. Spectrum-analysis and its remarkable results, the physical constitution of the sun and stars, the solar spots, nebulæ, comets, and meteors, are fully dealt with in the light of recent developments. The new and correct figures obtained for masses, distances, etc., based on the recent determination of the solar parallax, are given.

The mode of using both globe and telescope is explained; indeed, one great aim has been to render the volume as practical as possible. The fine Star-Maps of Arago, showing the boundaries of the constellations and the principal stars they contain, are appended to the volume. They answer every purpose of a large Celestial Atlas—without additional expense—this being the only text-book, as far as the Publishers are aware, in which such an advantage is presented. For those who have neither globe nor telescope, plain practical directions are given for finding the leading constellations and the principal stars visible in the United States, at certain hours, on different days throughout the year.

The illustrations of the book, some of which are from photographs and drawings by De La Rue, Guillemin, and various members of the Royal Astronomical Society, will speak for themselves. The text will by constant revision be made to keep pace with the progress of astronomical discovery.